THE CENTURY
POLITICAL SCIENCE SERIES

Edited by FREDERIC A. OGG, *University of Wisconsin*

Frederic A. Ogg and P. Orman Ray, INTRODUCTION TO AMERICAN GOVERNMENT, Ninth Edition, and ESSENTIALS OF AMERICAN GOVERNMENT, Fifth Edition.

L. Vaughan Howard and Hugh A. Bone, CURRENT AMERICAN GOVERNMENT.

Hillman M. Bishop and Samuel Hendel, BASIC CONCEPTS OF AMERICAN DEMOCRACY.

John A. Fairlie and Charles M. Kneier, COUNTY GOVERNMENT AND ADMINISTRATION.

Joseph P. Chamberlain, LEGISLATIVE PROCESSES: NATIONAL AND STATE.

Howard R. Penniman, SAIT'S AMERICAN PARTIES AND ELECTIONS, Fourth Edition.

Andrew C. McLaughlin, CONSTITUTIONAL HISTORY OF THE UNITED STATES.

Percy Thomas Fenn, Jr., THE DEVELOPMENT OF THE CONSTITUTION.

John M. Mathews, AMERICAN FOREIGN RELATIONS: CONDUCT AND POLICIES.

Graham H. Stuart, LATIN AMERICA AND THE UNITED STATES, Fourth Edition.

Pitman B. Potter, INTRODUCTION TO THE STUDY OF INTERNATIONAL ORGANIZATION, Fifth Edition.

Charles G. Fenwick, INTERNATIONAL LAW, Third Edition.

Frank M. Russell, THEORIES OF INTERNATIONAL RELATIONS.

William Anderson (ed.), LOCAL GOVERNMENT IN EUROPE.

Edward M. Sait, POLITICAL INSTITUTIONS: A PREFACE.

W. F. Willoughby, THE GOVERNMENT OF MODERN STATES.

Francis W. Coker, RECENT POLITICAL THOUGHT.

Raymond G. Gettell, HISTORY OF POLITICAL THOUGHT and HISTORY OF AMERICAN POLITICAL THOUGHT.

J. Mark Jacobson, THE DEVELOPMENT OF AMERICAN POLITICAL THOUGHT.

Anna Haddow, POLITICAL SCIENCE IN AMERICAN COLLEGES AND UNIVERSITIES, 1636-1900.

An Introduction to the Study of

INTERNATIONAL ORGANIZATION

BY

PITMAN B. POTTER

Grozier Professor of International Law, The American
University; Managing Editor, American Journal of
International Law

FIFTH EDITION

COMPLETELY REVISED AND EXTENDED

New York

APPLETON-CENTURY-CROFTS, INC.

TO

THE MEMORY OF

MY MOTHER

LOUISA A. POTTER

WITH

GRATITUDE AND RESPECT

Preface

In the preface to the original edition of this work it was indicated that three objectives had been sought in its preparation: (1) exposition of the nature of existing international institutions, (2) explanation of their establishment and evolution, and (3) appraisal of their value for the purposes for which they had professedly been created. These remain the principal aims of the present edition with a fairly even distribution of emphasis among them, and adequate care to base any judgments of value upon the effectiveness of given institutions in respect to their professed objectives rather than upon any purely personal preferences.

The difficulties encountered in the years 1920-22 in keeping account of and properly appreciating current developments in international organization have not diminished twenty-five years later. The present constitutes another of those periods of rapid growth of international institutions such as that which followed World War I.

Moreover the attitude taken at that time, namely that recent developments in international organization were by no means new in general character, and presumably by no means final, has been amply confirmed by subsequent events. The League of Nations has come and gone, and although we now have the United Nations, its ultimate fate—and perhaps its immediate future—are clearly uncertain. Meanwhile the historic institutions of international organization and the basic principles of that activity remain. This volume has always been intended not merely as a textbook for use in college and university instruction, summarizing the facts and generally accepted conclusions concerning current phenomena, but as an analytical treatise, based largely on primary materials and contacts, of the fundamentals of the subject.

A few additional points may usefully be made concerning the approach to the subject followed in this volume. Great emphasis is placed upon the historical or evolutionary aspect of the subject. There is ample justification for this inasmuch as, in spite of the long history of international organization, that activity is still in its youth if not exactly its infancy. It is not possible to treat the subject in a strictly analytical-systematic manner, as in the case of a more mature and complete system. At the same time, and for the same reason, it is most useful to introduce general views of the subject, where they are attainable, along with the evolutionary treatment itself. This will explain the combination of general political science and the many historical references to the nineteenth century, World War I, the interwar period, and World War II which is characteristic of the presentation in this work.

Concretely, it should also be noted that the treatment in Chapters I-X is based predominantly on the international situation prior to the establishment of the League of Nations. Chapter XI is introduced at that point by way of a summary and because it is believed that the student can better appreciate the history of international organization after he has become somewhat familiar with present conditions than if he were offered such an historical picture at the beginning.

A comparable problem arises in connection with the discussion of the functions of international institutions. It is useful to distinguish the structural from the functional aspects of international organization. At the same time, in spite of the structural reference implicit in that formula, and its use as the designation of the whole field of study, no inference is to be drawn that major attention, much less exclusive attention, is to be devoted to the structural aspects of the subject. To some extent the functions of international institutions are discussed throughout the treatment, as the titles of various chapters and sections will indicate. The subject is then summarized in Chapter X with special attention to certain major problems.

Similarly for the questions of international "government," efforts for the preservation of peace and security, and international law. Enforcement of international obligations has an important place in the general field but is far from constituting the whole subject. Peace and security may constitute the most important objectives of international coöperation and control, but international organization cannot be presented merely in that light in view of its manifold other functions. Finally international law is an important tool of international organization but by no means coterminous or synonymous with it, and confusion between them must by all means be avoided. All of these problems are discussed more fully in the text.

The order of treatment of various topics in this edition will be found to vary somewhat from the order followed in previous editions. As time passes the author learns, or believes that he learns, more concerning the nature of various international institutions and the proper relations among them, both theoretical and practical. It is not believed that these alterations will cause serious difficulty although the problems of principle to which they relate are far from unimportant.

I wish to take this opportunity to express my gratitude to the staffs of the libraries of the Division of International Law of the Carnegie Endowment for International Peace and of the School of Social Sciences and Public Affairs of The American University for many expert acts of assistance in the preparation of this edition, and to various officers and offices in the United States Department of State and the Secretariat of the United Nations for help in procuring materials and information. I wish to thank Mrs. Anna Stern very sincerely for ready and competent assistance with data and manuscript in the tedious process of preparation. Finally I owe deep appreciation to my wife, Dr. Margaret Hardy Potter, for constant discussion of problems of theory as well as practical assistance with manuscript and proofs. Needless to say any and all mistakes and defects are to be blamed on me alone.

P.B.P.

Contents

PART III

GENERAL INTERNATIONAL ORGANIZATION

APPENDIX A

DOCUMENTS ILLUSTRATING INTERNATIONAL ORGANIZATION

CONTENTS

PAGE

APPENDIX B

AN INTRODUCTION TO THE STUDY OF
INTERNATIONAL ORGANIZATION

CHAPTER I
Introduction: Nature of International Organization

The student of international phenomena may be impressed at first most forcibly by any one or more of those phenomena. Which of such phenomena will spontaneously claim his chief attention will depend upon his own subconscious prepossessions—economic, legalistic, psychological, political,—upon chance, or upon his deliberate estimate of their relative importance. If, however, he desires to approach his study in the best scientific manner, he will turn his attention first to those overt phenomena, whatever they may be, which appear most clearly upon the surface of international life, and then proceed from these, by analysis and evaluation, to any more subtle and obscure elements in the problem and to any questions of social value therein revealed. He may, of course, discover that the phenomena with which he started constitute in fact the most useful terms in which to cast his study of international affairs, or he may find them to have been of only trivial importance.

Those phenomena which appear most clearly in the foreground of international affairs today are the agencies, national and international, which are utilized in the conduct and regulation of international transactions, and the forms of procedure—in a broad, not a technical sense of that term—employed for that purpose. By their numbers, by their activity, and by their professions or implications of effectiveness and importance, these agencies and forms of procedure seem, at least, to constitute the principal features of international reality today. It is, therefore, with these that the student may well begin.

His first discovery, upon analyzing the phenomena mentioned, will be that they rest upon certain deeper relations which have been built up in recent periods among the nations of the modern world. They come into existence, survive, and they operate, as a result of some kind of underlying community among the nations themselves, not because of any life or purpose inherent in these agencies and processes as such. Even when—to anticipate—international institutions aim at composing conflicts among the nations their chief significance is to reveal the international need for peace and order.[1]

It is to this subliminal unification of the nations, whatever its type

[1] On the other hand, to assert that the objectives of international coöperation, and not the machinery therefor, should have all our attention (Peter Edson in *The Washington Post*, April 15, 1945) is to overlook the fact that for attainment of the objectives the machinery may be necessary.

(technological, economic, or political) or its extent, and in spite of its largely subconscious character, and to the aggregate of procedures and organs for expressing that unification, including its formulation in law, that the name of international organization may best be given.[2] Any degree of international unity or community which would supersede national interest, policy, and action would satisfy this concept, as, for example, a mere international custom, or an international agreement (followed, perhaps, by national actions in accord therewith); it is not necessary to the concept, as commonly understood and as here employed, that any strictly international organ should be involved. On the other hand, the phrase is often used, and without great error, to refer to the agencies and procedures deliberately set up as the expression of a more fundamental international organzation. Etymologically it would be more accurate if the term "institutions" were to be employed in this connection, inasmuch as this would cover any established procedure as well as any established organ, but the terminology of the matter had begun to crystallize before World War I and it is now too late to change. The term is relatively new in common speech and in formal political science and its emergence signifies a revolution in practice and thought upon international questions.

The science of international organization is, in other words, relatively new. International relations in general have been observed and studied, in a more or less unscientific way, for over two thousand years, and international law has been studied as a branch of general jurisprudence for well over three centuries, but the scientific study of international organization as such dates from the latter part of the nineteenth, or the early years of the twentieth, century. As already indicated, such a study must be historical and descriptive to begin with, then analytical, then normative. As such it can provide great assistance to mankind in the conduct of its affairs; the study of international relations in terms of international politics, or with reference to the economic aspect of things, or even from the point of view of international law, is relatively narrow and subordinate to the study of the processes by which national and international economic and political motives are expressed, reconciled, enacted into law, and carried out. The science of international organization is logically the over-all science in the political field.

It remains to analyze further the bases, the general nature, and the end of, as well as some of the more general problems involved in, this fundamental international development before proceeding to study it in detail.

Further investigation of the bases upon which, and the ways in which, the agencies of international organization come into existence reveals certain objective factors or conditions of fact—nations, international intercourse,—and certain elements of felt need or purpose—national and

[2] On the origins of this term see article by the author in *American Journal of International Law*, Vol. 39 (1945), p. 803.

international interests and policies,—as the foundations thereof. International organization grows up or is created by means of, and in response to, these factors.

Thus there exists in the world a group of some seventy of that type of human group or community which we know as the nation. These nations exist in widely divergent physical—geologic, geographic, and climatic—situations, and are composed of more or less divergent racial and cultural strains. As a result the nations individually develop divergent needs and interests, and these divergent needs and interests give rise to divergent foreign policies or programs of action toward other nations. Apart from any inherent ill will or pugnacity, which may or may not constitute the chief reason or need for law and government among nations as among individuals in the state, and apart from any scarcity of the good things of life which may constitute the reason for economic organization and justice among the states or in the individual state, the mere element of factual variety among the nations leads to a divergence of interests and desires and policies which is of critical importance. Variations in local situation are more important in producing variations of interest and demand, and hence a need for social control, among states than among individuals.

These divergences become manifest and are felt whenever and wherever the nations come into contact—through adjacent boundaries, resident or traveling aliens, trade—and as a result of international communications of all kinds. Among the individual nations physical contacts create the most elementary form of international community and also constitute the most urgent occasion for the reconciliation of divergent national policies dealing with these same items.

Now the policy programs of the nations consist of intentions of affirmative action (the export of goods, acquisition of territory), negative action (as not making alliances or guarantees), and prevention of action by others (as defense against invasion), and cover most if not all of the interests of the nation. The nations feel that they must make these policies effectual. When international contact takes place the question becomes urgent. Some policies require only toleration from other nations, while others need active coöperation, if they are to be effectuated; in the latter case the ultimate step would be international adoption of the given policy or the formation and acceptance of international policy, or international law, and execution thereof. It is to permit these steps to be taken that the international community organizes itself legally and governmentally.

For this purpose the procedure and agencies of international organization must facilitate communication of information and policy and opinion by one nation to another, agreement, and concurrent and joint action. Communication, agreement, and coöperation are the fundamental forms of action which international organization must facilitate, in order that national policies may, if possible, be reconciled one with another, socially synthesized (internationalized), and executed.

The effort to harmonize national policies may be made at two distinct stages: in the process of formation by the states or in the process of execution. The latter is the more difficult task, though the one which occurs most obviously to the nations; the former is more delicate but constitutes a very real function of international organization. Finally, such harmonization may be accomplished by facilitating expression and spontaneous adjustments of policy and action on the part of two nations, or by inducing modifications of policy and action (expansion, contraction, diversion) at a price, by promoting a process of bargaining or exchange of concessions in international conference. The latter process becomes so complicated, in its machinery and procedure, that the essence of the process is almost forgotten and the international organization alone is noted. The results will be losses and gains of benefits by the nations involved, on one hand, and formation and execution of international law, on the other.

The concentration of attention upon the machinery and the procedure of official international action,—upon international organization,—however, seems to be justified not merely as an initial step of inductive science but also for deeper reasons. International organization constitutes the central corpus or body of international phenomena today; organization and procedure constitute, respectively, the anatomy and the physiology of the international body politic. This seems clear if this phase of international relations is compared with certain other aspects of international life.

For example there are those who would concentrate attention upon psychological aspects of the situation—economic motives, religious emotions—and the means of dealing with these psychoses, such as education, religious exhortation, even the song and dance. There are others who would stress unofficial international interest and organization rather than the actions of the sovereignty-bound states. Of the nature and value of private international organization, so-called, much more will be said later, but for the moment it is to be noted that the two positions just cited are in fact one, apart from a question of technique. Official international organization does or may take into account economic and sentimental motives and deal with them; those who stress these aspects of the situation really desire to see action taken in individual states or by unofficial agencies with the purpose of altering the ideals and feelings of the men and women behind or beneath the governments of the world, upon issues of national and international policy. To this, of course, there can be no objection, but the way in which certain forms of official international coöperation—especially diplomacy and conference—may be used not only as tools of, but as the means of generating, a spirit of international coöperation among governments and their representatives, should also not be forgotten, especially since the conduct of international affairs still lies largely in the hands of officials remote from the people, and the people are still largely indifferent to these issues. It should further be remembered that forming men's minds to coöperate with other nations is of little value unless the facilities for coöperation are provided, and provided in advance of a need for them. Finally it seems dangerous to rely upon a technique of emotion in view of the unstable nature of emotion; pacifist and patriot may in turn sway the citizen or official, depending upon gifts of persuasion and the chance to get in the last word; although appealing to his mind may be more difficult, conclusions based upon fact and reason are more likely to resist assault, and these elements are all on the side of the internationalist.

It might be possible, of course, to formulate a science of international affairs in terms of an analysis of the motives or desires of the individual state, its offerings to other states, and the satisfactions obtained. Such an analysis might still justify and sustain the creation and operation of international organizations, in view of the benefits received in contrast to its costs. But here as in another field of social life, the scientific and dialectical burden of proof or interpretation incurred by starting from the extreme individualist viewpoint, as a means for arriving at an understanding of the social phenomena of the age, seems out of proportion to the effort necessary by use of another method. Taking the social institutions as a point of departure, we can analyze out the motives and satisfactions of the individual state with much greater facility and no less accurate results.

The relative importance of organized as against unorganized international coöperation has also to be considered. Nations do coöperate from time to time without the use of set forms of procedure and without creating or using any common organs, and even, perhaps, without adopting common legal foundations or limitations for their action. Contributions of famine relief by one nation to another would provide an example. And such coöperation has its value. It is, however, very slight in extent, very unstable in duration, very ambiguous in quality. It is organized international coöperation which counts most and in organized international coöperation it is the institutions—organs and procedures— which form the distinctive element and which determine to a large degree the effectiveness of the action. These institutions embody and reflect the motives of the nations, their most strongly felt convictions. They are, moreover made up of living and striving individuals who embody vital human and national and international purposes and demands. As between organs and procedure, indeed, it is, contrary to what might be expected, the former which are more dynamic and creative. Both react back to intensify the motives they express. Any doubt as to the relative importance of this aspect of international phenomena will quickly yield to careful reflection.

What has just been said holds true still more for any comparison between international organization on one side and, on the other, international commerce and communications ("international intercourse"),
or between international organization and the relations of conflict or
coincidence among national foreign policies ("international politics")
before any process of harmonization has been undertaken. These phenomena constitute in part the more immediate basis, as they constitute
the more immediate need, for international organization, but they represent a lower level, a more elementary form, of international life in its
impingement on human welfare. They must be given incidental attention
but not made the center of such a study.

International law, on the other hand, belongs within the field of international organization. Its nature and rôle must be thoroughly examined
though it turns out to cover fewer aspects of international life, while
being more precise in form, than its parent activity. It covers aspects of
international community life only remotely connected with international
organization (as nationality or citizenship), while it has little to say
on some phases of that subject (as conference) where practice still
varies and has not yet crystallized into law. At other points they coincide, as where international law defines the powers of international
courts and commissions. In a sense international law is a tool of international organization; on the other hand, the law defines the forms and
agencies and powers of the latter, giving juridical form and organization
to the latent or potential international community. Much more will have
to be said on this complex relationship later, but the two are at least
not to be identified or confused, and, of course no merely legalistic
treatment of the general subject should be permitted.

So rapidly is the structure of international organization growing today
and so pretentious are some of its ambitions that a still more advanced
concept has made its appearance among students in this field and a still
more pretentious label, namely international government. It does not
seem that the complete substitution of this concept or term for the older
is justified. Government means control, international government must
involve control of one or more nations by one or more other nations,
acting individually or in groups. Such control is neither logically nor
practically impossible; national sovereignty may be reconciled with international authority by the doctrine of original agreement—states may
agree voluntarily to a later involuntary control by international authority,
though this must be discussed more fully later.[3] Moreover we have
some such control among the nations today.[4] But it is still so slight in
amount that it is impossible to regard it as the whole story or the main
or characteristic element in the situation. Tactically it may be wise for

[3] Below, Chap. IX. B.
[4] See discussion by the writer and another in *Political Science Quarterly*, Vol.
XXIV, No. 4, and Vol. XXV, No. 3, (November, 1930, and August, 1931).

friends of the cause to indulge in propaganda for international government or unwise to arouse feeling against it, but in either case it is unscientific. It is epistemologically and pedagogically sounder and more satisfactory also to center attention upon institutions and processes which are relatively discrete in comparison with the general process of government as a whole. Hence adherence to the title of the present volume.

Something was just said concerning conditions prerequisite to the development of international institutions, apart, for the moment, from motives and willingness to pay the cost thereof which are very important also and will be discussed later. Certain circumstances will powerfully stimulate, others will equally retard, development in this direction. In the absence of some very simple conditions, indeed, it is quite impossible for international intercourse itself to spring up, or a legal system to be devised for the accommodation of that intercourse. Under differing conditions international life develops a richness and intensity calling for an extensive legal system and a complicated set of governmental organs to take care of it. The principal prerequisites for the appearance and growth of international organization must, therefore, be noted at the outset.[5]

First, there must exist a number of separate states or nations or national states. That is, there must be available certain potential members of a community of nations. There could be no international intercourse, law, or organization if and whenever there should cease to exist in the world a number of free states. The existence of independent nations is absolutely indispensable to the existence of international organization. This is so obvious as to hardly require mention, but some of its implications are of great importance.

Two nations might conceivably develop such relations. But a multiplicity of units is desirable, rather than a bare plurality, for, just as multiplicity of specimens provides a better foundation for the development of general principles of law in the field of physical science, so the multiplication of independent states is conducive to a rapid growth of the law of nations. The body of the law is enriched with new and rapidly increasing materials, while a more urgent demand is created for some international organization to supervise and foster, on governmental lines, the increasing bulk of international intercourse.

One of the most beneficial results which could be expected from an increase in the number of the nations would be the reduction of the existing nations to something like a condition of equality and in consequence the removal of many present difficulties in the way of international coöperation. The greatest obstacles to such coöperation now are, on one side, the feelings of the larger states that they have more to gain

[5] For a discussion of this problem in relation to the United States see the author's article, "Nature of American Foreign Policy," in *American Journal of International Law*, Vol. 21, No. 1 (January, 1927), p. 53.

by "going it alone" and preserving a free hand than by joining in a world federation and that, if any organization is to be created, they are entitled to control it. When two or three "Super-Powers" dominate the scene the difficulties reach a maximum although we should resist rash despair here as well as rash optimism; the whole situation is uncertain and experimental. On the other side the smaller states fear that any international organization will prove merely a device for their enslavement, seeing that they cannot control it. In addition the larger states feel that they are called upon to bear a too heavy share of the burdens of international government. A multiplication, and consequent equalization, of the states would tend to remedy these difficulties. It might also remedy another grave deficiency in the international community, namely lack of a large mass of members situation in the middle between the few at the top and the scattering at the bottom.

This conclusion, it is true, runs counter to ideas held in some quarters. Unquestionably the multiplication of states makes the task of international coöperation more complicated and to that extent more difficult; and the creation of artificial states by the powers that be, for ulterior purposes, is to be condemned on all grounds. But the protest arises chiefly from those who believe that great states make for peace by their powers of domination, forgetting that these states also cling to the old diplomacy as a means of regulating international questions and hardly wish to see it replaced by judicial and legalistic methods, hoping rather to profit by skilful diplomatic maneuvering, by fishing in troubled waters. This is more difficult if the number of states is multiplied, while the legalistic method would be encouraged thereby. The protest springs also from a realization of the inadequacy of existing international governmental machinery as a means of holding the many new states in order. The remedy here, obviously, is not to destroy the new states, but to provide a sufficient international system.

At the same time a certain degree of homogeneity among the states of the world is equally necessary. It is a familiar observation of political science that a moderate amount of homogeneity is indispensable as a basis for law among units of any order. Some common denominators among the nations must be found in the intercourse among them. If there are no common interests and standards there can be no legal community. General recognition of this principle is evidenced by the idea of restricting the application of international law to the European nations, to the "civilized" nations, to Christian nations—a thought which persisted as long as it seemed that the differences between the members of these groups and states outside were so profound as to render impossible a common life between them. The idea that there is a peculiar "American" international law, exaggerated though it may be, testifies to the operation of the same influence. At this point arises the thought that a substantial international spiritual unity or community must precede any effective international organization and the denial that any such thing exists today. Again we can only admit the principle in general, suggest that the facts may be slightly more hopeful than the hyper-realists contend, and insist that the experiment must be made. The two elements—spiritual community and practical organization—interact one upon another moreover to produce results not anticipated by an over-simplified analysis.

The foregoing conditions are fundamental.[6] There could be very little international law or practice in a world of one great state, of a restricted number of states, or of states immeasurably at variance in character. Retardation in the growth of international law and organization in the past can often be traced directly to the suppression of independent states, to the limited number of precedents available on a given point, or, more often, to the fact that national practices and views have differed so widely that agreement was impossible.

Beyond these fundamental requirements lie certain others of less importance—still relating to the states themselves—which nevertheless have a considerable bearing on the growth of international law and government. Such are the conditions of stability, equality, territorial possessions, and general secular character in the states of the world.

Thus it is clear that intercourse and the elaboration of legal and institutional connections among the states will be rendered increasingly difficult if the rise and fall of states in the world is too rapid. New states must now appear mainly by the modification of older ones. If this process of modification is too swift it becomes difficult to determine at any one time the degree of independence, of separable existence, enjoyed by any given so-called state. Too much flux and flow, too rapid change in the political map of the world, is not conducive to the development of an orderly international system. As in all periods of great revolutionary disturbances, international chaos is the disastrous result. To some extent this means that peace and international order are prerequisite for international coöperation; this is obvious, of course, but it raises the question of how peace may be attained by international coöperation and the prerequisites therefor; all of this will be discussed later in its proper place.

Furthermore, it is exceedingly desirable that every state shall be free to manage its own affairs and able to do so effectively. If the peculiar individuality of each nation is to find expression, independent action is essential, and domination of one state by another impairs the operation of the process of free international coöperation. When powerful empires control the discretion of weaker neighbors the latter contribute little to the growth of the law of nations. Recognition of the unwholesomeness of such a situation has led to the adoption of the doctrine of

[6] Compare these desirable conditions with the so-called fundamental rights of states at international law set forth in the orthodox treatises on international law, as in Wilson, *Handbook*, § 23; for explanation of abbreviations see Appendix B, below.

state independence. It is maintained that, irrespective of relative power, the nations are entitled to live independent lives in so far as they so desire. The smaller nations must have freedom to live their own lives and to receive satisfaction for their national rights in the face of the more powerful members of the international community.

It is equally desirable, though not so often remembered, that all states must be able to conduct their affairs effectively both within their own boundaries and in relations with other nations if international coöperation is to be successful. At least half of the states of the world today are so defective in this respect as to present a serious obstacle to international peace and order. Weak states are continually complaining of threats to their independence from stronger states—and they have some reasons for doing so—but they are also guilty of seriously impairing the progress of international coöperation themselves by their irresponsibility and ineffectiveness. Too powerful and too arrogant states endanger world coöperation, but a certain sufficient degree of independence and strength must be possessed by any state which is to participate usefully in that process.

That a nation must possess a certain territorial domain in order to be a state at all seems to be generally admitted. Conceivably a system of nomadic or non-territorial states might give rise to a body of international law and a set of international governmental organs. Throughout all history, however, states or other organizations of people lacking a territorial basis have failed to contribute greatly to international life, or, indeed, have totally failed to hold a place in that life. To deprive a state of its territorial basis means to deprive it of existence.[7] Modern international law and diplomacy are the products of a system of territorial states, in contrast to an earlier system of personal jurisdictions.

Finally, if the law and practice of the nations is to reach its fullest fruition, the states must be general in character. That is, they must be comprehensive in their activities and aims and not exclusively religious, industrial, scientific, or esthetic. It is doubtful whether such groups of people could properly be regarded as states at all. In so far as states have only special interests, relations with other states are more difficult, being dependent on the chance that there will be other states with like special interests. The path is not long to a condition of direct opposition between highly sectarian states. What could a labor state find in common with an ecclesiastical state? Members of the community of nations with only special interests would contribute little to the law of nations outside of their own interests; Switzerland has not contributed to the development of maritime law nor Iran to that of the law of river navigation.

Given these characteristics on the part of the potential members of

[7] Compare the disappearance of the Papacy as an international entity after the disappearance of the Papal territorial holdings in 1870: *American Journal of International Law*, Vol. VIII (1914), p. 865 (Editorial comment).

the community of nations considered within themselves, certain external historical conditions are also requisite to the growth of any considerable system of international relations and government. First, there must be a sufficient degree of contact among the existing states, and, second, a science of international relations must be developed to explain existing conditions and suggest the elaboration of new legal and political institutions.

Of these, the first is more fundamental. Unless two states make contact they can have no economic, political, or legal relations one with another. National isolation results in paralysis of international growth. In proportion as means of communication—commercial, personal, scientific —increase and are exploited among the nations, the intercourse upon which the whole system is founded grows in volume and complexity. More needs arise for, and more facilities are provided for creating, an international legal and governmental system.

It is at this point that national policies and activities in commercial matters, and particularly in regard to tariff matters, become important. If a nation, or several nations, attempt to live independent and self-sufficient economic lives, if they adopt tariffs, quotas, or other measures making commercial intercourse with them difficult or impossible, or if they refrain from entering into such intercourse on their own part, one important factual basis of international coöperation between themselves and other nations will be removed and the process of international coöperation chilled at the outset. Perhaps some nation or nations may be able to take such a position and maintain it profitably, but the situation should be recognized for what it is. Nations must be willing to enter into intercourse and coöperation before that result can be attained. It hardly needs to be added that any dogmatic ideologies hostile to internationalism, if held by important nations, can be fatal at this point. It should also be noted that the different groups in the society of a normal state (professional and capitalist, upper, middle, lower middle, proletariat) do not react to the problems of international organization and coöperation in the same manner—apart from special interests; the response to such needs is definitely more hostile in the latter groups.[8]

The importance of the second condition ought not to be underrated, however. For want of a mature science of international relations the Greek state-system went down before Macedon and Rome. For want of an adequate science and art of international government, millions died on the plains of Europe in the years 1914-18 and again in 1939-1945. With all the materials for international organization present,—a numerous group of fully developed states, and states bound closely together by a rich international intercourse on the nonpolitical side,—the world still lacked a statesmanship equal to the tasks of insuring justice and keeping peace. Perhaps this is the most serious prerequisite of all, though it may

[8] Gallup, G. H., and Rae, S. F., *The Pulse of Democracy*, 1940, Chap. 17.

amount to not so much a preliminary requirement as a requirement for the thing itself!

Another aspect of this situation is seen in the concepts or doctrines of international relations dominant at the time. If doctrines of national sovereignty and independence and self-sufficiency predominate then international organization will be rendered doubly difficult. The doctrinal climate of the world makes a great deal of difference to the progress—or lack of progress—in international organization. The question of the willingness of the nations to create and maintain a system of international organization arises at this very point. There are involved also the motives of the nations in taking such action and of the individuals involved in international affairs.

Thus it is relatively simple for the detached student to make the functional analysis set out at the beginning of this chapter and to conclude that the function of international organization is to facilitate harmonization and execution of national and international policy and law. But there are involved also not merely nations or states as such, and their governments, but human beings acting as public officials or as mere private citizens of those states or even merely as individual human beings, and as such the motives of the individual may vary considerably from what would be appropriate to a mere member of the state. Many students would, indeed, criticize sharply the use of the state as the unit of all reasoning in this field, and hold that the reality is far more informal, complex and pluralistic.

It does not seem truly realistic however, to deny the unity of the state or the logical or practical justification for employing that concept in this context. States are composed of individuals and can act only through individuals, it is true. No laws or instructions are so complete as to eliminate opportunity for exercise of discretion by the official. Considerations of official duty and loyalty may be influenced by conscious or unconscious ideas of personal satisfaction, fame, or profit, in harmony or in conflict therewith. Nevertheless it is the end result that counts and we have to have someone to hold responsible in the end. What is more, state unity and control of official action are on the increase, rather than the opposite, today and we may safely reason upon the assumption of their reality and their reliability both in practice and in theory.

It does however mean that, even in their collective rôle of state or nation, a group of people may not be willing to pay the price of international order, justice and coöperation. While international coöperation grows as a result of certain general causes, men and nations undertake such action because of desires for satisfactions obtainable only from beyond the boundaries of the nation, and these desires may vary greatly among individuals and groups within the state and among these from time to time. International coöperation does not always seem to promise such satisfactions to all. Conflicting group interests within the state may make such actions impossible. Mixture of conscious and unconscious motives may confuse and balk state action. Indirect benefits may seem so speculative that immediate sacrifices therefor seem unjustifiable, waiving entirely any idea of altruism and looking at most only for generosity, international solidarity, or enlightened national interest as a motive of state action. Benefits of considerable import must be held out to the individual state which is invited to participate in international organization, and this depends upon the concessions offered by other states, upon the effective organization of the system, and upon the stage of evolution of international life. Impairment of national sovereignty and independence are feared and shunned. Democracy, product of the same period since 1789 which has produced internationalism, is peculiarly susceptible to appeals to crude nationalistic judgments as against considerations of indirect welfare from world peace and progress. Armament manufacturers, emotional nationalists, journalists, politicians, military and naval officers and veterans, likely to see these things in one light, check the influence of preachers and teachers and scientific students on the other side. All of this slows down the process of developing international organization greatly. From a scientific viewpoint this is pertinent and important only as a part of the general picture; from the point of view of the reformer it is critical.

A largely dialectical problem may arise here, the problem, namely, whether international organization is or is not intended to check and even suppress national policy. The answer seems quite clear if the situation is viewed dispassionately and in the large. International organization is intended to check national policy and action harmful to others but positively to satisfy and fulfill national policy which is not invidious in character. Even in the first case international action is calculated to fulfill the basic needs and policies of the nations.

Another consequence of the fact that states are composed of individuals is that these individuals, upon the creation of international authority, find themselves under two allegiances, which at times seem to conflict. This is nothing new, as it occurs within the individual state (local versus national citizenship), but it seems more acute here. Likewise such conflicts are apparent rather than real if the international legal system is at all coherent and consistent, but the situation seems very complicated nevertheless. It is, however, unavoidable.

Finally, the same state of facts leads to the result that international authority impinges now upon the state and now directly upon the individuals in the state. It would be possible, perhaps, for the states to insure that this should be avoided; actually they create international law and administration very frequently in such form as to apply to their nationals directly. This is regarded by some students as a beginning of world unity, world law, and world government, rather than international organization. It does not seem, at all events, that this difference detracts from the importance or effectiveness of the control exercised, and it is certainly a fact or a situation which must be taken into account in the study of actual international organization.

A more precise analysis of the functions to be performed by international organization is now in order. The process of harmonization and execution of policy is complicated not only with reference to the levels at which it may be accomplished and the process of harmonization itself, already discussed, but with reference to the formulation of international policy and its execution.

These processes may be regarded as analogous to, or even identical with, the making and execution of law in the individual state. We are familiar with a threefold division of governmental action into legislative, executive, and judical forms; the same analysis is applicable here. Closer inspection reveals that judicial action is essentially part of the executive or administrative function: declaration of what the law is and its application to a given situation; but this does not alter the original analysis greatly. In international organization the task is to secure enactment or adoption of international law (out of national policies synthesized into international), its revision as the needs of the time change, and to secure its execution or administration by national or international agencies, including, logically, enforcement if need be.

In terms of subject matters treated this process ranges widely. Promotion of the welfare of the nations in general and in specific cases is the general objective. This is to be accomplished in the first place by preventing aggression by one state upon another, and promoting security and peaceful settlement of controversies. It is to be accomplished mainly by erecting and constantly revising standards of conduct whereby justice shall be done among the nations, and seeing that these standards are observed. Finally, securing international coöperation where necessary for the service of mutual needs is the objective which completes the schedule; pacification or protection, the doing of justice, and promotion of coöperation constitute, respectively, the negative, the basic, and the affirmative tasks to be performed by international organization.

This analysis does not turn on any distinction between domestic and international questions. There are, in this day of foreign travel and residence and ownership of property abroad, few questions exclusively domestic in character; questions once so regarded are constantly becoming more and more international in their significance and treatment. The old distinction has not lost its meaning but it has lost its importance somewhat.

In point of fact the functions of international organization range over all aspects of human life and cover about the same range as is covered by the scope of activity of the individual state. Maintenance of order and safety, protection of life and property and the facilities of com-

munications and transit, promoting the development of those communications and of the economic and social (health, morals) welfare of the
nations—what are these but the age-old objects of the solicitude of
the state? The subjects treated are not capricious choices, they are the
natural questions for consideration by any government.

This situation may be summed up by saying that the international institutions attempt to serve the welfare of the national states, the individuals who compose them, and the international community itself, with
slowly increasing attention to the last two. This welfare includes physical
safety, physical well-being and material prosperity, but also spiritual
well-being and progress. On the whole this gamut of objectives of the
international institutions tends strongly to expand. There may be room
for discussion as to the priority of certain of these functions logically
and historically. Making law, it seems, must precede its application, yet
preserving peace—a primary function—seems more a task of execution
than of legislation and certain institutions of international organization—
conference, courts, administrative bureaus—seem to have appeared historically in an order which would be regarded as almost the opposite of
that which would have been anticipated on logical grounds. The explanation lies in the fact that the adoption of international policy and
law began in a form simpler than the conference, and its administration
was relegated to national agencies before international agencies were
available. Besides, not much law is needed as a basis for keeping the
peace—only the principle that the individual state shall not resort to violence. Apart from all this stands the fact that in respect of subject matters international organization did actually neglect its primary task for
a long time and proceed to other tasks and subjects less fundamental but
somewhat easier of treatment! On the other hand, the historical evolution of international coöperation has not varied from the logical order
of function enough to constitute a serious scientific problem.

What has just been said may be completed by a systematic statement
of the forms in which, or the stages by which, international organization
has appeared in the world.[9] This analysis will be referred to repeatedly
and deserves to be borne in mind from the beginning. International co-
operation in its simplest form takes the shape of diplomacy, or the representation of one state, its ideas and its wishes, toward another, by persons appointed by the former; negotiation, or the making of demands
and offers, is the peak of the diplomatic function. The conclusion of
treaties, or international agreement, follows; this function emerges from
that of the diplomat but constitutes something higher than representation or negotiation. Next comes international law, its formation and
application, the regulation of international affairs by general standards,
growing in part out of treaty agreement but in part out of diplomatic
and other interstate practice antecedent thereto. International law may

[9] See diagram on page 17.

seem more rudimentary than diplomacy, involving, as it does no international agents or institutions, and evolving simultaneously with diplomacy and treaty-making; fuller discussion of these relations will be
offered later.

These are three special pre-institutional types of international organization. They are followed by conference, administration, and adjudication, also special forms of international coöperation but carried on by
international organs—conferences, commissions, courts. Finally comes international federation, general and organic synthesis of all the preceding;
the factual unity of the beginning becomes the legal union at the end.

International organization, it should be understood, is not the only
possible type of world unity, nor the only process by which some degree of unified world polity has been attained in the past. Two other
forms of world unity are always to be reckoned with, namely, empire
and cosmopolitanism. The relations among these several types of polity
may be briefly stated.

The national state is the basic unit upon which all discussion must
proceed. That state was originally the product of the historical development of the fifteenth and sixteenth centuries, although the list of such
political entities has been steadily growing down to the present time. Its
salient characteristic is the binding together in a single governmental
organization of a group of people who, because they are kindred in
race, ideals, manners, religion, language, or customs, and live in a definite
territory, regard themselves as members of one nation and carry on their
national life under a single system of law and government.

On one side of the national state we have empire, which is the forcible
union and subjection in one state of the people of otherwise independent
nations. The imperial unit may be more or less extensive, more or less
world-wide. The need of an autocratic government to dominate the
structure usually brings into being a monarch, an emperor; and at the
heart of the empire stands the master nation which has subjugated
the remainder. The logical maximum of empire is a world state resting on
conquest and domination.

On the other side we find cosmopolitanism, which is the unification of
individuals throughout the world in one society on the basis of interests
common to them all as individuals.[10] The logical outcome of this process
would be a world community created by voluntary action; and in its
form of government it would tend toward anarchy, because of its emphasis upon the individual. Such a community might be organized into
a world state of any form, but presumably it would tend toward some
shade of popular government. We thus have here, within the field of
world politics, the contrast between authority and liberty which is so
familiar within the national state.

Standing between empire and cosmopolitanism we have international

[10] Further discussion below, Chap. III.

INTERNATIONAL ORGANIZATION

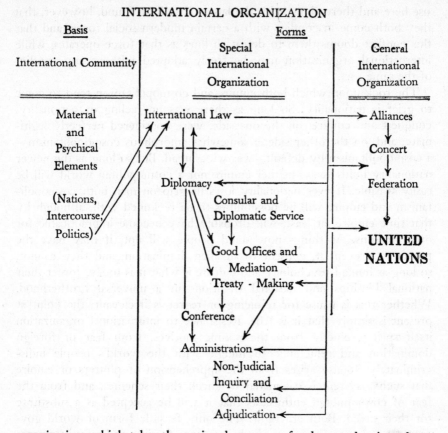

organization, which takes the national state as a fundamental unit and expects neither its subjugation nor its disappearance by the sublimation of the principle of nationality. International organization proceeds by the voluntary coöperation of separately organized nations. The result is a unity similar to that obtained by empire, but based on free consent and the preservation of national identity; or it is the unity attained under cosmopolitanism, but based on the action of national groups as such. International organization is not an inferior substitute for a unitary world state but a superior method of reconciling world unity and national liberty.

Examples of empire, or attempted empire, can of course, be cited from ancient to modern times. Examples of cosmopolitanism, or of tendencies toward it, extend from the days of Greek religion to modern science. Both programs are more or less discredited today as plans for world organization. But historically these modes of world order have ruled the scene with fully as much power and prestige and over periods fully as extensive as has international organization. It might seem more accurate, therefore, to regard these types as coördinate with international organization, as permanent forms of world government, available for

use here and there along with the latter. It will be found, however, that they both come in conflict with a certain modern social force, and that this conflict dooms them to defeat so long as that force operates, while international organization may be freely adopted without any conflict of the same sort.

The rock upon which both empire and cosmopolitanism tend to come to grief is nationality. So long as there was no feeling of nationality, conquest and empire, on the one side, were considered perfectly legitimate; and, on the other side, a somewhat amorphous cosmopolitanism,— a cosmopolitanism by default,—was widespread. But so long as the newer nationality holds sway, neither empire nor a cosmopolitan world will be easily feasible. If ever nationality loses its grip on man both cosmopolitanism and empire will be possibilities to be reckoned with, although by that time empire, at least, will probably have become impracticable for other reasons. As things now stand people will not, if they have the power to prevent it, consent to an alien domination; and they cannot, so long as human psychology and culture is what it is today, forget their national kinships and national traditions in a universal brotherhood. Whether this is cause for rejoicing or regret is irrelevant; the point at present is simply that it is true. Resistance to international organization itself springs chiefly from these same motives, from fear of foreign domination and reluctance to mingle with the world's people indiscriminately. It also arises from the apprehension of plotters of empire that such a system is calculated to check their schemes, and from the fear of cosmopolitan enthusiasts that it will be accepted as a substitute for their creed. Both are right. The only feasible form of world government today and the one which is at once feasible and safe, is international federation.

The possible modes of world organization just described are not, of course, entirely incompatible at any one time. Cosmopolitan society may develop within an imperial unit and still not develop so far as to threaten the stability of the empire as against outside influences. Indeed, the development of cosmopolitanism within an imperial state tends to remove internal sources of disruption. Austria-Hungary broke up largely because this process had not progressed sufficiently within her territories. Similarly, cosmopolitanism may develop under an international system without going so far as to threaten to obliterate national lines. In fact the strongest cause of internationalism is to be found in the previous development of a certain degree of cosmopolitan unity, calling for some measure of political and legal accommodation.

In like manner the methods of imperialism and of cosmopolitanism— force on one side and natural growth on the other—are not wholly absent from the field where an international federation is developing. Even in the case of empire there may be voluntary coöperation of distinct national units, as in the British Empire today, although it is doubtful

whether under these circumstances the concept of "empire" is truly applicable. Such development is most likely to take place not in compact continental empires but in transmaritime colonial empires whose geographical structure lends itself to political decentralization.

A more perplexing problem is encountered on the historical, or evolutionary, side of the subject. On one hand it is certain that a condition of relatively extensive social homogeneity immediately preceded the present condition of national differentiations. Medieval Europe knew a greater degree of social solidarity, at least in the cultural and religious aspects of life, than does contemporary Europe. On the other hand, there seems to be evidence today that cosmopolitanism—with or without imperialism—is developing, by a natural evolutionary process, as a condition to follow the nationalistic era; and, of course, Medieval cosmopolitanism was itself preceded by a period of nationalistic rivalries and conflicts which, in turn, followed the unity and cosmopolitanism of the Roman Empire, even as the latter followed a previous condition of national independence and competition in Italy and throughout the Mediterranean basin. There has heretofore been no permanent transition from one of these forms to the other. Neither can be classed, on the record alone, as primitive, and neither as ultimate. They would appear to be two modes of human life which might be expected to persist indefinitely. We do not have here a case of alternate progress and reaction; we have, rather, a case of more or less conflicting impulses toward variety and uniformity which are permanent conditions of life. And for their reconciliation, for preventing the constant oscillation from one to the other, from a too great unity, perhaps a forced unity, of the nations, to a too great degree of conflict, even to destructive war, international organization seems to provide the best structural device.

An effective international federation would also neutralize the more active tendencies toward either empire or cosmopolitan unity. The case of empire is specially clear. In spite of the easy assumption that "there have always been empires and there will always be empires," there is reason for hoping, and tentatively believing, that we have seen the end of the age of empire. Since 1789 nationality has become an unconquerable force. The fate of efforts at world empire in the past generation can hardly be reassuring to aspiring imperialists. The burdens—political and administrative—of far-flung empire are unsupportable. There is, indeed, today, no great, powerful, and close-knit empire; even present-day Russia is far from the rigidly controlled empire which she superficially appears to be. The future—the near future, at least—belongs to the national state of medium size; it is the unit in the present problem of world order.

This still leaves the future of cosmopolitanism uncertain. Is it to be a permanent aspect of human life on this planet, existing side by side with internationalism, as already suggested; is it to supplant internatonalism;

or is it, like empire, to pass? Despite a certain suggested parallelism with the case of empire, and notwithstanding things already said which tend to suggest the conclusion that cosmopolitanism will persist but that nationalism will persist also, it seems that the outcome will be still different. Cosmopolitanism seems likely to increase and finally overshadow internationalism. Both empire and international federation are forms of the process of unifying the human race in one community. One form is defective in being positively repulsive to nationality. The other is adequate to the final result when, but only when, it is gradually transformed, by the constant modification of its internal structure, so as to leave fewer and fewer matters to national jurisdiction and to expand the world jurisdiction more and more.

In the past the process of cosmopolitanization, if it may be so called, has been retarded by inadequate means of communication, by the political and social effects of sudden shifts of great masses of people from one section of the earth to another, and by the survival of primitive instincts of combativeness derived from earlier experience. Attempts to create a world state by voluntary federation or imperial compulsion have failed either because of the coercion employed or because the cosmopolitan basis was still inadequate. Within the past hundred years, however, the factors making for cosmopolitanization have multiplied and have been developed intensively to a degree never before known. Means of communication have increased enormously; population has become more mobile and at the same time—and largely for this very reason—less likely to shift suddenly and violently; theories and ideals of coöperation have tended to supplant those of rivalry and dissension. One might almost say that the cosmopolitanizing process has become conscious and deliberate. International organization might, of course, mean more or less reduction of differences and unification of culture among the nations,[11] depending upon whether or not they desired this result and could act effectively for its attainment, and this would depend not upon whether such a result would be beneficial to the world but whether it seemed advantageous to individual nations. But modes and conditions of international life and relations have received so much attention that one may dare hope that the collapses of earlier days—the disruption of the Roman empire, the anarchy of the fourteenth century, the catastrophes of 1914 and 1939, due largely to sins of neglect and unconsciousness—will be avoided in the future.

Whatever may be the ultimate form of the world community, however, and whatever be the variations observable in the history of the past, international federation is for all present purposes the one form of world order demanding study today. Demands for something approaching unitary world organization and government, often miscalled federal union, are out of all possible reach politically and probably the

[11] See below, Chap. XIX, C.

end is undesirable in itself. We must concentrate on that position in the scale of political evolution which is both attainable and most promising. To this we may now turn. Attention must be given, first, to the economic and social bases of international relations in modern times and to the nature of the national state-system, and afterwards to the institutions and methods of international organization, directly considered. Under the last heading are to be studied the institutions of modern diplomacy, treaties and international law, international congresses and conferences, international administrative bureaus and unions, arbitration and judicial settlement, and, finally, attempts to bring together all of these partial forms of international government under one federal league.

PART I

Bases of International Organization

CHAPTER II

The Nation States of the World

The primary unit of all international politics, international law, and organized international coöperation is the national state.[1] As has been pointed out, the essential feature of this entity is the element of legal authority which is exercised by the state over its members and the persons and things within its domain, and which is exercised externally, according to the terms of international law, to be explained later, toward or against other national states. It is not strictly necessary that a state should be a national state in the fullest sense of that term before it may participate in international organization, but the tendency toward identification of state organization with national unity is today so strong that the terms nation and state may be used interchangeably without great error; in certain connections it will be necessary to distinguish between the two.

There are about seventy nations in the world.[2] That number was larger a century or two ago; it may be larger again in the future; combination and disintegration, particularly the latter, are still going on among the nations. This estimate includes states which act independently in dealing with other states in international affairs, whether or not they belong to any particular international organization, and whether or not they have received formal diplomatic recognition by all other states. It includes certain units which are formally parts of the British imperial system but which belong to international unions in their own names and deal independently with other nations, such as Canada and Australia.

Much might be said concerning the origins of the nations. Political philosophers have speculated upon this subject for centuries, and have ascribed the origin of the state to divine authorization, to compact or contract among its members, and to other rather mystical sources. Sociologists have traced the origin of the state to the primitive tribe or clan or even to the elementary human family. Cynical realists have empha-

---

[1] On the subject matter of this chapter in general see literature cited, below, Appendix B, § 2.

[2] See list of states in the world as of 1939, on p. 26, reprinted, by permission, from *American Journal of International Law*, Vol. 38 (1944), Supplement, p. 136; this list should be analyzed by the student with reference to status, (Great Powers, second class powers, small states), size (area), location, race, economic situation, and other features. The best single manual for use in a study of the world state-system is the *Statesman's Year Book*.

PRE-WAR STATES LISTED BY POPULATION

Estimate as of December 31, 1939, from League of Nations Statistical
Yearbook, 1940-41, pp. 13-18

1.	China	450,000,000	37.	Ethiopia	5,500,000
2.	India	382,000,000	38.	Chile	4,940,000
3.	USSR	172,000,000	39.	Cuba	4,253,000
4.	United States	131,416,000	40.	Switzerland	4,206,000
5.	Germany	79,700,000	41.	Denmark	3,825,000
6.	Japan	72,520,000	42.	Iraq	3,700,000
7.	Great Britain	47,735,000	43.	Finland	3,684,000
8.	Italy	43,864,000	44.	Venezuela	3,650,000
9.	France	41,950,000	45.	Bolivia	3,400,000
10.	Brazil	40,900,000	46.	Guatemala	3,260,000
11.	Poland	35,090,000	47.	Ecuador	3,000,000
12.	Spain	26,000,000	48.	Ireland	2,946,000
13.	Mexico	19,038,000	49.	Norway	2,937,000
14.	Turkey	17,620,000	50.	Haiti	2,600,000
15.	Egypt	16,680,000	51.	Liberia	2,500,000
16.	Philippines	16,300,000	52.	Lithuania	2,442,000
17.	Yugoslavia	15,703,000	53.	Uruguay	2,147,000
18.	Thailand	15,600,000	54.	Latvia	1,951,000
19.	Czechoslovakia	15,239,000	55.	El Salvador	1,745,000
20.	Iran	15,000,000	56.	Dominican Republic	1,650,000
21.	Hungary	13,500,000	57.	New Zealand	1,642,000
22.	Rumania	13,300,000	58.	Estonia	1,122,000
23.	Argentine	13,132,000	59.	Honduras	1,090,000
24.	Canada	11,368,000	60.	Albania	1,064,000
25.	So. Africa	10,251,000	61.	Paraguay	970,000
26.	Colombia	8,986,000	62.	Nicaragua	883,000
27.	Netherlands	8,834,000	63.	Costa Rica	639,000
28.	Belgium	8,396,000	64.	Panama	570,000
29.	Portugal	7,620,000	65.	Danzig	391,000
30.	Greece	7,201,000	66.	Luxemburg	301,000
31.	Peru	7,000,000	67.	Iceland	120,000
32.	Afghanistan	7,000,000	68.	Monaco	24,000
33.	Australia	6,997,000	69.	San Marino	15,000
34.	Bulgaria	6,620,000	70.	Lichtenstein	12,000
35.	Sweden	6,341,000	71.	Vatican City	1,000
36.	Nepal	5,600,000			

sized the cases where strong leaders have built up the state by their military domination. It is probably possible to discover a degree of truth in all of these analyses—at least if we interpret divine authorization to mean that which was believed or alleged to be such. But it is not very important to decide among these various explanations inasmuch as the modern state savors little of the primitive state or its creative forces.

The states of the world today, do however, reflect in rather sharp colors the concrete historical processes by which they have come into being, and a knowledge of the more recent antecedents of those states contributes much to an accurate appreciation of their respective positions in international affairs today.[3] Certain states, such as Great Britain and France, have behind them a long experience of constitutional evolution, from feudal times to the present. Many more have a background of revolution against imperial domination, as have Poland and even the United States, not to mention all the Latin-American nations. And a few trace their origins far back to primitive times in Europe, Asia, or Africa, as do Hungary, Japan, and Ethiopia. A review of the constitutional origins of any state will reveal much regarding its present position in the world of nations.

The seventy nations which we regard as constituting the state-system of the world today, however, differ almost as much in their present qualities as in their past experiences, and their present qualities are much more important to us.

The most obvious difference to be noted among the nations is the difference in size. Yet this difference is both ambiguous and deceptive. Some nations are large in area, as are Russia and Canada, but Russia is also large in population while Canada is relatively small. Some nations are large in population, as are Italy and Japan, but relatively restricted in area. Some, such as India and China, are large in both area and population, but are far less important in international affairs than are states of much smaller area and population such as Germany and even Belgium. Area and population in themselves mean little, although they may be related to the real foundations of national importance, to be considered shortly.

Mention of Belgium raises a further consideration in connection with the area and population of the nations, however, and a consideration by reference to which a new classification of the nations may be made. Certain nations—less than ten out of the seventy, as a matter of fact—are nations which possess more or less extensive colonial domains in addition to their metropolitan territories, and colonial domains which are inhabited by many millions of people.[4] This phenomenon has important bearings not only upon the question of the size of the nations but also upon their whole position in international affairs.

There is no great need to review here the historical processes by which the great colonial empires of the world have been developed. Discovery and exploration and settlement of earlier days have been followed by military conquest and cession and retrocession among the colonial powers. The missionary and the trader have played their parts. Suffice it to say that half of the earth's surface and one third of its population are held by ten or a dozen nations in the status of colonial possessions of one form or another.

The colonies held by European, American, and Asiatic powers—for Europe has not alone been the seat of colonial powers—are located

[3] See here especially Bowman, Mallory, Renner.
[4] See Moon, *Imperialism*, with modifications resulting from World War II.

chiefly in Africa and Asia. But colonial holdings are to be found also in all parts of the American continents, in Australasia, and in the isles of the seven seas. They are very largely tropical and semi-tropical in latitude and in climate and general geographic and economic character. They are held today mainly for the sake of the products in raw materials and foodstuffs which they can provide to the metropolitan markets. Their administration is a heavy burden upon the metropolitan governments and the benefits obtained are enjoyed largely by private individuals and corporations. Nevertheless, in spite of much disillusionment regarding the benefits of imperialism, the colonial powers still insist upon retaining and even, perhaps, would like to expand their holdings.

The dependencies described vary greatly in their political or legal form and relations to the metropolitan Government and in their international status.[5] They vary from the leased territory which resembles a piece of real estate leased by one party to another, and which has no international status of its own, or from the crown colony, administered directly by the metropolitan government, and forming, to all intents and purposes, an integral part of the metropolitan state, to the autonomous colony or the international protectorate, which have at least the power of internal self-government and may possess a certain degree of independence in international affairs. To such a list might be added spheres of influence and vassal states and one or two other varieties of dependencies. There is presented here a whole field of material which no student of international affairs can safely neglect.

By far the most interesting problem in the field of colonial or dependency government is provided by the system of Trusteeships under the United Nations, touching, as it does, upon the questions of international control and the future of dependencies.[6] Further notice will be taken of this system later.[7] Under it a large number of former colonial territories are to be governed by the United States and other powers under United Nations supervision. Some of these territories have already gained their independence and others are expected to follow in the not too-distant future. There are thus suggested certain developments—international control and eventual independence—in colonial status which would radically alter the present situation.

Quite apart, indeed, from the system of Trusteeships and its implications there is no reason to doubt that certain processes which were observable in the history of the world state-system during the past century will come to an end. Everywhere colonial peoples and colonies tend to become more mature and to secure their independence from the metropolitan state by revolution or peaceful constitutional development. The

[5] See Willoughby and Fenwick, entire.
[6] See, in general, Wright, on the League Mandate system, antecedent of the new Trusteeships, cited in Appendix B, § 12.
[7] Below, Chap. XIII.

process will necessarily be slow—accelerating in pace, probably, as time goes on—but in the end the surface of the earth must come to be covered entirely by independent states, and, needless to say, by independent states in much greater numbers and of much greater variety than we know today. Before that time arrives both international law and organized international coöperation must attain a far more mature form than they now boast.

The sixty non-colonial powers of the world consist mostly of second and third class powers, and include all of the twenty Latin-American states and twenty of the thirty European states. The only Great Powers to be numbered among them are those (Germany, Italy, and Japan) which lost their holdings in World War I and II, unless we regard all of the Asiatic Russian territories as integral parts of Russia itself. They are in general very critical of colonial imperialism, having themselves, for the most part, escaped from imperial domination only in modern times. At the same time it must be admitted that they do not exercise great influence in this connection.

Mention has been made of certain "Great Powers" and of other states of inferior rank. This leads us back to a discussion of the states with respect to their size and importance in the world.

An impressionistic view of the situation would probably still reveal the presence of some seven "Great Powers," namely, the United States, Great Britain, France, Italy, Japan, Germany, and Russia. There could be no great doubt as to the inclusion in such a list of the first three. Germany, Italy, and Japan labor under certain diplomatic difficulties in their international relations at present, but remain potentially great powers, in spite of economic weaknesses in the Italian position and the remoteness of Japan from the center of general international affairs. There has been some inclination to rank the United States and Russia above the other Great Powers [8] but this seems absurdly excessive in the case of Russia, superficial appearances to the contrary notwithstanding.

An analysis of the positions of the members of this group will reveal the fact that they vary considerably in area and population and that the list does not contain either China or India. Further analysis will show that the Great Powers vary greatly in military and naval strength. In short, national power is based upon a number of factors and takes many forms. Area is important only if the land is rich in resources. Resources are effective only if effectively exploited. This can be done only by a numerous population and then only if that population is industrious and well trained. The wealth of the nation, even if thus produced, will be effective in international affairs in general only if the state is well organized and the people willing to support its policies in international action. In this case, on the other hand, armies and navies may be created as needed. National power is thus a culminating product of many factors

[8] W. T. R., Fox, *The Super-Powers*, 1944

and must vary as nations rise and fall in their spiritual life as well as in accord with sheer area and numbers.

It is ordinarily deemed difficult to judge of the relative advancement or backwardness of nations, a matter closely connected with what has just been discussed. Yet to ignore this difference among the nations would be to fail seriously in any effort to understand what goes on in the world. Conditions vary greatly among the nations in respect to literacy, health, and all other indexes of social and individual well-being. Outstanding qualities in the spiritual life of certain peoples, such as the peoples of China and India, may challenge our admiration, and cast doubts upon the validity of the tests of advancement just suggested. The thought that the black man of Africa has a soul just as surely as does his white brother in London must be retained. Yet the fact remains that China and India do not play decisive parts in international affairs, and that most of Africa is under the domination of European powers. In terms of international influence the peoples of Africa and Asia, with the exception of Japan, and, to a less degree, of course, but just as surely, the peoples and states of Latin-America, are limited in comparison with the peoples and nations of North America and Europe. This may or may not be discreditable; it is one of the most important facts of international relations.

It might be possible, perhaps, in a review of the factors which make for national power, as just stated, to accept the economic factors as decisive above all others, if we include under that label both natural resources and industrial capacity. The effective organization and conduct of the state is necessary to render national economic power effective in international affairs, and an ability to exercise its rights and discharge its obligations is indispensable. But where those qualities also exist it is the economic power of the nation which makes it influential in the society of its fellows. More and more even the fighting power of a nation in time of war depends upon this factor. Industry, commerce, and finance are among the principal bases of national might.

Now the nations vary greatly in their economic status. Certain nations are predominantly industrial, as is Belgium. Certain nations are predominantly agricultural, as is Argentina. A few nations rank high in commerce and shipping, as does The Netherlands. And a limited few, of which the United States is the best but not the only example, are important from the industrial, the agricultural, and the commercial viewpoint. It is such a nation, of course, which is in a position to lead a fully independent life of its own and to dominate the international scene if it desires.

The financial strength of a nation ordinarily corresponds to its general economic status. Some nations—the newer nations, the less mature nations (from an economic viewpoint)—are debtor nations because their governments and their peoples labor under the necessity of borrowing money from persons and corporations in other countries in order to finance the development of their country and its resources. The older nations are the creditor nations whose surplus of capital accumulations constitutes a reservoir from which loans may be made to backward countries, and which serves also as a powerful basis of the international influence of those nations. This particular factor in international relations can be exaggerated as to its importance, as is often done by economists who turn to a study of international affairs, but it is certainly one of the most important phases of the situation, and a phase of the international situation which is becoming more, rather than less, important as time goes on. It has long affected formal international organization.

It is obvious that the geographical location of a nation determines to a considerable extent its economic and social character. Colonial territories and the more backward nations are what they are partly at least because they are located in the tropical areas of the world, where human activity and development is difficult, and where, on the other hand, certain raw materials such as rubber and dyestuffs and certain food stuffs such as coffee and sugar are naturally produced. The status of such territories may thus be attributed in the last analysis to their geographical location, together with certain biological facts or influences, including the effect of climate on the human stock.

Conversely, it will be found that all of the important nations are to be found in the temperate zones of the world. In modern times no great nation has arisen except in the cooler and drier parts of the globe. Certain phases of the geographical distribution of the nations seem more arbitrary. Of the seventy independent nations of the world, nearly one-half are located in the small continent of Europe. In North America only two are located above the Rio Grande River, and only three above about 15° north latitude. Only nine, at the outside, are located in Asia; only four in Africa. Only eleven are located south of the equator, most of these being found in South America. Other peculiar phases of this situation may be discovered by a study of the world map. The distribution of the nations among the continents and zones of the world is one of the most important and interesting, yet one of the most frequently neglected, phases of world politics.

The causes of this situation are many. Some of them have just been noted, in the factors of climate and social geography. Historical evolution is of great importance also. The development of Mexico and the United States and Canada as huge federations of otherwise independent states illustrates this fact. The rivalries and dissensions among the European powers are also in point. And yet even in these cases it is probably necessary to trace the forces which have produced a paucity of states in one continent and a multiplicity of states in another to the early movements of people over the face of the earth, in Europe, and to the way in which the primitive peoples of North America were supplanted by not many, but by one or two, groups of European peoples. If Frenchmen and Germans and Italians had come to North America in as large numbers as the Spaniards and the English in the sixteenth and seventeenth centuries, the present simple state-system of the North American continent might not exist.

More important today than the causes of the distribution of the nations are the results. Europe is the center and the home of international relations, international law, and international organization. It is the headquarters, so to speak, of the colony-holding powers. Even the independent nations of North and South America are tied to Europe by historical and cultural bonds which exercise great influence upon international relations. It is only in Africa and Asia that native states or peoples are naturally in position to resist European domination as something entirely foreign. This is very noticeable in practical international relations, although the fact that the American nations also have for the most part secured independence only by revolution against European imperialism results in a situation where Europe seems to be faced on all sides by a hostile world. The United States and Japan, in America and Asia respectively, are likely to be able to march with the leading powers of Europe in the general practice of international affairs.

Much has been made at one time or another of the racial and religious differences among the nations. There are some twenty-five Latin nations, some ten Slavic nations, six or seven Anglo-Saxon nations so-called, and small groups of Germanic, Scandinavian, Mongolian, and Negro nations. From time to time this factor seems to play some slight part in international relations. But the part which it plays is a constantly decreasing one. In spite of sociologists and biologists of extreme views, and in spite of racial prejudices which are often very sharp and powerful, the fact seems to be that racial differences are fading or becoming confused, and are being increasingly ignored. Racial intermixture is going on as it always has gone on, and is going on more rapidly today than ever before, as it very probably will go on more rapidly still in the future, and this whether we like it or not, and as a result not of any deliberate adoption of the idea of one unified human race but of the entirely spontaneous and unavoidable movement and intermixture of individuals of all races all over the globe. More important still for the time being is the progress of the spread of a world culture and world-wide modes of thought and feeling, a matter to be discussed more fully later. Already today the differences among the nations in race and racial psychology are far less important than the differences of interest and policy which arise out of different geographic and economic conditions, as already cited.

All this is doubly true of religious differences. Theology and ritual are not as powerful in their hold on men's minds as they were even fifty years ago. The modern study of anthropology and comparative religion has revealed too much regarding the bases of theological beliefs and religious practices to permit the nations to clash seriously over such matters. Ecclesiastical organization and rivalry still provide dangerous grounds for international friction. But in fifty years more it will probably be possible, if, indeed, it is not already possible, to forget entirely this alleged fundamental difference among the nations.

The differences among the nations in juristic and political philosophy are more important. Governmental systems are tending to become everywhere similar in substance if not in form; democratic government, whatever its merits or defects, is occupying the ground, either in the form of republics or parliamentary monarchies, everywhere in spite of temporary dictatorships—themselves often merely special forms of democracy. But the differences among the theories or principles followed regarding the nature of the state, and the place of the individual in the state, are striking and important because they bear directly upon the conduct of international relations.

Thus the states of continental Europe, particularly the Latin states, tend to emphasize, on one hand, the authority of the state and the subordination of the individual, in view, largely, of their heritage of the law of ancient Rome, while Anglo-Saxon nations, and to a certain extent Scandinavian and Germanic nations, emphasize the liberty of the individual. Again the Latin nations tend to emphasize the concept of justice or equity in government and law, the Anglo-Germanic nations positive legislation. Cutting across this alignment is the difference between the older, more crowded nations, and the newer, more sparsely populated nations, as to the degree of state control of the individual which is necessary. Finally, in several nations—not alone in Russia—socialistic principles are making such headway as to produce a sharp difference between them and the nations still devoted to individualistic capitalism. Already we see sharp and deep conflicts among the nations on these points.

All of these differences among the nations emerge in their policies or programs of action one toward another. These policies must be reviewed in a later chapter.[9] Meanwhile they must be borne in mind in thinking of the state-system of the world. It is necessary to avoid two errors in this connection. It is necessary to avoid thinking of the seventy nations of the world as entirely similar in character, as so many entirely homogeneous units in a general system. It is also necessary to avoid the conclusion that they are so dissimilar that no unified system of law and organization can be developed among them; history shows this to be an exaggeration and the remaining chapters in this work should do likewise.

If space permitted we might well review here the various types of boundaries or frontiers which separate the nations, boundaries based on political events, geographic factors, economic considerations, linguistic differences, or military calculations. The geographical features which

[9] Below, Chap. IV.

really separate people are few—oceans, deserts, high mountains,—and most
state boundaries, internal as well as external, are extremely artificial and
unnatural. We shall have to include this problem in our study of the
state-system merely by reference.[10] There has been noticeable in recent
years some disposition to fix the location of boundaries by the mere
choice of the people concerned, rather than by reference to historic or
military considerations. But this practice has not gone very far as yet,
and it runs counter to the tendency toward objective scientific treatment
of governmental problems on grounds of geography and economics
which is somewhat noticeable also. It is still too early to discern the outcome in this direction.

[10] See Jones, entire.

CHAPTER III

International Intercourse, Private International Organization, Cosmopolitanism

Among the nations of the world the first and basic type of relationship and activity to develop is that interchange of commodities and cultural contributions in general which we call international intercourse. This activity leads into a form of international organization which is private or unofficial in character, and also into that form of worldwide culture and activity which we call cosmopolitanism.

It is impossible to indulge in any extensive description of modern international intercourse here.[1] Such intercourse takes the form of railway and steamship travel and trade; the exchange of postal matter, including parcel post matter; telegraphic and telephonic communication, by wire and by radio; financial transactions; news service; and the exchange of the products of art, literature, music, and science, in an ever increasing volume. An examination of any compilation of statistics concerning the activities of the nations and their peoples will reveal how widely and how deeply this development has already extended and how rapidly it expands year by year. Individuals in all nations are enabled to exchange ideas and commodities and even services by the many facilities provided by the modern world. Such intercourse is international only in being conducted across national lines but it constitutes a broad and substantial foundation for all the more mature forms of international relations.

One result is the appearance of private international associations of all sorts. To this we now turn.[2] Decades, and even centuries, before the national states were willing to join in any extensive formal coöperation, private persons were ready and eager to associate their activities across national frontiers. Private commercial and financial organizations crossing national boundaries date back to the early days of modern Europe, not to mention, for the moment, the great religious orders of a still earlier period, and while organizations conducted for direct pecuniary profit may later have to be left aside mainly for reasons of convenience they may be noted here as prototypes.

In the narrower sense, however, private associations have made their appearance in the world more recently and more slowly. Not until the nineteenth century did these private associations begin to multiply in the form in which we now find them. Prior to that time there had been

[1] See, below, Appendix B, § 3a.
[2] On private international associations see literature cited, below, Appendix B, § 3b.

35

private associations extending over various nations, but these earlier associations were not organized on the international principle. The later associations, while private and unofficial in composition, have taken the national state system as their foundation and structural standard. Indeed, it is chiefly in this sense that they are "international" at all.

Statistical information regarding the exact dates of organization of these associations is lacking. The reason is obvious: in their beginnings these bodies were relatively inconspicuous. Only at a later stage, when the association had attained a position of influence, was it given a place in the annals of international life.

A thousand or more such organizations exist today, apparently, and certain figures are available relating to the number of meetings held by these associations which reveal the state of affairs in this field with a fair degree of accuracy. Thus, during the decade 1850-59 there were held some eighteen meetings of private international bodies. During the decade 1880-89 there were over two hundred and seventy such meetings. During the first decade of the present century the number rose almost to the thousand mark, and when war broke out in 1914 meetings were being held at a rate which promised to exceed that of the preceding decade. Then the defects of official international organization permitted the breakdown of 1914 to occur and to interrupt the normal course of events. After World War I this activity was gradually resumed and expanded still further.[3]

In a very literal sense it is possible to say that these private associations cover every field, every nook and corner, of human endeavor. A comprehensive list of the private international organizations now covering the globe is a revelation.[4] Science is represented by the International Association of Medicine and the Institute of International Law; art by the International Institute of Public Art; religion by the Y. M. C. A., the World Church Alliance, and other bodies. In different fields we have the Olympic Games Committee, the International Congress for the Protection of Animals, the Interparliamentary Conference, and, in the world of industry and commerce, the International Congress of Chambers of Commerce, the International Association for the Legal Protection of

[3] Table of meetings of private international organizations 1840-1914:

1840-1849	10
1850-1859	18
1860-1869	64
1870-1879	139
1880-1889	272
1890-1899	475
1900-1909	985
1910-1914	458

"Historical Light on the League to Enforce Peace" in W. P. F., *Pamph. Ser.*, Vol. VI, No. 6, 22-23 (December, 1916), and Krehbiel, 136, citing *La Vie Internationale*, 1908-1909, I, 175. Statistics are lacking for the period 1919-1939; it is reliably estimated that such meetings occurred in the early 1930's to the number of 200-250 per year.
[4] *Handbook of International Organizations*, in general.

Laborers, various international labor and socialist bodies, and many private capitalist organizations. If we explore farther we encounter such oddities as the International Petrol Commission, the General Association of Hotel Keepers, the International Congress of the Deaf and Dumb, the International Association of Copper Chemists, and the International Cynological Federation. No important—or unimportant—aspect of human life is unrepresented.

There is much variety in form among these private international associations, but two types may be singled out with a fair degree of distinctness, namely, the federalistic association and the unified business concern.

The federalistic association is made up of national units, joined in a federal system, under a constitution defining the membership and structure of the association. The association holds conferences at intervals of a year or more—sometimes less—attended by delegates representing the national units; papers are read and there is general discussion of various subjects of interest to the members. The results are summed up in a set of printed proceedings, including, perhaps, a set of resolutions, copies of which may be forwarded to national governments and international organs if this seems useful. In addition, the association usually maintains a central office or bureau to look after its administrative and clerical work.

These wide-spreading associations built on the federalistic plan are, as has been said, of recent growth. More elementary in form are the great business houses with partners and share-holders in different nations, with branches all over the world, and with activities extending to all the continents and all the seven seas. It does not seem that these organizations —Standard Oil, North German Lloyd, Havas Agency—should be entirely disregarded in this study merely because they aim at direct pecuniary profit while other organizations only aim at indirect benefits; at the same time they are obviously in a class by themselves. The national state-system is respected by such organizations in their activities just as far as it is necessary to do so, but it is commonly merely utilized as a convenient tool.

The organization of capitalists and employers into world-wide trusts and syndicates has had its response in the development of the international trade union. Such is the World Federation of Trade Unions. It is not for any philosophical or idealistic reason that such bodies are created. No attachment to the abstract or humanitarian idea of international organization caused the employers and the bankers and the manufacturers to combine in one international association or another. International combination was perceived to be good business. So with the international labor bodies; a prosaic calculation of the advantage and benefits to be derived dictated their formation. The testimony here borne to the advantages of international coöperation is especially sincere.

As between the two, the employers and the financial and commercial interests have developed their organizations further and with more conviction than the workers. Nationalism is an affair of the middle classes largely, a bourgeois idea. The great capitalist has little of it to bother him, the common laborer likewise. But the latter may be aroused by appeals to his passions, and the skilled worker is petty bourgeois in his own way. At all events the international labor bodies are not as cohesive and do not run as smoothly as the international banking firms. Furthermore, it is the employers and financial and commercial chieftains who are able to prevail upon the official states to recognize them and to give them support. Where international coöperation is asked for in the name of labor it is not always regarded as reasonable and practical, but rather utopian. Economic considerations prompt the creation and development of international organization in the first place, and the relative economic power of different interests in society determines the share which each shall enjoy in the development of official international organization dealing with these matters.

There are no questions of power or authority to be raised in connection with the private international organizations. Questions of internal jurisdiction do exist—as between the component national bodies and the international associations—but no questions which project themselves into the realm of public law or affect the national states. For these organizations are not official, and they rest not upon a foundation of public authority but upon voluntary private coöperation.

There are significant differences of interest among the different classes of private international organizations.

The commercial concerns,—exporters and importers and shipping syndicates,—the international news agencies, and similar bodies, desire to see a rapid and extensive development of free international communication and trade. They thrive in proportion as international trade, travel, and communication are freed from nationalistic restrictions, vexatious discriminations, dangers of interference, and national monopolistic controls in the form of tariffs, exclusive patent and copyright laws, and similar devices. In a broad sense, they are all for free trade.

The international bankers, so-called, are in a similar position. Dealing as they do in international exchange and foreign credit, they desire to see the world credit structure developed and strengthened, and to that end they desire, above all, peace and order among the nations. An attempt was once made to show that certain world banking interests, by stimulating international jealousies, have managed to sell credit to many nations at once to finance war preparations one against another, thus creating an invisible empire of debt over them all.[5] This may or may not be true in general and it may have been true in the past. Certainly it can apply to few concerns today; certainly it is not applicable to the great majority of banking concerns dealing in international credit. And even

[5] See also works cited, below, Appendix B, § 10b.

where it is applicable the outbreak of war is not the thing desired, but the preparation for it, and the outbreak might still be dreaded for its effect upon existing national credit. Public financing for war and for military preparations is so gigantic today that private concerns do not, and could not, handle it except in a minor and auxiliary fashion. The states prefer to sell bonds in public at lower rates of interest than they would be compelled to pay to private concerns, thus also enlisting popular support and enthusiasm. At all events, everything goes to show that, in actual fact, the international banking houses are now internationalistic in their outlook.

Great manufacturing concerns, drawing upon world-wide sources of supply and selling in world-wide markets, take the same position. Freedom of trade and peace on the seas is their desire.

So for the labor organizations, especially in Europe. To mention but a single consideration, their members may have to depend on temporary migrations from country to country in search of work and they naturally want international protection in their wanderings.

On the other hand, manufacturing concerns enjoying a national monopoly of one sort or another, labor groups enjoying a similar fixed advantage over other groups, and banking houses confining their activities to national financial activities—in other words, organizations which are not so much international as polynational, with branches in different countries—are usually active in opposition to the development of internationalism and cosmopolitanism. They oppose free trade, free migration, and the establishment of international bureaus to control and adjust national competitive activities. International coöperation appears to them to be either positively dangerous or, at least, foolish and unnecessary, depending upon whether their advantage is natural or depends upon national legislation. All they demand in the international field is freedom to sell their goods abroad.

As a matter of fact, this small measure of freedom can hardly be obtained except by international reciprocity and agreement. And, finally, even industries enjoying nationalistic protection find it expensive to pay for such legislative protection and are often led to a manœuver which eventually lands them in the other camp. By the premises of the problem, there are competitive supplies of material and labor in foreign lands. The simplest remedy is, therefore, to set up a branch in that place and rise superior to the national state system. Indeed, such concerns not infrequently expand in this way and end by becoming powerful enough to dictate to the national government. Private international organization becomes so complete and adequate as to be able to dispense with official help. Indeed, as will presently appear, it may turn out to be profitable for the concern, because of its peculiar interests, to oppose official internationalism, itself indulging in private internationalism all the while. This is due to the fact that the states have neglected to keep up with the development of world civilization and have forced private interests to launch into the international field independently.

One other form of private international activity deserves passing notice. From time to time since 1850 there have been held at one important city or another a number of international expositions or world fairs, beginning with the exhibition at the Crystal Palace in London in 1851 and continuing at the present time. Paris, Vienna, Philadelphia, Brussels, Melbourne, Chicago, and numerous other cities have been the scenes of these huge international symposiums.[6] In addition, hundreds and thousands of smaller fairs have been held, especially in the cities of Europe, where exhibits from abroad are invited, although the fair is organized as a national event. Such were the fairs frequently held at Leipzig and Birmingham. The international expositions proper enjoy a semi-official standing and the national governments send official exhibits and encourage private exhibitors to participate on behalf of the nation. The result is a composite picture of world civilization at the time.

As has been pointed out, the motives underlying the formation of these private international bodies are motives of business advantage and pecuniary benefit. The result is that, once established, such associations make every effort to secure advantages for themselves and to secure satisfaction for the interests which they embody. This means, in most cases, bringing pressure to bear on the official national governments with this in view. The resolutions of the International Congress of Chambers of Commerce are not communicated to the President of the United States purely as a compliment, but in the hope that they may commend themselves to him for support. The international business house does not hesitate to carry its case to the government of the state in which it is located or to the governments of all the states in which it has active interests.

This sort of activity is of great present importance. The foreign policies of national governments are not a little influenced by the representations and pleadings of special international interests. The policy of the United States toward certain countries has in the past been influenced to some degree by the international missionary movement and by the international oil interests. The American attitude toward Russia at times has been influenced by both commercial and labor groups. Labor organizations have not been without their influence in the international relations of the past few years.

The most spectacular case of this kind is that of the international

[6] A partial table of such expositions follows:

1851 London	1880 Melbourne	1904 St. Louis	1933 Chicago
1855 Paris	1888 Melbourne	1905 Liége	1939 San Francisco
1867 Paris	1889 Paris	1910 Brussels	1939-1940 New York
1873 Vienna	1893 Chicago	1915 San Francisco	
1876 Philadelphia	1900 Paris	1926 Philadelphia	
1878 Paris	1901 Buffalo	1929 Barcelona	

armament firms. For a concern to maintain and operate factories for the manufacture of war materials in five or six nations at the same time and to continue to supply these materials to the different national governments while they are at war one with another, distributing the profits among its share-holders of one nationality or another, seems somewhat anomalous. For Englishmen to derive financial profit from ammunition sold to Germany seems dubious. The accusation is raised that war is encouraged by such concerns because of the sales it brings. Englishmen and Germans so interested are accused of bringing on war between their countries for the excess profits obtainable thereby. War scares are, it is said, worked up because of the extra contracts which result therefrom.[7]

A great deal of this criticism is undoubtedly sound, and the private manufacture of arms has been clearly recognized as "open to grave objections" on this score.[8] The most sensational charges have repeatedly been made, seldom denied, and proved to the hilt as far as anything can be proved by circumstantial evidence. And during World War I the French Government practically admitted that it had determined its military policy partly by reference to the representations of certain German-French iron interests holding mineral properties in Lorraine.[9] There is no room for doubt that private international concerns manufacturing arms have to some degree impeded the development of international peace and coöperation. To say that international peace societies have exerted an opposite influence is not to say very much, for the people engaged in the former sort of activity possess ten times the power and influence possessed by the peace people.

The activity of private international interests is going on continually. In all directions private international organizations were revived after World War I, were carried forward, or were organized to meet some new need. The same sort of revival is taking place today.

At times the private international activities here described develop into something quite unlike that from which they start. In such a movement there is present an element which constitutes a distinct departure from what has gone before. Private international bodies do not have a great deal of patience with the national state system. They tolerate it or utilize it as best they can. They are more concerned with association on the basis of the interest to be served—science, art, religion, business, or what not—and they are inclined to ignore national lines. As in the case cited above they often cut across such lines rather brusquely. They are inclined, that is, to develop a distinctly cosmopolitan outlook, which is a decisive turn in the evolution of world society.

This development serves to bring out very clearly the essential relations between internationalism and cosmopolitanism. On one hand pri-

---

[7] See literature, below, Appendix B, § 10, b.
[8] *Covenant of the League of Nations*, Art. VIII, Par. 5.
[9] Streit, *Where Iron is There is the Fatherland*, especially pp. 43-45.

vate interests are not averse to obtaining satisfaction through the mechanism of the national governments if this is possible, and they often call upon the latter for recognition, approval, and support, thereby manifesting a willingness to become part of the national and international system. But if satisfaction is denied the former position is likely to be resumed and the existing national states and governments will probably be ignored and even defied. Cosmopolitanism as a condition is, in point of fact, at once a support for and an encouragement to internationalism on one side and a threat and a menace on the other side. So long as the national governments strive by international coöperation to satisfy the substantive interests involved, the development of world trade, world science—world civilization, in short—can only stimulate and strengthen the system of national states and the fabric of international relations among them. Let the governments manifest an obstinate attachment to extreme nationalism, however, and attempt to ignore the facts, arrest the march of social and political evolution, and shut their eyes to the realities of world life today, and the world's life will simply pass by on its own course.

Most of the activity of the private international organizations just described touches, as has been seen, only remotely the official life of the states; the greater part of private internationalism exists and functions with scant reference to the system of national states. National lines are at times recognized for the sake of mechanical convenience, at times they are simply ignored as irrelevant to the business in hand, and at times they are deliberately set aside as antiquated obstacles to the proper and natural growth of world civilization. In other words cosmopolitanism bids fair to exert a profound influence upon the international relations of the future.[10]

Cosmopolitanism consists essentially of the action of one or more individuals in thinking and living according to tastes or aims apart from legal nationality. It leads to a unity based on elements which, except by accident, have little to do with nationality; it is a supernationality. The individuals join together for coöperative action in associations which do not greatly take into account the otherwise distinct nations. Such cosmopolitanism is, of course, quite distinct from internationalism. If completely developed, it would supersede internationalism entirely.

Cosmopolitanism may develop within one nation as well as among or above several nations. Ordinarily cosmopolitanism appears as liberation and unification of individuals legally members of distinct states but having interests in common irrespective of their diverse citizenship. In certain cases, however, as where a state diverges from the standard type of national state and embraces within its confines several nationalities, cosmopolitanism may be intra-national, or intra-state. This is notably true in all imperial states. Ancient Rome and the Holy Roman Empire of the

[10] On modern cosmopolitanism see literature cited, below, Appendix B, § 3c.

Middle Ages, to mention only two illustrations, produced a cosmopolitanism within their bosoms more pronounced and self-conscious than anything of the kind which the world was to know for some time afterwards. In that cosmopolitanism was found a measure of justification for the imperial domination. Under the sway of the Emperor unity of culture and feeling was achieved and the conflicts of national spirit were quieted. Unfortunately for the picture, however, this imperial cosmopolitanism was not entirely natural and spontaneous, but was imposed by authority from above; and such is an element frequently present in imperial cosmopolitanism. To be genuine, cosmopolitanism must come by a natural disappearance of nationalism, not by its destruction at the hands of imperial masters.

The cosmopolitanism of our day differs somewhat, as is obvious, in its bases and foundations, from that of earlier periods, and the prospects of its continuation and development are affected by that difference. Modern cosmopolitanism is built upon more solid foundations. Some of the older elements remain, but, in general, the world civilization of today is unlike that of Antiquity or the Middle Ages, and equally unlike that of eighteenth-century Europe.

To be sure, the "unity of Christendom" still means something, at least in continental Europe and Latin America. In Great Britain and North America it is felt to a less degree, as the religious temper becomes milder and secular ideals replace older feelings of piety and devotion. A similar phenomenon—a religious cosmopolitanism—exists in the Mohammedan world and in Buddhist Asia. But the distinct existence of these three great groups, and of the great subdivisions in the Christian world—Orthodox, Roman, and Protestant—lowers the importance of this effect. Religion is hardly strong enough, and certainly not sufficiently unified, in this day and age to produce a world society. Indeed, such cosmopolitanism as exists is somewhat cynical and skeptical of the religion which is too often tribal and nationalistic in its origin and employment.

Of legal unity Europe still knows something, at all events continental Europe west of Budapest. The Civil Law,—the law of Rome in modern form,—obtains in Madrid and Paris alike, in Berlin and in Bern, in Brussels and in Rome. Similarly, the Civil Law governs private rights and obligations in all of Latin America, in Louisiana, in Quebec. This, however, is only part of the story. As in the field of religion, so here it is necessary to note that Great Britain and North America are under the English Common Law, that Eastern Europe lives under Slavic law, and that many parts of Asia and Africa possess many indigenous legal systems of their own. Added to this is the fact that, even where supposedly common legal systems exist, the practice of constituent and statutory law-making has so worked upon and made over the historically received private law as to produce endless variations among the nations. And it is curious to notice that it is in connection with this particular legislative activity, which has largely destroyed the inherited comopolitanism based on the Civil Law, that a new legal cosmopolitanism may be expected as a result of deliberate imitation and concurrent legislative action. This leads us forward to the true bases of modern cosmopolitanism.

The principal element in modern cosmopolitanism, as it has developed since 1850, is a common economic and scientific culture.

The facts are familiar to every observer. With the introduction of steam and electricity, travel and the transportation of goods have become enormously easier, cheaper, and more rapid. The communication of information by post, telegraph, and telephone and the shipping of printed matter has been expanded and speeded up to a point unimagined a half-century ago. The commercial market of even the small manufacturer has become a world-market. Raw materials and labor come from places where they are plentiful to lands where exists the capital to put them to use; or capital, increasingly mobile in the hands of the international banking organizations, is transmitted in vast amounts to places where the materials and labor already exist. The manufactured product is carried by a world transportation system to all corners of the globe, so standardized and labeled that a merchant in Calcutta whose credit is attested by the credit agencies, and who probably maintains relations with an American house in New York, may buy automobiles in Detroit by post or telegraph and rely on the results of his action with some confidence. This means a new world, as compared with the world of the twelfth century, or even the world of the seventeenth.

The basic causes for this commercial revolution, comparable only with the commercial revolution of the thirteenth, fourteenth, and fifteenth centuries, are scientific inventions, such as steam locomotion on sea and land, and the electric telegraph. The railroad, the steamship, and the telegraph have reorganized the world.

With these must be grouped several other devices, of less importance by themselves, but influential as subsidiaries of the major inventions of Watt and Edison. Such are the decimal metric system, the standardization of time on the basis of Greenwich, England,—a result accomplished by formal international treaty, it may be noted,—the perfection of a system of maritime signals, and so on. The Gregorian calendar, long used generally in Europe and America, has finally been adopted in Russia and is establishing itself in Asia. The English, German, Spanish and French languages, especially English and Spanish, are making great headway in all parts of the world as the commonly accepted languages of commerce. These devices, and numerous others, all contribute to the support of a world economy possible only with free and complete communication and intercourse.

The results are manifest in many quarters, and are recognized by the most careful and competent authorities. The private scientific and economic associations just reviewed are based upon this foundation. As a result of these forces many private organizations and corporations are being recognized in public international law and treaty agreements and become units in the official international system. These acts of recognition in their turn help to intensify modern cosmopolitanism; the recognition of such world unity as exists leads to steps which increase that unity, and thus the whole process is accelerated.

The cosmopolitanism of our day is always making its appearance at unexpected places. In all directions this new cosmopolitanism of travel, communication, industry, commerce, and finance is developing and exerting an influence upon the international relations of the world. It is bound to go on increasing, as the means of communication become further perfected and the interchange of ideas and the generalization of world culture are intensified. It provides a firm basis for international coöperation. It also constitutes a threat that, failing international coöperation, the nations will be overrun against their will by a unified world civilization. Eventually, the cosmopolitan is heard to say, there will no longer be any "nations," even as there were none in Medieval Europe. Artificial political and legal distinctions—and the cosmopolitan is inclined to regard all political and legal distinctions as unreal—must be eliminated, and the world become one. If this is chimerical or undesirable, the alternative is international coöperation,—which itself, however, helps to develop cosmopolitanism!

CHAPTER IV

International Politics

After the phenomena of international intercourse, which have already been cited,[1] and the activities flowing therefrom, the simplest form of relationship which arises among the nations is that which may be designated by the term international politics.[2] Indeed, seeing that international intercourse is carried on chiefly by private individuals and groups of individuals, and gives rise merely to private international association and a cosmopolitan culture among individuals, it may be said that international politics constitutes the very simplest form of official international relationship. At the same time it should be remembered that official international political relations do originate very largely from the private international intercourse among the peoples of the various countries.

International politics is a form of relationship and activity which consists of the interactions, the relationships of conflict and coincidence, among the foreign policies of the nations, and the responses on the part of the nations to which these interactions lead. Every nation of importance is naturally led to formulate a program of action toward other nations; this program may be called the national program of foreign policy; and international politics arises from interacting foreign policies. It is somewhat amorphous and intangible and very complicated in content, but of utmost importance for the student of international organization, besides being of great interest in itself.

Two other phrases and the concepts to which they refer may usefully be distinguished here from the concept of international politics.

Thus we may profitably notice the more general idea of "international relations" in order to set it aside as too broad to be of service in a study of international organization. The "relations" among the nations are of all types, economic, political, and finally institutional. The economic and cultural relations of the nations we have noted under the title of international intercourse; their formal intergovernmental relations we shall study under the specific title of international organization or organized international coöperation. The political relations among the nations, visualized as conflict and coincidence of their national foreign policies, are what we study in this chapter.

Similarly we shall set aside the concept of "world politics." There is in fact little or no unity in the world of nations in matters of policy.

[1] Above, Chap. III, beginning.
[2] For references see, below, Appendix B, § 4.

The phrase might be employed to refer in the broadest possible way to all sorts of political matters in the world at large, such as questions of policy, comparative government and law, and inter-governmental coöperation, but as such it is entirely too indefinite to be of service. And although there are a few policies or principles of action, such as the principles of the balance of power and the open door in colonial territories, which may seem to be of general world significance, the fact is that most principles of political action in the world, including the two just mentioned, are items in the foreign policy programs of individual nations. The community of nations does not yet possess many principles of political action except such as have been incorporated into formal international law, which will be noted in due season. There are few accepted concepts of international ethics. The policies of the world of nations are national policies, and the politics of the world are international politics.

In order to obtain an adequate understanding of international politics we should begin by a study of the foundations of the foreign policy programs of the individual nations and pass thence to a survey of those programs themselves.[3] In the circumstances of the life of each nation [4] are to be found the sources and foundations of the programs of action toward other nations which each nation works out for itself. The physical and spiritual conditions of national life—land and resources, climate, people, culture and traditions—determine its foreign policies, with individual leaders and parties playing only a ministerial rôle in bringing these forces to articulate expression.

It is obviously impossible to attempt to give here any such survey. The student who desires to understand American foreign policy or Italian foreign policy, or the policy program of any country, must undertake an examination of the circumstances of national life in and for each country, and an examination of the policy program of each country by itself. We shall devote the remainder of this chapter to a study of the way in which the policies of various nations may come into conflict or coincide, and of certain questions and geographical areas on the earth with respect to which such clashes and coincidence are most likely to occur. In basic policies the nations are alike, as in protection of citizens abroad, and of these matters no more will be said; it is the cases of conflict which give rise to problems and make trouble.

Thus the policies of maritime nations are likely to clash with those of continental powers.[5] A nation which possesses an extensive coast line and a large mercantile marine, such as Great Britain, will desire to maintain a large navy. It will desire to see the rules of international law developed in such a way as to make defense of its coasts and utilization of the

[3] See article cited above, p. 7, n. 5, and references to literature therein, at pp. 61-64.
[4] Above, Chap. II.
[5] See Potter, *Freedom of the Seas*, Chaps. X-XI.

waters off its coasts by its own people secure. It will desire to see the rules governing maritime navigation developed so as to facilitate that activity. It will desire to see the rules of maritime warfare developed in such a way as to give full scope to its naval power in time of war.

The continental state, such as France, with extensive land frontiers and a large army, will desire to see the powers of the great naval state curtailed, the rights of belligerents on land extended, and the rules regarding international relations on land formulated in such a way as to protect its interests in that direction. No more fundamental cleavage in policy can be found among the nations than this cleavage between maritime and continental powers.

It is obvious that certain nations, such as the United States, being both great maritime states and great continental powers as well, must often be placed in an ambiguous position both as to their sympathies and antipathies toward other nations and as to the contents of their own policy programs. Continental states tend to be isolationist in policy, maritime states internationalist; from 1774 to the present time the United States has vacillated between these two points of view. In the presence of national weakness such a position is very dangerous; combined with national strength it is a source of maximum advantage.

Other such fundamental clashes of policy might be cited in great numbers. The overpopulated state, such as Italy, will have one policy regarding emigration and immigration; the underpopulated state, such as Brazil, another; at times two thickly populated states, such as Italy and pre-1914 Germany, will find that their policies of encouraging emigration from their own territories and immigration into the territories of other nations will clash because of their very similarity. Likewise two underpopulated states, such as Canada and Argentina, may be found rivaling one another to secure immigrants from other nations, who may, in turn, be opposed to permitting emigration to either. Nations which follow identical but non-competitive policies (relaxed passport restrictions, e.g.) for benefit of their own nationals may coöperate therein.

Space does not permit us to pass in review other such conflicts of policy. On the privileges of aliens, powers of diplomatic and consular agents, freedom of navigation and trade, customs tariffs, nationality, and a hundred other topics, the nations clash so sharply and deeply in their policies that it often seems doubtful whether any unified system of international law and organization is possible in the world.

We must notice, however, the fact that certain nations are naturally thrown together in matters of policy, and this not merely because they are both or all placed in the same circumstances of national life. All immigrant-receiving nations tend to have similar policies, it is obvious; even so, as has just been seen, such policies may clash. Similarly, nations placed in most diverse circumstances may find themselves thrown into one another's arms for special reasons; thus the agricultural nation and the industrial nation stand in a complementary relationship, one toward another, as do the United States and Cuba. Close relations of give and take may readily develop between such countries. The result may be a certain degree of hostility toward other nations which seek privileges in the ports or the markets of one or the other. When, in addition, as is frequently the case, the partners in such an alignment are unequal in power, and the dominant partner seeks to perpetuate the arrangement for its own profit, the resultant effect on general international harmony may be serious.

It is not to be imagined, of course, that national policies remain forever fixed. Nothing is more familiar to the persistent observer of international politics than to discover a nation demanding today what it repudiated yesterday, and the other way around. Nor is this to be attributed always to vacillations of purpose within the nation. The rise and fall of parties may, indeed, produce such results, and, quite apart from any artificial dogmas anent the desirability of continuity in foreign policy, nothing is much more disastrous for the smooth running of international political relations than arbitrary alterations in national foreign policy which are made as incidents in domestic party warfare. But the changes which take place in national foreign policies may be traced in a deeper sense to changes in the circumstances in the national life or in the international situation, the fundamental principles of national foreign policy remaining unchanged. Indeed, it may be discovered with little effort that in most of the problems which arise in its foreign affairs a nation is so bound by the fundamental principle of protecting and promoting the interests of its people in accordance with circumstances as they exist in the world, that not only are its principles predetermined for it in the beginning, but also the changes which must be made in these principles from time to time are determined for it as well.

A second basis of reference on which international politics might be studied is to be found in the individual great topics of international relations, such as raw material distribution, or disarmament.

The raw materials of industry and the supplies of food-stuffs available for human consumption are distributed very unevenly among the nations. Some have supplies of one sort of raw materials or food-stuffs, but not of another; some have materials but no food; others, food but no materials. The result is great variation among national policies on different phases of the problem of the distribution of raw materials and food.

Thus a nation with large mineral resources but no food will desire to control closely the exploitation and exportation of its minerals, and will attempt to secure full and free importation of food supplies. The nation with few raw materials will attempt to secure supplies of such materials, and perhaps, especially if lacking in food stuffs also, be disposed to move for international regulation of the distribution of such supplies, a step to which the nation which has plentiful supplies will be indifferent and even hostile if it desires to use its supplies in order to bargain for compensating benefits. The future will continue to witness many struggles on this matter, and many sharply conflicting points of view among the nations have already been revealed.

On no subject, probably, are clashes of national policy so sharp and bitter as on the problem of armaments. Formerly each nation was left to decide upon this question without international discussion, but in the past thirty years the topic has become a common theme of international debate and negotiation.

The conflicting views of the maritime and the continental nations have already been mentioned. The armament policies of nations located among many other nations in the heart of Europe, such as France, differ from those of nations located at some distance from that center of international conflicts, such as the Latin American countries. The policy of a nation with extensive trade connections and colonial holdings, such as Great Britain, differs from that of a nation whose whole life is or may be lived within its own boundaries, such as Russia. The nation which is still struggling to build up its economic life will economize on armaments; the older, wealthier nation need not do so. Finally, the very fact that other, greater, neighboring nations, which may be called on for aid in time of need, or whose larger armaments make any attempt to rival them impossible, exist, may lead smaller nations, such as Denmark, to abandon any serious attempt at heavy armament in just those circumstances wherein it would seem most natural and right.

The results are seen when any attempt is made to secure agreement among the nations for disarmament, however slight. Special interests are alleged in justification of existing armaments or as grounds for still greater armaments than those held at the time. Aspects of the international political situation are revealed the existence of which would never have been suspected unless brought to light in this way. It is probably safe to say that on this subject, even more than on migration or raw materials, are the clashes of national policy most acute.

It should be added that at certain points clashes of policy occur which seem almost wholly historical and adventitious in origin. Certain nations come to support certain policies and come to regard those policies as having a traditional sanctity just because they have been supported by that nation for a long stretch of time, as is the case with the French policy of friendship with Turkey. The fundamental material bases of those policies may usually be discovered by a thorough study of the situation. But the circumstances may have altered while the policy is retained, unreasonable as that may be. Or the policy may come to be regarded as having a certain moral value in itself, irrespective of the considerations which produced it. It is when we encounter clashes among policies of this sort that we seem to be in contact with international politics in its most characteristic form. Realistic views of the situation

are replaced by considerations of tradition, of national dignity and prestige, of international rivalry pure and simple. We then find the conflict
among the nations most unreasoning and uncompromising.

Finally, we should notice something which might be expected, the
influence of geography upon national policy being what it is, namely
that certain areas on the earth's surface are particularly important from
the point of view of international rivalry. A study of certain such regions
will serve to complete our introduction to the field of international
politics.

The whole continent of Africa constituted such a theater of international politics from 1870 to the outbreak of war in 1914, and does still
to a certain extent. Spain was pushing into the continent from the Northwest. France was pushing down from the North into the whole Sahara
region. She made contact with the British in Egypt and in the Sudan.
Britain and France and Belgium and Portugal were all struggling for
power in Central Africa. Later Italy began to assert herself in the North,
between France and Britain, and in the Northeast, while Germany interjected herself into the scene in the Southwest and East Central region.
The whole continent was the battle-ground of European national policies
of the simplest type, namely, policies of territorial aggrandizement.
While the situation has been stabilized to a certain extent today, there
are still scores of points on the map of Africa at which policies and activities conceived in London, Paris, Rome, and elsewhere, come into
conflict.

A similar situation exists and has long existed in the Far East, from
Sakhalin Island to Hongkong. Russia had thrust an arm across Siberia
to Vladivostok, Japan was laying hands upon Sakhalin, Korea, Man-
churia, and Mongolia. China was struggling to preserve her territorial
and political integrity, and Western European powers—Great Britain,
France, and others—were establishing scattered but extensive holdings
along the coast of that unhappy country from Port Arthur to Hongkong. Again the situation was produced not so much by the clash of
policies differing in aim and character as by the rivalry among the nations for opportunity to apply the same policies, namely policies of
economic exploitation, political domination, and territorial aggrandizement. Perhaps for that very reason the conflict was, as it still is to a
large degree, all the more serious; policies of different character may
conceivably be reconciled and adjusted, one to another, but the same
policy, when it is a policy which is exclusive and monopolistic in character, can hardly be applied by two nations at the same time and place.

It is quite true that in both Africa and the Far East a certain ameliora-
tion of the situation of conflict among the nations has been achieved.
Upon the more general aspects of this development more will be said
shortly. At present it will suffice to note that by such a process certain
areas, once highly contentious in character, may be given a more normal

tone. Just as certain items in the national foreign policy program may wax and wane in importance, and certain topics in international relations constitute matters of bitter contention at one time but not at another, so areas of conflict on the earth's surface may become more or less important in this respect as decades and centuries pass. The valleys of the Mississippi and the St. Lawrence provide illustrations of areas once of the utmost importance in international politics, now of little or no importance at all.

We have so far dealt with areas very wide in extent, and areas in which several nations come into conflict because of their various avenues of approach. Such areas resemble in nature the general world theater of international conflict, through the whole length and breadth of which this sort of thing is going on.

Of another character are the relatively isolated spots where two nations maintain some bitter conflict over a highly specific point. Alsace and Lorraine have provided one such case, although here, as is true in not a few of the cases such as we are now discussing, the highly specific conflict made part of a larger area of conflict as a whole. The Suez Canal, the Tyrolean passes, Gibraltar, the Rio Grande boundary, the mouth of the La Plata River provide better illustrations of this type of danger spot in political geography. Great Britain holds the Suez in order to secure her route to India, and she holds Gibraltar for similar reasons, in spite of opposition which has been offered at one time or another by Turkey, France, Germany, and Spain. Italy and Austria have clashed for decades at the Brenner pass; indeed for centuries this passage-way from Germanic Europe into the Italian peninsula has been a bone of contention in the international politics of Central Europe. And if the Rio Grande and the La Plata have not provided the world with scenes and events quite as dramatic as have the danger spots of the old world they have been none the less crucial in American international politics. It seems that it is such points as these, rather than the fields on which military engagements have been fought, that deserve the title of the international battlegrounds of the world.

More important still are certain areas of land or sea which are not as broad and general as those first discussed in this connection, but which are nevertheless broad enough to include more points of international friction than a single pass or waterway. We may notice two continental areas and two oceanic areas of this type, namely the Danube valley and the Rhineland, the Western Mediterranean, and the Caribbean. Of each something may be said briefly.

The Danube is the great artery of communication leading out from Central Europe to the Black Sea and giving access thence to the Mediterranean. Its fertile plains provide homelands for several distinct peoples: Czechs and Slovaks, Austrian Germans, Hungarians, Roumanians, Bulgarians, and Southern Slavs. Its mountain gateways and defensive boundary stretches are points of strategic advantage of great importance. For centuries Romans and barbarians, Hapsburg Germans and Hungarians and Slavs have fought over possession of different sections of its valley floor. Today, after the disappearance of the Austro-Hungarian Empire, it is the scene of a complex web of international political relationships which may lead to all sorts of unforeseen and important results. It is one of the great theaters of international politics in the modern world.

The Rhineland is an even more crucial area. Germany and France have faced one another across this historic stream since 843 A.D. when the empire of Charlemagne was divided. Switzerland relies upon the river to a large extent for an outlet for her products to the sea. And Belgium and The Netherlands lie on the lower reaches of the main stream and the Meuse, its tributary. In one sense the Rhineland is a great unified valley, and the peoples on its banks constitute a natural human group in this part of the world. In history, however, especially in the history of international political relations, the valley has a tragic significance as the scene of much warfare, constant rivalry, and permanent international tension. A thorough understanding of the various phases of German, French, and even British contacts along this line from Basel to the sea would constitute a liberal education in European international politics.

Of the Western Mediterranean too much could hardly be said with a view to explaining its significance in international politics. From the days of Rome and Carthage to the present it has constituted without a doubt the one greatest maritime theater of international rivalry in the world of nations. It is bordered by territories held by three great powers, if we include Gibraltar and Malta, held by Great Britain, and one second class power. The British line of communications cuts through from Gibraltar to Malta and thence to Suez. It is crossed by the French line of communications from Marseilles to Algiers, not to mention the French holdings of Corsica and her communications through Gibraltar to the Atlantic and to the Far East (French Indo-China) through Suez. Italy holds Sardinia and Sicily and sails forth from Genoa and Naples to the Atlantic and to the Northern shores of Africa. It has not been the scene of a great deal of naval warfare in modern times, but it is the scene of a nexus of international interests and policies of primary importance, great strength, and manifold ramifications.

With the significance of the Caribbean area all American students are somewhat familiar. That body of water touches the shores of fifteen independent nations or their dependencies, including colonies of Great Britain, France, and The Netherlands (Curaçao and other islands). It constitutes the approach to the Atlantic end of the Panama Canal. It provides the relatively narrow outlet from the Gulf of Mexico on the South. It is easily the most important theater of international political relations in the Western hemisphere, maritime or territorial. And it is bound to become more, rather than less, important as time goes on and the eleven Latin American states on its shores become more mature and powerful.

It would be possible to make similar introductory studies of various other areas on the earth's surface—the Baltic, the Australasian region, Tacna-Arica—but enough has probably been said to emphasize the importance of this basis of reference in international politics.

In conclusion we may inquire concerning the bearing which such forces have not only upon international law but also upon international organization, and the probable future of international politics in general.

It must be clear that every nation which boasts a foreign policy program at all—and it has often been said that only the more secure and powerful nations can support such programs—will attempt to carry out its policies in its diplomatic activities and its treaty agreements. It will attempt to influence the content of international law so that the rules of the law facilitate the satisfaction of its policies, as has already been indictated. And if this is not the easiest or simplest method of giving effect to foregn policy, as it is not, it is certainly, where successful, the most decisive or permanent in results. Foreign policies of the United States, many of them, have a solidity today, as a result of having been written into general international law, which they could have obtained in no other way.

Similarly a nation's foreign policy will express itself in that nation's attitude toward proposals for organized international coöperation. That policy may involve opposition to the expansion of such coöperation, as did the policy of Germany prior to 1914 and as has, in spite of professions to the contrary, the policy of Russia since 1917. Or it may mean support for such efforts, as did German policy from 1920 to 1933 and American policy before 1920. It may involve support for one type of such coöperation and hostility toward another—the United States has always preferred judicial to legislative forms of international organization. In any case international organization, like international law, feels the pressures of various angles and degrees of intensity which emanate from the foreign policy programs of the nations.

In proportion as such policies become embodied in international law and organization they cease to be merely national foreign policies, or national foreign policies at all. They are displaced by forms of international relationships at once broader than the individual nation, more general in their significance, and more stable. The clash of international politics is ameliorated. International law and international administration replace the give and take of the diplomacy of policy.

This is happening all over the world today. More and more matters of international rivalry are being given treatment in some more mature and formal manner. Institutions and forms of procedure in international coöperation are engulfing one after another of the great topics of international politics and reducing the importance of one after another area of international conflict. One item after another in the foreign policy programs of various nations is being transferred to the agenda of an international conference or the list of functions of an international commission. International politics tend to become obsolete, as international law and organized international coöperation become broader, deeper, and more effective.

CHAPTER V

International Law

Somewhat higher in the scale of official international relations than international politics, because it is both mutually binding and stable in character, and ultimately attaining a position among the various forms of international organization proper, is international law. In view of its more or less primitive and amorphous character, however, and the fact that it does not itself consist of an institution in the sense of an organized group of persons, we retain it under the heading of the bases of international organization, in which capacity moreover, it serves very clearly and significantly. International law may be defined as a system of general principles and detailed rules which define the rights and obligations of the nations one toward another. We shall examine its essential nature, its historic origin, and its development as a science, in the pages following.

The idea of law in the abstract is an idea of a fixed relationship between or among certain entities, such as one relationship between sunshine and water, which is that sunshine causes water to evaporate, or one relationship between a government and its subjects, which is that a government controls its subjects. If the relationship is known the law is known, if the relationship is stated or written out in human language the law is stated or written.

Obviously law may be merely a description of causes and phenomena, or scientific law, as in the two examples given above. Such descriptive law may relate to human entities—persons or groups of persons—or it may relate to non-human entities such as sun and water. In both cases the law may be merely natural law, that is, the law of the behavior of natural causes and phenomena, human or non-human. There is much interest today in, and much need for, a study of human behavior, including international behavior, from this viewpoint.

Law relating to human behavior may, however, take on another form. It may consist of conceptions of relationships among persons or groups of persons which those persons admit to be binding upon themselves in the sense that they have agreed to conform their actions thereto, and will therefore be logically subject to demands to that effect. Such law, which we may call volitional law in order to distinguish it from scientific law, must correspond with scientific law in order to be effective. No attempt to require people to do what does not seem reasonable to them can be very effective, although this involves problems too complex to be treated here. But even so the distinction between scientific law and volitional law is of paramount importance.[1]

The element of agreement creates such law. There are those who question the power of agreement to make law binding upon the sovereign state.[2] States do, however, regard themselves as living "under" international law.[3] And they regard this law as growing out of their consent to its authority. It is vain to seek the origin of law in the principles of nature prior to scientific or volitional recognition thereof, or, on the other hand, to seek the origin of law without going outside of the law itself to the social process creating it; to demand or assert a subliminal law of nature sanctioning the original agreement creating legal obligation is to persist in trying to explain law merely by more, or earlier, scientific law, while to explain law by "its own inherent nature" is to lapse into superstition.

International law arises out of international politics and the actions of nations one toward another which result. It is produced indirectly by those activities of international intercourse noticed earlier, and the essential nature of international intercourse has much to do with the content of international law. It comes into existence half-consciously, or without deliberate planning, although later it is revised and remolded by artistic effort.

The influence operating automatically or unconsciously to deduce international law from international practice flows from the demands of every nation for reciprocity and uniformity and equality in treatment by other nations, at least as minimum requirements. Each nation seeks treatment by other nations in accordance with its desires, primarily; but this by itself would not necessarily produce law, because the wants of a nation might fluctuate from time to time, thereby preventing the development of any constant or fixed relationships. Moreover, it may not always be possible for a state to secure treatment according to its wants. But what will be demanded as a minimum will be treatment as beneficial as that which is accorded to the nation with which the state is dealing, in specific transactions or in general international relations, and treatment as beneficial as that secured in the last similar instance, or treatment at least as beneficial as that accorded to other states in similar circumstances. The nations impose the principles of reciprocity, of uniformity, and of equality of treatment, and succeed in building international law on the basis of practice. It is often said that custom and usage—or uniform practice—constitute the basis of common law; what produces uniform practice

[1] Scientific international law, or international law as a scientific statement of international relations, must not be confused with the science of juristic international law (knowledge and statement of juristic international law), see below p. 58. On this whole theory see Potter, *Manual*, Pt. A., Chap. II.

[2] See Chap. IX. B., below.

[3] United States, Department of State, *Press Releases*, Weekly Edition, No. 240, 5 May, 1934, p. 245.

is the insistent demand for reciprocity, uniformity and equality. So far as the concept of and demand for justice denotes anything definite at all it seems to be treatment of at least this threefold quality.

These processes, described thus in the abstract, may seem somewhat unreal. In actual life they have operated for centuries, in all fields of international contact. They have produced an extensive body of international law which is still constantly being expanded by the same processes.

As is quite natural, the law is soon reduced to writing, or given formal statement. This occurs as part of the process of seeking equality and uniformity, as part of the process of the creation of the law, on the part of the states themselves. It occurs as part of the process of revising the law by deliberate arrangement. And it occurs as a result of the curiosity of students of international relations and international law who desire to discover what the law is and to give it statement, for their own intellectual satisfaction and in order to impart a knowledge of it to other students, as well as in order to provide the nations with statements of their rights and duties for use in practical international relations.

The process by which modern written international law and the science of juristic international law has been formed is somewhat curious.[4] It reminds one of the man who was made a physician in spite of himself. International law as now practised by the states of the world is largely the product of private scholarship, taken over later by the states more or less in spite of their natural instincts. Unlike the man in the story, however, the states have come to see to some extent the real value of what they have been persuaded to accept.

The ultimate foundation of international law is the sense of justice. However imperfect the vision which men have gained of what constitutes justice in general or justice among the nations in particular, and however imperfect the statements given to that principle as it is visualized, and the applications made of the rules as stated, no other conclusion is possible than that the nations expect the law to give every state its due. They are somewhat reluctant to have to do this, perhaps, but they come to it nevertheless. To intend otherwise were to undertake what in the long run would be impossible. Over no considerable period of time is it possible for a state to secure a greater share of this world's benefits than that to which it is entitled on a basis of its natural capacities as exercised in a reciprocal exchange of values with its fellows, in specific bargains or general treatment, and on the basis of uniformity and equality of treatment in similar circumstances.

This reasoning must not be misconstrued. Whenever it is suggested that considerations of justice have anything to do with the formulation of law the cynics and hyperrealists scoff at such naïveté.[5] There is, however, no thought here that the states indulge to any great extent in

---

[4] On history of international law see Potter, *Manual*, Pt. B, and Chap. XI, below.
[5] Sait, E. M., *Political Institutions*, 1938, pp. 269-270.

altruism; it is justice for themselves that they seek, or at most they may admit limitations on their demands which they conceive to be "fair" or likely to bring retaliation upon them if flouted. On the other side of the problem we have the facts of state practice, constituting the imperfect applications, the imperfect statements, and the imperfect visions of justice already mentioned. In actual life and in the actual operations of states it is state practice which seems to be decisive. What rights are accorded to a state depend definitely upon the rights recognized by fellow states in their actual dealings with that state.

The divergence which seems to be possible between justice and practice as sources of the authority of international law is to be bridged only by means of the doctrine of interstate consent. Justice being an ideal of right treatment and state practice being simply the operations of actual life, the basis of the law of nations would be a straddle, a hypothetical bridge, if no connection could be observed between the principles of justice and the rules of practice. The supreme reason for treating consent as the decisive basis of international law, apart from the fact that the states themselves so regard it, is no ethical principle but the fact that it provides the most reliable basis for the latter. In point of fact, students of international relations may be perfectly clear on this point: if justice is to be the source of international law it must be formulated by the members of the international community, and where these members do not formulate it expressly they do give expression to it in practice and there it may be discovered. The express provisions of international agreements declaring the law of nations, and the incidents of international practice, embody what the states of the world agree constitutes justice in their relations one with another. Not that there are three sources of authority—justice, consent, and practice—but that these three are one. As a typical preamble to an international agreement runs: "considering that justice demands a change in the boundary between the two states, the High Contracting Parties have agreed to the following articles."

This synthesis of justice and practice in the doctrine of consent makes the historical dissension between the philosophical school and the positivist school of international jurists unimportant and even unreal. There have been those who have considered that the law of nations ought to rest entirely upon justice and reason and have thereupon set forth their ideas as to what justice and reason demanded in international relations. There have been those who have held that the law of nations could only be found in positive state practice and that considerations of abstract justice and reason were irrelevant. The former have forgotten that it is not their ideas or their law on international relations which is sought, but the law of the nations upon their own relations one with another. The latter have forgotten that the nations maintain that they are acting upon the dictates of justice in that very state practice which seems to be so purely pragmatic and cynical in actuality. Where practice on a given point appears uniform for a long time among many states—the only situation which would permit generalization as to the rule of law involved—we may, moreover, be reasonably sure that the states have been correct in their attitude.

The desirable synthesis of the views of the positivists and those of the philosophers has been made only in recent times, and as yet very imperfectly. The two views must be reconciled and harmonized, not tolerated or propounded side by side. Where there is an express declaration of law by the nations, the rule embodies justice as agreed upon in law by the signatories. Where there is an established general practice, the law is thereby defined as the states evidently think that it should be. Where there is neither express declaration nor established practice the individual jurist is free to use his own judgment, but his conclusion must be based on the same elements, so far as they are present in the premises, and the only valid conclusions which he may draw are that the law is unsettled, that there is no (settled) law, that it is tending to become this or that, or that it ethically ought to be this or that.

For practical purposes it is necessary to have some clearer statement of the documentary sources from which a knowledge of current international law may be gleaned.

Most directly in point, of course, are documents embodying state practice, including national legislative acts and records of national administrative and judicial decisions on questions of international relations. When taken from one nation they may show practice divergent from commonly accepted international law; when collected from many nations they reveal the consensus—or lack of any consensus—of opinion on the points which are involved. Of greatest value and weight, however, are the texts of international settlements of various types, including the decisions of international courts, and international agreements.[6] The perfect documentary source is the text of an international agreement signed by many powerful states declaring international law on a certain point or series of points.

The processes by which the materials of treaty agreements enter into the composition of general international law vary in their simplicity and directness. Certain treaties or joint international declarations set forth international law directly and expressly, and leave no additional act necessary to this result. Such was the Declaration of Paris of 1856 which ended by declaring that, in naval war, "blockades, to be binding, must be effective." On the other hand, international law can be derived from certain economic or political pacts only by a process of induction, of inference, by indirection, and by a somewhat hazardous generalization from the specific instance to a common principle. Thus many treaties

[6] See, below, Chaps. VI. B. and VIII. B.2 for relations between treaties and international adjudication.

ceding territory in exchange for money payments imply that, in international law, territory may be acquired by purchase. A single case of the kind would not, however, be of any legalistic value. Thus, the guarantee by the United States of the territorial integrity of Panama in connection with the acquisition of the use and occupation of the Canal Zone could not be relied on as proving that states receiving concessions of that sort must guarantee the territorial integrity of the ceding state.

The same is true of treaties apparently in conflict with commonly accepted international law. So far as binding at all, they constitute exceptions to, not evidences of, the rules of common international law, just as national statutes make exceptions to the national common law. In the international field the repetition of such a treaty by many states will lead to an alteration in the rules of the common law itself based on the evidence afforded by these treaties.

The identity and numbers of the parties to a treaty are, however, of as much importance in the discussion of treaties as are the provisions of the treaty itself. Thus, the legalistic value of treaties and their effect on common international law depends to a great extent upon the number and importance of the signatory powers. A treaty between Siam and Haiti would not have much effect on the law of nations, even if it pretended to declare international law directly and in express terms. A treaty signed by ten or twelve leading states of the world would be more or less decisive on the subject with which it dealt, even if not cast explicitly in the form of a law-making treaty. According to the doctrine of sovereignty no state can legally be bound without its consent, and a given state could by express declaration refuse to be bound by the rules set forth in or deducible from the last-named treaty. But in the absence of such specific and explicit action or, what is the same thing, by common international law, other states would be presumed to agree to the rules accepted by the powers signatory to that treaty. It would be almost conclusive evidence upon the content of the current accepted law of nations on the subject with which it dealt. Not only would the doctrine of state sovereignty be ignored in so far as it is not covered by the theory of presumptive or implied consent; the doctrine of state equality, likewise involved in the case, would also be passed by in silence. The injured state may be partially conciliated and satisfied by the proposition that, while states may be equal in the right to enjoy such legal rights as they possess under common or conventional international law, they are not entitled to equal political power in the making of law or the control of international government. Leaving these problems of legal theory, it may be confidently concluded that treaties among several of the Great Powers specifically declaring rules of international law would contribute most effectively to the formation of general international law, even if these Powers did not through their agreements exercise any recognized internatonal legislative authority.

The law developed by international practice according to these processes presumes to cover the whole field of international relations. There are to be found in the law of nations [7] the most general principles regarding the nature of the state and the nature of sovereignty and of law, and likewise the most detailed rules regarding the enjoyment by diplomatic representatives of the recognized diplomatic immunities. The relations of states are treated as they exist in time of peace, in time of war, and under conditions of neutrality. The nature and attributes of the persons of international law, their rights and obligations, and the modes of action available for vindicating these rights and obligations are set forth. The nature and powers of the instruments of international government—courts and commissions and congresses—are described. On one hand, much attention is given to international transactions, rather than to substantive rights in the abstract. Thus there is much material descriptive of the methods whereby the international governing bodies—courts, commissions, and congresses—are created and operated; this is in effect international constitutional and administrative law. The presence of these subjects in works on international law is due to the absence of works dealing specifically with international government such as the one now in the hands of the reader, and it is bad both for international law and for international organization, for it detracts from the strictly legalistic character of the former and it obscures the independent existence of the latter. On the other hand, very little attention is given to international economic and cultural intercourse by comparison either with the amount of attention given to these matters in national law or with the amount given to purely political matters in international law; of recent years there has been a considerable change in this respect, but tariff legislation and the regulation of immigration, for example, are still left largely to national discretion. Finally we are witnessing today the early developments of an international criminal law, but discussion of this matter would take us too far afield at this point.[8]

Further comment upon the relations between international law and international organization may now be made. Among rigid students of the former there is some disposition to assert that there is no international organization of any moment except such as is embodied in international law, and that the two are therefore one. It is submitted that this is a too narrow conception of international organization. International law constitutes the standardized or normative phase of international organization, it is true, and in this relation deserves more attention from students of the latter than it receives. But the extensive descriptive portions of the science of international organization—as represented in the statement that arbitral tribunals are ordinarily composed of an odd number of persons, one or more of whom act as umpires between judges named by the

[7] See, in general, Potter, *Manual*, Pt. C.
[8] On international criminal jurisdiction see below, p. 163.

two disputants—are in fact very important, though not law. Much international organization or procedure rests upon no close legalistic basis, as the procedure in treaty-making. Even where some specific international organization rests upon some specific treaty it is not the law of the case but the practical aspects of the situation that count, not the rights and obligations of the parties or the organism but the actual composition and activities thereof. On the other hand all international law, even the portions dealing with territorial sovereignty and citizenship, may be regarded as dealing with international organization, albeit very remotely. Finally the latter science treats of the making and revision of international law, international law in its external aspects so to speak, and thus is broader than the latter.

Naturally enough, the multiplication of the documentary records of international law produces some confusion. As has been seen, this leads individual states to attempt to simplify matters by reducing the number and the complexity of their outstanding obligations. It also leads to efforts on the part of states or private individuals to digest or codify the law of nations for scientific convenience. In a sense all the writing of private scholars in this field is merely an effort at codification, for these scholars cannot make law; they can only record it and summarize it and reduce it to system and ordered statement. Some among them have recognized this by the titles adopted for their works; thus Fiore called his treatise "International Law Codified," and Field and Internoscia also called their compilations "codes" of international law.

Official codification has followed at a leisurely pace. After three centuries of private efforts in this direction, the states are beginning to make up in part for their indifference to international law in the past. For fully official codes, and codes which rest not merely upon the authority of one nation, we must turn to the great international conventions adopted by the states of the world in formal congresses and conferences, such as the Geneva Convention of 1864 setting forth the rules of law regarding the treatment of the wounded in the field. Such acts have multiplied further since the opening of the present century.[9]

From such acts of codification it is a slight step in point of form, although a tremendous stride in point of principle, to the action of legislation or the making of new law. The existing law is not only codified but also revised. Finally, entirely new law is adopted to supplement preëxisting law. This law relates to fundamental constitutional arrangements in the society of nations, such as the neutralization of Switzerland or Belgium, and also to the details of international procedure, such as the rules adopted at The Hague in 1907 for the conduct of war on land.[10]

[9] Specimen, below, Appendix A, Document No. 2. On codification in general see Potter, *Manual*, Pt. A., Chap. IX.

[10] On international legislation see below, Chap. X. A.

Such is the nature of international law, its origin and development, and its later treatment in private and public codes. Much might be said further regarding the functions of international agreements, or treaties, in relation to that law, and regarding its enforcement in daily life by the nations.[11] Many points of contact exist at which international law makes connection with international institutions of various types—courts, commissions, and conferences. Finally there arises the problem of possible joint international enforcement of international law. To all of these topics we shall turn in later chapters.[12]

[11] Potter, *Manual*, Pt. A, Chap. XIII.
[12] Below, Chap. X. A.

PART II

Special Forms
of
International Organization

CHAPTER VI

Diplomacy and Treaties

A1. *Consular Organization and Practice* *

A study of modern international institutions and practices must begin with an examination of the present status of the consular and diplomatic systems. The classification of international institutions as legislative, executive, and judicial, in the pattern of national government, cannot be applied with any success until a comparatively high stage in the evolution of international organization. Such a classification depends upon the idea of the regulation of international relations according to law. This law is to be made by legislative bodies, administered by executive agencies, or applied in litigation by judicial organs. Nothing of that character is found in primitive international relations; not until international relations attain a relatively advanced stage do such concepts enter the field of international affairs. Meanwhile international relations, not to be conducted by a legalistic method, are carried on by the method of personal representation and negotiation, the presentation of the views, offers, and demands of one government to or upon another. What is more, the development of more advanced types of international institutions, while it does reduce the scope of functions to be performed by diplomacy, does not entirely displace the latter, and the advanced institutions actually depend to some extent upon diplomacy for their operation.[1] And, as between the two sets of agents, diplomatic and consular, the latter take precedence in the structure of international organization.[2]

The essential cause which has produced the modern consular system is the need for some official governmental assistance to, and supervision over, the conduct of international intercourse by the private citizens of the various nations. To this is to be added the need for protection against illegal treatment.

All sorts of variations appear among the forms given by modern nations to their consular representation abroad. The idea of a multipartite consular convention, or organizing a world-wide consular civil service, has been put forward but has made little or no progress.[3] The organization and methods of operation of no two national consular services are exactly

* The footnotes in this chapter are numbered by the section.
[1] U. N. Charter, Ar. 33.
[2] For references see, below, Appendix B, § 6a (1).
[3] *American Journal of International Law*, Vol. 26 (1932), Supplement, p. 378.

alike. Therefore, to be accurate a description of the consular system must deal only with those fundamental matters where there is substantial uniformity among the nations. Moreover, it would be impossible to give anything but a very general survey of the consular system except by setting out at great length a mass of detailed material which has no general significance, and which could mean nothing apart from the circumstances and actions of the consular officials in individual cases. Leaving the detailed regulations of the different national consular services aside, therefore, we may turn to the principal elements in modern international consular activity as we know it.

It should be noted at the outset that every nation of political and, especially, of commercial, importance maintains consular officials in the territories of the other members of the community of nations. Under normal circumstances there is no state or quasi-state, whether it be able to claim and exercise diplomatic representation or not, whose business interests are willing to see it go without consular officials in the important markets and harbors of the world.

These consular officials reside in the various ports and other commercial centers of the nations to which they are accredited. Wherever industry and trade are active there are to be found consular officials from all other parts of the world; meanwhile, officials have gone out from that state to the regions from which raw materials are to be obtained or where finished products may find a market.

Each nation decides for itself upon the method to be followed in choosing persons to exercise consular functions abroad on its behalf, and some mode of selection is regularly provided for by law. The work naturally calls for an acquaintance with the various branches of international commerce, together with commercial and international law. Command of the language in common commercial use in the region to which the consul is to be sent is indispensable. In view of these facts it has been found advisable in several countries to establish schools for the preparation of candidates for the consular service or to make arrangements with private educational institutions for this work. The suitable candidates are then selected more or less by means of a series of technical examinations determining the fitness of the applicants for entrance into the lower and middle ranks of the service. The recruitment of the higher posts is generally left to promotion from the lower ranks.

Consular agents are grouped, for administrative purposes, into various classes. These naturally differ from one national service to another, yet, on the whole, there is a measure of uniformity here as in other phases of the system. Among the titles most frquently used are: Consul General, Consul, Vice Consul, and Consular Agent. There are also a great many consular clerks, often so called, and many consular officials of varying title and rank or, on the other hand, of quite special title and rank created to meet special circumstances.

Each consular office abroad has its proper territorial jurisdiction, which results in a districting and redistricting of each of the important nations, on the part of all the others, for this purpose. The idea that the United States, for example, is so parceled out, on the books of the British, French, Chinese and Argentine governments, may be a novel idea to an American citizen, but it is a commonplace of actual practice. The importance of the consular officer depends to a greater extent upon the importance of the district in which he is stationed than upon his rank or his relation to the other consular officials from his own nation who are stationed in the same country. At the same time the rank of the consular officer in charge will correspond, under ordinary circumstances, to the importance of the consular area. Finally, some effort is made to organize the consular officials abroad into a more or less complete hierarchy among themselves and in relation to the diplomatic service. The several districts and their incumbents are not left to depend entirely upon the home office without some coördination.

Ordinarily the field service is controlled by either the department of the national government dealing with foreign relations or the department of commerce. At one time or another, in one or another nation, the national consular officials have, however, been controlled by colonial departments or departments of the government dealing with naval affairs. This is due to the fact that consuls have sometimes been regarded by the country sending them out as colonial agents,—especially in the case of consuls sent into African and Oriental countries,—or as naval officers; early European and American consuls or diplomats were often military or naval officers. The control of the consul is still in an ambiguous position for the reason that his position as foreign agent of his national government would imply control by the diplomatic department of that government, while his work in connection with the foreign trade of his country would make it advantageous for him to be controlled by the commercial department.

In like manner the degree of control exercised by diplomatic officials over the consular officers from their own country who are stationed in the territory of the state to which the former are accredited varies greatly. In general it may be said that a certain amount of control exists, having been conferred upon the diplomatic representatives by the home government. On the other hand no diplomatic representative, at all events none but the very highest, and then only under instructions from the home government, could dictate to consuls in the same country the proper action for them to take on matters on which standing instructions have been provided.

Consular officers are coming to be paid mainly by salary. In earlier times they were frequently regarded as private commercial adventurers, sojourning abroad, who could be utilized and prevailed on to perform certain functions for their governments, or they were regarded as agents and representatives of private business interests or of the merchant community itself. They are now pretty generally regarded as public officers, agents of the state, and in no way private merchants. As a result, they are not required to perform their consular services out of a sense of honor or duty while supporting themselves by private business. Nor are they dependent for their pay, as was the case for many years, upon fees collected in the performance of their duties, although fees are still collected and go in part to the consul as pay. In so far as fees are still used, the government provides, for the protection of the consul—and his clients—tables of the fees which may be legally charged, in order that there may be no misunderstanding and hard feeling between the consul and his fellow nationals who come to him for his services. Similarly the consul is provided with fee stamps, the use of which prevents misunderstandings between him and the home government. Even with all precautions, however, the fee system is a source of constant annoyance to those who should receive nothing but help from the consul. It would be illogical to place the charge for consular service entirely upon the national treasury and to make no provision for special payments by those who in actual fact receive the special services of the consul. But the regulation and administration of the charges to be made is a perplexing problem.

As in the matter of recruitment of consuls so in the matters of promotion, retirement, and pensions, each nation follows its own bent. Other members of the international community are not interested except to obtain additional light on the best methods of managing their own consular services. These problems are wholly within the field of national administrative technology and impinge upon the international field only indirectly.

The difficulty of securing suitably equipped persons to accept consular posts, particularly some of the subordinate posts in the service, has led various nations to resort to the devices of merchant consuls and native consuls. The former are consuls who perform their official functions while engaging at the same time in trade for their private interest. As has been indicated, this practice was at one time the normal form of consular representation. Similarly the native consul, a person selected by a foreign state to act as its representative in the territory of his own nation, was a familiar figure in ancient times and was used, apparently, in the Middle Ages. To a certain extent the practice constitutes an independent historical source of the modern consular office. The native consul was, however, always wholly inadequate for the purpose in many parts of the world, as, for example, the Orient; and, even with all the exceptions to the doctrine of territorial sovereignty which modern states are accustomed to make in the interest of international coöperation, it is not to be expected that a nation will be content to entrust the protection of its interests abroad to an alien, particularly an alien who is a citizen of the country in which he is to perform that service. Accordingly the nations are increasingly willing to incur the additional expense involved in sending out their own citizens for purposes of consular action abroad, and they strive to avoid the handicap incident to the employment as a consul of a person who is subject to all the local regulations of his home country and city by confining their slight use of the native consul to the lowest ministerial and clerical posts in the service. Similarly the merchant consul, who is likely to confuse public office and private business, or to sacrifice one to the other, or to utilize official position—unconsciously, perhaps,—for personal profit, is eliminated as far as possible. These traces of more primitive forms of consular officers are gradually disappearing.

The consul is concerned in his daily work with a multitude of affairs relating to the state on whose behalf he acts. To perform this work he is given a certain measure of authority by the state which appoints him, and this authority is defined in a commission with which he is provided at the beginning of his mission. On the other hand, the permission to exercise the powers committed to him by his home government comes from the government of the state within whose jurisdiction he expects to exercise his functions and is embodied in a document called an "exequatur."

The reception of individual consular officers from other states is a purely voluntary matter on the part of each nation. However, consular intercourse is now so generally accepted by modern nations that refusal to participate in such interchange could fairly be regarded, and could only be explained, as a manifestation of an unfriendly disposition. At the same time it is useful, and it is a matter of common practice, for the nations to agree specifically one with another, in consular conventions or in special consular clauses in general commercial treaties, upon the terms under which they will exchange consular officials. The consular convention is thus the immediate foundation and legal basis of all consular intercourse.[4]

Once commissioned by the home state, and officially received by the foreign state, the consul carries on his work under several sets of rules.[5] The terms of his commission and his exequatur, together with the instructions from his home government in amplification of the former, are of most immediate importance to him in defining his powers and duties. Back of these stand the laws of the two nations concerned; these, in turn, must be read in the light of existing treaty agreements between the two states; in case of conflict the latter must prevail although diplomatic action may be needed to bring this about. Finally, above all stands the system of common international law to which the consul will often

[4] For a typical consular convention see below, Appendix A, Document No. 1.
[5] For material on legal aspects of consular office see *American Journal of International Law*, Vol. XXVI, No. 2 (April, 1932), Supplement, p. 189.

turn for information regarding his rights and obligations. The fact that the consul carries on his activity in the field of private interests and private property results in his being subjected to minute regulation by both the sending and receiving state. In practice, as can well be inferred, the individual consul is largely relieved of the necessity of referring to these different sets of legal principles and rules by having such matters cared for by the department of foreign affairs of his home government. He will receive from that source any information on these questions which he may desire.

The activities of a consul may be variously classified. He has certain duties relating to the persons and property of his clients, his fellow-nationals—or, rarely, others—who happen to be present within his consular area. He must keep a record, ordinarily, of such as are permanently resident there, and of transients who apply for services at the consulate. For all of these he must certify to births, marriages, and deaths, and even, if so authorized, perform marriages and draw up and attest wills. He may extend assistance to travelers who are out of funds, to the sick, to the poor. He aids in securing the burial of deceased fellow-nationals or in having their remains transported to the home country. He assists stranded sailors and wanderers of all sorts to return home. He must protect his clients, individuals or business concerns, from injustice in the local courts, in respect either of their persons or their property. This function is the modern version of the original power of the consul to determine litigation between fellow-nationals in the local district, a power of which traces remain in the West, and larger but decreasing portions in the East. He is called on to secure the release of fellow-nationals from unjust detention or compulsory military service, a duty which has fallen with special weight upon American consuls because of the number of returned naturalized Americans resident in all sections of Europe.

The consul is also of much service to fellow-nationals who are not present in his consular area but resident in the home country. Their property within his jurisdiction is in his general care; property interests acquired by inheritance will, for example, promptly be protected by him. The relevant and necessary evidence, both documentary and testimonial, must be secured by him, and, if need be, title must be proved before local probate courts. In all sorts of litigation connected with the local interests of business concerns at home the consul is called on for work in the courts in his consular district. Finally, and perhaps most important of all, the consul collects, compiles, and transmits to the home government all possible information regarding local export and import markets and, working with and through the diplomatic representative of his nation stationed in the capital of the country in which he is located, information regarding political events and conditions. This service of information is, as far as it goes, the foundation for international commerce as fostered by the official activities of the nations.

On behalf of the home government, as such, the consul performs certain quasi-diplomatic duties. He is called on to watch over and insist upon the execution of commercial treaties and other international agreements with the state in which he is stationed, in so far as these depend for their execution upon the local authorities. He is called on to act in demands by his government for the extradition of fugitives from justice, under existing extradition treaties. In case of inability on the part of the diplomatic representative from the home country to carry on his work a consular officer of higher rank may be temporarily and specifically charged with such work. Finally the original condition of affairs, where the consul was in full power as a diplomatic representative, is reflected in a few cases today where diplomatic and consular representation is united in one officer.

The consul, it must be noticed, is a national official, commissioned to act for the state. He is not accredited as a representative of his own government to another government, it is true, but, at the very least, the consul is an official of the state from which he is sent, in spite of the attempt still made in some quarters to interpret his position as that of a private representative of the national business interests—and as such he may be called on to take quasi-diplomatic action at times.

In his administrative capacity the consul has a very burdensome list of duties. He must endorse cargo manifests, crew lists, and other documents for merchant vessels about to sail for ports in his home state. He must interview, often at great effort, emigrants about to depart from their home country for settlement in his state, endorsing or "visé"-ing their passports (or not) and thereby enforcing the national immigration laws as far as possible at that stage. Finally, he acts as a judicial officer in many petty maritime cases and commercial disputes, and takes depositions of evidence for use in the courts of the home country. Here, as elsewhere, the consul performs functions which rise above the level of diplomacy and touch upon the higher realms of international administration; this is also true of the diplomat himself, as we shall see.

To enable him to perform his duties unhindered the consul is accorded certain immunities of person and property. These include unrestricted communication with his home government and his colleagues in the consul and diplomatic services of his country. This freedom of communication extends to the right to have access to his fellow-nationals at the time in the country, especially when they are under arrest. He is frequently held to be immune from taxes on his person and his personal property and from detention or prosecution for either civil or criminal offenses except criminal acts of a very serious nature. He may maintain an office and archives which are inviolable, and he may extend this inviolability to property of deceased nationals by sealing it. The degree of immunity enjoyed by the consul, in such matters as taxation and military and jury duty, for example, depends largely on whether he is a merchant and a native or a consul with no local interests except his official work. In the latter case he is free from control by the local authorities in all respects pertinent to the conduct of his consular duties. It is, however, one of the disadvantages of the merchant consul and the native consul that such immunities cannot readily be secured by them.

To guide the consular official through the maze of law defining his powers and duties and also his various privileges and immunities his home government usually provides him with certain forms of consular litera-ture, in addition to his commission and instructions, although he may, of course, provide himself with this material. He should have a working library on the various subjects of international commerce and law, commercial law and general international law, and the law of the nation where he is stationed. He should have reliable manuals or guides upon consular law, or those portions of public and private international law likely to be of special service to consuls. He may profitably possess published collections of consular precedents and cases. He will find use-ful a formulary for consular officers, in addition to the table of forms given in his instructions. He should have a set of the general instructions issued to the diplomatic service of his own country. Finally, the con-sulate, which should be maintained permanently by the state whose repre-sentative is to occupy it, and maintained, thereby, on a higher level than would be possible if it were left to each succeeding representative to provide a consular establishment, should be equipped with the ordinary geographical and statistical materials such as maps, tables of values, weights, and measures, and dictionaries and encyclopedias indispensable to effective office work.

The tenure of office of the consul may come to an end in various ways. He may resign and his resignation be accepted. Death may terminate his work. On the other hand, outside causes may bring his stay to a close, temporarily or permanently. Such, for example, is the effect of recall by his home government or the cancellation of his exequatur by the receiving government. The outbreak of war between the two nations will ordinarily lead to one or both of these steps, although it is con-ceivable that neither nation might move to terminate consular relations between them. Even in that case the effect of war would be to suspend the treaty on which that intercourse rested. This is of critical importance. International organization in the form of consular activity is continuous in normal times; in time of war it is almost always suspended. It might be contended, with some reason, that the very time when official inter-national communication is most needed is in a period when disputes arise between nations, and that in time of war there are many subjects which need settlement between the belligerents in the course of the war. This reasoning will be found to apply more forcibly to diplomatic repre-sentation. As matters stand, however, and particularly in the consular field, the legal nature of war, with its stoppage of trade, is held to preclude the continuation of international communication of this type in view of all the circumstances.

Surveyed as a whole, the consular system suggests several conclusions. The total result is an enormous and elaborate web of official bonds connecting the various members of the international community.[6] That web is growing in complexity and in toughness with each year. Further, the basis of the service is to be found in the quite simple desire for private commercial profit, for personal benefit and convenience. The simple and plain facts of international commerce and international travel are the reasons for consular representation, not any sophisticated and fine-spun theories of international relations. The creation, maintenance, and improvement of the consular service is a result of the demand of the commercial and traveling public, and any substantial curtailment of it would meet emphatic protest from that quarter. Since the dawn of international relations, in ancient, Medieval, and modern times, the nations have found it useful and even indispensable to provide themselves with some such arrangements. Any system of international organization to be developed today or in the future must take care of the interests now entrusted to the consular service or carry the present system along with itself.

2. Diplomatic Organization and Practice

The term "diplomacy" is employed by many persons to mean many different things. So diverse are the ideas back of this common term that no possible progress can be made in scientific discussion until some understanding has been reached upon the sense in which it is to be used.

In various discussions of the subject there are included, beyond the simpler forms of diplomacy, a description of the forms and procedures of international congresses and arbitral tribunals, much international law pure and simple, and the subject of treaty negotiation proper. At the same time all mention of the consular system is often omitted. It does not seem best to follow such a plan here. The last topic has, indeed, already been studied as part of diplomacy in the sense of the content of this chapter. Furthermore, we shall consider international conferences, commissions, and courts separately later, as institutions standing by themselves. For our purposes, therefore, the field is now narrowed to the subject of individual diplomats and their activities.[1] This is a strict interpretation of the term "diplomacy," and might be called diplomacy proper, in contrast to various forms of diplomatic activity which, by reason of their complexity and formality, become something distinct from simple diplomacy, deserving attention in their own names. The term

[6] See below, Appendix A, Document No. 3, and statistics in *American Journal of International Law*, Vol. 26, as cited, p. 376.
[1] See literature cited below, Appendix B, § 6a (2).

is used in the title to this chapter in an intermediate sense, believed to be the most satisfactory, in view of all facts.

Even with the narrower definition of the subject, it is well to take notice of two or three things which ought to be carefully set off from diplomacy proper. One is foreign policy and another is foreign relations or foreign affairs. The former phrase refers, as already explained, to national programs of action in international relations, to national motives or purposes or objectives to be carried out through the existing framework and procedure of the national foreign service. The phrase "foreign relations," on the other hand, refers to the totality of events and actions transpiring among nations or between one nation and the other members of the existing state-system. Neither of these things is diplomacy proper; the phrases diplomatic policy or diplomatic relations may be used in the place of "foreign policy" and "foreign relations," but the simple term "diplomacy" should be reserved for use in referring to the organs and practices whereby the nations carry on their political affairs one with another through individual personal representatives of different types.

There is one topic, however, which is commonly omitted from discussions of the general subject of diplomacy, but which should at least be noted in this connection. This is the department of the national government which has control of the nation's foreign service, consular and diplomatic. The department of foreign affairs—by whatever name it may be called—ordinarily has the control of the consular service, although this may be shared with the department of commerce or some other department of the central government. Invariably it has control of the diplomatic service, and as such it deserves to be included in any review of the machinery of diplomacy.

It is the function of the department of the national government dealing with foreign affairs to recruit, classify, instruct, and control the field force of the foreign service; and a monopoly of this control is ordinarily created on its behalf by national law.

Moreover, it is the task of the foreign office to provide such a mechanism of administrative divisions or sections or bureaus at the capital of the nation as can take care of the various sorts of business arising in the course of a nation's foreign relations. The members of the field force must rely upon the equipment and ability of the department of foreign affairs. The field force depends for its original composition and the constant maintenance of its personnel and equipment upon this department of the home government. Defective organization and defective administration at home means ineffectiveness and a failure abroad. Many of the failures and positive sins in diplomacy which are attributed to diplomatic representatives abroad really flow from causes beyond their control, in the foreign office at home.

To study, in detail, the department of foreign affairs here is, however, both unnecessary and impossible.[2] Suffice it to say that the standard principles of administrative organization and practice are defied only at the peril of the national interest. There must be unity of control over, and consistency of action among, the various bureaus of the department. There must be ample provision of distinct administrative units to care for the distinct varieties of work to be done. There must be as clear a demarcation between the determination of policy and routine administrative work as is practicable, and unqualified employees must be prevented from interfering in the business of policy formation. In short, the national government must provide an adequate administrative machine to support the consul and the diplomat abroad. The foreign affairs departments and the foreign services of the nations, taken together, still constitute the foundation and the pillars of organized international cooperation, and as such must be maintained in good condition.

The task of recruitment likewise belongs entirely to the national authorities. Each nation adopts the means which it prefers to secure competent diplomatic representatives. The diplomats form part of the national civil service and may be regulated as all other parts of the civil service are regulated with respect to methods of selection, treatment,—including salaries and pensions, leave, discipline, and so on,—and retirement. Whether an examination system is to be used in judging candidates for admission to the diplomatic service is to be decided by each nation for itself. Whether adequate salaries are to be paid, and whether any provisions are to be made for retirement and pensions, is likewise to be decided by the national governments. The nations observe the experiences of one another as various methods are tried from time to time, and a process of imitation is going on whereby the procedure followed in all countries tends to become the same. But in all countries likewise the source of changes is the national policy of each state.

Certain general reflections, however, may well be set forth here.

It is obvious, for example, that the principal diplomatic representatives of a nation must be loyal in matters of policy to the officials at home in control of national foreign policy. The diplomatic representative abroad largely determines the success or failure of the national policy. No set of instructions can possibly be so complete as to dispense with the need for discretion and judgment on the part of the representative in the foreign capital; and in the exercise of this discretion and judgment it is essential that the diplomat be in harmony with his superior officer as to the foreign policy to be pursued. The success of the national policy for the time being, whatever it may be, requires consistency and unity above and below in the foreign service, for it is an elementary rule of the art of administration that control must be effective from above. Nothing can insure that result in the field of personal diplomatic negotiations except subtle and delicate personal and political loyalty toward

[2] Norton, cited below, Appendix B, § 6a(2), does this for the period 1920-1930.

the foreign office chief from the diplomatic representative abroad. This is one point where the primitive traits of this ancient institution emerge most clearly; primitive or not, the personal element in diplomacy cannot be disregarded with safety. Whether the desired result is to be attained more readily by a system of appointments at discretion or by appointment as a result of technical examinations is another matter.

It is none the less desirable that heads of missions should possess those qualities of tact and manner which are conducive to smooth diplomatic negotiations. The bearings of a machine are not improved by being rough and unpolished. The appearance of strength and integrity is superficial, and the smooth and effective operation of the machine is retarded. Diplomatic representatives who have the task of actually conducting conversations and negotiations of various sorts are engaged in a form of personal intercourse, and certain personal qualifications are therefore pertinent in their selection. The ability to subordinate feelings and prejudices and personalities to considerateness and reasonableness and common decency is indispensable. We do not want weak or insincere or dishonest diplomats, however polished they may be. Equally, we do not want egregious boors for diplomats however strong and sincere and honest they may be. Honesty and sincerity can be found in combination with decent manners and considerateness.

Below the grade of the principal diplomatic representatives personally engaged in negotiations there are, however, large numbers of diplomatic agents to whom rules almost the opposite of those just stated apply. Personal manners and political beliefs are of little consequence in a mere technician or a law clerk in an embassy. The task of the members of the staff in a diplomatic establishment—except when assigned to representative work proper—is mainly to supply information to the head of the mission and to carry out administrative details. They have little contact work and little political or discretionary power. Expert training in history, law, economics, and, above all, the science of government and diplomacy, is what is required in such persons. Candidates for these posts may best be selected by a system of technical examinations, a procedure which might be intolerable for heads of missions. Likewise, it is in regard to such positions that permanence of tenure, experience in the service, promotion for merit, and other salutary administrative practices may be, and ought to be, adopted. With respect to heads of missions these practices have less or no value, and under certain circumstances would be clearly injurious. When questions of policy and of discretion no longer arise in the work of the diplomat he may be made a purely technical administrative officer; that is not the condition today and the diplomat at the head of a mission must continue to be chosen with this in mind. For technical members of the establishment, however, the opposite is true.

The future may see a considerable change in the relations between these two classes of diplomatic representatives. This depends upon what happens to international relations in general. If international organization develops very far, so that international assemblies or councils for the regulation of international relations preëmpt the field, in which the nations are represented by persons who are sent there to debate and vote rather than to negotiate, then only routine administrative details will be left to the resident diplomat. In that case he might well be merely a legal clerk or agent. Furthermore, if and in so far as the development of telegraphic communication narrows the discretion of the foreign representative and gives the home office control over him, the same result will follow. National representatives in the new international legislative bodies would enjoy the national confidence such as is accorded to elected representatives, and in the second case legal and business ability would be desirable. But in neither case would political attachment to a personal superior be in point.

A purely international aspect of the question of the selection of diplomats arises in the requirement that diplomatic representatives must be personally acceptable to the governments to which they are to be accredited. This leads to the practice of obtaining the consent of a foreign government to the appointment of a certain individual as diplomatic agent to that country before making the selection definite and before dispatching him upon his mission. The United States did not always follow this practice, but, on the contrary, contended that any American citizen must be acceptable to any foreign power which consented to enter into diplomatic relations with us. In part, that attitude was an expression of national pride and sensitiveness which was not entirely dignified and considerate; in part, however, it was a premature attempt to minimize the personal element in diplomacy. It has been largely abandoned now, because it has come to be seen that the rule of personal acceptability is in harmony with the actual nature of diplomacy, whether we like it so or not, and also because the equalitarianism and excessive nationalism of an earlier period have yielded to common sense. Here, as in the types of person to be chosen just discussed, the future of the rule is dependent upon the course of events in general international relations.

Just as a state will at times employ natives or citizens of a foreign country for consular representation on its behalf in the territories of their own country, so various nations have from time to time employed foreigners as diplomatic representatives either in the foreigners' own country or in a third country. The latter case raises only one question, namely, the ability of an alien to act loyally and effectively on behalf of the state. The former practice raises, further, and in an acute form, the question of conflicting loyalties to native land and client state. Most states now refuse to receive their citizens as diplomatic representatives of foreign powers, and except for backward states with a dearth of diplomatic talent, the practice has generally gone out of use.

After the foreign service force has been recruited the next task is that of classifying its members.

Broadly speaking, the foreign service as a whole must itself be sub-divided and the first step is the establishment of separate consular and diplomatic services. This separation is not wholly logical or satisfactory, and presents many difficulties. The line between the commercial and legal work entrusted to the consul and the political work of the diplomat is hard to locate in the abstract and is in practice rather vague and imaginary. In the result, consuls, as has already been pointed out, partici-pate in quasi-diplomatic work in connection with treaties and extradition proceedings, while diplomats are deeply concerned with commercial and financial relations among the nations. Further, we find cases where the consular and diplomatic offices are combined. There exists just enough confusion between the two branches of the foreign service to show its latent unity, and indications are not wanting to suggest that the two branches may in the future be brought together in one service.[3]

The diplomatic service proper, like the consular service, is classified into several ranks corresponding roughly to the regulations adopted by the European nations in 1815 and 1818 at Vienna and Aix-la-Chapelle.[4] The principal ranks are those of Ambassador (with which are to be classed the nuncios and legates of the Pope), Envoys Extraordinary and Ministers Plenipotentiary (all one), Ministers Resident, and Chargés d'Affaires. In addition, there are various special diplomatic representatives called Agents, Attachés, Secretaries, Counselors, and what not. The typical diplomatic establishment consists of a chief of mission holding one of the four principal ranks, together with a varying number of Sec-retaries, Attachés, and clerks. There is more freedom in the use of titles and styles for the subordinate positions than for the principal officers, and there is nothing to prevent a nation from inventing its own nomen-clature for its subordinate diplomatic agents.[5]

The respective rank of the principal diplomatic representatives for-merly had an important bearing upon their powers and upon their ability to conduct their business; rights of representation and of negotiation hinged upon the formal status of the foreign representative. At present this is still true but to only a very limited extent. Ambassadors and Min-isters are accredited to heads of states, while Chargés are accredited to the Secretary of Foreign Affairs. Ambassadors alone are held to repre-sent the sovereign personally. But all this signifies little in practice. The rank of a diplomat relates chiefly nowadays to ceremony and precedence. Indirectly, the effect on the real business of diplomacy is perceptible,

[3] For effort of the United States in this direction, see comment by E. C. Stowell in *American Journal of International Law*, Vol. 22 (1928), p. 606, and Stuart, pp. 185-190.

[4] Text, below, Appendix A, Document No. 2.

[5] For a plea (as yet unheeded) for still further internationalization of diplomacy see Bourquin, p. 49.

since priority in precedence often means an advantage in negotiations. The surface effect and appearance also in matters of ceremony and precedence is not without importance also.

Furthermore, the relative rank of the diplomatic representatives resident in a given capital depends in part upon the standing of the states which they represent. This is largely a result of the rule of reciprocity in rank whereby two states entering into diplomatic relations—and the establishment of such relations is always the result of a bipartite international agreement—arrange to exchange diplomatic representatives of equal rank. Thus the Great Powers are represented in one another's capitals by Ambassadors, generally speaking, and the smaller powers by Ministers. The effect of this rule or procedure is, however, sometimes curiously adverse to its intention. The Great Powers will not send diplomats of first rank to the very small nations and therefore accept merely Ministers or Envoys from them in return. It is a case of reducing the rank of the representatives exchanged to correspond to the level of the lower of the two powers. But the small nation may be exchanging diplomats of first rank with another small nation which regards it as an equal. The result is to place the Great Powers in a position of equality with the secondary powers, in the capitals of some small states, a result precisely the opposite from that aimed at by the rule.

What this means is evident. Rank alone tells little about the significance of the representative to the government to which he is accredited. The power behind the representative, not his official title, determines his influence. On the other hand, rank, having lost ground as a factor in determining the legal powers and political influence of diplomats, has continued to mean something in a ceremonial way in spite of the doctrine of state equality. If the states themselves are to be considered formally as equals, the only ground for precedence among their representatives is the relative rank of the latter. It is not surprising to find that salutes and all sorts of social privileges are standardized on this basis in so far as they survive at all today.

The present tendency is to get away from these discriminations as far as practicable. To avoid disputes over precedence, rather than to work out a system of precedence accurately reflecting some scale of real power and influence, seems to have been the principal object of the nations since 1815. The most important step in that direction is the adoption and spread of the twin devices of the alphabet and the alternat in actions involving several nations or their representatives. According to these forms of procedure, the nations involved take their places in a roll call, a seating plan, or a table of signatures by virtue of the position occupied in the alphabet by the initial letters of their names. In the case of a signed document it is arranged that each power shall retain that copy on which it appears at the head of the list of signatories, the various copies having been signed in such manner that each power signs once in the first position, once in the second position, and so on.[6] The order of signing may be settled by lot equally well, and the alternat employed in connection therewith. The motive and the net result of all this is, of course, to eliminate considerations of rank among representatives and among nations, so far as any effective application of it goes. The world seems to be tending toward the goal marked out by America, namely, the abolition of discriminations in rank among nations and diplomatic representatives and the employment of one uniform diplomatic title or office by all nations, albeit the title or rank of ambassador.

The diplomatic representative receives his authority from his appointment by his home government and his reception by the government to which he is accredited. His letter of credence is the formal evidence of his appointment to the representative office at a certain capital. In addition, a "full-power" may be provided for the ordinary work of the office or for special tasks committed to his charge. These documents are for the information of the foreign government and form the basis for the relations which are to be set up with the newly arrived diplomat. If all is agreeable to the power in question he will be formally received by the sovereign, the chief executive, or the Minister of Foreign Affairs and diplomatic relations between the two states will be thus established.

The diplomat receives oral instructions from his home government before setting out on his mission, and he carries with him general regulations and special instructions in writing. Furthermore, he receives from his foreign office a constant stream of advice and instructions which control his actions in the conduct of his office. These documents constitute his version of the credentials handed to the foreign government, and correspond to the latter in scope and authority. Needless to say, they are fuller and more precise than the latter.

The work of the diplomat at his post defies precise or complete definition. He must conduct negotiations with the government to which he is accredited; he must observe and report what is going on about him; and he must perform certain functions on behalf of his own state toward fellow-nationals who apply to him for passports, take part in the complex and delicate practice of extradition, and, in general, perform services not unlike those performed by the consul. He has also, in fact, administrative, petty judicial, and, as we shall see, even semi-legislative functions to perform. This leaves the main work of the diplomat to be described by elliptical general terms such as "representation," "protection," "pro-

[6] If Argentina, Brazil, Chile, and Denmark were to sign a document in English by alphabet and alternat, the result would be as follows:

Copy retained by Argentina:	Copy retained by Brazil:	Copy retained by Chile:	Copy retained by Denmark:
Argentina	Brazil	Chile	Denmark
Brazil	Chile	Denmark	Argentina
Chile	Denmark	Argentina	Brazil
Denmark	Argentina	Brazil	Chile

motion," and "administration," terms which must be filled out by each student according to the dictates of his own imagination. What is to be negotiated and what is to be observed cannot be defined in advance, yet they constitute the heart of the problem.

In the actual conduct of negotiations the diplomat enters a complicated and delicate field of action. Some efforts may be made to instruct him concerning the "manner of negotiating," but the business is too complicated and too subtle to be completely reduced to formal rules. The diplomat must rely upon his own tact, his own feeling, his own common sense to help him in his work. Much has been written cautioning the young diplomat against haste, against the use of flattery and bribery and falsehood and other shallow and therefore ineffective methods of action. Such advice is sound enough. The difficulty is to apply the principles when needed, and to recognize the situations where they are needed; in this nothing but the sound judgment and sensitive wisdom gained by experience in dealing with persons and politics can serve. So long as international relations are conducted by personal representation this is bound to be true.

The same must be said concerning the whole matter of style and ceremony. Not all of the mannerisms and rules of the etiquette of diplomacy are essential. Not all of them are, on the other hand, superfluous or irrelevant. The amount of such formalism has greatly decreased in the past century, and particularly in the past generation. With the advent of republican states and civilian diplomats the use of ceremonial costume, long deprecated by the United States, has declined perceptibly. The greater part of the punctiliousness and formality which does remain is due to an effort for precision and accuracy in a field where the materials dealt with and the issues involved are very complex and indeterminate and where the competitive national interests involved are great in magnitude and at the same time ill-defined. Propriety and form are an integral part of substantive right especially where procedure is still in the stage of personal negotiation.

The matter of written documents is similarly important; the art of literary composition constitutes an intimate part of diplomacy. Indeed, the term diplomacy is derived from *diploma*, which was a document in the form of a sheet of paper folded into two leaves; a certain famous collection of early treaties has the phrase "containing diplomas (*continens diplomata*)" in its title. The written record remains, once it is made, and it behooves the signers of a document to exercise the most scrupulous care about its wording. To say that two powers "are not prepared to act" (now) is not to say that they "will not act" (next year), and many apparent euphemisms and circumlocutions in diplomatic documents reflect what are often very genuine attempts to say just what is meant, and no more and no less. It is undeniable that diplomatic writing contains much bombast, and is often guilty of evasion, and worse. But it is equally true that much of the criticism of diplomatic diction is due to shallow inattentiveness to exactness in detail and to childish lack of thought upon the subject.

Some part of the difficulties attendant upon the composition of satisfactory documents in diplomacy is due to differences of language. So long as Latin could be used by all diplomats the situation was relatively simple. To some extent this situation was perpetuated by the general adoption of French in the seventeenth century in the place of Latin as the international diplomatic language. French possesses qualities of range, accuracy, and flexibility or delicacy which make it valuable on its intrinsic merits as a diplomatic medium, and the language of Louis XIV has never entirely lost its position in the world of international relations. Matters of this sort change, however, in response to considerations of what appear to be practical utility. The French is now being abandoned by certain nations and English or Spanish or some other common language is being employed, even where English and Spanish are not native tongues. Thus German speaking countries employ German in dealing one with another, Japan and Russia employed English at Portsmouth in 1905, and the South American states commonly employ Spanish in negotiations among themselves. Documents are sometimes drawn up in two or more languages in parallel columns. In such cases one of the versions may be regarded as the standard text, or, indeed, two texts may be accorded equal authority and potential discrepancies left for adjustment as they appear, a very objectionable practice. In many cases the merits of the French have been foresworn without commensurate convenience and benefit. It is absolutely impossible to produce two texts of a given document in any two different languages with identical meanings. Even single texts yield to varying interpretations; how much greater the difficulty when two or more national tongues are used!

The outcome of this question of language cannot be foretold, but the solution may partake of three elements. The leading national languages are likely to continue to compete one with another for preference in international dealings and to be recognized by different nations at different times according to present practice. By the generous use of translators and interpreters this way of doing business may be made to yield results which, if not wholly satisfactory, will at least be tolerable. Secondly, the study and use of foreign languages by people in general is likely to increase with the increase of international travel and communication. Along with this, we may see important changes as a result of the incorporation into one language of terms and forms in use in another; a process of amalgamation is steadily going on which tends to make the different languages more nearly alike. Finally, we may well see some serious effort to develop an artificial international language. To historically-minded persons such a suggestion seems ridiculous and in some way or other weak and futile. It bears on its face the appearance of artificiality. Notwithstanding all this, the circumstances of the case seem to justify the conclusion. If telegraphic codes, scales of weights and measures, signal systems, and other artificial media of communication have been successfully devised and put into use under similar circumstances the course of events is not likely to be different in the field of language.[7]

It should be added here that the diplomat is often utilized as a delegate to international conferences or a member of international court or commission, not always with good results. Such practices must be considered later in the treatment of those institutions.

The individual diplomat is not alone in the foreign capital; he is a member of a group of representatives from all countries who, collectively, form the "diplomatic corps" at that capital, comparable with the consular corps, already mentioned, but much more important. His relations with his colleagues will depend somewhat upon his position in the corps; if he is a newcomer he will be expected to defer, socially and in matters of precedence, to his colleagues; if he is an older member he will enjoy some influence in matters properly of concern to the corps as such.

The standing and powers of this somewhat amorphous body depend upon local court or governmental regulations. The diplomat of highest rank and longest tenure is commonly the "dean" of the corps but he does not exercise any substantial authority over the other members. Questions of diplomatic privilege form the chief concern of the corps as such, and its dean and the members would protest as a unit against any mistreatment of one of their number. At times joint action is taken by the ministers present in a certain capital on some substantive point in international relations, as when the diplomatic agents in Peking protested in 1921 against any interference by the Chinese Government in the administration of the customs revenues in China according to the standing agreements between China and the Powers.

As in the case of the consular system, the result of this practice of international exchange of representatives is to cover the world with a web of bilateral bonds running among the capitals of all the nations. These bonds are less numerous than in the case of the consular system, but they are of greater legal and political significance. They have for centuries in the past constituted the main form of existing international organization, and for some time to come they will remain the most common avenue of intergovernmental communication.[8]

Given this diplomatic system, it remains to be noted that international law attempts to define in some measure the powers and privileges attaching to the members thereof.[9] The rules already reviewed, relating to diplomatic amenities and the forms of diplomatic procedure, are part of

[7] See Guérard, entire.
[8] See the tables, below, Appendix A, Document No. 3.
[9] See draft in *American Journal of International Law*, Vol. XXVI, as cited, p. 15

what might be called the technique of diplomacy. The law of legation, on the other hand, deals with the right to send diplomatic representatives in the first place, and with the very practical question of the rights of diplomatic representatives in relation to the law and officials of the state where they are stationed. The law of legation is principally international law, though national laws, statutory and administrative, deal with the subject also.

The primary rule to be noted is that, as a general thing, only an independent state may send or receive diplomatic agents; indeed, the right of legation is frequently used as the supreme test of a state's independence. There are, however, many cases which are difficult to classify on this assumption. Certain states of the German Empire held a limited right of legation previous to 1918. Bavaria even attempted to deal with Berlin by diplomatic note as with a foreign power at one time in 1920-21. The British Dominions have been accorded the privilege of sending Ministers to Washington. The Pope exercises a right of legation in certain states of Europe and Latin America, and in February, 1921, there appeared the novel spectacle of the Papacy appealing diplomatically to the League of Nations on certain international questions! Yet on the whole the principle is sound, and what we should do in the above cases is to admit that the German states, Canada, the Papacy, and the League are or have been independent members of the existing state-system to the degree in which they act freely in international relations. Various international organizations enjoy that status today.

The members of the community of nations do not, however, exchange diplomatic representatives upon the basis of the principles of common international law alone. Each exchange is based upon express consent in the form either of a treaty or some simpler agreement. The reception of diplomatic representatives from other states is a legal obligation resting upon each member of the community of nations, and refusal would constitute a valid ground for complaint. But the manner, and even the simple fact, of discharging that obligation is commonly decided by special agreement between the interested parties. The further step of agreement upon the individual to be sent and received has already been noted.

Once received by the foreign power, the diplomat is accorded certain immunities from jurisdiction in view of his position and functions. International law defines the immunities which the receiving state is bound to accord to the foreign representative, and the national laws set forth these rules with a view to their application in the courts of the nation. These immunities comprise the ancient privileges of personal inviolability and independence of personal action, including freedom from arrest for acts under civil or criminal law. The diplomat enjoys the same relief from customs duties and personal taxes, witness duty, and other similar burdens, as does his colleague, the consul, but in a more definite manner and to a greater extent.

The original view of these immunities seems to have been that they were necessary in view of the impropriety and discourtesy of enforcing upon a foreign sovereign or his agent the local law; no state was entitled to impose its own will upon another state, equally sovereign, or its head or diplomatic representative. It is now seen that these privileges are essential to the effective operation of the system of diplomatic representation, and that they must be supported and defined with a view to that desirable end, irrespective of any theory of sovereignty.

One result of this change of view as to the foundation of diplomatic immunities is seen in the alteration of the rules of the law of nations on the subject of asylum in legations and embassies. The right of extending asylum to fugitives, formerly claimed by foreign representatives and reluctantly conceded to them in view of the doctrine that the embassy was foreign territory enjoying exterritorial status, has been curtailed in various ways. Particularly significant is the combination of the holding that a foreign representative must not receive and accord asylum to fugitives from justice with the principle that the grounds and buildings of the embassy are inviolable, even when so used. The reasons for this ambiguous position are found in the conflict between the desire to accord as much immunity to the diplomatic establishment as is necessary for its effective operation and the unwillingness to accord any unnecessary immunity to it. Likewise the diplomat may worship his own gods in his own way in his own chapel, and fellow nationals are free to join him in this worship; however, he must not make this a cause of disturbing the public peace.

All of these privileges are regulated, as has been said, by local law. The home government of the diplomat will instruct him regarding the immunities which he is to claim for himself and these will correspond to the privileges accorded by his own government to foreign representatives in its territory, including those from the state to which he is accredited. By this process of reciprocity practice on diplomatic immunities is generalized until the common rules of international law on the subject appear as a summary of the practices of all the nations. Meanwhile the diplomat is controlled exclusively by his own government in respect to the special costume which he shall wear, if any, the way in which he shall conduct the internal affairs of the embassy, and the reception of gifts and decorations at the hands of the government to which he is accredited. The result is that the rules governing the operations of the diplomatic system are found in general international law, written and unwritten, and in the national legal systems of all the states, including in the last the various codes of administrative regulations issued for the guidance of the national civil servants. The diplomat, hardly less than the consul, needs to be provided with manuals and guides wherewith to inform himself on the vast amount of law and procedure connected with the conduct of his office.

Finally, a diplomatic mission may be terminated in several ways. The person holding the mission may die, retire automatically by virtue of age, resign, or be recalled to make way for a new appointee. These are entirely matters of national law and have no bearing on international relations. Of real importance in the international field, however, is the recall of the head of the mission, leaving affairs in charge of a subordinate —here the mission is not interrupted,—or a discontinuance of the mission entirely by withdrawal of all diplomatic representatives. So much a part of normal international relations is the exchange of diplomatic representation that such action is construed as unfriendly and possibly the prelude to war. More striking and emphatic in tone, but of less consequence internationally, is dismissal of a diplomat by the receiving state. In such a case, although continuance of diplomatic representation between the two countries is not interrupted, diplomatic relations between them are bound to be gravely disturbed. It is of some significance that the institution of international representation is stable enough to persist through an episode of this kind.

It should be added that the diplomat, like the consul, while a national agent has an international status. He has certain general functions conferred upon him by international mandate. It has been noted that consuls and diplomats participate in the formulation and application of international law; they thereby become part of the whole system of international organization and, in view of the incompleteness of the higher forms of that system, one of its main foundations. They even participate, and that very extensively and actively, in that process of international harmonization and synthesis of national policies which is so close to the basis of all international action and which international conferences have such difficulty in performing.

Diplomacy has been the object of much criticism at many points in the past and particularly after World War I. Secrecy, intrigue, excess of nationalist zeal,—or, on the other hand, excess of appeasing zeal,— idleness, snobbery, reactionary political philosophy and technique—such are the charges leveled at the institution. The charges are often exaggerated but have some foundation. Some of the traits criticized have been imposed by the anarchic conditions of international life but improvements can be made and are being made. Certainly the loose talk about "abolishing" diplomacy cannot be taken seriously.[10]

3. *Good Offices and Mediation*

It is conceivable, perhaps, that international relations might proceed smoothly from month to month and from year to year merely by means of the ordinary practices of diplomacy and consular action. If no other

[10] See literature cited below, Appendix B, § 6, a (2), especially Reinsch, Ponsonby, Krock.

complicating factors were introduced in the problem these forms of international coöperation might perhaps be sufficient. As a matter of actual experience, however, they are not sufficient to meet all the needs of the situation. The reason for this is the appearance of what may be called the international dispute. The international dispute arises precisely because the procedures of diplomatic and consular action are inadequate to provide for the management of all future and contingent relationships between nations, and, because, in turn, once the dispute has made its appearance the inadequacy of diplomatic and consular action to resolve the difficulty and settle the dispute is accentuated at each succeeding stage.

Direct diplomatic negotiation is not, indeed, always inadequate to settle an international dispute, and, where successful, it constitutes the first and simplest method of removing the trouble which its own negligence or incapacity has allowed to develop. What happens here is that the machinery and practice of diplomacy as it is ordinarily conducted catches up with its task. It removes the dispute between the two nations by securing a diplomatic agreement of one sort or another, including, as one of the possible forms of settlement, an international treaty,[1] as described below.

This simple method of dealing with the international dispute is not, however, capable of resolving the more difficult and complicated questions which arise between nations. The technique of such a method is too primitive; it does not possess resources of procedure and treatment adequate for the task. No action is available to the contending parties but to continue to put forward their own views of the facts and the principles and to urge their claims and try to secure satisfaction of their interests by bargains and demands, persuasions, threats, or arguments. What is needed is an entirely new approach to the questions in dispute, and, particularly, an approach from a point of view, a right, and an interest, radically different from that of either of the two contending parties. That method and that approach have been found in the practices of good offices and mediation. These two forms of diplomatic practice serve to prepare the way for arbitration or judicial settlement proper.[2] Each of these forms of action has its peculiar nature and function, and it is worth while to exert some care to draw clearly the distinctions between them. Both good offices and mediation begin within the field of simple diplomacy, and in the end they go very far beyond that field and get well over toward adjudication. On the other hand, both stop short of true adjudication, and good offices stop very far short of that point. The use of one or the other may pave the way for adjudica-

---

[1] Below, p. 95; on relations between diplomacy and treaty negotiations see, below, Sec. B.

[2] See literature cited, below, Appendix B, § 6b. On arbitration and adjudication see, below, Chap. VIII. B. 2.

tion. Equally well, the use of one or the other may achieve a settlement of the dispute and render a resort to adjudication unnecessary.

The proper occasion for the exercise of good offices or mediation is the existence of the dispute between two nations respecting their rights and duties toward one another. War may be impending, and may possibly be averted by these means. Or a war which is already being waged may be brought to a close by securing an agreement between the parties. This agreement may be an agreement on the merits of the case,—the most definitive result which can be hoped for,—or it may be an agreement for adjudication on the merits, pending which, or in view of which, hostilities are to be postponed or suspended or even terminated entirely. In any case the result will almost certainly take the form of a treaty, since a dispute so important as to have reached the stage of mediation or adjudication can hardly be settled in any less formal manner. In the circumstances described the resulting treaty will very often be a treaty of peace or an arbitration convention. Mediation in time of peace is, naturally, the commoner of these forms of action, but there have been many cases of good offices or mediation in the termination of wars.

Whether the action in question is to be called "good offices" or "mediation" depends upon the distance to which the parties to the dispute are willing to go in adopting a new method for settling their quarrel. For what really happens is that the disputant nations are assisted in composing their dispute for the sake of general peace. This assistance comes from a state or states not party to the dispute, and whether it amounts to good offices or mediation depends upon the distance to which the third party is allowed to go in extending assistance in the premises. It is this presence of a third party, acting on a mandate from the disputants, plus the fact that the merits of the dispute are now under consideration, which raises mediation above the level of good offices.

Good offices consist merely in providing a neutral meeting place where representatives of the disputing nations may meet together to discuss anew, perhaps under the presidency of the third party, the subject matter of the dispute, or in receiving and then transmitting to the other party written proposals and counter-proposals dealing with the question in dispute. In such a case the third party refrains from giving any opinion or advice upon the substance of the question, and confines its activities to the mechanical steps just described. From this point on, therefore, the action does not possess any resources beyond those of ordinary diplomatic discussion. It does, however, serve to renew discussions when the parties themselves have drawn apart, and in this way may affect the future course of the dispute considerably. It is undertaken in the hope that renewed or continued discussion may result in some agreement. It is based on the supreme truth that conference is indispensable in such situations and that the more conference the better, so long as any issues remain open between nations.

In mediation we reach an entirely different sort of thing.[3] Here the third party takes up for consideration the substance of the dispute itself and attempts to discover a solution. This is, of course, of far more significance and, potentially, at least, is of far more service, than merely enabling the parties to continue trying to find a solution themselves. The mediator enters into much more intimate relations with the nations in dispute than does the party who merely extends good offices. The mediator must therefore possess the confidence of the parties in greater measure. There must be no suspicion that the mediator is attempting to secure a certain solution for motives of immediate self interest in that particular solution. The mediator must necessarily enter into discussion with both parties; or, if the parties meet face to face for discussions between themselves, the mediator must, in the very nature of the case, meet with them and enter into the discussions, whereas in the case of good offices the third party may never meet the disputants or either of them. The mediator may even sign the treaty which embodies the settlement reached, as did the American Secretary of State, "in the character of mediator," in the settlement of the war between Spain and Peru, Chile, and Ecuador in 1871. The mediator may thus become, to a greater or less degree, perhaps merely by implication, a guarantor of the settlement.

It is worthy of note that in good offices and mediation, and especially in the latter, there appears, for the first time, the case of the designation of an agency, and the giving of specific instructions thereto, upon an international, rather than a national, mandate. Diplomatic representatives are agents designated by individual nations. Even the diplomatic corps is, at best, a composite of national agents. Except for the general international consent back of the existence and activities of diplomatic agents as such, no truly international authority is exercised by them. The power whose good offices or mediation are accepted by other states, however, acts as an agent or official representative of two or more nations directly.

Good offices are, very naturally, offered more easily and accepted more readily than mediation. Once begun, however, good offices may develop into mediation, if the third party is led to take up the substance of the question at issue between the parties. Thus Theodore Roosevelt began in 1905 by merely extending his good offices to bring Japan and Russia together at Portsmouth to try to reach an agreement for a settlement of the conflicting interests at stake in the war. At a later point he was led to interest himself in the terms of the settlement, and in the final event he practically decided the terms of the settlement. Similarly, in the following year he began by persuading France and Germany to go into conference on their claims concerning Morocco, and ended, in 1906, by drafting the main item in the settlement reached at Algeciras.

[3] See article in *Encyclopedia of the Social Sciences*, Vol. X, p. 272, for further detail.

As in all other fields of international relations, the terminology of this body of procedure is somewhat unsettled, even after three centuries of practice. Thus the formula "good offices" is occasionally used to describe the diplomatic action taken by one state toward another for a purpose apart from any dispute between the latter and a second or third state. Likewise a power exercising "good offices" is sometimes spoken of as an "intermediary" in the case. Finally, the two sorts of action are at times confused for sheer want of knowledge or want of care in the use of terms.

To be of any service the mediator must be neutral and impartial. The parties to the dispute are naturally very suspicious of any outsider who enters the scene and undertakes to find a settlement of their quarrel. Only if the mediator gains nothing by the result, and where both parties are and remain equally satisfied with the settlement, will the mediator escape all suspicion and insinuation. The gratitude of the parties will only be earned where both feel that they have secured benefits from the settlement. What is probably the most remarkable case of mediation on record, when all the circumstances are borne in mind, came about when, in 1918, Germany, through Swiss good offices, in effect asked the United States, an enemy state, to act as mediator to secure mutually acceptable terms for an armistice and preliminaries of peace with the Allies.

The mediator will not, of course, be led to undertake such an ungrateful task without reason, and yet that very reason may well affect the formula of settlement proposed to the parties. As a rule, the third state is led to act in such cases by national interests which demand protection. Indeed, it would hardly seem proper for a third state to take action in the premises unless it had some substantial interests to defend. Mere idle meddling would be intolerable and entirely void of that essential basis of all legitimate diplomatic action, the necessity of defending substantial interests of the state. Such a requirement is not difficult to satisfy today, however, in view of the enormous material interests which all nations have at stake in seeing the general peace preserved and war averted. There is the general humanitarian interest in averting war which is shared by all peoples in varying degrees, and there are also special interests of particular nations which have to be safeguarded. Nations which may, as prospective neutrals, expect to see their commerce injured if war breaks out, and nations which fear lest they themselves be drawn into such a war have reason for promoting a settlement on general grounds. This is the common basis for joint international action to mediate a quarrel likely to lead to war. In such a case, also, the action may be affected because one possible solution rather than another is desirable in the interests of peace. Thus Theodore Roosevelt, because he was primarily interested in seeing Japan and Russia reach any solution which would end the war, was interested almost as much in seeing that the solution reached was just in order that it might really end the war and not be merely temporary. That meant that at the time of the settlement he was compelled to oppose first the Russian views and then those of the Japanese.

Beyond its interest in the restoration and maintenance of peace, however, a nation may very well be interested in seeing one solution rather than another adopted by the parties because of the indirect advantages to be had by that nation from one solution and not from the other. In the case of neighboring states such a condition is almost certain to exist. And if it does exist the third nation will commonly regard that desired solution as just on general grounds and feel free and even "compelled" to promote such a settlement for the sake of all concerned.

It is not to be assumed that the contending parties are unaware of this situation. Indeed, in earlier times all efforts at mediation were regarded as nothing but indirect efforts at self-aggrandizement. They were therefore viewed with grave suspicion by the parties in dispute. With the growth of the cost of, and consequent desire to avoid, international war, and with that development of wider international relations which, in actual fact, has made the just solution of a given dispute that solution which accords most with the interests of third states, this instinctive hostility has somewhat diminished. Nevertheless, the action is not so simple and natural and free from suspicion that it can be admitted without a careful definition of its legitimate scope and procedure.

To begin with, the third party normally possesses no jurisdiction over the question in dispute or over either of the parties. They cannot, therefore, be summoned to meet and settle the dispute by discussion, nor can any solution be imposed upon them. Even where the action is to be taken by two or more third parties, or by the family of nations in general, no such jurisdiction exists at common international law. Granted that, in the interest of the general peace and of general justice, or in its own special interests in peace and justice, a third party or a group of third parties has a right to attempt to secure a settlement under such circumstances, precisely what may be done with that end in view remains to be carefully defined.

The simplest case of all occurs where both parties to the dispute request a third state to extend its good offices or to act as mediator. The latter may then freely accept the request and perform the task as skilfully as may be. In rare circumstances, as where no peaceful or just solution seems possible of attainment and the attempt at mediation can lead only to further embitterment and to the useless involvement of the third power, the latter may decline the request.

An intermediate stage is found—and in many ways this is the most natural form of procedure—where only one of the disputing parties requests good offices or mediation, in view of its own inability to secure satisfaction either by diplomacy or war. The third party still has no jurisdiction over the second disputant or over the issue. Assuming that the request of the first disputant is to be acceded to, the third party may only turn to the party of the second part and offer to extend good offices or to act as mediator in accordance with the request of the first party. The second party is under no obligation to accept such an offer, and will accept or reject the offer as circumstances dictate. Here are to be considered the possibility of securing satisfaction by persisting in direct diplomacy or war, the desirability of getting some settlement at once, and of conciliating the opponent and the would-be mediator. If the offer be rejected there is nothing more to be done. If it be accepted the subsequent course of events is clear from the previous case.

The third case arises where there is no request from the disputants. Here the would-be mediator may, if circumstances seem propitious, as already outlined, offer to both parties at once or to first one and then—if accepted—to the other, to furnish good offices or to act as mediator. The offer may be accepted by both disputants or rejected by one or by both. In either of the last two cases the effort fails. Thus Theodore Roosevelt's first attempt to extend his good offices to Russia and Japan was balked by the attitude of Japan alone. In all of these cases mediation may be offered, accepted, or undertaken, upon certain conditions previously stipulated by the disputants, or by the third party, and these conditions must then be observed in all future negotiations unless repealed. In the same way, the disputants and the mediator alike may, at any stage of the proceedings, lacking an agreement to the contrary, withdraw and terminate the whole affair.

Under certain circumstances these normal principles may be varied considerably, apart from any specific international treaty agreements touching the matter. In cases of civil war or colonial revolt the request of the rebellious group for mediation may not be accepted as freely as that of a state whose independence has already been recognized. The quarrel is in law a domestic matter, and in most cases the very issue is that independence the establishment of which could alone make mediation by a third power legitimate and even an offer of mediation welcome to the mother country. Napoleon III was suspected of desiring to promote the separation of North and South when he suggested mediation during the Civil War in the United States. This does not entirely preclude the use of good offices and mediation in such situations, but it does mean that their range of application and their value is strictly limited.

On the other hand, there are situations where the "third party" possesses a basis for action which gives greater authority to the "offer" than inheres in such action in ordinary circumstances. Such a situation exists where a common superior possesses a right to come forward and invite, or to come forward and compel, the parties to accept good offices or mediation to settle their dispute. Such action was taken in times past by Rome, by the Papacy, by the Emperor, and, in certain cases, by the Great Powers of Europe. This is not free international practice at all but, so far as admitted or tolerated, is constitutional government. Where not admitted voluntarily and justified on that basis, but imposed by force, it is intervention. In that case it must be justified, as any intervention must be justified, not by reference to any general right of intervention but to the special circumstances of each case, the necessity of self-defense or equally cogent interests; of "armed mediation" there can be none in normal circumstances.[4]

It will be noted that, under ordinary conditions, acceptability, not justice, is the quality sought by the mediator in the formula of settlement. The object is peace; the mediator is not a judge. For the higher form of settlement other procedure is needed, namely, adjudication. Yet it may be suggested that immediate justice between the parties may result as frequently from the attempt to find a settlement acceptable to both parties as from the decision of an arbitrator who knows that his award must be accepted, right or wrong, but who has a very inadequate body of legal principles to guide him in his action.

Such is mediation, which, with good offices, extends the range of diplomacy until it makes contact with the international dispute, and with adjudication, yet which remains, largely, diplomacy in character and in the details of its operation. It remains diplomacy in spite of the fact that here at last a person or body of persons, internationally empowered and instructed specifically as to what they shall do, functions in reference to the merits of the situation. This is the extreme advanced point reached by purely diplomatic activity before it becomes something else.

B. *Treaties*

The ordinary work of the diplomatic representative consists in making representations relating to current questions at issue between his own state and the state to which he is accredited. These representations may be presented orally, in conversations with the Secretary of Foreign Affairs of the state to which the representative is sent, or in writing, by exchanges of diplomatic notes. In the former case the element of personal intercourse is predominant, and the action is transitory and leaves little trace of itself behind, unless a memorandum of the views put forward in the conversation is drawn up and signed by the participants. In the latter case the correspondence remains to serve as a record of the transaction; though here also, in the absence of a signed statement summarizing the exchange of views, the chance for uncertainty as to the real positions of the participants is great, and the degree of inconclusiveness and impermanence in this form of action is therefore also considerable. This is all the more inconvenient when the discussions have concerned not some special case, as, for example, the citizenship of a

---

[4] Just what may properly be done here is strictly a question of international law; see Potter, *Manual*, Arts. 23 and 155.

certain individual, but a general question, such as the principles which the two states agree to follow in the future in settling disputed cases of citizenship.

Moreover, these processes of representation and negotiation must lead to agreement, to the giving and taking of rights and obligations, if they are to be of much value. The parties then exchange declarations of their common or reciprocal intentions. The representation of views and the presentation of demands and offers must conclude in acceptance by both parties of a certain solution if they are to be fruitful, in other words, in the conclusion of a treaty. Indeed, the noun "treaty" seems to have been formed on the basis of the verb "to treat," used to describe diplomatic negotiations; when diplomats treat with one another a treaty is or may be the result. The treaty is of such a distinctive character, however, and has developed to such an extent on its own account, apart from its parent practice, that it deserves study by itself. The conclusion of treaties and their analysis and generalization among the states is a distinct branch of modern international coöperation.[1]

It is to be noted, first, that the usual object of the interstate treaty is to provide for certain and definite action in the future whenever a given type of question shall arise—a question of citizenship, of commercial privileges, of extradition—without the necessity for special interstate agreement every time upon the merits of the case. So far as the process of treaty making is successfully extended, therefore, the practice of diplomacy is rendered logically superfluous. The greater the number of questions which are settled in advance by treaties, the fewer will be left for settlement by diplomacy as they arise, assuming, of course, that the treaty is faithfully executed on both sides.

This elaborate extension of treaty making is preceded by a much simpler stage where the treaty itself has for its object merely the settlement of a concrete case. Such, for example, is the treaty providing for the sale of a given piece of territory. This simplest type of treaty is hardly more than a special compact or a contract promising a specific performance, in contrast to the treaty concluded upon a general subject to operate continuously into the future. The latter approaches general legislation in its nature, especially when it is concluded among several states and deals with subjects in a general and comprehensive way. Thus the treaty, which begins within the range of simple inconclusive diplomacy, ends in one of the advanced and final stages of international government.

Under ordinary circumstances treaties are concluded by the regular diplomatic representatives permanently accredited between or among the states concerned. For such a purpose the standing powers and instructions of the diplomatic representatives are often adequate; a regular diplomatic representative would not hesitate, if a sufficient occasion de-

[1] For literature on conclusion of treaties see, below, Appendix B, § 6b.

manded, to enter into treaty negotiations on the basis of his standing instructions. In most cases, however, special authorization and instructions are needed by the representative abroad; and, even if he enters into negotiations for a treaty with the state to which he is accredited, he will communicate with his home government for authority and instructions to continue the discussion, and he will be able to sign an agreement, in the absence of such special authority, only subject to approval, that is, upon the understanding that the agreement is to be referred to the home government for ratification. In these days of swift communication and when treaties must frequently be submitted for approval to representative bodies in any case, before being made effective, the diplomat finds few occasions for such unauthorized action, while, on the other hand, all treaties are, in actual fact, signed subject to ratification.

When special "powers" are issued to diplomats for the conclusion of treaties, these documents perform the function performed by the credentials of the diplomatic representative in ordinary cases. The "full-power" serves to identify the diplomat personally, and to describe the scope of his authority for the current negotiation. It ordinarily authorizes him to sign on behalf of his state. Indeed, it is of little value if it does not do so. Formerly full-powers pledged ratification by the state, provided the agreement made did not exceed the limits of discretion intrusted to the agent. But there would be no obligation resting upon a state which had given authority to its agent merely to arrange for an exchange of prisoners, to ratify an agreement for, let us say, the exchange of territory.

While the conclusion of ordinary treaties may be left to members of the regular diplomatic service, special treaties of great importance, such as treaties of peace and general international conventions among more than two states, are ordinarily concluded by delegates or commissioners specially chosen for the negotiations in hand or for representation at the conference where the convention is to be drawn up. The press of business upon the regular diplomatic service and the fact that specially qualified agents are, or are not, available, are considerations which determine whether or not special agents shall be utilized for the purpose. Where special agents are used they are given diplomatic rank, for the time being, to facilitate their work, and are provided with credentials and instructions in diplomatic form. They become, for the time and the purpose, diplomatic agents, even where they are acting as delegates to an international conference or congress.

The term "negotiation" should, as indicated, be confined to the first stage in the making of a treaty. In this stage of the proceedings the proposals of the negotiating parties are put forward, discussed, harmonized, and tentatively agreed upon. The next step, and a crucial one, is to draft a treaty or convention embodying the agreements in substance already projected, and to do this in such manner that the text will be satisfactory to the parties. Finally, the treaty must be signed. This completes the preliminary work of the diplomats and includes everything that can possibly be considered part of the negotiation of the treaty; even the drafting and especially the signing of the agreement might well be excluded from the concept of negotiation. The treaty then passes to the home government for examination and action.

Treaties signed by the diplomatic representatives are now quite widely submitted to the representative bodies for approval [2] before becoming effective. Whether this needs to be done is purely a matter of national Constitutional law in each state, although things are in such a position now that states are not likely to feel great confidence in the binding effectiveness of treaties not so submitted; and in the near future international law may hold that such action is necessary, just as it now holds that treaties may be concluded on behalf of the states only by duly authorized persons, and just as ratification by the formal head of the state is held to be necessary, whether based on the consent of a representative body or not. Few treaties fail to provide, in one of their articles or clauses, for ratification within a given period of time.

The original object of this ancient rule requiring ratification by the head of the state was to protect the latter against the faults of a diplomatic agent, primarily as to action in excess of the legal power conferred upon the agent, but also as to mistakes of policy. Hence this power of ratification, like the power to select diplomatic representatives on behalf of the state in the first place, and the power to consent to ratification, if such a step is required by the national Constitutional law, is conferred by the provisions of national law upon one of the national organs of government.

Finally, limits are at times set by national laws and constitutions as to the range of subjects upon which treaties may be concluded by the government, or upon the disposition which may be made of certain subjects by the government in treaty agreements. Thus the government may be forbidden to alienate national territory by treaty, or to change the form of national government, or to impose burdens upon the national revenue, without consent of the popular chamber. This whole matter—the range of the powers enjoyed by the government and the permissible modes of exercising these powers, the so-called "treaty-making power"—is ordinarily dealt with quite fully in the national constitution. [3]

The step of ratification has taken on a new significance in recent times as a result of the action of public representative bodies in seizing upon that occasion as an opportunity to exercise control over the execu-

[2] Not ratification, for which see below. Thus in the United States the Senate does not and can not ratify treaties, careless use of terms by the Supreme Court or anyone else to the contrary notwithstanding. The result is that the President may (and does at times) decline to ratify even after Senate approval: Mathews, p. 500.

[3] For limits set by international law upon such treatment, and discussion of the problem in general see article in *American Journal of International Law*, Vol. XXVIII (1934), p. 456.

tive officers and the diplomatic representatives of the state. For such action raises immediately the question of any duty to ratify.

It may be stated definitely at once that there is no obligation of ratification where the agreement actually signed exceeds the powers of him who signed it, be he a diplomatic representative or Secretary of State or President. More than that, there may be a constitutional inability and duty not to ratify in such circumstances. Where there has been no excess of power in a legal sense there is some room to maintain that a state, in selecting a diplomatic agent, commits its advantage or disadvantage to his judgment, discretion, and skill. In actual practice, all states, having this second opportunity to reflect upon the policy involved in the proposed agreement, do not hesitate to take it and to reject treaties on grounds of policy. This most frequently happens, of course, when the Executive who negotiated the treaty and the Legislature or representative body to which the treaty is submitted for approval have divergent views as to the desirable national policy. In such cases the only thing to be said is that the ordinary rules of representation in government must be applied. If the Executive is not at the time truly a national representative in principle or in fact or neither, while the Legislature is, no one can complain if the latter will not accept treaties signed by the former, unless the principle of public responsibility in government is to be given up. If both arms of the government are in theory representative, yet disagree in policy, it is evidently a case where the mechanism of representation is defective, leaving divergent mandates standing to conflict with one another. If the conflict be due to changes of public opinion in the passage of time, the case is the same but it must also be recognized, in such cases, that reconsideration of policy is not, by itself, a procedure which can be condemned. In none of these cases can it reasonably be argued that the action of the representative body deserves to be ignored, or that it would be better if that were possible.

In view of the very real difficulty of this problem, attempts are made to take care of the situation in advance. The agents chosen to negotiate the treaty are at times selected with the advice or consent—tacit and implied or explicit—of the body which is later to be called upon to ratify the treaty. Thus some degree of accord between the home government and its agent is assured, not only in point of law, but in point of policy. Such a procedure is rather desirable. Second thoughts are useful, and the value of two independent judgments upon a treaty is unquestioned, but this must not be sought at too great expense of consistency and effectiveness in state action. If the public assembly is to have the final word on the treaty the first word ought not be said in indifference to or defiance of the policy of that body. And the whole situation is greatly alleviated by stipulating ratification at discretion by the home government. In view of the fact that the ratifying body can hardly hope to control foreign representatives in practice, even though their appointment be subject to its approval, in view of the fact that their instructions must naturally come from the executive, such a solution seems to be inevitable. Control by the legislature of the selection of representatives to negotiate treaties would undoubtedly have some effect, but not a great deal. The practice of subjecting international agreements to public approval is not going to decrease; on the contrary, it is going to increase; and it remains to adjust matters in view of that movement by a device in the mechanism of treaty negotiation to take care of it.[4]

A similar line of reasoning is to be applied to "reservations" to treaties on the stage of ratification. Reservations which merely interpret the provisions of the treaty text present no difficulties; but this is merely to raise the question whether a given reservation is simply interpretative, that is, whether it serves merely to bring out the agreed meaning of the text, or whether it constitutes a change in the agreement as understood at the time by one or more of the parties. The net result is that if a state desires to make reservations it does so at its peril, while, if the co-signatory allows such reservations to stand, it, in turn, may suffer thereby. It is impossible to say either that a reservation made has no effect unless explicitly agreed to by the other parties or that, if merely allowed to stand unchallenged, it has the effect of altering the obligations of the treaty for the state making the reservations. The law of nations has not reached a point where these detailed problems are settled. The test to be applied is the test of joint agreement or mutual consent between or among the parties to the treaty; just what will constitute evidence of consent in the matter of ratifications with reservations remains to be settled in the special circumstances of the case, checked and reënforced by the risk of counterclaims and refusals to perform the obligations of the treaty in the future. Where reservations or amendments, including changes in the text and essential modifications of meaning, are stated by one party and accepted by the other, all difficulty is removed.

After ratification by the parties severally, evidences of this action are exchanged.[5] This exchange of ratifications is the definitive step in the conclusion of the treaty and gives it binding force upon the contracting states. A publication or promulgation of the treaty usually follows and renders it binding, subject to the Constitutional law of each state and common international law, upon the citizens of each of the contracting states, and, so far as may be by international law, upon third states. It will be noted that the range of binding effect of the treaty increases at each stage, from signature through ratification and exchange to promulgation. Signature binds the government, ratification and exchange of ratification binds the state, promulgation binds the people of the state individually.[6]

---

[4] Example below, Appendix A, Document No. 5a and b.

[5] Example below, Appendix A, Document No. 5c.

[6] On the possibility of a sovereign state being bound by treaty see above, Chap. V and below, Chap. IX 3.

The effect of treaties upon third states or states not parties to the agreement varies with the nature of the treaty and the action or inaction of these states. On the one hand the doctrine of the legal independence of states forbids any two states to impose legal obligations upon a third state without its consent. On the other hand, outside states may become parties to a treaty by giving such consent. Between the two extremes, and especially in the binding effect of these acts, there are many variations.

States not parties to a treaty may be invited to adhere to the agreement or to accede to its terms, and this invitation may be extended by separate diplomatic action or in the text of the treaty or in both ways. The distinction between accession and adhesion is slight, and the two terms are often confused. By accession a state becomes a party to the treaty, while by adhesion it simply recognizes the terms as agreed to by others and pledges to respect them. In one case the third state enters into the juridical system created by the treaty; in the second case it does not, but agrees to respect this set of arrangements as existing between other states which have already signed the document. This distinction is of importance where the treaty is of such character that accession would involve the new state in obligations to do certain things, as, for example, to participate in an exchange of military or economic statistics among the signatories. Where a cession of territory by one state to another is involved, third states could hardly, in the nature of the case, do more than adhere to the treaty and this would mean merely taking note of its effects.

In the absence of accession or adhesion third states are merely under obligation to take notice of the existence and effect of the treaty between the contracting powers. The results, in point of fact, are the same in the end, in the case of treaties such as those for the cession of territory, as though the state had formally adhered thereto. Likewise for treaties embodying and declaring rules or codes of international law; third states may in the nature of the case be compelled to accept them as evidences of the common law of nations in spite of the fact of not being signatory thereto, as in the case of the Declaration of Paris in 1856. Further, non-signatories may by independent action adopt the rules of law embodied in such treaties without joining in the signature of the treaty itself, as did the United States, in part, with respect to that same Declaration of Paris. It is hardly too much to say that the effect of treaties upon non-signatory states depends more upon the contents of the treaty in question than upon the formal action or inaction of these states. With the great increase of the number of treaties of a law-making character, this is doubly true. Treaty-making is becoming increasingly legislative in character, both within the individual states and in their relations to one another. It is a far cry to the age when treaties were merely contracts between personal sovereigns negotiated on their behalf by personal agents, and could in the nature of the case bind only the signatory parties.

Several questions arise in connection with international treaties which are of an essentially legal nature, as, for example, the rights of states signatory to the treaty by virtue of the terms of the agreement. These questions lie in the field of strict law, rather than in that of international governmental practice. Nevertheless, certain questions of this sort arise directly out of the process of treaty conclusion, and these problems cannot therefore be overlooked in any study of that process.

As has already been suggested, the scope of the treaty signed by the agents of the states must conform to the scope of the powers entrusted to them. Any agreement in excess of the powers conferred upon them can have no binding force unless it is conferred by some additional action of the state, such as ratification in spite of the extended scope of the agreement. The agent cannot commit his principal to obligations which are beyond his powers, although the latter may make good the defect by himself accepting those obligations.

Again, the principal cannot be held bound by agreements made by his diplomatic agent where the latter has, in the course of the negotiations, been subjected to fraud or duress to compel him to sign. The state as such may be "compelled" to accept a treaty at great disadvantage to itself by reason of the fact that the only alternatives open to it are still greater disadvantages or sufferings. But in such a case the state has lost its freedom of choice as a matter of fact at an earlier point of time, by allowing itself to be put in such a position that it can be confronted with the alternatives of conquest or agreement to pay an indemnity; as a matter of law, its choice is still free as between the alternatives presented. In the case of the agent, he has no choice when confronted with fraud or a threat of death; or, even if it is insisted that the same freedom to choose exists in his case as exists in the case of the state whose territory and capital have been occupied, the only choice that he actually has is between his own interests and those of the state. For this reason he is not properly capable of binding the state by such a choice.

Finally, the treaty as negotiated cannot abrogate the accepted rules of international law. Treaties may be concluded with the direct purpose of revising the accepted rules of international law, and two states may agree to act in their relations with one another in a manner at variance with these rules. But such a treaty can have no binding effect in respect of third states, nor will the rules of international law be revised for them without their consent as a result of that treaty. The utmost to be gained in such cases is that third states will recognize that its obligations exist as between the signatories. This they must admit, but may, on the contrary, enter a legitimate protest where their rights are adversely affected by a treaty contrary to commonly accepted international law.

The validity of treaties is affected not only by the manner and conditions under which they are concluded, but also by the course of subsequent events. And these may easily lead to the total disappearance of the treaty or its replacement in whole or in part by a new agreement.

The simplest mode in which a treaty may pass out of the system of effective international agreements is by the fulfilment of its terms or expiration according to a time limit set in those terms; it is sometimes said of the former that it persists as an executed treaty but this does not alter the situation greatly. By such a process treaties are lapsing continually, and if this were the only force operating in the field the existing treaty system would be seriously depleted with the passage of time, and only such treaties would remain as stipulated obligations which were still unperformed or were permanent and continuous in their nature.

Such a result is forestalled by the constant replacement of expiring treaties by new agreements. Old treaties are constantly revised, in whole or in part, and thus the treaty nexus is carried along continuously. The multiplication of state rights and obligations as a result of the repeated conclusion of single treaties leads to a condition of confusion and complexity which in itself calls for a process of constant revision and consolidation. States are from time to time compelled by this factor to pause, take stock of their outstanding treaties and treaty rights and obligations, and attempt to consolidate these rights and obligations and render them uniform and consistent. This leads to a renewal or revision of old treaties and it may also lead to the abandonment of old treaties by mutual agreement without any further steps, as well as to the replacement of old treaties by entirely new ones.

Treaties or parts of treaties may likewise come to an end by the action of the beneficiary in renouncing rights accorded by the terms thereof. This would not of itself give a right to release from obligations incurred by the treaty and could only take place under ordinary circumstances in connection with one-sided treaties. These are rare, and the case where a state is willing to renounce treaty rights while not securing a release from the corresponding obligations is rare. Hence this mode of terminating treaties or treaty obligations is unusual.

Finally, treaties may be terminated by a process of denunciation. One of the parties may denounce a treaty according to provisions found in the text of the instrument itself. Or one of the parties may denounce the treaty according to the rules of common international law. This may take place when it is discovered that there are defects in its original validity due to action by the negotiators in excess of their powers or due to duress applied to the negotiators. The proper stage at which to act upon such facts is that of ratification, and ratification may be taken to cover any such facts as those which are known at the time. But newly discovered facts of this nature will likewise justify and—what is more important for our purposes—probably lead to denunciation later. Beyond this, denunciation will be likely to follow upon the failure of one party to perform its obligations under the treaty, and also such a change in circumstances in either of the states parties to the agreement or in general international relations (*rebus non sic stantibus*) as to make the treaty dangerous to the existence of one of the parties or to invalidate the exchange of benefits upon which it is based. The denunciation in such a case will give a right of compensation to the other party for benefits actually conferred and for loss of compensating benefits, but no state can hope to hold another to treaty obligations apart from some substantial degree of mutual benefit or in circumstances endangering the safety of the state. Indeed, it is this very reason, turned in the other direction, that entitles the second party to compensation upon denunciation by the first; substantial equity and not the mere letter of the law must be satisfied.

By these processes treaties are made, revised, abandoned, replaced, and extended, and the web of international treaty obligations is kept in reasonable repair and effectiveness. As will have been observed, several trends or tendencies have appeared in the character of treaties in recent decades. Treaties have passed from mere contracts to something like statutes or even constitutions (the contract treaty still remaining the most numerous type, however), have tended to become longer and more comprehensive, have more signatories, be more detailed in treatment of any given topic, go into more non-political fields, and so on. The result is an imposing body of treaty law running among the nations.

The treaty nexus may be studied as it stands at any given point in time; and an analysis of existing treaty rights at any given point in the past gives a fairly adequate understanding of the existing state system and the existing system of international practice at that time. Moreover, despite the fact that, with each advancing decade, and almost with each new treaty made, some old treaty passes out of effective existence as a statute of binding obligation,—so that the vast majority of all the treaties on record are now obsolete, and only the more recent ones, such as have not expired and have not been superseded or abrogated by succeeding compacts, are directly effective,—these older treaties are not of merely historical interest. For the provisions which they contain furnish evidence regarding the principles upon which the nations may be presumed to desire to regulate their relations, in the absence of any conventional agreements in effect to the contrary. In other words, they provide the materials from which the rules of the historic common international law may be inferred by a process of induction. Finally, it is with the external aspects of this net-work of treaties in which the modern states of the world are and have been constantly enlaced that we are chiefly concerned, and not with the contents of those treaties; for this purpose the treaty system of a decade ago is as useful for study as that of today.

From an inspection of published collections of treaties [7] it appears that modern states have concluded tens of thousands of treaties with

[7] See references in Appendix B, § 6b.

one another since the dawn of international relations. In view of the nature of the material, it is, of course, impossible to render such data precise within two, or even three, figures. All of the collections contain many national statutes, decrees, and other acts besides treaties proper. There are many duplications, and doubtless not a few treaties have been entirely lost from their pages. Nevertheless the general result is sufficiently reliable to be dependable for the simple inferences which may be made from it. And the mere fact of bulk deserves attention if nothing else could be said. Here is a vast body of treaty practice and treaty law which forms a solid element of international organization on its own account.

The existing body of international conventions may be analyzed in several ways. The agreements among the nations may be classified according to form and also according to subject matter, and each method yields its own peculiar results. Of the two, the former classification is simpler and reveals more regarding the mechanics of international practice.

The "treaty" proper is the basic type of international agreement and is an agreement in full form and style between two or more states, independent at least for the purposes of that particular treaty.[8]

There is, however, great confusion in actual practice in the descriptive terms used to refer to various international compacts. The usage of daily language cannot be accepted uncritically. The term treaty may be used either generically, to refer to all sorts of international agreements, or, more specifically, to denote the typical, formal, international compact. It is in the latter sense that it is used here.

A treaty, or, rather, the text of a treaty,—although there is no such thing as an unwritten treaty, and the term refers to the document in which the agreement is recorded rather than to the agreement itself,—may be analyzed into various parts.[9] First comes the preamble, which declares that the parties named have, through their agents, as named, agreed to the following articles for a certain purpose, also named. Then follows the body or text of the treaty, usually divided into articles, and even, on occasion, into chapters, sections, clauses, paragraphs, and so on, giving the substance of the agreement. Articles dealing with the general principles of the agreement come first, followed by special articles which apply these principles. At the end are often found articles dealing with the way in which the agreement is to be carried out, and, perhaps, articles providing for guarantees of execution. At the end also come provisions concerning ratification and the exchange of ratifications and the date when the agreement shall be effective. This completes the body of the treaty, and the statement follows that this agreement has been made at a certain place and on a certain date and has been signed by the

[8] Specimens, below, Appendix A, Nos. 1, 4, and others.
[9] See Document No. 1, in Appendix A, below.

participants. Finally come the signatures and seals of the agents. There may be annexed to the treaty any number of appendices or schedules containing details of rates or similar material which operate in execution of the principles of the treaty, but which it has not been thought best to include even among the special articles.

Much labor has been spent upon the art or science of interpreting treaties. But such work is part of rhetoric or logic rather than of international relations and, in any case, refers to the subject matter of the treaty rather than to the form. Regarding the latter, as just described, the chief difficulty concerns the act of signing and sealing the document. The giving of guarantees is rapidly disappearing now, but the problems connected with the powers of the signers are not diminishing in numbers or in complexity. As greater care is now taken in the assumption of international obligations by treaty, and as opposition to secret treaties increases and likewise the demand for public approval of treaties concluded by the executive arm of the government, this question is rendered more difficult than ever. The rules regarding the power to sign are partially principles of Constitutional law and partially principles of international law pure and simple. What we have to note is the procedure in the case.

The negotiators are identified and their powers defined by their credentials and full-powers. The identification and declaration of powers in the preamble must lie within the limits of the former. Further, the treaty itself must lie within the limits of these full-powers. And, finally, the signatures and seals must correspond with the declarations of personal identity contained in the credentials. The seals used by the signers are not state seals, but private personal seals used for purposes of identification. Needless to say, they are not necessary in a day when personal signatures are adequate for these purposes, but they repay attention because they reveal the fact that the negotiators sign primarily as individual persons, and only indirectly as state officials. The question of due powers may, therefore, always be raised, and if raised must be settled by reference to the credentials and full-powers just described.

There are many varieties of international agreements beside the "treaty" proper. The term "convention" has been used in various ways in modern treaty practice to describe international agreements. On the one hand, it has been used in reference to international agreements of secondary importance, such as cultural conventions, and therefore of somewhat informal style—sub-treaties, if they may be so termed. On the other hand, the term has been used to refer to great international agreements signed by several nations, in full form, such as the Hague Conventions. Evidently there is some confusion here. The real distinction seems to run between agreements upon subjects of a political character and agreements upon subjects of a governmental or administrative character. Thus we always have "treaties" of peace, of alliance, of cession, but "conventions" regarding postal service, and "conventions" for the exchange of consular representatives. Even that distinction is not consistently followed, and the two terms are often used interchangeably.

Various other forms of international compact are in use. A "declaration" is a joint statement of international law as it is understood by the parties or a statement of the policy which they intend to pursue on a given subject, or a mixture of both. Such was the Declaration of Paris of 1909 relating to the rules of naval warfare. A *compromis d'arbitrage* is an agreement to arbitrate on certain terms a certain dispute which has arisen between the parties; it is to be contrasted with the "treaty of arbitration" which provides for the use of arbitration by the parties in disputes which may arise in the future.[10] The term "protocol" is used to describe either memoranda or records of discussions, articles drawn up in explanation of the terms of the main body of the treaty, or records of an exchange of ratifications to a treaty.[11]

It will appear that some of these distinctions are distinctions of substance as well as of form. Other classes of international agreements are definable in the same way. Thus a "capitulation" is a military agreement for surrender of one of the parties, and "the capitulations" are, or were, treaties between Western Powers and Turkey or other Eastern states relative to privileges of citizens of the former while in the East. The connection between the substance and the form of international agreements is not arbitrary, even including the distinction between treaties and conventions. The more important subjects are dealt with in formal treaties and conventions, while agreements upon questions of minor importance are embodied in less formal pacts called by various names, such as "agreement," "arrangement," "exchange of notes," *procès verbal*, "additional article," and *modus vivendi*.

One important aspect of this practice is found in the fact that such informal agreements, where the participants feel free to rely on them, may be concluded by executive officials, even subordinate executive officials, with less ostentation than would be involved in the conclusion of a full treaty, and even, perhaps, without the process of parliamentary confirmation which is often necessary in that case. Where legislation is necessary for the execution of the agreement the check of the representative body exists in that form, of course. Still, the loophole is and must be very large under the circumstances.

Two other forms of international agreements remain to be noted, one a very minor form and one a very significant form.

The executive agreement without posterior ratification deserves to be compared with the executive agreement based upon prior national statute. In all states today there has grown up a practice of enacting statutes dealing with matters arising in international relations, such as tariff laws

[10] Now being superseded: p. 159, below.
[11] Below, p. 328.

and postal service legislation, while providing in the text of such legislation for discretion by the executive authorities in applying the law to goods or mail coming from other states. Agreements are thereupon made with other states for reciprocal remission of tariff duties or the division of postal charges by the parties. This practice constitutes a fertile source of international agreements.[12]

Lastly, the "final act" is the ultimate treaty form.[13] This term refers to the concluding agreement reached in an international conference where several treaties or conventions have been signed and which recites the circumstances and objects of the conference, indicates the course of events in the conference, and lists the results achieved in the form of separate conventions. The final act does not contain a minute record of the proceedings of the conference and merely lists by name the agreements concluded, and it does not add anything in substance to what has already been accomplished, but, in point of form it is the most striking and solemn international agreement.

Before reviewing the various classes of international treaties by reference to the subjects with which they deal it will be well to set aside entirely two great classes of "treaties," so-called.

Many leading European and American states have concluded agreements with native tribes or semi-civilized people dealing chiefly with the cession of territory, but also with such matters as the payment of tribute, the rendering of services of one sort or another, and commercial relations. The United States concluded some five hundred "treaties" of this kind with the Indian nations prior to 1871, when the practice came to an end. These compacts deserve to be called treaties only in a formal sense. They have been so regarded in our jurisprudence and Constitutional government, but clearly they do not rest upon the essential assumption of treaty negotiations, namely, the independence of the contracting parties. The treaty form was used for tactical purposes, to save the faces and consciences of the European settlers and to assimilate the process of dispossessing the Indian nations to the accepted system of the European law of nations, and also for the superior moral and psychological effect in the eyes of the Indian of this form of action in contrast to a simple notice to him to vacate. The pretense of free consent was considered, apparently, to have a certain argumentative value and the question of constitutional jurisdiction was avoided, while placing the immediate burden of enforcement upon the Indian chiefs who had signed the "treaty."

In the second place, notice should be taken of the "Concordats" concluded by the Papacy with various states with the purpose of protecting the interests of the Roman Church in the territories of those states.

---

[12] See volume by McClure cited below, Appendix B, § 6b.

[13] Final Act of International Civil Aviation Conference, below, Appendix A, Document No. 6c.

While these agreements take the form of treaties or conventions they deal almost exclusively with religious and ecclesiastical matters and hence do not relate to the normal subject matter of international relations. And we cannot, in view of all the facts of the case, regard the Papacy as a state in all the implications of the term; such agreements are to be regarded rather as agreements between states and a private, or, at most, a quasi-state organization than as treaties in international law.

With the subject matter of the great majority of individual treaties neither the student of diplomacy nor of law has much concern. The cession of this piece of land, the granting of this or that commercial privilege, the settlement of this or that claim are not, in themselves, of more importance for common international law or the elaboration of international coöperation than are the contents of private contracts for the private or public law of the state where they are made. Given the methods of diplomatic negotiation and the legal rules concerning consent, interpretation, and termination, and the nations may agree with one another upon tariffs or territories at their pleasure. Of course, the student of law is interested in the classification of treaties as executory, executed, declarative, and so on, according as they provide for future performance, create a new legal status, or declare a given rule of law or line of policy. This again relates rather to legal forms than to subject matter, and does not alter the conclusion stated. This is all the more true because of the fact that as yet there seem to be few bars to the conclusion of individual treaties between the members of individual pairs of states contrary to common international law.

While not interested in the specific content of given treaties, however, the student of law and diplomacy finds it convenient to classify treaties according to the general nature of the subjects dealt with. They may be classified as treaties of peace, treaties of alliance, treaties of cession, boundary treaties, treaties of commerce, consular conventions, and so on through dozens of groups, covering all conceivable aspects of international relations.[14] For few questions arise in the life of the nations which have not been the subjects of international treaty agreement. Or, on the other hand, treaties may be grouped into two great classes, namely, treaties dealing with legal and governmental subjects and those dealing with concrete topics having no implications for international law or organization. Of the former class are treaties declaring rules of international law and conventions establishing international courts or commissions or conferences;[15] of the latter class are those ceding a piece of territory for a certain purchase price.[16] The former are of vital significance for the student of international government, the latter have little

---

[14] Text of one of the most important of modern treaties of peace is given, below, Appendix A, Document No. 4.

[15] Declaration of Paris, 1856, below, Appendix A, Document No. 5b.

[16] Treaty between the United States and France for cession of Louisiana, 1803.

more to do with that subject than a private horse trade has with national Constitutional law.

It is, of course, difficult to draw the line between these two classes of treaties with complete precision. It is still more difficult, in many cases, to classify a given treaty, because of the mixture of elements to be found in its provisions. The treaty of arbitration is easy to classify, and likewise the treaty agreeing to the cession of a given piece of territory. The treaty of commerce, however, may include provisions for the remission of tariff duties and also provisions for the exchange of consular representatives, and while the former have no special significance for international law or government, the latter have.[17] Even the treaty of cession, the purest type of non-legal treaty, may contain statements of the grounds for the cession in point and thereby take on an added significance.[18]

It would be of no special service to recite here a list of the different varieties of treaties by subject matter. Among the more important, beside those already named, are treaties of guarantee, treaties of navigation, treaties dealing with laws of copyright and patent, the settlement of claims, the protection of property, and jurisdiction over aliens, including the related subjects of naturalization and citizenship and extradition.[19] In the past century and a quarter there has, however, occurred a notable change in the predominating character of treaties, so far as their subject matter is concerned. A collection of treaties of the early eighteenth century bears the title "collection of treaties of alliance, of peace, of truce." Of late years there have been fewer such political treaties or treaties dealing with personal and formal diplomatic questions and more treaties dealing with legal, economic, and governmental affairs. There have been fewer treaties of alliance, marriage treaties, and treaties relating to the privileges of rulers and princes, and more agreements dealing with questions of international law, providing for the extradition of fugitives from justice, the settlement of pecuniary claims, the exchange of commercial and postal facilities, and the establishment of international judicial or administrative organs.

A secondary result is to be seen in the increase in the number of treaties signed by more than two powers, or what may be called general international acts. This is attributable to the fact that it is natural for

[17] Treaty of commerce and navigation between the United States and France, 1800, Arts. VI, IX, X.

[18] Treaty between the United States and Mexico for cession of territory and payment therefore, 1853, Art. IV.

[19] Treaty of guarantee between the United States and Panama, 1903; treaty of navigation between the United States and Denmark, 1857; treaties on patent and copyright between the United States and Japan; treaty on settlement of claims between the United States and France, 1880; treaty of amity and commerce between the United States and China, 1844, Art. XIX; treaty on naturalization between the United States and Ecuador, 1872; treaty of extradition between the United States and Bavaria, 1853.

several states to combine in law-making treaties while it was not natural to expect them to combine in treaties of the older type, creating special and exclusive privileges, or establishing special ties of marriage or alliance against hostile dynasties between friendly royal houses. The more recent international agreements are of a broadly coöperative character in contrast to the narrow competitive agreements of an earlier age.

The character of the treaty nexus is thus being altered within itself. Not only is the web of treaty obligations growing greater in magnitude and internal complexity; it is also growing firmer and more stable in quality. Bargains on concrete questions of no permanent significance are being superseded by what looks very much like international legislation on legal and governmental matters of general and continuing interest. Just as personal diplomacy is converted into something far more significant for the problem of international government by its metamorphosis into treaty making, so also the latter takes on a new and far more significant nature by the reorientation of its outlook as to subject matter. To this is to be added the changing characteristics of the process of treaty making, whereby treaties between two parties are increasingly supplemented by treaties concluded in international conferences among several nations. The transition from personal contract to general legislation is here seen in all its detailed steps.[20]

When the contents of the treaties concluded among the nations are examined more closely the relations between provisions found there and the whole body of national and international law appear to be very ambiguous. Treaties have been classified in the preceding pages as legal and governmental, on the one hand, and economic and political, on the other. Disregarding the latter class henceforth, it remains to define the processes by which the provisions of a treaty stating a rule of law to which the signatory parties have agreed becomes effective. This investigation leads in two directions. On the one hand it leads to an inquiry into the relation between the law of treaties, if it may be so called, and national law; on the other side it leads to the problem of the relation between treaties and international law and administration. The second question has already been considered in our discussion of international law; [21] to the first question we now turn.

It is obvious from an inspection of the text of many international treaties that their provisions, although stated as rules of law, and sometimes precisely because they are stated in that form, need further action in order to be effective. The general principles, and even the comparatively detailed rules, of a treaty may need elaboration in statement and in the explanation of their precise meanings. In any case they need to be carried into practical execution. Treaties sometimes relate merely to the state as such; thus, a treaty recognizing the independence of one of

[20] See, further, below, Chap. X. A.
[21] Above, Chap. V.

the contracting parties would need no elaboration upon that point, and it would call for no direct application in actual life. The effect intended is an effect in the field of theory and abstract law, and it is accomplished by the very act of concluding the treaty. In the case of a treaty providing for reciprocal commercial rights for citizens of the contracting states, however, there is a need for further legal statement and also for practical application in actual life. After all, the individual is the ultimate unit of political and legal action, and most treaties call for results in the realm of the individual citizen. In this great range of cases additional action is necessary in national law and government to carry out the treaty. Let us note those cases carefully and in some detail before proceeding any further.[22]

Certain types of treaties may be carried out by the simple action of executive officials without further coöperation from other governmental bodies and without any change in the national law. A treaty signed by the United States recognizing the independence of the cosignatory state would, as indicated, constitute such recognition. Furthermore, even if the agreement contained also a pledge to receive diplomatic representatives from that state, it could be carried out by the President alone, under his constitutional power to conduct our foreign relations.

Where, however, the action needed must be taken by subordinate officials who have no discretion and who must act solely in accordance with instructions from superior officers, such a procedure is impossible. In such cases some further action is necessary in order to set the machinery of the national government in operation.

In certain of these cases, again, the chief executive might carry the treaty into execution by issuing the necessary instructions to subordinate officials. This would be true, for example, where no statutory or Constitutional provisions existed to control executive and administrative action in that field. Such situations are relatively rare and can be found in the United States only in the field of foreign relations. Thus the President could instruct the Secretary of State to issue an exequatur to a certain individual in execution of a consular convention with a given state, without reference to any statute or other legal standard.

In most of these cases, however, action by subordinate administrative officials depends on authorization from the legislature, because the chief executive is unable to issue new instructions to his subordinates for the execution of the treaty in the face of national legislation to the contrary or in the absence of appropriate legislation. Even in the United States, where treaties become an integral part of the law of the land, and where a treaty acts to repeal previous statutes in conflict with it, this is true, especially as regards the payment of money from the treasury, and in the case where legislation contravenes a prior treaty. In these cases favor-

---

[22] On the relation of treaties to national law see literature cited, below, Appendix B, § 6b.

able or supporting legislation by Congress is needed, or, at the very least, careful abstention from hostile legislation.

If the executive is somewhat dependent upon the legislature for its power to act in execution of national treaty engagements, the judiciary is doubly dependent upon both the legislature and the executive branches. What the "political" departments of the government do or say as respects the nature and extent of the obligations of a treaty will be accepted by the judicial department as final in many cases, particularly as to the effectiveness or ineffectiveness of the treaty as a whole, the annexation of territory by treaty, and, as above, the actual administrative operations under the treaty. In another sense, however, the courts have more opportunity and power to carry into execution treaty obligations than do the other two departments of the government. Thus where the requisite action has been taken by these departments it is to the courts that the matter comes in the last instance if there be any doubt or dispute about it. Again, where no such action is necessary the courts are, in a number of nations, free to act upon the treaty directly, applying the treaty in litigation between private parties wherever it is in place. This is true especially in the United States, because of the Constitutional position of treaties in the national legal system, as already defined. It is not true, however, that this posture of affairs is wholly exceptional, and it seems fairly certain that the drift of things is toward this solution of the problem of the application of treaties. With the growth of the practice of subjecting treaties to national representative bodies for approval in legislative form, this method of action is bound to spread. Thus all branches of the national government will gain increased authority in carrying into execution the national treaty obligations.

Such a result is earnestly to be desired. As matters now stand in the field of international coöperation, a treaty depends for its execution largely upon the national governments of the signatory parties. Whether it is executed or not, and the terms on which it may be executed, are matters of comparative national Constitutional law and government. Failure of a national government to act means that the treaty fails of execution. There is, of course, a distinct moral obligation to act, and this obligation is not only moral but also legal, in the sense that it is supported by the accepted principles of international law. It is not, however, with certainty enforceable by a signatory state in any judicial tribunal, national or international, and it lacks a perfect binding force in operation. The national courts cannot attempt to compel the legislature to act in execution of the treaty. The legislature could perhaps compel the executive and the judiciary to act by the processes of statutory legislation or impeachment, but if the legislature, the repository of the national discretion, sees fit to refuse to carry out the national obligations, no adequate legal or governmental redress is available to the other state. In default of execution the signatory state not satisfied with the performance of the other party to the treaty may legitimately put forward diplomatic protests and seek compensation for value received and for any losses incurred. But the fact remains that in order to be finally effective a treaty must be incorporated into the national legal systems of the signatory states and thus made binding and operative in the hands of the executive, legislative, and judicial organs of the state.

There is one other aspect of this situation which deserves at least passing notice. So far we have been discussing treaties calling for action which is left by national law to national officials and regulated by that law in certain ways. But a treaty may expressly stipulate for certain action to be performed in a certain way by certain officials, all at variance with existing national law, statutory or Constitutional; this is occurring more and more frequently today. Conservative opinion holds that in such circumstances the state must change its law before the treaty can become effective. Sound theory would seem to indicate that the treaty of its own force modifies the local law, and in a number of recent cases international treaties providing for changes in administrative procedure in individual countries have been carried out without legislation, but as this is an extremely complex and difficult legal problem it will have to be left with this brief reference.[23]

[23] See, further; article cited in note 2, above, and *The First Decade*, p. 267.

CHAPTER VII

International Conference

The most vital defect in the international organization of the past has been the difficulty of securing international conference where, and especially when, it was needed. Why was this difficult, why was it a serious defect, and how has it been remedied?

International conference [1] grows out of the joint consideration and discussion, by the representatives of at least two states, of matters of interest common to both. Whenever the representatives of two states meet together to discuss an international difference, however, it is their hope and expectation that they will come to some agreement, and agreement, not mere discussion, is assumed to be their aim. Conferences of two nations, moreover, naturally lead on to conferences of several nations, as the problems of international life become generalized and expanded so that they affect more than two states. Eventually we reach the conference in which thirty or forty independent nations, perhaps the states of the whole world, participate. Bi-party conferences become tri-party and multi-party conferences as the interests of all states become further and further interwoven.

International conference in its simplest form is merely personal diplomacy as already studied. Whenever the Ambassador of a foreign state visits for business purposes the Minister for Foreign Affairs in the capital where he is stationed we have an international conference. The action takes on its full significance, however, when the conference is specially arranged before it takes place, when the questions for discussion are previously defined, and when the discussions in conference are conducted by representatives specially named for the purpose. If, in addition, the conference includes several nations, as just suggested, the action is still more significant. Although it will involve a certain amount of anticipation of things to come it may be pointed out here that the states pass on from diplomacy to conference because of belief in the superior values mechanical and psychological of the latter. Conference is more flexible and more rapid than diplomacy, both as to the subjects and participants which are included. It tends to reduce the formal aspects of negotiation and extend the elements of human contact and appreciation. At the same time it is far from a certain cure, as some seem to fancy, for all world problems.

Like personal diplomacy of the simpler form, the international con-

[1] See literature, below, Appendix B, § 7.

ference may end in one of two ways. A formal international treaty of one type or another may be signed; or the results may be left in the form of memoranda or minutes of the discussions. The more important the conference and the questions there discussed, the more likely it is that a formal treaty will at least be attempted, although the conference held deliberately for a mere exchange of views must not be excluded or denied all value.[2] Likewise, where extensive agreements are reached in conference and definite decisions are taken, the results will be put in treaty form. Inconclusive conferences on unimportant topics are recorded only in minutes or memoranda of discussions.

When the treaty form is adopted for expressing the result the conference reaches its highest point of significance, and also the highest point of development possible for any of the special forms of international organization. For this is legislation, constituent or regulatory. It is creative law-making. The representation of national policies and the making of demands and settlement of disputes is a comparatively simple thing; the conclusion of special contractual agreements regarding international relations, while it initiates the process of legislation, carries us but little further; the settlement of disputes by arbitration on the basis of existing law, and the administration of international business according to existing law,—to anticipate again—are not revolutionary, as far as the substance of international rights is concerned. But the revision and amendment of international constitutional and customary law by deliberate discussion and agreement reaches the center of international coöperation. Petty lawmaking is to be found in all of the other special fields of international government; here legislation is the principal business, and the development of the law of nations, the practice of diplomacy, the negotiation of treaties, and international arbitration and administration are all, in turn, amenable to its control.

This is to state the function of conference in the international field in terms of its formal results. Beneath the legislation which it produces, however, lies another function or achievement of international conference which should be emphasized still further. This is the synthesis or harmonization of divergent national policies, so important, as has been pointed out already and as will be seen at every step of the way, in the operation of organized international coöperation. International administration can operate only if a basis of international law or policy has been provided, and that can be accomplished only if conflicting national views have been reconciled and common international policy achieved. To some extent this can be done and is done outside of, and prior to the advent or application of, international organization, or at least in the early stages of that process, by diplomacy. But if it is to be done most effectively and in connection with more advanced forms of international

[2] Example in *The New York Times*, May 18, 1946, p. 6.

coöperation, it is in and by the conference that it must be achieved.

The subjects dealt with by international conferences range over the whole field of international relations. The decisions taken may relate to constitutional questions of deep and lasting moment to all nations, such as the decision to establish a compulsory court of arbitration. At times they relate to comparatively trivial concrete questions affecting two states only, such as the cession of a bit of property by one state to another. The more critical questions, both constitutional and practical, arise in conferences held at the termination of wars, and we shall encounter at that point the whole general problem of peace and war and of the relation between peace and international organization.

No distinction need be made, probably, between the terms "conference" and "congress." It was once felt that a "congress" must be more formal, more important, and more general, than a "conference." But in view of the practice of speaking of the gatherings at The Hague in 1899 and 1907 as the "Hague Conferences" and of the gathering in Paris in 1919 as the "Peace Conference of Paris," this distinction vanishes. No international meetings were ever more formal, more important, or more general than these. It sometimes appears that the term "conference" is given to gatherings of diplomats for the discussion of political questions, while the meeting of experts and administrative officials on legal and scientific matters is called a "congress," as in the cases of the Postal Congress and the Pan-American Scientific Congress. Here again, however, numerous Health Conferences and the Pan-American Financial Conferences rise to confound all attempts at differentiation by reference to the actual use of these terms in the names of international bodies. Indeed, there seems to be a tendency to get away entirely from the rather flowery and pompous term "congress" and to stick to the simpler, more direct, and more accurate designation.

At times, the term "peace" is also used ambiguously in this connection. A "peace conference" is, curiously enough, a conference which meets in time of war to settle questions connected with the war. It derives its name from its object, which is the reëstablishment of peace. The conferences at The Hague in 1899 and 1907, on the other hand, are commonly referred to as the "Hague Peace Conferences" for a similar reason, namely, that they were aimed at the more effective maintenance of peace, although, unlike most "peace conferences," they were not called at the close of hostilities to define the terms of peace between belligerents. Now every international conference is a peace conference in a sense, for it aims in some degree at the maintenance of international peace. It seems best therefore to classify international conferences more carefully, as conferences in time of peace and conferences for the termination of war.

International conferences in time of peace deal with a multitude of subjects, and the differences among them mean little. The conference either deals with the problems before it in terms of general policy and law or moves on to those points where questions of principle have been settled and administration alone is at issue.

International discussions on political questions are older than the conferences on legal or administrative questions, for the reason that such a conference is not much more than simple diplomatic negotiation. By the same token such conferences tend to diminish in number as international relations are subjected to legal regulation. The result is that when we reach the later nineteenth century, and the period of multipartite international conferences proper, the meetings which deal with purely political or diplomatic problems are relatively few.

Frequently, especially since the development of "public international law," such questions take on also a legal aspect. Thus, the conference held at London in 1871 regarding the Black Sea question issued a declaration concerning the inviolability of treaties. More frequently, however, legal questions arise in connection with the details of current international practice, and a conference must be held to revise and codify the rules of international law relating to the conduct of war, the treatment of wounded in time of war, or the neutralization of certain sections of territory or certain bodies of water. It is worth noting that most of the early conferences on legal subjects dealt with the laws of war, just as the first treatises on the law of nations dealt with this subject. The reason is the same in both cases, namely, that war is the earliest and most critical form of international contact. The question of neutralization, again, harks back rather directly to the political sphere, inasmuch as the proposal to neutralize a given body of water can hardly be based on any established legal grounds and inevitably affects one nation or another adversely. Thus the neutralization of Belgium and Luxembourg resulted from the actions of the conferences, political in character, convened at London in 1830 and 1867. The Conference of Brussels in 1874 and the Hague Conferences of 1899 and 1907 were conferences on legal subjects, as also were the London Naval Conference in 1908-1909, and many others.

The provision of international administrative service (including adjudication) for some subject of international interest, or for legal principles and rules adopted relating to that subject, follows in second place; administration must wait upon legislation. Conferences with this objective in view have also increased in number. The Hague Conferences may be classed here in part, the conference held at Rome in 1905 for establishment of the International Institute of Agriculture is another example, and there are numerous others. Of course political and legal issues arise here, just as administrative issues arise in the conferences devoted chiefly to legal problems, but the principal character of the conference is not altered thereby. Subsequent conferences are held for revision of the conventions and regulations underlying such organizations and for reviewing the services rendered. The conferences themselves take on a quasi-administrative atmosphere.

Speaking broadly, the second group of problems yield solutions more satisfactory from all points of view than do those of the first. Technical questions can be subjected to statistical treatment and the knowledge and opinions of technicians can be utilized; moreover, business is business, and neither eternal wrangling nor false pride nor national sentiment count as heavily in the business world as in the world of diplomacy. Legal questions might possibly be treated in a scientific manner also, and professional lawyers and jurists might be called in for assistance. But the definition of general rules to govern all cases arising in the future is a delicate task for an international conference, and hence legal problems are not as easy of solution as they might be expected to be. When we get back into the world of political and diplomatic relations conditions are worse than they are in the administrative sphere. There are no fixed points to go upon, no generally accepted principles to apply, and not only is every delegate an expert—in his own estimation—but national desire, rather than inherent reason and right or the general interest, governs the outcome. In the field of administration national greed is not unknown, but neither are considerations of common benefit, mutual protection, and good business for all.

The form given to the results of the conference varies with the subjects discussed, as well as with the extent and definiteness of the conclusions reached. When it is desired to adopt rules covering a certain problem the matter is commonly disposed of by an international convention, which constitutes for the future a code of the law of nations on the subject with which it deals. Such were the Hague Conventions relating to the Rules of War.

As has been said, the settlement in such cases may be a specific bargain for territory or an indemnity payment, or it may consist of the declaration of a general principle. The former type,—a mere contractual bargain,—resulted from the Conference at Hanover in 1861 regarding the Stade Toll. The latter type of settlement resulted from the Conference in London in 1871 respecting the Inviolability of Treaties and Navigation of the Black Sea. Such treaties or declarations as the latter, dealing with political problems, and at the same time attempting to provide a permanent rule of public law as a solution to govern similar cases in the future, approach the acme of difficulty and importance in the field of international legislation. They approximate international constitution making. The one thing more important and more fruitful is the closely allied task of establishing international governing bodies to exercise authority over the states in the future according to principles now defined in advance. Such action followed from the numerous conferences for the creation of international administrative bureaus in the later nineteenth century and early twentieth.

It will be apparent that single international conferences may well perform various functions. The Congress of Vienna, for example, was primarily a conference for the definitive termination of war, yet it was also a conference in time of peace striving to prevent future war. It dealt with purely legal questions,—diplomatic rank,—with economic questions, and with political problems. It created an administrative bureau, it defined certain principles of the public law of nations in Europe, and it produced certain political results still evident in the state-system of Europe today.

The form given to the decisions of the international conference is not the only thing influenced by the nature of the problems discussed. The organization and methods of action of the conference are subject to the same influence. This will appear as we examine the way in which the conference meets and sets about its work.

International conferences met historically only upon invitation. There were relatively few conferences with serial sessions. There was little certainty that a conference would be held at any time. In the normal course of events few conferences meet at all, conference is still regarded as an abnormal event.[3] The burden of proof is upon any one suggesting a conference at any time, because of the absence of any conviction that a continuous series of regular conferences is needed. No state has any recognized right to call the nations to a conference and the community of nations has no recognized right to summon its members to an assembly. The proposal which was made at the conference at The Hague that such conferences should meet continuously at regular intervals in the future was considered a radical proposal indeed.

The situation just described is changing today but the traditional attitude still survives. Even where, as in the United Nations and the Union of American States and in various international administrative unions, so-called, regular sessions of conferences are provided, those meetings still seem slightly abnormal. Why is this? Why has conference seemed, in the past, such an exceptional kind of action?

In part the answer is that conference was, in sheer numerical fact, exceptional; not many conferences had been held, precedents and practice were lacking, and the action seemed very rare. In the second place there were no, or few, agreements for the holding of conferences; this explained the first phenomenon to some extent and tended to perpetuate it; it also left proposals for a conference without support in law.

These facts must be traced back, however, to psychological causes. The underlying reasons for lack of conferences or agreements for conference were lack of appreciation of any need for conference and fear of the consequences of round-table discussion of international affairs. Conference was not as necessary, as a feature of international coöpera-

[3] See French press release of April 10, 1946, in *The Washington Post*, April 11, 1946.

tion, fifty years ago as it is today, with greatly increased interpenetration of national interests; but diplomatic and official appreciation of the value of conference has always lagged behind the facts. With this has gone timidity, hesitation,—fear, and even hostility,—to such a dangerous proceeding.

This is not intended to imply that conference is always effective and may be indulged in upon all possible occasions. Indeed an unsuccessful conference usually retards international coöperation. Certain conditions are prerequisite to the success of a conference and in their absence conference cannot safely be attempted. Thus a fairly definite question must be presented if success is to be hoped for; a conference on the general state of the universe would not be very helpful. The question must be one on which agreement is possible; a conference on racial equality would be difficult and dangerous. Adequate preparation of agenda and data,—preferably by a central bureau,—selection of personnel qualified by their equipment of information and suitable personal qualities, clear formulation of national policies but with a reasonable degree of willingness to compromise, these are indispensable. Adequate housing and equipment, facilities for personal and social intercourse,—even an agreeable climate and landscape!—, all such factors do in sober reality contribute to or detract from the possibilities of success. The success at Locarno in 1925, the failure at Geneva in 1927, and the difficulties at London in 1933, together with many other recent cases, illustrate the meaning of these principles.

This situation gives the nation which initiates the conference an enormous tactical advantage. The agenda or program of discussions at the conference must be decided. What shall be discussed and what shall not be discussed depends in the first instance upon the proposal of the "august initiator" of the conference.[4] Frequently the acceptance or rejection by other nations of the invitations issued to them by the nation suggesting the conference depends upon the views held by the former as to the general advisability of the meeting and as to their own advantage in discussing the subjects proposed. Frequently they will make reservations concerning the proper range of discussion in the forthcoming conference, thereby excluding certain topics from its jurisdiction. Frequently the agenda as originally proposed will be modified, in view of preliminary objections from the nations invited to attend the conference, and in order to obtain their consent to participate.

This power of defining the agenda before the beginning of the conference also gives great prestige and influence to the nation initiating the conference, an advantage enhanced by the fact that the conference will usually be held in the territory, and at the seat of government, of this state. It is likewise an occasion of suspicion. If a certain nation moves for a conference on a certain subject it may be assumed that it is for

[4] Proposals for Hague Conference of 1907, below, Appendix A, Document No. 5.

certain definite national advantages that the move is made. (So Napoleon III was continually under suspicion because of his frequent suggestions for European conferences; he was suspected not only of having an ax to grind in each particular case but of desiring to secure a sort of diplomatic domination over Europe as a whole.) The other nations, therefore, come prepared to combat the demands of the nation which is chiefly sponsoring the conference. Because of the way in which the agenda is drawn up there can hardly be a set of openly competing programs when the conference meets and this is an unhealthy thing in itself. Furthermore, competition or opposition which is stifled makes itself felt in a silent suspicion and mistrust and an opposition "on general principles." Where preliminary national views have been canvassed fully in advance something like competing party programs exist at the outset and it is generally agreed that such a procedure helps enormously for the members do not then need to lose time in discovering each other's beliefs and demands.

The nation calling the conference is free, in the nature of the case, to invite such other states as seems best, subject to the danger of giving offense by failing to invite this or that state, and to the danger of opposition to the results of the conference from non-participants. A nation initiating a conference on maritime law and failing to invite Great Britain would encounter both British resentment and futility in the result. In such a case other states would in all probability refuse to attend, for the same reasons.

Membership in the conference itself is limited to accredited representatives of states which have been invited to attend and which have accepted. This limitation is enforced through a system of credentials. Delegates carry commissions and powers identifying them as representatives of this or that nation, and these credentials are inspected by a credentials committee at the beginning of the conference. It may be added that universally persons chosen are named by executive appointment rather than by popular election, and that they are usually middle-aged male diplomats, although this is all a matter of practice, not law, and on such points the states are free to do as they please.

The membership of the conference having been decided, it remains to select the presiding officials and the secretariat. Here again the state holding the conference has an enormous advantage, for that bane of international relations, precedence and diplomatic courtesy, decrees that the presiding officer and the chief secretary shall be chosen from among the representatives of the local state. When the deliberations of the conference are also conducted in the language of that nation the result is complete. The secretarial force, working with all the conveniences which the local government can place at its disposal, largely controls the documentation and the record of the conference, and the chief secretary controls the secretarial force. Even where no effort is made to abuse its power, the state calling the conference exerts an enormous influence on the conference through these simple facts.

The conference meets in full session at the beginning and may hold plenary sessions thereafter as often or as seldom as seems best. It ordinarily closes with one or more plenary sessions. In the intervals come many sittings of committees and commissions, in which experts are heard and matters are thrashed out in detail for reference to full sessions of the conference for final decision later. The conferences on legal and technical questions employ the committee system and make use of experts more extensively than do those on political and diplomatic problems; in the latter the principal delegates insist on keeping things largely in their own hands. It is partly for this reason that there seems to be ground for speaking of the former bodies as "congresses" and the latter as "conferences."

Debate is, of course, far freer in the committees than in the full sessions, especially among the experts in attendance at committee meetings, who are interested in the subject matter under debate and have fewer scruples about international delicacy and sensitiveness. Speeches at the plenary meetings are stilted, formal, flowery. The real argumentation in the conference, so far as there is any at all, comes in committee meetings. Steam-roller methods are not uncommonly employed in the plenary sessions to put through bargains made outside, either in committees or still further out in the corridors or the conference chambers. This is especially true where the plenary sessions are public and where committee meetings are—as is frequently the case—confidential. This may not be true where the conference is concerned with economic problems, where committee meetings have been public, and where a fight in committee crops out again on the floor in plenary session. All of this is quite like the situation in national legislative bodies, only in greater degree. To criticize the methods of doing business in international conferences is, of course, to criticize the common methods of legislation in all ranks of political organization—international, national, provincial, and municipal. That criticism may, however, be applied to international conferences with special aptitude. There seems to be something in the nature of the subject matter and in the traditions of the profession which encourages this particular sort of thing in international circles.

Members of the conference are not ordinarily free to vote according to their best judgment on proposals coming before them but are bound by restrictions from their home governments. They are instructed delegates, not discretionary representatives. As a further result the votes are not so much counted as weighed. That is, the vote of a delegate is not regarded simply as one vote, but as evidence of the support of his government, whatever that be, great or small, strong or weak. The vote, moreover, is not given so much upon the basis of arguments or facts brought out in the conference as upon grounds of national policy maintained and asserted by the home government, not present at the conference at all.

The requirement of unanimity weakens the value and effect of committee decisions unless all members of the conference are represented on all committees. In that case the value of committee work is lowered by being made more cumbersome and difficult. The committee becomes a miniature conference, with all the power—potentially—and all the difficulties, of a conference. The only solution is a prior agreement among the nations in conference to be bound by a majority or a two-thirds vote on decisions to be taken in the course of the conference. Such a vote would preserve the doctrine of consent and at the same time remove the necessity for unanimity at every step and on every point in the discussion. Whether the nations are ready for such a step, and whether, on the whole, it would be wise, are other questions. Its effect on the procedure of international conferences cannot be doubted.

A similar result flows from the general practice of equality of representation in international conferences. The smaller states would generally refuse to go into conference with the larger ones if they were compelled to admit that the larger states possess some degree of jurisdiction over themselves as of right. Yet nothing could be more unjust and unscientific than to give the few hundred thousand citizens of Costa Rica equal power in international legislation with the forty million citizens of France. And in actual practice, of course, the votes of different nations count differently in the results in the sessions of the conference. What is needed is a system of proportionate representation in international bodies which will rest on facts, not upon an outworn metaphysic of public corporations; [5] until such a change is made the larger states, in their turn, will resist passage from unanimity to majority rule.

The conference ends with the signing and sealing of the treaty, as described in connection with treaty negotiations.[6] The fact that only signatories are bound by the treaty derogates somewhat from its significance. But for those who sign, and in so far as the signers do not impose reservations upon their signatures, the effect is to bring into existence new rules of international law, assuming, of course, as we must assume, that the national states will ratify the actions of their agents. The delegates accept the new instrument for their constituents as do members of representative bodies in the national states, at least in national states where legislation is subject to executive approval. This is the central process in international regulation.

The origin of international conferences in time of peace was found to lie in deliberate efforts to take thought for the morrow and to preserve the peace in the future by international arrangements made in advance of the actual need for them. Conferences for the termination of

[5] Article by Sohn in *American Journal of International Law*, Vol. 40 (1946), p. 71.
[6] For Final Act of a conference see, below, Appendix A, Document No. 6c.

war are quite different. Such conferences, called "peace conferences" by reason of the object directly in view, namely, the restoration of peace, are actually held in time of war and originate in the practical necessity for clearing up the problems at issue between or among two or more states whose interests have clashed and whose peaceful relations have actually been interrupted by the outbreak of war.[7]

It would be possible, of course, for belligerents merely to stop fighting, and to go on into the future without concluding a formal treaty of peace, and this has happened several times in the modern history of international relations. Such a method of terminating war, known as "simple cessation of hostilities," is, however, very unsatisfactory to all concerned. The belligerents themselves are left in doubt regarding each other's intentions. Hostilities may be resumed without warning. A constant attitude of defense and suspicion is rendered inevitable. Neutrals, again, or states which would be neutral if war actually existed, are left uncertain regarding their rights and duties toward the belligerents.

Finally, the status of occupied territory is ambiguous. The termination of war by the conquest or complete subjugation of one party by the other might leave no room for doubt. Even here, however, both logic and convenience require some formal notice to the world by the conquering power declaring its intention respecting the conquered territory. And where merely a portion of the territory of an opposing belligerent has been occupied it is doubly desirable for the status of that territory to be defined and made known to all the members of the society of nations. Where hostilities have long ceased and positive acts of peaceful intercourse have been performed by the recent enemies, third states must conclude that the war is over and, according to the rule of *uti possidetis*, that the occupied territory has passed under the sovereignty of the state whose forces are in possession at the termination of hostilities. Obviously, however, it would be better for all concerned if the belligerents would clear up all questions outstanding between them in a formal and explicit agreement or treaty of peace. The superior convenience of such a settlement has led to the practice of conference for the termination of war.

Such conferences are somewhat older than elaborate conferences in time of peace. Indeed, they are as old as international relations themselves, since war and the termination of war are equally as old. From the immemorial dawn of tribal and interstate conflict belligerents have met together, quite naturally and simply at first, deliberately and ceremoniously later, to patch up the broken fabric of their normal relations one with another. And in spite of the knowledge that the peace to be made will not, in all probability, be permanent, in spite of the memories and feelings of war which still dominate men's minds, such meetings have never failed to appeal mightily to the peoples suffering from the hostilities, and in some degree even to the cynical professional diplomat, who

[7] On peace conferences see literature cited, below, Appendix B, § 7.

could but suspect that this was only one of the many pacifications hailed as complete and definitive at the time only to be proved hollow and transitory in the event.

Certain notable changes have, however, come over the typical peace conference in the past century. Of these, three deserve notice here.

First, there has occurred what might be described as a generalization of the peace conference in respect to the parties who are concerned and who are therefore invited to participate. Originally the peace conference included only the belligerents, and in the great majority of cases only two belligerents. This form of peace conference still persists, of course, and is illustrated best by a case where the belligerents come in contact and conduct their conference to a successful conclusion without aid from any third state, as happened at the end of the war between France and Prussia in 1871. In modern times, however, there has appeared a tendency to expand the peace conference to include several, and indeed many, powers. This has been attributable partially to a second tendency, discernible still further beneath the surface of events, whereby wars have changed from "special" wars between two parties to "general" wars involving several parties. This has resulted, in the main, from the increased degree to which the interests of all nations are interwoven in modern times, and, more especially, from the practice of forming alliances for the furtherance of these interests. So long as all of the participants in the peace conference are belligerents, there is no sharp break with the traditional theory. Very early in modern international relations, however, it was felt to be advisable to call in states which had been neutral in the war, in view of the extent to which their interests were involved in the general settlement. This happened at Westphalia in 1648, at Vienna in 1815, at Paris in 1856 and again in 1919, to name only four famous general peace conferences, and it marks a new stage in international constitutional development.

In like manner the questions treated in peace conferences have been generalized. Originally the questions at issue between the belligerents in the war were, alone, put in discussion. With the expansion of the area of conflict, however, the necessity for keeping in view many collateral questions affecting the belligerents, and also states with whom the belligerents were in mutual relationships, became evident. Inasmuch as the object of peace conferences soon came to be that of making a permanent peace, and not merely patching up the current dispute, this necessity grew greater. In the end what was involved was a general review and settlement of all outstanding international disputes, a general pacification. The peace conference thus approached more nearly the nature of the conference in time of peace, that is, an international constituent assembly of general jurisdiction. The traditional rule to the effect that only questions at issue between the belligerents come within the jurisdiction of the conference is still put forward by neutrals desiring to block consideration of questions affecting them and by belligerents desiring to avoid certain embarrassing problems. None the less the tendency described is unmistakable in practice, and in view of the fact that the conference has no authority to settle any questions except by the consent of the participants, and that such a method of settlement may as well be applied to collateral questions as to the main issues of the war, the traditional rule is to be regarded merely as one of convenience.

Such general peace conferences as are here under discussion have tended to decrease in number recently. Inasmuch as this implies a decrease in the frequency of general wars, no one can deplore the diminution in this form of international organization or practice. The reasons for this change, however, are more complicated, and deserve further attention at this point.

General wars have, indeed, decreased in frequency since 1815, and, in fact, since the beginning of the eighteenth century. But this is due to increasing efforts to preserve the peace and to the special use of conferences in time of peace to settle outstanding questions likely to lead to war, a procedure which thus indirectly tends to diminish the number of general peace conferences which are necessary. It is due further to another device which is of still greater significance, of greater significance even than the general conference at the termination of a war, and which also constitutes the third way in which peace conferences have been generalized in recent decades.

As was pointed out above, the settlements made at the conclusion of hostilities have not always been the embodiments of pure justice and wisdom. This has led not only to the holding of conferences in time of peace to devise in advance a settlement of better quality than that of the settlement to be attained at the end of a possible war, but also to the holding of conferences in the ensuing state of peace to revise settlements already made at the end of a preceding war. Such was the Congress of Aix-la-Chapelle in 1818; such, more clearly, was the Congress of Berlin in 1878; and the action of Russia, Germany, and France in 1895, regarding the Treaty of Shimonoseki between China and Japan, was of the same type. It was largely the failure of the Powers to take such action respecting the Balkan settlement of 1913 that prepared the ground for the events of 1914. The peace of 1919 was subjected to revision by Inter-Allied conferences already during the years 1920 and 1921, but alas the process of revision was allowed to lapse in the late 1920's and early 1930's. Considering this development along with the establishment of the conference in time of peace to prevent war, it is possible to say that peace conferences are being generalized, not only as to parties involved and questions discussed, but also as to the time when they are held. In addition, it may be observed that such conferences for revision of peace settlements attest further the interest taken by states not parties to the war, especially the Great Powers, where a settlement has been made by minor powers which appears to them defective from the point of view of their own interests or the balance of power and the general peace.

In organization and procedure, peace conferences do not differ materially from conferences in time of peace, and a brief review of the subject will therefore be sufficient.

A peace conference convenes as the result of either direct negotiations between the belligerents or action by a third state in providing a means of bringing the belligerents into conference. Participation is, of course, wholly voluntary, and depends upon calculations of the results which it may be possible to obtain from such a conference in contrast to those to be obtained by continuing the war.

The membership of the peace conference has already been discussed. It should be recalled that at times the conference is attended by a mediator, if it happens that the war has been brought to an end through the action of a mediator. This is very likely to happen where the mediator has been led to take action in order to defend certain national interests, and especially where the mediation has been performed by one or more of the Great Powers in defense of their own interests or the general welfare, and where the small powers, belligerents in the war, have been compelled to accept such mediation. In all cases, however, the belligerents must be present; a peace conference without them, even with mediators or conciliators—or conquerors—present, would be "Hamlet" without the Prince.

The range of subjects discussed, or the jurisdiction of the conference, has also been described in another connection. A further set of considerations must, however, be added here.

It should be noted, first, that the jurisdiction of a peace conference must be defined in terms of subjects or questions, not in terms of parties or territory. The conference has no legal power over any territory or property, nor has it authority over any persons or states. More particularly still, the powers victorious in the war do not gain thereby any degree of legal authority over the vanquished nor over his possessions.

In the second place the territory of one belligerent occupied by another is not thereby acquired in full sovereignty, even where the whole of the territory of the enemy is so occupied. In this case only a cessation of resistance and an at least tacit consent—albeit "forced" consent—to annexation or absorption in the conquering state, accompanied, probably, by a proclamation of the annexation by the latter or some overt act testifying to the same intent, will be effective in the eyes of other states. In the former case only cession in an international agreement or consent to the retention of the partially occupied territory by the state at the time in possession will be effective. This is one of the chief reasons for holding a conference between the belligerents at the end of the war.

Military victory, moreover, gives to the successful belligerent no legal authority to dictate terms to his defeated enemy. It is doubtful whether peace can ever be successfully founded upon dictation; it is certain that a treaty cannot, in its very nature, be dictated by one state to another. Perhaps the conquered need not be taken into conference, but his consent must be secured, to render valid any changes which affect his rights under the existing status. A state may find it necessary to accept certain changes and to agree to certain terms of peace, in order to avoid certain other results, such as military occupation of its territories, loss of life, or what not. But, after all, some alternative is present in such a situation, and freedom of choice, in a sense necessary to satisfy the doctrine of sovereignty, is preserved. Nor is this merely an imaginary freedom, for a state might prefer to go on with the war; cases have been known in which states have refused to bow the knee even when all seemed lost. The choice of agreeing to the proffered terms or continuing to resist is always present, at least in form.[8]

From a strictly mechanical viewpoint, peace conferences are ordinarily organized much as are conferences in time of peace.[9] They are based on credentials and full-powers and, ordinarily, upon the principles of equality of representation and voting power, and they operate by unanimous consent. Presiding officers and numerous secretaries are chosen, plenary sessions and sessions in committee are held, and the results are put in the form of a treaty and signed.

Peace conferences are not, however, usually as well organized or as well conducted as are conferences in time of peace. They are composed of diplomats in the narrowest sense of that word, and the personal element plays a very great part in the negotiations. They are smaller in membership; they do not make use of committees and commissions as fully as do the conferences in time of peace; they operate more secretly; they go less upon grounds of law and economics and statistical data generally, and more upon grounds of "policy," national ambition, and the personal opinions of the negotiators. There is more dickering behind the scenes, extra-conference agreements are more numerous, and there is more subterranean "accommodation" all along the line. Not common and permanent advantages, but exclusive, direct, and immediate, even if temporary, national advantages, are pursued. There is no fixed program or agenda to be followed and everything depends on the turns in the negotiations from day to day. The result is that the atmosphere is very unwholesome and not conducive to the production of a sound settlement. Indeed, the questions are not commonly approached as problems to be settled by joint efforts to discover sound solutions, but as contests in which each nation must seek to outwit the other in securing satisfaction. Another way in which this may be viewed is to note that there is no one present to represent the general interest of the society of nations.

[8] Discussed further, below, Chap. IX. B.
[9] For regulations governing organization and procedure of a large conference see, below, Appendix A, Document No. 7, at p. 344.

CHAPTER VIII

International Administration and Adjudication *

A1. *International Administration: Description and Analysis* †

At the other end of the scale from international legislation stands international administration. Whereas the former consists of the creation of law, the latter consists of its execution or application. It is the final step in organized international coöperation or international government where that function exists.

It is here also that some of the most critical questions concerning international organization in general become most acute. The great variety of structures and functions observable in international administration seems to challenge and threaten to defeat any sound generalization, although the international administrative bodies of different size and function resemble one another far more than international conferences of extreme types. The vast amount of data available seems to challenge mastery and assimilation. The problem of appraisal is both more urgent and also more difficult here than elsewhere in international organization. None of these difficulties seem insurmountable, however, and we must simply proceed to do the best we can.[1]

The sense in which we employ the term administration in this discussion is indicated above. We shall try to avoid using the term to mean merely the conduct of affairs, as it is sometimes used in familiar speech. Similarly we shall assume that it is law which is being administered, and not merely policy, although it must be admitted that this position cannot be maintained invariably, while being a more salutary, if no more realistic, position in the international than in the national field, all things fairly considered.

On the other hand the law to be administered may at times be national rather than international law, and the essence of international administration lies not in the source of the law administered but in the source of the mandate of the administrator or administrators. To satisfy our conception this must consist of a delegation of power from two or more states. It may be added that such a delegation may be made to a person

* The footnotes in this chapter are numbered by the section.

† I am deeply indebted to the Brookings Institution for the opportunity given me in 1941-42 to study the subject of international administration in its recent manifestations under particularly favorable conditions in Washington, D.C.

¹ For literature see below, Appendix B, Section 8.

who is already a national official—who then becomes to that extent an international official also.[2]

In this discussion two or three minor forms of international organization will be omitted and one major special form postponed for separate consideration. Thus, according to our hypotheses, consular and diplomatic activity, especially the former, approximates international administration, in spite of its highly nationalistic character, and international conferences share to some degree in this function, in their supervisory activities and their action on appointments, for example. Private international agencies do a great deal of work which is pseudo-administrative in character. Finally international adjudication turns out on closer inspection to constitute international administration also, and very close to the principle of our definition, but where such emphasis is placed upon one element of administration, namely finding and interpreting the law, that it must be set off by itself. The first three types of activity are, however, too far down in the scale of importance to deserve much space here[3] while the fourth is so important and so special in character as to deserve separate treatment.[4]

As already suggested, there exist a surprisingly large number of specimens of international administration in the world today, as there have existed a large number for the past seventy-five years.[5] Statistics are sadly lacking here but it is probably entirely safe to say that some two or three hundred agencies, with international mandates and an existence sufficiently independent of any other agency or system to justify their being considered separately, exist in the world today. Some of these are small (Inter-American Trade-Mark Bureau) and some large (International Labor Office), some entirely isolated (International Ice Patrol) and some integrated with a larger system like the United Nations (as is UNESCO). A whole world of fact and principle concerning the origins and the development and decline of these agencies which exist here can be touched upon only briefly, without more than a mention of the technically very difficult problem of the exact dates of origin and demise of a given agency.

The core of international administration is an agency deputized for that function by the members of a union of states. In practice the agency may be called a bureau or commission or board or council or by any one of a dozen names. It may also vary in personnel from one person on part time to several hundred or even several thousand persons on full time,

---

[2] See word chart on p. 133.

[3] So for financial and other "advisers" sent by one country to another; see Buell, R. L., "International Advisers," in *Encyclopedia of the Social Sciences*, Vol. VIII, p. 155; also military occupation, especially under the UN.

[4] Below, Sec. B.

[5] See Handbooks in general prepared by the League of Nations, Ruth D. Masters, and the United States Department of State; below, Appendix B, § 8a (1). The present treatment is based upon a list of several hundred agencies compiled by the author in 1941-1942 and revised and amplified subsequently.

although the average agency may be thought of as consisting of twenty or thirty persons. At times, though rarely, the agency will maintain branches outside of its central core; and of course the larger agencies (United Nations Secretariat, for example) will be subdivided and organized internally in a very complicated way. The variations in nomenclature and in numbers of personnel make very much less difference than might be imagined in the nature and functions of the international administrative agencies.[6]

Just above the agency there may be stationed a supervisory body to watch over its operations on behalf of the member states; such is the Governing Body of the International Labor Organization, which also acts as the executive council of the union; in most cases supervision is relegated higher up—to the conference of the union or the member states themselves.[7] Next in the ascending scale come one or more representative bodies or conferences which form the legislative and constituent organs; in most unions there will be only one such body. The formation of policy and exercise of leadership reposes on this level, which is really not a phase of administration but of legislation, though very important for the success of the former; it is very necessary at the beginning and may be useful later also.

Above the representative body just mentioned, or, to change the figure somewhat, at the top of the whole structure, are the members of the union composing it. This is commonly a union of states although in recent days dependencies, government departments, and even private groups or individuals, from below or within the states on one side, and superstate organizations on the other, have been permitted to mix with states as members thereof; this is a problem of federal union rather than administration.[8] The union in question is often called by that name but sometimes it is not designated at all. These unions are often referred to elliptically as "administrative unions" with the intention of emphasizing what is felt to be their distinguishing trait, namely possession of an administrative organ. The union may be entirely simple in its internal structure or the members may be arranged in regional groups or in strata of one kind or another. However this may be, at bottom the real basis of international administration is to be found in the needs, interests, and desires of the human beings who make up the states or other political entities, members of the union, the geophysical and social conditions which create these reactions, and the public policies to which they lead.

[6] At times (rarely) distinctly judicial organs are found attached to the administrative agencies: Hudson, *Tribunals*, Chap. XIX; Domke, "Settlement of Disputes in International Agencies," in *The Arbitration Journal*, New Series, Vol. 1, No. 2 (Summer, 1946), p. 145, n. 2; at other times the agencies themselves perform this function: International Bureau of the Universal Postal Union, in *Agencies*, p. 299.

[7] At times supervision is delegated to one member state, acting on behalf of the rest; this does not seem to be a very progressive device: Inter-American Trade-Mark Bureau, in Masters, p. 186.

[8] Below, Chap. IX. C.

Formally international administrative agencies are created most frequently by treaty agreement. At times the constitutive action is less formal, consisting of conference resolution or mere diplomatic communication, and two or three rare cases of agencies created by practice are to be found. All of this takes place normally in time of peace but war neither eliminates all existing agencies nor fails to produce its own crop of new agencies, both for the conduct of hostilities and for the liquidation of the situation, and this both among allies and across belligerent lines.

In connection with these considerations it should be noted that international administrative agencies may be merely bipartite and temporary in character or multipartite and permanent. The bipartite agencies (International High Commission of the United States and Canada, for example) are not necessarily unimportant and do not differ perceptibly in character from the multipartites; temporary agencies are for the time being on a par with permanent agencies, apart from the fact that some agencies last longer than intended while some do not last as long. Other things being equal, permanent multipartite agencies are most significant; at times this type is regarded as alone being important in this field, but this seems an exaggeration; it would, for example, exclude the thousands of temporary bipartite boundary commissions which have functioned from time to time throughout the history of international relations.[9]

The geographical aspect of international administration, with its rivalry between universalism and regionalism, deserves notice here.[10] Many —probably most—agencies rest upon an assumption of universality of membership (the principle of being open to all states); some are frankly regional (Union of American States). Many of the former consist chiefly of European states with one, or a few, overseas countries. At times eligibility for membership is made to turn on political complexion rather than location, [11] but this is a reactionary attitude on the whole. The merits of universalism as against regionalism cannot be argued here; regional unions seem to deserve a reasonable place in the picture [12] though universalism, at least as an overall coördination, gains ground daily. Finally it must be noted that the field of operation of an agency is much more important than its membership and that these may not be identical; to this we shall return later.

The question of the seat of the agency likewise would repay study.[13]

[9] For emphasis on permanence as the crucial test see Schmeckebier, p. vii; on boundary commissions see Jones, as cited.

[10] See article by the author in *American Political Science Review*, Vol. XXXVII, No. 5 (October, 1943), p. 850.

[11] Resolutions of General Assembly of the United Nations, UN Doc. A/64/Add. 1, p. 65.

[12] See Mrs. Roosevelt's "My Day" for 11 December 1946; "Of course for this (IRO) to be a truly international organization all the nations of the world ... should be included."

[13] Jenks, as cited below, Appendix B, Section 8a.

The merits of certain continents, countries, cities, and quarters of cities, and of certain types of buildings and equipment: all these considerations are of serious importance for the success of international administration.

The personnel of international administrative agencies constitutes one of the most crucial elements in the problem.[14] As has been seen, it varies enormously in volume; it also varies enormously in quality. In the past no great attention was paid to modes of selection of this personnel and still today, except in the largest agencies (United Nations Secretariat), no great use is made of merit system tests, general principles of selection, and so on. The language factor intervenes, moreover, to distort any merit system which might be contemplated: persons must be obtained who can use the official language or languages of the agency even if that means leaving abler persons aside. The political influence of governments cannot always be evaded here, and no rigid quota system is practical; citizens of smaller states or even persons of plural nationality and cosmopolitan background may be more useful than nationals of Great Powers. Finally no concerted thought or action has been given to the matter of training,[15] which goes on, in the main, in individual states; at least one international institute for such training exists, however, and others are projected.[16] Of course much of the training of international administrators must be obtained, as in the national field, after admission to the service.

The problems of supervision and control in international administration resemble those problems in national administration very closely, with special variations.[17] Assignment of work, checking up on performance, discipline,—these aspects of administration are perennially present; rates of pay, hours, leave, retirement,—these problems likewise have to be faced; all are complicated by variations of nationality and language and customs and standards of living among the nations and their peoples. National feelings being what they are, loyalty to the international agency is not entirely easy to obtain.[18] International administration not necessarily providing a permanent career, the idea of retirement to reënter national service—a very dubious proceeding—inevitably arises. And dismissal is an even more acute issue here than in the national field.

One other aspect of the structure of international administrative in-

---

[14] In general see Ranshofen-Wertheimer, pp. 239-370.

[15] See minutes of conference on training for international administration held in Washington, D.C., on August 21-22, 1943, under auspices of Carnegie Endowment for International Peace, recorded by the Endowment.

[16] *Institut Universitaire de Hautes Etudes Internationales*, Geneva, Switzerland; the Institute operates under Swiss law and is affiliated with the University of Geneva but it has a very cosmopolitan staff and student body and complete freedom of action.

[17] Below, p. 143.

[18] See the League experiment with a declaration of loyalty: Ranshofen-Wertheimer, p. 245.

stitutions lies in their relations to other international institutions and entities although this problem involves also questions of activity or function. The problem has been badly neglected in the past but is now receiving much more attention.[19] It is important in avoiding duplication of effort, promoting coöperation, and enriching the organization and operation of the agencies in various other ways. The relations between regional and universal organizations arise here and also those between organizations with general jurisdiction (UN) and the more highly specialized agencies (FAO). Beyond this lie questions of relations with states and governments members but also non-members and the general public,[20] including the informational, educational, and propagandist activity on the part of the agencies.

Relations between or among the many international administrative bodies may be attempted on a plane of voluntary consultation and coöperation or on a basis of structural coördination or consolidation. The former are easy to suggest or require, but inconclusive when achieved, the second difficult to secure, not entirely simple to operate, but potentially much more effective. Such relations may be built up by free agreement or imposed from above; the latter method would be most effective but is not often possible, in view of the voluntary nature of most international organizations, except in the process of proliferation under a general organization.

The relations between the international agencies and the government members and non-members of the union are too complicated to be set forth here.[21] Relationships of service to the states in return for support, subject to control, are standard. At times these relationships are formalized through subdivisions of foreign offices or permanent contact officers at the seat of the agency.[22] Even with non-member states agencies maintain coöperation at times quite comparable with those maintained with members.[23] At times member states attempt to exercise power over non-members,[24] but such an effort is of dubious practical value as well as dubious legal validity. Finally the agencies actually try to serve the general public and private organizations within the limits of their authority and the nature of the situation.

International administrative agencies are set up and maintained, of course, for the services which they can perform, and all of the structural

[19] Articles by W. R. Sharp in *International Organization*, Vol. I (1947), p. 460, and references; also report by H. B. Calderwood for Institute on World Organization, Washington, D. C.

[20] For a study in the relations of international agencies and the public see Gay and Fisher, cited below, Appendix B, § 8a; also article by the author in *Public-Opinion Quarterly*, Vol. II (1938), p. 399.

[21] W. H. C. Laves, "The United Nations: Reorganizing the World's Governmental Institutions," in *Public Administration Review*, Vol. V (1945), p. 183.

[22] P. B. Potter, *Permanent Delegation to the League of Nations*, Geneva, 1930.

[23] U. P. Hubbard, *Coöperation of the United States with the League of Nations, 1931-1936*, New York, 1937.

[24] Covenant, Art. 17; Charter, Art. II, par. 6.

aspect of the matter is secondary to this. And the services to be performed consist of doing certain things, in certain ways, to certain bodies
of subject matter, in order to accomplish certain ends. We shall consider
these questions in the following order: aims or objectives, subject matters, procedures.

The objectives of international administration are chiefly the concern
of the states establishing this activity, but the personnel called upon to
carry out the activities of the institution may, and indeed must, give
some attention to this question. It is here that administration of policy
seems legitimate. By the same token it is permissible for students of
social problems to record the state of affairs at this point and also to comment reasonably thereon.

The benefit or welfare of the member states may be set down as the
general objective of international administration; from the texts of scores
or hundreds of international instruments it is abundantly clear that this
is the object of international administration rather than anything more
abstract or altruistic. On the other hand this general statement leaves a
number of points concealed. Is the welfare of the international community, or of the human race, not involved, not to mention that of individuals and groups below the level of the state? And what about advantages for the agency itself? Actually these aspects of the situation
have been sadly neglected in the past although they are now being
given extensive and serious and express consideration by various students
in various countries.

International administration also may and does serve both the spiritual
(in the broadest sense of the term) and the material welfare of its beneficiaries. It deals with practical economic interests but also with science
and art; the former appeared somewhat earlier in the history of this
activity and the impression is commonly held that such subjects constitute the whole of the field but that is far from the case, as will appear in
greater detail in a moment.

Another criticism made at times concerning the aims of international
administration holds that it does little or nothing for the maintenance
of peace, and is therefore of only secondary importance in international
affairs. In point of fact the agencies which we are discussing do have
few tasks to perform in connection with the maintenance of peace—in
regard to disarmament, suppression of aggression, and so on—unless one
includes the judicial type of administration omitted here.[25] This, however, is attributable to the failure of the states to confer such tasks on the
agencies; there is every reason to believe that the latter could be very
active in this connection if given a chance. In addition the agencies do
contribute greatly to the development of international solidarity by their
work in international communications and other matters and hence indirectly to peace. And we may leave the question of the relative im-

[25] Below, Sec. B (2).

portance of peace and other international objectives for consideration in its own place later.[26]

Similarly international administration is said to be too closely pre-occupied with the existing status and not sufficiently creative. Again this is true in bare fact but not if examined in relation to the whole situation. Actually many of the personalities in the agencies are dynamic crusaders who would be only too glad for a chance to reform the world. Again it is the states which—or who, for states are people, fundamentally,—who deny this opportunity to the administrators. The fact is that this is not the job of administration but of legislation and we should not complain if a governmental institution is true to its character.

Many observers of international administration feel that subject-matter provides the most convenient and significant approach to that problem. By subject-matter is intended various frameworks or contexts of human experience such as health, law, trade, and so on. These subject-matters obviously elaborate and explain the ends or aims of international adminis-tration; health work is a central sector of service for national and indi-vidual welfare. On the other hand it appears that in fact international agencies do not vary greatly either in structure or in function in relation to the subject-matter treated; the same forms and functions occur in scientific and artistic work as in armaments and penalogy.

To state the matter simply, international administration ranges over the whole gamut of human life from astronomy to zoölogy, and touches upon some seventy or eighty other miscellaneous items in between.[27] In any such analysis of subject-matters much overlapping and duplication will be observable.[28] One of the most striking differences among interna-tional organizations is that between the organization with general juris-diction (as to subject matter) and the highly specialized agency. The occurrence of numerous methodological items (which could as easily be transferred to other groups) will also be noted, and the eternal problem of political and non-political subjects.[29] A statistical and historical summary of these matters would not be without interest; it would reveal that both the oldest and the most numerous agencies are to be found in the field of communications, the least numerous and newest in law and government—although again the two areas are not entirely discrete—further revealing the defective character of the subject-matter approach. Nevertheless this type of survey has a certain value of its own.

What the agencies do in reference to these different subject-matters may be discussed under the heading of "procedure" although here also two or more different levels are to be borne in mind. By procedure is

[26] Below, Chap. X. B.
[27] See classified list on p. 140, based strictly on statements made by the agencies themselves.
[28] As the items of physics and science in Group I.
[29] See discussion, "Note on the Distinction between Political and Technical Ques-tions," in *Political Science Quarterly*, Vol. L, No. 2 (June, 1935), p. 264.

Subject Matters of International Administration

I. SCIENCE AND ART

Astronomy
Biology
Chemistry
Cinematography
Documentation
Electricity
Exploration
Expositions
Geodesy
Geography
Historical monuments
History
Hydrography
Intellectual coöperation
Language
Linguistics
Literature
Mathematics
Meteorology
Museology
Nature (protection of)
Pedagogy
Physics
Science
Seismology
Statistics
Weights and measures

II. COMMUNICATIONS AND TRANSIT

Aviation
Communications and transit
Highways
Inland waterways
Maritime navigation
Navigation
Postal communications
Radio communications
Railway transport
River navigation
Telegraphic communications
Telephonic communications

III. ECONOMICS AND FINANCE

Agriculture
Banking
Cheese
Coffee
Currency
Customs

Economic entomology
Economics
Epizootics
Finance
Forestry
Insurance
Intercourse
Refrigeration
Rubber
Sugar
Tea
Tin
Trade
Whaling
Wheat
Wine

IV. HEALTH AND MORALS

Alcoholic liquors
Children
Criminology
Drugs
Health
Labor
Nosology
Pharmacology
Prisoners of war
Refugees
Relief
Slavery and slave trade
Women

V. LAW AND GOVERNMENT

Armaments
Arms (traffic)
Boundaries
Copyright
Defense
Government
International law
International organization
Passports
Patents and trademarks
Peace
Penal and penitentiary matters
Plebiscite
Police
Private law
Public administration
Sanctions
Security

meant not merely method or technique (the questionnaire method, for example) but the larger aspects of agency operation as well (as research or investigation). In addition the question of area will have to be reconsidered as promised. Finally the question here is not merely that of the power or degree of authority of the agency but how it works; as will appear later the problem of coercive action is not very important in this sphere.

The activities of the international administrative agencies may be grouped under two broad headings, those performed chiefly within the agency itself and those performed on the outside (toward member states or others).[30] Under each heading will be found numerous items which can again be grouped in one case under three rubrics, namely custodial work, secretarial work, and the management of persons and plant, and, in the second, under informational, advisory, and executive action, the last item including, along with the characteristic element of enforcement measures, a certain amount of judicial action (the taking of decisions) and even of legislative action (adoption of regulations).[31] The internal activities are not wholly confined within the agency,—correspondence is not, for example,—and some of the external activities call for a good deal of internal work both in their preparation and their execution. It is further noticeable that the first group of procedures is more nearly ministerial or non-discretionary in character, the second somewhat broader in the matter of policy. All agencies have a great deal of the former type of work to do; only a few rise to the true executive level. Of course many other aspects of this situation would repay notice if time and space permitted, including the relative importance of the different types of action, the trends observable today, and so on, but this brief discussion will have to suffice; perhaps one word of caution may be permitted: no hasty judgments should be adopted concerning the relative significance of secretarial, informational, or executive services.[32]

At times international administrative agencies are instructed by convention to "prepare international conferences" on the subject treated or to "assure execution of the convention" or do other jobs equally difficult. Such provisions are highly eliptical, in part referring to the detailed functions cited above, and in part a combination of optimism and irresponsibility on the part of the states.

The activities of certain agencies are carried on all over the world, as those of the International Labor Office; those of other agencies, such as the International Bureau of the Universal Postal Union, are carried on in one spot but take effect everywhere. It is obvious that the area of operations may or may not correspond with the area of membership:

[30] See word chart on p. 142.

[31] At times the agency, in this case often called a commission, tends to move over from administration toward legislation entirely: League *Handbook*, p. 204.

[32] See below, p. 144.

FUNCTIONS AND PROCEDURE OF INTERNATIONAL ADMINISTRATION

A. *Internal; Ministerial*
  I. Custodial
    a. Property (land and buildings; equipment)
    b. Archives and records
    c. Libraries; museums
  II. Secretarial
    a. Records (making), including accounts
    b. Registration (treaties; patents)
    c. Filing
    d. Correspondence
    e. Translating (and interpreting)
    f. Editing and publishing
    g. Drafting
  III. Management
    a. Of personnel, including

  recruitment and treatment
    b. Of plant, including printing and distribution

B. *External;* Semi-discretionary
  IV. Information
    a. Reception or collection
    b. Analysis and interpretation
    c. Distribution
  V. Advisory
    a. Recommendations
    b. Promotion and education
  VI. Executive
    a. Decisions
    b. Regulations
    c. Enforcement (non-physical and physical)

the International Wine Office, with membership limited to Southern Europe chiefly, carries on world-wide activities while some agencies with world-wide membership perform, perhaps among others, very local functions, such as the government of a bit of territory. On the whole the trend here is toward universalism also, with due attention to the regional tasks in coördination under general supervision.

This leads us to the final problems of the financial support of the agencies, supervision and control, and their conversion or termination.

International administrative agencies, or rather the organizations of which they are part, are supported, as are international organizations of other types, mainly by contributions from member states.[33] These contributions or dues are usually fixed by agreement but at times this function is delegated to the agency. In smaller agencies equality of contributions is not uncommon but in larger systems levies proportioned to capacity to pay are laid upon the members; in a few cases states have been allowed to choose the number of units of contribution which they will assume. Other sources of revenue for the agencies are voluntary donations from states, very large at times, and also sales of publications, fees for services, and interest on bank deposits or profits on exchange, although these latter are rather trivial. Donations from individuals or from private philanthropic foundations, again very large at times, are by no means unknown; this raises the old question of private influence on public

[33] On financial aspects of international administration see Jenks in Grotius Society, *Transactions*, Vol. XXVIII, p. 87. Data on this question are not given much attention in agency reports.

authorities. In a few cases agencies have been allowed to impose and collect fines and levy what look very much like taxes.[34] Finally agencies may be authorized to float loans though this is rare.

On the expenditure side the agencies are called upon chiefly to pay salaries,—those of agency staffs; compensation of delegates to representative bodies is provided by the states,—but have some expenses for plant and equipment, supplies and so on. Their budgets range from a few hundred dollars a year [35] to several millions; again it might be objected that such variation precludes any generalization but the situation does not differ on this point from that found in national government where budgetary science embraces both huge departments and tiny committees. What is more interesting is the fact that historically there has not been very much controversy over the financial aspect of international administration [36] and little evidence of that connection between contributions and control or influence which is felt to be so dangerous in national government. Finally it must be remembered that some agency budgets form parts of the budgets of larger systems and that in this case the problem of control becomes quite real.[37]

Not much needs to be added to what has already been said concerning the control of international administrative agencies.[38] Again the problem has been less acute than it would have been if the agencies had possessed more power. Finally it must be added that the states and governments and diplomats have not commonly been sufficiently versed in the science of public administration to perform the function of supervision very competently.

The states do not always support the agencies which they have created very effectively either in financial matters or by compliance with their orders or requests. At times this reaches the level of outright opposition. Indeed the same chronic tug of war goes on here as goes on between government and governed in all fields. This may lead to efforts to modify the agency or even terminate it. There is a vast process of conversion of international administrative agencies going on all the time, some of it more or less simple factual change, some of it elaborate reorganization on the basis of calculated planning. The effects of war, already alluded to,[39] have to be dealt with at this point also. One peculiar aspect of the situation is found in the same chronic resistance to revision here as is

[34] In the case of territorial administration this is commonplace: Wambaugh, p. 60.

[35] Some agencies have no budgets at all, expenses being borne by the states: Pink, p. 40, and Sayre, p. 73.

[36] For an exception see International Ice Patrol, manuscript studies in library of the Carnegie Endowment for International Peace, Washington, D. C.; such controversies are increasing with increase in the size of agency budgets.

[37] Study by present author in *American Society of International Law Proceedings,* *1931,* pp. 103-105.

[38] Above, p. 136.

[39] Above, p. 135.

observed in connection with international legislation.[40] There is also evident a disposition to place too much emphasis on structural matters in this connection. All of this involves rather an appraisal of international administration, however, and to this we now turn.

2. *International Administration: Appraisal*

Mere description and analysis of international administration would leave the most important questions concerning such institutions untouched. These institutions must be evaluated or appraised with reference to the functions which they are professedly created to perform.[1] And although fragments of such appraisal have been introduced already in discussion of other institutions, it is in connection with the international administrative union, which constitutes in itself a more or less complete epitome of international organization, that such an appraisal can best be made on a general and comprehensive scale.[2]

There can be little doubt, in the first place, that these institutions, particularly the administrative agencies proper, have for the most part justified their existence. A considerable number have not been successful but the great majority have commended themselves sufficiently to the states to be maintained and developed and imitated widely. The old preference for remitting the administration of international legislation to individual signatory states has not entirely disappeared but the opposition to creating international agencies for the purpose mentioned has declined with the observed helpfulness of the latter.

On the other hand the governments have not changed very much on the score of planning their administrative arrangements in advance nor have those arrangements (as a result) improved much in respect to their more or less improvised and haphazard character. No extensive or elaborate advance planning is, probably, possible in this field, but something more might be done by adequate study of the subject in general as preparation for occasions when action is required. Even this has been shunned by the governments hitherto though it is encouraging to observe an improvement in this respect recently.

When it comes to actually securing an agency to do a job the nations also still seem to prefer to set up a new agency rather than confer additional work on an existing institution. They also have, in the past, disliked to establish structural or functional relations between a new agency and agencies already existing, thus producing further chaos and con-

---

[40] Below, p. 211.

[1] Rather than on the basis of mere personal preference; the appraisal which follows rests upon direct observation and a study of the record by the writer but also on systematic and carefully recorded interviews with some one hundred experienced international administrators.

[2] The present section consists of a severe condensation of an extensive unpublished manuscript of the author.

fusion. Finally they have not always supported the agencies created as well as they should have—on grounds both of logic and practical interest—which in turn intensifies the disorder. It is not clear that any change is imminent on this score but a considerable change can be noted in regard to relations among the agencies, large and small, new and old.

In the past few years the whole situation and numerous specific agencies have, of course, been strongly affected by war-time conditions. In some cases the effect has been to weaken the agency, if it existed prior to 1939. In other cases it has been to give added impulse to an old agency or to bring into existence a new agency entirely. In the course of time these effects, negative and positive, may be expected to fade, but for the time being they are still strong. As unexpected as it may seem, the predominant effect of World War II on international administration will probably prove to be positive rather than negative or indeed has already been so.

One way in which this development may be liquidated beneficially would be for war-time agencies or war-time functions of older agencies to be converted into more significant items in terms of the objectives served. The agencies should be set to serving the normal peace-time interests of the states and the international community and the range of ends or aims served in the past could very beneficially be expanded. The charge that international administration serves only secondary and material ends should be met by the development of more significant jobs for the agencies.

It goes almost without saying that the agencies have been restricted too severely in the past in serving humanity and human beings apart from the sovereign state. Happily that also is changing today but the resistance is still serious. Similarly in the point of subject-matter, while the old opposition to international regulation of "domestic questions" had begun to wane some time ago today there is some recrudescence of opposition on that score, provoked in part precisely by the evidence that that barrier was giving way. Now it is true that this is largely and indeed basically a problem of international legislation but it is at the level of administration that the impact of international action on national interest is felt most acutely.

Existing agencies, or the unions which support them, could be criticized for being rather exclusive as to membership by anyone who held broad views in this matter. In the overwhelming majority they are composed of sovereign states and exclude anything else, although enough exceptions are observable to show that this is a matter of choice, not necessity. On the other hand, it does seem that any great extension of membership to dependencies, departments, private groups, or individuals would lead to a great deal of confusion and blur the line between public authority and its absence pretty badly. The agencies should be able to serve individuals but probably at least formal and voting membership in their supporting unions is just as well confined to governments, although this may well include dependencies as well.

No great amount of either criticism or commendation can be voiced concerning the geographical aspects of union membership. There is some inclination to exaggerate the universal character of some institutions and some disposition or overemphasize the regional character of others. The actual arrangements do not vary greatly from what is desirable but there is some unsound theorizing and interpretation thereof.

It is here that the criticism of international organization as a general form emerges and the plea for something higher in type, something at least approaching unitary world government, appears. It is in connection with administration that this plea holds most meaning. To judge by the record of the reactions of people and governments, existing international institutions do not fall far below what is desired and would be accepted and supported today, although limited improvements could certainly be made at any time. The advocates of unitary world government admit themselves that such a consummation is unattainable at present; they seem mistaken in believing it to be desirable. The value of the tactic of promoting the unattainable is still another question.[3]

In view of the generally uniform structure of international administrative unions, it might safely be inferred that no serious criticism can fairly be levelled against that structure. The points of variation—employment of one or two representative bodies, or of a distinct supervisory body, or a judicial body—are too detailed to permit discussion here.[4] And while various opinions are held concerning the enormous variations in the numbers of personnel of the agencies, the considerations applying to the problem are so numerous that no simple favorable or unfavorable judgment is possible. Few agencies of the ordinary international administrative type are now clearly either overstaffed or understaffed.

In the past the most obvious structural defect in international administration has resided in the lack of organic connection between or among the many coexisting agencies. With this has gone a similar lack of coordination of activities even without structural connection. The agencies themselves have done something to remedy this defect, for which the states or governments have been chiefly to blame, but even they have not always been without guilt at this point. As already indicated, some improvement is noticeable in this matter today but it will take a very long time and enormous effort to accomplish any very extensive improvement here.[5]

---

[3] "The Tactic of Progress in International Government," in *Journal of Comparative Legislation and International Law*, Third Series, Vol. 17 (1935), p. 260.

[4] One principle should, it seems, be emphasized here: the technical experts and the statesmen should be separated, on the administrative and political levels respectively; the former should, as an experienced international administrator puts it, be on tap but not on top.

[5] See references above, p. 137, note 19.

The most varied judgments can and must be passed upon the quality of the personnel of international administration. Many of the persons involved are of the finest type of public servants, and many are saints and crusaders as well. Others are incompetent and traitorous to the principles of international government. Many are colorless employes. In any case the character of international administrative personnel is more the result of accident or the operation of general influences than it is of any careful recruitment policy, let alone preparatory training. And of course the agencies have not been entirely free from political pressure either at the time of selection of personnel or later, although this particular issue has not been felt as acutely in international administration, as in the national field.

In all matters of management and discipline, of course, the nationality element in the situation tends to render international administration much more difficult than local administration. On the whole the agencies have not suffered too much, however, in connection with job assignment, efficiency control, and discipline in general because of differences of nationality among staff members, officials, or employes. To some degree this has resulted from the coöperative zeal among the personnel just cited; to some extent it has resulted from the low level of authority exercised by and within the agencies for the most part. But both of these factors are likely to change in the future and this problem deserves increased attention.

Finally much more attention is required by the problems of compensation, hours, leave, retirement and so on. Variations in standards of living and fluctuations in exchange rates, differences among national patterns of work-and-play behavior, the often remote location of the agency from the homes of most of its personnel, and various other elements complicate the situation tremendously. Failure to provide adequate retirement arrangements leads to even greater evils than follow upon such failure in the national sphere, such as retirement from international service to enter (or reënter) national service, much more objectionable than similar action in a national federal union because of the more highly competitive international situation. The proper solution is obvious but drastic.

When we enter the sphere of their activities and methods the agencies are open to greater criticism, partly because these are matters for which they are as much to blame as the states and which they could alter very largely by themselves.

Thus it seems that the international administrator has exaggerated the necessity for avoiding any initiative on his own part and has failed to exercise leadership where that was clearly needed and was quite feasible. It is true that states are very sensitive on this point and that the general theory of administration tends to support the position taken; also we should hardly wish to see reproduced in the international sphere that effort to usurp power recently so familiar in national administration. But with these features in mind it would still surely be possible for the international administrator to exercise more leadership than he has and it would surely be useful. It must be added that this judgement has recently received official approval.[6]

In a closely related matter the agencies have not been quite so cautious, namely the adoption of regulations and their interpretation. Unless restricted to purely informational or advisory functions the average international administrative agency has been commendably ready to elaborate regulations governing the matter entrusted to its care; it must be added that no great opposition to such action has been forthcoming from the states! The explanation seems to lie partly in a happy ignorance of the limited nature of administration strictly defined, on one side, and an assumption by the governments that if a bureau (more probably a "commission" in this case) is set up to handle a given matter it may and must be expected to make rules about it at the very least.

In a seemingly much less crucial matter the agencies have been more backward and have also become involved in more trouble when they did venture forward. This is the matter of publicity and promotion. There would seem to be no more normal activity for an agency assigned to the service of public health on the international level than to carry on a campaign for public education on this line. Yet few agencies have done this to any great extent and the states have revealed a somewhat surprising sensitiveness on this score. The first phenomenon is traceable to the indifference of most international administrators in matters of public relations, the second to the dogma that policy and influence upon policy are exclusively matters of state concern. Surely a change must be brought about here for the sake of international administration itself not to mention its clients.

On the culminating issue of executive action, the taking of decisions and their enforcement, the agencies can hardly be either praised or blamed. On these points they are so closely regulated by the states that they have little margin for discretion, for either improvement or for failure to act properly. In the taking of decisions there has seemed to emerge a slight expansionist tendency akin to that noted in the matter of regulations. In the matter of enforcement the agency is practically powerless to exceed its mandate (if any) and indeed is commonly unable to carry out its mandate (to "assure the execution of this convention" for example) for lack of adequate facilities.

As for the area of their operations the agencies themselves do not appear to have sinned greatly or greatly served. The timidity already mentioned has balanced the natural aggrandizing tendency of all wielders of power and the result has been that the agencies have abided by their charters. Nor can it be said that those charters have been drawn too

[6] Landis, Chap. II, on administrative usurpation; on recent approval of administrative leadership see UN Charter, Art. 99.

broadly or too narrowly by the states; area of operations is certainly not one of the more controversial issues in international administration.

Not so in the matter of the location of headquarters, branch or field operations, and plant. These again are questions in which the states must be held responsible rather than the agencies for any good or bad results which appear, but whoever is to blame the effects are highly uneven. The heavy concentration of headquarters of agencies in one continent, and in three countries, and in a similar number of cities, is at least challenging; the absence of a single international capital is the heart of this problem. The opposition of the governments to branch and field operations by the agencies is possibly understandable but clearly unfortunate. And the failure to provide the agencies with adequate buildings and adequate equipment and adequate supplies is not only undignified but also disloyal and finally very poor economy.

Closely allied is the financial issue, and here again it must be said flatly that the states have tended to starve the agencies. This is the major point to be made at this juncture although precisely in that connection it might also be argued that it would probably be helpful if the raising of funds were shared by the states with the agencies in some degree, as by allowing them to expand their revenue-producing activities or even to levy supplemental charges in case of need. On the expenditure side no great criticism is to be made; the agencies have not committed many notable mistakes nor have the states been unduly restrictive. If anything this whole aspect of international administration has been allowed to drift along without great attention. It is probable that this will change with increase in the size of international administrative budgets but it is to be hoped that some of the characteristics of the present era will survive in the new age.

With changes in the relations among international administrative agencies the terms of the problem of supervision and control will alter. Hitherto there has been too little inclination to provide effective supervision or carry it out, and the objectionable delegation of this function to one government has already been cited. It should be interjected that the agencies themselves have encouraged such neglect by, in general, performing their often harmless tasks in such a way that supervision seemed superfluous. All this will certainly change with increased powers, increased budgets, and so on. Perhaps also there can be adopted some revised set of principles under which international administration can operate more effectively than under the seventeenth-century dogmas all too prevalent in international affairs, notably the dogmas of state equality and the exclusiveness of the two spheres, the national and the international. But there will above all be felt a necessity for organizing control so that the international community as such can be heard in the matter, so that interested states can receive adequate attention for just complaints, and so that ordinary human beings can also obtain an audience in matters of individual rights, where these are intrusted to international administration, and on all sorts of public questions in general with many of which they are deeply concerned.

How far it will be possible to go in reorganizing and improving international administration is a matter for conjecture. The record indicates that it will not be necessary to stand absolutely still but it also indicates that revolutionary change is not likely to be successful, if attempted, atomic bomb or no atomic bomb. It is to be hoped that the pace of international reform can be accelerated, as, indeed, seems to have been true in the past thirty years. The whole problem, of course, is one of alteration, remodeling, and adaptation or readaptation. Rarely if ever is the step taken of wiping the slate clean and starting afresh. Even in the recent case of the League of Nations and the Permanent Court of International Justice the new institutions are, largely in fact in both cases, and also in theory in the case of the new court, remodelings of the old. The need for consolidation of the preëxisting agencies is as pressing today as ever and indeed more pressing; likewise the need for considering the situation carefully before proceeding to create new agencies and new systems.

It is hoped that this exceedingly condensed review of the marginal problems of international administration will have served to emphasize three points. One is the complex and rich character of international administration itself and the many issues calling for consideration in connection with its future. A second is the way in which international administration symbolizes and summarizes international organization in general and brings the general activity to a head. And the third is the way in which the problems of international organization and administration epitomize the generic problems of human society and government in and among the nation states.

B1. *Inquiry and Conciliation*

It is common, of course, in the analysis of governmental powers in the national sphere, to set off adjudication as a third type of power in addition to legislative and executive or administrative power, and as distinct from the latter. At least this is common in Anglo-American countries, and the reason is largely accidental and historical; in civil law countries judicial action is more commonly regarded as a branch of administration or the application of the law. As between the Anglo-American and the Continental view the latter appears to have both logic and experience in its favor, and even Anglo-Americans frequently recognize this, in speaking about the "administration of justice" and in other ways, although they tenaciously adhere to their historic position at the same time. On the other hand, judicial administration is so highly specialized, not to say peculiar, in nature, that it deserves separate treatment and has, therefore, been placed in this section apart from ordinary international administration.

The essential element of judicial administration lies in the fact that it is concentrated upon the settlement of disputes, disputes which arise mainly over the content of the law in general and its meaning as applied to a given situation and the consequences thereof. Discovery of the law, its interpretation in general or as applied in specific cases, and the drawing of appropriate conclusions as to rights, obligations, penalties, and so on constitute the essence of the judicial function. To that activity, its organization and operation, we now turn.

At this point we should, however, take note of two types of international administration which arise—as the international administration which we have been considering so far, does not, to any great extent, —in or from ordinary diplomacy, but attain a higher status by virtue of the way in which they are organized and carried on, "administered" in fact. We are all the more justified in doing so because these two forms of action inaugurate the treatment of the international dispute, even if they do not deal with the strictly legal aspects of the situation to any great extent. They lie just between non-contentious international administration and adjudication, rising above the latter to deal with disputes but remaining below the latter in not dealing with the dispute in terms of law. They are by name inquiry and conciliation.

The simplest method of dealing with the international dispute beyond diplomatic negotiation, and one which leads to the first international institution or organ beyond the rudimentary consular and diplomatic corps, is inquiry or the use of a commission of inquiry.[1] Inquiry itself, or investigation of the facts of a situation, is, of course, present in all international controversies or diplomatic representations between one nation and another, but here the inquiry is conducted by each party for itself. The commission of inquiry rests upon a different principle, is organized and conducted in a different manner, and leads to a different result.

The commission of inquiry is based in theory upon two phenomena familiar to all who have studied international relations. On the one hand, it is undeniably true that much of the difficulty of settling international disputes amicably derives from the initial difficulty of establishing a statement or version of the facts to which both parties will agree. On the other hand, this difficulty perpetuates itself by allowing passions to be roused on either side which not only obstruct agreement between the parties on points of principle but also prevent a clear settlement of the facts in the case in preparation for agreement on points of principle. Even given goodwill on both sides to start with, it would still be of little avail, and would often be destroyed very shortly, by claims and counterclaims on questions of fact.

Thus the first task of the mediator—to be studied later—is often that

---

[1] On inquiry see literature cited below, Appendix B, § 8b (1).

of allaying international tension and getting agreement upon the facts. It may then appear that, the facts being what they are, the solution follows almost automatically as a result of gradual agreement of the parties on the law and equity of the case. Seeing that such a task is useful when performed by a mediator, the nations have in very recent years developed the commission of inquiry to perform the same function, while abstaining from any treatment of the substance of the dispute in principle. The commission is to take over the function of ferreting out the facts and providing time for passions to cool and for consideration of the merits of the case.

Here we meet an international governmental body, an organ empowered and fully instructed by several (two or more) states. The diplomatic corps would constitute such a body if it were more fully organized and functioned more effectively. The international conference possesses a certain amount of such authority but relatively little. In the commission of inquiry there is no doubt on this score. Here we have a body of persons acting as a unified international governmental institution, and in the evolution of international institutions it antedates the non-judicial agencies discussed above.

The commission of inquiry is organized by the appointment of representatives by the disputing parties, with or without an umpire, with provisions for majority votes or unanimous consent as the parties may prefer. The questions examined are questions of fact, and the final settlement and political considerations are removed from the scene. The members of the commission are chosen primarily for their expert scientific ability, rather than from the diplomatic forces. The atmosphere of the commission is, therefore, more conducive to calm and able discussion than it might otherwise be. For that reason a surprising degree of unanimity can be obtained in the decisions of the commission.

Following the report of the commission on the facts, the parties are free to settle the question of principle or of rights, and to act upon the application of the result to the facts as found. The fact that the report of the commission is known may make difficult an agreement upon the principles or law to be applied, since the outcome would be a foregone conclusion. This situation may be avoided only by prior agreement upon the principles. This step, however, is, in turn, likely to influence the decisions or discussions of the commission in the same way, although not to the same extent. In the former case the report of the commission leaves the definitive settlement open, and there may be a need for good offices or mediation or arbitration on top of the work of the commission. For that matter, mediation may be used to induce the disputants to accept a commission of inquiry or arbitration in the first place. Still further, in the second case the commission may amount to a court of arbitration. The "questions of fact" and "questions of law" are not, of course, always distinct or even distinguishable, in these cases, and the commission almost inevitably tends to include legal questions in its work. In this manner a "commission of inquiry" which sat in Paris in 1905 upon an Anglo-Russian dispute over the action of a Russian fleet in firing on English fishermen in the North Sea during the Russo-Japanese War found on the facts and also upon the liability of the parties arising out of the facts. Such action serves to show the relation between the commission of inquiry and arbitration, but is likely to bring suspicion on the commission of inquiry as a court of disguise.

A further development in the practice of mediation leads to a result still further up the scale. This is conciliation or the council of conciliation.

Mediation is weak in that a third state which proffers such service is almost inevitably suspected of ulterior motives or at least regarded as interfering in a matter of no immediate concern to itself. It is also weak in being carried out by an individual state, enjoying, as such, little greater prestige than the individual states parties to the dispute. Resort to mediation is voluntary and precarious, an offer of mediation is suspect, and performance of mediation lacks confidence and authority. The remedy is to be found in an agreement for mediation or conciliation if and when the need arises, and the creation of a permanent general mediation or conciliation commission to be held available for this purpose.

Conciliation so-called, then, is mediation in essence. Being performed by a commission or council it is called by a different name, and the procedure does, of course, have certain qualities of its own. Perhaps being viewed not from the standpoint of the third state but with reference to the objective or from the viewpoint of the detached observer helps to explain the emphasis upon the understanding to be attained between the disputants. At all events the practice is essentially the same.

On the other hand, conciliation by a commission consisting in the main of representatives of the parties, with only an umpire, so to speak, from a third state, and based upon a bilateral agreement,[2] while evidently rising above the level of episodic practice to that of permanently organized and institutionalized practice, is evidently inferior to the practice of conciliation by an agency resting upon a multi-lateral agreement and manned by agents of two or three or more neutral parties. In the matter of recourse or submission the two forms of conciliation may be on a par; in the matter of confidence and authority they are not. Mediation, like good offices—and inquiry—grows out of simple diplomacy, but the further it grows above its roots the more effective it will be.

It must be recalled that inquiry by itself contributes in only a limited degree to the settlement of international disputes, taken by itself. It must be, as indeed it very conveniently may be, combined with mediation or conciliation, or with arbitration or adjudication, to be of most value. When conciliation is thus filled out it, in turn, provides a certain degree,

[2] See Commissions in Department of State *Register*, Jan. 1, 1932, p. 285.

but also only a limited degree, of assistance in the settlement of international difficulties. It is peculiarly useful for political disputes, being flexible where rigid legalistic methods would be less useful. On the other hand, its object is peace by compromise, not justice by law. It is easier to secure pledges for submission to inquiry or conciliation than to adjudication, and, what is more important, and not by any means the same thing, actual submission. The same highly desirable element of delay and emotional deflation, febrifuge of war, is provided as by arbitration. But it also must be combined with, or used as a path leading toward, adjudication to produce most lasting results.

It will be obvious that the most important step to be taken in connection with the practice of inquiry, good offices, mediation, and conciliation is to place such functions in the hands of permanent commissions with power to take the initiative in the face of international disputes, and to summon the disputants to inquiry, to further discussions between themselves, to mediation, or conciliation. Acceptance of mediatory recommendations might be left to voluntary action by the parties. But the inauguration of such action and response to it should be made automatic and obligatory to be most effective. Steps of this sort are being taken in many quarters today, as we shall see. And when so organized, mediation, or conciliation, as it is now called in such circumstances, is probably the most valuable means available for composing disputes and preserving peace among the nations.

Neither inquiry nor conciliation provides a means of settling international disputes unless the solution worked out in diplomatic discussions or proposed by the conciliators is acceptable to both parties, and it will command the assent of both parties only if it appears to offer to them the maximum of advantage obtainable in that particular case at that particular time. The parties may conceivably take account of the advantages of a peaceful settlement instead of war. They may, indeed, take account of any indirect or remote advantages to be derived by the acceptance of a settlement of the current dispute which is less favorable on its merits than they would desire to accept. In international relations, however, with the constant rise and fall of national power and advantage and the constant shifting of support to one party or another in the diplomatic game, the nations are not very prone to seek the indirect advantages which might come by the support of legal principles calculated to bring a general benefit in the long run. They are prone to seize the immediate advantage and take a chance on being able to do the same thing in whatever circumstances may arise in the future. Thus it is that the formula proposed by the conciliator must be acceptable not so much because it conforms with general principles which might be acceptable in themselves for constant application to all cases at all times but because it represents concrete benefits at the time in the case in hand.

The result is to diminish considerably the value of conciliation as an

international practice. Conciliation is the sort of task which, being performed, may easily have to be performed all over again at once, not because of any change in the subject matter of the dispute but because of
changes in the relative positions of the parties and their opportunity to
demand greater things for themselves. Each conciliation is a new task,
not to be performed by reference to any preceding act of the same sort
or any principles or rules of law, unless the results of the application of
such rules or the rules themselves appeal at the time to the parties as
desirable. This prevents the use of artificial or antiquated legal rules
or principles, just because they have once been established, and irrespective of their intrinsic justice. In this way, as has been pointed out, conciliation may secure greater substantial justice and equity in certain cases
than a more legalistic settlement. The result in the total number of cases,
however, is to produce instability, uncertainty, and disorder, and to allow
free rein to capricious political claims which take no account of any general principles of law.

This is partly accountable for the reluctance often felt by third states
to undertake the task of conciliation. The mediator has no fixed rules
which he is free to follow in proposing a settlement. Not that there are
no such rules of law or equity in existence which could be called on to
settle the dispute. There may not, indeed, be any such generally accepted rules applicable to the case; many aspects of international relations are still in that position. Even where such rules are available,
however, the conciliator dares not depend upon them for fear that the
parties will not agree with him or with each other on the merit of the
rules or the results of their application. To the world in general, interested in seeing a peaceful, a permanent, and, to that end, a just settlement,
this objectionable fact presents itself even more sharply.

2. *Adjudication*

The attempt to remedy this defect in the practice of conciliation leads
to the use of arbitration. The conciliator, anxious to be free to devise a
solution which shall avoid war at the present and avoid it for good and
all if possible, so far as this particular case is concerned, may ask to be
freed from the necessity of too solicitously conciliating the particular
demands put forward at the time by the parties. He may then be authorized to apply existing principles of law and equity to the case by a prior
agreement of the parties to accept the result of his mediation. Agreed
mediation results in setting up the mediator as judge of the dispute. This
is arbitration in all but name. Indeed, at one time in the history of arbitration the judges were called indifferently "arbitrators" and "amicable
mediators."

Arbitration [1] may be formally defined as the settlement of international

---

[1] On international adjudication see literature cited, below, Appendix B, § 8b (2).

disputes by judges chosen by the parties. Several elements in this concept deserve special notice.

Arbitration is judicial settlement and henceforth will be referred to as adjudication. It is administration, administration of law in the most acute form. It is settlement by a person or persons acting in a judicial capacity, called by the usual term "judge", attempting to decide by reference not to the claims of one or the other of the parties, for those conflicting claims, indeed, constitute the dispute itself, but by reference to some standard common to both parties and external to the particular dispute. That standard may be merely one of general convenience—convenience to the parties and to the community at large—or it may be one of philosophical justice, as conceived by the arbitrator and as presumed by him to be conceived by the parties. Where the arbitrator or international judge is able to discover legal rules, rules, that is, which have actually been accepted at some time in the past as such by the parties, which are applicable to the case in hand, he will not hesitate to utilize them, even where those rules have not been accepted generally by the family of nations. For, although acting on the basis of a pledge by the parties to accept his award, he knows that the award must in fact be accepted and carried out by the parties if it is to be effective. It would, therefore, injure his standing with the parties to hand down an award not capable of being justified by reference to previous declarations made by them. Arbitral awards were based less upon legal grounds historically but this was due to paucity of law rather than to the inherent character of the institution. Whether the arbitrator decides the case by equity or by law, he is acting in a judicial capacity, and where legal foundations are not used in the process it is because they do not exist. The deficiencies of the system of international law, however, should be kept distinct from the supposed deficiencies of arbitral procedure.

Note may be profitably taken at this point of the fact that adjudication often seems to be an earlier form of international government than legislation, or even administration. Logically, of course, the making, the administration, and the explanation or interpretation of law would have to follow in that order. Historically it appears otherwise. Judicial settlement began at a time when as yet there was available merely a very limited volume of customary law and special compacts between individual states. The revision of the law and its elaboration have come much later. In fact adjudication appeared only after some law-making had been accomplished, though formal and conventional legislation had not yet appeared. It had also been preceded by administration by individual states, pending true international administration.

Adjudication or arbitration might be conceived, and should be conceived in part, as a form of action available to one individual state for use against another in order to secure satisfaction for its rights. It is not to be conceived merely as a form of organized action which occurs or is available in the international community for settlement of disputes, a phase of administration of the law. Or, if it be a phase of administration of the law [2] it is a phase or form of action which may be set in motion by the individual state. In this sense it ranks along with national diplomatic representation, retaliation by legislative and administrative action (tariffs, arrests, or such), or military action. Administration or invocation of the law is not, among the nations, merely—or mainly as yet—a matter of action by a common administrative agency, but rather a matter of complaint and demand and pressure by the aggrieved state; adjudication, or a demand for adjudication which may or may not be sound, is one tool available for that task on the part of the states.

Likewise it should be remembered that while we are talking in the main of interstate adjudication, adjudication of cases where states are parties, there is a whole branch—indeed a whole world—of international adjudication where this is not entirely the case. This is claims adjudication, or the adjudication of claims preferred by nationals of one country against the governments or sometimes the nationals of other states where adequate remedies are not available through the national courts of the latter.[3] This subject is regulated in detail by many rules and practices. Hundreds and thousands of such claims adjudications occur for every one of the other type. And perhaps it is here that the most powerful and promising seeds of a mature system of international adjudication are being sown.[4] But the principles involved do not differ from those controlling the other type of activity and it is the latter which seems to raise the problems of international adjudication most clearly to view.

The arbitrator or judge is not left to his own resources respecting the standards to be applied in settling the case submitted to him. The parties to the dispute commonly agree at the time of the submission on the standards to be applied in the case, and this provides the arbitrator with his necessary basis of settlement. Where the parties simply agree to a settlement "according to the principles of international law and equity" the arbitrator is left much latitude. On the other hand, if the bases of settlement are closely specified by the parties, the arbitrator will depart from them at his peril, even where the bases agreed upon seem to him to be out of accord with common international law. In order to secure a settlement according to common international law a submission in general terms is preferable.

Implicit in these conditions regarding the basis for the decision of the arbitrator lies the most significant principle governing the practice of international adjudication, namely, the principle that the jurisdiction of the arbitrator and all that this involves is derived from the express consent of the parties, exercised in a choice of particular judges for a

[2] Above, pp. 131-133.
[3] See Hudson, *Tribunals*, Chap. XVI.
[4] See, below, p. 163.

particular case to be decided at a particular time and place. There exists no general arbitral jurisdiction based upon general agreement of the community of nations, covering all the issues, or even any special group of issues, submitted in advance of their appearance to any court of continuous sessions. The arbitrator is usually chosen by the parties at the time, and the issue to be settled by him, as well as the time and place of the hearing and the standards to be applied in reaching the decision, are defined at the same time. This is the essence of international arbitral settlement.[5]

Considerable variation is possible among the methods adopted in making up the arbitral tribunal. A single arbitrator may be chosen by agreement. Each party may first select one or more judges and then an umpire may be chosen by agreement. The umpire may be chosen by lot or by the judges already named, or by third and fourth powers who have been named by the parties. All of this procedure is settled in the agreement for submission.

In each case submitted to adjudication, therefore, the critical legal step is the agreement to submit the case. This agreement is ordinarily embodied in what is called a *compromis d'arbitrage* or arbitral convention, one of the special forms of international treaties. It is in this document that provisions are found controlling the choice of arbitrators, the scope of the question, the time and place of the trial, the procedure at the hearing,—including the languages to be used, the forms or argument and counter-argument to be permitted, the submission of evidence, and whatever else is necessary. The bases of the award are here specified and the document closes with provisions for the rendering of the award, provisions for carrying out the decision and, perhaps, provisions guaranteeing execution. This is the simplest and most primitive basis for an international adjudication.

Where a dispute involves several nations the agreement for arbitration may, of course, be signed by more than two parties. In that case the relative positions of the parties in the trial will be defined in the text.

Very different from the agreement for the adjudication of a dispute which has arisen, and providing the machinery and rules for this adjudication, is the arbitration treaty proper, which provides for the submission in the future of disputes between the parties as they arise. Such an agreement may cover all varieties of disputes, or it may cover only a certain list of disputes described in general terms, or it may cover all disputes outside of a certain specified list of exceptions. In any case the object is to provide in advance for the submission of a question to adjudication without leaving for discussion, at the time when the dispute arises, the question whether it shall be submitted or not. When a dispute has actually arisen between two nations the atmosphere is not suitable

---

[5] See, below, pp. 266-267, for modification of this and other aspects of the situation treated in this section.

for the conclusion of an agreement to arbitrate, even though the question be such that in general—apart from the current case—there would be no hesitation to submit it to adjudication.

The agreement in advance to submit certain questions to adjudication upon occurrence may take several forms. The earliest form was the arbitral clause, a clause inserted in a treaty dealing with commercial or territorial or any other subjects, providing that if disputes should arise in the future over the meaning of terms of the treaty or any questions arising out of the treaty, these disputes should be submitted to adjudication.

The arbitral clause was followed by the bipartite permanent arbitration treaty as just described, covering different questions of one sort and another, apart from any particular treaty. This is the prevalent type of arbitration treaty today.

The third stage is the multi-lateral or general arbitration treaty, providing for the submission to adjudication in the future of all disputes of a certain sort arising among the parties, and signed by a large number of states. This type of arbitration treaty is a little in advance of general usage today.[6]

For this, in the technical language of diplomacy, is "compulsory" or "obligatory" arbitration, the second term being preferable, for reasons soon to appear. By this it is meant that, once such a treaty is concluded, the signatory states are under legal obligation to submit certain cases to adjudication when they arise. Of course, this obligation arises from a sovereign act of consent made at an earlier time, and is therefore a self-assumed obligation. In that sense it is not obligatory but voluntary. But at the time of the dispute the legal obligation is real and—what is, perhaps, more important—is felt very keenly in the state of opinion existing at the time of the dispute.

On the other hand, even the existence of such a treaty does not necessarily avoid the necessity for a special agreement at the time of submission. This is attributable to the fact that the issue must be defined more precisely than can ever be done in advance by a general treaty, that judges must be chosen, times and places for the hearings selected, and all the many details of procedure arranged. There are few permanent courts, no forms of action, no sufficient code of procedure; and no way exists for making good these deficiencies except by special agreement at the time. This means that a large part of the force of any agreement in advance to arbitrate certain cases as they appear is destroyed. Not until, in addition to the promise in advance to arbitrate a specified set of cases as they arise, there exist a standing court, a prearranged method of initiating the action, and a previously established code of procedure ready for instant use, does the need for the special agreement at the time disappear or find satisfaction.

[6] See treaty signed in Washington on 5 January, 1929.

There is, however, another aspect of this situation to be noted, and another problem to be faced by the student of international adjudication. During the past fifteen years we have had an enormous increase in the number of agreements for arbitration, many of them giving the parties power to hale one another into court by unilateral action; at the same time we have had no appreciable increase in arbitration or actual submission of cases! Why this anomaly? The explanation is very complicated. Defects in the existing system of international law and arbitral procedure, desire not to offend another state by invoking obligatory adjudication, preference for diplomatic settlement to avoid arbitration, —such are a few of the factors operating in the premises. It will be interesting and important to watch the developments, or lack of developments, along this line.

The questions specified for submission to adjudication vary greatly. No question is incapable of submission to a mediator, of course, for he may devise a formula of settlement in reliance solely upon his own ideas of convenience and expediency, apart from any law or formal equity, so long as he can secure its acceptance by the parties. Where legal standards are to be used in the settlement, however,—and agreements to arbitrate generally specify that such standards are to be so used,—the range of questions capable of submission is immediately restricted to those on which there exist accepted rules or principles of law or equity, namely justiciable questions. Such are questions of treaty interpretation, which, as has been pointed out, was the earliest type of question submitted to adjudication. Such, likewise, are questions arising under national statutes and accepted rules of international law. Yet the great difficulty here resides in the number of questions of large importance which arise in international relations for whose settlement there are no legal standards available.

Turning to the other side of the question, certain types of questions were once commonly excepted from the scope of pledges to arbitrate future disputes and these categories still have some importance in this connection. They were or are questions of honor and of vital interest, questions affecting the national independence, domestic questions and questions involving the rights of third powers. These exceptions could, of course, be used as disguises for a reluctance to arbitrate based on other grounds. "National honor" in particular could be employed to cover anything which it was desired to withhold from arbitration. The terms are so general that they were—like all general terms—subject to abuse although historically they were not very frequently abused.

The exception of national honor is not without foundation and has its analogy in the law governing relations among individuals. What is to be treated as a matter of national honor is, however, a question of fact. More important is the fact that conceptions of what affects the national honor are constantly changing. The national sensitiveness of the early modern period, of the seventeenth and eighteenth and early nineteenth centuries—which made so much ado about questions of diplomatic precedence, which cast suspicion on the offer of good offices and mediation—is fading to a more prosaic and sensible mood. Nations with a practical outlook are not likely, in this unsentimental age, to hold out on this ground very long. The exception is already unimportant.[7]

Similarly with questions which affect the vital interests, the independence, the very existence of the state. No state could submit to arbitration a question likely to result in a decision that it had no right to exist. The state can hardly be asked to incur serious risk of disastrous consequences, even for the sake of the general benefits of peace and order, as long as it has an opportunity to protect itself by exceptions to the obligation to submit to adjudication—afterward it will be too late to make any such reservation. Again the important thing is not to try to deny the principle itself, for the principle is sound, but to notice that its consequences are not as extensive in application as they once were. As the state system becomes more and more stable, and the nations are more and more firmly established, the questions which in reality do threaten their existence are fewer and fewer. With the development of a legal system defining national rights more fully, less is left to political manœuvering. With the continued existence of certain states side by side, relationships spring up which cut down the zone of undefined potentialities between them. A new state may have its existence menaced, and, what is more, may feel that its independent existence is menaced, by questions which an older state would accept as arbitrable with far more safety and equanimity. This is not merely speculative. States of recent origin are conspicuously apprehensive about events and actions in the territories of their neighbors which are not of sufficient importance in the eyes of the older and more firmly established states to justify in the minds of the latter the feelings of the weaker states.

The exception of the domestic question is far more important. At any one time international law leaves certain matters to the jurisdiction of the national state. Such matters are hardly suitable for international adjudication in the absence of international law regulating them, as already indicated. What would be dangerous to the progress of international adjudication would be to leave determination of what is a domestic question to the state, which could then raise difficulties, though not necessarily succeed in obstructing international action in every case arising. It may be argued that to allow the preliminary question to be decided by an international court, on the other hand, tends to nullify the exception, but it can be replied that to pass upon the scope of their own jurisdiction is a power almost universally granted to courts and that this task is certainly performed by courts with less bias and thirst for power than by the national governments. As the Permanent Court of Interna-

[7] Habicht, p. 993.

tional Justice said, the range of the "domestic question" is constantly changing—constantly contracting, it might have said.

As for questions affecting the rights of third parties, the situation is again somewhat different. Such questions are likely to increase rather than decrease as time goes on; at the same time it is well agreed that the rights of third parties may not, as a matter of principle, be settled by decisions between others. The solution lies, obviously, in two directions. The third parties may be invited to join in the case, or may even be brought in under standing treaties of arbitration. Or secondary arbitration cases may be instituted to settle issues derived from the decision in the first. After all, this is an exception relating not to the subject matter of questions submitted to adjudication but to the parties to the cases submitted. It argues a defect, not in the nature of adjudication, but in the existing mechanism of conducting cases.

In actual practice numerous states have agreed to arbitrate all international questions. There is revealed in such action a curious mixture of cynicism and idealism, of practicality and romanticism. Considerations of national honor and pride are put aside for the sake of getting a settlement without the expense and waste of war. In the enthusiastic support of the peace ideal, the limitations of arbitral practice due to the insufficiency of the legal materials available, are overlooked. At all events, the tendency seems to be to eliminate the traditional exceptions as described and to take care of the real interests formerly covered by those exceptions in some other way. It may be added that the preliminary question of the propriety of submission may itself be arbitrated if the parties are so disposed.

Finally, as regards the questions submitted to adjudication, it should be recognized that there is a vast difference between conflicting rights of states submitted to arbitral tribunals and private claims submitted to international commissions. The former are the questions which attract attention. The latter bulk large in actual practice. Even in the latter case, of course, the nations whose citizens have claims against each other and against the governments act on behalf of their citizens and make these claims their own in arranging for the creation of mixed commissions to evaluate them and often to adjudicate upon them. Moreover, the principles of national liability determining the settlement of the various claims presented are principles of public law. Without the latter, and the action of the states as such, no hearing and settlement could be had on the claims. But, granted the provision for hearing and settlement, the claims actually settled are claims of private individuals.

In practice there is often a close intermixture of public and private law in cases submitted to arbitral courts. In the end the commission is led to try to settle the cases coming before it by any law applicable— public or private international law, Anglo-American or Civil law, or what not. And the further we go in that direction the more evident does it become that arbitration is, as far as circumstances permit, judicial settlement.

The whole problem of the status of the individual before international courts is now in process of reorganization. The traditional hostility to such a development, incompatible with claims commission practices, may itself be modified. Development of international criminal jurisdiction, of the war crimes type exercised at Nuremburg and elsewhere of a more general type, would affect the situation. Provisions for international protection of individual rights would presumably have similar results. Altogether very important developments may be expected along these lines.[8]

The decision of an international tribunal is made universally by majority vote. This phenomenon is so universal and yet so fundamental in its bearing on the principles of international law and organization, with special reference to national sovereignty, that it cannot be overemphasized. Further reference will be made to it later in our discussion of international federation.[9]

Once the court's decision is rendered, it is subject to no appeal. The reason is to be found in two facts. There is no other tribunal to which, as of right, the case may be carried. There is no superior court; all international courts are supreme courts.[10] In the second place, the parties have pledged themselves to accept the decision, duly made according to the convention of submission. The pledge of acceptance having been given, the rendering of the award makes it part of the treaty itself and of final effect; state sovereignty has been satisfied by the original agreement, now the state is bound.

In point of fact, few judicial awards have been rejected by the participants. One reason is to be found in the fact that by the time a state is willing to submit to adjudication the chief desire is to secure a settlement of some sort or other, and this is the chief reason for that willingness. This leads to the mutual pledge of acceptance and to its almost automatic observance, thus eliminating any problem of enforcement.

In order for this rule to operate, however, the award must have been duly made. An award made in excess of the authority conferred by the parties submitting the case is not binding; nor is an award touching questions not submitted, or based upon considerations not open to the court acting under the convention of submission. Likewise, an award obtained by coercion or fraud upon arbitrators or counsel, the use of threats or of dishonest documentary or oral evidence, would have no binding force. It is commonly said that in such cases the parties may ask for a revision

<hr />

[8] Hudson, *Tribunals*, Chaps. VI, XV, XVI; convention for creation of International Criminal Court: League Document C.547(1). M.384.(1). 1937.

[9] Below, p. 189.

[10] For proposals looking toward establishment of international courts of appeal, see Hudson, *Tribunals*, pp. 82-83, 125-126.

of the award. It would be more to the point to say that the case may be resubmitted to a new tribunal for a new decision. The original award has no legal existence. It is not appealed, revised, or overruled. It is of no importance at all.

Such is the nature and the form of international arbitration or adjudication. For a knowledge of the existing agreements for submission of cases to international judicial settlement, the student must turn to treaties in force among the nations of the world at any one time.[11] We shall later take notice of the new International Court of Justice which forms part of the general system of the United Nations and which constitutes the highest point yet reached in the development of this form of international coöperation.

The importance or value of adjudication in international government has been much disputed. For some students it constitutes the highest point attained in that process. For others it is relatively weak in view of its reliance on existing law and its inability to deal constructively with the more dangerous political problems which lead to war. Certainly we must eschew the attitude of regarding arbitration as a panacea for all international troubles. And certainly there is a need for many improvements if international adjudication is to render its maximum possible service to international order and progress.

[11] As of the end of 1932, for example; see De Wolfe, entire.

PART III

General International Organization

CHAPTER IX

International Federation

A. *Alliances, the Balance of Power, International Concert* *

Successive imperial movements in Europe from the fifteenth to the twentieth centuries [1] constitute the second of the three principal lines of development in the history of the modern state-system.[2] Yet they have all failed. St. Helena, Doorn, and the bunker in the Chancellery in the Wilhelmstrasse where the Nazi dictator perished,—these are symbols of the defeat of imperial power and pretensions. There may be schemes of empire in the minds of some dreamers still, but in actual fact the world is back where Europe stood in the fifteenth century, and no great strong empire dominates the liberties of the free national states of Europe, nor, indeed, of any part of the world. The explanation lies in one aspect of the third thread of modern international history, namely, in the development of international alliances and the principle of the balance of power to which we now turn.

We have seen how, following upon the appearance of independent states in the world, came first the development of the community of nations on the material side and then the slow appreciation of that situation by the states and the expression of this consciousness in elementary forms of coöperation, such as diplomatic representation, treaty agreement, and the development of a system of international law. Underlying these activities grew a certain sense of unity or union of the states concerned, even of continuing unity, though it was not expressed in any common organs of coöperation. There follow more elaborate and organic forms of coöperation, the international conference and the administrative agency, including the international court, and here the element of interstate union is much more apparent, particularly in the creation and maintenance of the administrative agency. Even here, however, the states in union do not always commit themselves to ultimate executory action for the accomplishment of the objects of the union, but often trust to voluntary respect for the rulings of the conference, the bureau, or the court.

* The footnotes in this chapter are numbered by the section.
[1] On the imperial movement in modern Europe see Schevill, as cited below, Appendix B, § 9a.
[2] The first being the appearance of independent national states, for which see Chap. II, above, and the third the development of international organization itself.

The simplest form of international union approaching the higher forms of international government is the alliance, or union of two or more states for common executive action.[3] Only independent states can so commit themselves, of course, and the commitments as to objects and methods must for practical reasons be defined in a treaty or other equally formal agreement. These objectives and methods may vary somewhat and even resemble those contemplated in the practice of diplomacy, treaty negotiation, and international conference. The arrangement may be made for a long or short period of time. There will usually not be any common organ of coöperation set up, as there is in some of the simpler forms of coöperation; the states rather prefer to retain the action in their own hands when it partakes of this serious executive nature. But the crux of the institution is precisely the pledge of executory diplomatic, administrative or military action by the states in union.

Two points deserve special notice here.

The first point is that the alliance is an authentic step in the process of international federation. This is recognized in many notable documents. The Constitution of the United States provides that no state shall make any "treaty, alliance, or confederation."[4] The gradation from alliance to confederation is a natural one. The treaty of friendship and commerce concluded in 1778 between the United States and France on the same day which saw the conclusion of the military alliance between those two states spoke of the parties as "the confederates."[5] An alliance and a treaty are to be distinguished mainly in that ordinarily a treaty does not provide for common or joint action by the parties for execution of the agreement, while an alliance does provide for such action whatever the content of the agreement.

In the second place the alliance may be distinguished from the federation in the full sense of the word by the fact that there is no common organ of government. The activities of the allies are coördinated but not unified, and they are coördinated, usually, not by a permanent organ but by diplomatic consultations in each case.

The objects of alliances are as manifold as the interests which states may have in common, and, as in the case of the subject matter of treaty-negotiation, no purpose is to be served by a long enumeration of those objects, by the pedantic enumeration, as has often been done, of treaties of alliance and guarantee, of treaties of alliance and assistance or subsidy, and so on. Nor would it be profitable to dwell upon the different varieties of alliances by reference to the motives which lead to their original formation, and to speak of alliances of blood, of faith, of interest. All alliances are alliances of interest and the interests are too many to be listed singly. A few of the more important and more common objects

[3] On alliances in general see literature cited, below, Appendix B, § 9a.
[4] Art. I, § 10, ¶ 1.
[5] Art. XXIII.

may be noted, as well as a few general inferences regarding the whole matter.

In the first place, it is an elementary rule of sound policy to provide at the outset a clear and specific statement of the objects sought by the alliance. Alliances in general terms are often called alliances "pure and simple." Such alliances are, on the contrary, neither pure nor simple. They are bound to be sources of continual disagreement between the parties. They are "entangling alliances" above all others. They are agreements of indefinite liability for the parties and are certain to cause friction and misunderstanding later. Moreover, the objects as stated in a treaty of alliance must in fact coincide with the real interests of the parties, for otherwise they will be ineffective when the time comes to invoke the obligations of the pact. The parties will not support with men and money the fanciful objects stated in the text.

The commonest purpose of the alliance is to provide for coöperation by military action in self-defense. It is not uncommon to deride the idea that an alliance may be purely defensive. As to that it may be said, first, that, in point of fact, it is a simple matter to point out alliances which have operated entirely in that rôle. Moreover, in so far as defensive alliances tend to become more positive in character this is due to causes much deeper than the alliance itself. Parties to a defensive alliance engage to protect one another in what they believe to be their legitimate rights and interests. That this leads to offensive action at times, and, more commonly still, to stronger action by the parties in defining and pressing for the satisfaction of these rights, in reliance upon the support of the alliance, is due to the fact that international government is still so rudimentary as to leave so very largely to individual nations the business of defining and obtaining satisfaction for their rights. It is this which induces in the defensive alliance its seeming aggressive character, just as the same factor tends to make war always offensive in actual fact unless attention is focused on the mechanical question as to which party first undertakes military action.

The objects of alliances are commonly stated in the preambles of the treaties creating them. Often there is a profession of solicitude for the maintenance of peace and justice by means of the alliance. This is, in part, but another reflection of the situation just described. It is also true that for the real character of the alliance recourse must be had to the body of the treaty, just as it is true that many treaties, if their texts are examined, prove to be in fact alliances although perhaps not called so by name. But it may safely be averred, further, that the professions of solicitude for the maintenance of peace and justice by means of the alliance are not by any means contrary to the facts and this for a very definite reason, namely, that practically every alliance aims at support of a condition of balance of power, without which there can be, in reality, neither peace nor justice.

Before turning to this subject of the balance of power, however, two other matters are to be considered, namely, the legal aspects of alliances and the question of membership.

In common with all treaties, treaties of alliance involve many questions of law respecting the original power of the signatories to conclude the treaty, the duration and binding effectiveness of the pact, the scope of the obligations assumed, and the effect of the treaty upon other treaties and other parties. Because of the fact that definite action, and military action at that, is commonly called for, the question of the scope of the obligation of the treaty, of the appearance of the occasion for action under the treaty, called the *casus fœderis*, is especially vital. It is, however, a strictly legal question, and the student must be referred for its adequate treatment, as well as for treatment of all the various legal questions relating to alliances, to the special volumes upon the legal aspects of treaties of which there are now an ample number.[6]

As to membership, alliances may be bilateral or multilateral, dual, triple, quadruple, and so on. They may also be "general" in form, including, that is, a substantial number of all the states of Europe, or of the world. At this point we begin to reach the final stages of the development of alliances as instruments of international government. It requires a broader and more general interest to bind three states together than two, four than three, and so on. Likewise it requires a more permanent interest to create an alliance of long term than an alliance for a short period, and it requires a permanent interest to justify an alliance for an indefinite term. It requires a very general and a very permanent object to establish a permanent general alliance, an international federation. Such an object, again, is found in the maintenance of the balance of power. To that we now turn.

The concept of the "balance of power" relates to the powers and positions of the states in the political scene in Europe, in Asia, or in whatever region it is applied.[7] A balance of power would exist where no state was in a position to dictate to other states. Out of this concept a rule of law might be made, to the effect that no state may legally claim or hold such a position. Or the matter might be stated as a practical probability: no state will be allowed to obtain and hold such a position. Finally, we might turn the idea into a statement of policy: no state should be permitted to attain such a position, and such a balance must be preserved as will prevent such a result.

Even if embodied in a principle of law, which it is not, the formula would leave much to be desired. It is rather broad in character and would be very difficult to apply. It appears to imply that states may not legally expand in power and possessions and political influence, which is not the case. On the other side the formula does reflect a familiar and

---

[6] See for example McNair as cited below, Appendix B, § 9a.

[7] On the balance of power see literature cited, below, Appendix B, § 9a.

an accepted principle namely that no state may, of right, lay down the law for others. It consists of an attempt to insure the maintenance of that principle by action in the world of physical facts. It is not a principle or rule of law but a rule of action designed to reinforce and vindicate the law from the outside.

The formula as a statement of probability is of more value. Surveying the long course of international relations from ancient times to the present, it is clear that the states will not, if they can prevent it, permit such a predominance on the part of one state as will endanger their own liberties. As a scientific statement of habitual and characteristic behavior, as a law of the descriptive type, it is well supported by the evidence.

It is as a rule of policy, however, that the doctrine may be regarded to best advantage. On the surface it is a rule of national policy, serving as a guide for each individual state. At a second stage it is an international policy, a generally recognized principle of public interest. As both it has been proclaimed and supported consistently from the earliest times. It is generally felt to be necessary as a practical support for the observance of public law; in the absence of an international police for the vindication of the law, free combinations for security are necessary.

The concept of the balance may take any one of several distinct forms which vary considerably among themselves in value.

The simplest form of the balance is found where two states are somewhere nearly equal in power, and are, by force of circumstances, balanced one against another so that neither possesses a predominance over the other. This form of balance is most unstable and precarious. In its mechanical aspect it resembles a see-saw, or the beam of a pair of scales, which will tip violently if a slight weight is cast into one side of the balance. It is bound to result in an agonizing competition between the parties to prevent one from securing advantages over the other. It leads to the practice of "partition" whereby the rivals, by a "calculus of lands and souls," divide equally the possessions of a weaker neighbor and thus grow in greatness yet preserve the balance. It leads to attempts, on one side and the other, to secure the protection of alliances, counter-alliances, and cross-alliances, resulting in a veritable "nightmare of alliances," haunting the minds of all parties and creating a super-sensitive and suspicious atmosphere among them.

Some improvement is made in the second form of the balance, where a third state, not permanently allied to either of the rivals, holds the balance of power between them. This state, acting from time to time as a make-weight, has the power to exert a moderating influence upon the other parties and to reassure each that he will be protected in his legitimate interests. On the other hand, the situation leads these rivals to curry favor continually with the third state and it allows the third state itself to maintain its supremacy by dividing the rivals and playing upon their fears, and to assume an attitude of dictation checked only by the possibility that the rivals may make common cause against the dictator. While greatly superior to the primitive form of the balance, in view of the presence at the fulcrum of a stabilizing weight which may always serve to redress the balance, it is not entirely satisfactory.

The desirable form of the balance is found where three or more states are substantially equal and are not grouped in any particular or exclusive alliances one with another. This is the mechanical form of the equilateral triangle or, if the comparison is permissible, of the equilateral polygon. There is at once greater stability and greater flexibility in this form of balance than in the simpler forms. It is not so easily upset, because it has the capacity to adjust itself more readily to stresses and strains from without and within. There is a condition not so much of balance as of general equilibrium. Where these conditions exist, among not merely three but four or five or a larger number of states, the ideal condition exists. We then find ourselves back upon the familiar principle that a condition of general equality among the states is what is most to be sought. We also find ourselves demanding that exclusive alliances shall be dropped, as they tend to destroy the general equilibrium. The latter demand, however, leads to a more detailed consideration of the relations between the alliances described in preceding paragraphs and the principle of the balance of power.

The essential connection between alliances and the balance of power is found in the fact that alliances are commonly formed in order to resist the imperialistic efforts alluded to briefly at the beginning of this chapter, and to preserve the balance of power.[8] Two endangered states will combine for mutual aid in defense against conquest by the powerful neighboring nation which is felt to threaten the security of both. In such circumstances neither the object in view nor the method employed seems to merit aught but approval and encouragement. In such a situation both the balance of power sought and the defensive alliance employed for that purpose seem sound and progressive for both local national interests and general international welfare.

If approval can be expressed for such methods when used under such circumstances it is still easier to approve the expansion of the defensive alliance, which has been formed to maintain a balance, into the general concert, in order to achieve a condition of international equilibrium. Our remaining discussion of alliances and balance will turn upon this phase of the problem or the formation of a general international concert and the preservation of international equilibrium and order by various means of international control.

Every experience with efforts at imperial conquest in Europe has served to reinforce all the convictions concerning the necessity for a just and stable distribution of power there which have been developing

[8] For example see, below, Appendix A, Document No. 11.

since the beginning of modern times. The most elaborate and the most successful efforts made at universal European empire have been defeated only by a system of defensive alliances, which have approximated a league of public safety for the reëstablishment of equilibrium and national freedom in Europe. The principle of the balance of power, far from being dropped, has in the most serious situations been placed for enforcement and administration in the hands of something like a continuing, or constantly recurring, organ of international government, instead of being left to individual states or temporary alliances for its defense and support.[9]

It is the fashion in many quarters to criticize the idea of the general alliance or the international concert and its activities, along with the principle of the balance of power itself. Such criticism must be reexamined here to discover its true value, for the principles of the concert and of the balance are present in current efforts at international government just as they were a century ago.

It will be noted, first, that opposition to the concert and to the balance has usually arisen from hostility to the perversion by the concert of the principle of balance to serve some ulterior designs of the individual parties to the concert, and from aversion to the methods employed by the former for the maintenance of the latter. This leads us deeper, however, into the question whether such equilibrium could ever be maintained, and how it could be maintained, without stifling legitimate national activities and national growth. This question will answer itself if we examine more closely the nature of the methods employed for preservation of the balance.

The principal agency of international control used by the concert is intervention.[10] Of course, when any difficulty arises the first step is conference, with or without participation by the offending parties, and conference is followed by a recommendation regarding the action to be taken in the interests of peace and order. Such recommendation, if adopted, could be embodied in an agreement which would settle the matter once and for all. But in the last resort collective intervention with the possibility of use of military or naval force—intervention which might take the simple forms of invasion and occupation, or the more subtle form of pacific blockade [11]—is always in the background. A threat might be sufficient, but whether force be actually employed or only threatened, the juristic nature of the proceeding is the same.

Now according to common or customary international law, individual nations are free to follow their own policies in spite of the views of other nations, except in so far as they have limited themselves by the

[9] For text of the Holy Alliance see, below, Appendix A, Document No. 12.

[10] On intervention see references, below, Appendix B, § 9a. Intervention is, of course, employed by individual states also; it is to be judged here in its rôle as a tool of international concert.

[11] On pacific blockade see Hogan, entire, as cited, below, Appendix B, § 9a.

adoption of certain customary or conventional rules and principles for the regulation of international relations. Each state is free to judge for itself of the nature of those limitations and their effect upon its own action. No state may define the rules of law for another, but may only demand respect for what it regards as those rules, threatening various actions if the demand is not met, actions which may vary from economic retaliation to the most serious steps known to international law. The aggrieved state is entitled, in the last resort, to go to war for the satisfaction of what it believes to be its rights, and the first state is, from the beginning, under legal obligation to satisfy those rights, properly defined. Does this apply to the concert and intervention for the maintenance of the balance?

It is certainly true that any international concert enjoys, and can enjoy, no right of general supervision over the actions of individual states. It could not, as of right, claim any such wide jurisdiction over even its own members. Much less could it claim such jurisdiction over outsiders. Nor could it, all the more, claim any general right of intervention to make good such supervisory jurisdiction. On the other hand, in so far as the concert or its members merely demanded the observance of established rules of international law it would be wholly within its rights, even when it threatened to back up that demand by physical force. Moreover, the individual states to whom such a demand was addressed would be under legal obligation to submit to that demand. It is frequently forgotten that in demanding its rights—providing that what is demanded really is an established right—a state is not assuming to dictate to another, but is simply acting under a system of law deriving its authority from other, broader, sources, including the consent of the state upon whom the demand is made, as previously given.

Does this mean that the maintenance of the international equilibrium commits us to the suppression of all change in the state-system? Is not such a task impossible? How can we prevent the increase of power of a progressive state, the break-up of mature or even decrepit states? How can we ever hope to regulate and control national mutations in the interest of world peace and order, even if we discard the fallacy of organic national growth and death and hope for greater stability as humanity matures?

If the problem had to be faced in just this form it would be impossible of solution. If order and change were necessarily conflicting elements in the international problem the outcome would be a perpetual chaos. Conditions of national life will change even while those states which stand to benefit by the established order attempt to prevent such change, as they probably realize themselves.

The solution of the seeming conflict between international order and equilibrium and the fact of change lies in the practice of constant reorganization by consent. Every settlement, every international order is in some measure unjust, unbalanced, almost as soon as it is made. It must be rectified and the balance corrected by constant revision, not by force but by consent applied in the recognition of new and changing facts.

The concert may succeed where the alliance failed because it makes provision for changes in the existing state-system in accord with the needs of the time. Permitting and promoting rational revision is the crucial test of any system of international coöperation.[12] The "order" to be sought is not any particular status but any order based on reason, justice, and consent. If the concert can attain this aim it will succeed and deserve to succeed.

What of the record of the concert in practice? Can it be maintained that the concert preserves a condition of equilibrium and that it goes upon the basis of consent? If a balance existed before the achievement of independence by some new state did not this action destroy that balance? If the balance was lacking until the action of the concert was taken in each case,—and that action will, it may be mentioned, usually be undertaken only after the initial movement is made by some interested state or national group,—did the concert not tolerate conditions of instability more frequently than it attempted to remedy them? And can the sort of "consent" yielded by the parent state be made the basis of any firm assertions or conclusions whatever?

The leading question implies a misconception of the nature of the balance or equilibrium of power. What is to be maintained is not any given status or alignment but such a status or distribution of power that each group may be in a position freely to live its own life. This means that as time passes a given status—a given distribution of territory or population, of allegiance and sovereignty—may become obsolete and press for change. The balance or equilibrium of things is then to be served, not by a vain attempt to preserve the existing, or, rather, the preëxisting, balance, but by revising the legally established order. What the concert commonly does is to redefine the balance; it does not destroy a condition of balance in favor of a condition of unbalance, but rather it supplants an increasingly inadequate formula of equilibrium with a new and accurate formula; it does not deliberately tolerate conditions of unbalance, but moves to remedy them when evidence appears that such conditions existed. The concert does not, indeed, engage in preventive action as freely as it might. This is due mainly to the lack of uncertainty of its jurisdiction and to the tradition that international coöperation should take place only upon direct and immediate provocation, not for general purposes. But when problems have once arisen, it may attempt to devise solutions which will last, and it may have the courage and judgment to recognize the facts and act upon them.

This may appear to amount to commending the concert for accepting every change that comes along; it may appear to reduce the task of main-

[12] See Potter, *Article XIX.*

taining the balance of power to the job of keeping pace with the upsets which constantly overtake that mythical condition. In the sense that the decisive facts in the problem are to be found outside the realm of diplomacy, politics, and law, and that the existing political and legal balance is either upset or not upset as a result of economic and social forces working independently of it, this is true. The task of law and government in this problem is to register and embody the forces of a non-political nature,—the course of population, the alterations of wealth, of intelligence, of national feeling. The balance of power in the sense of the actual distribution of power will always be what in fact it is, and no diplomatic legerdemain can alter the facts of nature very much or for very long.

The suggestion is probably true also in another sense. It must, apparently, be admitted that it is finally impossible to prevent the expansion and development of any given state which is in a natural position to develop its power and might. If the preservation of the international equilibrium depended upon the stifling of natural national growth it would be both an unrighteous and a futile task. How then can the equilibrium be preserved? If states are to be allowed to develop as they can, and new states to come into being if natural forces demand it, how can we prevent a disruption of the public peace and order, and consequent danger to the rights and interests of existing states? The answer to these questions may be found by again observing the behavior of the concert, particularly upon the question of obtaining the consent of the interested states to the necessary changes in the existing state-system, in the international arrangements of the time.

The consent of the interested states may be obtained by the concert by a process which may be described as the funding or generalization of interests or rights, accompanied by a correlative funding or generalization of power. Turkey felt that she would be injured by the creation of an independent Greece, and hence was led to refuse consent, and to oppose it; and she would have had a right to oppose it, and, probably, would have been able to oppose it successfully, if the question had been allowed to remain a Greco-Turkish question alone. But when it was asserted and recognized that the question of Greek independence, with all that it involved, interested all the Powers and affected their peace and safety and the public peace and justice of Europe generally, the way was open to take care of the problem so as to take into account all interests. Turkish consent could be obtained—that type of consent which emerges from a balancing of alternatives in all such situations—by bringing forward considerations which would set the Turkish loss in one direction off against gains in another direction, such as continued support from the Powers which would otherwise be lost. Turkish rights had to be considered in conjunction with the rights of the Powers to act in defense of their own peace and safety. Turkish power to deny Greek demands had to be weighed in conjunction with the power of the whole concert of interested powers.[13]

So it is in general, in all cases where such a change is involved. The concert must express the conflicting interests of national groups the coexistence of which is exactly what makes it necessary for the individual state to socialize or internationalize its policy. If the prospective change means an expansion of power for one state, such as would have to be considered a threat to neighboring states, the same method of generalization of interests would have to be employed to take care of the situation. Thus, assuming that the concert had been able to function properly in 1908 when Austria-Hungary annexed Bosnia and Herzegovina, what would have happened? The question would have been recognized to be one in which the rights and interests of all the nations were involved and in whose settlement they therefore had a right to a voice. And if the annexation appeared to be dictated by sound principles of international political relations,—if, for example, it had been based upon the economic interests and the desires of the people of Bosnia and had been recognized and agreed to as such,—the consequent expansion of power for Austria-Hungary would have worn a different aspect. Such an expansion with the consent and approval of the concert would not be the menace which it would be in contrary circumstances. It is arbitrary, artificial, and forced expansions of power which disturb the natural distribution of forces in the state-system and provide incitement and precedents for similar forced expansions in the future, that are dangerous to the peace and safety of other states. A great state based upon natural facts, not upon arrogant imperialism, composed of contented instead of rebellious peoples, is not a menace to its neighbors. Moreover, the concert, functioning as such, would be ample enough and powerful enough to assimilate and take up into its complex constitution the expanded Austria-Hungary. No such effect could be hoped for if the individual states, or even limited combinations of those states joined in the old type of alliances for mutual defense, were left to face the new Austria-Hungary depending on their own strength alone. Finally, if the expansion were not dictated by sound principles the concert would be in a position effectively to veto the expansion where individual states or limited alliances would not be—and in the actual conditions of Europe in 1908 were not—so able.[14]

The final form of international combination for preserving the equilibrium of power is, therefore, the general international concert; and the

[13] The Greco-Turkish case is best discussed in Holland, 4-13. The consent of Turkey was obtained, ostensibly, in 1829, by military action, war *pleno jure*, by Russia (Holland, 11); this action must be considered, however, in connection with the activities of France and Britain in conference with Russia.

[14] For description of the Bosnian case as it actually worked itself out see Seymour, 179-182.

final form of the equilibrium itself is at the same time to be found in the generalization of power in this international concert.

The initial step to be taken by the concert in all cases, as has been seen, is discussion or conference, with or without the participation of the state or group involved in the question under examination. The next step is to intervene diplomatically and make recommendations in the premises.[15]

The concert might, however, go on to support its diplomatic intervention by force of arms. This it need not do very frequently. But diplomatic intervention, whether or not carried out by force of arms, if successful, must produce certain results in the realm of politics and law, such as consent to a cession of territory, or the granting of certain rights to certain persons. The next step is to attempt to render these results permanent. For this purpose the members might resort to the device of the guarantee, embodied in a treaty of guarantee or in a clause in the treaty of settlement.[16] Such a treaty defines the rights guaranteed,— for example, rights of jurisdiction, commercial or fishing rights, or dynastic rights and privileges, and the action to be taken for the protection of that guarantee. As in the case of ordinary alliances—for this, in fact, closely resembles an alliance—the execution of the guaranty bond is a delicate and often awkward matter. Much doubt may be raised regarding the obligations of the parties to act under the treaty, and to act singly or in concert; for guarantees may be unilateral or mutual, single or collective, joint or several. Waiving such questions of application, however, the treaty of guarantee, as used by the concert, and embodying as it does a clear right to intervene for its execution in the future, is the next to the very last word in the creation of international control.

If any criticism is to be made of the treaty of guarantee, it is that automatic action for enforcement is not obtainable, and that the enforcement of the guarantee depends upon the interest and willingness of the guarantors to act when the time comes, and not upon any broader basis, such as action by all states. For this reason more definite results may be obtained where it is possible to create by an executed agreement a status which then remains fixed and recognized by all the world. The merit of such a step is that an air of accomplished fact is given to the situation and all the world is made party to the settlement. This is peculiarly true where all states derive certain benefits from the status created.

Among the varieties of status which may be created and guaranteed are, first, territorial possessions and independence. Such a guarantee extends only to existing possessions and the existing degree of inde-

---

[15] For a typical act of intervention and recommendation by the concert see, below, Appendix A, Document No. 13.

[16] On treaties of guarantee see references, below, Appendix B, § 9a. For example see, below, Appendix A, Document No. 14.

pendence and does not cover new additions of territory or new rights subsequently acquired. It need not prevent voluntary changes in the existing status. It involves an approval of that status, and, indirectly, it implies a ruling upon the proper bases of territorial jurisdiction in general; and it depends for its success in the end upon the justice of the status guaranteed. Yet even a supremely just status needs recognition and support against isolated parties who may oppose it; territory and independence may need defensive action for their protection in the future, for they may be attacked by outside parties, or even by one of the guarantors themselves. If carried to its logical extreme and applied generally, this method would lead to nothing more—and nothing less— than coöperation by all states for mutual defense, a general international guarantee of existing possessions and independence against violent attack.

Where the status created is of a different type, different, and perhaps better, results may be expected. Thus the status of territorial neutrality, which is usually created mainly for the purpose of protecting certain states from attack, may be calculated to enlist at least the defensive efforts of those states. Neutralization as applied to strategic areas, such as Switzerland and Luxembourg, is a form of stabilization which rests upon the real necessities of certain imperiled countries and will enlist their support for its defense.[17]

The most advanced type of status to be guaranteed by the nations,— most advanced because most directly useful and most exacting for its maintenance,—is internationalization, or the opening of territory or of certain rights to the use of all nations. Thus the high seas, after being claimed in whole or part by various nations for centuries, are internationalized by common international law and practice, as are the principal international straits. International rivers are being increasingly placed in the same condition by treaty agreements; the same is true in some degree for such canals as those at Kiel, Suez, and Panama. The public maritime highways of the world are thus made a symbol of public international authority.[18]

Similarly, colonial territories are being placed in a condition where all states may enjoy equal opportunities therein for investment and trade. How this attempt will work out in the future remains to be seen. But, whether or not it is successful as an application of the principle, it constitutes another effort to establish international control in the field of otherwise free international competitive struggle. In all parts of the world to which this treatment is applied the door is declared open and national monopoly forbidden. In these cases, moreover, the parties benefited by the arrangement are so increasingly numerous, and the

[17] On status in general and neutralization in particular see references below, Appendix B, § 9a; for example of neutralization see case of the Aaland Islands in League of Nations, *Treaty Series,* Vol. IX, p. 211.

[18] On international waterways see references below, Appendix B, § 9a.

benefit is so real, that a violation or overturn of the status created is less and less likely.

It should be noted, in passing, that in the end neutralization and internationalization come to be much the same thing. Guaranteed neutrality usually involves a surrender of certain rights of offensive and defensive military action by the guaranteed state and an acceptance of protection from the guarantors, that is, a subjection of that state to a more or less limited international régime. Moreover, perfect neutralization is obtained only when all states join in the action; and this intensifies the status established. Where the process of neutralization is applied to uninhabited territories, or to bodies of water, it amounts to opening these areas to free international use, which, again, is internationalization. It may also be mentioned that it has been found useful to neutralize certain territories in the process of bringing them under the control of international administration. The destruction or removal of unilateral national rights over a territory or a water area is almost certain to result in the substitution of affirmative international jurisdiction over it; and as international coöperation develops further this type of action will probably be resorted to with increasing frequency wherever it seems useful.

In recent years—for the past fifty years—the international concert has been, in spite of its embodiment in formal league and union, largely ineffective. The agencies of conference and intervention, guarantee, neutralization, and internationalization, have been of little use in preserving public order and justice in the world. On one hand, there has developed an increasing interest in, and knowledge of, international affairs, and a strong desire in certain quarters to promote some form of international concert and control. While the traditional opposition to any general right of intervention, based upon the doctrine of state independence, has been maintained, the idea of the responsibility and authority of the leading powers for the peace and order of the world has grown stronger and stronger. On the other hand, certain forces have come into operation which have more than equaled this development and nullified its effects. It remains to examine what, in general, are the forces which have defied the best efforts of the concert and all its agencies of international control.

At the center of the resistance is the simple and familiar force of nationalism which has been encountered so frequently in the course of this study, both as a friend and a foe of international organization. National consciousness and the nationalist spirit are still so strong among certain nations, independence and power are still so heady for some nations, that there is often little patience with ideas of the common international welfare, or even with notions of permanent if indirect national benefit as against immediate if temporary advantage; and hence there is little genuine desire for effective international organization. Contrary to common impressions, it is just in the smaller states that nationalism is at times found in its worst forms. A secure and satisfied nationalism is a stable factor in international relations and a good basis for international coöperation, but an insecure and even romantic nationalism is not.

The excesses of the nationalistic spirit have led to a reaction against it in the minds of many students of world affairs in recent years; that reaction has already been discussed as it has leaned· toward cosmopolitanism. They have led also to a supersophistical reaction in· favor of empire as a means of bringing peace and order in a too, too nationalistic world. This reaction likewise has been noted. During recent years both of these reactions have found vigorous expression.

In the decade or so before World War· I, during the years 1914-1918, and between 1919-1939, nationalisms old and new, European and Asiatic, if not also African and American, burst forth in a way to make international regulation appear an impossible task and yet a task all the more needed just because of this situation. The present situation is, of course, largely a product of World War II, as that period was largely a product of preceding conditions. Both of these facts being so, it is not fanciful but strictly necessary to seek the origins of the difficulties of contemporary international coöperation and control in the nationalistic forces which first produced the cataclysm of 1914.

The operation of the force of nationalism in bringing on the catastrophe of 1914 was indirect. The war did not come as a direct result of rebellion in Poland or Bohemia or Ireland. It came directly as a result of Austrian and German and Russian and French imperialism. Yet empire, in its German and Austrian embodiment, at least, was, on one hand, the product of an earlier nationalistic development and, on the other, was merely given its current form by those in a position to profit from a use of its power in conflict with newer nationalist movements which they, in turn, sought to stifle. Germanic nationalism had become nationalistic imperialism. The monarchs of Berlin and Vienna were attempting to use nationalism for imperialistic objects, as had Napoleon a century before. Ironical and paradoxical as it may seem, empire was to be built upon the foundation of nationalism.

Closely allied to this development was the movement of commercial imperialism which bulked so large in the same generation. Commercial imperialism may, of course, be discovered in the colonizing movement of the seventeenth century. But with the increase of population at home, the improvement of means of transportation, and the development of the machine processes of manufacture, the demand upon the newer territories of the earth for food, raw materials, and markets became so overmastering as to lead to a great wave of commercial imperialism in the years after 1878, such as is best exemplified in the partition of Africa. An attempt was made at the Berlin Conference in 1884-85 to apply to this movement the methods of concert, and more success was attained than might have been expected,—more, also, than could have been hoped for ten or twenty years later. Yet the best that can be said is that the precarious balance was preserved by a process of partition without much reference to anything but financial profits and national power. The fundamental forces at the bottom of things were left untouched.

Such empire is better, of course, than empire over advanced peoples. It is even possible to talk with sincerity of carrying civilization to the backward races, and to arouse the noblest as well as the lowest minds in the cause. Even the laboring class will respond to the idea of coloring further sections of the map red or white or blue, and popular support may readily be secured for a war to carry democratic liberties and the benefits of progress to oppressed and backward peoples. Something of this motive entered into the American war with Spain. A sort of popular or democratic imperialism may be developed, working upon the basis of the democracy of the revolution, even nationalistic imperialism utilizes revolutionary nationalism as its motive power.

Rising still higher in the scale, nationalism turns into pan-nationalism, —pan-Slavism, pan-Germanism and so on. Such movements range from pan-Germanism, with its admixture of commercialism, militarism, and dynastic imperialism, to Anglo-Saxonism, with its reliance upon sentiment and voluntary coöperation for mutual assistance. Yet all alike, in one degree or another, present difficulties and obstacles to the concert and have retarded international organization in general. They may offer quicker and more certain returns in the way of international coöperation for those nations and peoples participating in them, but in the end they tend to obstruct general international friendship and coöperation.

No mention has here been made of certain types of state expansion which have grown up along with these principal movements of nationalistic and commercial imperialism, such as the thirst for protectorates and for spheres of influence, the Monroe Doctrine, and the Japanese policy in the Far East. All such activities have tended in the past to prevent free international coöperation. Concrete evidence of this is found in the fact that it is felt to be necessary to recognize the Monroe Doctrine, the basis of the mildest of these movements, as an exception to the full application of all current programs of world organization. In reviewing the agencies of, and the obstacles to, international organization and international coöperation as they have developed in the past half-century, such devices must be placed in the same class with territorial conquests and imperial domination generally. The Monroe Doctrine escapes from this class in so far as it is merely the proclamation of a policy on the part of the United States to prevent conquest or intervention in Latin America. In so far as it amounts to a claim to a general sphere of interest in those regions, it is on a par with Japanese desire for hegemony in China or British domination in Southern Asia as a hindrance to full and free international coöperation. Even so, the United States may prefer to maintain the Doctrine and let the world and world harmony go by the board. She should, however, face the problem squarely and settle it with open eyes.

No great changes took place on the score of nationalism and imperialism, or balance and concert, during the period 1919-1939 or 1939-1947. Nationalism did not increase greatly nor did it decline. There seems to have been some decline of imperialist motives in France and Great Britain, and even the National Socialist program and the Soviet program have differed in character rather sharply from those of older empires,— perhaps for the worse!—but Italian and Japanese imperialism was clear and strong. The United States has certainly become more assertive and dominating but in curiously hesitant and indirect and even inept ways. In spite of the very confused and possibly dangerous character of the international situation it cannot be denied that the world has passed beyond the situation of 1914 when six or seven frankly rival empires confronted one another unabashed. That change has been brought about by the evolution of international mores, not by international organization, but the results have been registered and to some degree sanctified in contemporary international law and organization.

We have now reviewed the nature and development of international alliances and concerts in modern times, and their more or less ineffective efforts to provide a system of international control. These efforts inevitably suggest the creation of a formal international league or federation, and to that subject we now turn.

B. *National Sovereignty and International Federation*

In earlier chapters attention was directed to the nature of the modern state-system, and to four special forms of international organization namely, diplomacy and treaty-negotiation, international conference, administration, and adjudication. Some attention was there given to the relations which exist among different members of this series, as, for example, between treaty-negotiation and international administration. But it was also found that, except by the accidents of history, or by virtue of the way in which they are employed, these institutions are not coordinated into any one system of international government. They are, indeed, coördinated and employed by the foreign offices of individual nations as one body of diplomatic machinery, capable of serving the national interests. When so used, however, they constitute an arm of national service, not a system of international government. Only by deliberately assuming the world point of view can they be so regarded.

To gather these activities together into one system of international government would thus be the next step forward. To do this it would be necessary to unite the national states upon which these practices at present rest in one federal system and thereby unify the activities of these states in their relations one with another. This is international organization in the most precise and significant meaning of that phrase. It is the step for which international concert clearly paves the way.

Such a step, however, raises the fundamental question of the position of the national state and of the juristic nature of the relations among the national states today. It brings us in touch with the most difficult problem in international organization, namely, the reconciliation of international organization with national sovereignty.[1] Of course the element of federal union is latent in all rudimentary forms of international organization, and is very prominent in international administrative unions, but even in the latter case it is not emphasized greatly.

Much effort is being expended today in attempting to evade or circumvent the classical doctrine regarding the sovereignty of the state. These efforts are being put forth, first, by those persons who desire to curb the state in its relations with individual citizens and groups of citizens within the state, and who are impatient with severe theory at any point and feel that all rigid and simple doctrines in political science belie the rich complexity of life. Such are the pluralists in the political philosophy of constitutional government. These efforts are also being made by people who desire to curb the state in its relations with other states, and who believe that the classical doctrine is untenable in view of actual practice and the facts of contemporary world relations. Among these are internationalists and pacifists of all types, emotional or scientific, practical or theoretical.

It is doubtful whether this attitude is either courageous or prudent. The classical doctrine of state sovereignty must either be met directly and those who hold it satisfied by direct replies, or the theory must be simply ignored. If it is mentioned at all in relation to international federation, it must be given an adequate hearing; to mention it only to evade the issue is worse than to ignore it entirely.

It is plain, moreover, that the issue cannot safely be ignored. For practical political reasons this is impossible in view of the fact that those in power in the states of the world adhere more or less to the orthodox theory and are supported in their position by the peoples of those states. In the immediate future, at least, the idea of national sovereignty will not be scrapped and must be met by anyone advocating development of international federation. For a good many states at the present time the need for such a federation is so great, and is felt so keenly, and the influence of abstract forms of political theory is so weakened in the practice of everyday government, that not much is said or heard regarding state sovereignty as an obstacle to international organization. But in the United States the issue is sharply raised and must be met, whether the reasons for raising it are of one type or another, flowing from partisan politics or from patriotic solicitude for the national welfare. Moreover,

[1] On juristic theory of international federation see literature cited, below, Appendix B, § 9b.

the issue, so long as it is not definitely settled, may be raised by politicians everywhere whenever the tactics of the diplomatic battle demands it.

Evasion is the less justifiable when the path of direct attack seems plain. It does not appear to be at all impossible to reconcile the concepts of international federation, international federal government, world government, world state, super-state—making the concept as strong as possible—with the doctrine of state sovereignty, as long as we keep scrupulously in mind the exact steps in the process of creating such an international federation or world state.

It will be profitable to begin by reverting to the most elementary stages in the development of international organization, the stages of personal diplomacy and the negotiation of treaties. In those early phases two or more states, none of which owe any degree of allegiance one to another or to any state or body of states, enter into a practice of discussing matters of common interest through the medium of personal agents. Disputes are settled and arrangements made for the future by voluntary agreements recorded in more or less formal diplomatic documents, the most formal of which is the treaty proper. Such agreements derive their authority from the voluntary participation of the two or more states entering into them.

These elementary proceedings are not felt to constitute a violation of state sovereignty; they are entered into continually by states which do not admit any loss of sovereignty and are not regarded as having suffered such loss. And rightly so. The action of making a diplomatic agreement or concluding a treaty is sometimes described as the acceptance of a self-imposed limitation upon sovereignty. No state may dictate the terms of a settlement or a treaty to another, and consent alone can create an agreement which is admitted to be binding and which in fact has that effect. Willing acceptance creates its effectiveness originally; this result then acquires factual status; finally all parties concerned can rely thereon. The treaty is, therefore, certainly not more than a self-imposed limitation. It is, indeed, only partially that. It is at least as much a positive action of sovereignty in asserting a demand and securing recognition of it. It must be considered an act of self-expression or self-direction as much as an act of self-limitation. The rule that only sovereign states may conclude treaties may be mentioned in confirmation of the general acceptance of this position in international law.

The case of the state "compelled" to accept a treaty "by force" has already been mentioned.[2] Here, as where it is said in all similar situations in human affairs that we do not wish to do a certain thing but that we must, what we really mean is that we would not wish to do a certain thing if facts were not as they are, but, that, things being as they are, we do, after all, prefer to sign on the dotted line. We have a choice which any reasonable person, living under the common conditions of human

2 Above, p. 102.

life, would, indeed, decide in only one way, but his decision would be needed to make the choice; in proportion as conditions have varied from the normal the decision also must vary. Being reluctantly willing to sign is not being glad to sign but it is consent.

When the treaty has been concluded, however, and after it has continued in operation for some time, the situation appears, superficially, to have changed. When a state is held to performance of a treaty obligation incurred twenty or thirty years before it may appear—to that state, and to some presumably disinterested students of the matter—that state sovereignty has been lost.

To such a conclusion there are several replies.

First, as in the initial negotiation of the treaty, so here, it is to be noted that all states come to stand, in the course of events, in precisely this position, and yet their public representatives do not consider that they have lost their sovereignty, nor are they considered by the public officials of other states to have suffered such impairment. This certainly proves that such a conclusion is not warranted in the minds of the high priests of state sovereignty themselves.

Again, it is to the source and creation of the current obligation that we must look, not to its incidence. The obligation flows, and can only flow, from the original agreement of the state; it can be referred to no other state or body of states. This, by itself, is sufficient to satisfy the doctrine of sovereignty. The state may appear to be bound to act against its present will; if so, it is a case of one act of the state's own will, made at a previous point in time, overriding a possible later act of will, and the doctrine of sovereignty certainly does not pretend to bar such a process within the total area of operations of the will of the state.

Third, it is not even accurate to say that a state is bound against its present will. What happens is that the state acts upon the dictates of a general policy, rather than those of a specific present desire. It wills to act to respect the bond of this treaty, rather than to express a policy of commercial discriminations. Or it acts upon the will to preserve the friendship of the cosignatory party, or the will to secure advantages corresponding to the concessions rendered, or upon some similar ground. Again, it is one act of the state's own will overriding another; but both are acts of will of the same state.

Finally, although this is less essential to the validity of our conclusion, the state is not bound by its original agreement except just so far as the conditions which led to that original consent persist and thereby justify the assumption that that act of consent is continued. In so far as conditions change and render the arrangement unjust, there arises a right of denunciation for the state suffering from the effect of the alteration of circumstances, apart from any explicit provision in the treaty for denunciation upon notice, the so-called principle of *rebus non sic stantibus.* Such action may precipitate a discussion of the question of fact as to whether this principle is really applicable, that is, whether conditions have, in point of fact, so changed as to render denunciation permissible, but that does not affect the validity of the principle. Indeed, the principle is so firmly established as to give rise to fears for the strength of treaty obligations; there certainly is no room for a contention that sovereignty is lost by the conclusion of a binding treaty.

Suppose, however, that conditions have not changed, yet one of the states party to the treaty desires to denounce the treaty, and, not acting upon any higher will of this or any previous period (such as a provision in the treaty for denunciation on notice, or a new agreement to supersede the treaty in question), denounces the treaty or proclaims that national safety compels it to disregard its obligations under the treaty. What is to be said in such circumstances?

The fact is that the state in question is within its rights in refusing to be bound by the treaty. It is liable to make adequate amends for not carrying out its pledge, but it is not compelled to carry out that pledge in such circumstances. The liability for compensation is in the nature of an equitable adjustment for benefits received and certainly provides little ground for a claim that sovereignty has been lost by the state liable.

The state whose rights under the treaty have been denied is in a different position. Without action and without consent on its part, its rights are denied respect. The important point, however, is that they are not destroyed. In many cases this may even be admitted by the state refusing to carry out the terms of the treaty, or, at all events, not explicitly denied; the principal point of the recalcitrant state in the situation now under discussion is that, although it is under certain legal obligations, it cannot safely perform them. If it did not, at least in principle, admit the validity of the obligations, there would be no cause for taking the position described. In any event, the rights which are unsatisfied remain intact, and if they cannot at present be enforced, this is due in part to a deficiency of international government, not of legal right. It is not sovereignty and legal rights, but courts and executives for the enforcement of those rights, that are inadequate.

If, now, we turn to the third and succeeding stages in the development of international organization these conclusions will be applicable to the end.

From diplomatic settlements and practice in general customary or common international law was developed by the states of Western Europe in the generations following the Renaissance, and this law has been extended to America, Asia, and Africa in more recent times. This common international law is held to be binding upon the individual state. Is this not a loss of sovereignty?

Once more the test of usage is to be applied. The states, or those in a place to speak for them, while recognizing the binding force of common international law, do not admit a loss of sovereignty thereby. Nay, they do not even suggest that there might be any such result. Sovereignty does not preclude subjection to law. It precludes only subjection to law made by another, to law dictated from an external source, subjection to the will of another.

Such subjection is not present in common international law. That law is based upon the consent of the members of the society of nations as evidenced by the diplomatic records, treaties, arbitral decisions, and so on, which they have left behind. Even national judicial decisions—in cases of prize, admiralty, criminal, civil, and constitutional law—and also national diplomatic and legal instructions and opinions, are valuable as showing the consent or agreement yielded by the states to various rules of the law.[3]

When a rule which has received the specific consent of a certain state is invoked against that state, the case is, therefore, entirely simple; the binding force of the rule flows from the prior consent, and no sovereignty is impaired. Suppose, however, that a commonly accepted rule is invoked against a state which has not specifically consented to it or has definitely repudiated it.

In the first alternative the rule is binding and derives its binding effect from the action of the state in joining the society of nations. The state sought, received, and accepted admission into that international community under the commonly accepted standards of admission. One of these is responsibility under common international law to the other members of the community of nations. The new state is now bound by that law as a result of its own assumption of the obligation covering all the commonly accepted rules of the law.

In the second alternative the rule is not binding, international law permitting individual states to refuse to be bound by individual rules of the law within the limits set in the immediately preceding paragraph. If the state had simply refused to act in accordance with the rule, while not denying its binding force, nothing would be proved one way or another, as was seen in the case of the treaty whose terms were defied by a signatory party. If, likewise, the state yields "unwilling" obedience to the rule, while denying its legal validity, the case is on a par with that of the treaty obeyed under similar circumstances. If we agree with the state's own contention that the rule is not binding, no problem of loss of sovereignty is, of course, left. If we deny that contention our denial will be based upon the reasoning of the preceding paragraph but the liberty of decision of the state on the validity of this particular rule remains intact. If we attend simply to the action of the state itself it might appear at first that we have "unwilling obedi-

[3] See, on these matters, and the doctrine of consent, what is said, above, Chaps. V and VI.B.

ence," a supposedly sovereign state constrained to act against its will. The reality of the matter is that the state does desire, does will, to obey the rule, in order either to keep in line on the general issue of obedience to international law or to avoid retaliation or for similar purposes. This is not a "fiction," as it has been called; the fiction is the "unwillingness" which in fact does not prevent the action. Obedience proves consent, if not consent to the rule as binding at least consent to observe it at the time; actions speak louder than words.

It ought not to be overlooked that the idea that a state is "compelled" to do a given thing is susceptible of infinite variation to suit the needs of the moment. In the situation where an opportunity is presented to the state to secure a great advantage at little cost the diplomats will often say "we were compelled to act quickly," or something of the same sort. The compulsion in such cases is not fanciful. It is just as real as the compulsion bearing upon an individual to get in out of the rain, a compulsion to act for one's best interests. But it does not derive specifically from any outside human source; it derives from the general posture of affairs, human, political, or natural and non-political, and, more specifically, from the reaction of the individual or state to that situation. In such situations the state may always be observed debating the issue with itself. The fictitious character of the compulsion reaches its maximum when a state says "we are compelled" and really means "we want (but wish to pretend that it is not our choice)." Finally it should be noted that very rarely are original agreements for the establishment of international organization set up in this manner, that is, imposed by force.

In like manner the effort to deny a prior act of consent is often real, sincere, and deserving of respect. But it does not affect our argument. A state may wish that it had not become party to a certain prior agreement but may be unable to get out of it. That means only that acts of will are often the result of poor judgment or ignorance and that, nevertheless, the hands of the clock cannot be turned back. The unwelcome effect and the binding force is in the march of events and in the part in that process played by this state as the result of a decision made some time ago, not in the will of the other state which is now in position to profit by present conditions. The doctrine of sovereignty does not pretend to prevent prior agreements or stay the march of time.

When international arbitration and administration and conference are reached the process becomes still more complicated, yet it is no less clear. Let us state the conclusions briefly for each of these forms of international government in turn.

Where two or more states agree to a conference wherein decisions shall be taken by majority vote, the binding force of the decisions taken flows indirectly from the original agreement.

Where two or more states agree to create an administrative commission and to abide by its actions, in practice the binding force of the subsequent action of the commission derives from the original convention creating the commission and giving it authority.

Where two or more states agree to submit a dispute to arbitration and to abide by the result the result is binding because of the original agreement to submit the case.

In no instance is there any loss of sovereignty. These cases are vivid because of the fact that the representatives of a given state may vote openly for one thing, and the settlement actually reached by the conference, the administrative ruling, or the arbitral decision may be exactly the opposite. The state is then bound, not in the absence of any expression of will, but, apparently, contrary to a clear expression of will. Yet there is no loss of sovereignty, for the binding force of the decision flows not from any legal authority inhering in the wishes of the majority by virtue of its own existence, but in the agreement originally made to use the device of the majority vote to decide questions in the court, the commission, or the conference. Without such agreement the majority vote would have no value. Given that agreement, the majority vote takes on a value it would not otherwise have. The clear expression of the present will of this state must be checked up against the equally clear expression in the past of a general will still operative in the present case.

If all this be true, there is no obstacle in national sovereignty to the creation of an international federation with legislative, executive, and judicial functions, for that result would be obtained by merely gathering together into one system the various organs or institutions of international government already existing on independent foundations. To effect this integration is, indeed, one elementary end for which an international league is serviceable today. From this action to the extension of the machinery and the powers of the league to any desired extent by the creation of new organs of government and the delegation of new powers to these new organs or to organs already in existence, is merely a matter of quantitative expansion. So long as the process of expansion and intensification goes on by means of the original form of action, the consent of the members of the league, the power of the league may be increased indefinitely without violating the sovereignty of any state. By what may be called the doctrine of the original agreement, we may reconcile national sovereignty and the world state. If this appears to reduce sovereignty to a vassal condition, if it appears to amount to the subjugation of sovereignty, the phenomenon is startling only because of a common neglect to observe the things which sovereignty may, and often does, do with or to itself, and because of failure to realize that what we have here is merely a case of sovereign power acting upon itself.

At this point three supplementary questions will naturally be raised, and all deserve attention. First, have we not committed ourselves to the principle of unanimity, and is that not an almost unsurmountable handicap to effective international federal government? Second, why is this concession necessary? Finally, is the doctrine of original agreement powerful enough to support the creation of a fixed or perpetual union of states?

The necessity for unanimity lies in the fact that, in their original condition, states stand toward each other in a condition of entire independence. In the absence of any agreement among them no state has any right or jurisdiction over another. There are no natural grounds of superiority or supremacy giving any state or states the right to lay down the law for another. This condition is often described by saying that all states are equal, and in this sense the principle is sound, and has received universal assent. It may be maintained that there is a common bond of humanity and natural justice connecting the states of the world. It may also be argued that reasons of natural justice imply or demand the supremacy of greater and more advanced nations over lesser and backward ones. It is also true that, until the principles of that natural justice are recognized and defined by agreement among the states, it can have no effective contact with human affairs, no binding force upon international relations; and in this process of defining natural justice, and until it is defined, no state or states have any ground for jurisdiction over others.

This means, indeed, that the initial establishment of any international government, and the initial creation of any bonds of authority among the nations, demands unanimous consent, and that any international federation must lack all jurisdiction over the nations which do not participate in its formation. This is unescapable, in the nature of the case, whether it be bad or good, although it does not exclude that disingenuous "forced consent" already described. It may also be suggested that too much impatience is at times manifested in this connection by persons who desire to make headway quickly, without being required to secure from all concerned consent for the schemes or actions which they propose. The real trouble is not so much in the unanimity rule as in the inability or unwillingness of the peoples to come to accord on subjects of common interest. In other walks of life much "unanimous consent business" is carried along successfully. Unanimous consent at the initial stage is neither an unreasonable nor an impossible requirement.

Where the need for unanimity is an intolerable burden is in the later operation of international government, in its application to concrete questions. But the necessity for an initial unanimity does not involve a like necessity beyond that point. There is no reason in law or jurisprudence why the members of a group of states should not provide by original agreement for the operation of any organs of the federation which they are in the act of creating by three-fourths votes, two-thirds votes, or simple majority votes. Thereafter the decisions of the league need not be unanimous; yet all members will be bound thereby, and, at the same time, no violation of state sovereignty will take place, because of the continuing effect of the original agreement, which is an integral element in the authority of each subsequent decision.

Suppose, however, that the federal agreement is made for an indefinite period, and that no method is provided for withdrawal from the league or for amendment of its terms. Does not this result in a loss of sovereignty by the member states?

To this question several replies are to be made.

In the first place it may be observed that many simple treaties have been concluded in the past without any provision for a definite period of operation and without any provisions for withdrawal or denunciation. Yet they have certainly not been regarded as involving a fatal loss of sovereignty.

In the second place we must not forget that such treaties are susceptible of denunciation by the principle of altered circumstances, and there is no juristic reason why that process could not justifiably be applied to a treaty creating a federal league.

Third, it is not to be overlooked that, even if there were a loss of sovereignty, it would be a voluntary surrender of sovereignty, not its destruction or violation at the hands of another state or states. Now the doctrine of sovereignty does not insist that all sovereign states which ever come into being shall remain in existence forever. It merely requires that so long as a state exists as such and desires to continue to exist as such it shall be free from outside interference. Voluntary surrender of sovereignty is therefore entirely compatible with the doctrine of sovereignty. It has been said that slavery is no less slavery because entered willingly. If we can escape the emotional nuance surrounding such a declaration it will appear that the essence of slavery is precisely the element of compulsion, and that where freedom of choice exists in taking up certain duties—indefinite in extent, and, perhaps, running into an indefinite future,—precisely that element of compulsion is lacking. It may also be added that such a voluntary surrender not only escapes the description "violation of sovereignty" at the time. It also makes improbable any violation of sovereignty in the future by bringing about the consolidation of that sovereignty, or, rather, by merging it, in practice, in the common power of the league considered as a juristic unit.

The issue must, however, be met still more directly. Does such an agreement really involve a loss of state sovereignty, in spite of official opinion, without reliance on the rule of *rebus sic stantibus,* and admitting that surrender, not violation, is in question? It does not seem so, for various reasons.

It should always be remembered that the critical stage at which the test must be made is not the resultant situation, but the stage of the original agreement. Why? Because the whole question relates to the foundation or basis of authority, and that can be discovered only by going back to the process of creation. Without such a method of analysis the simplest treaty or diplomatic agreement would be susceptible of being interpreted as a destruction or loss of sovereignty, the simplest contract as slavery. And when such a method is employed the voluntary character of the original agreement covers and obliterates absolutely any apparent compulsion emerging at a later stage—and this even into a perpetual future.

A most illuminating and vivid, yet very simple, example is to be found in the case of an international agreement, without time limits, not to exercise the treaty power, not to make a certain sort of treaty, such as a treaty of peace. Such agreements are familiar in the history of international relations. Both of the objectionable elements are present: permanence, and, apparently, a surrender of a peculiarly essential sovereign power. Yet such agreements have not been regarded as destructive of the sovereignty of the contracting parties or as involving a loss or surrender of that sovereignty, nor can they soundly be so regarded.

Furthermore the unalterable character of the agreement, and not merely the content of the agreement which is made unalterable, is itself the result of the will of the state. The element of irrevocability and permanence, like a specific promise to pay money, derives its juristic reality from the continuing sovereign power of the state which for its own self wrote that element into the agreement. It cannot then result in a loss of that sovereign power, for such a· result would deprive the agreement of its own authority upon this particular point. The permanence of the arrangement depends upon the persistence of sovereignty in the states which decree that it shall be permanent.

Finally, the unalterable membership in the union, the unalterable specific terms of union, and the duties assumed by the member state, are likewise embodiments of the sovereignty of that state, not acts of surrender. Construe them as such, and all the foundation for their future authority is destroyed. What the state has done is to perform a permanent action of sovereign power, to achieve a perpetual act of sovereignty, as when an individual chooses to become a member of some association. Other states have done the same thing, and these simultaneous acts bring into existence, as a joint product, a federal league wherein are funded and exercised for the future the united sovereign powers of all the constituent states.

At times it appears that it is precisely this process of practical coöperation which is really opposed by the supporters of the doctrine of state sovereignty; oftentimes it seems that the doctrine is used merely to cloak with an ideal moral value a policy of opposition to international coöperation, of national action for immediate and exclusive national advantage. For this reason it has seemed necessary to argue at some length the issue of national sovereignty. It might occur to some students of the problem that if the advantages and benefits of international organization in the concrete are such as to justify its adoption then any conflict which is apparent between such a step and the preservation of national sovereignty shows that the latter is a useless, and even harmful, doctrine. As we have seen, however, neither the violation of national sovereignty by others nor the voluntary surrender of sovereignty by the state itself is involved in the creation of a federal union. The original agreement, on the contrary, preserves, during the term of its life, the sovereignty of the state which enters the league.

Comparable with the supposed conflict between national sovereignty and international authority is the conflict of allegiances which may be imagined by the individual who is subjected to both national and international jurisdiction. This is not an uncommon situation wherever federal state organization is involved, however, and it need not be exhaustively discussed here. Reconciliation of such apparently conflicting allegiances is not beyond the capacity of federal political and legal principle.[4]

C. *Constitution of International Federation*

The repeated proposal of projects for international federation since the dawn of modern times furnishes evidence of a general and persistent conviction that a more comprehensive scheme of international government is needed. The multiplication of such proposals in the nineteenth century and in the opening years of the present century indicated an intensification of that conviction. It is worth while to make an analysis, at this point, of the foundations of that belief and of the purposes of those bringing forward various schemes for international federation.[1]

The basic idea underlying all such plans is the simple and elementary truth that the nation is not, as such, a self-sufficient unit, and that there is a constant and general need for interstate coöperation in all phases of world affairs. That idea is so simple and so commonplace that it is usually passed over in silence. It deserves, however, to be put in the very forefront of any discussion of the problem of international federation.

More specifically, the cause which led to the elaboration of various schemes for international federation was the insufficiency of the existing system of international coöperation. Even if the need for coöperation among the nations be granted, there would be no occasion for devising and publishing a plan for world federation if the historically existent set of institutions and practices were not very inadequate to the needs of the case. The system of international coöperation in the past has been too loose, too disjointed; the world has remained unorganized too long and too widely. The alliances of the sixteenth, seventeenth, and eighteenth centuries, and the system of the balance of power of which they were the embodiment; the Holy Alliance, the Concert of Europe, and

4 Stimson, Bk. II, Ch. 3.
1 On projects for international federation see literature cited, below, Appendix B, § 9c.

even the coöperation of the nations for arbitral and administrative purposes, have been judged and found wanting. By their meager fruits it is known that they have not, and, by their nature it is seen that they cannot, possess the power to provide a very satisfactory coöperative system. The alliances of earlier days and the principle of the balance of power did not prevent international relations from breaking down in repeated wars, and they did not provide that state of justice, order, and safety which the world needed. The Holy Alliance constituted a certain slight advance in the right direction, and the Concert of Europe embodied the essential principle which must be acted on if any results are to be had, and for some years gave that principle adequate expression in a few rather narrow cases. And the latter part of the past century saw the development of certain organs of international government of still greater import.

When the situation between Austria and Serbia developed as it did in 1914, however, these steps did not suffice. The critical test of those critical days and weeks brought out clearly the fact that the existing system of international government was defective and incapable of conducting international relations past such a storm. It is true that the situation was such in 1914 that it may appear unduly exacting to demand a system of international control capable of taking care of such a crisis. And yet, after all, the situation appears to have been not utterly uncontrollable. A solution or a method of securing a solution was very nearly obtained at one stage of the crisis. And the important point is that, whether or not a solution could have been obtained in that crisis or in any similar crisis, the best, and, indeed, the only practicable method for obtaining that solution was not available. The existing scheme of international government was deficient at the most vital point in that it neither provided in advance for any international conference to take up such a conflict as that which arose between Austria and Serbia, nor offered any sure method of obtaining such a conference. The solution was left to depend completely upon the possibility of securing the consent of the parties to the dispute to an international conference on the question after the dispute had arisen and when the atmosphere was of precisely that character to leave the parties least inclined to compromise and conciliation. The proposals for international federation which appeared in 1915 and 1916 reflect this revelation of a condition of international anarchy. The effort to solve this problem by or in the League of Nations in 1919-1939 came much closer to success.[2] Much was done to develop the various special types of organized international activity and something was done to coördinate these activities in one coherent system. Finally notable progress was made in the direction of collective action for peace and security, in view of the incompleteness of precedents

[2] On details see below, Chapter XII. Formally the League continued to exist at the very least until April 18, 1946.

in this field, although it was, of course, here that the League finally broke down. Now another effort is being made, in the United Nations, to achieve the same ends, but under conditions made much more difficult by both technological and political developments of recent years.[3] The function of international federation in drawing together special forms of international organization and action has also been given much more attention that it was under the League of Nations.[4]

On the other hand, the serious student of the problem of world government realizes that this condition of anarchy can be cured only by taking into consideration the conditions which have produced it. The simplest solution which might suggest itself is the concept of the world state. Yet, except in so far as the proposed world state should be organized in a federal form, such a plan would be fantastic. Most of the nations are too immature politically for such a venture and people are too firmly attached to their national states to be willing to see them swallowed up in a unified world state. If nationalism is so powerful as to present an obstacle to the simpler forms of international coöperation, how much more of an obstacle does it present, not only to cosmopolitanism, as has been seen, but, still more, to the establishment of a unified and centralized world state! Federation is the only practicable form of world political organization. Even that may not be practicable. Certain it is that nothing higher in the scale of state forms would be practicable. Some appear impatient with a world organization which retains as its foundation the national state-system. Such a position, it must be said, with all due respect, is somewhat naïve in so far as it is sincere. To scorn international federation and cry after a unified world state is to deny support to an attainable improvement over the present anarchy, and waste it upon an unattainable ideal, whatever one may think of that ideal.[5]

This, then, is the case for international federation: the nation is insufficient by itself and some system of international coöperation is needed; the previously existing system of international government is inadequate to the needs of the case; a unified world state is impossible. The conclusion is obvious.

Moreover, we have the benefit of much actual experience in the practice of interstate federation. It is possible to review the record of interstate federation in the past and learn therefrom not only its practicality but its essential prerequisites, its weaknesses and its potentialities for service. This experimentation has gone on within single nationalities and also among states of distinct nationality.[6]

[3] For details on the United Nations see below, Chapter XIII.
[4] See Charter, Arts. 57, and 63.
[5] For statement of contrary view, see Reves, especially Chap. XI.
[6] On interstate federation see literature cited, below, Appendix B, § 9c. Space does not permit discussion here of the similarities or differences between national and international federal unions; in the judgement of the author the differences, while

The most elementary antecedent condition of affairs for the formation of a federal union is found, of course, where several independent states exist side by side.[7] A federal union is even then to be created or attempted only where the mass of interests common to all the states is so great as to demand common organs of government to take care of them. Particular interests must remain in the hands of the local states. The burden of proof is upon anyone proposing federal union, an obligation to show that a central government is needed in addition to the local governments, a central government beyond any coöperative efforts which may be made by concurrent state action, by alliances, or by any form of association short of federal government.

There are no objective mechanical means of measuring this mass of common interest. It is possible for the student to compute the amount of commerce which goes on among the states of the group in question, to record the amount of interstate travel and communication in existence among them, and to picture the degree to which a cosmopolitan or interstate life has developed. When that is done some light will, indeed, have been thrown upon the advisability of creating a federal union. The final decision, however, depends upon the judgment of advantage and disadvantage in the minds of those who live in the various states. After all, it is impossible to anticipate exactly the net result of convenience and inconvenience which will flow from creating or failing to create a federal union. Those who are to live under the union must decide, more or less at a venture, as to its probable utility.

Not uncommonly the decision is made in a manner even less precise than this. Where a condition of cosmopolitanism has begun to develop among the members of a group of states the simpler forms of interstate association—diplomacy, treaty negotiation, alliances—will already have made their appearance. The question then presents itself in a familiar form, namely, whether or not the loose forms of association existing shall be converted into a federal government. More frequently still the degree of association increases imperceptibly until federal government is reached unconsciously.

The problem then becomes a purely scientific one, namely, to discover whether or not federal government has actually made its appearance. To a certain extent this is wholly a problem of terminology, but it is of a degree of importance not usual in problems of terminology. After all, federalism may be the decisive first stage in the organization of a single state and deserves to be identified carefully as it occurs.

---

important, are wholly factual and capable of being duly respected. See Wheare, pp. 1-54. The United Nations was assimilated to the United States in character by a very careful lawyer and student of such problems, Lester H. Woolsey, in Hearings before a subcommittee of the Committee on Foreign Relations of the United States Senate on 12 July, 1946.

[7] Compare, above, Chap. I, p. 7.

The most useful test which can be employed to discover the existence of a federal government—most useful partially because of its ease of application—is the test of established organs of government. Where there is no established common organ of government there is no federal government of any degree, as in the case of the alliance. Where there is a common organ of government, no matter how limited its power, there exists a federal government for the purposes defined by the powers entrusted to the common governmental body. Thus the international administrative union exercising governmental power appears to be a federal state to the extent of the substantive jurisdiction entrusted to its care.

A distinction can, secondly, be drawn between a lower and a higher, a looser or tighter, type of federal union, or between confederation and federation, as it is sometimes expressed, depending upon whether the states in the union have surrendered their sovereignty or retained it, including reference to the temporary or permanent character of the union, already discussed. This test is not very reliable or satisfactory. It is distinctly worth while to differentiate higher from lower types or degrees of federal union but the question is definitely one of degree. States surrender or suspend or waive their sovereignty indirectly and by implication in or at single points very frequently and indeed continuously but they seldom, even when establishing permanent unions of broad jurisdiction and great power, expressly renounce their sovereignty in its entirety. It may be hazarded that they—at least the leading powers—are not prepared to do so and that to demand such a step would be idle and injurious to reasonable progress in international order and coöperation.

A third test, which serves to mark the culmination of federation, relates to the incidence and source of governmental power. If the authority of the established organ of government falls only upon the states which are members of the union in their official capacity the union remains strictly federal in character. When the common organs of government operate directly upon the individual members of the states of the union without action by the individual states as such, the last stage of federal development has been passed, and something else is setting in. So long as the states remain in existence and the authority of the central government rests upon their consent—as revealed by the character of the provisions in force for amending the federal constitution—the federal character of the union remains. If the central government should, in addition to exercising its power directly upon the people of the union as a whole, draw its power directly from the people of the entire union, irrespective of state lines, the federal character of the union gives way to that of the unified state.[8]

The reassuring thing about all this is that the steps described are all

---

[8] This standard for the transition from a federal to a unitary system is erroneously used at times to distinguish federal union from something more rudimentary; Streit, *Union Now*, in general.

optional, in so far as any steps in human life are optional. All powers enjoyed by a federal government are delegated to it from the members of the union. That is not accidental, nor is it peculiar to one federal system or another. It is necessarily true in the nature of the case. In the beginning there is no central government. It must be created and it must be endowed with life and power. Hence the expansion and intensification of its powers are dependent upon action, upon tacit acquiescence at the very least, by the members of the union. Even if the members should at once by constitutional grant confer upon the central government all powers in so many words, such a step would still remain an action of delegation and therefore subject to revision or revocation.

Once a federal union has been created by constitutional action, these questions of revision and revocation, of constitutional amendment and withdrawal from membership, become the most critical phases of the situation. The degree of permanence of the union depends, apparently, on a denial of the right of withdrawal. So long as a right of withdrawal upon notice is allowed, the life of the union is potentially limited to the extent of the notice period. The powers enjoyed by the central government are potentially subject to destruction by the action of constitutional revision. A permanent and firmly established federal union should have, apparently, a constitution not subject to amendment and a membership not subject to diminution by withdrawal.

A little reflection, however, will serve to qualify those conclusions. It is, it must be admitted, of great importance in the creation of a federal union to have the processes of constitutional change and of withdrawal clearly defined and not left to interpretation and implication. The United States suffered her greatest constitutional crisis through the failure of the fathers to take up and settle explicitly in the text of her fundamental law the vital question of secession. The right should be definitely denied or affirmed and the conditions under which it may be exercised should be explicitly stated. This is very far from saying that, in the interests of permanence, such a right should be denied. To deny such a right is to risk the appearance of converting the federal government from servant into master, as far as the individual state is concerned, albeit a master voluntarily accepted in the first instance. To deny the possibility of constitutional revision appears to convert the government from servant into master for all the members of the union. This may not be wholly disastrous, if the original action in creating the federal union and in defining the nature of the government was supremely wise. But it imposes upon the federal state and government the burden of not only the current difficulties of state practice at any one time but the cumulative difficulties of all time, seeing that it is impossible to cure a fault when once that fault arises, or to escape from its consequences. Besides, where withdrawal is impossible, where even revision in coöperation with other member states is impossible, it is rather hazardous to rely upon the original act of consent as evidence of the voluntary character of the union. The states of the union in such case appear to become not much more than provinces in a state whose power they cannot escape.

Beyond these fundamental problems of structure, however, rise the more practical questions of governmental action from day to day, the question of the distribution of powers. Assuming that the member states retain their discretion in granting or withholding powers from the federal government, the theory of sovereignty is amply cared for. But the practical questions of utility and convenience which demand settlement are not to be avoided in any way.

The principle to be followed is as simple as its application is difficult. Such powers are to be given to the central government as will enable it to care for those interests which led originally to the formation of the union. Such matters as the regulation of interstate commerce should thus naturally go to the central government. The remaining subjects—those which do not affirmatively call for regulation from the center—naturally remain where they were in the first place.

It is easy to render this problem of distribution difficult by assuming that it is necessary or desirable to traverse the whole field of governmental power and to decide deliberately in advance upon each item of power, as to whether it should go to the central government or the states. In practice this is not what happens, nor is it necessary or natural. What does happen is that certain powers or subjects cry aloud for transfer to the central jurisdiction, others seem to require such a transfer, but merit further study, while still others are by general consent allowed to remain within the local jurisdiction. As in the original delegation of power in the abstract, so in the definition of jurisdiction in the concrete, the burden of argument is on him who suggests that a certain power be conferred upon the central government.

That burden will be heavy or light as the circumstances of the case change with time. The advisability of conferring a given power on the central government changes from decade to decade. In a sense this development through history is the sum and substance of the problem of the distribution of powers. There seems to be a general tendency, as time passes,—as population increases in each state and in the union, as communication becomes more active and extensive,—for more items of government and power to deserve to be transferred to the central government.[9] The process of centralization seems to be general, continuous, and persistent. History records no example of a federal union in which this process has not manifested itself, hardly any where the process has been reversed.

On the other hand, there are very few cases in history where the centralizing tendency in federalism has led to the supercession of this

[9] See Potter, P. B., "The Expansion of International Jurisdiction," in *Political Science Quarterly*, Vol. XLI, No. 4 (Dec., 1926), p. 546.

form by unitary government. We are inclined to think of federal union as a compromise form, a temporary makeshift, to be supplanted eventually by the unitary state form. A compromise federalism certainly is, but it may be a permanent compromise, and not a temporary form at all. It may harbor values which are so great and so deep that it can survive indefinitely, especially in the international sphere.

As may easily be imagined, the definition of jurisdiction cannot be so clear that disputes over jurisdiction between the central government and the local governments will not arise. Hence the urgent necessity of providing some institution or some method for settling such disputes. In view of the fact that, as time passes, the central government is led constantly to aggrandize itself at the expense of the local governments, this is especially necessary. A body of some sort qualified to decide upon conflicts of authority is indispensable unless disputes regarding jurisdiction are to be threshed out in the field of usage and practice at the risk of great excitement and violent disturbances.

Granted that the federal system is created on due cause, that the power conferred upon the central government is of the proper amount, and that the problems of revision, of withdrawal, and of conflicts are duly cared for, federalism is, considered as a mechanical device, the highest form of state organization, particularly if mixed with unitary elements. It is more adaptable to local impulses than a unitary form, and it offers the means of greater power than is possible in a unitary state unless the latter is to become so huge as to become unmanageable. The federal system reconciles local variety and general uniformity. It harmonizes central government and local individuality, power and freedom, unity and mutiplicity. It marshals the powers of many states without imperial conquest. It performs in the sphere of interstate relations the great synthesis of authority and liberty which is the heart of the problem of government.

This is not to deny that difficulties are involved. Federalism is a complicated and delicate political form, where it is not positively cumbersome and awkward. A federal state moves slowly and may be disconcerted where a unitary state would be confident. The larger the federation the greater these difficulties. In a competition of wits and strength the unitary state may easily have the best of it at the start and in all the tight places, even if the federal union boasts some unitary elements.

This implies, of course, that the unitary state would be more effective as a state, and, judging by absolute standards, this must be admitted at once. The unitary state, where it is feasible, the unitary state in its proper place, is more effective than the federal union. The important thing for us is that international conditions are not ripe for the world unitary state. We thus come back to the original proposition. If all variety and local feeling were to vanish, the centralized or unitary state would be in perfect place. With things as they are, it is not only impossible but highly undesirable. A mixture of federalism and the unitary world state is the only available form.

It is not surprising, therefore, that students who have attempted to devise plans for world government in the past have generally adopted the federal form on which to build their plans. Since the thirteenth century, at least, various schemes have been brought forward for leagues and associations of nations, in more or less conscious emulation of the leagues of classical Greece. These schemes may now be briefly examined.

It would be worse than useless, however, to review here the details of the plans of Podiébrad, Crucé, Franklin, Ladd, and others.[10] In their details these various plans betray the idiosyncrasies of their authors and are based on generous but impractical hopes rather than sound statesmanship, and they are deceptive in what they imply regarding the conditions of the problem. Moreover, no single plan is of decisive importance, inasmuch as no one of these various plans has ever been adopted as such by the states. The chief value which these schemes have today for the student of international organization is the light which they shed, in their main outlines, upon the development of the idea of world government since the Renaissance.[11]

These plans have commonly been based upon one or more of four rather distinct foundations, namely, selfish national advantage, historical development in international relations, previous plans of the same sort, and abstract reason. These foundation principles may best be examined in the reverse of the order as named.

Every would-be architect of world government naturally professes to aim at justice and, through justice, peace; and in a large measure every reformer who has suggested a plan for international federation really has tried to serve these ends. However, when the ends of justice and peace are sought directly the result is likely to be unfortunate. The ideal of peace by itself induces on the part of its possessor a quietism and a willingness to accept almost any settlement for the sake of peace. The ideal of justice, on the other hand, taken by itself, leads to a meddlesome dissatisfaction with all things as they are, which is as bad on its side as is quietism on the other. In the end, plans which attempt to serve these abstract ideals directly are incoherent and unstable.

The simplest method which can be adopted for the correction of such errors is the comparison of plans which other students have worked out in previous ages. In recent years a great deal has been done in collecting, analyzing and collating the classic projects for international federation worked out in the past. A most valuable form of such activity is found in the practice of scrutinizing the plans for international courts and conferences which have previously been proposed or adopted when the occasion arises for creating a new court or conference.

[10] On classic projects see literature cited, below, Appendix B, § 9c.
[11] See Ledermann and ter Meulen especially.

The action last described carries us over into the second method of drawing up such plans, namely, building the new edifice of international government not upon paper plans, but upon the actual historical development of international federation in the past. We have had many examples of international federation in the past, most of them incomplete in respect of their fields of jurisdiction and their functions. International federation has been tried for dealing with all sorts of special subjects, and by all sorts of special procedures—judicial, administrative, legislative (although in the first and last cases the court and conference have overshadowed the underlying federation)—and these experiments provide very valuable guidance in the development of international federal union of general jurisdiction and general functions. Thus, the creation of the Permanent Court of Arbitration in 1899 and the revision of the plan in 1907 were both based upon a study of prior courts of arbitration and the working of such courts, including the Hague Court itself between 1899 and 1907, and both Great Britain and the United States, in preparing for the Peace Conference of 1919 collected much data on international negotiation, administration, and conference in the past.[12] The results have such a high degree of reliability, in comparison with schemes not based on actual experience, that this method is clearly the one to be preferred.

To connect the proposed plan too closely with actual political life, however, is to fall again into error. Several plans for international federation proposed in the past have amounted to not much more than schemes for the aggrandizement of the power and prestige of the nation in which they have originated. Such was the—not improperly named—Great Design attributed to Henry IV. It is, of course, not to be assumed that a given plan for international federation is necessarily bad because it satisfies the interests of a given nation. No nation will accept such a plan unless it does serve the national interest. The only requirement which can be made is that the national interest which is served shall be a noncompetitive interest, one which can be satisfied without injury to other states. But when a plan for international organization is put forth directly with the calculation that it will serve the national interest the probabilities are that the plan will not be of great value from the point of view of other states and of the common international welfare.

Beyond the nature of the motives for its formulation, however, the value of any plan for international federation depends also upon the exact provisions which are written into the proposed international constitution. These will presumably reflect one or more of the different foundations upon which the plan may be based. But, after all, it is in the text of the plan that the decisive virtue lies. Here also the projects put forward in the past have varied considerably.

[12] Somewhat less attention was given to prior experience by the leading powers in 1944-1945; see below, p. 258.

The earlier projects were very simple and highly unified. Later plans have been more comprehensive and more analytical. Recent proposals cover, as any feasible proposal must cover, institutions for the making of law, for its administration, and for its interpretation in case of doubt. Conferences, commissions, and courts are essential in any international government. Earlier projects not only contained no separate provisions for such bodies but ignored the distinction between the different varieties of work to be done by a world government. With the growing understanding of the process of government in general since the eighteenth century plans for international government have similarly improved in quality.

There is still some temptation to visualize world government in terms of some particular form of institutional organization. Thus, a few years ago arbitration or judicial settlement seemed to be the sum and substance of international reform and an international court the equivalent of international government. At another time "the world in alliance" or an international police was regarded as the essence of international coöperation. In recent years international administrative unions and bureaus were regarded as international governing bodies of the highest type. Later still international conference seemed to be most important. It cannot be too strongly affirmed that any adequate international association must include organs of all types, constituent and legislative, administrative, and judicial. The most recent projects for international federation respond favorably to this test.

Finally, all recent plans have recognized the need for control in operation and for adaptation as times and circumstances change. Earlier plans pretended to be panaceas to be adopted by the world intact and left as originally framed. In some cases the precious scheme was to be imposed upon the world by autocrats and maintained in place by their authority. Modern plans do not pretend to be infallible and are subject to amendment. They are, in the first place, to be adopted by voluntary action by the states of the world. They are, further, to be operated by responsible officials; their virtue is to depend on such operation rather than upon any magic quality of the scheme as adopted; and they are to be open to constant revision.

Needless to say, this last view is of great importance. Combined with the other changes in approach just described it has brought the proposal for international federation out of the realms of religion and speculative theory into practical politics. International federation is to be built up gradually, on the basis of what has gone before, to meet the actual needs of this international and cosmopolitan world, by the voluntary coöperation of the states in the paths of conference, administration, and arbitration, subject always to revision and control as the times require.

CHAPTER X

Functions of International Organization *

Without delving too deeply into problems of method or pedagogy, it may be recalled here that the student in this field of social and political science does encounter at the outset of his activities a serious problem of scientific procedure. He may be most impressed, at first sight, by the more obvious phenomena of the institutions which appear on the surface of international life, such as diplomacy, international conferences, international courts, and so on. He should begin his studies with these overt phenomena, proceeding from them to more delicate and obscure qualities lying beneath. It is, however, indispensable to recognize at the proper point that these institutions have certain functions to perform, that, indeed, they are called into existence to satisfy the need for those functions. International institutions having been discussed mainly with reference to their structure in the foregoing pages, it is now time to turn to the problems of functions underlying the organization of international institutions. These questions have, of course, been touched upon constantly in the course of the description and analysis of international institutions. What remains to be done here, therefore, is to summarize in systematic form, and to extend and complete, what has already been said.

The functions to be performed by international organization may be studied with reference both to the forms of action to be taken or performed and the nature of the objects to be sought and the subject matters to be treated. The functioning of international organization in the general field of governmental processes may be discussed first, and the interests of the states in various fields of social life may be stated later. The first involves a discussion of law making and administration, including enforcement, by international organization, and will be discussed in this section; the second involves, among other things, questions of peace and security and social welfare and will be treated in the section to follow.

A. *Procedure; International Legislation; Sanctions*

As has been pointed out already, international coöperation logically begins in conditions where the adjustment of conflicting national interests is to be made upon a special and temporary basis. Each case is to be treated in and by itself, relations with each country in and by them-

* The footnotes in this chapter are numbered by the section.

selves, and what is done at one time is not regarded as necessarily committing the states acting to any particular line of action in the future. Analytically it is clear that this must be so—the special case must precede the general rule, for men feel life before they know truth, and historically it has actually been so, and traces of this attitude survive today.

In this stage representation, negotiation, and special agreement, sought by means of personal diplomacy, must be the form of action to be taken. No question of the making or administration of general law or rules of action for the future is involved. The action of primitive international coöperation is, indeed, very formal, highly standardized, stereotyped and stylized, but it is formulated largely in pre-legal and even anti-legal terms. There is as yet no question of making and applying general rules for all parties in all cases at all times, but rather strong opposition to anything of the kind, in view of the great variations felt to exist among the parties, situations, and stages of international relations.

When this period or phase has been passed, the functions of international coöperation resemble very closely, if they do not entirely duplicate, the functions of national government. Analogy is proverbially weak as a scientific device, and there is no intention to employ any simple or any crude analogy here, but we may trace the evolution of the forms of action of international coöperation both in their own place and in their resemblance to the forms of action of national government.

In the sense of rules accepted by the parties as binding upon themselves international law does, as we saw, make its appearance as a phase or direct result of diplomacy. Treaty agreements constitute law for the parties. The legal element is injected into the action or product not by any abstract principle or metaphysical or ethical factor but by the act of will of the states. On the other hand, treaties are still very specific in parties and subject matter if not in period.

General international law makes its appearance first in the form of an amorphous fragmentary mass of rules and principles, based upon practice. Contacts at the frontier, in war, in trade, in travel and foreign residence, and in diplomacy lead to the formulation in the mind of one party of conclusions as to how the others may be expected to act, may be counted upon to act, and will demand that they be treated; these formulations being accepted as fixed and binding rules of conduct become law. Customary or common law is born.

By this time international adjudication or, as it is called in its earlier phases, arbitration, will have made its appearance. The conventional law of treaties and the rudimentary customary law will call for application or for definition and application in cases where its meaning is in dispute or its bearing on the situation is contested. Two difficult points are raised here.

In the first place the appearance of adjudication in the earlier years of international coöperation seems to antedate the appearance of international conference and to constitute an illogicality or an anomaly. How can application of law precede conference and legislation? The answer is, of course, that legislation, or law making, and conference are not synonymous and that there had been a good deal of law making before the times of formal international conference. International adjudication began on the basis of treaty agreements and customary law, and only later came to deal with law produced by conference legislation, unless conference is to be defined so loosely as to cover the bilateral transactions of primitive times.

The second problem concerns international administration. Adjudication is essentially an incident of administration or, at most, a form of administration. Whatever allowance is made for so-called judge-made law, for the function of the judge in spinning out from law already in existence further implications and inferences, the fact remains that the judicial function is performed solely upon the basis of a supposition of preëxisting law; certainly this is true in the international field. But again international adjudication seems to antedate international administration. It is the nineteenth century before international administration really emerges; arbitration records we have from 4000 B.C.

The discrepancy can be explained to some extent by finding a species of international administration latent in earlier practices. Administration of international agreements and common international law is remitted, in the earlier stages of international affairs, to national agents, including national courts, and is carried on by them very actively. And this may in an indirect way be regarded as international administration. What the national agencies may do and not do in this direction is defined or limited by international law and to some degree it may be said that the national agents are authorized to act in this capacity by the nations under the rules of the law of nations. It should, however, be remembered that these agencies are created by national action and act upon national instructions; the limits and even the authorization mentioned would have no effects without the national action; this is not international administration in its best sense.

The simple fact seems to be that, while adjudication must occur as an incident of administration of preëxisting law, not only may international law be made before conference in its most elaborate form makes its appearance but also international law may be administered by national agents in the earlier stages and international adjudication invoked to support their efforts or correct their errors rather than those of true international administrators. It may go on to the other task later if this proves to be possible.

Today, on the other hand, we have international legislation, international administration, and international adjudication, all three. They did not appear simultaneously, or even in logical order, they have not developed with equal rapidity, and they are not all of the same degree of maturity or effectiveness today, but they are available and can be utilized and developed as conditions permit.

Apart from the historical aspect of the situation, however, and apart from any close analogy with national governmental procedure, the question may be raised whether the functions of international coöperation, on its formal side, should be defined or interpreted in terms of the making and enforcement of law. Is social action—here international action—to be best organized or conducted in this manner, or, turning upon the present and past scene from the outside, is international coöperation best understood by attempting to analyze it in these terms?

International coöperation in its earlier development could not be understood scientifically or accurately appreciated if considered solely in terms of law making and administration, for the simple reason, so strongly emphasized above, that such coöperation did not take this form and can be made to fit the categories of this analysis only with great difficulty. To try to classify the treaty of the common type as a statute is to miss its essential character almost entirely.

On the other hand, the conformance of international coöperation to the familiar analysis is increasing today, and the time is not far distant, perhaps, when the traces of the earlier sort of thing will be as great curios as are today the same anachronisms in the field of national government. It is still too early to make the transition completely, and errors will be made by any student who does so. But the error of this type of approach to the study of international administration decreases year by year.

There are, of course, two or three types of action even in these later days of international coöperation which fit with special difficulty into any scheme or analysis based upon the juristic principle. These must be studied and treated by themselves even though the juristic analysis is employed for the main body of international coöperation and even though they bear some relation thereto. They are inquiry, conciliation, and recommendation. Inquiry and conciliation have been studied in some detail. They obviously do not turn to any great degree upon the existence or the content of law, although the mediator may strengthen his position by relying upon legal principle. They must be taken as phases of pre-legal international coöperation, or diplomacy. Recommendation, on the other hand, not unknown in the practice of national government, prominent in the functioning of international administrative organs, and not entirely different or divorced from mediation and conciliation, is intimately involved in the international legislative process. It constitutes a preliminary auxiliary step in that process, and at times in connection with international executive or administrative action.

If the scientific problem is in a state of flux the problem of social engineering involved is no less so. We are not, in this volume, concerned primarily with that aspect of the problem, but something may be said on the matter before dismissing it to the reformers.

In its broadest or most general sense international legislation as a form of action would consist of any international action creating legal rights and obligations.[1] In a very special and strict sense it should consist of international action such as that taken by legislative bodies in individual states. Similarly the products of such action, also referred to by the same phrase, might consist of all kinds of legal materials or only of formal statutes. In the broadest sense international law-making would thus consist of practice, agreement, or enactment—to mention only three main forms of international law-making action—; in the narrowest sense it would consist only of the last of these. Practice and the conclusion of treaties do create legal rights and obligations, as we have seen,[2] and therefore do not deserve to go unmentioned in even a brief discussion of international legislation. But they are so far down the scale as legislative instrumentalities, and the third form of action is so much more significant, that we shall deal almost exclusively with this last. We shall define international legislation as the enactment of international law by formal action of less-than-unanimous consent.[3]

This situation is not the product of any artificial or formal theory as much as it is the natural result of the facts of the situation. In absence of any special stipulation there is no ground for any exercise of authority by any one or more states over any other state or states. It is necessary to provide for such action, if it is desired, by special agreement. On the other hand it is obvious that provisions for majority rule will, inevitably, make possible a minority veto, and a veto which is more significant than the opposition of the lone dissenter, if it is permitted to block action for the members of the majority among themselves. Given the variety of conditions among the nations all of these modalities are indispensable, throwing the burden on those who would produce agreement and uniformity nevertheless.

Such action develops naturally in and from international conference. It emerges whenever an original agreement is adopted authorizing subsequent action by less than unanimity. The matters to be so treated may be merely procedural in character—leaving decision on the merits or substantive issues still open—, or they may be substantive in character and in that case the action to be taken may consist of the adoption of detailed regulations or may go the length of general statutory or even constitutional legislation. Such action will with difficulty be disengaged from diplomatic negotiation (and signature and ratification and all the rest) but may finally come to resemble its national analogue very closely.

[1] For references see, below, Appendix B, § 10a.

[2] Above, p. 60.

[3] The most useful brief treatment of the subject is found in the Introduction to Hudson's *International Legislation;* see also Gihl and Knudson, as cited below, Appendix B, § 10a.

The greatest obstacle to the development of international legislation is, of course, national reluctance to be restricted by international regulation. This reluctance is expressed by appealing to the principle of national "sovereignty" and "independence" and by claiming that certain subjects are exclusively "domestic" in character. Such obstructive tactics lose something of their force with every decade that passes, although they seem to ardent reformers the great obstacle to world peace and order.

The essence of international legislation is the synthesis of national policies in any given matter, the formulation of international policy, and its adoption as international law. International conference gives an opportunity for the communication of information and ideas among the states participating therein, which may lead to the more advanced type of action, but this is incidental. Similarly the conference may set up administrative facilities for carrying into execution the legislation adopted [4] but this also is a distinct matter.

Much or indeed the bulk of the problem of international legislation relates to the structure and procedure of international conferences, already discussed,[5] and we shall not repeat here what has already been said on that score. The most critical issues relate to the system of representation in the conference, employment of the committee system, parliamentary procedure, drafting, and majority voting; as already indicated, there seems to be a definite and rather pronounced drift toward proportionate (as against equal) representation, more use of committees, improved facilities for drafting, and toward majority (simple or qualified) voting, with corresponding effects on international legislation. There is also the prevailing trend, too obvious to need emphasis, and too general in character to require notice here perhaps, for international legislation to extend itself over vast ranges of all and sundry sorts of questions, a negation in strong terms of the "domestic questions" doctrine.

Two problems require special attention, however, one of form and one of subject matter, the problem of resolutions and that of revision.

In view of the continued restriction on international legislation in the strict sense of the term (adoption of binding law by less-than-unanimity) there is some temptation to take refuge in adoption by international conferences of numerous "resolutions" [6] which do not call for unanimity but which also do not have binding legal force.[7] Such a device is more or less an evasion but may help to build up the process of international legislation in the long run. For the moment it does not fulfill the requirements for creating binding international law.

The requirement of unanimous consent for international legislation

---

[4] See below, p. 212. For an interesting treatment of the "domestic question" see ITO Charter, Art. 21.

[5] Above, p. 122.

[6] Wilcox, pp. 263-285.

[7] See review by Kuhn in *American Journal of International Law*, Vol. XXII (1928), p. 228.

has the effect at times of retarding action in spite of large favorable majorities of the states concerned and in other cases of compelling resort to devices for achieving the desired result which distort the legislative process in an undesirable way without completely achieving the end desired. Persons who have participated in the international legislative process testify to these effects and objective evidence thereof is obvious in the process itself. Regrets and complaints are expressed that action is prevented by small minorities and by insistence on the unanimity rule. The superior efficiency of agencies which have dispensed with unanimity is openly exhibited. Abstention from voting and taking refuge in recommendations are only two of the devices adopted for evading unanimity. Modification of the unanimity rule is advocated with increasing frequency and considerable progress in that direction has recently been made. It is surprising that so much useful international legislation has been adopted in spite of the unanimity rule, but minor evasions and modifications will not suffice to cure the situation fundamentally.[8]

The problem of revision is a far larger problem than that of mere legislative procedure. Revision of multipartite international instruments—still assuming that they have been adopted by less-than-unanimous consent—presents little or no difficulty beyond those encountered in their adoption and is fairly common today. The most serious difficulty arises over the proposal to permit revision of existing treaties, often bipartite in character, by general international action. Something of the kind is needed to correct national resistance to equitable readjustment of international obligations to changing circumstances, but there is great opposition to conferring such power on any international body.[9]

For the rest the problem of international legislation is the problem of international conference, particularly the extension of procedure by less-than-unanimous consent. As already indicated, there has been a marked growth along these lines in the past thirty-five years, and radical proposals for international legislative bodies have been put forward recently.[10] As, however, this is the very crux and heart of the process of extending international authority, at least on the originating and creating side, we may expect to see the development proceed relatively slowly.

There is today in the field of national government some tendency to abandon the treatment of social problems by the legislation-administration formula. Social situations today seem so complex and delicate, and the legislative organization—including its personnel—and procedure so crude, that there has appeared a disposition to deal with problems of

[8] Riches, *Unanimity*, pp. 175, 211, 212, 214, 216.
[9] This is, of course, the so-called problem of "peaceful change," the thought being that provision must be made for changes in existing international arrangements by peaceful means in order to avoid attempts at change by war; see Dunn, and references. See also the author's study of Article XIX of the Covenant of the League of Nations, cited below, in Appendix B, § 10a.
[10] Streit, *Union Now*, pp. 187, 247.

public utilities, labor, or health, by means of commissions or boards having large discretion and acting in each case as circumstances dictate. The possibility of formulating law in general terms which will apply both with justice and practical effectiveness to the complicated and seemingly variable social situations of our day seems slender. To this is to be added a renascent, or perhaps it is only a persistent, opposition to government by coercion in some quarters, reëmphasis on individual liberty and conscience, and renewed advocacy of voluntary coöperation rather than coercive control. Are these not points of view or programs which must and perhaps should be taken into account in the development of international organization?

The fact is, however, that on both points international organization is so far behind that it has a long distance to go before becoming too rigidly legalistic or too authoritarian. The difficulty of formulating international law so as to fit the divergent and even obscure interests of the different nations of the globe has been emphasized already. Waiving the fact that the first of the two reforms mentioned does not involve an abandonment of the juristic process but its refinement, however, the fact is that there is still so much prelegal coöperation and still so little clear and firm recognition by law of, or at least of vigorous administration of law to protect, national rights, that what is needed is surely not less but more of that type of action. And as for the second point, the fact here also is that we have practically no international community coercion as yet. There can be opposition to the overdevelopment of international coercion within wide limits without interfering with a perhaps reasonable and useful degree of such action. This, however, brings us to another subject entirely.

The last step to be taken in developing the formal functions of international organization is the provision of community enforcement of national rights or of international law, the provision of community sanctions for international authority.[11]

It is, of course, impossible to discuss this question in any fullness here. It is the central, most significant and at the same time the most difficult problem in international organization. The principal angles of the problem may be indicated here, however, and the student given a start in the study of this fascinating question.

Thus the real question is not a question of sanctions or no sanctions. Sanctions—actions taken in order to induce or compel compliance with the law apart from considerations of mutual benefits to be derived therefrom—we have, always have had, and always shall have. Complete voluntary respect for law never has or will be relied upon by men or groups of men desirous of protection for their rights. The question is whether, in the international field, sanctions are to be left in the hands of indi-

[11] See summary analysis and bibliography in Potter, *Collective Security*, cited below, Appendix B, § 10a.

vidual states, limited, of course, in their use, but having some freedom to use force in this connection, or transferred to the international community. It might be recalled that experiments with even international sanctions of all types have been made in the past with varying degrees of success, so that the question is not one of an entirely new departure in international affairs.[12]

Second, the question is not solely one of the use of military force. Any influence compelling obedience to law on the part of a state in response to ulterior considerations is a sanction. Aversion to and fear of loss of life, liberty, or property as a result of possible action by another state or states is at the bottom of the opposition to sanctions, but the action which it is feared may have such results may vary from propaganda to seizure by military force. This, however, cuts both ways. It means that sanctions need not partake of the nature of physical action or military operations, and hence may remain milder in nature than is sometimes thought. It means, on the other hand, that "moral influence" is just about as much a sanction and a form of coercion as war, in so far as it is effective. Both advocates and opponents of sanctions fail to think clearly on this point.

Third, sanctions must be considered in connection with legal rights and they may be considered in connection with the whole range of such rights. It cannot be proposed to provide for sanctions operating apart from accepted principles of international law and procedure, for such action would be too capricious and arbitrary. On the other hand, there is no reason why sanctions should be applied merely in connection with rights of territorial security or rules for pacific settlement except that these interests are of paramount importance to the states of the world. In the principle of the thing and in the long run in practice sanctions must apply to all national rights; indeed, in the end,—when war and aggression are obsolete,—it will be only in connection with secondary rights, not security and peace, that sanctions will be important, and hence this may be considered the real or permanent sanctions problem, the real problem of international government.

Fourth, even if it were decided to attempt to organize and operate some system of international sanctions the question of the form of action to be taken is still critical. At least two possible forms of action may be distinguished, omitting all degrees of qualification and combination: concurrent or joint action by individual states or action by a unitary agency of the international community. Each proposed system has its own prospective difficulties and prospective advantages. Concurrent national action for bringing pressure upon the recalcitrant, or an international police force—which?

The question of the relative values of these two systems may be argued at great length. Whether one or the other method will be preferred will

[12] Wehberg, cited below, Appendix B, § 10a.

depend, of course, on calculations of prospective benefits and losses by individual states, confused by habits and traditions and emotional influences, deprived of full factual information, and repelled by the unknown consequences of such action. Voluntary coöperation seems to succeed fairly well, remarkably well at times; states recoil at being actually compelled to coöperate; [13] why press for sanctions? Yet at certain points resistance is encountered and this must increase as international regulation penetrates more deeply into national interests. Perhaps such action would inevitably degenerate into war and produce more suffering than even disregard for national rights. Yet no system of law or government which lacks sanctions for use in the extreme case where they may be needed can be sure of its authority.

The questions of value involved do not of course look alike to all nations. Strong nations are able to enforce their own rights, weak states need international protection; yet under any system of sanctions the stronger states would control the situation and the weaker would be at their mercy—tempered by law—even more than they are today. No less important is the reluctance of the stronger states to undertake the job of policing the world. European states feel the importance of the problem as ultra-oceanic states do not—the tenderloin and the suburbs again. States benefiting from the existing status want sanctions, states anxious for revision are opposed. States with the traditions of Rome are philosophically disposed toward sanctions, nations with traditions of Teutonic liberty are instinctively hostile. Military nations are not afraid of the concept, pacifist peoples shudder at it.

These are but the most general aspects of the problem. Many detailed considerations of the values involved must also be taken into account. But perhaps two conclusions may be suggested here. One is that no serious progress will be made in this direction unless revisionism is integrated with sanctions, unless provisions for constant revision of the existing status, including territorial possessions, are adopted in connection with guarantees of the present status. The other is that even if the politically and technically very difficult, and practically very dangerous, program for international military sanctions is adopted, there must be a strong development of international moral responsibility and pressure of some type—political, diplomatic, financial,—to strengthen the bonds of international obligation especially upon such vital matters as peace and security. Neither the states which are at a disadvantage under the existing status, nor other states which are asked to share in guaranteeing that status, are going to act in that direction until and unless present injustices are cured and facilities provided for doing the same in the future; on the other hand, something must be done in the direction of sanctions

---

[13] See Fite, entire, and review in *American Journal of International Law*, Vol. XXVI, No. 3 (Oct. 1932), p. 907.

and security, even if no international police be created, or the whole progress of international coöperation will be thrown backward.

As for analysis of international coöperation in terms of internationalization and synthesis of national policies, this is included in the analysis in terms of legislation. If the interests of the nations are to be converted into rights by being formulated in international law, and their policies thus satisfied, the process of harmonization must precede or form the preliminary stage of international legislation. It is also true that, short of this stage of the process, the harmonization of conflicting or divergent national policies must be achieved by diplomacy and conclusion of treaties, even if the more mature forms of synthesis and execution (legislation and administration) are not reached. Actually all of these aspects of the process of harmonization exist today side by side.

From a viewpoint based upon form of action taken, therefore, international organization, it may be said, does and must operate by pre-juristic methods and by juristic methods as well, including, though to a doubtful degree, sanctions or enforcement of law. The value and persistence and position, in the whole picture, of pre-juristic methods, the possibility and limits of the various juristic methods, and the value and practicability of international sanctions constitute serious questions for the future, and, indeed, not merely for the future but for the immediate present.

B. *Content; Subject Matters; Peace*

When we turn to the substance or subject matter of the functions or activities of international coöperation we are not left to such a great extent in the realm of theory or speculation. We have concrete social interests—health and prosperity, for example—with which to deal, and broad and prolonged experience in international coöperation for our guidance.

From purely logical principles we should expect that international organization would deal or attempt to deal with all of the normal subjects of national concern which have any international aspects. The interests of the international state should resemble those of the national state and the interests of the national state should be ministered to by the international organization. And we should expect certain interests to take precedence over others either in time or in point of importance. It remains to be seen whether these hypothetical expectations are borne out in fact.

The undisturbed existence of the state would seem to be its primary and fundamental concern; peace and security might be expected to constitute the first and greatest preoccupation of international organization. After this would follow interest in the minimum conditions of health and prosperity of the people, with progress in the enjoyable or happy life following afterwards. These major groups of interests involve many others, of course. Perfection of communications is needed to facilitate the conduct of public administration and also to promote prosperity. Moral or psychic welfare is part of health, and intellectual coöperation a part of the good life. Justice must be done, by the application of existing law and the revision of that law when needed, both for punishment of crimes against social order and welfare and also to distribute the wealth of society equitably. Do the functions of international organization play upon these subjects?

In general, as has been indicated in another connection, international coöperation does range over the whole gamut of international and national life. If there is any phase of human life not touched upon by international coöperation, because not touched upon by national government, that must be a very minute and remote angle of human life indeed.

International organization does not deal, however, or has not dealt, with the various interests of national life in the strict order of their importance. Failure to deal effectively with some of the major issues leaves time and energy for the minor matters it is true, but it also distorts the treatment of these same matters.

Thus international coöperation has not until recently attempted to satisfy the need of the state and the international community for peace, at least to any great extent. Perhaps the primacy of that need was not perceived or felt; perhaps in earlier days that interest was not paramount, if all nations were willing to abide by the fortunes of war for their existence, while they could also, perchance, benefit thereby. At all events it was not until relatively recent times that efforts have been made at preservation of peace by organized international action, by international coöperation.

And the provision of security was even more difficult, even further beyond the possible range of effective international action. For it involved sanctions and sanctions are, as we have just seen, still today a highly problematical function in international coöperation. Bipartite treaties of guarantee were signed, and even multipartite treaties, and some of these arrangements had some force and effect, but still today such guarantees seem, at least for any general participation, impossibly radical and advanced.

The result has been that international coöperation has passed on to other less difficult tasks such as promotion of social welfare—physiological and psychological welfare, economic prosperity, science, art, and what not. Some of these—health and prosperity—are obviously among the most important social interests of the nation, once it can, or if it could, depend upon its safety from attack and upon the perpetuation of peace; and, in so far as security and peace persisted, international coöperation in acting upon these matters was dealing with what were properly its chief tasks.

It is, however, in the problem of peace that most students of international organization are chiefly interested. Emotional reactions in many quarters concerning the horrors of war, coupled perhaps with ignorance regarding the values of international coöperation on economic and similar interests, led, in the past, to great exaggeration of the importance of peace as a condition of international welfare and the importance of efforts for the preservation of peace as a function of international coöperation. War was relatively rare and of minor import in the lives of individual states after the end of the seventeenth century; it became increasingly rare after 1815; it is bound, even apart from any activities to preserve the peace, to become obsolescent rather rapidly in the future for reasons internal to itself. It was relatively unimportant, even though it did occur, in the relations of the nations involved and certainly of minor importance—or the problem of maintaining peace was of minor importance—in comparison with the vast volume of international coöperation needed and practiced in connection with other international economic and human relations. But the prominence of the problem in the practice of international coöperation today necessitates its full discussion; it will occupy the remainder of this chapter.

It is not clear that the development of much more powerful means of destruction, including the atomic bomb, has so far altered this situation, although there would be many who would challenge very strongly such a position. We do not yet know how widely the atomic bomb can be produced or made effective, and certainly the paralyzed condition of Germany, Italy, and Japan in the present post-war period is traceable as much to pre-atomic weapons and to failure to permit normal economic, social, and political recovery as to the sheer effects of war—which were very slight in Italy and Japan. There is, however, no need to deny the desirability of eliminating war from international relations, even the imperative urgency of doing so. On this basis the discussion can proceed.

Peace may be conceived entirely as a negative thing, as the condition which exists when there is no war.[1] Even this simple description, however, requires some analysis, for "war" also is a concept not commonly analyzed and defined with precision. War may be defined as general military action by a state, undertaken for the purpose of vindicating what it believes to be its rights or interests against another state or other states. Direct action of a limited sort—retorsion, reprisals—may be undertaken for the defense of certain limited rights without bringing on a state of war in the full sense of the term. Forcible action may be undertaken by certain individuals or groups against others without the result of creating a state of public war. Finally, if joint military action is taken by several states for the purpose of vindicating international law or the general peace, we have something which does not deserve to be regarded as "war" in the usual sense of the term; no claim is made that such action

[1] On peace movements see literature cited, below, Appendix B, § 10b.

is taken for "altruistic" reasons, nor is it necessary for the conclusion, so long as the interests defended be public international interests.

Peace, then, while excluding international war proper, does not necessarily exclude all military action. The occurrence of sporadic outbursts of individual violence, of piratical marauding or civil rioting, does not disturb the peace from an international viewpoint. Likewise, the military action of an international organization for the enforcement of international law would not amount to a breach of the peace. On the contrary, such action would in reality constitute a step taken for the maintenance of ultimate peace. At the same time it is obvious that such action resembles war in a physical sense and must be kept at a minimum if physical peace is desired.

If no war means peace, then, obviously, peace might conceivably be brought about by each nation voluntarily abstaining from the use of military action to vindicate its rights, preferring peace to justice. Such a peace is not to be counted on in fact and would be seriously criticized by many from the moral viewpoint. A nation, like an individual, may, of course, calculate that the inconvenience and expense of enforcing its rights will be greater than the values to be obtained by that step, and decide to refrain from action. This may go the length of deciding that war is, in general, a method of action so terrible and expensive that no values which can be obtained through its use can conceivably compensate for the suffering and cost which it entails, or of deciding even to comply with all demands made upon it which cannot be warded off by diplomacy. To make war would then be rashness and folly. That is not what is at issue here. The undesirable thing is an attitude in making the foregoing calculation which gives undue weight to inconvenience and expense and trouble, which unduly fears the harsh realities of conflict and, in particular, undervalues the interests of right and justice.

We encounter at this point the vast polemical literature for and against war, describing it as useful, beneficial, and inevitable, or the opposite. That war is inevitable so long as certain conditions of mind and certain international social and political conditions persist is certain. The former are, however, changing notably in recent times; [2] the latter, as we now see, may soon be changed radically in certain particulars. As for the utility of war, that also must be considered not by itself but in relation to the alternatives available, in particular the alternatives in international procedure which have already been described. The absolute anti-force pacifist and the absolute pro-force militarist are equally anti-social in their mysticisms.

Granting, then, that for the nations to seek peace by sacrificing their rights would be demoralizing, how is the enforcement of those rights to

[2] See report of a questionnaire circulated among members of American Psychological Association, in *New York Times*, 8 Aug., 1932, p. 14, col. 4, and *Science Monthly*, Vol. XXXV, No. 4 (August, 1932), p. 142.

be reconciled with the maintenance of peace? Granting, further, as we must grant, that the nations are unwilling to surrender their rights generally for the sake of peace, how may the same problem be solved? There is presented here a task of political engineering deserving most intensive study. Peace cannot be attained by aspiration merely, by crying "let us have peace." The peace movement was once injured by nothing else as much as by the spread of a concept of peace typified by a milk-white dove bearing inanely before it a silly twig of olive leaves. Contrary to the old adage, it only takes one state to make war but it takes two, three—all—to keep the peace. It must be attained by international organization for the definition, administration, and, perhaps, the enforcement of the rights of individual states so as to relieve them of the necessity of self-help in this regard. Peace must be attained indirectly, and international organization may be regarded as the means to the end.

With this in mind, peace becomes not a weak condition of inaction and dissolution, but a condition where the adequate power of the community maintains the common law and common justice, and public order reigns. The peace of the public highway is the peace to be sought and, haply, obtained by international government. These general principles remain, however, to be worked out in detail, and it is most convenient to make the beginning in connection with the international conferences discussed in a preceding chapter.

It has been seen that war may be terminated by a simple cessation of of hostilities or by treaty. It was noted that the former method left matters in an inconvenient state of uncertainty. More important here is the fact that it leaves open many questions likely to lead to a renewal of war. For that reason the method of concluding war by treaty is of much greater value for preserving the peace, in that it provides for the mutual satisfaction of claims outstanding between the parties.

When this task is undertaken the peace conference is led, first of all, to revert to the causes which originally brought on the war. The discussion of international relations must be resumed where the discussion, and where those relations, speaking generally, were broken off by the advent of war subject to any modifications effected during the war.

The most natural question suggested by this obvious but commonly neglected fact is the question why, if this be so, the discussion was broken off originally, and what assistance has been derived from the intervening war in the settlement of the issues at stake. The reply is extremely complicated and varies with the nature of the issues.

In general terms, it may be said that diplomatic discussions are broken off and military action begun in such cases because of a failure on the part of the disputants to come to agreement, or, more specifically, the failure of one party to secure from the other a satisfactory degree of compliance with its demands by the use of diplomatic argument. But what is that "argument" the failure of which brings war? It is the presentation of alternatives from which the other state will, it is claimed, suffer as a result of refusing the demands of its neighbor. Those argumentative alternatives may be of many forms, such as warnings of the loss of reputation or the loss of favor in the eyes of the state making the demand, and of other states, resulting indirectly in material loss; physical attack by the state making the demand (or by others, or both), with the object of seizing the object of the demand, if that be feasible, or other things to be held for exchange; or with the object of securing power over the state resisting the demand—over its property, territory, people, and government—in order to compel satisfaction as the price of continued free existence. And, the arguments being unconvincing, the action threatened is taken in fact. So far as war does not come about merely amid excitement and confusion, this is the rational theory of the event.

It will be noted, however, that the value of war in the proper regulation of the current dispute is as remote from view as ever. When we examine the case again we find that what the first state has done is to take action having little or no bearing upon the merits of the issue in dispute. So far as that state is victorious in war, it secures satisfaction for its demands without reference to the merits of the issue; the issue is therefore not "settled" in any rational sense, but remains in dispute in the minds of the parties; for the second party has yielded not from conviction on the merits of the issue but as a price of continuing to enjoy some of the good things of life. If the second party is victorious the same result follows: the original demand is refused, with as little reference to the merits as in the preceding case. Now if the war should be a drawn battle, the only recourse is to resume negotiations where they were dropped, for no new factors have entered the situation at all. Where, as most often happens, there is a partial victory for one party, the situation is a mixture of cases one, two, and three, but in none of these cases does the war facilitate in any way the solution of the dispute on the merits.

It is partly for this reason that peace conferences, held at the conclusion of war, are of little value for the cause of international peace and justice. The atmosphere and temper of the time is, of course, bad. But more important is the fact that such conferences are based upon the situation at the time. They treat the disputes between the parties by reference to the perhaps temporary preponderance of military force of one power at the time, not by reference to the permanent conditions of power between, and the relative needs of, the two states. The result may easily be the reverse of what it should be in the interests of the common welfare, of justice, and, therefore, of permanence. They produce artificial solutions capable of being maintained only by the constant use of military force. They do not deal with the issue as it stood on the merits at the outbreak of war.

It is obvious, therefore, that the critical point, the point upon which attention must be focused in an effort to find a method of really solving international disputes, is the point where negotiations were broken off. New issues arise during the war, partly connected with the conduct of the war and partly independent of it. But when these issues come to be discussed in the peace conference it is similarly true that the subsequent conduct of the war has no more bearing upon the merits of those issues than upon the original issues. In attempting to deal with the problem of war or national action by military force to vindicate national rights we must revert to the nature of those rights or demands, or, in familiar terms, the causes of war.

The causes of war are, of course, too complicated for complete analysis here. The search for peace by the elimination of the causes of war must be a hopeless task. But in seeking peace by other means the nature of the causes of war is not unimportant. They may be described as falling under one or the other of two heads, either violations of legal rights or actions not covered by international law at all.[3] The former may take the form of maltreatment of citizens abroad, violation of territorial sovereignty, and many other actions. The latter are still more varied, consisting in commercial rivalry, political rivalry, and what not. The conclusions significant for our purpose flow from the twofold classification itself, not from the detailed description of the two classes.

What are the outstanding features of these two forms of the causes of war? The first is the failure to define legally the interests included in the latter group of causes, thus leaving great discretion to the individual state in its decision regarding supposed violations of its alleged "rights." It is a testimony to the respect for law among the nations that the "rights" demanded are invariably portrayed as legal rights wherever possible, but this effort is not in most cases very successful. The second is the freedom left to individual states to decide whether their legal rights have been violated. The third is a failure to provide the state with any means of enforcing even its legal rights except self-help and a toleration of self-help on the part of the states. It is to these features of the situation that international government must be applied if it is to accomplish anything for the cause of peace.

In accordance with this conclusion, the conferences held in time of peace with the purpose of preventing war turn first to the definition of the rights of the states participating in them. Such conferences have a greater chance of success than conferences at the end of war because the temper of the time is better, the alignment of the forces in the scene is normal, and the common interest may conceivably be kept in view. National advantage is here sought through the common advantage, benefit is now sought not at once but in the long run, and the attention is directed to the origin of disputes, not to the results thereof, as is not

---

[3] On causes of war see literature cited, below, Appendix B, § 10b.

true in conferences in time of war. By treaty agreements the rights of
the parties regarding territory, commercial privileges, and all the interests
at stake in the situation, are defined. The next step which needs to be
taken is the provision of machinery for adjudication upon those rights,
and the third step would be to provide for enforcement by the community of nations participating in the plan, in place of enforcement by
the individual state.

Historically something, but not a great deal, has been done on the first
point, in formally defining international rights. For the most part international law has been allowed to grow up by itself, and the task of recording and codifying it has been left to private scholars. Only in the
last fifty years have official conferences for the statement of the law met
with any frequency, and these have dealt principally with the conduct
of war. By far the greater part of the law of normal intercourse, covering the period when war is not being carried on, yet in which it originates, is left untouched. The reason for this, as well as the reason for the
same action by private scholars in recording first the common international law of war, is that the law has been set down, not so much deliberately with the object of effecting a world government and preventing
war in the future, as with the object of recording retrospectively the
methods of making war, of avoiding disputes concerning these methods,
and, if possible, of ameliorating these methods. At present the great need
for an effort to set forth the law of international relations in complete
and official form is better appreciated.

Provisions for the adjudication of disputed rights have also been made
in the past, as the history of arbitration shows, and the steps taken in
this direction, although not very well coördinated before the end of the
last century, have been more numerous and consistent than those taken
for the definition of the law. This is attributable to the fact that it has
seemed simpler to reconcile such a proceeding with the idea of state
independence than the declaration of law binding for the future, and
to the greater intrinsic difficulty of the latter task. It is intrinsically difficult to find legal formulas capable of doing justice to all parties. This
is the fundamental human obstacle to the development of international
law, the lack of such knowledge of international relations as would
enable us to write fairly and completely the law of those relations.[4] But
the movement for the judicial settlement of international legal disputes
is now well on its feet.

The last step to be taken in providing for peaceful world government
is to provide for community enforcement of international rights, and
prohibition of recourse to force by the individual state. This problem

[4] See Prince von Bülow's remark (made, probably, without complete candor),
"Germany has not found any formula that will meet the great diversity which char-
acterizes the geographical, the economic, the military, and the political positions of
the various countries," in reference to the proposals at The Hague in 1907 for
obligatory arbitration, in an address in the Reichstag, 30 April, 1907.

has already been discussed [5] and the discussion need not be repeated here.

The common expression of the peace movement consists not so much of a demand for this type of international government, however, as of an emotional attack upon the state system and interstate relations. The literature of the peace movement deals not so much with the practical methods of political engineering which might be used to reduce the chances of war as with the beauty of peace and the ugliness of war. A reproduction of the picture "The Spirit of '76" is placed beside a photograph of the mutilated and gangrened face and jaws of a wounded soldier and the title "The Glory of War" is placed under the two. To such an attitude the reply is direct: peace will not come and war will not disappear by wishing it so, by dwelling on the beauty of peace and the horror of war. More effective steps must be taken than mere denunciation and aspiration.

A solution for the problem especially favored by peace advocates is disarmament. It seems obvious that securing the surrender of their armaments by the potential belligerents would be about the most certain means of rendering war impossible which could be conceived. The difficulty is, however, precisely to secure that result. Neither weak states nor strong states seem willing to disarm in absence of protection for their alleged rights and interests, even though their own efforts toward this end may also be somewhat unreliable. Nor has increased danger from atomic weapons or their like changed this attitude as yet. Of course disarmament must be general, by agreement, and not merely disarmament by the most peacefully inclined, and it must be limited and supplemented by international police action; otherwise it will simply benefit the less peace-loving nations and open the door to international violence of various kinds, piracy and riots and common crime included. With these qualifications the proposal may still be promoted—especially for whatever benefits it might produce in the diversion of public expenditures to other ends.

A further result of partial disarmament, even by agreement, without an adequate sanctions system, would, incidentallly, be to place certain countries in position to do as they like in their corners of the earth without other countries, whose power to operate at a distance has been reduced, being able to check them; such was the position of Japan in the period 1925-40 as a result of the measures taken at the Washington Conference in 1921-1922. This means that such disarmament positively works against the maintenance of peace, and inasmuch as this intermediate stage can never be avoided disarmament without sanctions must be regarded as certainly and definitely inimical to peace.

This is confirmed when the factor of war potential is taken into account, that is, the power of a state to wage war apart from its standing army and navy, as embodied in its economic and industrial power and

[5] Above, Section A.

facilities. Disarmament, reduction of armed forces and armaments, must leave the country with greatest war potential supreme, and tempt it to embark on adventures, in absence of an effective security system. As a step toward peace disarmament as such is not only extremely difficult but deceptive as well.

Even the more enlightened nations are loath to take such a step. This brings us to the reason for the general unwillingness to disarm. That reason is found in the fact that national rights are still ill-defined, that no sure method of adjudication upon those rights except self-adjudication is available, and no method of enforcement but self-enforcement. We are back to the deficiencies of international government as the chief cause of huge armaments. The only method available for producing a state of mind in the nations such that they will be willing to disarm is to provide them with a system for securing definition, application, and enforcement of their rights without arms. It need not be pointed out again that this can only be done by a general international organization for the purpose.

If we return to the proposal for a mere limitation of armaments, the same conclusions apply, with even greater cogency. The amount of reduction possible would depend upon the forces needed to maintain peace and order on the seas and in civil society. The amount of reduction for each power would have to be carefully calculated in order to prevent many undesirable possibilities. Those states most willing to accept limitations would be precisely the ones which should not be asked or allowed to take such action. The states upon which the most severe limitations should be placed are the ones which it would be most difficult to persuade to accept any limitations at all. Finally, these facts are all accentuated because the deficiency of international government is felt, not in defining the maximum size of forces needed to preserve domestic peace, a matter in which the peaceful nation may need forces as great as any, but in deciding upon the possibility of any curtailment at all, just the point where the peaceful nation has the weakest case.

What is perhaps the greatest difficulty, however, would arise after it is agreed to accept some limitation of armaments. How great shall the reduction be? Shall it be the same for all states? How shall it be enforced? If the reduction is to be the same in all cases it must be less than the size of the armament of that one of the present powers whose armament is smallest; otherwise some state will be left without any forces for preserving domestic peace. In a general agreement for the limitation of armaments intended to include all nations this procedure would, of course, be ridiculous in its application to the Great Powers—another evidence of the unwholesome effect on international relations of the existence of gross inequality among the nations. Evidently, reductions must be unequal or the action must be confined to the Great Powers. But it is often smaller powers, with armaments excessive for their size and with less sense of responsibility, which precipitate international conflict; they are, moreover, among the states in position to gain most by the saving incident to limitation of armaments. Hence it appears that the proposed reductions may have to be unequal, a thing hard to present in an acceptable light to those powers now in a position of relative supremacy regarding their armed strength.

The whole matter is, moreover, very difficult to reduce to exact figures, and, of course, it must be reduced to exact figures, for after a certain stage general considerations are of absolutely no use. Probably the only sure basis for computing the armaments needed by individual powers is the force needed to maintain domestic law and order. Even here the relative maturity of society in one nation and another makes the adoption of a uniform standard impossible, though the experience of the past and the judgment of those responsible for the performance of the task are substantial foundations on which to build. This assumes—an assumption justified with difficulty in view of the facts—that a reliable unit of computation can be found. Perhaps a complex unit can be devised, a unit made up from the number of persons in the armed forces of a state, the number and caliber of arms in stock, the amount of ammunition on hand, the number and tonnage of vessels in commission, and other factors.

It is obviously impossible to settle such questions here. It is not difficult, however, to discover the truth that the very complexity of the problem makes a certain method of procedure inevitable. Some sort of a conference is needed to secure the primary adoption of any plan, as joint action is essential in the nature of the case. Careful conference is necessary for the selection of the particular plan to be utilized, and for the construction or selection of a unit of computation to be employed. Finally joint administration and enforcement are needed if the plan is to be carried out successfully. Inevitable ambiguities which will develop in the process of execution must be interpreted, attempts at evasion must be detected, and the whole matter must be watched over from the very beginning. If the administrative experience of national governments in similar situations is any guide, partial limitation of armaments would need such supervision even more than complete disarmament because it would be more complicated and easier to evade. Moreover, the work would never be entirely completed and such supervision would have to be maintained permanently. If any changes were to be made in the ratios of reduction, if any further progress in limitation of armaments were desirable and feasible, they could only be had by the same process of conference and coöperation which was necessary at first. And it does not need to be repeated that for the limitation, as for the abandonment, of armaments, a definition of national rights is essential to prepare the ground and that such a result can only be had by conference. Moreover, when we reflect that some joint administration of international rights would, on the one hand, be necessary to secure any consent to a limitation of national armaments for national use, and that it might, on the other hand, mean military coöperation for this purpose, it is not wholly fanciful to say that, when worked out in actual practice, national disarmament actually approaches the internationalization of armaments.

It may appear that the subject has been argued over much. If so, it will be useful to note, on one side, that peace is more imperative today than ever before, that disarmament is demanded as never before in modern times, and, on the other hand, that nationalism and resistance to international supervision were never more pronounced, at least on the part of several important states. The situation is one of the great internal conflicts of history: the desire for international peace against the assertion of national power. The conflict is real, and a choice must be made; either common peace or individual power may be enjoyed, not both.[6]

The discussion of the proposals for disarmament has, however, thrown the emphasis where it does not belong. The principal conclusion to be drawn in this section has been stated already, namely, that maintenance of permanent peace, as the chief function to be performed by international organization, is, in its essence, and depends for its existence upon, the definition and satisfaction of national rights through common international action by legislation, adjudication, administration, and enforcement on behalf of all members of the society of nations. That such a step would also be essential for the successful working of any plan for disarmament is collateral evidence of the soundness of this conclusion. If space permitted it would be simple to demonstrate also that the attempt made so earnestly during modern times to mitigate the severity of war and restrict its incidence was largely unsuccessful because it needed for its success precisely the method of procedure described for the effective limitation of armaments and was deprived of that procedure. That movement sometimes received the scorn of the pacifists who declared that war could not be tamed but must be destroyed. This resulted partly from their desire to accomplish the greater good and partly from a reluctance to take the procedural steps necessary to the end in view. This reluctance, further, was dictated somewhat by temperament, and also by an unwillingness to be mixed up in international politics which was quite innocent and understandable in many ways but wholly irreconcilable with the end in view. Nothing is more ridiculously inept than the combination of pacifism or opposition to war and national armaments, on one side, and a refusal to participate in organized international government on the other. And, while international peace and order probably will come as a result both of the negative movement for disarmament and peace and the affirmative movement to prevent the outbreak of war by settling international disputes likely to lead to war, it will certainly not come solely from the efforts to secure disarmament or restrict war on the part

---

[6] Again the relative responsibility of the "common man" for lack of progress in the effort for peace must be emphasized: see Angell, Butler, Gallup.

of those who dwell on the beauties of peace and the horror of war without provision for practical conference and coöperation for that end.

A word may be added concerning the probable success of the peace
movement in our times. The organization of international enforcement of
national rights and international protection of national security, suggested in this chapter and in a preceding chapter as being logically necessary to the maintenance of international peace and order, seems at present
a stupendous task. The maintenance of peace consequently seems to hang
upon the appearance of a conviction that war must be so costly to victor
and vanquished alike that it cannot be compensated for by any benefits
which could possibly be attained by resort to its use. When this view
comes to be held by the nations war will become obsolete as a result,
quite apart from the program of procedure discussed above. The costs
of war, in the broadest sense, are so high in our day that such a conviction is gaining ground rapidly. Education designed to mitigate the misunderstandings among men and nations would consume more time than
is available for saving the international civilization of the world from
the danger of destruction by war. But education designed to bring home
to men the costs of war may do much to stimulate the development just
referred to. Coupled with the development of organized international co-
operation for the regulation of official international business this movement may be decisive. Prophecy is hazardous, and undue optimism weak,
but the institution of war may even now be enjoying the climax preceding
decline.

CHAPTER XI

History of International Organization

The significance of current developments in international organization cannot be fully appreciated without due notice of the history of that activity. A distorted conception of the novelty of contemporary efforts at international control detracts from a balanced conception of the nature of that function and its effective action. Also the history of international organization has much to teach concerning both the steps to be taken in this field, if fruitful results are to be achieved, and the mistakes which are to be avoided. A brief review of the long story of international organization will amply repay the time and effort which it requires.[1]

The substantive or organic aspects of the matter demand attention more than the purely external or chronological aspects, of course. We are interested in the factors which caused organized international co-operation to appear in the world and which led to its development. We are also interested in the factors which at times tended to make it almost disappear. Finally we are interested in the way in which different forms of the activity led into one another and the state of affairs resulting. We shall, in drawing up this account, follow generally the scheme of things set out in other chapters, and consider more or less distinctly for each period (1) the condition of the international community, including international intercourse and cosmopolitanism, and common international law, (2) diplomacy and treaty-making, (3) international conference, (4) international administration and adjudication, and (5) international federation. No attention will be given to international politics, little evolutionary element being discernible there. On the other hand proper attention will be given to international legislation and sanctions, not, indeed, in each period but at appropriate points. Finally, for the purpose of this survey, the following periods will be observed: (a) Antiquity (to 500 A.D.); (b) the Middle Ages (500 to 1300 A.D.); (c) the Renaissance and early modern times (1300 to 1789); (d) modern times (1789 to the present). Some attention will be given in passing to the effects of war on

[1] This Chapter is based largely on a series of lectures (*Développement de l'organisation internationale, 1815-1914*) given by the author at the *Académie de Droit International* at The Hague in 1938: *Receuil*, T. 64, p. 75. On its position in this volume as a whole see above, in Preface, at p. viii. See also the first edition of this work (1922), Chaps. II-IV, V, VII, and pp. 156-160, 203-205, 208, 223-227, 271-275, 303-314, 321-323, 337-341, 417-437, 441-444, etc. There is no compact history of international organization in existence; for elements of the subject, in addition to the lectures mentioned above and the footnotes thereto see works by Phillipson, Walker, Garner, and Hershey cited below, Appendix B, § 11.

international organization. A few general comments will be offered by way of conclusions.

International organization in one form or another dates back just about as far as anything like distinct nations or states can be found, a need for some dealings with other political entities being about simultaneous with the appearance of such entities individually. Actually traces of diplomacy, treaty-making, and arbitration date back several thousands of years, and, in Egypt, Southern Asia, and the Far East, antedate the civilization of Greece and Rome by several millennia.[2] Such activity originated, obviously, not in any abnormal or isolated cause but as an incident of the life of whatever rudimentary national groups existed at that time in the areas named.

This raises a point much emphasized later by some observers and one not irrelevant to present discussions of international organization. There could be, it has been said, no international institutions in antiquity in the absence of national states, a product of a much later time. If this be true all talk of pre-Greek international organization is hazardous, or even of any international organization prior to the Renaissance. This seems to to be an unduly narrow view. The essence of international law and organization is the regulation of relations among otherwise independent communities, and whether these partake entirely of the social entity known as the national state today seems largely irrelevant. As we shall see, this is doubly pertinent in connection with international federal unions today. We shall examine briefly the interstate organization found in ancient times without putting too fine a point on its "international" character.

The states of Northern Africa and Asia prior to 1000 B.C. were too scattered and their relations too fragmentary to give rise to any common institutions and practices except those of an equally fragmentary character. They are interesting as our earliest prototypes of modern institutions but they did not constitute any considerable body of practice at the time. We shall not pause on them further, but confine our attention to Europe and the Western Hemisphere until the very end of our survey.

In Greek times an interstate community developed in the Peninsula itself, in Asia Minor, and on the shores of the Black Sea, the Aegean, and the Mediterranean, as far west as Gibraltar, almost ideally adapted to the development of interstate organization.[3] Over five hundred independent city-states, of substantially equal size, and with many common bonds of race and culture, developed a lively body of intercourse in trade and travel and foreign residence. An ideal combination of heterogeneity and homogeneity existed for the birth of interstate practice and organization.

The results were indeed forthcoming. Something closely resembling modern consular service made its appearance, although the proxenus

---

[2] Hershey, Chap. III; Wegner, p. 2.
[3] Phillipson, Chap. I.

was a citizen of the state in which he acted rather than of the appointing state.[4]

Diplomacy was a familiar matter although apparently the resident diplomat was not.[5] Many treaties were concluded and we have the texts of many examples; few of the treaties were multipartite in character, but of course that has been true elsewhere until very recent times.[6] On the other hand the international conference was not a frequent event, being confined largely to the settlement of war or operation of international leagues. Arbitration, however, was in common use and again we have many specimens for study.[7] Finally the Greek city states developed the federal league to a high point, including limited legislative organs and executive and administrative organs (common treasuries and military forces), and almost attaining the level of the full federal state.[8]

The Greeks failed, however, to work out a union sufficiently broad and strong to resist the Macedonian and the Roman and they therefore went down in defeat. This may perhaps be regarded as the greatest lesson in this field given by the Greeks to later times: perfection in detail availed little when the fundamental problem of interstate union was not solved on a universal scale.

In early Italy conditions resembled those in primitive Greece and the results were much the same. The beginnings of free interstate coöperation were in evidence down to the time of the early Republic.[9]

As soon as Rome began to conquer the Italian peninsula, however, and then the Mediterranean basin, and then the known Western world, free interstate activity and organization began to disappear.[10] A rich body of trade and travel existed, of course, but before long a consolidated Roman rule supplanted the coexistence of numerous independent states. A cosmopolitanism probably broader and deeper than that of either Periclean Greece or the Hellenistic age matured but it was not a basis for free interstate coöperation but its substitute.

Similar results followed in the field of the more formal institutions. The Romans took over diplomacy and treaty-making from the Levant but they did not improve upon it and they largely converted, not to say perverted, it to domestic constitutional, imperial ends.[11] Interstate conferences were as infrequent as ever. Arbitration was, it is true, practiced to some degree but also as a device of superior government rather than of free interstate coöperation.[12] Finally the Romans made little or no experiment with interstate federal union after the establishment of the

[4] *Ibid.*, Vol. I, p. 147.
[5] *Ibid.*, Chap. XIII.
[6] Egger, in general, especially Chaps. II and III; Phillipson, Chap. XV.
[7] Raeder, in general; Phillipson, Chaps. XX and XXI.
[8] Phillipson, Chap. XVI.
[9] Hershey, § 34 and notes thereto; Phillipson, Vol. I, p. 102.
[10] *Ibid.*
[11] Phillipson, Vol. I, pp. 106-110.
[12] Raeder, Chap. III, Part C, Nos. 3-6.

early monarchy. Free international organization did not lie within the limits of Roman genius or preference.

At the end of the Roman period (500 A.D.) little remained of the accomplishments of the Greeks, or of their predecessors, or of the Romans, along these lines. The achievements of these early peoples had been of considerable stature and even very striking in quality at various points. But they had lacked in theoretical foundation and appreciation, they had lacked emotional sympathy, and they had lacked in continuity. The result was that by the end of the Roman period,—indeed long before that time,—imperial conquest and domination had snuffed out all prior developments of a contrary character and little but a memory was bequeathed to Medieval Europe along these lines.

For nearly a thousand years little happened in this field. The chaotic condition of the political organization of Europe, or its disorganization, and the lack of any great body of international intercourse, meant that no foundation existed for even simple diplomacy or arbitration. Even the development of the feudal system, while it brought a certain amount of order to the scene, did not provide sufficiently independent and freely coöperating units to constitute a suitable foundation for international organization.[13] It is true that traces of diplomacy and treaty-making persisted even during the Dark Ages but, while this is significant in itself, those traces were very thin and fragmentary.[14] Arbitration was similarly fragmentary and subordinate, in spite of some encouragement by Pope and Emperor,[15] and, except for Church diets,—which do not deserve to be entirely disregarded in this context, it is true, nor the real but restricted cosmopolitanism of the life of the Church,—interstate or international conferences were almost totally absent.[16] Even in the end of the fourteenth century Europe was little further ahead along this line than it had been in 400 A.D. or 400 B.C., in spite of brilliant but isolated and irregular advances at times in the past.

It is true that by the later fourteenth century beginnings had been made upon a revival of institutionalized international activity, and that still more important steps lay just ahead. At the end of the eleventh century the foundations of the modern consular office were laid in Levantine trading cities.[17] From the tenth century onward treaty-making manifested a definite increase in volume and a beginning of the trend from personal contract toward interstate statute.[18] And some increase of arbitration at the behest of higher feudal, imperial, and even ecclesiastical authorities was noticeable.[19]

[13] Hershey, § 40. On this whole period see R. F. Wright, as cited below, Appendix B, § 11.
[14] Wright, pp. 93, 109.
[15] Hershey, § 44, and note; Wright, p. 83.
[16] *Ibid.*, §§ 41, 42, and Wright, p. 51.
[17] Ravndal, cited below, Appendix B, § 11.
[18] See earlier items in the du Mont collection cited below, Appendix B, § 11.
[19] Moore, *Arbitrations*, Vol. V, pp. 4825-4851 (a translation of Merighnac).

What was more important, large beginnings were soon made not only in restoring European overland trade and travel but also in promoting exploration and settlement overseas and in the whole art and practice of navigation.[20] From the fourteenth century onward the national state, at the time such a valuable foundation for interstate organization, whatever it might become later, began to assert itself.[21] In the fifteenth century the resident diplomat made his appearance, as a result of Italian and French genius in this sphere.[22] Finally a slight trend is noticeable at that time in the direction of increased mediation or conciliation, though not of arbitration.[23] Although the effects were less extensive than might have been expected international organization also experienced a certain degree of rebirth. It remains only to mention that in the later Middle Ages a number of leagues of trading cities, of which the Hanseatic League was only one, though the most vigorous, produced phenomena reminiscent of the days of the Latin and Greek confederacies.[24]

It was, of course, some time before the European state system took on its modern forms. A considerable number of the larger feudal principalities and kingdoms did, however, become sufficiently stable and powerful to play important parts in interstate relations in and after the period of the Renaissance.[25] A still limited, though increasing, number of large consolidated states had appeared by the time of the Thirty Years War so that the Peace of Westphalia (1648) constituted a veritable confirmation of the modern European state system which still persists today. As order grew on land, moreover, and the technique of navigation improved at sea, the volume of trade and of travel among the European countries and overseas to the colonies expanded and by the eighteenth century an impressive body of cosmopolitan civilization had come to prevail in Europe and to flow out from Europe to America; Africa and the Orient remained, except for minute areas, dark and untouched for many decades still.[26]

Consular service naturally grew rapidly as a result of these developments although a set-back was felt a little later as a result of the expansion of diplomacy proper. Permanent resident diplomatic representation had been inaugurated in the middle of the fifteenth century, and the extremely active character of international—there need be no hesitation in using that term after 1648—politics, and the still somewhat limited character of international intercourse, both operated to limit consular activity. Treaty-making of course increased greatly in volume and complexity and the great collections of texts of treaties began to make

[20] Day, in general, as cited below, Appendix B, § 11.
[21] Best related in Hill, as cited, and Muir, pp. 33, 37, 126.
[22] Hill, Vol. II, p. 152.
[23] Hershey, § 44.
[24] Walker, pp. 116-117.
[25] Hershey, § 52.
[26] Day, as already cited.

their appearance.[27] Arbitration likewise increased somewhat in frequency, although neither here, nor in the matter of conference or some other items to be discussed in a moment, did international institutions develop as rapidly in this lively nationalistic period as might have been expected. International federal union also lagged; the medieval leagues of trading cities waned and no more advanced type appeared to take their place.

The developments in international organization between 1789 and 1914 exceeded everything that had gone before in both quantity and quality. The state system of Europe matured and spread all over the Western Hemisphere and to considerable sections of Asia and Africa, if only in the form of dependencies.[28] An enormous volume of now very diversified communications and intercourse developed which sustained and impelled the development of international institutions more vigorously than ever before.[29] And a modern economic and scientific and cultural cosmopolitanism appeared which is far broader and more substantial than either the somewhat mystical religious unity of the Middle Ages or the polite literary and artistic cosmopolitanism of the eighteenth century, also, like its medieval counterpart, found only in the limited upper strata of society.[30]

The effects on diplomacy and treaty-making do not need to be described. The expansion which took place here equalled and exceeded all that had happened previously.[31] The nations even got around to official standardization of diplomatic ranks [32] and if they did not succeed in working out any multipartite consular convention they did, by comparison and by imitation, work out a very elaborate and remarkably well standardized consular system on a bipartite basis. Finally treaty-making and treaty-collecting doubled the performance of the preceding period until by the beginning of the present century there was a strong demand here too for standardization and collective action.[33] The great multipartite convention on such matters as health and river navigation and other phases of communication became common.[34]

Several agreements of exceptional range and importance were concluded for the submission of cases to arbitration just as the modern period opened.[35] These were followed by an expansion of this practice, still rather moderate but steady, down to the last quarter of the nineteenth

[27] Myers, *Manual.*
[28] Moon, in general.
[29] Most readily tapped in a common manual such as the *World Almanac;* see, in edition of 1947, pp. 368-386, 750, 756, 789, etc.
[30] Marvin, Chaps. V-IX.
[31] See data given concerning consuls in *American Journal of International Law,* Vol. XXVI (1932), Supplement, p. 201.
[32] Below, Appendix A, Document No. 2.
[33] Myers, as cited.
[34] Hudson, *Legislation.*
[35] Ralston, §§ 140, 175, etc.

century and then there occurred a truly rapid development culminating
in the creation of the Permanent Court of Arbitration at The Hague in
1899 (revised in 1907).[36] In the meantime the Claims Commission, for
adjudicating claims of individuals against foreign governments, was also
developed and utilized to a very extensive degree.[37] By 1914 international
judicial settlement so far exceeded the institution of the preceding periods in Europe and in Antiquity in practice if not in theory as to suggest the imminence of something very different in character and in
function.

Finally the states got around again to the establishment of federal
unions. Of course a number of national federal unions were formed,—
the Swiss and American examples dating back to the thirteenth and the
eighteenth centuries.[38] Students of these matters are not yet in accord,
however, upon the degree of similarity between this phenomenon and
international federation, though the two often seem identical, and it is
to professedly international unions that we refer here. Such institutions
as the Universal Postal Union, the Metric Union, and the Pan-American
Union [39] reintroduced the problem of international federation in a manner and to an extent unknown since Greek times. By the beginning of
the twentieth century the nations might have been presumed to be ready
for any kind of federal union which the circumstances might require
although down to that time international organization had consisted
mainly of a scattering of special institutions exhibiting little general constitutional pattern.

It will be noted that the unions just mentioned appeared in connection
with the activity studied earlier under the name of international administration; indeed these unions were often referred to as administrative
unions in view of the emphasis placed on that feature of activity in their
operations, although they also contained organs for legislation and often
adjudication.[40] This may serve to draw attention to the fact that international administration made its appearance in a serious and general form
only in the nineteenth century.[41] Of course international law, so far as
it existed at all, and treaty agreements had to be applied all through the
past, but this function was commonly remitted to the governments signatories thereto. It is also true that arbitration or adjudication is a form
of administration of law but it is a very special form. Finally it is true
that bipartite boundary commissions have been employed for centuries
and do constitute a genuine case of true if limited international administration. It was, however, only in 1804 and 1856 and 1865 and so on that
multipartite agencies for this work began to be created and only after

[36] *Ibid.*, §§ 218-225.
[37] Hudson, *Tribunals*, Chap. **XVI**.
[38] The old historical survey by Hart still seems the best (below, Appendix B, § 9e).
[39] Reinsch, entire.
[40] See above, Chap. VIII. A, p. 131.
[41] One such agency began to develop in practice in 1792: Stuart, *Tangier*, p. 31.

1875 or 1880 that they became numerous. By 1914 a whole new field of international organization was in being.[42]

International law has been referred to several times in the course of this review. The fact is that present-day international law is the creation of the past seven hundred years, its beginnings being discernible chiefly in thirteenth century Europe.[43] It is true that the Romans and the Greeks and even the ancient Egyptians, Persians, Hindus, and Chinese knew the idea of law between nations or peoples.[44] Cicero may be quoted concerning the "law of nations" as it was called until very recent times, and plain antecedents of the system can be traced back to the dim dawn of human history. On the other hand, there was little or no continuity between these ancient prototypes and modern international law, and numerous differences existed between it and them, particularly between the Roman law of nations and our own. The modern system grew up in the period of the Renaissance, on the basis of Roman law, feudal and canon law, international practice—diplomacy and war,—and ethical philosophy.[45] It was written up by various jurists in the period from 1400 to 1650, grew rather slowly from the time of Grotius to the middle of the nineteenth century, and then expanded rapidly and richly down to 1914.[46] It covered the relations among states in time of peace and the laws of war and neutrality and embodied the results of practice and treaty-making and both private and official codification. Just prior to World War I rather remarkable strides had been made in codifying preëxisting law, particularly on the conduct of war but on other matters also, and in extending the law to many matters not previously covered.[47]

International legislation has enjoyed a less prominent and indeed less assured position. It will be recalled that we reserve this term for rules of law adopted by less than unanimous consent, as by simple majority, on the basis of an original agreement authorizing such action. The term was first applied, and is still applied, to the familiar multipartite convention on matters of public health, communications, and so on, but this seems to be a rather loose usage. That sort of thing developed greatly during the latter part of the nineteenth century while adoption of international regulations by majority vote came somewhat later. Even the adoption of non-binding resolutions was relatively rare in international conferences prior to 1875 or 1900. The development has still not gone very far and the term itself still provokes criticism or objection on the part of the conservatives but there is no doubt that it is on the way;

[42] Best summary in Hill, cited above, p. 000.

[43] See summary in this author's *Manual Digest*, pp. 102-111.

[44] Same, pp. 93-102.

[45] Walker, §§ 49-70.

[46] Potter, *Manual Digest*, pp. 111-124 and "International Law in the Twentieth century" as cited below, Appendix B, § 5.

[47] See above, p. 63.

radical proposals for true international legislative bodies have been made but have not yet come to fruition.[48]

Nevertheless the same period was remarkable for the development of the international conference in time of peace.[49] Conferences at the end of war were common historically; the international legislature still lies in the future; conferences to maintain the peace or deal by agreement with large international political problems—the Near East, Central Africa, Chinese questions, Morocco—became an established institution from 1850 onward. Many such meetings were also held, of course, in the course of operation of the administrative unions, already mentioned, for the adoption and revision of the basic instrument of the unions and also for the enactment and revision of their relations. Prior to 1875 any government which proposed an international conference was sure to be suspected of ulterior aims; after 1920 this attitude, while it had not been entirely supplanted, had been greatly weakened, particularly by the holding of conferences in series, called automatically by a central secretariat. At the same time there had been an enormous improvement in the organization and procedural methods and technique of international conference.[50]

Finally the recent emergence of the problem of "sanctions" must be noted.[51] Historically states attempted to coerce one another if the need arose, to secure respect for their rights or satisfaction for their interests. At times they joined together for this purpose, but the idea of general international community action of this type for support of general international law and security was rather remote. In the nineteenth century, however, the Concert of Europe made such an idea familiar on the political side and a number of international administrative unions, strangely enough, were provided with enforcement powers in connection with the opposite type of subjects (health and communications). At last proposals for international police action, and even an international police force, were made, in support of territorial security, disarmament, and other objects. Down to 1914 this seemed to be a very drastic and radical proposal but it was so fundamentally sound that within a very short time, as international relations go, the idea was accepted and attempts were made to apply it. At no other point have the force and tempo of international evolution been greater or more obvious; indeed this seems to be the climax of the whole growth of international control.

The effects of World War I on this historical process were, of course, important and interesting but by no means simple or entirely disastrous and this may be given as the effect of war on international organization in general. Diplomacy and treaty-making are temporarily interrupted by war,—between the belligerents,—but nothing more. International law is

[48] See discussion above, pp. 211.
[49] See literature cited below, Appendix B, § 10a(1).
[50] Pastuhov, entire.
[51] The best general survey is still probably that of Davies, as cited below, Appendix B, § 10a(2); see also Potter, *Collective Security*.

in part (the law of peace) left untouched, in part more or less shattered, or, in the sequel, vindicated and extended. Conference and legislation are suspended temporarily but renewed with increased vigor at the close of hostilities. Adjudication likewise. International administrative agencies vary greatly in the effects which they suffer on the outbreak of war. Those operating solely between the belligerents, on various aspects of international intercourse, are liquidated for the time being, in law and in fact. Others, operating in and among other states, are left entirely intact. Some agencies actually have their work increased. At times new agencies are created as a result of the outbreak of war, among belligerents on one side, for waging war or building the peace. The whole matter is obviously too complicated and delicate to be dismissed thus briefly. Above all else at the end of war a survey of what has happened is needed and a sober decision on what is to be done for the future.[52]

In general retrospect a few observations may be made upon this historical picture. In spite of the neglect of, and even the hostility toward, the historical background of international organization on the part of the contemporary advocates and practitioners thereof, certain valuable lessons may be learned from this history. It would be extremely helpful if they could be borne in mind in trying to promote this activity in the years which lie ahead of us.

Thus the story is a long one. Six thousand years ago people were engaged in the pacific settlement of interstate disputes by arbitration. Surely something is to be learned from that story. Specifically, if working with that device did not, in all those centuries, produce greater results in the direction of permanent international peace and justice then surely that must reveal something concerning the capacities of that institution. On the other hand this record should put an end to the shallow and cheap attitude of present-day reformers which would ignore the experience of the past and the lessons which it has to teach concerning the useful and the useless moves to be made in the development of international organization.

Even the irregularities of the recorded evolution should be given due attention. There have been tremendous ups and downs in this story. There was something like international law in use among the Romans around the beginning of the Empire, but seven or eight hundred years later this had almost entirely disappeared. The consular officer was a very important figure toward the end of the twelfth century but greatly overshadowed by his diplomatic colleague in the early sixteenth century. This clearly suggests that evolution in this field may be very uneven and that alternations of, or oscillations in, volume and in scale must also be anticipated. They need also not be taken too seriously; the low estate of international federal union in the seventeenth and eighteenth centuries

[52] See Treaty of Versailles, Arts. 282-295.

merely allowed matters to drift until the great expansion in this field which set in during the late nineteenth century.

Even complete blank spots in the record should not be regarded as too decisive. The almost complete absence of multipartite international administration prior to the nineteenth century does not now seem final. The relatively late origin of true international law did not seriously impede its development when it did appear. The gap in the history of the codification of international law between March of 1930 and the present time need not be regarded as a conclusive indication of the death of that movement. Such gaps are disquieting; that is, they make one wonder why they happen or what may happen of a similar character in the future, but they obviously do not at any given time indicate with any certainty that any particular activity will not be resumed and even carried to a point of development higher than it had ever reached before.

All of this means in general that there has been a considerable lack of continuity in the development of international organization. There has been a long historical development back of current efforts but it does not seem to mean very much in concrete detail—while constituting a severe condemnation of any neglect of the past by any Johnnie-come-lately's. There have been many ups and downs and many blank spaces. There has been a notable lack of continuity in general and in the several subdivisions of the field, at least until late in the nineteenth century. The extension and intensification of the movement in this field in the last quarter of the nineteenth century served to gather together many straggling threads and scattered fragments from sixty centuries of experimentation. It remains to be seen whether the future holds any such relapse as took place in these matters from 150 B.C. to 500 A.D. or indeed from that time onward to 1500 A.D.

Finally the cumulative revolutions of 1900, 1920, and 1940 (roughly) must be registered. The events of the end of the nineteenth century and the early years of the present century did not, in content, really exceed greatly what had been accomplished in the preceding generation, but the steps now taken are more self-conscious, deliberate, and articulate. The developments of 1875-1900 were obscure, unheralded, and unsung; they were even denied in principle. In 1899, 1900, 1904, and 1907 international organization was put forward in so many words as a desirable thing. Then came a relapse which lasted for ten years or more when again a revolution had to be staged in favor of a League of Nations and all the accompanying developments (1918-1928). The peak of this development came just before the economic collapse of 1929; perhaps we should say that this collapse brought that movement to an end. At all events there was another reaction and only in 1942 could the forward movement be taken up again. The volume and force of the present movement seem to dwarf anything that has gone before but we should be sufficiently chastened by this historical review to approach present developments with suitable humility. It is true that the long history of international organization made the creation of the League of Nations in 1919-1920 appear not surprising but surprisingly late. It is true that after the events of 1936-1941 the recreation of the League under another name seems to have been inevitable and wholly in accord with international needs. Nevertheless nothing is certain—in matters of detail at least— in this field and all further action will still be an historical experiment.

CHAPTER XII

The League of Nations

Little explanation or excuse is necessary for spending a reasonable amount of time and attention at this point on the League of Nations, although that institution has now formally passed into history. The League effort or experience constituted such an important passage in the history of international organization, and made such important contributions to the science and art of that now indispensable human activity, that on these grounds alone it would deserve attention. In addition it provided, obviously, the most direct precedents for the United Nations organization of today, and deserves attention in this connection also. We shall examine the origins, nature, and development of the League, its functions and its organization, and then try to appraise its contribution to the practice of organized international coöperation and examine the process by which it passed over into the United Nations.

A. *Origins; Nature; Development*

I. ORIGINS

On 25 January 1919 a proposal to establish a League of Nations, (as the prospective institution was already known), was introduced in the Inter-Allied Conference, as the first phase of the Peace Conference of Paris was called, a resolution to this effect was adopted by the Conference, and a Commission, headed by President Wilson, was created to draft a "constitution" for the new organization.[1] Back of this action lay a rather extensive body of developments, general and special, leading to such a result. The nature of the League as finally created flowed almost as much from these factors as from the formal action taken in the ensuing four months. They may therefore profitably be reviewed here before passing to the drafting of the Covenant.[2]

It is not to be doubted that certain projects for international organization which had been produced from the thirteenth century onward, in both Europe and America, had had some influence in paving the way for the League of Nations.[3] These projects—Sully's *Grand Design,*

---

[1] Miller, Vol. I, pp. 76, 81, and Vol. II, p. 695. On substitution of the term Covenant for Constitution, see same, Vol. II, docs. 28-30.

[2] For an interesting picture of the situation in 1916 see Bourne, as cited below, Appendix B, § 12.

[3] See Wymer and Lloyd, in general, especially pp. 31-81.

William Ladd's *Plan*, and the rest—did not, in their own time, exercise much if any immediate influence on the course of practical politics, but they undoubtedly had a certain effect on the mind of the average individual and even the average statesman. Their cumulative effect certainly counted for something in the establishment of the League of Nations in 1919.

Of much more concrete importance were the so-called international administrative unions of the nineteenth century and the Concert of Europe.[4] Both the former and the latter have already been discussed in some detail above, in their contributions of the non-political and the political sides of international relations respectively they played rather different roles in international relations but both provided important precedents for the League and both extended down into the twentieth century, to the outbreak of World War I, and to the very eve of the League of Nations itself.

The third element consisted of the peace movement in Europe and America (dating from the period of the American and French revolutions), to socialist and labor movements and organizations, and women's groups, coming down to the time of World War I.[5] Neither the pacifists, the socialists, the laborites, nor the women gave much attention to the detailed problems of international organization and procedure; indeed they rather looked down on this sort of thing in contrast to their ideals of peace and human welfare, but they undoubtedly did strengthen the demand for a stable and fruitful international order.

The most powerful and acute impulse in the direction of the establishment of the League of Nations was generated in this country, beginning in the winter of 1914-1915, in the form of a private group calling itself the League to Enforce Peace.[6] It was actually an association to promote the establishment of a League of Nations whose chief function should be that indicated. The organization numbered persons of different political parties among its members, some of them distinguished publicists and former public officials, educators, and so on. They reasoned that, while we had had a great deal of international law and even international adjudication in the past, what we really needed was enforcement machinery and action. Propaganda in favor of such a step was carried on all over the country and, after nearly provoking him into open and explicit opposition, the members of the organization had the pleasure of seeing President Wilson adopt their program in May of 1916, and from that time onward they had only to create as much support as possible for the official American policy.

Drafts of a Covenant began to appear in the Spring and Summer of 1918, first a British, then one or more American, and finally a number

---

[4] Above, pp. 173-178.
[5] Bourne, pp. 249-261, 268-272, and elsewhere.
[6] The story is told best in Bartlett, Chap. II, but see also documents in Marburg.

of French, Italian, and German plans made their appearance before the Peace Conference convened.[7] Of these only the American and British drafts played any large part in the formulation of the Covenant. A combination of the official British draft and the official American draft (President Wilson's latest revision, to be exact), made after the Conference had convened, became the basis of discussion in the Commission created to draft the Covenant, and contributions from other sources were almost negligible, with one important exception, the plan for colonial mandates.

The Covenant was drafted in the ten days between February 3 and February 13 and revised, after the public criticism which followed its publication on February 14, between March 18 and April 11. It was adopted by the Conference on April 28 and was first signed as Part I of the Treaty of Versailles on June 28. It became Part I of other peace treaties signed in 1919-1921 and went into force on January 10, 1920, with the exchange of ratifications of the Treaty of Versailles.[8]

2. NATURE

As thus created the League of Nations was something of a novelty but much more a recapitulation of experience. Some of the more significant aspects of the nature of the League may be noted, in part as a basis for later comparison with the United Nations.

The name of the institution had no great historic precedent; indeed it seems to have had no precedent at all. It was an obvious formula, however, and was coined by the League to Enforce Peace. It was quickly taken up and seemed to reflect the idea widely held concerning the nature of the institution to be created. The French version, Société des Nations, tended to imply greater unity in the organization, while the German version, Völkerbund, retained the English emphasis, combined with a characteristic reference to "peoples." It is entirely probable that the name or names employed to designate the organization influenced the attitudes taken toward the institution by people in different countries.

Similarly the term "Covenant" was used to designate the fundamental instrument of the League in order to rise above the level of a mere treaty but also to remain below the level of a Constitution—which term was actually proposed and rejected. Here, however, the French version, Pacte, remained faithful to the original, even reproducing somewhat the aura of moral piety surrounding Mr. Wilson's English or Scottish term, while the Germans used the same term, Satzung, which they use for any Constitution. Again the psychological and political influence of the choice of words made here is not negligible.

In structure and drafting the Covenant was not too bad, not too good.

[7] Miller, Vol. I, Chap. I and Vol. II, pp. 238, 246, 744.
[8] Miller, Vol. I, pp. 118, 279, 439, 493.

It began (Arts. 1-7) with articles dealing with the membership and organs of the League, went on (Arts. 8-22) to deal with functions and procedure (organization also in Arts. 9, 14, 22), and ended (Arts. 23-26) with miscellany and amendment procedure. It was quite brief and general, leaving much to be worked out (and fought over) in practice, though certain details (the plural form of a word in Art. 14; a particularly —even deliberately—inept term in Art. 19) became matters of great consequence. Bad phraseology occurred here and there, but rarely, and the French and English texts, though equally authoritative under a concluding provision of the Treaty of Versailles, at times failed to correspond (as in Art. 8). It cannot be claimed, however, that the League was seriously hampered in operation by any or all such defects.

In its general character the League of Nations was a loose federal union, with a few traits of unitary power. The States Members of the union created certain common agencies and delegated to them certain powers, for performance of certain functions according to certain procedures. There was no pretense that the authority of any League organ derived from any higher or more unified source. On the other hand, while the League organs dealt in general with Member States in the exercise of their powers, certain League agencies were given power to deal with individuals in the Member States directly; this was done in the Covenant itself (Art. 23) and in many other instruments concluded in respect to League activities in various fields.[9]

By this time it will be apparent that by the phrase "League of Nations" at least three distinct things might be meant. Reference might be meant to the States Members of the League, to the legal obligations (no pun intended) set up among them, or to the organs of the League and their methods and techniques. In actual operation all three of these aspects of the League were important and interacted one upon the other. But it will be most important when we come to analyze the operation of the League, and particularly to appraise its success and failure, to have these three elements distinctly in mind.

Structurally the League consisted of the Member States, an Assembly, a Council, a Secretariat, a number of both temporary and permanent auxiliary organizations more or less organically attached to the League through the Secretariat, a varying number of both temporary and permanent conferences and commissions existing and operating under the Assembly and (or) the Council, the autonomous Permanent Court of International Justice, and the equally autonomous International Labor Organization.[10] In addition a certain number of international organizations outside of the League, some of them created long before 1919 and some under League auspices, were linked to the League in one degree or an-

---

[9] Greaves, pp. 105, 181, 227.

[10] The Court and the Labor Organization are not under consideration further in this chapter unless specifically named.

other.[11] Large numbers of persons were involved in these organs and organizations either as delegates of States or as individuals appointed or employed by the League.

Functionally the League tried to secure two major ends, namely (1) peace and security and (2) social welfare, by procedures and techniques which became fairly well developed and standardized in the course of twenty-five years. To all of these points we shall return more fully later.

3. DEVELOPMENT

The League did not, of course, present the same aspect, or even amount to the same thing, in all of the years of its career. A review of the various phases of League history, its general ups and downs, so to speak, will be helpful in appreciating the problems which that organization had to face and which any similar organization may have to face again.

The years from 1920 to 1929 were years of almost steady growth and increasing effectiveness for the League of Nations.[12] In the first place the mere structure of the organization expanded and developed both externally and internally during this period. The Secretariat grew in size from early beginnings in London, even prior to January 1920, to the maximum size of seven or eight hundred persons, accompanied by corresponding internal evolution and sub-organization, far beyond what the framers of the Covenant had anticipated or what had been indicated in the Covenant.[13] At the same time the non-political activities of the institution—the welfare activities, so to speak—developed enormously. The political activities—in the field of pacific settlement, minority protection, mandates supervision, and armaments—were also set on foot although without the same extensive expansion and with less definitive results. The web of treaty engagements among the Member States relating to all sorts of matters, including pacific settlement of disputes, grew in volume and in detail. It is probably quite accurate to say that the peak of League growth and promise was reached in the year 1929, after the beginning of an attack on international economic problems in 1927, the General Act for Pacific Settlement of International Disputes in 1928, and the completion, in 1929, of preparations for a conference on the codification of international law, not to mention the continued preparations for a disarmament conference.

Unfortunately the threat of reversal had already become apparent and early in 1930 a conference on international economic coöperation felt the first effects of the economic crash which had already begun in the

[11] See study by present writer, "The League of Nations and other International Organizations," in *Geneva Special Studies*, Vol. V, No. 6 (1934).

[12] The only history of the League is that of Knudson, but another is in preparation by Mr. Frank Walters, formerly of the Secretariat.

[13] League Budget for 1930, in *Official Journal*, Vol. 10, No. 10; Myers, p. 46, Note 94.

United States. The Codification Conference at The Hague in March of that year was also a rather spectacular failure. In the following year the Manchurian case broke upon the League and, while the nature of League failure to check Japan in that case was concealed for a time,—by a deliberate abstention from sanctions action to stop Japanese aggression,—the situation was ominous. Again the opening of the Conference on Limitation of Armaments was deceptively promising in 1932 but the success of the National Socialist coup in Germany in January of 1933 was fatal. German withdrawal in 1934 followed Japanese action on the same line, and in 1935 came the Italian aggression in Ethiopia.

In short the record of the League became increasingly bad from 1930 to the outbreak of World War II in 1939, with only isolated items— admission of Russia in 1934, perhaps, and courageous action to expel the same state in 1939 on account of her attack upon Finland—to redeem the general picture. Economy measures taken during—and under cover of—the economic depression maimed the Secretariat and timid measures born of fear of Axis threats in Spain and elsewhere intensified the general defeatist effect. Of course isolated actions in applying sanctions against Italy and providing for suppression of terrorism, not to mention continued constructive action in the non-political field, should not be overlooked, but the fact is that from 1930 to the outbreak of World War II the League cause was going down hill. Belated and timid efforts at League reform in 1936-1938 would perhaps have been encouraging if they had held any real promise of success but unfortunately they did not. The fundamental issues involved in Ethiopia, the Rhineland, Spain, and finally Czechoslovakia and Austria were never effectively dealt with under League auspices, not to mention the attack upon Poland and the outbreak of war itself in 1939.

The period 1939-1946 saw the culmination and inevitable consequences of the preceding period of decline. During the war a good deal of useful work on the non-political side was continued, and should not be entirely forgotten.[14] On the other hand the migration of certain branches of League activity overseas, including the International Labor Organization, the dispersal of the Permanent Court of International Justice upon the occupation of the Netherlands by Germany in 1940, and the severe restriction of such League action as remained in Switzerland, were both more or less disastrous in themselves and also symbolical for the future. As we shall see, the abandonment of the League in 1944-1945 turned upon special political considerations rather than upon any serious calculation of the possibility of utilizing the League as the basis for postwar international organization, but in view of the progressive collapse which dated back for a decade and a half before that time it is not difficult to agree that herculean efforts would have been needed either to

[14] *Report on the Work of the League During the War*, League Document A. 6. 1946.

return to the promising days of 1929 or to remedy the serious defects in League organization and practice which had been evident even then.

B. *Functions; Structure*

I. FUNCTIONS

As already indicated, the functions of the League of Nations were, by the Preamble of the Covenant, related to two objectives, namely the preservation of peace and security and the promotion of social welfare; in the Preamble the second objective is described as "the promotion of international coöperation" but the reference is, in view of the historical background, quite clear. After all, international coöperation was also to be sought for the preservation of peace and security, but this is not what was meant here, and while peace and security also are essential for social welfare they were almost never mentioned in that light. It is also interesting to note that maintenance of peace and security was given first place in this statement of objectives; this was entirely in keeping with the mood of the time and the chief cause for surprise lies in the fact that the framers of the Covenant mentioned coöperation for social welfare at all.

A problem concerning the prospective beneficiaries of the international coöperation mentioned arises here as arises in the general problem of international organization and administration, already discussed.[15] Undoubtedly the framers of the Covenant had in mind the welfare of the individual nations primarily but also that of the international community as such and even the welfare of private individuals. We shall take note of such extension of the field of international service under the League as we proceed.

In order to promote these objectives the League found it necessary, of course, to go into various aspects of human life, individual and collective, known as "subject matter." On this score it is quite simple to summarize the story of the League: the League dealt, first and last, with all sorts of subject matters or all aspects of human life. The framers of the Covenant had no anticipation of such a development, and within five years of its establishment timid delegates were protesting against such expansion on both the political and non-political sides,[16] without, in the sequel, much result. It is also true that excessive caution led to undue delay in developing League activity in the economic sphere, but it is doubtful whether, even if the League had been really active in this sphere from the beginning, as it was not, it could have done anything to prevent the collapse of 1929-1931. In any case it is impossible to attribute much of whatever ineffectiveness and failure must be ascribed to the League to

---

[15] Above, pp. 137-138.
[16] League of Nations, *Official Journal*, Special Supplement 44, p. 47.

either undue expansion or unjustified neglect of any particular subject matter problem or problems. Even the so-called "domestic question," as already defined, amounted to little as a handicap on effective League action, though this is a legal problem rather than one of a subject matter.

In handling the various problems and subjects the various League organs made use of various forms of procedure, various methods or techniques. These were in the main imposed by the character and indeed in part by the very terms of the Covenant and other instruments concluded from time to time, but they also developed in the course of League experience and in view of all the circumstances of the international situation. In any case these forms of procedure were extremely important, indeed they were just about the most crucial element in the whole system.

Investigation, discussion, agreement, and administration constituted the main forms of action taken by or under the League of Nations. A great deal of the first (inquiry, research, analysis) was necessary in view of the novelty of many of the international problems which had to be met; it also constituted a means of compensating for lack of greater authority higher up the scale and a basis for the voluntary coöperation which had to be relied upon in its stead. Discussion occupied a no less prominent place in the activities of the League; the Fascist taunt anent government by palaver (rather than dictation) at Geneva had much foundation. Agreement was necessarily the basis for almost all League law-making in view of the very restricted scope of League powers of legislation by majority vote,[17] although the presence of a limited amount of that element should not be overlooked. Finally the agreements reached had to be carried out, and here League procedure split into two parts; in part agreements were remitted to Member States for administration, with or without League supervision,—as in the case of labor conventions [18] —, and in part they were handed over to League agencies themselves for execution as in conventions for suppression of traffic in dangerous drugs. It was, finally, in this connection that the question of enforcement or sanctions arose [19] and here two or three points must be made very sharply. Enforcement powers were not entirely absent from the League system but they were very limited. They were not restricted entirely to action by Member States, although in the main they were. Much—indeed the vast bulk—of successful League action proceeded without any exercise of such powers; on the other hand the decisive failure of the League in 1936-1939 arose from the lack of effective sanctions power.

It should also be noted that these different types of action were available in differing degrees to different League organs. Inquiry was carried on chiefly in the Secretariat and affiliated organs, largely for the benefit

[17] Riches, *Unanimity*, who, however, emphasizes the growth of opposite trends.

[18] See the extremely interesting study of this problem in general in Berthoud, cited below, Appendix B, § 12.

[19] See Highley, Chaps. I-IV.

of the Assembly and the Council and the Member States, although these latter were somewhat inclined to neglect the results of the vast amount of expert research carried on. Discussion went on principally in the Assembly and Council and other representative bodies but was not entirely absent from various administrative organs such as the Mandates Commission. Agreement was a job for the Member States, and if they could not or would not agree, as happened at times, much of the potential benefit of the preceding operations was lost. Finally if any administration of conventions was to be performed by the League itself this task fell to the Secretariat or some special administrative agency such as the High Commissioner for Danzig; supervision of Member State administration was divided among the Secretariat and special administrative organs, the Assembly, and the Council. If any sanctions were to be applied that supreme action would rest with the Member States except in special cases where such a task had been asigned to the Permanent Central Opium Board or the Saar Valley Constabulary. We shall return to some debatable aspects of this situation later.

2. STRUCTURE

The general structure of the League organization has already been mentioned. Without as yet attempting to appraise fully the value of that institution we may now pass to more extended examination of some of its details.

Thus it should be noted that 61 states became members of the League at one time or another. The maximum membership at any one time was 59. Only 4 states withdrew from membership prior to 1938; only one state (Russia) was ever expelled. The intentions of the framers of the Covenant, namely that all autonomous states and dependencies should become members, failed of achievement mainly in the continued absence of the United States and the absence of Russia for fifteen years; two or three other states entered rather late also. On the other hand, the membership of the League was expanded rather rapidly in its first five or six years and perhaps some "states" were admitted as members which were hardly suited to that role. In the matter of membership the League was far from perfect and there is no question that the difficulties encountered by it in several matters in later years flowed from these defects in large part.

The Assembly was the largest and most impressive single organ of the League (apart from the Secretariat taken as a whole).[20] It consisted potentially of 186 delegates and an undefined number of alternates (sitting in absence of delegates); in view of incomplete delegations and absences it was ordinarily a body of some 100 persons. Among these delegates politicians, diplomats, and administrative officials predominated,

[20] Burton, entire, especially pp. 375-383.

with a few educators, writers or journalists, and laymen in addition. A small number of delegates were women. The Assembly had its own officers and a set of standing committees and commissions, the latter corresponding with the main problems to be considered. On the whole the Assembly commanded a good deal of respect from 1924 onward, its shortcomings being traceable in the main to the limitations of its powers in the Covenant, which it succeeded, indeed, to some extent in overcoming so as to dominate the League scene.

The Council, on the other hand, varied from a theoretical nine persons at the beginning, with the Great Powers in a majority, (actually, because of the absence of the United States the alignment at this time was four to four), to a maximum of fifteen at the end, with several intermediate stages, at none of which were the Great Powers in a majority. In view of the very limited application of the rule of majority and the lack of solidarity among the Great Powers this was not, perhaps, tremendously important, but it is worth remembering for the future. The Council was, of course, in part a policy forming and in part an executive body. It never quite made its position in the League system clear or, perhaps, entirely respected, this in part because of the prominence of the element of power politics evident in its operations. It made little or no use of standing committees, the committees of three, dealing with minority problems, coming nearest to such a result. And in spite of what may well have been the intention of the framers of the Covenant, and in spite of its freedom of action and domineering attitude during the first year or two of the League history, the Council soon rather completely and explicitly subordinated itself to the Assembly. At the end an effort had been inaugurated to divide the Council in two,[21] along the line separating its political from its non-political activities, but this proposed reform also came too late.

It would hardly be justifiable to retrace the structure of the League Secretariat here in any great detail, apart from the fact that this structure passed through more than one reorganization in the course of League history. Through these various changes the main features remained constant: a High Directorate at the top, consisting of the Secretary General, a Deputy Secretary General, and from two to four Under Secretaries General; the considerable body of professional staff, consisting of Directors and Assistant Directors of some ten or twelve Sections, with Members of Sections under them; and a large body of employes of all kinds (clerical, manual, and so on). The total number of persons involved rose to nearly eight hundred in 1930, including nationals of 60 countries, and including many women. The Sections varied greatly in size, according to their work, but this was to be expected. What was more serious was a certain amount of overlapping in functions among the Sections, and a still more serious lack of coördination from above. The Secretary

[21] See the so-called Bruce Report in League Document A. 23. 1939.

General and most of the members of the staff adhered to the orthodox conception of the rôle of the administrator and refrained from any great amount of initiative; this tended to avoid the worst consequences of the lack of vigorous coördination but also provided ground for the charge that the League was ineffective largely for lack of adequate leadership on the part of precisely those individuals best qualified to give it.[22]

The affiliated organizations and congeries of conferences, commissions, and other agencies attached to the Secretariat or operating under the Assembly or Council were somewhat varied in form and in their relationships to the League, not to mention their functions. The larger organizations (Health, Intellectual Coöperation, and others) tended to resemble the League in general structure a good deal, although this was probably traceable mainly to the fact that any political organization must have members and a law-making organ and executive or administrative agencies. The relations between these organizations and the League were even more controversial and in more than one case there was stubborn opposition to any close relationship with the League and movements for severance of such relationship once established. Perhaps nothing more was involved in these cases, or in the numerous other cases where conferences or commissions under the League seemed to suffer from defects of organization or operation, than the chronic difficulties of any administrative system, especially an expanding system, difficulties requiring constant attention and constant reform for their proper adjustment. But the situation was made worse by the fact that not many of the persons concerned knew much about the science and art of public administration, or were willing to approach the situation in any but a highly political and personal manner, and by the opposition of numerous governments to any reforms except such as would result in political advantages for themselves, or, perhaps, just simply to any reforms at all.

It is also permissible and indispensable to add that the difficulties of the various League organs, both political and administrative, can be attributed to failure of Member States, in many cases, to send capable and loyal delegates to meetings, and to the failure of the Secretariat (influenced in part by the Member States) to solve the problems of recruitment, organization and management, and discipline of personnel completely. Of course no political organization ever completely solves these problems but again the two basic weaknesses of League organization and operation were present to cause deep and spreading harm, namely the exceptional and peculiar difficulties of all problems of political organization and administration in the international field, as compared with the national field, and the ignorance, indifference, and even hostility of most diplomats and Continental European or European-

[22] L. Zimmern, Chap. IV.

trained officials toward the body of experience and analysis now available in the fields of political science and public administration.

C. *Appraisal; Liquidation*

1. APPRAISAL

There can, it would seem, exist no doubt concerning the utility of a genuine effort to appraise the success of the League of Nations and discover the reasons therefor. No false scruples over the formation of value judgements in social science and no excessive reluctance to become involved in the old pro-League anti-League controversy should stand in the way. We have, indeed, an almost unique case study in international organization at our disposal here and should derive from it all lessons for the future which it can yield.[23]

It is obviously necessary, above all else, to distinguish between two major fields of League activity before seeking to reach a conclusion concerning the effectiveness of that institution. We may say at once that in the fields of public health, communications and transit, social problems, intellectual coöperation, labor, and even economics and finance, the success of the League was much greater than it was in matters such as the settlement of disputes, armaments, security, and minority protection. As we have seen, it would be inaccurate to describe these two groups of questions simply as non-political and political, respectively, in view of the presence of strong political elements in the first group and also of the existence of solid technical problems in the second. We must remember that there are in reality two levels of treatment of any subject, the policy-making or legislative level and the administrative, but it would also be a mistake to overlook the fact that League action was much more effective even on the policy-making and legislative level in the first group of topics than in the second. Perhaps we may best designate the two groups of problems as the security group and the welfare group, waiving the fact that security is obviously an aspect of welfare; we thus return to the definition of League aims in the Preamble to the Covenant.

Whether the degree of success attained by the League in either field is to be rated high or low obviously depends greatly upon the standard of measurement employed. If we measure League achievement by what could have been desired and was actually hoped for by many people when the League was established the results in both security and welfare clearly fell far short. If we measure even by what was indispensable to order and well-being among the nations the results also fell short in both

[23] Perhaps the most helpful attempt in this direction is to be found in the volume called *World Organization: A Balance Sheet*, published by the Institute on World Organization, in Washington, D. C.; see also works by Davis, Dell, and others cited below, Appendix B, § 12.

fields, although just how far the action taken missed its objective, how close action under League auspices came to saving the peace of the world, will never be known and the margin of failure was probably much narrower than is supposed, in view of the disastrous consequences of that somewhat near miss. In the field of social welfare, moreover, it was only in economic matters that League action fell far short of adequacy, being nearly adequate indeed in many other matters in that sector. Finally it is perfectly plain that if measured by what other international organiza-- tions had accomplished in the past the League performance, even in the security field, rates very high, indeed higher than that of any other international institution, with the exception of a very few highly special and limited agencies.

It is also worth recalling that the success of the League varied somewhat by reference to different periods, as already indicated. Accomplishments in welfare work were small in the years 1920-1924 while many disputes among the nations were settled and other progress made in security matters. Toward the end (1931-1939) the work in welfare matters was at its peak just when League security efforts were collapsing. Above all we must distinguish between different elements of the League system in making this appraisal. Attributing the failure to solve the international problem—particularly the security problem—to "the League of Nations" in general comes perilously close (sometimes more or less intentionally) to inveighing against international organization as such.[24] This will properly lead us into an analysis of reasons for such success or failure as was encountered in the end.

The International Labor Organization may be said to have enjoyed a large measure of success. It did not—rather has not, because it still continues—revolutionized labor conditions throughout the world, but this must be traced in large part to its lack of true legislative power. It did, however, promote much salutary labor legislation in individual states and it accomplished much more than is appreciated in the direction of research and information, and more than is known in adjusting relations between employers and employees.

Similarly the Permanent Court of International Justice was an almost unqualified success in its field. There was no serious criticism of its decisions or opinions. Again the Court was prevented from making its maximum contribution to international peace by the limitations imposed upon its jurisdiction in both the rendering of advisory opinions and judgments. But it is hardly saying too much to assert that the Court was the most clearly successful League organ within the limits set for it.

The Secretariat and affiliated organizations on one hand, like the conferences and administrative agencies functioning under the Council and Assembly, cannot be appraised in general terms. Certain of the latter accomplished little or nothing—such as the Economic Conference in Lon-

[24] Hoover and Gibson, especially Chap. XIII, at pp. 260-261.

don in 1933;—others were quite effective, such as the Permanent Mandates Commission. The Secretariat itself was far from a failure; [25] indeed it ranked near the other end of the scale; its officials and staff did about all that they were asked to do, or even more; they could probably have done more if they had been allowed, although they probably could not have saved the day in view of the stern restraint imposed upon them, and attempts made at times to show that the Secretariat did, could have, or should have, really run the League seem somewhat wide of the mark.[26]

The League Council probably comes off with least credit in this assessment. As a tribunal it was not free from politics; as an administrative agency it was neither impartial nor expert; as a leader in matters of policy it was neither generous nor courageous. This unfortunate situation is not to be traced exclusively to Great Power predominance; as has been seen, the Great Powers never numerically dominated the Council. It is traceable to the assumption, which was made from the beginning, that in the Council the politics of national rivalry should be the dominating note, an assumption never made, in almost identical circumstances, in the Assembly.

The Assembly, indeed, acquired a repute almost exactly the opposite of that of the Council.[27] It had been named first in the Covenant but it had been kept in the background during the whole of the first year of the League, or even its first two years. It had not been given true legislative power nor—explicitly, at least—power over the Secretariat, let alone the Council. Nevertheless by 1924 the Assembly came to dominate the scene. This was not traceable, it seems, merely to the greater number of small states represented in that body, some of whom were more stupid and vicious than any of the Great Powers. It was traceable to the difference between the general atmosphere, method, and technique of the Assembly and the corresponding aspects of the Council, a result of the larger number of states, and particularly states of moderate size and true social outlook—middle class states—represented in the former. In the latter the prevailing pattern of behavior was that of diplomatic negotiation; in the Assembly it was that of inquiry, debate, and agreement, and the moral tone of the Assembly was appreciably higher thereby. On the other hand the Assembly clearly failed to exploit its advantage and develop its powers as fully as it might have. One of the two great tragedies of the League experience lies in the fact that the Assembly just fell short of maximum effectiveness.

The ultimate culprits in the failure of the League were the Member States. It was not the League of Nations but the Nations of the League which failed, in so far as there was failure. The legal obligations, or the legal theory, of the organization was defective on this side, perhaps, but

[25] Raushofen-Wertheimer, Part V.
[26] L. Zimmern, Morley.
[27] Burton, especially p. 382.

this did not preclude action by the members for effective promotion of security and welfare beyond what was required of them; it is probably true that they lived up to their obligations in the main, but they certainly failed to live up to the ideals or the principles or the clear implications of the Covenant. The techniques of the Council and numerous conferences and even of the Secretariat were too "diplomatic," but this was mainly because of the attitude taken by the Governments of the Member States. So for the too frequently biased behavior of not only delegates but also administrative officials. Certainly the League did not fail because of any major defects in its general structure or even defects in the structure of individual organs. For what it is worth the conclusion can be adopted almost without qualification that the League failed—especially in the maintenance of peace and security—because its leading members, France and Great Britain, failed to support it with sufficient vigor in the Manchurian and the Ethiopian cases.

Of course, the absence of the United States may be cited as an important element in the situation, and this is only proper, especially in the Manchurian case, where the notorious unwillingness of this country to back up brave words with brave deeds was rather influential in restraining British action.[28] On the other hand lack of American support certainly cannot be cited as a reason for failure to press sanctions action upon Italy in the Spring of 1936, where the German threat and French and British hesitation based thereon, turned the tide. Finally it was not so much the absence of Russia from the League until 1934 as her presence after that date,—thus giving to anti-Italian and anti-German action a pro-bolshevist tinge which rendered it highly unacceptable in many quarters,—that added further difficulties in this situation.

As a matter of fact the League failed—in so far as it failed—because the peoples of Germany, Italy, and Japan preferred to support their Governments in careers of imperialistic conquest, and because the peoples of England, France, and the United States discouraged their governments from taking effective action early enough to stem the tide of Axis aggression. The peoples and governments of totalitarian states were more responsible for the destruction of international order under League auspices than those of the liberal states, but the latter must bear a large share of negative blame. The people were aided and abetted in this myopic and cowardly course by politicians and journalists more addicted to exploiting dominant psychoses than to exercising intelligent and courageous leadership for general and permanent national welfare. Of course the deleterious influence on League effectiveness of the economic collapse of 1929-1931 was extremely serious at the time, and had much to

---

[28] "As I explained to the British Foreign Minister, its main purpose (that of a proposed joint declaration in favor of observance of the Nine-Power Treaty) was to make clear our faith in and intention to live up to the covenants of the Nine-Power Treaty...." (!); Stimson, pp. 163-164.

do in preparing the way for ultimate Italian Fascist and German Nazi attack on the international order in 1936, but the attack when made had little to do with economic difficulties and the failure of political leadership in League countries had less. But this is to such an extent the common aspect of international relations that we do not need to expand upon it further here.

2. LIQUIDATION

Immediately upon the outbreak of war in 1939 students of international organization in practically all European countries and in many countries in the Western Hemisphere, the Far East, and elsewhere began to study the problems of post-war reorganization. There was something slightly ridiculous, somewhat pathetic, but also decidedly encouraging in the outburst of activity of this type in the Winter of 1939-1940. The failure of the League reform movement, in 1936-1939, and the direction of attention to this general problem by the International Studies Conference (indirectly under the League) meeting in Bergen in 1939, intensified this orientation.

The result was that much more work, and much better work, was done on this problem in 1939-1945 than in the years 1914-1918. The volume of discussion and analysis of post-war problems was enormous in this country.[29] Even after the extension of German domination in the Spring of 1940 a good deal of work was done in numerous European countries, some in Germany and Italy, and this not entirely under Axis control. The persons engaged in these studies included, in contrast to the state of affairs in 1914-1948, many of the most competent and public-spirited citizens of the leading nations. And finally the governments of the leading United Nations countries, again in contrast to the state of affairs in 1914-1948, encouraged this activity and professed a desire to benefit by it. The millennium seemed just around the corner.

The question of what to do with the League of Nations was inescapable.[30] Should it, at one extreme, just be ignored, or, on the other, maintained intact? In between came ideas of formally replacing the League with another body or of utilizing a reformed League as the basis of post-war international organization. The first two extreme solutions were necessarily excluded by the facts: something had to be said and done about the League, for it could certainly not just be carried along without change. As between the second pair of alternatives it was the idea of displacing the League by a new institution which won out. There were several good arguments in favor of perpetuating a reformed League, several against such action. The League existed, it had an established organization and technique (not to mention plant), and vindication of

[29] *Postwar Planning in the United States,* editions of 1943 and 1944, pp. xiv, xvi.
[30] Chapter by present writer in *Problems of the Post-War World,* New York, 1945, "The League, A League, or What?."

the League would be a moral step of great significance; on the other hand the process of reform would necessarily be very complicated and difficult and the aura of failure clinging to the League was very strong. There was perhaps a slight margin of reason in favor of utilizing the League rather than beginning all over again. But the decision was made on grounds of national policy; Russian and American opposition were decisive in the matter. The Russians had been expelled from the League for aggression upon Finland, they had for fifteen years stigmatized the League as a stronghold of capitalist imperialism, and then had participated in some of its activities, and later joined, almost solely for narrow or even exclusive nationalistic reasons, rather than common good,—certainly to an extent not true of other Member States; this is the crucial question regarding national attitudes toward international organization, not simple support for or opposition thereto. In addition the Russians had a long-standing feud with bourgeois Switzerland on both ideological and practical grounds. Finally, President Roosevelt was reluctant to reopen the controversy of 1919-1920 in this country, in spite of altered opinion concerning our participation in international organization. It was on these grounds rather than on the merits of the League that it was decided to set up a new institution in its stead.

The League and its officials had little or nothing to do with the framing of the Charter of the United Nations, and, indeed, were studiously ignored in this connection—in a rather childish manner, it may be suggested, especially at the Dumbarton Oaks stage. On the other hand many individuals who had taken direct part in League activities were at the Conference at San Francisco and probably influenced the framing of the Charter somewhat; of that more later. So for the participation of actual or past League personnel in the practical establishment and subsequent operation of the United Nations: it has increased slowly.

The next step necessary was, of course, the negotiation of one or more agreements for transmission to the United Nations of the assets of the League, and the liquidation of the latter, although this process would necessarily be somewhat prolonged. After the decision to displace the League had been taken, and the difficulties of setting up a new organization in the American scene had been experienced, there was a reaction in favor of the League tradition and at one point the Russians, of all people, seemed to be leading a "back-to-Geneva" movement; this was blocked not so much by official American opposition as by the offer, at a strategic moment, of several million dollars of Rockefeller money to hold the United Nations headquarters in New York. The League certainly appeared more worthy and dignified in its last days than it had in the catastrophes of 1936-1939.

Much more remains to be said, of course, than is said here, in order to explore fully the story of the League of Nations and its contributions to international organization. Whereas friends of the League were inclined in the early years to exaggerate its novelty and its excellence there undoubtedly arose a disposition in the later years of league history to undervalue its capacities and its actual contributions. There is no shadow of doubt that the League of Nations, prior to its liquidation on April 18, 1946, made far greater contributions to the progress of international organization than any other institution in history, while being, in a certain sense and in a certain specific situation, history's most colossal failure and disappointment. The United Nations will do well to equal the record of the League on the credit side; heaven forbid that the new system should result in a collapse as dramatic and disastrous as that of the League—or the League group—in the years 1936-1939; heaven forbid, for that matter, that any international situation should develop which would call for action such as that which the League was called upon to provide in 1936-1939. The situation has changed to such an extent that it is no longer possible to calculate the probable success of the new organization closely on the League precedent. To that new situation and new organization we now turn.

CHAPTER XIII

The United Nations

A. *Origins; Nature; Structure*

If the League of Nations was not to be revived and reformed as the center of future international organization following World War II something obviously had to be prepared to take its place. In 1918 the governments of a few individual states, large and small, had, as we have seen, worked out projects for a League of Nations, not to mention the numerous unofficial projects prepared at the same time.[1] On the other hand there was virtually no international consultation on the subject, incredible as that may seem, prior to the meeting of the Peace Conference of Paris. If this default, which greatly enhanced the difficulties encountered in drafting the Covenant, was not to be repeated something must be done in the way of preliminary consultation. As has already been pointed out, much work on post-war planning has been carried on by unofficial persons and groups from September of 1939 onward, but governmental action was needed also.[2]

This was provided in the Dumbarton Oaks (Washington) Conversations of August 21-October 7, 1944, sponsored by the United States and Great Britain, and including Soviet Russia and China. The results of these Conversations were published on October 9, 1944, under the name of the Dumbarton Oaks Proposals, and constituted an official four-power basis for discussion in the later framing of the United Nations Charter.[3]

The Dumbarton Oaks Conversations, while they supplied a lack keenly felt in 1918-1919, also constituted a case of Great Power politics and domination which could not be mistaken. The Great Powers alone were represented, the United States and Great Britain and Soviet Russia dominating the scene, and China being admitted largely on sufferance. The persons taking part were mainly high-level diplomatic representatives of these Powers rather than technical experts or persons (1) who had been closely identified with previous international institutions or (2) who were possessed of a strong theoretical grasp on the problems at issue;

[1] Above, p. 241.

[2] Above, p. 255. See also H. Reiff, "Transition from League of Nations to United Nations," in *Department of State Bulletin*, Vol. 14, pp. 691, 739.

[3] Text in *American Journal of International Law*, Vol. 39, No. 1 (January, 1945), Supplement, p. 42. For all UN developments see *Chronology* issued periodically by UN Department of Public Information.

THE UNITED NATIONS 259

in any case the experts were kept in a thoroughly innocuous position. Intense secrecy prevailed and the whole affair had the air of a negotiation of competitive national political advantages, as indeed it was, rather than a candid consideration of the wisest lines along which to organize the international community for general welfare. Perhaps this was inevitable and only what could have been expected in war time and in view of the special attitudes taken particularly by the United States and Soviet Russia, but the occasion must be recognized for what it was.

The Dumbarton Oaks Proposals were naturally greeted with widespread and in certain quarters violent criticism.[4] They attempted to turn the hands of the clock back and at several points they were clearly reactionary in comparison with the League of Nations. Great Power domination was greatly intensified and extended. The principle of national sovereignty was proclaimed far more broadly and strongly than it had been in 1919. References to international law and justice were even rarer and vaguer than in the Covenant. The operation of the new system was left very widely to the discretion of the Powers in an alleged effort to escape an alleged legalism in the League, actually in order not to tie the hands of the Powers or engage them too definitely in advance. Little or no reference, however weak, was made to revision of treaties nor to several other matters which were said to be still under consideration.

At other points the Proposals promised to improve upon the League, as in a more effective organization of enforcement,[5] more effective protection for the administrative personnel,[6] specialization in economic and social matters and an improved system of supervision of dependencies,[7] protection of individuals rather than minority groups,[8] and, of course, adhesion by the United States and Russia. Some of these were real improvements; two seem at least debatable; and the last point relates not to the system as such but to external political considerations on the basis of which, as already pointed out, America and Russia refused to accept the League, not on its merits.

Numerous students and friends of international organization demanded the repudiation of the Proposals emanating from the Dumbarton Oaks Proposals as a giant hoax,[9] pointing out all of the objectionable features mentioned and others beside. The disillusionment was immensely greater than it had been when the first draft of the Covenant was published in 1919, although the two points of time or evolution in the process are not strictly comparable. It was obvious, however, that this was in one sense

---

[4] *American Journal of International Law*, Vol. 39 (1945), pp. 95, 97, 101, 103, 295, 318; Summers, R. E., *Dumbarton Oaks;* F. Morley in *Human Events*, Vol. I (1945), p. 128.

[5] *Charter*, Chap. VII.

[6] Art. 100, ¶ 2.

[7] Chaps. IX-XIII.

[8] Arts 55 (c), 62 (2) and (3).

[9] Frey, V., "The Little War before the Last; a 'realistic' appraisal of Dumbarton Oaks," in *New Europe*, Vol. 5, No. 2 (February, 1945), p. 4.

a counsel of despair, for repudiation of the Proposals would have resulted in chaos and probable failure to get anything to take their place for an incalculable space of time. The three dominant figures—Roosevelt, Churchill, and Stalin—were in no mood and in no need to turn back at that time. It was a question of going forward along the lines of the Proposals, revised and improved as much as possible, or risking getting no post-war general international organization at all for an incalculable period.

The criticism of the Dumbarton Oaks Proposals did serve, particularly in the United States, to pave the way for modifications at the United Nations Conference on International Organization which was held at San Francisco from April 25 to June 26, 1945. The United Nations had decided to draft the world constitution without waiting for a peace conference; we are thus given a chance to judge whether keeping such an instrument free from the peace treaties constitutes any great gain or not. The three (perhaps the five) (rather the two) Great Powers were still dominant in the scene but they were now subject to extensive and lively criticism from forty other governments. They were also faced with slightly more independent criticism from their technical advisers (still carefully chosen for their tact though they were). More important still, they were subject to observation and indirect criticism from public opinion in the world at large and in the United States in particular, as a result of representation at San Francisco of the press and of hundreds of private organizations, national and international, devoted to peace and progress, probably the most remarkable manifestation in history of unofficial public opinion influencing official action in the international field. The Powers entered the Conference in somewhat chastened mood; Roosevelt was dead and Churchill tottering; finally a bipartisan delegation had been appointed to represent the United States which, while at certain points it may have done more harm than good, at least helped to moderate any sharp American demands at San Francisco.

The organization which emerged in the United Nations Charter is in general another League of Nations or loose federal union.[10] No unitary world state emerged, as, indeed, it was clear after Dumbarton Oaks would not be the case, and as we have suggested should not be; the UN is another example of that political form of maximum stability and effectiveness, the mixture of federal union and unitary state,—of order and variety, whether the proportions be properly adjusted or not. The doctrine of the sovereign equality of states is flaunted as its basic principle though at numerous points both elements of this idea are flouted in practice; perhaps this is preferable to the practice in the Covenant of keeping discreetly silent about the whole matter, but this seems doubtful. It is further said that membership is to be limited to peace-loving states but subsequent events indicate that here, as in the League, and perhaps

[10] For comparison of Charter and Covenant see Eagleton in *Department of State Bulletin*, Vol. 13, p. 263.

inevitably, membership will be granted or withheld largely on partisan political grounds; on the other hand UN membership rose to 57 states in the first two years of the new organization in comparison with the League maximum at any one moment of 59. The Charter is silent concerning withdrawal and if this silence could be relied upon the union might be regarded as tighter than the League, but a permission to withdraw was professedly given at San Francisco in such general terms as to virtually reverse this.[11] At most points the organs of the UN have only powers of recommendation, but at a number of points they do have powers of decision and command exceeding anything in the League system.[12] Majority voting is accepted for the making of decisions much more widely than in the League, both for the General Assembly and various Councils (Security, Economic and Social, Trusteeship). As promised by the Proposals the UN has, on paper at least, a more powerful system of enforcement and more discretion in its use, as in everything else, checked only by the retention of requirements for unanimity, specifically Great Power consent, at numerous important points. Finally the Charter may be amended somewhat more effectively than the Covenant,[13] again subject to Great Power veto, though there seems to have developed already that typical campaign against reform or revision which contributed so largely to the fatal ruin of the League.

The main organs of the UN, in the order named in the Charter,[14] are the General Assembly, the Security Council, the Economic and Social Council, the Trusteeship Council, the International Court of Justice, and the Secretariat. It is somewhat remarkable to find the Assembly placed at the head of this list in view of the emphasis later placed on the Security Council; one may venture the comment that this was lip service, as far as the Great Powers were concerned, and also that many a true word is spoken in a jest—the experience of the League may well repeat itself here. The subdivision of the League Council into alleged political and non-political organs is, of course, a major change, although it had already been projected in 1939;[15] which of these Councils will outshine the other remains to be seen although from the Charter there could be no doubt about the intentions of the framers. Elevation of the organ dealing with dependencies (the old League Mandates Commission) to the rank of principal organ is striking but the sequel remains to be observed. The frank inclusion of the Court is refreshing and reassuring in contrast to the disingenuous attitude taken on this point in the Covenant and in League practice. On the other hand the omission of the International Labor Organization, an integral part of the League system, relegating it to the ranks of the Specialized Agencies, is interesting although it

[11] Goodrich and Hambro, pp. 86, 104.
[12] Arts. 41, 42, 87 (c), 99.
[13] Arts. 108, 109.
[14] Art. 7 (1).
[15] Above, p. 149.

should be said that this harmonizes entirely with ILO developments in recent years.[16] Finally the placing of the Secretariat at the end of the list, while justified logically by the fact that the latter is not a representative but merely an administrative branch, suggests the comment that this organ is, as in the League, likely to come to count for a great deal more than perhaps one or two of the Councils.

Needless to say, numerous other organs were anticipated by the Charter and in part provided for in so many words. Among these the Military Staff Committee, with possible regional subcommittees,[17] intended to assist the Security Council, and the Regional Security Agencies,[18] also related, if somewhat less intimately, to the Security Council, may be mentioned, although the latter should probably be classified as affiliated agencies rather than UN organs. Commissions to deal with Human Rights, Economic and Employment questions, Transport and Communications, Narcotic Drugs, the Status of Women, and other matters, were created under the Economic and Social Council (indirectly under the General Assembly) very early.[19] An Atomic Energy Commission was created under the Security Council and the Assembly,[20] a Committee on the Progressive Development of International Law and its Codification under the General Assembly.[21] Thus the familiar process repeats itself.

The General Assembly, in principle consisting of five representatives from each Member State, will probably be somewhat larger than the League Assembly, even if, as is also likely, the smaller states do not send full delegations. Its personnel will probably be largely the same in character and quality as that of the League Assembly, with probably, as time passes, a little less of the diplomatic character and somewhat more of that of popular representation, even though still selected by Departments of Foreign Affairs. Finally the General Assembly is staffed by the familiar President and Vice Presidents and even the familiar six standing committees on Political and Security questions; Economic and Financial questions; Social, Humanitarian, and Cultural questions; Trusteeships; Administrative and Budget matters; and legal questions, each Committee consisting of one representative from each Member State attending the General Assembly.

The Security Council, Economic and Social Council, and Trusteeship Council consist respectively of eleven (five permanent—the Great Powers —and six elective), eighteen, and an uncertain number (probably around ten) members chosen in appropriate ways. The Court consists as before of fifteen judges, elected, also as before, by the General Assembly and

[16] International Labor Office, *Future Policy*, cited below, App. B. § 12.
[17] Art. 47 (4).
[18] Chap. VIII.
[19] Dolivet, Chap. V.
[20] See its first two reports: UN docs. AEC/18/Rev./ and AEC/26.
[21] Discussed in *American Journal of International Law*, Vol. 41 (1947), Supplement.

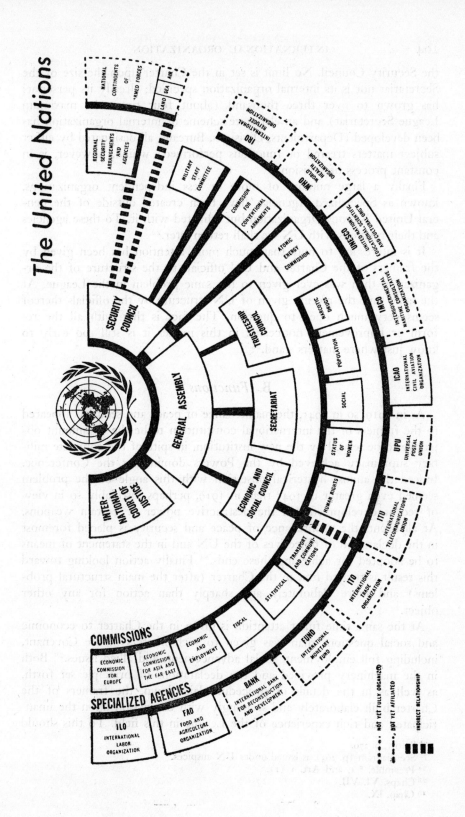

the Security Council. No limit is set in the Charter upon the size of the Secretariat nor is its internal organization specified; already its personnel has grown to over three thousand (about four times the maximum League Secretariat) and an elaborate scheme of internal organization has been developed (Departments, Divisions, Bureaus, all designated by either subject matters treated or functions performed) which, however, is in constant process of revision.

Finally a large number of more or less independent organizations, known as Specialized Agencies, have been created outside of the general United Nations Organization but affiliated with it. To these agencies and their relations with UN we shall return later.[22]

It is interesting to note that much more attention has been given by the framers of the Charter and UN officials to the structure of the organization than was ever given to the same problem in the League. At the same time the picture given of UN structure by the officials thereof seems very much open to question. The fact is that with all the reform or improvement noticeable in this matter it is still too early to know just where matters stand.[23]

B. *Functions*

As in 1919, so in 1945, the maintenance of peace and security appeared to the framers of the international constitution to be the paramount objective to be served by the new institution, in spite of the complete military supremacy achieved by the Powers dominating the Conference. Indeed the almost hysterical obsession with this angle of the problem seemed even greater in 1945 than in 1919, perhaps justifiably so in view of recent developments in the destructive power of certain weapons. At all events the maintenance of peace and security is placed foremost in the declaration of objectives of the UN and in the statement of means to be adopted for achieving these ends.[24] Finally action looking toward this result is treated first in the Charter (after the main structural problems) and more elaborately and sharply than action for any other object.[25]

At the same time fuller attention is given in the Charter to economic and social questions than was given to such matters in the Covenant, including full employment, social advancement, and allied issues.[26] Both in the machinery provided and the declarations of principle set forth, as well as in the details of procedure laid down, the framers of the Charter built elaborately and seemingly with conviction upon the unanticipated and rich experience of the League in this field. To this should

[22] Below, p. 270.
[23] See diagram (p. 263) as issued under UN auspices.
[24] Preamble, ¶ 1, and Art. 1 (1).
[25] Chaps. VI, VII.
[26] Chap. IX.

perhaps be added the expanded provisions for dependency administration under the trusteeship system and the truly radical provisions for international protection of human rights, not to mention international cultural relations, although the first is highly political in character if not the second also.[27] The somewhat anomalous position of the labor question in this elaborate arrangement has already been alluded to.

There would, of course, be no purpose to be served by trying to indicate the so-called "subject-matters" to be dealt with by the UN. Within the broad categories employed in defining the functions of the General Assembly and the Economic and Social Council ("international coöperation in the economic, social, cultural, educational, and health fields [matters]") [28] anything from agriculture to zoölogy could easily be accommodated. This was probably not consciously in the minds of the framers but the result is the same and after that formula no subject is likely to arise which can be excluded as exclusively domestic in character.

The procedures available to organs of the United Nations for treating these problems and these subjects are not, in general, as advanced, in comparison with League procedures, as are some of the structural arrangements and functional definitions in comparison with their prototypes. At one point and one point only do UN procedures register an unmistakable progress.

Thus while some friends of international government hoped and even expected that something like true legislative power would be conferred upon the new organization or its representative assembly, this was not done. It is true that the General Assembly may act by simple majority in most cases and by two-thirds majority in others,[29] but the provisions for Assembly action usually refer to recommendations,[30] elections (of Security Council members for example),[31] or decisions (such as expulsion of Members of the UN) [32] and nowhere is that body authorized to adopt statutes on any aspects of international relations. It is barely possible that the Assembly may succeed in developing such power by usage, in spite of the legal presumption against such power in absence of express authorization, and in spite of the opposition which would inevitably be encountered, at least at first, just as the League Assembly developed a function of preparing and sponsoring multipartite conventions ("international legislation"?) in similar circumstances.[33] On this issue time alone can give a reply.

At this point it may be noted that under United Nations auspices the

[27] Chaps. XI-XIII; Art. 1 (3).
[28] Arts. 13 (1b), 62 (1).
[29] Art 18 (1) and (2).
[30] As in Art. 14.
[31] Art. 23 (1).
[32] Art. 6.
[33] Burton, as cited above, Chap. XII.

effort for codification of existing international law, particularly common international law on basic political or juridical matters derived from practice, and the development of the law, notably by legislation on marginal social matters, explored unsuccessfully under the League of Nations, has been resumed.[34] The problem is a terribly difficult one but cannot be neglected; it is now being approached with full appreciation of its difficulty and with some improvement in methods.[35]

In most phases of administration the powers of the organs of the UN are identical with those of the League—investigation and recommendation, to sum them up in two words. The vast bulk of the activities of the organization are to be carried on by such methods supplemented by the agreement and coöperation of the Members. In this sense the UN is merely a vast enterprise in voluntary international coöperation, although this is not to be taken necessarily as condemnation.

What has just been said applies to the activities of UN organs in relation to Member States. Many activities contemplated by the Charter, notably those to be carried on by the Economic and Social Council and the Specialized Agencies, will apply to individuals in one way or another,[36] thus injecting the unitary element of world government into the system, and here it is possible that administrative action of a more authoritative kind may come to be provided, as can be done in such circumstances with greater success. But in dealing with Member States as such the UN organs possess little real power of dictation or compulsion.

Even in the activities of the Security Council for pacific settlement of disputes that body lacks all power of dictation, and, indeed, lacks much of the power of the League Council in the same situation.[37] This is a special point where avoidance of legalistic regulation in favor of discretionary adjustment was attempted. It is barely possible that history will be reversed and that such a technique will prove adequate for settlement of acute international disputes, but it will indeed be somewhat surprising if this comes true.

The same issue arose, of course, in the revision of the Statute of the Permanent Court of International Justice for use as the basis of the UN Court (International Court of Justice). Again the effort was made, as in 1920, to insert a provision for obligatory submission of cases to the Court, or to allow one state to bring action before the Court against another state so as to require the latter to appear as defendant.[38] Again the most stubbornly independent states refused to accept such an obligation and again resort was had to an optional clause whereby individual states could accept the jurisdiction of the Court as obligatory as between

[34] Above, note 21.
[35] For comment see *American Journal of International Law*, Vol. 41 (1947), pp. 631-634.
[36] Art. 62 (2).
[37] Arts. 34, 36, 37.
[38] *Statute*, Art. 36 (2)-(5).

but which are more tangible and manageable than peace by security police.

This raises the question of what an international organization should accomplish in general. Should it merely canalize and facilitate control of the situation by the dominant Great Powers—with a minimum of violence and injustice? Or should it make or facilitate maximum advances in general international welfare, including freedom from violence, given the existing distribution of power, which may not be very different from the foregoing concept except for the emphasis upon what it is hoped the Great Powers can be led to do? In either case the League and the UN have contained large possibilities, the UN probably greater potentialities than the League, and this whichever of the two statements of the function of such a system is adopted. It seems clear that, the United States and Russia apart, the nations are now ready for a far more advanced system of international organization than either the League or the UN; perhaps even the United States is so ready; perhaps Russia can be led to be. The United States is trying to lead the UN, as the Russians tried to exploit the League, but for a sound international program.

And this raises the final problem of procedure or technique to be contemplated in this context. In order that a system of voluntary coöperation among governments shall operate fruitfully the participants must assume that the members of the international community will seek whatever benefits are to be obtained in common with other members of the community, in, needless to say, increments reasonably proportioned to need, to contributions made, or to some other measure. There can be no effort at monopoly of benefits or power, let alone at the actual elimination of rivals. There must be a generous exchange of concessions and genuine coöperation, there must be full and honest exchange of information and ideas (in other words publicity), there must be free inquiry and discussion, and there must be no abuse of dialectical tactics, such as exaggerated resistance on detailed application after pretending to accept in principle. The parties must be willing to indicate candidly the positions which they are taking and give notice of any change. Decisions must be reached by free agreement and the parties must be loyal to their promises and carry out faithfully any agreements made. Some arrangements must be made for the decision of public issues by less than unanimity, but adequate limits must be set on the power of the majority as well as on individual power. The members must be willing to submit to reasonable supervision and control under law, and in accordance with impartial judicial decisions in case of controversy. No government which, because of emotional fixations or doctrinal dogma, adheres to opposite views and practices, can be a helpful Member. If such discrepancies exist the choice of trying to get on with the program or declaring it impossible is presented. The latter decision would obviously be very serious in the case of the UN, if not necessarily catastrophic. Probably the sound strategy is to make every effort to operate the system while remaining continually and acutely on guard against any deception and any effort to take advantage of the situation to gain ground in the competitive struggle or to gain time advantage.[43] The possibility of winning over the dissident Member or Members to sound attitudes and methods should be exploited fully in the meantime. These alternative lines of action are each difficult in itself and extremely difficult to adjust to one another, but no other course of action seems open. After all, the job of establishing and developing and operating a system of organized international coöperation or of world government is inevitably a complicated and difficult one. It is rendered more difficult today by the circumstances of the present post-war period; it undoubtedly is rendered somewhat more feasible by the perception, widespread among people and governments today, of its necessity.

In this connection it is worth noting that efforts are being made under the UN to build up relations with non-governmental organizations for the cultivation of public opinion favorable to the UN and its program as was never done—indeed, as was egregiously scorned,—under the League. Similarly, an effort is being made, not always sensibly or intelligently, but in the main seriously, to employ properly and effectively the UNESCO for a similar end, in contrast to the inadequate use made under the League of the Institute of Intellectual Coöperation.

C. *Specialized Agencies*

The United Nations was born, in more senses than one, during World War II. In the first place the group of nations which were banded together for defeat of the Axis, or the Triaxis, came into being in 1941-1942, after the United States had been forced into the war by the Japanese attack at Pearl Harbor and subsequent declarations of war by Germany and Italy.[44] There was some question whether this war-time union, formed for waging hostilities, could suitably and satisfactorily be converted into a peacetime organization for normal international coöperation; as we have seen, this end was accomplished through an elaborate process of reorganization so that the question did not finally arise in the simple form. And in the second place a number of special United Nations organizations, now known as the Specialized Agencies, were created from 1943 onward, to supplement the general United Nations Organization. A brief notice of these Agencies in themselves and a consideration of some general aspects of the situation, especially of relations between the special organizations and the general, is now in order.

The recent United Nations Relief and Rehabilitation Administration

---

[43] *American Journal of International Law,* Vol. 40 (1946), p. 304.
[44] Declaration of 1 January 1942: *Department of State Bulletin,* Vol. VI, No. 132 (3 January 1942), p. 3.

(UNRRA) was the first such Agency to be created (November, 1943).[45] It was also intended to aid in the prosecution of the war, by giving relief to populations in United Nations countries suffering from the war, and later to aid in rehabilitation or even post-war reconstruction in these countries. The second element in the program of UNRRA was always somewhat controversial, and the organization suffered from the beginning by being involved, rightly or wrongly, but inevitably, with domestic political quarrels in the United States, by far its largest contributor. The Agency unquestionably did enormous service of a relief character, spending some $3,000,000,000 before its termination in June, 1947, although there was apparently room for some criticism of its internal organization and operation. The relief part of its program was to be taken up by another agency discussed below, and the rehabilitation part by another.

The second Agency to be created was the Food and Agriculture Organization of the United Nations (FAO). An Interim Commission in the same field had been created in May, 1943, by a conference at Hot Springs, Virginia, and the permanent Agency came into being in October, 1945.[46] Its objectives relate mainly to the nutritional needs of the consumer although it inevitably gives considerable attention to the farmer and other producers of food (fisheries). A forestry division carries on the tradition of international action in that field.[47] Its Constitution and methods set the pace quite noticeably for those of other Agencies which followed. It finally replaces the old although never entirely satisfactory or efficient International Institute of Agriculture in Rome.[48]

A mammoth conference was held at Bretton Woods, New Hampshire, in July, 1944, to plan for an International Monetary Fund (IMF) and an International Bank for Reconstruction and Development (IBRD).[49] Constitutions for these institutions were signed and finally went into force in March, 1946. The Fund is intended to promote a stabilization of currencies and international exchange rates and so to promote international trade and employment, the Bank to facilitate reconstruction in war-torn countries and elsewhere by loans against suitable security. Because of their highly special functions these Agencies enjoy also rather highly special organizational and procedural features. Because of their highly dynamic functions likewise they both face opportunities for exercise of great influence and acute controversies in the exercise of this power. The Bank for International Settlements, part of the League System, is replaced by these Agencies, particularly the former.

[45] Agreement of 9 November 1943; same, Vol. IX, No. 222 (25 September 1943), p. 211, and same, No. 229 (13 November 1943), p. 317.

[46] See note in *American Journal of International Law*, Vol. 38 (1944), p. 708. For current developments in all of the Agencies consult the quarterly *International Organization*.

[47] Constitution, Art. 16.

[48] FAO, *Report of the Second Session of the Conference*, 1946, p. 60.

[49] IMF, *Report of Executive Directors*, 1946; IBRD, *Second Annual Report*, 1946-1947.

Likewise in 1944 (1 November) a conference held at Chicago provided for an International Civil Aviation Organization (ICAO) which finally came into being in 1947; a Provisional Organization (PICAO) functioned during the interval.[50] ICAO is to supplant the comparable organization set up in 1919,[51] and another comparable Pan-American agency. PICAO made a great deal of progress in its time and the permanent organization obviously has an extremely important field of operation. The structure of ICAO is not particularly unusual nor its methods of operation. It has, however, been especially troubled by one aspect of the relationship problem which will be mentioned later.

In November, 1946, the United Nations Educational, Scientific, and Cultural Organization (UNESCO) came into being, having been projected by a draft Constitution signed in London one year earlier.[52] UNESCO replaces the International Institute of Intellectual Coöperation of the League system. It is based on the somewhat dangerous ellipsis that "wars begin in the minds of men" but apart from this it obviously has very useful services to perform, in the long run making for peace, perhaps, but in any case enriching the lives of the peoples. Its Constitution and organization and methods are in the nature of things bound to be more elaborate and varied than those of FAO or ICAO, for example. At one point it is very likely to encounter certain difficulties formerly experienced by the International Studies Conference of the International Institute of Intellectual Coöperation, namely at the point where liberty of thought and expression and information are demanded for private scholars, free from state control.[53]

A World Health Organization (WHO) was authorized by the United Nations Economic and Social Council by a resolution adopted on 15 February 1946, and a Constitution was signed on 22 July 1946, in New York.[54] An Interim Commission operated pending the going into effect of the Constitution. WHO replaces both the Health Organization of the League of Nations and the old International Office of Public Health in Paris. The term "World" in its title or name, rather unusual in such cases, is intended to emphasize its world-wide character and relationship to the people of the world.[55]

It was mentioned earlier that the International Labor Organization (ILO) must now be treated as a Specialized Agency, in view of its detachment from the defunct League and failure to incorporate it in any other manner in the UN system. It has, on the other hand, a Constitution

[50] UN *Doc.* E/456 and accompanying report.
[51] Tombs, L. C., *International Organization in European Air Transport*, p. 83; Mance, *Air*, pp. 16, 89.
[52] *Department of State Bulletin*, Vol. XIII, No. 334 (November 18, 1945), p. 802.
[53] UN *Doc.* E/461, pp. 17, 20.
[54] See article by W. R. Sharp in *American Journal of International Law*, Vol. 41 (1947), p. 509.
[55] *Ibid.*, p. 510.

and patterns of behavior of its own [56] and a record of rather successful operation going back to December, 1919. It also has a fuller and more experienced personnel and program than any of the newer Agencies. It is distinctly in a class by itself.[57]

Finally creation of an International Trade Organization (ITO) was authorized by the United Nations Economic and Social Council on 18 February 1946, although it had been planned in 1945 by the United States as a continuation of the Trade Agreements program.[58] A Constitution was drafted in London in October and November, 1946, and revised in New York in January and February, 1947. A conference held in Geneva from April to August of that year put the Draft Charter in form [59] for a United Nations Conference on Trade and Employment in Havana in November where the final text was drafted and signed.

Similarly a Constitution for an International Refugee Organization (IRO) was approved by the United Nations General Assembly on 15 December 1946 and operations were begun in meetings held in Geneva and Lausanne in February-July, 1947.[60] This is the organization intended to take over UNRRA relief work with special reference to refugees and displaced persons.

Several general observations are imposed by the various features of this situation.

In the first place the old question of why such Specialized Agencies should be created instead of conferring the functions to be performed by them upon the general UN arises. Why complicate the system and duplicate general arrangements and expense? There are two major reasons in the minds of those responsible, whether or not the reasons be entirely sound. The general organization and its delegates and officials and personnel could not take on all of these additional activities, or at least not without greatly increasing administrative personnel and the time to be devoted to UN meetings, steps not to be contemplated with confidence. In addition such an expansion of UN in size and power would not be regarded by the Members with entire equanimity. Furthermore it is desired to obtain highly specialized persons for both the representative and the administrative organs of these Agencies and instinct leads naturally under these circumstances to creation of special institutions.

Secondly it is worth noting that these institutions are called Agencies; they are Specialized as to subject-matter, of course, but the implications of the second term may not be so clear. These Agencies are in fact, as the general UN is not, examples of the international administrative

[56] Revised text issued by International Labor Conference, Montreal, 1946.
[57] Above, note 16.
[58] United States, Department of State, *Draft Charter for the International Trade Organization of the United Nations*, 1947, p. 3.
[59] Same, p. 8.
[60] United Nations, *Docs.* Prep/27, 90, 126.

agencies studied earlier,[61] whose chief function is the administrative one, although the conference or representative organs associated with them (or with which they are associated), and the legislative or policy-determining activities of the latter, are not to be disregarded. It will be recalled that the international administrative agencies were the most effective among historical international institutions. It will also be recalled that the technical organizations and administrative branches of the League were its most successful departments. Perhaps history will repeat itself in the UN. Perhaps that explains further the multiplication of these agencies. Such a situation is probably to be expected until the states are willing to confer on general international organizations like the UN powers which they rather freely confer on special organizations, although experience in national government suggests that even then the latter may be the most effective units.

The relationships to be developed between the Specialized Agencies and the UN constitutes a major problem of international statesmanship.[62] As in the case of regional organizations, whatever the value of the special institutions the situation would be difficult and dangerous unless adequate measures for coördination of the various elements could be worked out. This is a problem for searching analysis in principle and for careful application in practice. If the Specialized Agencies are created by the UN suitable coördination should be possible, but if it be a question of coordinating with the UN an Agency created independently the task is more difficult. The resultant position or relationship desired may vary from that of subordination to, and command by, the UN to equalitarian collaboration. Finally whatever relationship is established in principle must be carefully watched lest personnel become unfaithful thereto.

Already difficulties have arisen on more than one of these points. Political decisions concerning membership in UN organs have troubled ICAO; indeed Soviet Russia has repeated, in relation to UN, her performance in relation to the League; while professing great interest in the general organization she has held aloof from the more concrete agencies. The IMF and IBRD have found it extremely difficult to work out satisfactory relations with UN. The ILO is jealous of any control or coördination whatever, and for obvious reasons; the position of the International Court of Justice, another hold-over from League times in reality if not in form, is much more satisfactory although the most significant aspect of this situation lies in the reason for this independence: it is not a legislative or administrative institution but a purely judicial organ.

In detail, and beyond membership, general structure, and policy, problems relating to budgets, personnel, supplies, and similar matters are unescapable. Complete financial freedom or autonomy cannot, probably,

[61] Above, Chap. VIII A.
[62] See references given above, p. 137, note 19.

be granted, but serious interference by UN with any Agency by means of budget control would be very debatable. Uniform rules of recruitment, appointment, tenure, payment, and so on might be practicable but much discretion must be left to Agencies in respect to higher personnel. It might be possible to consolidate purchase of supplies, equipment, and even to arrange joint housing facilities but obviously no rigid position can be taken on such special and concrete issues.[63]

In short we are here at the margin of our problem. The UN is another new experiment in general international organization. It is surrounded by a number of new special institutions which are familiar in general type but nevertheless completely new in their concrete selves. The problem of coördination of international institutions is old but very badly neglected, as we have seen; here is an excellent opportunity for exploring and exploiting its suitable solution.[64]

[63] Calderwood, as cited.

[64] For summary of the second session of the General Assembly (1947) and its achievements, especially creation of a "Little Assembly" or Interim Committee, see *United Nations News*, Vol. II, No. 12 (December, 1947), and official *United Nations Weekly Bulletin*, Vol. III, No. 24, 9 December 1947. For quarterly summaries of UN activities, see *International Organization* (magazine). For severe criticism of UN see F. Morley in *Human Events*, No. 185, Aug. 13, 1947, and for typical reform movement see *The New York Times*, July 10, 1947, p. 6.

CHAPTER XIV

Summary and Conclusions

It seems desirable to glance backward over the treatment of the problems of international organization offered in the preceding pages in order to summarize the principal facts of the situation, the principal inferences to be drawn from those facts, and to note the principal conclusions to be adopted for the present and the immediate future.

The dominant fact to be noted both from such an historical survey of the field as could be offered in a mainly analytical and systematic treatment, as well as from a survey of the present situation in all its ramifications, is that international organization is an institution of long standing rather than a creation of the past thirty years, and a phenomenon of broad scope rather than something confined to any one institution such as the League of Nations or the United Nations. There has been much international organization throughout history, long before the League was created; there is much today outside of the United Nations. The transition from the League to the United Nations and the imminent possibility that the United Nations may soon have to be replaced by something else affords ample confirmation for this observation and for the emphasis placed upon it.

The inference is obvious. More attention should be given by the student of organized international coöperation and control to the basic facts, the history, the fundamental principles, and the general aspects of the subject than to any one institution or to the current details of international politics. Many international institutions exist at any one time and they also come and go constantly and quite frequently. The policies of the powers, largely but by no means exclusively those of the Great Powers, do affect the establishment and operation of international institutions, but it is the long-run policies of the nations which are most important in this connection, not their passing politics, and exaggerating and catering to the latter can only lead to scientific error and practical disaster.

A clever English economist is reported to have quipped, in connection with a plea for attention to long-run phenomena and causal factors in his own field, that in the long run we should all be dead. This is doubtless true, and true of political scientists as well as economists, but it is doubtful whether it justifies the demand for immediate and immediately acceptable solutions of problems of international or world organization. The supposed solutions obtainable are likely to turn out to be no solutions at all. Those who plunge in for this sort of tactic appear simply to lack perspective and perhaps the capacity to endure disappointment and still persist in the effort. The English gentleman in question is himself now dead, the problems which he attacked are still unsolved, but, contrary to his philosophy, it is those who adhered and still adhere to more basic and permanent principles who still have the possibility of solving them.

In the first instance this means that the older institutions of diplomacy and treaty-making, including the consul and good offices and mediation, international conference and the beginnings of international legislation, international administration, both uncontested and that involving adjudication, not to forget the auxiliary devices of inquiry and conciliation, must all be thoroughly studied and developed outside of the limits of any general international organization like the United Nations as well as within such an organization. Specific embodiments of basic forms of international action come and go, but those basic forms have gone on for thousands of years. It is at least doubtful whether the world of nations will discover a permanent general international political institution within the next few years or even decades. The union of states known as the United States has been singularly fortunate (perhaps the good fortune was in large part earned by an unusual exercise of wisdom and generosity, but the result is the same) in going a long way in solving the problems of federalism with only two tries at a constitution, one major civil war and a few amendments. Most federal unions go through many experiments in this development and there is every reason to believe that the world community of states will suffer the same fate. Meantime less general and centralized institutions will have to serve the necessities of the situation.

Finally it is quite clear that in so far as anything of this sort is achieved or even approximated it can only come from profound understanding of the basic principles of federal union as they have been evolved in the experience of the states with alliances, international concert, and the whole interplay of state sovereignty and federal unification, leading to the obsolescence of the former and the evolution of some measure of unitary government. It is of little value, alas, to yearn for a good world, and agitate for drastic steps, and denounce the pedagogic mind—identified here with the pedestrian mind—unless the poetic fire is guided and even tempered by political science. For what is involved here is statecraft, state-building and the operation of state machinery; that the state is to be an international or a world state does not render the need for attention to the teachings of experience any less pressing! Improvisation and compromise to accommodate alleged immediate political necessities cannot safely flout thorough analysis and precedent and example repeated through the long history of international relations. If political delegates feel it necessary to cater to misguided government policies in this context the informed and judicious student can only grieve and bide his time; if his advice is rejected he can at the very least only refuse to agree with folly born of ignorance and short-sightedness and selfishness; certainly he must refrain from aiding and abetting such folly.

On the functional side the main observation to be made would stress the fact that political questions or subjects, and particularly the problem of peace and security, do not by any means constitute the whole problem of organized international coöperation and government. The enormous growth of the League on the erroneously so-called non-political side, when founded by governments acutely preoccupied with the problem of peace and security and the still more pronounced development of the same kind taking place in the United Nations today in face of even more acute preoccupation with the problem of peace, are ample confirmation here if any were needed (as it should not be on the heels of the long history of the matter). Everything possible should be done to solve the problem of peace and war, of course—more so today than ever in view of the catastrophic character of war psychologically and economically as well as physically. But in the meantime all effort available should be devoted to treatment of other international problems both for their own sake and for the contribution which can thereby be made indirectly to the solution of the problem of peace, without, however, indulging in the disingenuous and unsound attempt to justify attention to labor and nutrition and such problems on the ground that they must be solved in the interests of peace. Just how the appropriate division of labor necessary in this connection is to be worked out can hardly be foretold in complete detail but doubtless can be solved empirically or experimentally. All this is necessary, but that which is distinctly necessary, is to dispel the artificial and incredibly unrealistic view that the political security problem can reasonably be allowed to monopolize all attention or complete priority.

Much attention has already been given to the position of international law in this field and it is only necessary here to recall the main outlines of that position. International law does embody much international organization and action although it also deals with numerous aspects of international relations, such as territorial sovereignty, which are only indirectly connected therewith. On the other hand there are numerous aspects of international organization, such as the normal composition of the personnel of an international conference, which, while important and discoverable and susceptible of description, are pure political science and not law. It seems impossible and highly objectionable to identify the two or to interweave them to any great extent or to confuse them— which is the most likely result. International law of all kinds—customary and conventional and statutory—is in desperate need of revision, codification, and development today. In the development of international organization much new international constitutional law must be written.

But it is highly desirable that the different tasks involved in the two fields be carried on with a maximum appreciation of their special characteristics, their special techniques, and their mutual interrelationships at all times.

In conclusion one can only stress again the incontestable importance of this supreme application of political science and art or statecraft, the construction of the world state on federal lines. It is an assignment on which men have labored since national groups first appeared in the morning of human history although only during the past two thousand years has the undertaking been appreciated very fully or explored at all completely. Tremendous pressure for solution of the problem has been generated in the past one hundred years, with greatly increased tempo in the past generation, and tremendous strides forward have been made in the same time. Today, it is probably safe to say, only the rigid dogmas of the Marxian social and political philosophy really stand in the way of revolutionary accomplishment in this direction, due allowance made for chronic nationalism, although one cannot be sure just how far American opinion and sentiment would be willing to go if this obstacle were removed. Just how far it is desirable to go in the direction of world federal organization is itself, of course, a question to be considered carefully as progress is made in that direction. With this outer margin of the problem ever in mind, present possibilities prudently in view, and historical experience in the background, the process of developing international organization marches normally onward.

Documents Illustrating International Organization

1. CONSULAR CONVENTION BETWEEN THE UNITED STATES OF AMERICA AND THE REPUBLIC OF THE PHILIPPINES, 1947 [1]

The President of the United States of America, and the President of the Philippines, being desirous of defining the rights, privileges, exemptions and immunities of consular officers of each country in the territories of the other country, have decided to conclude a convention for that purpose and have appointed as their plenipotentiaries:

The President of the United States of America:

His Excellency Paul V. McNutt, Ambassador of the United States of America, and

The President of the Philippines:

His Excellency Elpidio Quirino, Vice President and concurrently Secretary of Foreign Affairs of the Republic of the Philippines.

Who, having communicated to each other their respective full powers, found to be in good and due form, have agreed on the following Articles:

ARTICLE I

1. The Government of each High Contracting Party shall, in respect of any consular officer duly commissioned by it to exercise consular functions in the territories of the other High Contracting Party, give written notice to the Government of such other High Contracting Party of the appointment of such consular officer and shall request that recognition be accorded to such consular officer. The Government of each High Contracting Party shall furnish free of charge the necessary exequatur of any consular officer of the other High Contracting Party who presents a regular commission signed by the Chief Executive of the appointing country and under its great seal, and shall issue to a subordinate or substitute consular officer who is duly appointed by an accepted superior consular officer or by any other competent officer of his Government, such documents as according to the laws of the respective High Contracting Parties shall be requisite for the exercise by the appointee of the consular function; provided in either case that the person applying for an exequatur or other document is found acceptable.

2. Consular officers of each High Contracting Party shall, after entering upon their duties, enjoy reciprocally in the territories of the other High Contracting Party rights, privileges, exemptions and immunities no less favorable in any respect than the rights, privileges, exemptions and immunities which are enjoyed by consular officers of the same grade of any third country and in conformity with modern international usage. As official agents, such officers shall be entitled to the high consideration of all officials, national, state, provincial or municipal, with whom they have official intercourse in the

[1] Congressional Record, Vol. 93, No. 105 (June 4, 1947), p. 6477; see above, Chap. VI, A1.

territories of the High Contracting Party which receives them. It is understood that the term "consular officers", as used in the present Convention, includes consuls general, consuls and vice consuls who are not honorary.

3. Upon the death, incapacity, or absence of a consular officer having no subordinate consular officer at his post, any secretary, chancellor or assistant, whose official character as an employee in the consulate may previously have been made known to the Government of the High Contracting Party in whose territories the consular function was exercised, may temporarily exercise the consular functions of the deceased or incapacitated or absent consular officer; and while so acting shall enjoy all the rights, privileges, exemptions and immunities that were granted to the consular officer.

4. A consular officer or a diplomatic officer of either High Contracting Party, a national of the country by which he is appointed and duly commissioned or accredited, may, in the territories of the other High Contracting Party, have the rank also of a diplomatic officer or consular officer, as the case may be, it being understood that permission for him to exercise such dual functions shall have been duly granted by the Government of the High Contracting Party in the territories of which he exercises his functions.

ARTICLE II

1. Consular officers, nationals of the High Contracting Party by which they are appointed, and not engaged in any private occupations for gain within the territories of the country in which they exercise their functions, shall be exempt from arrest in such territories except when charged with the commission of an offense designated by local legislation as a crime other than a misdemeanor and subjecting the individual guilty thereof to punishment by imprisonment. Such officers shall be exempt from military billetings, and from service of any military or naval, administrative or police character whatsoever, and the exemptions provided for by this sentence shall apply equally to employees in a consulate who are nationals of the High Contracting Party by which they are employed, and not engaged in any private occupation for gain.

2. In criminal cases the attendance at court by a consular officer as witness may be demanded by the plaintiff, the defense or the court. The demand shall be made with all possible respect for the consular dignity and the duties of the office, and when so made there shall be compliance on the part of the consular officer.

3. In civil cases, consular officers shall be subject to the jurisdiction of the courts in the territories of the High Contracting Party which receives them. When the testimony of a consular officer who is a national of the High Contracting Party which appoints him and who is not engaged in any private occupation for gain is taken in civil cases, it shall be taken orally or in writing at his residence or office and with due regard for his convenience. The officer should, however, voluntarily give his testimony at court whenever it is possible to do so without serious interference with his official duties.

4. Consular officers and employees in a consulate shall not be required to testify in criminal or civil cases, regarding acts performed by them in their official capacity.

ARTICLE III

1. The Government of each High Contracting Party shall have the right to acquire and hold, lease and occupy land and buildings required for diplomatic or consular purposes in the territories of the other High Contracting Party, and shall have the right to erect buildings on land which is held by

or on behalf of such Government in the territories of the other High Contracting Party for diplomatic or consular purposes, subject to local building regulations.

2. No tax of any kind, national, state, provincial or municipal, shall be levied in the territories of either High Contracting Party on the Government of the other High Contracting Party, or on any officer or employee of such other High Contracting Party, in respect of land or buildings acquired, leased, or occupied by such other High Contracting Party and used exclusively for the conduct of official business, except assessments levied for services or local public improvements by which the premises are benefited, provided the right of each High Contracting Party to tax the owner of property leased to the other High Contracting Party is not hereby abridged.

ARTICLE IV

Consular officers and employees in a consulate, nationals of the High Contracting Party by which they are appointed or employed, and not engaged in any private occupation for gain within the territories in which they exercise their functions, shall be exempt from all taxes, national, state, provincial and municipal, levied on their persons or property, except taxes levied on account of the possession or ownership of immovable property situated within the territories in which they exercise their functions or taxes levied on account of income derived from property of any kind situated within such territories. Consular officers and employees in a consulate, nationals of the High Contracting Party by which they are appointed or employed, shall be exempt from the payment of all taxes, national, state, provincial and municipal, on the salaries, allowances, fees or wages received by them in compensation for consular services.

ARTICLE V

1. All furniture, equipment and supplies intended for official use in the consular offices and official consular residences of either High Contracting Party in the territories of the other High Contracting Party shall be permitted entry into such territories free of all duty.

2. Consular officers of either High Contracting Party and members of their families and suites, including employees in a consulate and their families, shall be exempt from the payment of any duty in respect of the entry into the territories of the other High Contracting Party of their baggage and all other personal property, whether preceding or accompanying them to a consular post, either upon first arrival or upon subsequent arrivals, or imported at any time while assigned to or employed at such post.

3. It is understood, however,

(a) that the exemptions provided in paragraph 2 of this Article shall not be extended to consular officers and members of their suites, including employees in a consulate, who are not nationals of the High Contracting Party by which they are appointed or employed, or who are engaged in any private occupation for gain within the territories of the other High Contracting Party;

(b) that in the case of each consignment of articles imported for the personal use of consular officers or members of their families or suites, including employees in a consulate and their families, at any time during their official residence within the territories in which they exercise their functions, a request for entry free of duty shall be made through diplomatic channels; and

(c) that nothing herein shall be construed to permit the entry into the territory of either High Contracting Party of any article the importation of which is specifically prohibited by law.

ARTICLE VI

1. Consular officers of either High Contracting Party may place over the outer door of their respective offices the arms of their country with an appropriate inscription designating the nature of the office, and they may place the coat of arms and fly the flag of their country on automobiles employed by them in the exercise of their consular functions. Such officers may also fly the flag of their country on their offices, including those situated in the capitals of the respective countries. They may likewise fly such flag over any boat, vessel, or aircraft employed in the exercise of their consular functions.

2. The quarters where consular business is conducted, all consular correspondence in transit under official seal, and all papers, records, and correspondence comprising the consular archives shall at all times be inviolable and under no pretext shall any authorities of any character of the country in which such quarters or archives are located invade such premises or make any examination or seizure of papers or other property in such quarters or of such archives. When the consular officers are engaged in business within the territories in which they exercise their functions, the consular files and documents shall be kept in a place entirely separate from the place where private or business papers are kept. Consular offices shall not be used as places of asylum. No consular officer shall be required to produce official archives in court or to testify as to their contents.

ARTICLE VII

1. Consular officers of either High Contracting Party shall have the right, within their respective consular districts, to apply to or address the authorities, national, state, provincial, or municipal, for the purpose of protecting the nationals of the High Contracting Party by which they were appointed in the enjoyment of rights accruing by treaty or otherwise. Complaint may be made for the infraction of those rights. Failure upon the part of the proper authorities to grant redress or to accord protection shall justify interposition through the diplomatic channel, and in the absence of a diplomatic representative, a consul general or the consular officer stationed at the capital shall have the right to apply directly to the Government of the country.

2. Consular officers of either High Contracting Party shall, within their respective districts, have the right to interview, to communicate with, and to advise nationals of their country; to inquire into any incidents which have occurred affecting the interest of such nationals; and to assist such nationals in proceedings before or relations with authorities in the territories of the other High Contracting Party. Consular officers of either High Contracting Party shall be informed immediately whenever nationals of their country are under detention or arrest or in prison or are awaiting trial in their consular districts and they shall, upon notification to the appropriate authorities, be permitted without delay to visit and communicate with any such nationals.

3. Nationals of either High Contracting Party in the territories of the other High Contracting Party shall have the right at all times to communicate with the consular officers of their country. Communications to their consular officers from nationals of either High Contracting Party who are under detention or arrest or in prison or are awaiting trial in the territories of the

other High Contracting Party shall be forwarded without delay to such consular officers by the local authorities.

1. Consular officers in pursuance of the laws of their respective countries shall have the right, within their respective consular districts:

(a) To take and attest the oaths, affirmations or depositions of any occupant of a vessel of their country, or of any national of their country, or of any person having permanent residence within the territories of their country:

(b) To authenticate signatures;

(c) To draw up, attest, certify and authenticate unilateral acts, translations, deeds, testamentary dispositions and contracts of the nationals of the High Contracting Party by which the consular officers are appointed; and

(d) To draw up, attest, certify, and authenticate unilateral acts, deeds, contracts, testamentary dispositions and written instruments of any kind, which are intended to have application, execution and legal effect principally in the territories of the High Contracting Party by which the consular officers are appointed.

2. Instruments and documents thus executed and copies and translations thereof, when duly authenticated by the consular officer, under his official seal, shall be received as evidence in the territories of either High Contracting Party as original documents or authenticated copies, as the case may be, and shall have the same force and effect as if drawn by or executed before a notary or other public officer duly authorized in the territories of the High Contracting Party by which the consular officer was appointed; provided, always, that such documents shall have been drawn and executed in conformity with the laws and regulations of the country where they are designed to take effect.

1. In case of the death of a national of either High Contracting Party in the territories of the other High Contracting Party, without having in the locality of his decease any known heirs or testamentary executors by him appointed, the competent local authorities shall at once inform the nearest consular officer of the High Contracting Party of which the deceased was a national of the fact of his death, in order that necessary information may be forwarded to the persons concerned.

2. In case of the death of a national of either High Contracting Party in the territories of the other High Contracting Party, without will or testament whereby he has appointed a testamentary executor, the consular officer of the High Contracting Party of which the deceased was a national and within whose district the deceased made his home at the time of death, shall, so far as the laws of the country permit and pending the appointment of an administrator and until letters of administration have been granted, be deemed qualified to take charge of the property left by the decedent for the preservation and protection of such property. Such consular officer shall have the right to be appointed as administrator within the discretion of a court or other agency controlling the administration of estates, provided the laws governing administration of the estate so permit.

3. Whenever a consular officer accepts the office of administrator of the estate of a deceased countryman, he subjects himself in that capacity to the jurisdiction of the court or other agency making the appointment for all necessary purposes to the same extent as if he were a national of the High Contracting Party by which he has been received.

ARTICLE X

1. A consular officer of either High Contracting Party shall within his district have the right to appear personally or by authorized representative in all matters concerning the administration and distribution of the estate of a deceased person under the jurisdiction of the local authorities, for all such heirs or legatees in the estate, either minors or adults, as may be non-residents of the country and nationals of the High Contracting Party by which the consular officer was appointed, unless such heirs or legatees have appeared, either in person or by duly authorized representatives.

2. A consular officer of either High Contracting Party shall have the right, on behalf of the non-resident nationals of the High Contracting Party by which he was appointed, to collect and receipt for their distributive shares derived from estates in process of probate or accruing under the provisions of workmen's compensation laws or other like statutes, for transmission through channels prescribed by his Government to the proper distributees, provided that the court or other agency making distribution through him may require him to furnish reasonable evidence of the remission of the funds to the distributees, it being understood that his responsibility with respect to remission of such funds shall cease when such evidence has been furnished by him to and accepted by such court or other agency.

ARTICLE XI

1. A consular officer of either High Contracting Party shall have exclusive jurisdiction over controversies arising out of the internal order of private vessels of his country and shall alone exercise jurisdiction in situations, wherever arising, between officers and crews, pertaining to the enforcement of discipline on board, provided the vessel and the persons charged with wrongdoing shall have entered the territorial waters or territories within his consular district. Consular officers shall also have jurisdiction over issues concerning the adjustment of wages of the crews and the execution of contracts relating to their wages or conditions of employment, provided the local laws so permit.

2. When acts committed on board private vessels of the country by which the consular officer has been appointed and within the territories or the territorial waters of the High Contracting Party by which he has been received, constitute crimes according to the laws of the receiving country, subjecting the persons guilty thereof to punishment by a sentence of death or of imprisonment for a period of at least one year, the consular officer shall not exercise jurisdiction except in so far as he is permitted to do so by the laws of the receiving country.

3. A consular officer shall have the right freely to invoke the assistance of the local police authorities in all matters pertaining to the maintenance of internal order on board vessels of his country within the territories or the territorial waters of the country by which he has been received, and upon such request the requisite assistance shall be given promptly.

4. A consular officer shall have the right to appear with the officers and crews of vessels of his country before the judicial authorities of the country by which he has been received for the purpose of observing proceedings or of rendering assistance as an interpreter or agent.

ARTICLE XII

1. A consular officer of either High Contracting Party shall have the right to inspect within the ports of the other High Contracting Party within his

consular district, the private vessels of any flag destined to and about to clear for the ports of his country, for the sole purpose of observing the sanitary conditions and measures taken on board such vessels, in order that he may be enabled thereby to execute intelligently bills of health and other documents required by the laws of his country, and to inform his Government concerning the extent to which its sanitary regulations have been observed at ports of departure by vessels destined to its ports, with a view to facilitating entry of such vessels.

2. In exercising the right conferred upon them by this Article, consular officers shall act with all possible dispatch and without unnecessary delay.

ARTICLE XIII

1. All proceedings relative to the salvage of vessels of either High Contracting Party wrecked upon the coasts of the other High Contracting Party shall be directed by the consular officer of the country to which the vessel belongs and within whose district the wreck may have occurred, or by some other person authorized for such purpose by the law of such country and whose identity and authority shall be made known to the local authorities by the consular officer.

2. The local authorities of the country where the wreck has occurred shall immediately inform the consular officer, or such other authorized person, of the occurrence. Pending the arrival of the consular officer or such other authorized person, the local authorities shall take all necessary measures for the protection of persons and the preservation of the wrecked property. The local authorities shall intervene only to maintain order, to protect the interests of the salvors, if the salvors do not belong to the crew of the wrecked vessel, and to ensure the execution of the arrangements which shall be made for the entry and exportation of the salvaged merchandise and equipment. It is understood that such merchandise and equipment shall not be subjected to any customs or customhouse charges unless intended for consumption in the country where the wreck has occurred.

3. When the wreck occurs within a port, there shall be observed also those arrangements which may be ordered by the local authorities with a view to avoiding any damage that might otherwise be caused thereby to the port and to other ships.

4. The intervention of the local authorities shall occasion no expense of any kind to the owners or operators of the wrecked vessels, except such expenses as may be caused by the operations of salvage and the preservation of the merchandise and equipment saved, together with expenses that would be incurred under similar circumstances by vessels of the country.

ARTICLE XIV

Honorary consuls or vice consuls of either High Contracting Party, as the case may be, shall enjoy those rights, privileges, exemptions and immunities provided for in Article I, Paragraph 1, Article II, paragraph 1, Articles VI, VII, VIII, IX, X, XI, XII, XIII, and XIV of the present Convention, for which they have received authority in conformity with the laws of the High Contracting Party by which they are appointed; and they shall enjoy in an case all the rights, privileges, exemptions and immunities enjoyed by honorary consular officers of the same rank of any third country.

A consular officer shall cease to discharge his functions (1) by virtue of an official communication from the Government of the High Contracting Party by which appointed addressed to the Government of the High Contracting Party by which he has been received advising that his functions have ceased, or (2) by virtue of a request from the Government of the High Contracting Party by which appointed that an exequatur be issued to a successor, or (3) by withdrawal of the exequatur granted him by the Government of the High Contracting Party in whose territory he has been discharging his duties.

1. The present Convention shall be ratified and the ratification thereof shall be exchanged at Manila. The Convention shall take effect in all its provisions immediately upon the exchange of ratifications and shall continue in force for the term of ten years.

2. If, six months before the expiration of the aforesaid period of ten years, the Government of neither High Contracting Party shall have given notice to the Government of the other High Contracting Party of an intention to terminate the Convention upon the expiration of the aforesaid period of ten years, the Convention shall continue in effect after the aforesaid period and until six months from the date on which the Government of either High Contracting Party shall have notified to the Government of the other High Contracting Party an intention to terminate the Convention.

In faith whereof the above named plenipotentiaries have signed the present Convention and have affixed thereto their seals.

Done in duplicate at Manila, this fourteenth day of March in the year of our Lord one thousand nine hundred and forty-seven and of the Independence of the Republic of the Philippines the first.

For the Government of the United States of America:
[SEAL]   *Paul V. McNutt.*
For the Government of the Republic of the Philippines:
[SEAL]   *E. Quirino.*

2. REGULATIONS OF VIENNA, 1815, AND OF AIX-LA-CHAPELLE, 1818, CONCERNING DIPLOMATIC RANK [1]

In order to prevent in the future the inconveniences which have frequently occurred, and which may still occur, from the claims of Precedence among the different Diplomatic characters, the Plenipotentiaries of the Powers who signed the treaty of Paris have agreed on the following Articles, and think it their duty to invite those of other Crowned Heads to adopt the same regulations:

Diplomatic characters are divided into three classes:
That of Ambassadors, Legates, or Nuncios.
That of Envoys, Ministers, or other persons accredited to Sovereigns.
That of Chargés d'Affaires accredited to Ministers for Foreign Affairs.

---

[1] United States, *Department of State, Diplomatic Instructions,* § 18; see above, Chap. VI, A2.

ARTICLE II

Ambassadors, Legates, or Nuncios only shall have the Representative character.

ARTICLE III

Diplomatic characters charged with any special mission shall not, on that account, assume any superiority of rank.

ARTICLE IV

Diplomatic characters shall rank in their respective classes according to the date of the official notification of their arrival.

The present Regulation shall not occasion any change respecting the Representative of the Pope.

ARTICLE V

There shall be a regular form adopted by each State for the reception of Diplomatic Characters of every class.

ARTICLE VI

Ties of consanguinity or family alliance between Courts confer no rank on their Diplomatic Agents. The same rule also applies to political alliances.

ARTICLE VII

In Acts or Treaties between several Powers that admit alternity, the order which is to be observed in the signatures of Ministers shall be decided by ballot.

ARTICLE VIII

It is agreed between the Five Courts that Ministers Resident accredited to them shall form, with respect to their Precedence, an intermediate class between Ministers of the Second Class and Chargés d'Affaires.

3. UNITED STATES FOREIGN SERVICE AND FOREIGN DIPLOMATIC REPRESENTATIVES AND CONSULAR OFFICERS IN THE UNITED STATES

a. (1) United States Foreign Service; sample posts, 1947 [1]

AUSTRALIA

Canberra, Australia.   Robert Butler, appointed ambassador extraordinary.
                              Llewellyn Vernon Toyne, agricultural attaché, vice
                                  consul.[2]
                              Douglas Jenkins, Jr., second secretary.
                              Martin B. Dale, acting cml. attaché.[3]
                              James M. Gilchrist, Jr., third secretary.

[1] United States, Department of State, *Foreign Service List, January 1, 1947*, pp. 2-3, 19-22, 37-39.
[2] Resident in Sydney.
[3] Assigned also as vice consul at Sydney; resident in Sydney.

(MA & NA).

Brig. Gen. Admund B. Sebree, military attaché.
Capt. Benjamin F. Tompkins, naval attaché and naval attaché for air.
Col. Ralph L. Michaelis, military air attaché.
Col. Jacob S. Sauer, asst. military attaché.
Maj. Seaton F. McDaniel, asst. military attaché.
Comdr. Brendan J. Moynahan, asst. naval attaché and asst. naval attaché for air.

Adelaide, South Australia
(C).
Knowlton V. Hicks, consul.

Brisbane, Queensland (C).
William L. Peck, consul.
C. William Cowles, vice consul.

Melbourne, Victoria (C).
Richard F. Boyce, consul general.
Helen E. Wessels, cultural officer.
Armistead M. Lee, vice consul.
Ralph H. Hunt, vice consul.
Herbert Leggett, vice consul.
E. Eleanor Booth, librarian.
James B. Lindsey, vice consul.
Martin G. Blackmun, consul.

Perth, Western Australia.
(C).
Rudolph W. Hefti, vice consul.

Sydney, New South
Wales (CG).
Orsen N. Nielsen, consul general.
Oville Brown, special representative.
Charles H. Derry, consul.
Robert S. Burlingame, public-affairs officer.
Webster Powell, attaché.
Martin B. Dale, vice consul.[4]
Delano McKelvey, vice consul.
Donald W. Lamm, vice consul.
Rupert Prohme, asst. public-affairs officer.

Sydney, New South
Wales (CG).
Forrest N. Daggett, vice consul.
Lyle C. Himmel, vice consul.
Alexander C. Johnpoll, vice consul.
Elizabeth M. Bond, librarian.
Evelyn M. Schwarztrauber, vice consul; econ. analyst.
Robert C. Arnold, vice consul.[5]
Joanne V. Winn, vice consul.
Eva Bryan Wilson, vice consul.

FRANCE AND POSSESSIONS

Paris (E)

Jefferson Caffery, ambassador extraordinary and pleni-potentiary.
Daniel J. Reagan, counselor of embassy for econ. affairs.
Hugh S. Fullerton, counselor of embassy; consul general.
Douglas H. Schneider, public-affairs officer.
Gerald A. Drew, first secretary; consul.
Walter N. Walmsley, Jr., first secretary; consul.
James C. H. Bonbright, counselor of embassy.
Thomas C. Wasson, first secretary; consul.
Ben Thibodeaux, agricultural attaché.
Charles J. Little, sr. econ. analyst.
Barton P. Jenks, attaché.
George M. Abbott, first secretary; consul.

[4] Assigned also as acting cml. attaché at Canberra.
[5] Resident in Canberra.

Charles H. Ducoté, asst. cml. attaché.
John N. Plakias, attaché.
Howard B. Railey, civil air attaché.[6]
Richard Eldridge, attaché.
Samuel E. Perkins, attaché.
William Edward Share, attaché.
Russell S. McClure, attaché.
Arthur P. Muelberger, sr. econ. analyst.
Manuel Sanchez, publications officer.
George L. Picard, provincial officer.
Turner C. Cameron, Jr., sr. econ. analyst.
Sylvain R. Loupe, communications officer.
Norris B. Chipman, second secretary; consul.
Ivan B. White, second secretary; consul.
Douglas MacArthur, 2d, second secretary; consul.
Elim O'Shaughnessy, second secretary; consul.
Robert M. Taylor, second secretary; consul.
Robert L. Buell, second secretary.
Howard C. Rice, Jr., librarian.
Walter Smith, second secretary; consul.
Jean A. Graffis, information officer.
Leslie Snowden Brady, acting cultural officer.
John R. Wood, vice consul; attaché.
William M. Gibson, sr. econ. analyst.
Ridgway B. Knight, special asst.
John Henry Kelly, econ. analyst.
Norman S. Jacobs, press officer.
Harold Kaplan, asst. information officer.
John H. Tobler, acting press attaché.
Sabin J. Dalferes, vice consul.
Richard E. Funkhouser, asst. petroleum attaché.[7]
Simon J. Copans, radio officer.
Alfred H. Lovell, Jr., second secretary; vice consul.
John G. Hrones, vice consul.
Cyrus B. Follmer, vice consul.
Agnes Schneider, vice consul.
William S. Patten, econ. analyst.
E. Allen Fidel, econ. analyst.
Laurence J. Daymont, vice consul; special disbursing.
  agent.
Perry Hager Culley, admin. officer.
Ernest L. Eslinger, vice consul.
Claude T. Lanier, admin. officer.
Leslie A. Weisenburg, vice consul.
Keeler Faus, third secretary; vice consul.
Florence Palmer, attaché.
Gordon J. Wright, third secretary; vice consul.
Cabot Sedgwick, third secretary; vice consul.
Francis Henry Colombat, third secretary; vice consul.
Adele Dix, vice consul.
Harry H. Bell, third secretary; vice consul.
Richard Sears, Jr., third secretary; vice consul.
John X. Carrier, third secretary; vice consul.
Richard C. Desmond, third secretary; vice consul.
Richard H. Stephens, third secretary; vice consul.
Harry R. Zerbel, third secretary; vice consul.
Leonard R. Morey, vice consul.
Marcelle Henry, press officer.

[6] Assigned also to Luxembourg and Brussels.
[7] Assigned also to Bern, Brussels, and Luxembourg.

Robert J. Moore, vice consul.
Robert M. Schneider, vice consul.
Melville E. Osborne, vice consul.
Edward J. Krause, vice consul.
Donald Bloomingdale, attaché.

(MA & NA).   Brig. Gen. Foster J. Tate, military attaché.
Capt. Roscoe H. Hillenkoetter, naval attaché and naval attaché for air.
Col. Francis B. Valentine, military air attaché.
Col. Thomas W. Hammond, Jr., asst. military attaché.
Col. Robert F. Hyatt, asst. military attaché.
Lt. Col. Paul Birdsall, asst. military attaché.
Maj. E. R. Warner McCabe, Jr., asst. military attaché.
Maj. Thomas W. Sharkey, asst. military attaché.
Maj. John S. Wood, Jr., asst. military attaché.
Capt. Stephen J. Campbell, asst. military attaché.
Capt. Edward H. Germann, asst. military attaché.
Lt. Col. Robert D. Van Auken, asst. military air attaché.
Capt. Francois C. B. Jordan, asst. naval attaché and asst. naval attaché for air.
Lt. Comdr. John G. Williams, asst. naval attaché and asst. naval attaché for air.
Lt. Comdr. Bernard Steele, asst. naval attaché and asst. naval attaché for air.
Lt. Comdr. James C. Longino, asst. naval attaché and asst. attaché for air.
Lt. Paul F. Brine, asst. naval attaché and asst. naval attaché for air.

Bordeaux (C).   Wainwright Abbott, consul general.
Elmer S. Dorsay, public-affairs officer.
Frank Cussans, vice consul.
Donald S. King, vice consul.
Walter W. Wiley, vice consul.
Julia Louise Wooster, vice consul.

Cherbourg (C).   George D. Whittinghill, vice consul.

Le Havre (C).   James E. Parks, consul.
Reinhard W. Lamprecht, vice consul.
Arthur Potter Allen, vice consul.

Lyon (C).   Russell M. Brooks, consul.
Robert M. Sheehan, vice consul.
Joseph J. Montllor, vice consul.

Marseille (C).   Hervé J. L'Heureux, consul general.
George E. Rehm, public-affairs officer.
Boies C. Hart, Jr., consul.
William H. Christensen, consul.
Edward S. Parker, vice consul.
Thomas D. Bowie, vice consul.
Walter M. Walsh, vice consul.
Leonard G. Bradford, vice consul.
William H. Friedman, vice consul.

Nice (C).   Hartwell Johnson, consul.[8]
Sheldon B. Vance, vice consul.[8]
Charles B. Beylard, vice consul.[8]

Strasbourg (C).   Richard W. Byrd, consul.
Edwin D. Crowley, vice consul.

Algiers, Algeria (CG).   Harold D. Finley, consul general.
Roland K. Beyer, vice consul.

[8] Assigned also to Monaco.

John T. Black, public-affairs officer.
Joseph F. Walker, vice consul.
Howard Brandon, vice consul.
Harrison L. Dick, vice consul.
John H. Randolph, vice consul.
Jack C. Spinx, vice consul.

Dakar, French West Africa (CG).
Hasell H. Dick, consul general.
Robert Grinnell, consul.
Hubert H. Buzbee, Jr., vice consul.
William S. Krason, vice consul.

Hanoï French Indochina (C).
James L. O'Sullivan, vice consul.
Edwin C. Rendall, vice consul.

Martinique, French West Indies (C).
Frederick D. Hunt, vice consul.
Angelo D. Valenza, vice consul.

Nouméa, New Caledonia (C).
Robert L. Brown, vice consul.
Charles S. Reed, 2d, consul.

Saigon, French Indochina (CG).
Joseph A. Robinson, public-affairs officer.
Charles T. Caddock, public-affairs officer.
Albert W. Stoffel, vice consul.
Richard J. Coughlin, vice consul.
Jeanne R. Skewes, public-affairs asst.

Tahiti, Society Islands, Oceania (C).
Scudder Mersman, vice consul.
Robert F. Fernald, consul general.

Tananarive, Madagascar (C).
George Gregg Fuller, consul general.
Jerome R. Lavallee, vice consul.

Tunis, Tunisia (CG).
Donald A. Dumont, vice consul.
L. Pittman Springs, vice consul.
Thomas T. Turner, vice consul.

GERMANY

Berlin (Office of the United States Political Adviser on German Affairs).[9]
Robert D. Murphy, United States political adviser.[10]
Donald R. Heath, counselor of mission.
Loyd V. Steere, counselor of mission.
Edward J. Kerrigan, director of European relay bases.
Marshall M. Vance, counselor of mission; consul general.
Warren M. Chase, Foreign Service officer.
William P. Cochran, Jr., Foreign Service officer.
Francis Deak, civil air attaché.[11]
Jacob D. Beam, Foreign Service officer.
Horace H. Smith, Foreign Service officer.
Gerald A. Mokma, consul.
William Bruce Lockling, attaché.
Thomas J. B. Wenner, attaché.

MEXICO

México, D. F. (E).
Walter Thurston, ambassador extraordinary and plenipotentiary.
Raymond H. Geist, counselor of embassy.
Merwin L. Bohan, counselor of embassy for econ. affairs.
S. Walter Washington, first secretary; consul.
Maurice L. Stafford, consul general; first secretary.
Jacob Barnard Gibbs, agricultural attaché.

[9] This office performs consular functions.
[10] With the personal rank of ambassador.
[11] Assigned also to Belgrade, Bern, Bucharest, Budapest, Praha, Sofia, and Vienna; resident in Bern.

R. Horton Henry, first secretary; consul.
Dorsey Gassaway Fisher, first secretary; consul.
Lew B. Clark, cml. attaché.
Morrill Cody, cultural officer.
William A. Conkright, sr. econ. analyst.
Alfred M. Barlow, attaché.
Charles B. Parker, sr. econ. analyst.
Forrest K. Geerken, second secretary; consul.
William F. Busser, second secretary; vice consul.
Walter J. Linthicum, second secretary; consul.
Douglas Flood, second secretary; consul.
Dixon Donnelley, press officer.
Horace Harper Braun, econ. analyst.
Minedee McLean, second secretary; vice consul.
Marvin A. Derrick, admin. officer.
J. Paxton Haddow, asst. information officer.
James C. Powell, Jr., vice consul.
Don Stoops, asst. agricultural attaché.
Albert E. Pappano, third secretary; vice consul.
Juan de Zengotita, third secretary; vice consul.
Scott Lyon, third secretary; vice consul.
John Wallace Hill, admin. asst.
Frederick R. Mangold, econ. analyst.
Philip D. Sumner, vice consul.
Robert L. Hunter, vice consul.
W. John Wilson, Jr., vice consul.
William L. Brewster, third secretary; vice consul.
Dwight Dickinson, third secretary; vice consul.
John N. Smith, third secretary; vice consul.
Raymond Bastianello, vice consul..
Frederick D. Sharp, 3d, third secretary; vice consul.
Armando E. Vargas, vice consul.
Richard M. Hughes, third secretary; vice consul.
Ana M. Gomez, jr. econ. analyst.
Hugh Veltman, vice consul.
Taylor G. Belcher, vice consul.
Mildred A. Johnson, vice consul.
Robert L. Shields, vice consul.

(MA & NA).

Brig. Gen. James W. Spry, military attaché and military air attaché.
Capt. Albert E. Jarrell, naval attaché and naval attaché for air.
Lt. Col. Thomas J. Riggs, Jr., asst. military attaché.
Lt. Col. Maurice C. Holden, asst. military attaché.
Lt. Col. Joseph G. Duncan, asst. military attaché.
Capt. Edward J. Walsh, Jr., asst. military air attaché.
Lt. Comdr. William A. Savin, asst. naval attaché and asst. naval attaché for air.
Lt. Comdr. Leslie E. Geer, asst. naval attaché and asst. naval attaché for air.

Agua Prieta, Sonora (C).

William Clarke Vyse, consul.
Chester H. Kimrey, vice consul.

Chihuahua, Chihuahua (C).

H. Claremont Moses, vice consul.
Charley L. Rice, vice consul.

Ciudad Juárez, Chihuahua (C).

Stephen E. Aguirre, consul.
Edward S. Benet, vice consul.
Harry K. Pangburn, vice consul.
J. D. Lambeth, vice consul.
Lionel S. Mordecai, vice consul.
William A. Campbell, vice consul.

Guadalajara, Jalisco (C).	James E. Henderson, consul.
	Henry T. Unverzagt, vice consul.
	Walter E. Kneeland, vice consul.
Guaymas, Sonora (C).	Edward C. Webster, Jr., vice consul.
Matamoros, Tamaulipas (C).	Cyril L. F. Thiel, consul.
	Givon M. Parsons, vice consul.
Mazatlán, Sinaloa (C).	Arthur V. Metcalfe, vice consul.
Mérida, Yucatán (C).	Stephen C. Worster, vice consul.
Mexicali, Baja California (C).	William A. Smale, consul.
	Howard L. Walker, Jr., vice consul.
Monterrey, Nuevo León (C).	James P. Moffitt, consul general.
	Myron H. Schraud, vice consul.
	Douglas Henderson, vice consul.
	Anthony E. Starcevic, vice consul.
	William A. Carsey, vice consul.
Nogales, Sonora (C).	Ben Zweig, vice consul.
	Antonio Certosimo, vice consul.
	Frank C. Niccoll, vice consul.
Nuevo Laredo, Tamaulipas (C).	V. Harwood Blocker, vice consul.
	Gerald G. Jones, vice consul.
	Abraham Vigil, vice consul.
Piedras Negras, Coahuila (C).	Earl Wilbert Eaton, vice consul.
	Harold C. Wood, vice consul.
Reynosa, Tamaulipas (C).	Henry G. Krausse, vice consul.
	Weston A. Hall, vice consul.
San Luis Potosí, San Luis Potosí (C).	F. Ridgway Lineaweaver, consul.
	Elias G. Garza, vice consul.
Tampico, Tamaulipas (C).	Harold B. Quarton, consul general.
	Samuel A. McIlhenny, Jr., vice consul.
Tijuana, Baja California (C).	Francis C. Jordan, consul.
	Willys A. Myers, vice consul.
	Francis M. Withey, vice consul.
	Leonard E. Thompson, vice consul.
Torreón, Coahuila (C).	Stanley G. Slavens, consul.
	John G. Oliver, vice consul.
Veracruz, Veracruz (C).	Ilo C. Funk, consul.
	Ernesto S. Guaderrama, vice consul.

a. (2) Description of Consular Districts [1]

AUSTRALIA

Adelaide, South Australia
   The State of South Australia and the Northern Territory.

Brisbane, Queensland
   The State of Queensland.

Melbourne, Victoria
   The State of Victoria, and Tasmania.

Perth, Western Australia
   The State of Western Australia.

Sydney, New South Wales
   The State of New South Wales; the Territories of the Commonwealth (the Federal Capital Territory, the Territory of Papua, the Territory of Norfolk Island, and the Mandated Territory of New Guinea); the Mandated Territory of Nauru; and the New Hebrides.

   [1] *Foreign Service List,* as cited, pp. 61, 63-64, 68-70.

FRANCE AND POSSESSIONS

Bordeaux
   The Departments of Ariège, Basses-Pyrénées, Charente, Charente-Inférieure, Corrèze, Creuse, Deux Sèvres, Dordogne, Gers, Gironde, Haute-Garonne, Haute-Vienne, Hautes-Pyrénées, Landes, Lot, Lot-et-Garonne, Tarn-et-Garonne, Vendée, and Vienne.

Cherbourg
   The Departments of Calvados, Côtes-du-Nord, Finistère, Ille-et-Vilaine, Manche, Mayenne, Morbihan, and Orne.

Le Havre
   The Departments of Eure, Nord, Pas de Calais, Sein-Inférieure, and Somme.

Lyon
   The Departments of Ain, Allier, Cantal, Côte-d'Or, Haute-Loire, Haute-Savoie, Isère, Jura, Loire, Puy-de-Dôme, Rhône, Saône-et-Loire, and Savoie.

Marseille
   The Departments of Ardèche, Aude, Aveyron, Bouches-du-Rhône, Drôme, Gard, Hérault, Lozère, Pyrénées-Orientales, Tarn, Var, Vaucluse, and the island of Corsica (Corse).

Nice
   The Departments of Basses-Alpes, Hautes-Alpes, Alpes-Maritimes, and the Principality of Monaco.

Paris
   The Departments of Aisne, Aube, Cher, Eure-et-Loire, Indre, Indre-et-Loire, Loir-et-Cher, Loiret, Loire Inférieure, Main-et-Loire, Marne, Nièvre, Oise, Sarthe, Seine, Seine-et-Marne, Seine-et-Oise, Yonne, and in Africa, French Equatorial Africa (comprising Chad, Gabon, Ubangi-Shari, and Middle Congo), and Cameroons (French Mandate).

Strasbourg
   The Departments of Ardennes, Bas-Rhin, Doubs, Haute-Marne, Haut-Rhin, Haute-Saône, Meurthe-et-Moselle, Meuse, Moselle, Vosges, and the Territory of Belfort.

Algiers, Algeria
   All of Algeria (including the Territories of the South).

Dakar, French West Africa
   All of French West Africa (including the Colonies Dahomey, French Sudan, French Guinea, Ivory Coast, Mauritania, Niger, and Senegal, and the Circumscription of Dakar), and Togoland (French mandate).

Hanoï, French Indochina
   The State of Tonkin, the State of Annam which includes the Provinces of Quang Tri, Quang Bing, Ha Tinh, Ngaean, and Thanh Hoa, and in the State of Laos the Provinces of Savannakat, Kham Mon, Vientiane, Tran Ninh, Luang Prabang, Huz Panh, Haut Mekong, and Muong Hou.

Martinique, French West Indies
   All of French West Indies and French Guiana.

Nouméa, New Caledonia
   All of New Caledonia and dependencies (including the Wallis Archipelago, the Loyalty Islands, the Huon Islands, Futuna, and Alofi).

Saigon, French Indochina
The States of Cambodia, Cochinchina, in the State of Annam the Provinces of Binh Thuan, Khanh Hoa, Kon Toum, Binh Dinh, Quang Ngai, Quang Nam, and Thua Thien, and in the State of Laos the Provinces of Khong, Bassac, Attopeu, and Saravanne.

Tahiti, Society Islands
The Society Islands, Austral Islands, Marquesas Islands, the Tuamotu Archipelago, and the Gambier Islands.

Tananarive, Madagascar
The island of Madagascar (together with the Comoro Islands, the Glorious Islands, and the islands of Nossi Bé and Ste. Marie, and Kerguelen, Crozet, St. Paul, Amsterdam, and other island dependencies of Madagascar) and Réunion Island.

Tunis, Tunisia
All of Tunisia.

MEXICO

Agua Prieta, Sonora
That part of the State of Sonora bounded on the west and south by a line drawn from the international boundary at 110° west longitude, due south to the Naco-Cananea railway, thence along that railway to Cananea (the railway and Cananea included), thence in the following directions which are true, south to the latitude of Mututicachi, east to the meridian of 110° west longitude, south to the parallel of 29° north latitude, and east to the Sonora-Chihuahua boundary.

Chihuahua, Chihuahua
That portion of the State of Chihuahua lying to the south and east of a line drawn from the Sonora boundary through Madera to Sauz (both towns included); thence northeastwardly through, and excluding, San Antonio on the Río Grande.

Ciudad Juárez, Chihuahua
That part of the State of Chihuahua lying to the north of a line drawn through Madera to Sauz (both towns excluded); thence northeastwardly through, and including, San Antonio on the Río Grande.

Guadalajara, Jalisco
The part of the State of Zacatecas lying to the south of latitude 22°, all of the State of Jalisco except that portion lying north of 22° north latitude and east of the meridian of 103°30′ west longitude, and the State of Colima.

Guaymas, Sonora
That part of the State of Sonora lying south of latitude 29°, and the southern territory of Baja California (south of latitude 28°).

Matamoros, Tamaulipas
That part of the State of Tamaulipas lying north of latitude 24° north, except the portion that lies west and northwest of a line drawn from a point at latitude 24° north, longitude 99° west of Greenwich, due north to the boundary of Nuevo León, and except the portion that lies north and northwest of a line drawn from the international boundary at 97°40′ west longitude in a southwesterly direction to El Chapul (excluded) and thence to Laguna de Indios (in the State of Nuevo León).

Mazatlán, Sinaloa

The States of Sinaloa and Nayarit, and that part of the State of Durango lying west of a line drawn from the point on the Zacatecas-Durango boundary where it is intercepted by the Tropic of Cancer, thence drawn due west to the meridian of 105° west longitude, thence to St. Gregorio (excluded) and to Guanacevi (excluded) and thence due northwest to the Durango-Chihuahua boundary.

Mérida, Yucatán

The States of Campeche and Yucatán and the territory of Quintana Roo.

Mexicali, Baja California

That part of Baja California north and east of a line drawn from the intersection of the international boundary and the meridian of 116° west longitude due south to the parallel of 32° north latitude, and thence to a point on the west shore of the Gulf of California at latitude 30° north; also that part of the State of Sonora lying west of 113° west longitude.

México, D. F.

The States of Querétaro, Hidalgo, Pueblo, Tlaxcala, Morelos, México, Michoacán, Guerrero, and the Federal District; and that part of the State of Oaxaca west of a line drawn from the point common to the boundaries of the States of Oaxaca, Veracruz, and Pueblo, in a southeasterly direction to a point at 96° west longitude and 17° north latitude, and thence due south to the Pacific Ocean.

Monterrey, Nuevo León

The State of Nuevo León, except the portion that lies north and northwest of a line drawn across the State through Golondrinas and Parás, leaving Golondrinas within, and Parás without, the Monterrey consular district, and except that part of the State that lies to the northeast of a line drawn from El Chapul (in the State of Tamaulipas) westwardly to Laguna de Indios and to China (both excluded), thence to Agualeguas (included), and thence to Ciudad Mier (in the State of Tamaulipas); that part of the State of Tamaulipas lying west and northwest of a line drawn from a point at latitude 24° north, longitude 99° west of Greenwich, due north to the Nuevo León boundary; that part of the State of Coahuila bounded on the north, west, and south, by a line drawn from the Nuevo León boundary westwardly through a point just south of Monclova to but excluding Cuatro Ciénegas, thence southwardly to and including Parras, thence southeastwardly to a point on the Zacatecas boundary, just west of Lavaderos, and thence along the Zacatecas boundary to the point common to Coahuila, Nuevo León, and Zacatecas; and that part of the State of Zacatecas that lies east of a north-south line drawn through and including Mazapil.

Nogales, Sonora

That part of the State of Sonora bounded on the east, south, and west by a line drawn from the international boundary at 110° west longitude, due south to the Naco-Cananea railway, thence along that railway to Cananea (the railway and Cananea excluded), thence in the following directions which are true, south to the latitude of Mututicachi, east to the meridian of 110° west longitude, south to the parallel of 29° north latitude, west to the meridian of 113° west longitude, and thence north to the international boundary.

Nuevo Laredo, Tamaulipas

That part of the State of Tamaulipas that lies north and northwest of a line drawn from the international boundary through Ciudad Mier (excluded) to

Agualeguas (in the State of Nuevo León); and that part of the State of Nuevo León lying north and northwest of a line drawn across the State, through Golondrinas (excluded) and Parás (included).

Piedras Negras, Coahuila
That part of the State of Coahuila lying north and east of a line drawn from the Chihuahua boundary, each along the parallel of 28° north latitude to a point directly north of Tanque (included), thence southeasterly to La Reforma (excluded) and to Cuatro Ciénegas (included), and thence by a straight line through a point just south of Monclova to the Nuevo León boundary.

Reynosa, Tamaulipas
That part of the State of Tamaulipas bounded on the east by a line drawn from the international boundary at 97°40' west longitude in a southwesterly direction to El Chapul (included) and thence to Laguna de Indios (in the State of Nuevo León), and bounded on the west by a line drawn from the international boundary through Ciudad Mier (included) to Agualeguas (in the State of Nuevo León); and that part of the State of Nuevo León lying to the northeast of a line drawn from El Chapul (in the State of Tamaulipas) westwardly to Laguna de Indios and to China (both included), thence to Agualeguas (excluded), and from Agualeguas to Ciudad Mier (in the State of Tamaulipas).

San Luis Potosí, San Luis Potosí
The State of San Luis Potosí, except that portion lying to the east of a line drawn due north and south through, but excluding, the town of Tamazopo (approximately in longitude 99°25' west of Greenwich); the States of Aguascalientes and Guanajuato, that part of the State of Zacatecas lying to the south of the Tropic of Cancer, and to the north of the parallel of 22° north latitude, and that part of the State of Jalisco lying to the north of latitude 22° but east of the meridian of 103°30' west longitude.

Tampico, Tamaulipas
That part of the State of Tamaulipas lying south of latitude 24°; that part of the State of Veracruz lying northwestward of the Río Cazones; and that part of the State of San Luis Potosí lying to the east of a line drawn north and south through, and including, the town of Tamazopo (approximately in longitude 99°25' west of Greenwich).

Tijuana, Baja California
That part of Baja California north of latitude 28° and south and west of a line drawn from the intersection of the international boundary and the meridian of 116° west longitude due south to the parallel of 32° north latitude, and thence to a point on the west shore of the Gulf of California at latitude 30° north.

Torreón, Coahuila
Those parts of the States of Coahuila, Durango, and Zacatecas lying within the following boundaries: The parallel of 28° north latitude from the Chihuahua boundary east to a point directly north of Tanque (excluded); thence southeasterly to La Reforma (included) and to Cuatro Ciénegas (excluded); thence southwardly to Parras (excluded); thence southeastwardly to a point on the Zacatecas boundary, just west of Lavaderos, and thence along the Zacatecas boundary to a point directly north of Mazapil, Zacatecas; thence directly south on a line through Mazapil (excluded) to the Zacatecas-San Luis Potosí boundary; thence southwestwardly on the Zacatecas-San Luis Potosí boundary to the Tropic of Cancer; thence due west on the Tropic of

Cancer to the Zacatecas-Durango boundary and continuing due west along the Tropic of Cancer in the State of Durango to the meridian of 105° west longitude; thence to St. Gregorio (included) and to Guanacevi (included) and thence due northwest to the Durango-Chihuahua boundary; thence following the Chihuahua-Durango boundary to the point where they touch the Coahuila boundary; thence north along the Chihuahua-Cuahuila boundary to latitude 28°.

Veracruz, Veracruz

The State of Veracruz, except the part lying northwestward of the Río Cazones; the States of Chiapas and Tabasco; and that part of the State of Oaxaca eastward of a line drawn from the point common to the boundaries of the States of Oaxaca, Veracruz, and Puebla, in a southeasterly direction to a point at 96° west longitude and 17° north latitude, and thence due south to the Pacific Ocean.

b. **Foreign Diplomatic Representatives in the United States,**
sample posts, 1947 [1]

HONDURAS
EMBASSY OF HONDURAS

Credentials presented by the Ambassador
May 4, 1943

Señor Dr. Don Julián R. Cáceres, Ambassador E. and P., 4715 Sixteenth Street (telephone, Georgia 5855).[2]
Señora de Cáceres.
Captain Juan Da Costa, Military Attaché, 1433 Decatur Street (telephone, Georgia 7333).
Office of Embassy, 4715 Sixteenth Street (telephone, Georgia 9318).

FRANCE
EMBASSY OF THE FRENCH REPUBLIC

Credentials presented by the Ambassador
January 1, 1945

Mr. Henri Bonnet, Ambassador E. and P., 2221 Kalorama Road (telephone, Dupont 2666).
Madame Bonnet.
General Maurice Mathenet, Military Attaché, 3750 Fordham Road (telephone, Woodley 7985).
Madame Mathenet.
Mr. Francis Lacoste, E.E. and M.P., 2815 Woodland Drive (telephone, Adams 3721).
Madame Lacoste.
Mr. Armand Berard, E.E. and M.P., 18 Grafton Street, Chevy Chase, Maryland (telephone, Oliver 0025).
Madame Berard.
Mr. Raymond Dreux, Commercial Counselor, 3010 Cleveland Avenue (telephone, Michigan 8265).
Madame Dreux.
Captain Pierre Lancelot, Naval Attaché, 1825 Q Street (telephone, Michigan 3092).

---

[1] United States, Department of State, *Diplomatic List, May, 1947*, pp. 20, 27-30, 120-121, 137.
[2] E.E. and M.P. from July 18, 1939 to May 4, 1943.

Colonel William Breyton, Air Attaché, 3512 Albermarle Street (telephone, Emerson 3151).
Madame Breyton.
Mr. Christian Valensi, Financial Counselor, 2819 Twenty-ninth Street (telephone, Columbia 3037).
Madame Valensi.
Colonel Albert J. P. Le Bel, Assistant Military Attaché, 1654 Thirty-fourth Street (telephone, Columbia 5822).
Madame Le Bel. Absent.
Mr. Raymond Treuil, Commercial Counselor.
Madame Treuil.
Mr. Pierre Siraud, Counselor, 1061 C Thirty-first Street (telephone, North 7753).
Mr. Arnauld Wapler, Counselor, 28 East Bradley Lane, Chevy Chase, Maryland (telephone, Wisconsin 8410).
Madame Wapler.
Mr. François Charles-Roux, Counselor, 3009 Thirty-fourth Street (telephone, Woodley 8871).
Madame Charles-Roux.
Mr. Claude Levi-Strauss, Counselor.
Madame Levi-Strauss.
Mr. Jean Baube, Counselor, 2311 Connecticut Avenue (telephone, North 1874).
Madame Baube.
Lieutenant Colonel Raymond J. Cann, Assistant Military Attaché, 3218 Nineteenth Street (telephone, Adams 6445).
Madame Cann.
Commander Gilbert Monier, Assistant Naval Attaché, 4130 Garrison Street (telephone, Emerson 7023).
Madame Monier.
Lieutenant Colonel Albert Ladousse, Assistant Air Attaché, 1614 Crittenden Street (telephone, Randolph 8867).
Madame Ladousse.
Mr. Ernest Castan, Commercial Attaché, 4805 Sedgwick Street (telephone, Emerson 6887).
Mr. Jean Pierre Benard, First Secretary, 1606 Twentieth Street (telephone, Hobart 2846).
Madame Benard.
Mr. Marcel Flory, First Secretary, 1606 Twentieth Street (telephone, Hobart 2846).
Madame Flory.
Lieutenant Pierre Rouliot, Assistant Naval Attaché, 2311 Connecticut Avenue (telephone, Hobart 2047).
Madame Rouliot.
Mr. Pierre Dupont, Second Secretary, 2535 Belmont Road (telephone, Adams 0990).
Madame Dupont.
Mr. Jean-Claude Winckler, Second Secretary, 3601 Poeter Street (telephone, Ordway 2830).
Madame Winckler.
Mr. Henri Claudel, Attaché, 119 East Woodbine Street, Chevy Chase, Maryland (telephone, Oliver 1475).
Madame Claudel.
Mr. Pierre Basdevant, Attaché, 3724 Jocelyn Street (telephone, Ordway 1920).
Mr. Jean Beliard, Attaché, 2407 Fifteenth Street (telephone, Adams 5592).
Office of the Naval Attaché, 1759 R Street (telephone, Decatur 8300).
Office of the Military Attaché, 1759 R Street (telephone, Decatur 8300).
Office of the Air Attaché, 1759 R Street (telephone, Decatur 8300).
Office of the Commercial Counselor, 2129 Wyoming Avenue (telephone, Decatur 8400).
Office of the Financial Counselor, 1822 Massachusetts Avenue (telephone, Decatur 8300).
Office of Embassy, 2535 Belmont Road (telephone, Adams 0990).

LEGATION OF SWITZERLAND

Credentials presented by the Minister
October 10, 1939

Mr. Charles Bruggmann, E.E. and M.P., 2920 Cathedral Avenue (telephone, Hobart 4247).
Madame Bruggmann.
Mr. Max Grässli, Counselor, 3218 Woodley Road (telephone, Ordway 0260).
Madame Grässli.
Lieutenant Colonel Max Waibel, G.S.C., Military and Air Attaché, 3215 Cathedral Avenue (telephone, Hobart 1815).
Madame Waibel.
Mr. Werner Fuchss, Commercial Counselor, 115 Albermarle Street, Westmoreland Hills, Maryland (telephone, Oliver 7494).
Madame Fuchss.
Mr. Emile Bisang, Counselor, 4607 Connecticut Avenue (telephone, Woodley 4868).
Mr. Eric Kessler, Counselor, 3202 Cleveland Avenue (telephone, Emerson 2939).
Madame Kessler.
Mr. André Boissier, First Secretary, 2442 Massachusetts Avenue (telephone, Hobart 7969).
Madame Boissier.
Mr. Ernst Schneeberger, First Secretary, 5415 Nevada Avenue (telephone, Emerson 4794).
Madame Schneeberger.
Mr. Guy de Keller, Second Secretary, 4 Carvell Circle, Westmoreland Hills, Maryland (telephone, Oliver 0614).
Madame de Keller.
Captain Henri Morier, Assistant Military and Air Attaché, 3125 Cathedral Avenue (telephone, Emerson 9582).
Mr. Paul R. Jolles, Attaché, 2800 Woodley Road (telephone, Adams 3012).
Mr. Jürg Niehans, Attaché, 2737 Cathedral Avenue (telephone, Adams 1137).
Office of Military and Air Attaché, 3215 Cathedral Avenue, Annex (telephone, Hobart 1815).
Office of Legation, 2900 Cathedral Avenue (telephone, Hobart 1815).

ETHIOPIA
LEGATION OF ETHIOPIA

Credentials presented by the Minister
May 15, 1946

Ras H. S. Imru, E.E. and M.P., 2134 Kalorama Road.
Madame Imru.
Miss Ruth Imru.
Miss Judith Imru.
Mr. Gatahoun Tesemma, First Secretary.
Mr. Petros Sahlou, Second Secretary.
Office of Legation, 2134 Kalorama Road (telephones, Adams 2281 and 2282).

c. Foreign Consular Officers in the United States, sample posts, 1947 [1]

BRAZIL

California.	Los Angeles	Affonzo Barbosa de Almeida Portugal, consul.
		Vinicius de Moraes, vice consul.
	San Francisco.	José Cochrane de Alencar, consul general.

[1] United States, Department of State, *Foreign Consular Offices in the United States, April 1, 1947,* pp. 4-5, 16-20, 43.

Heraldo Pacheco de Oliveiro, consul.
Joao Baptista Pinheiro, consul.
Roberto Barthel Rosa, vice consul.
Carlos Fernandes, vice consul (honorary).
>For Arizona, California, Idaho, Montana, Nevada, Oregon, Utah, Washington, and Wyoming.
>For Alaska, the Territory of Hawaii, and the Philippine Islands.

Canal Zone.	Panamá, Panamá.	Paulo Germano Hasslocher, consul general.
Florida.	Miami.	Alfredo Polzin, consul general.

Miguel Alvaro Osorio de Almeida, consul.
Armindo Branco Mendes Cadaxa, vice consul.
>For Florida and Georgia.

Georgia.	Savannah.	Henrique Oswaldo de Miranda, honorary vice consul.
Illinois.	Chicago.	Nelson Tabajara de Oliveira, consul.

Victor Ricardo Parr de Araujo, vice consul.
>For Illinois, Indiana, Iowa, Kansas, Michigan, Minnesota, Missouri, Nebraska, North Dakota, South Dakota, and Wisconsin.

Louisiana.	New Orleans.	Fernando Nilo de Alvarenga, consul.

Adolpho Justo Bezerra de Menezes, vice consul.
>For Alabama, Arkansas, Louisiana, Mississippi, and Tennessee.
>For United States possessions in the Caribbean Sea.

Maryland.	Baltimore.	Armando Fleury de Barros, honorary consul.

Pablo Alegre, honorary vice consul.
>For Delaware and Maryland.

Massachusetts.	Boston.	Jayme Azevedo Rodrigues, consul.

Lauro Escorel Rodrigues de Moraes, vice consul.

New York.	New York City.	Walder Lima Saramanho, consul general.

Sotero Cosme, consul.
Zilah Mafra Peixoto, consul.
João Augusto de Araujo Castro, consul.
Carlos Federico Duarte Goncalves da Rocha, vice consul.
Lauro Muller Netto, vice consul.
>For Connecticut, Maine, Massachusetts, New Hampshire, New York, Rhode Island, and Vermont.

Pennsylvania.	Philadelphia.	Pedro de Alcantara Nabuco de Abreu, Jr., consul.

Paulo de Oliveira Versiani Cunha, vice consul.
>For Delaware, Maryland, New Jersey, Ohio and Pennsylvania.
>For the District of Columbia.

South Carolina.	Charleston.	A. Beauregard Betancourt, vice consul (honorary).

William Porter Cart, acting vice consul (honorary).

Texas.	Dallas.	J. Kirby McDonough, honorary consul.

Charles Stewart Barry, Jr., honorary vice consul.
Harold M. Young, vice consul (honorary).

	Houston.	Edison Ramos Nogueira, consul.

>For Kansas, New Mexico, Oklahoma, and Texas.

	Port Arthur.	José Maria Delamare Garcia, honorary consul.

Waldemar Paula Ramos Ortiz, vice consul (honorary).

Lawrence McCurley, consular agent (honorary).

| Virginia. | Norfolk. | Pedro Eugenio Soares, consul. |

For North Carolina, South Carolina, Virginia, and West Virginia.

| Washington. | Seattle. | Robert C. Bullwinkel, vice consul (honorary). |

Ross Whitfield Sutherland, consular agent (honorary).

GREAT BRITAIN

| Alabama. | Mobile. | John Ritchie Macpherson, vice consul (honorary). |
| California. | Los Angeles. | John Eric Maclean Carvell, consul general. |

George Wellington Irving, vice consul.

Donovan Harold Clibborn, vice consul.

Thomas McDonald, vice consul.

George Alexander Anderson, vice consul.

For the counties of Imperial, Kern, Los Angeles, Orange, Riverside, San Bernardino, San Diego, San Luis Obispo, Santa Barbara, and Ventura.

For Arizona.

| | San Francisco. | Cyril Hubert Cane, consul general. |

Ayrton John Seaton Pullan, consul.

Walter Hollis Adams, vice consul.

Ernest William Owen, vice consul.

David Laurence Mears, vice consul.

For California (except the counties included in the jurisdiction of the consulate at Los Angeles) and Nevada.

| Canal Zone. | Panamá, Panama. | John Dee Greenway, consul general. |

William Kingsley Smith, consul.

Stephen Patrick House, vice consul.

For the Canal Zone.

| Colorado. | Denver. | Herbert Stanley Marchant, consul. |

Cyril Ward, vice consul.

For Colorado, Utah, and Wyoming.

| District of Columbia. | Washington. | Gavin Robert Rankin, consul. |

Frank George Waters, vice consul.

For the District of Columbia.

| Florida. | Jacksonville. | Francis Joseph White, vice consul. |
| | Miami. | John Campbell Thomson, consul. |

Lewis Arthur Oates, vice consul (honorary).

For Florida East of Apalachicola River.

| | Tampa. | Henry Russell Henshaw, vice consul. |
| Georgia. | Atlanta. | Morgan Charles Garnet Man, consul. |

Tom Bolton, vice consul.

For Georgia and South Carolina.

For Tennessee east of the Tennessee River.

| Hawaii, Territory of. | Honolulu. | John Chevalier O'Dwyer, consul. |

Harry Lewis Dawson, vice consul.

For the Territory of Hawaii.

| Illinois. | Chicago. | Wilfred Hansford Gallienne, consul general. |

Kenneth Bumstead, consul.

John Roland Kay, vice consul.

Walter Henry Williams, vice consul.

Herbert Thomas James Crean, acting vice consul.

For the Illinois counties of Adams, Boone, Brown, Bureau, Calhoun, Carroll, Cass, Champaign, Christian, Clark, Coles, Cook, Cumberland, De Kalb, De Witt, Douglas, Du Page, Edgar, Ford, Fulton, Greene, Grundy, Hancock, Henderson, Henry, Iroquois, Jersey, Jo Daviess, Kane, Kankakee, Kendall, Knox, Lake, La Salle, Lee, Livingston, Logan, Macon, Macoupin, Marshall, Mason, McDonough, McHenry, McLean, Menard, Mercer, Montgomery, Morgan, Moultrie, Ogle, Peoria, Piatt, Pike, Putnam, Rock Island, Sangamon, Schuyler, Scott, Shelby, Stark, Stephenson, Tazewell, Vermilion, Warren, Whiteside, Will, Winnebago, and Woodford.

For the Wisconsin counties of Columbia, Crawford, Dane, Dodge, Grant, Green, Iowa, Jefferson, Kenosha, Lafayette, Milwaukee, Ozaukee, Racine, Richland, Rock, Sauk, Vernon, Walworth, Washington, and Waukesha.

For Iowa and Indiana.

Louisiana.   New Orleans. Albert Spencer Calvert, consul general.

Brian Godden, vice consul.

For Alabama, Louisiana, Mississippi, and Tennessee except that part east of the Tennessee River.

For Florida west of the Apalachicola River.

Maryland.   Baltimore. Harold Braham, consul.

Joseph Todd Mulvenny, vice consul.

James Telfer Hyslop, vice consul.

For the West Virginia counties of Barbour, Berkeley, Brooke, Grant, Hampshire, Hancock, Hardy, Jefferson, Marion, Marshall, Mineral, Monongalia, Morgan, Ohio, Pendleton, Pocahontas, Preston, Randolph, Taylor, Tucker, Webster, and Wetzel.

For Maryland, North Carolina, and Virginia.

Massachusetts.   Boston. Bernard P. Sullivan, consul general.

William John Parkyns, vice consul.

For Maine, Massachusetts, New Hampshire, Rhode Island, and Vermont.

Michigan.   Detroit. Daniel Francis Horseman Brickell, consul general.

Leslie Hammersley Williams, vice consul.

For the Ohio counties of Allen, Ashland, Ashtabula, Auglaize, Belmont, Carroll, Champaign, Clark, Columbiana, Coshocton, Crawford, Cuyahoga, Darke, Defiance, Delaware, Erie, Fairfield, Fayette, Franklin, Fulton, Geauga, Greene, Guernsey, Hancock, Hardin, Harrison, Henry, Hocking, Holmes, Huron, Jefferson, Knox, Lake, Licking, Logan, Lorain, Lucas, Madison, Mahoning, Marion, Medina, Mercer, Miami, Monroe, Montgomery, Morgan, Morrow, Muskingum, Noble, Ottawa, Paulding, Perry, Pickaway, Portage, Preble, Putnam, Richland, Sandusky, Seneca, Shelby, Stark, Summit, Trumbull, Tuscarawas, Union, Van Wert, Wayne, Williams, Wood, and Wyandot.

For the southern peninsula of Michigan.

Minnesota.	St. Paul and Minneapolis.	——, consul. Dennis Willoughby Day Heathcote, acting vice consul. For the Wisconsin counties of Adams, Ashland, Barron, Bayfield, Brown, Buffalo, Burnett, Calumet, Chippewa, Clark, Door, Douglas, Dunn, Eau Claire, Florence, Fond Du Lac, Forest, Green Lake, Iron, Jackson, Juneau, Kewaunee, La Crosse, Langlade, Lincoln, Manitowoc, Marathon, Marinette, Marquette, Monroe, Oconto, Oneida, Outagamie, Pepin, Pierce, Polk, Portage, Price, Rusk, Saint Croix, Sawyer, Shawano, Sheboygan, Taylor, Trempealeau, Vilas, Washburn, Waupaca, Waushara, Winnebago, and Wood. For Minnesota, North Dakota, South Dakota, and the upper peninsula of Michigan.
Missouri.	Kansas City.	James Humphrey Cotton Minchin, consul. Sydney Mittens, acting vice consul. For Kansas, Nebraska, Oklahoma, and Kansas City (Missouri).
	St. Louis.	Alfred Stanley Fordham, consul. William Milne Guthrie, vice consul. For the Illinois counties of Alexander, Bond, Clay, Clinton, Crawford, Edwards, Effingham, Fayette, Franklin, Gallatin, Hamilton, Hardin, Jackson, Jasper, Jefferson, Johnson, Lawrence, Madison, Marion, Massac, Monroe, Perry, Pope, Pulaski, Randolph, Richland, St. Clair, Saline, Union, Wabash, Washington, Wayne, White, and Williamson. For Arkansas, for that part of Kentucky and Tennessee west of the Tennessee River, and Missouri except Kansas City (Missouri).
New York.	Buffalo. New York City.	Angus Somerville Fletcher, consul. Francis Edward Evans, consul general. Randle Reid-Adam, consul. Ronald Sinclair, consul. Douglas John Brett Robey, consul. Dennis William Hennessy, vice consul. Joseph Stanton Goodreds, vice consul. Gawin Wild, vice consul. Peter Mennell, vice consul. Walter Frederick James, acting vice consul. John Oliver Wright, acting vice consul. Dudley Francis Preece Williams, acting vice consul. Nigel Oliver Willoughby Steward, deputy consul general. For Connecticut, New Jersey (except the counties of Atlantic, Burlington, Camden, Cape May, Cumberland, Gloucester, Ocean, and Salem), and New York.
Ohio.	Cincinnati.	Gerald Fraser Tyrrell, consul. Peter Gordon McDonald, vice consul. For the Ohio counties of Adams, Athens, Brown, Butler, Clermont, Clinton, Galia, Hamilton, Highland, Jackson, Lawrence, Meigs, Pike, Ross, Scioto, Vinton, Warren, and Washington.

For the West Virginia counties of Boone, Braxton, Cabell, Calhoun, Clay, Doddridge, Fayette, Gilmer, Greenbrier, Harrison, Jackson, Kanawha, Lewis, Lincoln, Logan, Mason, McDowell, Mercer, Mingo, Monroe, Nicholas, Pleasants, Putnam, Raleigh, Ritchie, Roane, Summers, Tyler, Upshur, Wayne, Wirt, Wood, and Wyoming.

For that part of Kentucky west of the Tennessee River.

	Cleveland.	Edward James Hobbs, acting consul.
Oregon.	Portland.	James McDonald, consul.
		Humphrey Campbell Dickson Neilson, vice consul.
Pacific Ocean.	(Tonga).	Charles Walter Trevor Johnson, consul.

For the islands under United States possession in the Pacific Ocean south of the Equator.

Pennsylvania.	Philadelphia.	Hugh Charles McClelland, consul general.
		Theodore Harold Fox, vice consul.
		Peter Joseph Nolan, vice consul.

For the New Jersey counties of Atlantic, Burlington, Camden, Cape May, Cumberland, Gloucester, Ocean, and Salem.

For Delaware and Pennsylvania.

	Pittsburgh.	———, consul.
		Alexander McQuaker Galbraith, acting consul (honorary).
Puerto Rico.	San Juan.	Arthur Henry Noble, consul (honorary).
		Edward Henry Osborne Thorne, vice consul.

For Puerto Rico.

Texas.	Dallas.	Lewis Bernays, consul general.
	Galveston.	Stewart Hunter Evans, vice consul (honorary).
	Houston.	Eric Arthur Cleugh, consul general.
		Leslie Bland Dufton, vice consul.
		Charles Mortimer Cree, vice consul.

For New Mexico and Texas.

Virgin Islands.	Frederiksted.	Miles Merwin, vice consul.
	Charlotte Amalie.	———, consul.
		Henry Leopold O'Neal, acting vice consul.

For the islands of St. Croix and St. Thomas.

Virginia.	Norfolk.	James Guthrie, consul.
		Andrew Ian Pye, vice consul.
Washington.	Seattle.	George Edgar Vaughan, consul.
		Herbert Raymond Guyler White, vice consul.

For Idaho, Montana, Oregon and Washington.

For Alaska.

UNION OF SOVIET SOCIALIST REPUBLICS

California.	Los Angeles.	Evgeni Pavlovich Tumantzef, vice consul.

For the counties of Imperial, Los Angeles, Orange, Riverside, San Bernardino, San Diego, Santa Barbara, and Ventura.

	San Francisco.	Konstantin Alekseevich Efremov, consul general.
		Victor Vassilievich Afanasiev, vice consul.

For Arizona, California, Colorado, Idaho, Montana, Nevada, New Mexico, Oregon, Utah, Washington, and Wyoming.

For the Territory of Hawaii.

| New York. | New York City. | Yakov Mironovich Lomakin, consul general. Mikhail Ivanovich Fedosimov, vice consul. Mikhail Ivanovich Sorokin, vice consul. For Connecticut, Delaware, Illinois, Indiana, Iowa, Kansas, Maine, Massachusetts. Michigan, Minnesota, Missouri, Nebraska, New Hampshire, New Jersey, New York, North Dakota, Ohio, Pennsylvania, Rhode Island, South Dakota, Vermont, and Wisconsin. |

4. TREATY BETWEEN THE UNITED STATES AND MEXICO CONCERNING THE UTILIZATION OF THE WATERS OF CERTAIN RIVERS, 1944 [1]

The Government of the United States of America and the Government of the United Mexican States: animated by the sincere spirit of cordiality and friendly cooperation which happily governs the relations between them; taking into account the fact that Articles VI and VII of the Treaty of Peace, Friendship and Limits between the United States of America and the United Mexican States signed at Guadalupe Hidalgo on February 2, 1848,[2] and Article IV of the boundary treaty between the two countries signed at the City of Mexico December 30, 1853 [3] regulate the use of the waters of the Rio Grande (Rio Bravo) and the Colorado River for purposes of navigation only; considering that the utilization of these waters for other purposes is desirable in the interest of both countries, and desiring, moreover, to fix and delimit the rights of the two countries with respect to the waters of the Colorado and Tijuana Rivers, and of the Rio Grande (Rio Bravo) from Fort Quitman, Texas, United States of America, to the Gulf of Mexico, in order to obtain the most complete and satisfactory utilization thereof, have resolved to conclude a treaty and for this purpose have named as their plenipotentiaries:

The President of the United States of America:

Cordell Hull, Secretary of State of the United States of America, George S. Messersmith, Ambassador Extraordinary and Plenipotentiary of the United States of America in Mexico, and Lawrence M. Lawson, United States Commissioner, International Boundary Commission, United States and Mexico; and

The President of the United Mexican States:

Francisco Castillo Nájera, Ambassador Extraordinary and Plenipotentiary of the United Mexican States in Washington, and Rafael Fernández Mac-Gregor, Mexican Commissioner, International Boundary Commission, United States and Mexico; who, having communicated to each other their respective Full Powers and having found them in good and due form, have agreed upon the following:

I. PRELIMINARY PROVISIONS

ARTICLE I

For the purposes of this Treaty it shall be understood that:

a "The United States" means the United States of America.

b "Mexico" means the United Mexican States.

[1] United States, Department of State, *Treaty Series*, No. 994.
[2] [Treaty Series 207; 9 Stat. 922; 18 Stat. (pt. 2, Public Treaties) 492.]
[3] [Treaty Series 208; 10 Stat. 1031; 18 Stat. (pt. 2, Public Treaties) 503.]

c "The Commission" means the International Boundary and Water Commission, United States and Mexico, as described in Article 2 of this Treaty.

d "To divert" means the deliberate act of taking water from any channel in order to convey it elsewhere for storage, or to utilize it for domestic, agricultural, stock-raising or industrial purposes whether this be done by means of dams across the channel, partition weirs, lateral intakes, pumps or any other methods.

e "Point of diversion" means the place where the act of diverting the water is effected.

f "Conservation capacity of storage reservoirs" means that part of their total capacity devoted to holding and conserving the water for disposal thereof as and when required, that is, capacity additional to that provided for silt retention and flood control.

g "Flood discharges and spills" means the voluntary or involuntary discharge of water for flood control as distinguished from releases for other purposes.

h "Return flow" means that portion of diverted water that eventually finds it way back to the source from which it was diverted.

i "Release" means the deliberate discharge of stored water for conveyance elsewhere or for direct utilization.

j "Consumptive use" means the use of water by evaporation, plant transpiration or other manner whereby the water is consumed and does not return to its source of supply. In general it is measured by the amount of water diverted less the part thereof which returns to the stream.

k "Lowest major international dam or reservoir" means the major international dam or reservoir situated farthest downstream.

l "Highest major international dam or reservoir" means the major international dam or reservoir situated farthest upstream.

ARTICLE 2

The International Boundary Commission established pursuant to the provisions of the Convention between the United States and Mexico signed in Washington March 1, 1889 [4] to facilitate the carrying out of the principles contained in the Treaty of November 12, 1884 [5] and to avoid difficulties occasioned by reason of the changes which take place in the beds of the Rio Grande (Rio Bravo) and the Colorado River shall hereafter be known as the International Boundary and Water Commission, United States and Mexico, which shall continue to function for the entire period during which the present Treaty shall continue in force. Accordingly, the term of the Convention of March 1, 1889 shall be considered to be indefinitely extended, and the Convention of November 21, 1900 [6] between the United States and Mexico regarding that Convention shall be considered completely terminated.

The application of the present Treaty, the regulation and exercise of the rights and obligations which the two Governments assume thereunder, and the settlement of all disputes to which its observance and execution may give rise are hereby entrusted to the International Boundary and Water Commission, which shall function in conformity with the powers and limitations set forth in this Treaty.

The Commission shall in all respects have the status of an international body, and shall consist of a United States Section and a Mexican Section.

[4] [Treaty Series 232; 26 Stat. 1512.]
[5] [Treaty Series 226; 24 Stat. 1011.]
[6] [Treaty Series 244; 31 Stat. 1936.]

The head of each Section shall be an Engineer Commissioner. Wherever there are provisions in this Treaty for joint action or joint agreement by the two Governments, or for the furnishing of reports, studies or plans to the two Governments, or similar provisions, it shall be understood that the particular matter in question shall be handled by or through the Department of State of the United States and the Ministry of Foreign Relations of Mexico.

The Commission or either of its two Sections may employ such assistants and engineering and legal advisers as it may deem necessary. Each Government shall accord diplomatic status to the Commissioner, designated by the other Government. The Commissioner, two principal engineers, a legal adviser, and a secretary, designated by each Government as members of its Section of the Commission, shall be entitled in the territory of the other country to the privileges and immunities appertaining to diplomatic officers. The Commission and its personnel may freely carry out their observations, studies and field work in the territory of either country.

The jurisdiction of the Commission shall extend to the limitrophe parts of the Rio Grande (Rio Bravo) and the Colorado River, to the land boundary between the two countries, and to works located upon their common boundary, each Section of the Commission retaining jurisdiction over that part of the works located within the limits of its own country. Neither Section shall assume jurisdiction or control over works located within the limits of the country of the other without the express consent of the Government of the latter. The works constructed, acquired or used in fulfillment of the provisions of this Treaty and located wholly within the territorial limits of either country, although these works may be international in character, shall remain, except as herein otherwise specifically provided, under the exclusive jurisdiction and control of the Section of the Commission in whose country the works may be situated.

The duties and powers vested in the Commission by this Treaty shall be in addition to those vested in the International Boundary Commission by the Convention of March 1, 1889 and other pertinent treaties and agreements in force between the two countries except as the provisions of any of them may be modified by the present Treaty.

Each Government shall bear the expenses incurred in the maintenance of its Section of the Commission. The joint expenses, which may be incurred as agreed upon by the Commission, shall be borne equally by the two Governments.

ARTICLE 3

In matters in which the Commission may be called upon to make provision for the joint use of international waters, the following order of preferences shall serve as a guide:

1. Domestic and municipal uses.
2. Agriculture and stock-raising.
3. Electric power.
4. Other industrial uses.
5. Navigation.
6. Fishing and hunting.
7. Any other beneficial uses which may be determined by the Commission.

All the foregoing uses shall be subject to any sanitary measures or works which may be mutually agreed upon by the two Governments, which hereby agree to give preferential attention to the solution of all border sanitation problems.

II. RIO GRANDE (RIO BRAVO)

ARTICLE 4 [7]

. . . .

ARTICLE 5

The two Governments agree to construct jointly, through their respective Sections of the Commission, the following works in the main channel of the Rio Grande (Rio Bravo):

I. The dams required for the conservation, storage and regulation of the greatest quantity of the annual flow of the river in a way to ensure the continuance of existing uses and the development of the greatest number of feasible projects, within the limits imposed by the water allotments specified.

II. The dams and other joint works required for the diversion of the flow of the Rio Grande (Rio Bravo).

One of the storage dams shall be constructed in the section between Santa Helena Canyon and the mouth of the Pecos River; one in the section between Eagle Pass and Laredo, Texas (Piedras Negras and Nuevo Laredo in Mexico); and a third in the section between Laredo and Roma, Texas (Nuevo Laredo and San Pedro de Roma in Mexico). One or more of the stipulated dams may be omitted, and others than those enumerated may be built, in either case as may be determined by the Commission, subject to the approval of the two Governments.

In planning the construction of such dams the Commission shall determine:

a The most feasible sites;

b The maximum feasible reservoir capacity at each site;

c The conservation capacity required by each country at each site, taking into consideration the amount and regimen of its allotment of water and its contemplated uses;

d The capacity required for retention of silt;

e The capacity required for flood control.

The conservation and silt capacities of each reservoir shall be assigned to each country in the same proportion as the capacities required by each country in such reservoir for conservation purposes. Each country shall have an undivided interest in the flood control capacity of each reservoir.

The construction of the international storage dams shall start within two years following the approval of the respective plans by the two Governments. The works shall begin with the construction of the lowest major international storage dam, but works in the upper reaches of the river may be constructed simultaneously. The lowest major international storage dam shall be completed within a period of eight years from the date of the entry into force of this Treaty.

The construction of the dams and other joint works required for the diversion of the flows of the river shall be initiated on the dates recommended by the Commission and approved by the two Governments.

The cost of construction, operation and maintenance of each of the international storage dams shall be prorated between the two Governments in proportion to the capacity allotted to each country for conservation purposes in the reservoir at such dam.

[7] Technical passages omitted; omissions indicated by periods.

The cost of construction, operation and maintenance of each of the dams and other joint works required for the diversion of the flows of the river shall be prorated between the two Governments in proportion to the benefits which the respective countries receive therefrom, as determined by the Commission and approved by the two Governments.

ARTICLE 6

The Commission shall study, investigate, and prepare plans for flood control works, where and when necessary, other than those referred to in Article 5 of this Treaty, on the Rio Grande (Rio Bravo) from Fort Quitman, Texas to the Gulf of Mexico. These works may include levees along the river, floodways and grade-control structures, and works for the canalization, rectification and artificial channeling of reaches of the river. The Commission shall report to the two Governments the works which should be built, the estimated cost thereof, the part of the works to be constructed by each Government, and the part of the works to be operated and maintained by each Section of the Commission. Each Government agrees to construct, through its Section of the Commission, such works as may be recommended by the Commission and approved by the two Governments. Each Government shall pay the costs of the works constructed by it and the costs of operation and maintenance of the part of the works assigned to it for such purpose.

ARTICLE 7

The Commission shall study, investigate and prepare plans for plants for generating hydro-electric energy which it may be feasible to construct at the international storage dams on the Rio Grande (Rio Bravo). The Commission shall report to the two Governments in a Minute the works which should be built, the estimated cost thereof, and the part of the works to be constructed by each Government. Each Government agrees to construct, through its Section of the Commission, such works as may be recommended by the Commission and approved by the two Governments. Both Governments, through their respective Sections of the Commission, shall operate and maintain jointly such hydro-electric plants. Each Government shall pay half the cost of the construction, operation and maintenance of such plants, and the energy generated shall be assigned to each country in like proportion.

ARTICLE 8

The two Governments recognize that both countries have a common interest in the conservation and storage of waters in the international reservoirs and in the maximum use of these structures for the purpose of obtaining the most beneficial, regular and constant use of the waters belonging to them. Accordingly, within the year following the placing in operation of the first of the major international storage dams which is constructed, the Commission shall submit to each Government for its approval, regulations for the storage, conveyance and delivery of the waters of the Rio Grande (Rio Bravo) from Fort Quitman, Texas to the Gulf of Mexico. Such regulations may be modified, amended or supplemented when necessary by the Commission, subject to the approval of the two Governments. The following general rules shall severally govern until modified or amended by agreement of the Commission, with the approval of the two Governments:

. . . .

e Flood discharges and spills from the upper reservoirs shall be divided in the same proportion as the ownership of the inflows occurring at the time of such flood discharges and spills, except as provided in subparagraph (c) of this Article. Flood discharges and spills from the lowest reservoir shall be divided equally, except that one country, with the consent of the Commission, may use such part of the share of the other country as is not used by the latter country.

f Either of the two countries may avail itself, whenever it so desires, of any water belonging to it and stored in the international reservoirs, provided that the water so taken is for direct beneficial use or for storage in other reservoirs. For this purpose the Commissioner of the respective country shall give appropriate notice to the Commission, which shall prescribe the proper measures for the opportune furnishing of the water.

ARTICLE 9

a The channel of the Rio Grande (Rio Bravo) may be used by either of the two countries to convey water belonging to it.

b Either of the two countries may, at any point on the main channel of the river from Fort Quitman, Texas to the Gulf of Mexico, divert and use the water belonging to it and may for this purpose construct any necessary works. However, no such diversion or use, not existing on the date this Treaty enters into force, shall be permitted in either country, nor shall works be constructed for such purpose, until the Section of the Commission in whose country the diversion or use is proposed has made a finding that the water necessary for such diversion or use is available from the share of that country, unless the Commission has agreed to a greater diversion or use as provided by paragraph (d) of this Article. The proposed use and the plans for the diversion works to be constructed in connection therewith shall be previously made known to the Commission for its information.

c Consumptive uses from the main stream and from the unmeasured tributaries below Fort Quitman shall be charged against the share of the country making them.

d The Commission shall have the power to authorize either country to divert and use water not belonging entirely to such country, when the water belonging to the other country can be diverted and used without injury to the latter and can be replaced at some other point on the river.

e The Commission shall have the power to authorize temporary diversion and use by one country of water belonging to the other, when the latter does not need it or is unable to use it, provided that such authorization or the use of such water shall not establish any right to continue to divert it.

f In case of the occurrence of an extraordinary drought in one country with an abundant supply of water in the other country, water stored in the international storage reservoirs and belonging to the country enjoying such abundant water supply may be withdrawn, with the consent of the Commission, for the use of the country undergoing the drought.

g Each country shall have the right to divert from the main channel of the river any amount of water, including the water belonging to the other country, for the purpose of generating hydro-electric power, provided that such diversion causes no injury to the other country and does not interfere with the international generation of power and that the quantities not returning directly to the river are charged against the share of the country making the diversion. The feasibility of such diversions not existing on the date this Treaty enters into force shall be determined by the Commission, which shall also determine the amount of water consumed, such water to be charged against the country making the diversion.

h In case either of the two countries shall construct works for diverting into the main channel of the Rio Grande (Rio Bravo) or its tributaries waters that do not at the time this Treaty enters into force contribute to the flow of the Rio Grande (Rio Bravo) such water shall belong to the country making such diversion.

i Main stream channel losses shall be charged in proportion to the ownership of water being conveyed in the channel at the times and places of the losses.

j The Commission shall keep a record of the waters belonging to each country and of those that may be available at a given moment, taking into account the measurement of the allotments, the regulation of the waters in storage, the consumptive uses, the withdrawals, the diversions, and the losses. For this purpose the Commission shall construct, operate and maintain on the main channel of the Rio Grande (Rio Bravo), and each Section shall construct, operate and maintain on the measured tributaries in its own country, all the gaging stations and mechanical apparatus necessary for the purpose of making computations and of obtaining the necessary data for such record. The information with respect to the diversions and consumptive uses on the unmeasured tributaries shall be furnished to the Commission by the appropriate Section. The cost of construction of any new gaging stations located on the main channel of the Rio Grande (Rio Bravo) shall be borne equally by the two Governments. The operation and maintenance of all gaging stations or the cost of such operation and maintenance shall be apportioned between the two Sections in accordance with determinations to be made by the Commission.

III. COLORADO RIVER

ARTICLE 10

. . . .

ARTICLE 11

. . . .

ARTICLE 12

The two Governments agree to construct the following works:

a Mexico shall construct at its expense, within a period of five years from the date of the entry into force of this Treaty, a main diversion structure below the point where the northernmost part of the international land boundary line intersects the Colorado River. If such diversion structure is located in the limitrophe section of the river, its location, design and construction shall be subject to the approval of the Commission. The Commission shall thereafter maintain and operate the structure at the expense of Mexico. Regardless of where such diversion structure is located, there shall simultaneously be constructed such levees, interior drainage facilities and other works, or improvements to existing works, as in the opinion of the Commission shall be necessary to protect lands within the United States against damage from such floods and seepage as might result from the construction, operation and maintenance of this diversion structure. These protective works shall be constructed, operated and maintained at the expense of Mexico by the respective Sections of the Commission, or under their supervision, each within the territory of its own country.

b The United States, within a period of five years from the date of the entry into force of this Treaty, shall construct in its own territory and at its expense, and thereafter operate and maintain at its expense, the Davis storage dam and reservoir, a part of the capacity of which shall be used to make possible the regulation at the boundary of the waters to be delivered to Mexico in accordance with the provisions of Article 15 of this Treaty.

c The United States shall construct or acquire in its own territory the works that may be necessary to convey a part of the waters of the Colorado River allotted to Mexico to the Mexican diversion points on the international land boundary line referred to in this Treaty. Among these works shall be included: the canal and other works necessary to convey water from the lower end of the Pilot Knob Wasteway to the international boundary, and, should Mexico request it, a canal to connect the main diversion structure referred to in subparagraph (a) of this Article, if this diversion structure should be built in the limitrophe section of the river, with the Mexican system of canals at a point to be agreed upon by the Commission on the international land boundary near San Luis, Sonora. Such works shall be constructed or acquired and operated and maintained by the United States Section at the expense of Mexico. Mexico shall also pay the costs of any sites or rights of way required for such works.

d The Commission shall construct, operate and maintain in the limitrophe section of the Colorado River, and each Section shall construct, operate and maintain in the territory of its own country on the Colorado River below Imperial Dam and on all other carrying facilities used for the delivery of water to Mexico, all necessary gaging stations and other measuring devices for the purpose of keeping a complete record of the waters delivered to Mexico and of the flows of the river. All data obtained as to such deliveries and flows shall be periodically compiled and exchanged between the two Sections.

ARTICLE 13

The Commission shall study, investigate and prepare plans for flood control on the Lower Colorado River between Imperial Dam and the Gulf of California, in both the United States and Mexico, and shall, in a Minute, report to the two Governments the works which should be built, the estimated cost thereof, and the part of the works to be constructed by each Government. The two Governments agree to construct, through their respective Sections of the Commission, such works as may be recommended by the Commission and approved by the two Governments, each Government to pay the costs of the works constructed by it. The Commission shall likewise recommend the parts of the works to be operated and maintained jointly by the Commission and the parts to be operated and maintained by each Section. The two Governments agree to pay in equal shares the cost of joint operation and maintenance, and each Government agrees to pay the cost of operation and maintenance of the works assigned to it for such purpose.

ARTICLE 14

In consideration of the use of the All-American Canal for the delivery to Mexico, in the manner provided in Articles 11 and 15 of this Treaty, of a part of its allotment of the waters of the Colorado River, Mexico shall pay to the United States:

a A proportion of the costs actually incurred in the construction of Imperial Dam and the Imperial Dam-Pilot Knob section of the All-American Canal, this proportion and the method and terms of repayment to be determined by the two Governments, which, for this purpose, shall take into consideration the proportionate uses of these facilities by the two countries, these determinations to be made as soon as Davis dam and reservoir are placed in operation.

b Annually, a proportionate part of the total costs of maintenance and operation of such facilities, these costs to be prorated between the two countries in proportion to the amount of water delivered annually through such facilities for use in each of the two countries.

In the event that revenues from the sale of hydro-electric power which may be generated at Pilot Knob become available for the amortization of part or all of the costs of the facilities named in subparagraph (a) of this Article, the part that Mexico should pay of the costs of said facilities shall be reduced or repaid in the same proportion as the balance of the total costs are reduced or repaid. It is understood that any such revenue shall not become available until the cost of any works which may be constructed for the generation of hydro-electric power at said location has been fully amortized from the revenues derived therefrom.

ARTICLE 15

. . . .

IV. TIJUANA RIVER

ARTICLE 16

In order to improve existing uses and to assure any feasible further development, the Commission shall study and investigate, and shall submit to the two Governments for their approval:

(1) Recommendations for the equitable distribution between the two countries of the waters of the Tijuana River system;

(2) Plans for storage and flood control to promote and develop domestic, irrigation and other feasible uses of the waters of this system;

(3) An estimate of the cost of the proposed works and the manner in which the construction of such works or the cost thereof should be divided between the two Governments;

(4) Recommendations regarding the parts of the works to be operated and maintained by the Commission and the parts to be operated and maintained by each Section.

The two Governments through their respective Sections of the Commission shall construct such of the proposed works as are approved by both Governments, shall divide the work to be done or the cost thereof, and shall distribute between the two countries the waters of the Tijuana River system in the proportions approved by the two Governments. The two Governments agree to pay in equal shares the costs of joint operation and maintenance of the works involved, and each Government agrees to pay the cost of operation and maintenance of the works assigned to it for such purpose.

V. GENERAL PROVISIONS

ARTICLE 17

The use of the channels of the international rivers for the discharge of flood or other excess waters shall be free and not subject to limitation by either country, and neither country shall have any claim against the other in respect of any damage caused by such use. Each Government agrees to furnish the other Government, as far in advance as practicable, any information it may have in regard to such extraordinary discharges of water from reservoirs and flood flows on its own territory as may produce floods on the territory of the other.

Each Government declares its intention to operate its storage dams in such manner, consistent with the normal operations of its hydraulic systems, as to avoid, as far as feasible, material damage in the territory of the other.

ARTICLE 18

Public use of the water surface of lakes formed by international dams shall, when not harmful to the services rendered by such dams, be free and common to both countries, subject to the police regulations of each country in its territory, to such general regulations as may appropriately be prescribed and enforced by the Commission with the approval of the two Governments for the purpose of the application of the provisions of this Treaty, and to such regulations as may appropriately be prescribed and enforced for the same purpose by each Section of the Commission with respect to the areas and borders of such parts of those lakes as lie within its territory. Neither Government shall use for military purposes such water surface situated within the territory of the other country except by express agreement between the two Governments.

ARTICLE 19

The two Governments shall conclude such special agreements as may be necessary to regulate the generation, development and disposition of electric power at international plants, including the necessary provisions for the export of electric current.

ARTICLE 20

The two Governments shall, through their respective Sections of the Commission, carry out the construction of works allotted to them. For this purpose the respective Sections of the Commission may make use of any competent public or private agencies in accordance with the laws of the respective countries. With respect to such works as either Section of the Commission may have to execute on the territory of the other, it shall, in the execution of such works, observe the laws of the place where such works are located or carried out, with the exceptions hereinafter stated.

All materials, implements, equipment and repair parts intended for the construction, operation and maintenance of such works shall be exempt from import and export customs duties. The whole of the personnel employed either directly or indirectly on the construction, operation or maintenance of the works may pass freely from one country to the other for the purpose of going to and from the place of location of the works, without any immigration restrictions, passports or labor requirements. Each Government shall furnish, through its own Section of the Commission, convenient means of identification to the personnel employed by it on the aforesaid works and verification certificates covering all materials, implements, equipment and repair parts intended for the works.

Each Government shall assume responsibility for and shall adjust exclusively in accordance with its own laws all claims arising within its territory in connection with the construction, operation or maintenance of the whole or of any part of the works herein agreed upon, or of any works which may, in the execution of this Treaty, be agreed upon in the future.

ARTICLE 21

The construction of the international dams and the formation of artificial lakes shall produce no change in the fluvial international boundary, which shall continue to be governed by existing treaties and conventions in force between the two countries.

The Commission shall, with the approval of the two Governments, establish in the artificial lakes, by buoys or by other suitable markers, a practicable and convenient line to provide for the exercise of the jurisdiction and control vested by this Treaty in the Commission and its respective Sections. Such line shall also mark the boundary for the application of the customs and police regulations of each country.

ARTICLE 22

The provisions of the Convention between the United States and Mexico for the rectification of the Rio Grande (Rio Bravo) in the El Paso-Juárez Valley signed on February 1, 1933,[8] shall govern, so far as delimitation of the Boundary, distribution of jurisdiction and sovereignty, and relations with private owners are concerned, in any places where works for the artificial channeling, canalization or rectification of the Rio Grande (Rio Bravo) and the Colorado River are carried out.

ARTICLE 23

The two Governments recognize the public interest attached to the works required for the execution and performance of this Treaty and agree to acquire, in accordance with their respective domestic laws, any private property that may be required for the construction of the said works, including the main structures and their appurtenances and the construction materials therefor, and for the operation and maintenance thereof, at the cost of the country within which the property is situated, except as may be otherwise specifically provided in this Treaty.

Each Section of the Commission shall determine the extent and location of any private property to be acquired within its own country and shall make the necessary requests upon its Government for the acquisition of such property.

The Commission shall determine the cases in which it shall become necessary to locate works for the conveyance of water or electrical energy and for the servicing of any such works, for the benefit of either of the two countries, in the territory of the other country, in order that such works can be built pursuant to agreement between the two Governments. Such

---

[8] [Treaty Series 864; 48 Stat. 1621.]

works shall be subject to the jurisdiction and supervision of the Section of the Commission within whose country they are located.

Construction of the works built in pursuance of the provisions of this Treaty shall not confer upon either of the two countries any rights either of property or of jurisdiction over any part whatsoever of the territory of the other. These works shall be part of the territory and be the property of the country wherein they are situated. However, in the case of any incidents occurring on works constructed across the limitrophe part of a river and with supports on both banks, the jurisdiction of each country shall be limited by the center line of such works, which shall be marked by the Commission, without thereby changing the international boundary.

Each Government shall retain, through its own Section of the Commission and within the limits and to the extent necessary to effectuate the provisions of this Treaty, direct ownership, control and jurisdiction within its own territory and in accordance with its own laws, over all real property—including that within the channel of any river—rights of way and rights *in rem*, that it may be necessary to enter upon and occupy for the construction, operation or maintenance of all the works constructed, acquired or used pursuant to this Treaty. Furthermore, each Government shall similarly acquire and retain in its own possession the titles, control and jurisdiction over such works.

ARTICLE 24

The International Boundary and Water Commission shall have, in addition to the powers and duties otherwise specifically provided in this Treaty, the following powers and duties:

a To initiate and carry on investigations and develop plans for the works which are to be constructed or established in accordance with the provisions of this and other treaties or agreements in force between the two Governments dealing with boundaries and international waters; to determine, as to such works, their location, size, kind and characteristic specifications; to estimate the cost of such works; and to recommend the division of such costs between the two Governments, the arrangements for the furnishing of the necessary funds, and the dates for the beginning of the works, to the extent that the matters mentioned in this subparagraph are not otherwise covered by specific provisions of this or any other Treaty.

b To construct the works agreed upon or to supervise their construction and to operate and maintain such works or to supervise their operation and maintenance, in accordance with the respective domestic laws of each country. Each Section shall have, to the extent necessary to give effect to the provisions of this Treaty, jurisdiction over the works constructed exclusively in the territory of its country whenever such works shall be connected with or shall directly affect the execution of the provisions of this Treaty.

c In general to exercise and discharge the specific powers and duties entrusted to the Commission by this and other treaties and agreements in force between the two countries, and to carry into execution and prevent the violation of the provisions of those treaties and agreements. The authorities of each country shall aid and support the exercise and discharge of these powers and duties, and each Commissioner shall invoke when necessary the jurisdiction of the courts or other appropriate agencies of his country to aid in the execution and enforcement of these powers and duties.

d To settle all differences that may arise between the two Governments with respect to the interpretation or application of this Treaty, subject to the approval of the two Governments. In any case in which the Commissioners do not reach an agreement, they shall so inform their respective governments reporting their respective opinions and the grounds therefor and the points upon which they differ, for discussion and adjustment of the difference through diplomatic channels and for application where proper of the general or special agreements which the two Governments have concluded for the settlement of controversies.

e To furnish the information requested of the Commissioners jointly by the two Governments on matters within their jurisdiction. In the event that the request is made by one Government alone, the Commissioner of the other Government must have the express authorization of his Government in order to comply with such request.

f The Commission shall construct, operate and maintain upon the limitrophe parts of the international streams, and each Section shall severally construct, operate and maintain upon the parts of the international streams and their tributaries within the boundaries of its own country, such stream gaging stations as may be needed to provide the hydrographic data necessary or convenient for the proper functioning of this Treaty. The data so obtained shall be compiled and periodically exchanged between the two Sections.

g The Commission shall submit annually a joint report to the two Governments on the matters in its charge. The Commission shall also submit to the two Governments joint reports on general or any particular matters at such other times as it may deem necessary or as may be requested by the two Governments.

ARTICLE 25

Except as otherwise specifically provided in this Treaty, Articles III and VII of the Convention of March 1, 1889 shall govern the proceedings of the Commission in carrying out the provisions of this Treaty. Supplementary thereto the Commission shall establish a body of rules and regulations to govern its procedure, consistent with the provisions of this Treaty and of Articles III and VII of the Convention of March 1, 1889 and subject to the approval of both Governments.

Decisions of the Commission shall be recorded in the form of Minutes done in duplicate in the English and Spanish languages, signed by each Commissioner and attested by the Secretaries, and copies thereof forwarded to each Government within three days after being signed. Except where the specific approval of the two Governments is required by any provision of this Treaty, if one of the Governments fails to communicate to the Commission its approval or disapproval of a decision of the Commission within thirty days reckoned from the date of the Minute in which it shall have been pronounced, the Minute in question and the decisions which it contains shall be considered to be approved by that Government. The Commissioners, within the limits of their respective jurisdictions, shall execute the decisions of the Commission that are approved by both Governments.

If either Government disapproves a decision of the Commission the two Governments shall take cognizance of the matter, and if an agreement regarding such matter is reached between the two Governments, the agreement shall be communicated to the Commissioners, who shall take such further proceedings as may be necessary to carry out such agreement.

VI. TRANSITORY PROVISIONS

ARTICLE 26

During a period of eight years from the date of the entry into force of this Treaty, or until the beginning of operation of the lowest major international reservoir on the Rio Grande (Rio Bravo), should it be placed in operation prior to the expiration of said period, Mexico will cooperate with the United States to relieve, in times of drought, any lack of water needed to irrigate the lands now under irrigation in the Lower Rio Grande Valley in the United States, and for this purpose Mexico will release water from El Azúcar reservoir on the San Juan River and allow that water to run through its system of canals back into the San Juan River in order that the United States may divert such water from the Rio Grande (Rio Bravo). Such releases shall be made on condition that they do not affect the Mexican irrigation system, provided that Mexico shall, in any exent, except in cases of extraordinary drought or serious accident to its hydraulic works, release and make available to the United States for its use the quantities requested, under the following conditions: that during the said eight years there shall be made available a total of 160,000 acre-feet (197,358,000 cubic meters) and up to 40,000 acre-feet (49,340,000 cubic meters) in any one year; that the water shall be made available as requested at rates not exceeding 750 cubic feet (21.2 cubic meters) per second; that when the rates of flow requested and made available have been more than 500 cubic feet (14.2 cubic meters) per second the period of release shall not extend beyond fifteen consecutive days; and that at least thirty days must elapse between any two periods of release during which rates of flow in excess of 500 cubic feet (14.2 cubic meters) per second have been requested and made available. In addition to the guaranteed flow, Mexico shall release from El Azúcar reservoir and conduct through its canal system and the San Juan River, for use in the United States during periods of drought and after satisfying the needs of Mexican users, any excess water that does not in the opinion of the Mexican Section have to be stored and that may be needed for the irrigation of lands which were under irrigation during the year 1943 in the Lower Rio Grande Valley in the United States.

ARTICLE 27

The provisions of Article 10, 11, and 15 of this Treaty shall not be applied during a period of five years from the date of the entry into force of this Treaty, or until the Davis dam and the major Mexican diversion structure on the Colorado River are placed in operation, should these works be placed in operation prior to the expiration of said period. In the meantime Mexico may construct and operate at its expense a temporary diversion structure in the bed of the Colorado River in territory of the United States for the purpose of diverting water into the Alamo Canal, provided that the plans for such structure and the construction and operation thereof shall be subject to the approval of the United States Section. During this period of time the United States will make available in the river at such diversion structure river flow not currently required in the United States, and the United States will cooperate with Mexico to the end that the latter may satisfy its irrigation requirements within the limits of those requirements for lands irrigated in Mexico from the Colorado River during the year 1943.

VII. FINAL PROVISIONS

ARTICLE 28

This Treaty shall be ratified and the ratifications thereof shall be exchanged in Washington. It shall enter into force on the day of the exchange of ratifications and shall continue in force until terminated by another Treaty concluded for that purpose between the two Governments.

In witness whereof the respective Plenipotentiaries have signed this Treaty and have hereunto affixed their seals.

Done in duplicate in the English and Spanish languages, in Washington on this third day of February, 1944.

FOR THE GOVERNMENT OF THE UNITED STATES OF AMERICA:

Cordell Hull	[SEAL]
George S. Messersmith	[SEAL]
Lawrence M. Lawson	[SEAL]

FOR THE GOVERNMENT OF THE UNITED MEXICAN STATES:

F. Castillo Nájera	[SEAL]
Rafael Fernández MacGregor	[SEAL]

PROTOCOL [1]

The Government of the United States of America and the Government of the United Mexican States agree and understand that:

Wherever, by virtue of the provisions of the Treaty between the United States of America and the United Mexican States, signed in Washington on February 3, 1944, relating to the utilization of the waters of the Colorado and Tijuana Rivers and of the Rio Grande from Fort Quitman, Texas, to the Gulf of Mexico, specific functions are imposed on, or exclusive jurisdiction is vested in, either of the Sections of the International Boundary and Water Commission, which involve the construction or use of works for storage or conveyance of water, flood control, stream gaging, or for any other purpose, which are situated wholly within the territory of the country of that Section, and which are to be used only partly for the performance of treaty provisions, such jurisdiction shall be exercised, and such functions, including the construction, operation and maintenance of the said works, shall be performed and carried out by the Federal agencies of that country which now or hereafter may be authorized by domestic law to construct, or to operate and maintain, such works. Such functions or jurisdictions shall be exercised in conformity with the provisions of the Treaty and in cooperation with the respective Section of the Commission, to the end that all international obligations and functions may be coordinated and fulfilled.

The works to be constructed or used on or along the boundary, and those to be constructed or used exclusively for the discharge of treaty stipulations, shall be under the jurisdiction of the Commission or of the respective Section, in accordance with the provisions of the Treaty. In carrying out the construction of such works the Sections of the Commission may utilize the services of public or private organizations in accordance with the laws of their respective countries.

[1] Treaty Series, No. 994, p. 50.

This Protocol, which shall be regarded as an integral part of the afore-mentioned Treaty signed in Washington on February 3, 1944, shall be ratified and the ratifications thereof shall be exchanged in Washington. This Protocol shall be effective beginning with the day of the entry into force of the Treaty and shall continue effective so long as the Treaty remains in force.

In witness whereof the respective Plenipotentiaries have signed this Protocol and have hereunto affixed their seals.

Done in duplicate, in the English and Spanish languages, in Washington, this fourteenth day of November, 1944.

FOR THE GOVERNMENT OF THE UNITED STATES
OF AMERICA:
E. R. Stettinius, Jr.   [SEAL]
Acting Secretary of State
of the United States of America

FOR THE GOVERNMENT OF THE UNITED MEXICAN STATES:
F. Castillo Nájera   [SEAL]
Ambassador Extraordinary and Plenipotentiary
of the United Mexican States in Washington

5. RATIFICATION OF A TREATY

a. **Resolution of United States Senate Consenting to Ratification of a Treaty** [1]

Resolved (two-thirds of the Senators present concurring therein), That the Senate advise and consent to the ratification of Executive A, Seventy-eighth Congress, second session, a treaty between the United States of America and the United Mexican States, signed at Washington on February 3, 1944, relating to the utilization of the waters of the Colorado and Tijuana Rivers and of the Rio Grande from Fort Quitman, Texas, to the Gulf of Mexico, and Executive H, Seventy-eighth Congress, second session, a protocol, signed at Washington on November 14, 1944, supplementary to the treaty, subject to the following understandings, and that these understandings will be mentioned in the ratification of this treaty as conveying the true meaning of the treaty, and will in effect form a part of the treaty:

a That no commitment for works to be built by the United States in whole or in part at its expense, or for expenditures by the United States, other than those specifically provided for in the treaty, shall be made by the Secretary of State of the United States, the Commissioner of the United States Section of the International Boundary and Water Commission, the United States Section of said Commission, or any other officer or employee of the United States, without prior approval of the Congress of the United States. It is understood that the works to be built by the United States, in whole or in part at its expense, and the expenditures by the United States, which are specifically provided for in the treaty, are as follows:

1. The joint construction of the three storage and flood-control dams on the Rio Grande below Fort Quitman, Texas, mentioned in article 5 of the treaty.

2. The dams and other joint works required for the diversion of the flow of the Rio Grande mentioned in subparagraph II of article 5 of the treaty, it being understood that the commitment of the United States to make ex-

[1] Treaty Series, No. 994, p. 53.

penditures under this subparagraph is limited to its share of the cost of one dam and works appurtenant thereto.

3. Stream-gaging stations which may be required under the provisions of section (j) of article 9 of the treaty and of subparagraph (d) of article 12 of the treaty.

4. The Davis Dam and Reservoir mentioned in subparagraph (b) of article 12 of the treaty.

5. The joint flood-control investigations, preparation of plans, and reports on the Rio Grande below Fort Quitman required by the provisions of article 6 of the treaty.

6. The joint flood-control investigations, preparations of plans, and reports on the lower Colorado River between the Imperial Dam and the Gulf of California required by article 13 of the treaty.

7. The joint investigations, preparation of plans, and reports on the establishment of hydroelectric plants at the international dams on the Rio Grande below Fort Quitman provided for by article 7 of the treaty.

8. The studies, investigations, preparation of plans, recommendations, reports, and other matters dealing with the Tijuana River system provided for by the first paragraph (including the numbered subparagraphs) of article 16 of the treaty.

b Insofar as they affect persons and property in the territorial limits of the United States, the powers and functions of the Secretary of State of the United States, the Commissioner of the United States Section of the International Boundary and Water Commission, the United States Section of said Commission, and any other officer or employee of the United States, shall be subject to the statutory and constitutional controls and processes. Nothing contained in the treaty or protocol shall be construed as impairing the power of the Congress of the United States to define the terms of office of members of the United States Section of the International Boundary and Water Commission or to provide for their appointment by the President by and with the advice and consent of the Senate or otherwise.

c That nothing contained in the treaty or protocol shall be construed as authorizing the Secretary of State of the United States, the Commissioner of the United States Section of the International Boundary and Water Commission, or the United States Section of said Commission, directly or indirectly to alter or control the distribution of water to users within the territorial limits of any of the individual States.

d That "international dam or reservoir" means a dam or reservoir built across the common boundary between the two countries.

e That the words "international plants", appearing in article 19, mean only hydroelectric generating plants in connection with dams built across the common boundary between the two countries.

f That the words "electric current", appearing in article 19, mean hydroelectric power generated at an international plant.

g That by the use of the words "The jurisdiction of the Commission shall extend to the limitrophe parts of the Rio Grande (Rio Bravo) and the Colorado River to the land boundary between the two countries, and to works located upon their common boundary * * *" in the first sentence of the fifth paragraph of article 2, is meant: "The jurisdiction of the Commission shall extend and be limited to the limitrophe parts of the Rio Grande (Rio Bravo) and the Colorado River, to the land boundary between the two countries, and to works located upon their common boundary * * *."

h The word "agreements" whenever used in subparagraphs (a), (c), and (d) of article 24 of the treaty shall refer only to agreements entered into pursuant to and subject to the provisions and limitations of treaties in force between the United States of America and the United Mexican States.

i The word "disputes" in the second paragraph of article 2 shall have reference only to disputes between the Governments of the United States of America and the United Mexican States.

j First, that the one million seven hundred thousand acre-feet specified in subparagraph (b) of article 10 includes and is not in addition to the one million five hundred thousand acre-feet, the delivery of which to Mexico is guaranteed in subparagraph (a) of article 10; second, that the one million five hundred thousand acre-feet specified in three places in said subparagraph (b) is identical with the one million five hundred thousand acre-feet specified in said subparagraph (a); third, that any use by Mexico under said subparagraph (b) of quantities of water arriving at the Mexican points of diversion in excess of said one million five hundred thousand acre-feet shall not give rise to any future claim or right by Mexico in excess of said guaranteed quantity of one million five hundred thousand acre-feet of water.

k The United States recognizes a duty to require that the protective structures to be constructed under article 12, paragraph (a), of this treaty, are so constructed, operated, and maintained as to adequately prevent damage to property and lands within the United States from the construction and operation of the diversion structure referred to in said paragraph.

b. (1) Act of Ratification by the President of the United States [1]

HARRY S. TRUMAN

President of the United States of America

TO ALL TO WHOM THESE PRESENTS SHALL COME, GREETING:

KNOW YE, That whereas a treaty between the United States of America and the United Mexican States relating to the utilization of the waters of the Colorado and Tijuana Rivers, and of the Rio Grande (Rio Bravo) from Fort Quitman, Texas, to the Gulf of Mexico, was signed by their respective Plenipotentiaries in Washington on February 3, 1944, and a protocol supplementary to the said treaty was signed by their respective Plenipotentiaries in Washington on November 14, 1944, the originals of which treaty and protocol, in the English and Spanish languages, are hereto annexed;

AND WHEREAS the Senate of the United States of America by their Resolution of April 18, 1945, two-thirds of the Senators present concurring therein, did advise and consent to the ratification of the said treaty and protocol, subject to the following understandings, which understandings convey the true meaning of the treaty and will in effect form a part of the treaty, namely:

"(*a*) That no commitment for works to be built by the United States in whole or in part at its expense, or for expenditures by the United States, other than those specifically provided for in the treaty, shall be made by the Secretary of State of the United States, the Commissioner of the United States Section of the International Boundary and Water Commission, the United States Section of said Commission, or any other officer or employee of the United States, without prior approval of the Congress of the United States. It is understood that the works to be built by the United States, in whole or in part at its expense, and the ex-

[1] Text by courtesy of the Department of State.

penditures by the United States, which are specifically provided for in the treaty, are as follows:

"1. The joint construction of the three storage and flood-control dams on the Rio Grande below Fort Quitman, Texas, mentioned in article 5 of the treaty.

"2. The dams and other joint works required for the diversion of the flow of the Rio Grande mentioned in subparagraph II of article 5 of the treaty, it being understood that the commitment of the United States to make expenditures under this subparagraph is limited to its share of the cost of one dam and works appurtenant thereto.

"3. Stream-gaging stations which may be required under the provisions of section (j) of article 9 of the treaty and of subparagraph (d) of article 12 of the treaty.

"4. The Davis Dam and Reservoir mentioned in subparagraph (b) of article 12 of the treaty.

"5. The joint flood-control investigations, preparation of plans, and reports on the Rio Grande below Fort Quitman required by the provisions of article 6 of the treaty.

"6. The joint flood-control investigations, preparations of plans, and reports on the lower Colorado River between the Imperial Dam and the Gulf of California required by article 13 of the treaty.

"7. The joint investigations, preparation of plans, and reports on the establishment of hydroelectric plants at the international dams on the Rio Grande below Fort Quitman provided for by article 7 of the treaty.

"8. The studies, investigations, preparation of plans, recommendations, reports, and other matters dealing with the Tijuana River system provided for by the first paragraph (including the numbered subparagraghs) of article 16 of the treaty.

"(b) Insofar as they affect persons and property in the territorial limits of the United States, the powers and functions of the Secretary of State of the United States, the Commissioner of the United States Section of the International Boundary and Water Commission, the United States Section of said Commission, and any other officer or employee of the United States, shall be subject to the statutory and constitutional controls and processes. Nothing contained in the treaty or protocol shall be construed as impairing the power of the Congress of the United States to define the terms of office of members of the United States Section of the International Boundary and Water Commission or to provide for their appointment by the President by and with the advice and consent of the Senate or otherwise.

"(c) That nothing contained in the treaty or protocol shall be construed as authorizing the Secretary of State of the United States, the Commissioner of the United States Section of the International Boundary and Water Commission, or the United States Section of said Commission, directly or indirectly to alter or control the distribution of water to users within the territorial limits of any of the individual States.

"(d) That 'international dam or reservoir' means a dam or reservoir built across the common boundary between the two countries.

"(e) That the words 'international plants', appearing in article 19, mean only hydroelectric generating plants in connection with dams built across the common boundary between the two countries.

"(f) That the words 'electric current', appearing in article 19, mean hydroelectric power generated at an international plant.

"(g) That by the use of the words 'The jurisdiction of the Commission shall extend to the limitrophe parts of the Rio Grande (Rio Bravo) and the Colorado River, to the land boundary between the two countries, and to works located upon their common boundary * * *' in the first sentence of the fifth paragraph of article 2, is meant: 'The jurisdiction of the Commission shall extend and be limited to the limitrophe parts of the Rio Grande (Rio Bravo) and the Colorado River, to the land boundary between the two countries, and to works located upon their common boundary * * *.'

"(h) The word 'agreements' whenever used in subparagraphs (a), (c), and (d) of article 24 of the treaty shall refer only to agreements entered into pursuant to and subject to the provisions and limitations of treaties in force between the United States of America and the United Mexican States.

"(*i*) The word 'disputes' in the second paragraph of article 2 shall have reference only to disputes between the Governments of the United States of America and the United Mexican States.

"(*j*) First, that the one million seven hundred thousand acre-feet specified in subparagraph (b) of article 10 includes and is not in addition to the one million five hundred thousand acre-feet, the delivery of which to Mexico is guaranteed in subparagraph (a) of article 10; second, that the one million five hundred thousand acre-feet specified in three places in said subparagraph (b) is identical with the one million five hundred thousand acre-feet specified in said subparagraph (a); third, that any use by Mexico under said subparagraph (b) of quantities of water arriving at the Mexican points of diversion in excess of said one million five hundred thousand acre-feet shall not give rise to any future claim of right by Mexico in excess of said guaranteed quantity of one million five hundred thousand acre-feet of water.

"(*k*) The United States recognizes a duty to require that the protective structures to be constructed under article 12, paragraph (a), of this treaty, are so constructed, operated, and maintained as to adequately prevent damage to property and lands within the United States from the construction and operation of the diversion structure referred to in said paragraph."

NOW, THEREFORE, be it known that I, Harry S. Truman, President of the United States of America, having seen and considered the said treaty and protocol, do hereby, in pursuance of the aforesaid advice and consent of the Senate, ratify and confirm the same and every article and clause thereof, subject to the aforesaid understandings on the part of the United States of America.

IN TESTIMONY WHEREOF, I have caused the Seal of the United States of America to be hereunto affixed.

DONE at the city of Washington this first day of November in the year of our Lord one thousand nine hundred forty-five and of the independence of the United States of America the one hundred seventieth.

By the President:

Harry S. Truman

James F. Byrnes
Secretary of State

b. (2) Act of Ratification by the President of Mexico [1]

MANUEL AVILA CAMACHO,

PRESIDENTE CONSTITUCIONAL DE LOS ESTADOS UNIDOS MEXICANOS,

a todos los que las presentes vieren, sabed:

Que el día tres de febrero de mil novecientos cuarenta y cuatro, fué firmado en Washington, Distrito de Columbia, Estados Unidos de América, el Tratado de distribución de las Aguas Internacionales de los ríos Colorado y Tijuana y Bravo desde Fort Quitman, Texas, Estados Unidos de América, al Golfo de México;

Que el Tratado que se menciona fué aprobado según el Decreto respectivo de la Cámara de Senadores, en los siguientes términos:

"La Cámara de Senadores del Congreso de los Estados Unidos Mexicanos, en ejercicio de la Facultad que le concede la Fracción I del Artículo 76 de la Constitución Federal, decreta:

[1] Text by courtesy of the Department of State.

ARTICULO 1°.—Se aprueba el Tratado de Distribución de las Aguas Internacionales de los ríos Colorado y Tijuana y Bravo desde Fort Quitman, Texas, Estados Unidos de América, al Golfo de México, concertado el 3 de febrero de 1944, en la ciudad de Washington, D.C., entre los señores Doctor Francisco Castillo Nájera, Embajador Extraordinario y Plenipotenciario de México ante los Estados Unidos de América, e Ingeniero Rafael Fernández MacGregor, Comisionado Mexicano de la Comisión Internacional de Límites entre México y los Estados Unidos de América, en representación de los Estados Unidos Mexicanos, y los señores Cordell Hull, Secretario de Estado de los Estados Unidos de América, George S. Messersmith, Embajador Extraordinario y Plenipotenciario de los Estados Unidos de América en México e Ingeniero Lawrence M. Lawson, Comisionado de los Estados Unidos de América en la Comisión Internacional de Límites entre México y los Estados Unidos de América, en representación del Gobierno de aquel país.

ARTICULO 2°.—Se aprueba el Protocolo Adicional al citado Tratado, firmado el 14 de noviembre de 1944, en Washington, D.C., por los representantes autorizados de México y de los Estados Unidos de América.

ARTICULO 3°.—Se aprueban las aclaraciones que al texto del Tratado referido hizo el H. Senado de los Estados Unidos de América, al acordar su ratificación el 18 de abril de 1945 en todo aquello que se refiere a los derechos y obligaciones entre ambas Partes, México y los Estados Unidos de América. El Senado Mexicano hace punto omiso, porque no le corresponde calificarlas, de las prevenciones que atañen exclusivamente a la aplicación interna del Tratado dentro de los Estados Unidos de América y por sus propias autoridades, y que son las aclaraciones enunciadas bajo la letra a) en su primer párrafo hasta el punto anterior a las palabras "Queda entendido" y bajo las letras b) y c).

Lic. Esteban García de Alba, S.P.—Lic. Arturo Martínez Adame, S.S.—Ing. Augusto Hinojosa, S.S.—Rúbricas."

En tal virtud, yo, Manuel Avila Camacho, Presidente Constitucional de los Estados Unidos Mexicanos, en uso de la facultad que me concede la Fracción Décima del Artículo Octogésimo Noveno de la Constitución Política, ratifico, acepto y confirmo el Tratado que se menciona, y prometo, en nombre de la Nación Mexicano, cumplirlo y observarlo y hacer que se cumpla y observe, según el Decreto preinserto.

En fe de lo cual expido las presentes, firmadas de mi mano, autorizadas con el Gran Sello de la Nación y refrendadas por el señor Doctor Francisco Castillo Nájera, Secretario de Relaciones Exteriores, en la residencia del Poder Ejecutivo Federal, en la ciudad de México, a los dieciséis días del mes de octubre de mil novecientos cuarenta y cinco.

M. Avila Camacho

F. Castillo Nájera
El Secretario de Relaciones
    Exteriores

c. Protocol of Exchange of Ratification [1]

The undersigned, James F. Byrnes, Secretary of State of the United States of America, and Antonio Espinosa de los Monteros, Ambassador Extraordinary and Plenipotentiary of the United Mexican States in Washington, duly authorized thereto by their respective Governments, having met for the

[1] Text by courtesy of the Department of State.

purpose of exchanging the instruments of ratification by the Governments of the United States of America and the United Mexican States of the treaty between the United States of America and the United Mexican States relating to the utilization of the waters of the Colorado and Tijuana Rivers, and of the Rio Grande (Rio Bravo) from Fort Quitman, Texas, to the Gulf of Mexico, signed in Washington on February 3, 1944, and of the protocol supplementary to the treaty aforesaid, signed in Washington on November 14, 1944, and the instruments of ratification of the treaty and protocol aforesaid having been carefully compared and found to be in conformity with each other, the exchange took place this day in the usual manner.

The ratification by the Government of the United States of America of the treaty and protocol aforesaid recites in their entirety the understandings contained in the resolution of April 18, 1945 of the Senate of the United States of America advising and consenting to ratification, the text of which resolution was communicated by the Government of the United States of America to the Government of the United Mexican States. The ratification by the Government of the United Mexican States of the treaty and protocol aforesaid is effected, in the terms of its instrument of ratification, in conformity to the Decree of September 27, 1945 of the Senate of the United Mexican States approving the treaty and protocol aforesaid and approving also the aforesaid understandings on the part of the United States of America in all that refers to the rights and obligations between both parties, and in which the Mexican Senate refrains from considering, because it is not competent to pass judgment upon them, the provisions which relate exclusively to the internal application of the treaty within the United States of America and by its own authorities, and which are included in the understandings set forth under the letter (a) in its first part to the period preceding the words "It is understood" and under the letters (b) and (c).

IN WITNESS WHEREOF, they have signed the present Protocol of Exchange and have affixed their seals thereto.

DONE in duplicate in Washington this eighth day of November, one thousand nine hundred forty-five.

James F. Byrnes
Secretary of State
of the United States of America

Antonio Espinosa de los Monteros
Ambassador Extraordinary and Plenipotentiary
of the United Mexican States in Washington

d. Proclamation of a Treaty [1]

BY THE PRESIDENT OF THE UNITED STATES OF AMERICA

A PROCLAMATION

WHEREAS a treaty between the United States of America and the United Mexican States relating to the utilization of the waters of the Colorado and Tijuana Rivers, and of the Rio Grande (Rio Bravo) from Fort Quitman, Texas, to the Gulf of Mexico, was signed by their respective Plenipotentiaries

[1] Treaty Series, No. 944, p. 1.

in Washington on February 3, 1944, and a protocol supplementary to the said treaty was signed by their respective Plenipotentiaries in Washington on November 14, 1944, the originals of which treaty and protocol, in the English and Spanish languages, are word for word as follows:

. . . .[2]

AND WHEREAS the Senate of the United States of America by their Resolution of April 18, 1945, two-thirds of the Senators present concurring therein, did advise and consent to the ratification of the said treaty and protocol, subject to certain understandings, the text of which Resolution is word for word as follows:

. . . .[3]

AND WHEREAS the said treaty and protocol were duly ratified by the President of the United States of America on November 1, 1945, in pursuance of the aforesaid advice and consent of the Senate and subject to the aforesaid understandings on the part of the United States of America;

AND WHEREAS the said treaty and protocol were duly ratified by the President of the United Mexican States on October 16, 1945, in pursuance and according to the terms of a Decree of September 27, 1945 of the Senate of the United Mexican States approving the said treaty and protocol and approving the said understandings on the part of the United States of America in all that refers to the rights and obligations between the parties;

AND WHEREAS it is provided in Article 28 of the said treaty that the treaty shall enter into force on the day of the exchange of ratifications;

AND WHEREAS it is provided in the said protocol that the protocol shall be regarded as an integral part of the said treaty and shall be effective beginning with the day of the entry into force of the said treaty;

AND WHEREAS the respective instruments of ratification of the said treaty and protocol were duly exchanged, and a protocol of exchange of instruments of ratification was signed in the English and Spanish languages, by the respective Plenipotentiaries of the United States of America and the United Mexican States on November 8, 1945, the English text of which protocol of exchange of instruments of ratification reads in part as follows:

. . . .[4]

Now, THEREFORE, be it known that I, Harry S. Truman, President of the United States of America, do hereby proclaim and make public the said treaty and the said protocol supplementary thereto, to the end that the same and every article and clause thereof may be observed and fulfilled with good faith, on and from the eighth day of November, one thousand nine hundred forty-five, by the United States of America and by the citizens of the United States of America and all other persons subject to the jurisdiction thereof.

IN TESTIMONY WHEREOF, I have hereunto set my hand and caused the Seal of the United States of America to be affixed.

DONE at the city of Washington this twenty-seventh day of November in the year of our Lord one thousand nine hundred forty-five and
[SEAL]   of the Independence of the United States of America the one hundred seventieth.

Harry S. Truman

By the President:
   James F. Byrnes
      Secretary of State

[2] Text of treaty and protocol as above, pp. 308 and 321.
[3] Senate resolution as above, p. 323.
[4] Protocol of exchange of ratifications above, p. 328.

6. INVITATION, AGENDA, AND FINAL ACT OF INTERNATIONAL CIVIL AVIATION CONFERENCE, 1944

a. Invitation, 11 September, 1944 [1]

The Government of the United States has concluded bilateral exploratory conversations with a number of other governments which have displayed a special interest on the subject of post-war civil aviation, with particular emphasis on the development of international air transport.

These discussions have indicated a substantial measure of agreement on such topics as the right of transit and non-traffic stops, the non-exclusivity of international operating rights, the application of cabotage to air traffic, the control of rates and competitive practices, the gradual curtailment of subsidies, the need for uniform operating and safety standards and the standardization of coordination of air navigation aids and communications facilities, the use of airports and facilities on a non-discriminatory basis, and the operation of airports and facilities in certain areas. It was also generally conceded that international collaboration, probably by means of an inter-national aeronautical body, would be desirable in achieving and implementing the aforementioned objectives, although there was some diversity of opinion as to the extent of regulatory powers on economic matters which should be delegated to this international body.

The approaching defeat of Germany, and the consequent liberation of great parts of Europe and Africa from military interruption of traffic, sets up the urgent need for establishing an international civil air service pattern on a provisional basis at least, so that all important trade and population areas of the world may obtain the benefits of air transportation as soon as possible, and so that the restorative processes of prompt communication may be avail-able to assist in returning great areas to processes of peace.

The Government of the United States believes that an international civil aviation conference might profitably be convened within the near future, for the purpose of agreeing on an increase in existing services and on the early establishment of international air routes and services for operation in and to areas now freed from danger of military interruption, such arrangements to continue during a transitional period. This conference might also agree so far as possible upon the principles of a permanent interna-tional structure of civil aviation and air transport, and might set up ap-propriate interim committees to prepare definitive proposals. Definitive action on such proposals, based on practical experience gained during the interim period, might be taken either as a result of a later conference, or by direct approval of the governments without the necessity of conference.

This Government suggests that the international conference proposed for the immediate future could have the following objectives:

I. a The establishment of provisional world route arrangements by gen-eral agreement to be reached at the Conference. These arrangements would form the basis for the prompt establishment of international air transport services by the appropriate countries.

b The countries participating in the conference would also be asked to agree to grant the landing and transit rights necessary for establishing the provisional route arrangements and air services referred to above.

(It would be highly desirable if each delegation were sufficiently familiar with its country's plans for international air services to permit formulation

[1] United States, Department of State, *Publications* No. 2282, pp. 1-3.

of an international air transport pattern referred to in paragraphs (a) and (b) above.)

II. The establishment of an Interim Council to act as the clearing house and advisory agency during the transitional period. It would receive and consider recommendations from each of the working committees referred to in item III; it would report upon desirable revisions in routes and services during the interim period, subject to the approval of the countries served by these routes and services; it would maintain liaison with each of the participating countries; it would supervise studies and submit information to the interested governments concerning the development of air transport during the transitional period; and would make recommendations to be considered at any subsequent international conference.

III. Agreement upon the principles to be followed in setting up a permanent international aeronautical body, and a multilateral aviation convention dealing with the fields of air transport, air navigation and aviation technical subjects; and, for the purpose of developing the details and making proposals for carrying into effect the principles so agreed, the establishment of the following working committees, which would be under the supervision of the Interim Council:

a A committee to follow developments relating to the establishment of the routes and services to be established under item I, to correlate traffic data, to study related problems and to recommend desirable revisions in routes and services. This committee would also make studies and recommendations concerning the future pattern of these routes and services.

b A central technical committee, with subordinate sub-committees, which would work closely with the committee described in subparagraph (c) below, to consider the whole field of technical matters including standards, procedures, and minimum requirements, and to make recommendations for their application and adoption at the earliest practicable time.

c A committee to draft a proposal with respect to the constitution of a permanent international aeronautical body and a new multilateral aviation convention.

Having in mind the foregoing considerations as a basis for discussion, the Government of the United States extends a cordial invitation to your Government to participate in an international conference along the above lines, to take place in the United States beginning November 1, 1944; and in view of the time element would appreciate receiving an early response as to whether your Government can arrange to have a delegation at such conference.

This invitation is being extended to the following governments and authorities:

a all members of the United Nations;
b nations associated with the United Nations in this war;
c the European and Asiatic neutral nations, in view of their close relationship to the expansion of air transport which may be expected along with the liberation of Europe.

The Danish Minister and Thai Minister in Washington will be invited to attend in their personal capacities.

LIST OF GOVERNMENTS AND AUTHORITIES TO WHOM INVITATIONS WERE EXTENDED

Afghanistan	Guatemala	Poland
Australia	Haiti	Portugal
Belgium	Honduras	Saudi Arabia
Bolivia	Iceland	Spain
Brazil	India	Sweden
Canada	Iran	Switzerland
Chile	Iraq	Syria
China	Ireland	Turkey
Colombia	Lebanon	Union of South Africa
Costa Rica	Liberia	Union of Soviet Socialist
Cuba	Luxembourg	Republics
Czechoslovakia	Mexico	Uruguay
Dominican Republic	Netherlands	Venezuela
Ecuador	New Zealand	Yugoslavia
Egypt	Nicaragua	The Danish Minister in
El Salvador	Norway	Washington
Ethiopia	Panama	The Thai Minister in
French Delegation	Paraguay	Washington
Great Britain	Peru	
Greece	Philippines	

b. Agenda [1]

I. Multilateral aviation convention and international aeronautical body.

1. Formulation of principles to be followed in:

    a Drawing up a new multilateral convention on air navigation and re-lated subjects.

    b Establishing such permanent international aeronautical body as may be agreed on, and determining the extent of its jurisdiction.

2. Arrangement for and selection of a Committee on Multilateral Convention and International Body to serve during transitional period and to draw up definitive proposals for submission to the interested governments.

II. Technical standards and procedures.

1. Recommendations for setting up and adopting standards and procedures in the following fields:

    a Communications systems and air-navigation aids, including ground markings.

    b Rules of the air and traffic-control practices.

    c Standards governing the licensing of operating and mechanical personnel.

    d Airworthiness of aircraft.

    e Registration and identification of aircraft.

    f Collection and exchange of meteorological information.

    g Logbooks and manifests.

    h Maps.

    i Airports.

    j Customs procedure.

[1] Department of State, *Publication* No. 2282, pp. 6-7. Proposed to invited governments late in September, 1944; approved at Second Plenary Session of Conference, 2 November 1944.

2. Arrangements for and selection of a Technical Committee and subcommittees to serve during transitional period, and to draft definitive proposals for submission to the interested governments.

III. Arrangements covering transitional period: Establishment of air-transport services on a provisional basis.

1. Arrangements for routes and services to operate during a transitional period.

2. Drafting of agreements to implement the provisional route pattern and to guide operations during transitional period.

 a Landing and transit rights to permit establishment of provisional air services as soon as possible.

 b Right of technical or non-traffic stop.

 c Application of cabotage.

 d Use of public airports and facilities, on a non-discriminatory basis.

 e Frequency of operations.

 f Bona fide nationality of air carriers.

 g Control of rates and competitive practices.

3. Arrangements for and selection of continuing Committee on Air Transport to serve during the transitional period.

IV. Consideration of establishment of Interim Council to serve during a transitional period which might supervise the work of other committees functioning during this period; and performing such other functions as the conference may determine.

1. Recommendations concerning locale, composition, and scope of Interim Council.

2. Length of transitional period, mechanism for converting recommendations of Interim Council and its committees into permanent arrangements, and other arrangements covering the transitional period.

c. Final Act [1]

The Governments of Afghanistan, Australia, Belgium, Bolivia, Brazil, Canada, Chile, China, Colombia, Costa Rica, Cuba, Czechoslovakia, Dominican Republic, Ecuador, Egypt, El Salvador, Ethiopia, France, Greece, Guatemala, Haiti, Honduras, Iceland, India, Iran, Iraq, Ireland, Lebanon, Liberia, Luxembourg, Mexico, Netherlands, New Zealand, Nicaragua, Norway, Panama, Paraguay, Peru, Philippine Commonwealth, Poland, Portugal, Spain, Sweden, Switzerland, Syria, Turkey, Union of South Africa, United Kingdom, United States of America, Uruguay, Venezuela, and Yugoslavia;

Having accepted the invitation extended to them by the Government of the United States of America to be represented at an International Civil Aviation Conference;

Appointed their respective delegates, who are listed below by counttries in the order of alphabetical precedence: [2]

· ·

Who met at Chicago, Illinois, on November 1, 1944, under the Temporary Presidency of Adolf A. Berle, Jr., Chairman of the Delegation of the United States of America.

Henrik de Kauffmann, Danish Minister at Washington, and Mom Rajawongse Seni Pramoj, Thai Minister at Washington, attended the First Plenary

---

[1] Department of State *Publication* No. 2282, pp. 25-43.

[2] Names omitted.

Session in response to an invitation extended by the Government of the United States to be present in a personal capacity. The Conference, on the recommendation of the Committee on Credentials, approved the attendance of the Danish Minister and the Thai Minister at the remaining sessions of the Conference.

Warren Kelchner, Chief of the Division of International Conferences, Department of State of the United States, was designated, with the approval of the President of the United States, as Secretary General of the Conference, and Theodore P. Wright, Administrator of Civil Aeronautics, Civil Aeronautics Administration, Department of Commerce of the United States, was designated Technical Secretary of the Conference.

Adolf A. Berle, Jr., Chairman of the Delegation of the United States of America, was elected Permanent President of the Conference at the Second Plenary Session, held on November 2, 1944.

Max Hymans, Chairman of the Delegation of France, and Kia-ngau Chang, Chairman of the Delegation of China, were elected Vice Presidents of the Conference.

The Executive Committee, composed of the Chairman of the respective Delegations, and presided over by the Temporary President of the Conference, appointed a Steering Committee of the Conference, with the following membership: [3]

. . . .

STEERING COMMITTEE

The Temporary President appointed the following members of the General Committees constituted by the Conference:

COMMITTEE ON NOMINATIONS

COMMITTEE ON CREDENTIALS

COMMITTEE ON RULES AND REGULATIONS

On November 30, 1944, the Coördinating Committee was appointed by the Executive Committee, with the following membership: [4]

. . . .

COÖRDINATING COMMITTEE

The Conference was divided into four Technical Committees. The officers of these Committees, as elected by the Conference, and officers of the Subcommittees established by the Committees, are listed below: [5]

. . . .

COMMITTEE I

MULTILATERAL AVIATION CONVENTION AND INTERNATIONAL AERONAUTICAL BODY

Subcommittee 1.—*International Organization*

Subcommittee 2.—*Air Navigation Principles*

Subcommittee 3.—*Air Transportation Principles*

[3] Names omitted.
[4] Names omitted.
[5] Names omitted.

COMMITTEE II

TECHNICAL STANDARDS AND PROCEDURES

Subcommittee 1.—*Communications Procedures; Airways Systems*

Subcommittee 2.—*Rules of the Air; Air Traffic Control Practices*

Subcommittee 3.—*Standards Governing the Licensing of Operating and Mechanical Personnel; Log Books*

Subcommittee 4.—*Airworthiness of Aircraft*

Subcommittee 5.—*Registration and Identification of Aircraft*

Subcommittee 6.—*Collection and Dissemination of Meteorological Information*

Subcommittee 7.—*Aeronautical Maps and Charts*

Subcommittee 8.—*Customs Procedures; Manifests*

Subcommittee 9.—*Accident Investigation, Including Search and Salvage*

Subcommittee 10.—*Publications and Forms*

COMMITTEE III

PROVISIONAL AIR ROUTES

Subcommittee 1.—*Standard Form of Provisional Route Agreements*

COMMITTEE IV

INTERIM COUNCIL

Subcommittee 1.—*Composition and Organization of the Interim Council*
Subcommittee 2.—*Powers and Duties of the Interim Council*

The Final Plenary Session was held on December 7, 1944.
As a result of the deliberations of the Conference, as recorded in the minutes and reports of the respective Committees and Subcommittees and of the Plenary Sessions, the following instruments were formulated:

INTERIM AGREEMENT ON INTERNATIONAL CIVIL AVIATION

Interim Agreement on International Civil Aviation, which is attached hereto as Appendix I.

CONVENTION ON INTERNATIONAL CIVIL AVIATION

Convention on International Civil Aviation, which is attached hereto as Appendix II.

INTERNATIONAL AIR SERVICES TRANSIT AGREEMENT

International Air Services Transit Agreement, which is attached hereto as Appendix III.

INTERNATIONAL AIR TRANSPORT AGREEMENT

International Air Transport Agreement, which is attached hereto as Appendix IV.

The following resolutions and recommendations were adopted:

I

PREPARATION OF THE FINAL ACT

The International Civil Aviation Conference

RESOLVES:

That the Secretariat be authorized to prepare the Final Act in accordance with the suggestions proposed by the Secretary General in *Journal* No. 34, December 4, 1944, and that the Coordinating Committee review the text;

That the Final Act contain the definitive texts of the instruments formulated by the Conference in plenary session, and that no changes be made therein at the Final Plenary Session.

II

DRAFT TECHNICAL ANNEXES

WHEREAS:

The largest possible degree of international standardization of practice in many matters is important to safe, expeditious, and easy air navigation; and

WHEREAS:

These matters typically involve problems of great variety and complexity, and require that much new ground be explored; and

WHEREAS:

Considerable progress has been made, during the discussions of the present Conference, in the development of codes of practice agreed upon as proper by the technicians participating in the discussions, but the time has been too limited, and the number of personnel able to participate directly too small, to permit carrying the discussions to final conviction of the adequacy or correctness of certain of the determinations here made;

The International Civil Aviation Conference

RESOLVES:

That the drafts of annexes for an international civil aviation convention, which are attached hereto as Appendix V, be accepted by the Conference, upon the bases that:

a The drafts as now presented shall be accepted by the participating States for immediate and continuing study;

b They shall be accepted as constituting models of the desirable scope and arrangement of the several annexes;

c The participating States undertake to forward to the Government of the United States (or to the Provisional International Civil Aviation Organization if it shall in the meantime have been established), by May 1, 1945, any recommendations which they may have for necessary additions, deletions, or amendments;

d The Government of the United States (or the Provisional International Civil Aviation Organization) will transmit such suggestions to the other participating States in anticipation of meetings of the technical committees to be established by the Provisional International Civil Aviation Organization for dealing with the subject matter of the various documents, such meetings to be held as soon as practicable thereafter for the purpose of ultimate acceptance of the annexes in final form for attachment to a convention.

e Meanwhile, in so far as the Technical Subcommittees have been able to agree on recommended practices, the States of the world, bearing in mind their present international obligations, are urged to accept these practices as ones toward which the national practices of the several States should be directed as far and as rapidly as may prove practicable.

III
TECHNICAL PERSONNEL

WHEREAS:

The development and maintenance of suitable international standards in matters relating to international air navigation will require constant analysis, by technically qualified personnel, of the development of the pertinent arts and of the various practices existing with respect thereto;

The International Civil Aviation Conference

RESOLVES:

That the Provisional International Civil Aviation Organization, as soon as possible after its organization, should employ in its Secretariat a suitable body of personnel, expert in the fields of aeronautical science and practice in which continuing study will be particularly needed; and that such technically qualified members of the Secretariat should be charged to analyze and report to the Provisional International Civil Aviation Organization on problems relating to the drafting of international standards and recommended practices and to conduct and report on such other studies as will promote the safe and efficient conduct of international air transportation.

IV
METRIC SYSTEM

WHEREAS:

A standard system of measurements in all rules and regulations pertaining to air traffic on international and intercontinental airways would greatly contribute to the safety of these operations; and

WHEREAS:

It is considered of high importance that figures used in rules and regulations and other data, with which air crews and other operational personnel have to deal in the preparation of and during flights over various countries, should consist of round figures which can easily be remembered;

The International Civil Aviation Conference
RESOLVES:

1. That in those cases in which it appears impracticable or undesirable to make use of the metric system as a primary international standard, units in

publications and codes of practice directly affecting international air navigation should be expressed both in the metric and English systems; and

2. That the Provisional International Civil Aviation Organization shall make further unification of numbering and systems of dimensioning and specification of dimensions used in connection with international air navigation the subject of continuing study and recommendation.

V

TRANSFER OF TITLE TO AIRCRAFT

CONSIDERING:

That the sale of aircraft to be used in international operations will render it desirable for the various governments to reach a common understanding on the legal questions involved in the transfer of title;

The International Civil Aviation Conference

RECOMMENDS:

That the various governments represented at this International Civil Aviation Conference give consideration to the early calling of an international conference on private international air law for the purpose of adopting a convention dealing with the transfer of title to aircraft and that such private air law conference include in the bases of discussions:

(a) The existing draft convention relating to mortgages, other real securities, and aerial privileges; and

(b) The existing draft convention on the ownership of aircraft and the aeronautic register,

both of which were adopted by the Comité International Technique d'Experts Juridiques Aériens (CITEJA) in 1931.

VI

ROME CONVENTION (MAY 29, 1933) RELATING TO THE PRECAUTIONARY ATTACHMENT OF AIRCRAFT

CONSIDERING:

That the expeditious movement of aircraft in international commerce is essential in order that the fullest advantage may be derived from the rapid means of communication afforded by aircraft;

That the seizure or detention of aircraft where the attaching creditor cannot invoke a judgment and execution obtained beforehand in the ordinary course of procedure, or an equivalent right of execution, affects the expeditious movement of aircraft in international commerce;

The International Civil Aviation Conference

RECOMMENDS:

That the various governments represented at this International Civil Aviation Conference give consideration to the desirability of ratifying or adhering to the Convention for the Unification of Certain Rules Relating to the Precautionary Attachment of Aircraft, signed at Rome on May 29, 1933, during the Third International Conference on Private Air Law, in so far as such governments have not already ratified or adhered to that Convention.

VII

RESUMPTION OF AND COÖRDINATION WITH THE SESSIONS OF CITEJA

CONSIDERING:

That the Comité International Technique d'Experts Juridiques Aériens (CITEJA), created pursuant to a recommendation adopted at the First International Conference on Private Air Law held at Paris in 1925, has made considerable progress in the development of a code of private international air law through the preparation of draft international conventions for final adoption at periodic international conferences on private air law;

That the further elaboration of this code of private international air law through the completion of pending CITEJA projects and the initiation of new studies in the field of private air law will contribute materially to the development of international civil aviation;

The International Civil Aviation Conference

RECOMMENDS:

1. That the various governments represented at this International Civil Aviation Conference give consideration to the desirability of bringing about the resumption at the earliest possible date of the CITEJA sessions which were suspended because of the outbreak of war, of making necessary contributions toward the expenses of the Secretariat of CITEJA, and of appointing legal experts to attend the CITEJA meetings; and

2. That consideration also be given by the various governments to the desirability of coordinating the activities of CITEJA with those of the Provisional International Civil Aviation Organization and, after it shall have come into existence, of the permanent International Civil Aviation Organization established pursuant to the Convention on International Civil Aviation drawn up in Chicago on December 7, 1944.

VIII

STANDARD FORM OF AGREEMENT FOR PROVISIONAL AIR ROUTES

WHEREAS:

The course of military events will free certain areas of the world from the interruption which the war has caused to civil air traffic;

WHEREAS:

The civil transport systems and facilities of many States have been reduced to a level which is far from adequate, but on the other hand there exist wide opportunities for utilizing the airplane, which has demonstrated its efficiency in rendering rapid transportation on a large scale basis, in bringing aid to needy countries and in hastening the return of normal trade and commerce;

WHEREAS:

The possibilities of air transportation are so great and at the same time so unpredictable, that it is desirable to promote early development in this field during a transitional period, in order to obtain practical experience for giving effect to more permanent arrangements at a later date;

WHEREAS:

Every State has complete and exclusive sovereignty over the airspace above its territory; and

WHEREAS:

It is desirable that there should be as great a measure of uniformity as possible in any agreements that may be made between States for the operation of air services;

The International Civil Aviation Conference

RECOMMENDS:

1. That each State undertake to refrain from including specific provisions in an agreement which grant exclusive rights of transit, non-traffic stop, and commercial entry to any other State or airline, or from making any agreement excluding or discriminating against the airlines of any State, and will terminate any existing exclusive or discriminatory rights as soon as such action can be taken under presently outstanding agreements;

2. That the clauses contained in the draft form of standard agreement hereinafter set out shall be regarded as standard clauses for incorporation in the agreements referred to above, it being understood that the right is reserved to the States concerned to effect such changes of wording as may be necessary in the particular case and to add additional clauses so long as such changes or additions are not inconsistent with the standard clauses, it being further understood that nothing herein shall prevent any State from entering into agreements with airlines of other States provided that such agreements shall incorporate the aforementioned standard clauses to the extent that these may be applicable:

FORM OF STANDARD AGREEMENT FOR PROVISIONAL AIR ROUTES

(1) The contracting parties grant the rights specified in the Annex [6] hereto necessary for establishing the international civil air routes and services therein described, whether such services be inaugurated immediately or at a later date at the option of the contracting party to whom the rights are granted.

(2) a Each of the air services so described shall be placed in operation as soon as the contracting party to whom the right has been granted by paragraph (1) to designate an airline or airlines for the route concerned has authorized an airline for such route, and the contracting party granting the right shall, subject to Article (7) hereof, be bound to give the appropriate operating permission to the airline or airlines concerned; provided that the airline so designated may be required to qualify before the competent aeronautical authorities of the contracting party granting the rights under the laws and regulations normally applied by these authorities before being permitted to engage in the operations contemplated by this Agreement; and provided that in areas of hostilities or of military occupation, or in areas affected thereby, such inauguration shall be subject to the approval of the competent military authorities.

[6] An annex will include a description of the routes and of the rights granted whether of transit only, of non-traffic stops or of commercial entry as the case may be, and the conditions incidental to the granting of the rights. Where rights of non-traffic stop or commercial rights are granted, the Annex will include a designation of the ports of call at which stops can be made, or at which commercial rights for the embarkation and disembarkation of passengers, cargo and mail are authorized, and a statement of the contracting parties to whom the respective rights are granted.

b It is understood that any contracting party granted commercial rights under this Agreement should exercise them at the earliest practicable date except in the case of temporary inability to do so.

(3) Operating rights which may have been granted previously by any of the contracting parties to any State not a party to this Agreement or to an airline shall continue in force according to their terms.

(4) In order to prevent discriminatory practices and to assure equality of treatment, it is agreed that:

a Each of the contracting parties may impose or permit to be imposed just and reasonable charges for the use of airports, and other facilities. Each of the contracting parties agrees, however, that these charges shall not be higher than would be paid for the use of such airports and facilities by its national aircraft engaged in similar international services.

b Fuel, lubricating oils and spare parts introduced into the territory of a contracting party by another contracting party or its nationals, and intended solely for use by aircraft of such other contracting party shall be accorded national and most-favored-nation treatment with respect to the imposition of customs duties, inspection fees or other national duties or charges by the contracting party whose territory is entered.

c The fuel, lubricating oils, spare parts, regular equipment and aircraft stores retained on board civil aircraft of the airlines of the contracting parties authorized to operate the routes and services described in the Annex shall, upon arriving in or leaving the territory of other contracting parties, be exempt from customs, inspection fees or similar duties or charges, even though such supplies be used or consumed by such aircraft on flights in that territory.

(5) Certificates of airworthiness, certificates of competency and licenses issued or rendered valid by one contracting party shall be recognized as valid by the other contracting parties for the purpose of operating the routes and services described in the Annex. Each contracting party reserves the right, however, to refuse to recognize, for the purpose of flight above its own territory, certificates of competency and licenses granted to its own nationals by another State.

(6) *a* The laws and regulations of a contracting party relating to the admission to or departure from its territory of aircraft engaged in international air navigation, or to the operation and navigation of such aircraft while within its territory, shall be applied to the aircraft of all contracting parties without distinction as to nationality, and shall be complied with by such aircraft upon entering or departing from or while within the territory of that party.

b The laws and regulations of a contracting party as to the admission to or departure from its territory of passengers, crew, or cargo of aircraft, such as regulations relating to entry, clearance, immigration, passports, customs, and quarantine shall be complied with by or on behalf of such passengers, crew, or cargo upon entrance into or departure from, or while within the territory of that party.

(7) Each contracting party reserves the right to withhold or revoke a certificate or permit to an airline of another State in any case where it is not satisfied that substantial ownership and effective control are vested in nationals of a party to this Agreement, or in case of failure of an airline to comply with the laws of the State over which it operates, as described in Article (6) hereof, or to perform its obligations under this Agreement.

(8) This Agreement and all contracts connected therewith shall be registered with the Provisional International Civil Aviation Organization.

(9) [Where desired, here insert provisions for arbitration, the details of which will be a matter for negotiation between the parties to each agreement.]

(10) This Agreement shall continue in force until such time as it may be amended, or superseded by a general multilateral air convention, provided, however, that the rights for services granted under this Agreement may be terminated by giving one year's notice to the contracting party whose airlines are concerned. Such notice may be given at any time after a period of two months to allow for consultation between the contracting party giving notice and the contracting parties served by the routes.

IX

FLIGHT DOCUMENTS AND FORMS

The International Civil Aviation Conference

RESOLVES:

That the Provisional International Civil Aviation Organization, when established, be requested to give consideration to the question of the publication of flight documents and forms in representative languages of areas through which major international air routes are operated.

X

RECOMMENDATION THAT CERTAIN MATTERS BE REFERRED TO THE INTERIM COUNCIL FOR STUDY

The International Civil Aviation Conference

RECOMMENDS:

That the matters on which it has not been possible to reach agreement between the States represented at this Conference, in particular the matters comprehended within the headings of Articles II, X, XI, and XII of Document 358 (Draft of a Section of an International Air Convention Relating Primarily to Air Transport), together with Conference Documents 384, 385, 400, 407, and 429, and all other documentation relating thereto, be referred to the Interim Council provided for in the Interim Agreement on International Civil Aviation drawn up at Chicago on December 7, 1944, with instruction to give these matters continuing study and to submit a report thereon with recommendations to the Interim Assembly as soon as practicable.

XI

PUBLICATION OF DOCUMENTATION

The International Civil Aviation Conference

RESOLVES:

That the Government of the United States of America be authorized to publish the Final Act of this Conference; the Reports of the Committees; the Minutes of the Public Sessions; the Texts of any Multilateral Agreements concluded at the Conference; and to make available for publication such additional documents in connection with the work of this Conference as in its judgment may be considered in the public interest.

XII

The International Civil Aviation Conference

RESOLVES:

1. To express its gratitude to the President of the United States, Franklin D. Roosevelt, for his initiative in convening the present Conference and for its preparation;

2. To express to its President, Adolf A. Berle, Jr., its deep appreciation for the admirable manner in which he has guided the Conference;

3. To express to the Officers and Staff of the Secretariat its appreciation for their untiring services and diligent efforts in contributing to the attainment of the objectives of the Conference;

IN WITNESS WHEREOF, the following Delegates sign the present Final Act.

DONE at Chicago the seventh day of December 1944, in the English language. A text drawn up in the English, French, and Spanish languages, each of which shall be of equal authenticity, shall be opened for signature at Washington, D. C. Both texts shall be deposited in the archives of the Government of the United States of America, and certified copies shall be transmitted by that Government to each of the governments represented at the Conference.

[Here follow the signatures of the representatives of all participating Governments.]

7. RULES OF PROCEDURE, UNITED NATIONS CONFERENCE ON INTERNATIONAL ORGANIZATION, APRIL 25-JUNE 26, 1945 [1]

a. Informal Memorandum on Possible Rules of Procedure, Doc. 25, April 23

I. ESTABLISHMENT OF COMMISSIONS, TECHNICAL COMMITTEES AND SUBCOMMITTEES

1. It is suggested that upon adoption by the Conference in plenary session of an organizational plan for the Conference, the President of the Conference would request the presidents of the commissions, in consultation with the Secretary-General of the Conference, to call the first meetings of their respective commissions as soon as possible. The secretary-general of each delegation would as soon as possible inform the Secretary-General of the Conference as to the commissions and technical committees on which his delegation desires to be represented and the name of the member or members designated in each case.

2. At the appropriate time the presidents of the respective commissions would request the chairman of the technical committees to call the first meetings of their respective committees.

3. Subcommittees would begin meetings when requested to do so by the respective technical committees.

II. SUBMISSION OF FORMAL PROPOSALS

Formal proposals which a delegation desires to submit to the Conference would be transmitted through the Secretary-General to the Steering Com-

---

[1] United States, Department of State, *United Nations Conference on International Organization*, pp. 69-83.

mittee or, upon authorization of the Steering Committee, to the Executive Committee. The committee to which such a formal proposal is transmitted should determine the procedure to be followed with respect to it, including its reference to a commission or technical committee. No such proposal should be discussed in the commission or technical committee to which it is referred unless the text has been distributed to all delegations not less than 24 hours preceding the meeting.

III. RIGHT TO ADDRESS THE CONFERENCE

Speakers should be recognized by the presiding officer in the order in which they have signified their desire to speak. The president, chairman, or rapporteur of a commission or committee might be accorded precedence for the purpose of explaining or clarifying the conclusions arrived at by a commission or committee.

IV. VOTING

1. Each delegation would have one vote in each body of the Conference on which it is represented.
2. Voting in Public Sessions and Meetings
In all public sessions and meetings of the Conference (in plenary sessions and public meetings of the commissions) voting on questions of procedure, it is suggested, would be by majority vote of the delegations present, and voting on a text or other substantive questions would be by two-thirds vote of the delegations present.
3. Voting in Closed Meetings
The voting procedure and rules in closed meetings of the Conference (in closed meetings of the commissions and in meetings of the technical committees), it is suggested, would be decided, on an *ad hoc* basis, by the body concerned.
4. The Conference should normally be a show of hands except that any delegation in any body of the Conference might request a roll call which would be taken by countries in English alphabetical order.

V. LANGUAGES

1. English, Russian, Chinese, French, and Spanish should be the official languages of the Conference.
2. The final text of the Charter will be prepared and opened for signature in each of the five official languages. If time does not permit the completion of the texts in each of these languages before the closing of the Conference, the texts which have not been completed by that time should be opened for signature at a later date.
3. The Dumbarton Oaks Proposals, supplemented by the Crimea proposal on voting procedure in the Security Council, would be issued in all five official languages as the first document of the Conference.
4. As a practical matter it would be helpful if English were to be used as the working language of the Conference. All Conference documents, records, and the official *Journal* would be issued in English. Upon request by the chairman of a delegation to the Secretary-General, the Secretariat would endeavor so far as possible, to issue important documents of the Conference (in addition to those mentioned in paragraphs 2 and 3 above) in other official languages as well as in English. For mechanical reasons, however, it is suggested that, apart from the documents mentioned in paragraphs 2 and 3, no

printing would be done in any language other than English and that requests for reproduction in typewritten form of important documents in languages other than English be held to a minimum. The Secretariat would be prepared to assist delegations in translating Russian, Chinese, French, or Spanish documents into English. In addition, the Secretariat would comply, so far as possible, with requests for assistance in translating draft texts or proposals into Russian, French, or Spanish.

5. Deliberation of the plenary sessions of the Conference and of the commissions should normally be conducted in English. Delegates speaking in other languages should, if possible, furnish an English interpretation or an English translation of their remarks. The Secretariat would provide assistance in interpreting from Russian, French, and Spanish into English at plenary sessions, and at other meetings so far as possible. English should also generally be used in the meetings of the technical committees and subcommittees. Delegates should provide their own interpreters to enable them to follow discussions in English.

VI. RECORDS

1. No stenographic transcript of proceedings would be kept except at plenary sessions of the Conference and at public meetings of the commissions.

2. For all other meetings the Secretariat would prepare a brief summary of the discussion and of the decisions reached.

3. Both stenographic transcripts and summaries of proceedings would be prepared first in provisional form for clearance, prior to general distribution, with the appropriate members of the bodies concerned. After corrections have been made the transcript or summary would be issued in final form.

VII. DOCUMENT CLASSIFICATION

The classification and distribution of each document would be determined by the body of the Conference which originates it.

There would be two classifications of documents:

1. *Unrestricted,* for distribution to all delegations, to accredited press, radio, and newsreel representatives, and to the public so far as the supply permits;

2. *Restricted,* for distribution only to delegations.

VIII. PUBLIC-INFORMATION POLICY

Plenary sessions of the Conference and meetings of the commissions would be held in public, subject to the reservation that the commissions in their discretion might hold closed meetings. In addition, principal officers of the Conference would hold regular meetings with the accredited press, radio, and newsreel representatives. The meetings of the technical committees and subcommittees would be closed.

IX. HOURS OF ASSEMBLY

1. Plenary sessions of the Conference would normally convene at 10:30 a.m. or 3.30 p.m. Meetings of the commissions and technical committees would normally be from 10:30 a.m. to 1:00 p.m. or from 3:00 p.m. to 6:00 p.m. Meetings could, of course, be arranged for other hours by decision of the bodies concerned.

b. **Alternative Proposals on Conference Voting Procedure, Doc. 141, May 8**

(TO FORM SECTION IV OF THE CONFERENCE RULES OF PROCEDURE)

I. ORIGINAL PROPOSAL

(Contained in the Secretariat's memorandum of April 23, with verbal modifications necessary to put it in final instead of proposal form)

1. Each delegation shall have one vote in each body of the Conference on which it is represented.

2. Voting in Public Sessions and Meetings

In all public sessions and meetings of the Conference (in plenary sessions and in public meetings of the commissions) voting on questions of procedure shall be by majority vote of the delegations present, and voting on a text or other substantive questions shall be by two-thirds vote of the delegations present.

3. Voting in Closed Meetings

The voting procedure and rules in closed meetings of the Conference (in closed meetings of the commissions and in meetings of the technical committees) shall be decided, on an *ad hoc* basis, by the body concerned.

4. The Conference should normally voted by a show of hands except that any delegation in any body of the Conference may request a roll call which shall be taken by countries in English alphabetical order.

II. ALTERNATIVE A

(Formula suggested by the Secretariat to provide for the possibility of voting on substantive questions in commissions and plenary sessions by majority instead of two-thirds vote under certain conditions)

1. Each Delegation One Vote

Each delegation shall have one vote in each body of the Conference on which it is represented.

2. Voting on a Question of Procedure

Any question of procedure put to the vote shall be decided by a majority of the votes of the delegations present and voting.

3. Voting on All Other Questions

All other questions (those concerning a text, an amendment, or other substantive matter) put to the vote shall be decided as follows:

a. In general committees, technical committees, and subcommittees, by a majority of the votes of the delegations present and voting. At the request of any delegation voting contrary to the majority, or abstaining, its views together with the views of the majority shall be reported to the appropriate superior body.

b. In commissions, by two thirds of the votes of the delegations present and voting, provided that, either on its own initiative or upon the request of any delegation presented to it through the president of the commission concerned, the Executive Committee may direct that any given question be decided by a majority of the votes cast.

c. In plenary sessions, by two thirds of the votes of the delegations present and voting, provided that the Steering Committee, after advice by the Executive Committee, may recommend to the Conference in plenary session that any given question be decided by a majority of the votes cast. In that event the Conference in plenary session, before voting on the substantive question referred to it, shall decide by a majority vote of the delegations

INTERNATIONAL ORGANIZATION

present and voting whether or not to accept the recommendation of the Steering Committee regarding the vote to be required.

4. Manner of Voting

The Conference shall normally vote by a show of hands except that any delegation in any body of the Conference may request a roll call, which shall then be taken by countries in English alphabetical order.

III. ALTERNATIVE B

(Formula suggested by the Secretariat to provide for the possibility of voting on substantive questions in commissions and plenary sessions by two-thirds instead of majority vote under certain conditions)

1. Each Delegation One Vote

Each delegation shall have one vote in each body of the Conference on which it is represented.

2. Voting on a Question of Procedure

Any question of procedure put to the vote shall be decided by a majority of the votes of the delegations present and voting.

3. Voting on All Other Questions

All other questions (those concerning a text, an amendment, or other substantive matter) put to the vote shall be decided as follows:

a. In general committees, technical committees, and subcommittees, by a majority of the votes of the delegations present and voting. At the request of any delegation voting contrary to the majority, or abstaining, its views together with the views of the majority shall be reported to the appropriate superior body.

b. In commissions, by a majority of the votes of the delegations present and voting, provided that, either on its own initiative, or upon the request of any delegation presented to it through the president of the commission concerned, the Executive Committee may direct that any given question be decided by two thirds of the votes cast.

c. In plenary sessions, by a majority of the votes of the delegations present and voting, provided that the Steering Committee, after advice by the Executive Committee, may recommend to the Conference in plenary session that any given question be decided by two thirds of the votes cast. In that event the Conference in plenary session, before voting on the substantive question referred to it, shall decide by a majority vote of the delegations present and voting whether or not to accept the recommendation of the Steering Committee regarding the vote to be required.

4. Manner of Voting

The Conference shall normally vote by a show of hands except that any delegation in any body of the Conference may request a roll call, which shall then be taken by countries in English alphabetical order.

IV. ALTERNATIVE C [1]

(Revision of the original proposal suggested by the Secretariat, applying the two-thirds voting requirement on substantive questions to all bodies of the Conference, instead of limiting it to public sessions and meetings)

1. Each delegation shall have one vote in each body of the Conference on which it is represented.

[1] The Executive Committee at its third meeting, on May 8, adopted alternative C with the addition of the words "and voting" to the end of each of the two sentences in paragraph 2.

2. Any question of procedure put to the vote shall be decided by a majority of the votes of the delegations present. All other questions put to the vote shall be decided by two thirds of the votes of the delegations present.

3. If there is a substantial degree of uncertainty prior to a vote on any given question as to whether that question is or is not one of procedure, the presiding officer of the body concerned shall submit the question to the Executive Committee, which shall decide.

4. The Conference shall normally vote by a show of hands, except that any delegation in any body of the Conference may request a roll call, which shall then be taken by countries in English alphabetical order.

c. Rules of Procedure,[1] Doc. 177, May 9

I. ESTABLISHMENT OF COMMISSIONS, TECHNICAL COMMITTEES AND SUBCOMMITTEES

1. Upon adoption by the Conference in plenary session of the Report of the Meeting of the Heads of Delegations To Organize the Conference, the President of the Conference will request the presidents of the commissions, in consultation with the Secretary-General of the Conference, to call the first meetings of their respective commissions as soon as possible. The secretary-general of each delegation as soon as possible will inform the Secretary-General of the Conference as to the commissions and technical committees on which his delegation desires to be represented and the name of the member or members designated in each case.

2. At the appropriate time the presidents of the respective commissions will request the chairman of the technical committees to call the first meetings of their respective committees.

3. Subcommittees will begin meetings when requested to do so by the respective technical committees.

II. SUBMISSION AND ALLOCATION OF FORMAL PROPOSALS

Formal proposals which a delegation desires to submit to the Conference shall be circulated to all delegations. All such proposals should be submitted before midnight, Friday, May 4, it being understood that drafting changes may be put forward at any time. Formal proposals received after Friday, May 4, can be accepted only upon authorization of the Executive Committee, before which body the Secretary-General will lay them. The Secretary-General will provisionally allocate all proposals submitted by the various delegations to the appropriate commissions and their committees.

III. COMMUNICATIONS FROM NON-PARTICIPANTS IN THE CONFERENCE

Communications from governments, organizations, and individuals not participating in the Conference which are sent to the Secretariat will be distributed to the delegations only if, in the discretion of the Secretary-General, they are relevant to the subject-matter of the Conference and if the facilities of the Secretariat are available to handle them without delay to official work.

IV. RIGHT TO ADDRESS THE CONFERENCE

Speakers shall be recognized by the presiding officer in the order in which they have signified their desire to speak. The president, chairman, or rap-

[1] This document is still to be submitted to the Conference in plenary session. [Footnote in the original; the document was never submitted to a plenary session and consequently was never approved.]

porteur of a commission or committee may be accorded precedence for the purpose of explaining or clarifying the conclusions arrived at by the commission or committee.

V. VOTING

1. Each delegation shall have one vote in each body of the Conference on which it is represented.

2. Any question of procedure put to the vote shall be decided by a majority of the votes of the delegations present and voting. All other questions put to the vote shall be decided by two thirds of the votes of the delegations present and voting.

3. If there is a substantial degree of uncertainty prior to a vote on any given question as to whether that question is or is not one of procedure, the presiding officer of the body concerned shall submit the question to the Executive Committee, which shall decide.

4. The Conference shall normally vote by a show of hands, except that any delegation in any body of the Conference may request a roll call, which shall then be taken by countries in English alphabetical order.

VI. LANGUAGES

1. English, Russian, Chinese, French, and Spanish shall be the official languages of the Conference.

2. English and French shall be the working languages of the Conference.

3. At plenary sessions of the Conference addresses in English or French shall not be interpreted into the other language unless the speaker so requests, but a translation will appear subsequently in the verbatim minutes.

Delegates shall be free to use any other language besides English or French, but in this case they shall provide interpretations thereof into either English or French at their choice. Interpretations will be provided by the Secretariat into the other of these two languages if the speaker so requests. As regards meetings of commissions, technical committees, and subcommittees, interpretations from English into French and from French into English will be provided. Delegates shall be free in these bodies also to speak in any other language, but shall provide their own interpretations into either English or French at their choice; the Secretariat will provide interpretations into the other of these two languages if the speaker so requests.

4. The Dumbarton Oaks Proposals, as supplemented at the Crimea Conference and by the Chinese proposals agreed to by all of the sponsoring governments, will be issued in each of the five official languages as the first document of the Conference.

5. The final text of the Charter will be prepared and opened for signature in each of the five official languages. If time does not permit the completion of the texts in each of these languages before the closing of the Conference, the texts which have not been completed by that time shall be opened for signature at a later date.

6. All Conference documents, records, and the official *Journal* will be issued in the two working languages of the Conference.

7. The following categories of documents will be published (i.e. issued in printed, mimeographed, hectographed, or other appropriate form) upon request in any or all of the five official languages in addition to English and French.

    a. All proposals presented to the Conference or its subordinate bodies;

    b. All decisions of plenary sessions, commissions, or committees;

    c. Summaries or records of meetings of the committees or subcommittees.

VII. RECORDS

1. No stenographic transcript of proceedings will be kept except at plenary sessions of the Conference and at public meetings of the commissions.

2. The Secretariat will prepare a brief summary of the proceedings in other meetings.

3. Both stenographic transcripts and summaries of proceedings will be prepared first in provisional form and be subject to correction. After corrections have been made the transcript or summary will be issued in final form.

VIII. DOCUMENT CLASSIFICATION

There will be two classifications of documents:

1. *Unrestricted*, for distribution to all delegations, to accredited press, radio, and newsreel representatives, and to the public so far as the supply permits;

2. *Restricted*, for distribution only to delegations.

IX. PUBLIC-INFORMATION POLICY

Plenary sessions of the Conference and meetings of the commissions will be held in public, subject to the reservation that the commissions in their discretion may hold closed meetings. In addition, principal officers of the Conference will hold regular meetings with the accredited press, radio, and newsreel representatives. The meetings of the technical committees and subcommittees will be closed.

X. HOURS OF ASSEMBLY

1. Plenary sessions of the Conference will normally convene at 10:30 a.m. or 3.30 p.m. Meetings of the commissions will normally take place at 10:30 a.m. and 2:45 p.m. For the technical committees there will be four sittings each day, at 10:30 a.m., 2:45 p.m., 5:00 p.m., and 8:30 p.m. At each of these hours three committees will normally convene. If the work of technical committees, or their subcommittees, makes it essential for them to hold special meetings at hours differing from the established schedule, they should consult with the Office of the Executive Secretary.

d. Conference Procedure on Drafting Final Charter. Doc. 243, May 11

(THIS DOCUMENT WAS APPROVED BY THE STEERING COMMITTEE AT ITS THIRD MEETING, MAY 10)

1. Responsibility for preparing the final Charter shall rest upon the Coordination Committee as an agent of the Executive Committee. In this connection, the Coördination Committee's main responsibilities, under the Executive Committee, shall be as follows:

    a. to determine the general outline and type of charter to be drafted,

    b. to examine the drafts received from the technical committees with a view to eliminating inconsistencies between them, in consultation if necessary with the committees concerned or by referring the matter to the Executive Committee;

    c. to recommend to the Executive Committee the final draft of the Charter as a whole or in parts.

2. There shall also be established, under the Executive Committee, an Advisory Committee of Jurists, consisting of a small number (five or six members) which shall be responsible for reviewing the texts prepared by the Coördination Committee and eventually the whole text, from the point of view of terminology, in accordance with the procedure set forth in paragraph 5 below.

3. In the event of a disagreement between the Coördination Committee and the Advisory Committee of Jurists, there shall be a joint meeting of the two to resolve the difficulties, and if necessary consultation shall be had with the technical committees concerned. If such joint meeting fails to resolve such disagreements, then the matter shall be referred to the Executive Committee.

4. The technical committees of the Conference shall embody their decisions on points for which they are responsible in the form of drafts.

5. Subsequent procedure shall be as follows:

a. These drafts shall be submitted by the technical committees to the Executive Committee, which shall refer them to the Coördination Committee.

b. The Coördination Committee, after its review of the drafts, shall refer them to the Advisory Committee of Jurists, which shall, after its review, refer them back to the Coördination Committee for final review and submission to the Executive Committee.

c. The Executive Committee shall refer the drafts submitted to it by the Coördination Committee to the respective commissions, which, after having examined and approved them, will in turn submit them to a plenary session of the Conference.

6. This procedure does not prejudice the right of commissions at any stage to review the activities or recommendations of their respective technical committees.

e. **Suggested Procedure for Conducting Committee Meetings. Doc. 332, EX-SEC/8, May 13**

(MEMORANDUM TO THE DELEGATIONS FROM THE SECRETARIAT, MAY 13)

(The following rules of procedure relating to discussion, to motions, and to the appointment of subcommittees have been widely applied in connection with international conferences in the past. At the suggestion of several delegations these rules are brought to the attention of delegations by the Secretariat as an aid to the conduct of committee discussions)

Rules for Discussion

1. The chairman may call a speaker to order if his remarks are not relevant to the subject under discussion.

2. If, in the course of discussion, a member rises to a point of order, he shall be given the floor immediately and such point of order shall be immediately decided by the chairman. If exception is taken to the decision of the chairman, the point should be referred by the chairman to the Executive Committee. Pending a decision by the Executive Committee, the decision of the chairman shall stand.

3. On motions pertaining to procedural matters the chairman may limit the debate to two speakers for and two speakers against the motion. On motions to close debate permission to speak for or against the motion shall not be accorded to more than two speakers on each side with a time limit of five minutes for each speech.

4. The chairman may limit the time of speeches of the delegates at any point in the debate.

Motions

1. Any delegate may move motions, subject to Section II of the Conference Rules of Procedure; [2] motions shall not be voted upon unless seconded.

2. A motion, other than privileged motions, in paragraph 4 below, should be submitted in writing in one of the working languages of the Conference and handed in to the secretary of the committee before the motion is voted upon.

3. When a number of motions are before a meeting, the chairman shall determine the order in which they shall be discussed and put to the vote, subject to the following provisions:

(*a*) If an amendment striking out or altering certain words in a proposal is moved, the meeting shall first vote on whether the words in question shall stand as part of the proposal. When an amendment is moved which adds to a proposal, the amendment shall be voted on first, and, if it is adopted, the amended proposal shall then be voted on.

4. The following motions, in the order named, shall have precedence over all other motions:

(*a*) a motion to adjourn the sitting;
(*b*) a motion to close debate on a particular question;
(*c*) a motion to postpone consideration of the question;
(*d*) a motion to refer the matter to subcommittee.

Officers of Subcommittees

1. The Chairman shall nominate chairmen, rapporteurs, and members of subcommittees or drafting committees as may be required, subject to the approval of a majority of the committee members present and voting.

f. Suggested Measures to Expedite the Work of the Conference. Doc. 468, May 20

I. SUGGESTED TIME-TABLE

A. The general aim should be to complete the work of the technical committees by the end of the present week.

B. The work of the technical committees is subject to review by the commissions at two stages: prior to and subsequent to the redrafting of the committees' proposals by the Coördination Committee. So far as review at the first stage is desired, meetings of the Commissions for this purpose might begin in the course of the present week and continue into the next. It would seem preferable that such meetings should take place after the technical committees concerned have completed a substantial part of their task and have disposed of their major issues.

C. Commission meetings during the week beginning May 28 would presumably be concerned to an increasing extent with the second stage of the commissions' work, namely, the approval of the proposals as revised in Charter language by the Coördination Committee.

D. When all the commissions have approved the Charter texts referred to them by the Coördination Committee, the entire Charter should be reviewed by the Steering Committee prior to its presentation to the final plenary sessions.

E. It is hoped that the final plenary sessions might take place in the first

[2] Above, p. 344.

week of June and that two sessions (perhaps held on the same day) might suffice to complete the work of the Conference. At these sessions the commissions would report their respective portions of the Charter and the entire Charter would be approved and signed.

F. Measures designed to facilitate the attainment of this time schedule are outlined in II and III below. These measures involve an amplification of the procedures laid down in Documents 243 and EX-SEC/8.

II. PROCEDURE FOR PREPARING THE CHARTER

A. Proposals adopted by the technical committees—even if these proposals form only part of a chapter or section—should be reported immediately to the Coördination Committee, which will examine them in relation to the Charter as a whole and redraft them in Charter form.

B. Such proposals may, at the same time, in the discretion of the committees concerned in consultation with the president of their commission, be reported directly to the commission for review of substance. Meetings of the commissions for this purpose should be held under conditions which will permit an adequate discussion and review of the committees' reports. The committee rapporteurs should make it clear that the text under discussion is preliminary and subject to (1) coördination with texts adopted by other technical committees, and (2) redrafting into Charter language by the Coördination Committee. Should the commission introduce changes in the technical committees' proposals, these changes should be reported forthwith to the Coördination Committee through the Secretariat.

C. Proposals which have been redrafted in Charter form by the Coördination Committee should be reported to the commissions concerned by the rapporteurs of the technical committees within which the texts originated.

D. In order to limit the number of plenary meetings required to approve the acts of the Conference, (1) the commission rapporteurs should not be required at those meetings to read in full such texts as have previously been read and approved in commission meeting, and (2) there should be no discussion of or statements concerning the substance of the texts approved, full opportunity for discussion and statements having been afforded in the commission meetings. (As a further measure to avoid prolonging the closing sessions, the Secretariat is studying appropriate procedures whereby the delegations can be afforded opportunity, if they so desire, to make concluding statements through the medium of the Conference *Journal* and through the public press.)

E. It is suggested that the acts of the Conference should be limited to the Charter, the Statute of the International Court, and an annex to the Charter establishing a commission with administrative powers to function during the interim period prior to the first meeting of the Assembly. This presupposes the avoidance of resolutions which would pre-judge the future policy of the Organization or deal with matters not directly related to the acts of the Conference.

III. MEASURES TO EXPEDITE THE WORK OF THE TECHNICAL COMMITTEES

A. Wherever uncertainty concerning the jurisdiction of different committees arises, solution should be worked out by the presidents of the commissions and the chairmen of the committees concerned, either directly or by setting up joint subcommittees.

B. Some time-limit for speeches in committees appears desirable. As regards debate on motions of procedure, it is suggested in Document EX-SEC/8 that debate be limited to two speakers on either side. As regards debate on questions of substance, the following procedure is now proposed:

(1) A delegate may not speak more than twice on any one question, with a limit of 10 minutes on the first and 5 minutes on the second occasion. (The chairman might apply this rule with some discretion where the discussion involves a matter of major importance.)

(2) When two delegates have spoken for a motion and no speaker wishes to take the opposite point of view, the chairman should put the motion to a vote immediately.

(3) In order to conserve time, a delegation might, in lieu of an oral statement, file a written statement of its position for inclusion in the permanent archives of the Conference and, where requested, for summarization in the permanent committee records.

C. The attention of all committees is called to the suggested rules of procedure for conducting committee meetings, contained in Document EX-SEC/8. The rule with respect to motions for the closing of debate indicated in paragraph 3, under "Rules for Discussion", in that document might be supplemented by the following:

Any member of the committee may at any time move that the debate be closed. It should be within the discretion of the chairman to accept such a motion if he considers the question before the committee has been sufficiently debated. A motion for the closure of a debate should be put to the vote forthwith without discussion, and if the motion is carried, the previous question before the committee should then forthwith be put to the vote without further discussion.

D. Where several delegations have agreed to amalgamate amendments or to put forward a joint proposal, they should, so far as possible, arrange among themselves that only two speakers should speak in favor of the common proposal. The other delegations concerned would retain their right to file statements in the manner suggested under B (3) above.

E. When a committee has requested an authoritative interpretation of a given proposal or amendment and when such interpretation has been given by a delegation and has been adopted by the Committee, that interpretation should then be set forth in the report of the rapporteur.

g. Recommendations Concerning Conduct of Commission Meetings; Doc. 593, May 26

(MEMORANDUM TO ALL DELEGATIONS FROM THE SECRETARIAT, MAY 26.)
DOC. 593, MAY 26

The following recommendations were considered and approved in a meeting of the officers of commissions and committees on Friday, May 25, as a means of facilitating the conduct of public commission meetings. The objective is to provide a maximum freedom of expression at these meetings, yet to achieve the orderly and expeditious completion of the business of the commissions.

It is recommended that:

(1) Delegations should be given opportunity in the commission meeting to make statements either for or against proposals reported by a committee to the commission and voted on in the commission. It is not generally con-

sidered useful, however, to repeat in the commission meetings the debates which have been thoroughly heard in Committee meetings.

(2) Reasonable time limitations should be placed upon the debate in commission meetings. To this end, it is recommended that the rules limiting debate in committee meetings (as set forth in Doc. 468, ST/9) [1] be adopted for commission meetings. As provided in those rules, the president of the commission would normally call for a vote if two speakers have been heard in favor of a proposal and no one wishes to speak against the proposal. The president might apply this rule with some discretion where the discussion involves a matter of major importance.

(3) If delegates wish to propose in commission meetings amendments which have previously been considered but defeated in committee meetings, they should be permitted to do so. In such cases, the delegates should notify the president of the commission and the executive officer of the commission not later than 8 p.m. on the day prior to the scheduled commission meeting of their desire to introduce such proposals.

(4) Essentially new proposals, not previously discussed in committee meetings, will not be introduced in commission meetings.

(5) At least one day shall elapse between a committee meeting at which a report to the commission is approved and the commission meeting at which the report is presented, in order that all delegates may have an opportunity to study the report. So far as possible delegates should notify the president of the commission and the executive officer, by 8 p.m. the previous day, of their intention to speak at the commission meeting. Delegations may so far as possible, in the discussions in commission meetings, present their points of view in written texts to be read by the delegate concerned. The Secretariat requests that copies of such texts, and translations therof, be supplied in advance to insure the reading of satisfactory translations at the meetings.

(6) Individual interpretations stated by delegates at commission meetings will not be incorporated in the report of the commission rapporteur unless they are in accord with the sense of the meeting.[2]

(7) The rules stated in the above paragraph will apply to commission meetings, regardless of whether the commission is considering—

(a) proposals reported from committees but not yet put into Charter language by the Coördination Committee;

(b) texts in Charter language, referred from the Coördination Committee, which may or may not have been discussed previously in the commission.

(8) In the interest of conserving time, the report to be made to the plenary sessions might be considered in the same commission meeting at which the Charter texts referred from the Coördination Committee are discussed.

(9) There should be general uniformity in the procedures of all four commissions.

(MEMORANDUM TO ALL DELEGATIONS FROM THE SECRETARIAT, JUNE 19) DOC. 1098, JUNE 19.

Paragraph (6) of Doc. 593, EX-SEC/11, is clarified to read as follows:

(a) Interpretations adopted by a committee and included in its report to a commission will be automatically included in the commission report to the plenary session, if they are adopted by the commission.

(b) Interpretations proposed at a commission meeting will be incorporated

---

[1] Above, p. 353.

[2] See following document.

in the report of the commission to the plenary session if such interpretations are presented to the commission for approval and adopted by a two-thirds majority. Any interpretation stated by one or more delegations, but not presented for action by the commission, will be recorded in the minutes of the meeting, but will not, of course, be regarded as expressing the views of the commission and will not be included in the report of the commission to the plenary session.

8. CONVENTION OF THE INTERNATIONAL BUREAU OF WEIGHTS AND MEASURES, 1875 [1]

His Excellency the President of the United States of America, His Majesty the Emperor of Germany, His Majesty the Emperor of Austria-Hungary, His Majesty the King of Belgians, His Majesty the Emperor of Brazil, His Excellency the President of the Argentine Confederation, His Majesty the King of Denmark, His Majesty the King of Spain, His Excellency the President of the French Republic, His Majesty the King of Italy, His Excellency the President of the Republic of Peru, His Majesty the King of Portugal and the Algarves, His Majesty the Emperor of all the Russias, His Majesty the King of Sweden and Norway, His Excellency the President of the Swiss Confederation, His Majesty the Emperor of the Ottomans, and His Excellency the President of the Republic of Venezuela, desiring international uniformity and precision in standards of weight and measure, have resolved to conclude a convention to this effect, and have named as their plenipotentiaries the following: [2]

· ·

ARTICLE 1

The high contracting parties engage to establish and maintain, at their common expense, a scientific and permanent international bureau of weights and measures, the location of which shall be at Paris.

ARTICLE 2

The French Government shall take all the necessary measures to facilitate the purchase, or, if expedient, the construction, of a building which shall be especially devoted to this purpose, subject to the conditions stated in the regulations which are subjoined to this convention.

ARTICLE 3

The operation of the international bureau shall be under the exclusive direction and supervision of an international committee of weights and measures, which latter shall be under the control of a general conference for weights and measures, to be composed of the delegates of all the contracting governments.

ARTICLE 4

The general conference for weights and measures shall be presided over by the president for the time being of the Paris Academy of Sciences.

[1] Malloy, *Treaties*, Vol. II, p. 1924. This constitution was slightly modified by an agreement of 6 October 1921: League of Nations, *Treaty Series*, Vol. 17, p. 47.
[2] Names of delegates omitted.

ARTICLE 5

The organization of the bureau, as well as the formation and the powers of the international committee, and of the general conference for weights and measures, are established by the regulations subjoined to this convention.

ARTICLE 6

The international bureau of weights and measures shall be charged with the following duties:

1st. All comparisons and verifications of the new prototypes of the meter and kilogram.

2d. The custody of the international prototypes.

3d. The periodical comparison of the national standards with the international prototypes and with their test copies, as well as comparisons of the standard thermometers.

4th. The comparison of the prototypes with the fundamental standards of non-metrical weights and measures used in different countries for scientific purposes.

5th. The sealing and comparison of geodesic measuring-bars.

6th. The comparison of standards and scales of precision, the verification of which may be requested by governments or by scientific societies, or even by constructors or men of science.

ARTICLE 7

The persons composing the bureau shall be a director, two assistants, and the necessary number of employés. When the comparisons of the new prototypes shall have been finished, and when these prototypes shall have been distributed among the different states, the number of persons composing the bureau shall be reduced so far as may be deemed expedient.

The governments of the high contracting parties will be informed by the international committee of the appointment of the persons composing the bureau.

ARTICLE 8

The international prototypes of the meter and of the kilogram, together with the test copies of the same, shall be deposited in the bureau, and access to them shall be allowed to the international committee only.

ARTICLE 9

The entire expense of the construction and outfit of the international bureau of weights and measures, together with the annual cost of its maintenance and the expenses of the committee, shall be defrayed by contributions from the contracting states, the amount of which shall be computed in proportion to the actual population of each.

ARTICLE 10

The amounts representing the contributions of each of the contracting states shall be paid at the beginning of each year, through the ministry of foreign affairs of France, into the *Caisse de dépöts et consignations* at Paris, whence they may be drawn as occasion may require, upon the order of the director of the bureau.

ARTICLE 11

Those governments which may take advantage of the privilege, open to every state, of acceding to this convention, shall be required to pay a contribution, the amount of which shall be fixed by the committee, on the basis established in article 9, and which shall be devoted to the improvement of the scientific apparatus of the bureau.

ARTICLE 12

The high contracting parties reserve to themselves the power of introducing into the present convention, by common consent, any modifications the propriety of which may have been shown by experience.

ARTICLE 13

At the expiration of twelve years this convention may be abrogated by any one of the high contracting parties, so far as it is concerned.

Any government which may avail itself of the right of terminating this convention, so far as it is concerned, shall be required to give notice of its intentions one year in advance, and by so doing shall renounce all rights of joint ownership in the international prototypes and in the bureau.

ARTICLE 14

This Convention shall be ratified according to the constitutional laws of each state, and the ratifications shall be exchanged in Paris within six months, or sooner, if possible.

It shall take effect on the first day of January, 1876.

In testimony whereof the respective plenipotentiaries have attached their signatures and have hereunto affixed their seals of arms.

Done at Paris, May 20, 1875.[3]

. . . .

APPENDIX NO. I

REGULATIONS

ARTICLE 1

The international bureau of weights and measures shall be established in a special building, possessing all the necessary safeguards of stillness and stability.

It shall comprise, in addition to the vault, which shall be devoted to the safe-keeping of the prototypes, rooms for mounting the comparators and balances; a laboratory, a library, a room for the archives, work-rooms for the employés, and lodgings for the watchmen and attendants.

ARTICLE 2

It shall be the duty of the international committee to acquire and fit up the aforesaid building and to set in operation the work for which it was designed.

In case of the committee's inability to obtain a suitable building, one shall be built under its directions and in accordance with its plans.

[3] Signatures omitted.

ARTICLE 3

The French Government shall, at the request of the international committee, take the necessary measures to cause the bureau to be recognized as an establishment of public utility.

ARTICLE 4

The international committee shall cause the necessary instruments to be constructed, such as comparators for the standards of line and measures, apparatus for the determination of absolute dilatations, balances for weighing in air and in vacuo, comparators for geodetic measuring-bars, &c.

ARTICLE 5

The entire expense incurred in the purchase or construction of the building, and in the purchase and placing of the instruments and apparatus, shall not exceed 400,000 francs.

ARTICLE 6

The estimate of annual expenditures is as follows:

A. For the first period—during the construction and comparison of the new prototypes—

(a) Salary of the director	15,000 fr.
" of two adjuncts, at 6,000 fr. each	12,000
" of four assistants, at 3,000 fr. each	12,000
Pay of door-keeper, (mechanic)	3,000
Wages of two office-boys, at 1,500 fr. each	3,000
Total for salaries	45,000
(b) Compensation to men of science and artists, who by direction of the committee, may be employed to perform special duties, keeping of the building in proper order, purchase and repair of apparatus, fuel, light, and office-expenses	24,000
(c) Compensation of the secretary of the international committee of weights and measures	6,000
Total	75,000

The annual budget of the bureau may be modified by the international committee as necessity may require at the suggestion of the director, but it shall in no case exceed the sum of 100,000 francs.

The contracting governments shall be notified of any modifications that the committee may think proper to make within these limits, in the annual budget fixed by the present regulations.

The Committee may authorize the director, at his request, to make transfers from one subdivision of the allotted budget to another.

B. For the period subsequent to the distribution of the prototypes:

(a) Salary of the director	15,000 fr.
" one adjunct	6,000
Pay of a door-keeper, (mechanic)	3,000
Wages of an office-boy	1,500
Total	25,000

(b) Office-expenses 18,500
(c) Compensation of secretary, international committee 6,000

Total 50,000

ARTICLE 7

The general conference mentioned in article 3 of this convention shall be at Paris, upon the summons of the international committee, at least once every six years.

It shall be its duty to discuss and initiate measures necessary for the dissemination and improvement of the metrical system, and to pass upon such new fundamental metrological determinations as may have been made during the time when it was not in session. It shall receive the report of the international committee concerning the work that has been accomplished, and shall replace one-half of the international committee by secret ballot.

The voting in the general conference shall be by states; each state shall be entitled to one vote.

Each of the members of the international committee shall be entitled to a seat at the meetings of the conference. They may at the same time be delegates of their governments.

ARTICLE 8

The international committee mentioned in article 3 of the convention shall be composed of fourteen members, who shall belong to different states.

It shall consist, at first, of the twelve members of the former permanent committee of the international commission of 1872, and of the two delegates who, at the time of the appointment of that permanent committee, received the largest number of votes next to the members who were elected.

At the time of the renewal of one-half of the international committee, the retiring members shall be, first, those who, in cases of vacancy, may have been elected provisionally during the interval occurring between two sessions of the conference. The others shall be designated by lot.

The retiring members shall be re-eligible.

ARTICLE 9

The international committee shall direct the work connected with the verification of the new prototypes, and, in general, all the metrological labors, as the high contracting parties may decide to have performed at the common expense. It shall, moreover, exercise supervision over the safe-keeping of the international prototype.

ARTICLE 10

The international committee shall choose its chairman and secretary by secret ballot. The governments of the high contracting parties shall be notified of the result of such elections.

The chairman and secretary of the committee, and the director of the bureau, must belong to different countries.

After having been formed, the committee shall hold no new elections and make no new appointments until three months after notice thereof shall have been given to all the members by the bureau of the committee.

ARTICLE 11

Until the prototypes shall have been finished and distributed, the committee shall meet at least once a year. After that time its meetings shall be held at least biennially.

ARTICLE 12

Questions upon which a vote is taken in the committee shall be decided by a majority of the votes cast. In case of a tie, the vote of the chairman shall decide. No resolution shall be considered to have been duly adopted unless the number of members present be at least equal to a majority of the members composing the committee.

This condition being fulfilled, absent members shall have the right to authorize members who are present to vote for them, and the members thus authorized shall furnish proper evidence of their authorization. The same shall be the case in elections by secret ballot.

ARTICLE 13

During the interval occurring between two sessions, the committee shall have the right to discuss questions by correspondence.

In such cases, in order that its resolutions may be considered to have been adopted in due form, it shall be necessary for all the members of the committee to have been called upon to express their opinions.

ARTICLE 14

The international committee for weights and measures shall provisionally fill such vacancies as may occur in it; these elections shall take place by correspondence, each of the members being called upon to take part therein.

ARTICLE 15

The international committee shall prepare detailed regulations for the organization and the labors of the bureau, and shall fix the amounts to be paid for the performance of the extraordinary duties provided for in article 6 of this convention.

Such amounts shall be applied to the improvement of the scientific apparatus of the bureau.

ARTICLE 16

All communications from the international committee to the governments of the high contracting parties shall take place through the diplomatic representatives of such countries at Paris.

For all matters requiring the attention of the French authorities, the committees shall have recourse to the ministry of foreign affairs of France.

ARTICLE 17

The director of the bureau and the adjuncts shall be chosen by the international committee by secret ballot.

The employés shall be appointed by the director.

The director shall have a right to take part in the deliberations of the committee.

ARTICLE 18

The director of the bureau shall have access to the place of deposit of the international prototypes of the meter and the kilogram only in pursuance of a resolution of the committee and in the presence of two of its members.

The place of deposit of the prototypes shall be opened only by means of three keys, one of which shall be in possession of the director of the archives of France, the second in that of the chairman of the committee, and the third in that of the director of the bureau.

The standards of the class of national prototypes alone shall be used for the ordinary comparing work of the bureau.

ARTICLE 19

The director of the bureau shall annually furnish to the committee: 1st. A financial report concerning the accounts of the preceding year, which shall be examined, and, if found correct, a certificate to that effect shall be given him; 2d. A report on the condition of the apparatus; 3d. A general report concerning the work accomplished during the course of the year just closed.

The international committee shall make to each of the governments of the high contracting parties an annual report concerning all its scientific, technical, and administrative operations, and concerning those of the bureau. The chairman of the committee shall make a report to the general conference concerning the work that has been accomplished since its last session.

The reports and publications of the committee shall be in the French language. They shall be printed and furnished to the governments of the high contracting parties.

ARTICLE 20

The contribution referred to in article 9 of the convention shall be paid according to the following scale:

The number representing the population, expressed in millions, shall be multiplied by the coefficient three for states in which the use of the metrical system is obligatory;

by the coefficient two for those in which it is optional;

by the coefficient one for other states.

The sum of the products thus obtained will furnish the number of units by which the total expense is to be divided. The quotient will give the amount of the unit of expense.

ARTICLE 21

The expense of constructing the international prototypes, and the standards and test copies which are to accompany them, shall be defrayed by the high contracting parties in accordance with the scale fixed in the foregoing article.

The amounts to be paid for the comparison and verification of standards required by states not represented at this convention shall be regulated by the committee in conformity with the rates fixed in virtue of article 15 of the regulations.

ARTICLE 22

These regulations shall have the same force and value as the convention to which they are annexed.[4]

. . . .

[4] Signatures omitted.

APPENDIX NO. 2

TRANSIENT PROVISIONS

ARTICLE I

All states which were represented at the international meter commission which met at Paris, in 1872, whether they are contracting parties to the present convention or not, shall receive the prototype that they may have ordered, which shall be delivered to them in the condition guaranteed by the said international commission.

ARTICLE 2

The principal object of the first meeting of the general conference of weights and measures shall be to sanction these new prototypes and to distribute them among the states which shall have expressed a desire to receive them.

In consequence, the delegates of all the governments which were represented in the international commission of 1872, as likewise the members of the French section, shall, of right, form part of this first meeting for the sanction of the prototypes.

ARTICLE 3

It shall be the duty of the international committee mentioned in Article 3 of the convention, and composed as provided in Article 8 of the regulations, to receive and compare the new prototypes one with the other, in accordance with the scientific decisions of the international commission of 1872, and of its permanent committee. Such modifications may, however, be made as may in future be suggested by experience.

ARTICLE 4

The French section of the international commission of 1872 shall continue to have charge of the labors intrusted to it in the construction of the new prototypes, with the co-operation of the international committee.

ARTICLE 5

The cost of manufacturing the metrical standards prepared by the French section shall be reimbursed by the governments interested, according to the cost-price per unit which shall be fixed by the said section.

ARTICLE 6

The immediate formation of the international committee is authorized, and that body, when formed, is hereby empowered to make all necessary preparatory examinations for the carrying into effect of the convention, without, however, incurring any expense before the exchange of the ratifications of the said convention.[5]

. . . .

[5] Signatures omitted.

9. CONVENTION FOR THE PACIFIC SETTLEMENT OF INTERNA-TIONAL DISPUTES SIGNED AT THE HAGUE, 1907 [1]

His Majesty the German Emperor, King of Prussia; [etc.]:

Animated by the sincere desire to work for the maintenance of general peace;

Resolved to promote by all the efforts in their power the friendly settlement of international disputes;

Recognizing the solidarity uniting the members of the society of civilized nations;

Desirous of extending the empire of law and of strengthening the apprecia-tion of international justice;

Convinced that the permanent institution of a tribunal of arbitration, ac-cessible to all, in the midst of independent Powers, will contribute effectively to this result;

Having regard to the advantages attending the general and regular organi-zation of the procedure of arbitration;

Sharing the opinion of the august initiator of the International Peace Con-ference that it is expedient to record in an international agreement the prin-ciples of equity and right on which are based the security of States and the welfare of peoples;

Being desirous, *with this object, of insuring the better working in practice of commissions of inquiry and tribunals of arbitration, and of facilitating recourse to arbitration in cases which allow of a summary procedure,*[2]

Have deemed it necessary to revise in certain particulars and to complete the work of the First Peace Conference for the pacific settlement of interna-tional disputes;

The high contracting Parties have resolved to conclude a *new* Convention for this purpose, *and* have appointed the following as their plenipotentiaries:

(*Here follow the names of plenipotentiaries.*)

Who, after having *deposited* their full powers, found in good and due form, have agreed upon the following:

PART I. THE MAINTENANCE OF GENERAL PEACE

ARTICLE I

With a view to obviating as far as possible recourse to force in the relations between States, the *contracting* Powers agree to use their best efforts to in-sure the pacific settlement of international differences.

PART II. GOOD OFFICES AND MEDIATION

ARTICLE 2

In case of serious disagreement or dispute, before an appeal to arms, the *contracting* Powers agree to have recourse, as far as circumstances may allow, to the good offices or mediation of one or more friendly Powers.

[1] *United States Statutes at Large,* Vol. XXXVI, p. 2199; see above, text, Chaps, VI and VIII.

[2] Italics indicate changes in the Convention as drawn in 1907.

ARTICLE 3

Independently of this recourse, the *contracting* Powers deem it expedient *and desirable* that one or more Powers, strangers to the dispute, should, on their own initiative and as far as circumstances may allow, offer their good offices or mediation to the States at variance.

Powers strangers to the dispute have the right to offer good offices or mediation even during the course of hostilities.

The exercise of this right can never be regarded by either of the parties in dispute as an unfriendly act.

ARTICLE 4

The part of the mediator consists in reconciling the opposing claims and appeasing the feelings of resentment which may have arisen between the States at variance.

ARTICLE 5

The functions of the mediator are at an end when once it is declared, either by one of the parties to the dispute or by the mediator himself, that the means of reconciliation proposed by him are not accepted.

ARTICLE 6

Good offices and mediation undertaken either at the request of the parties in dispute or on the initiative of Powers strangers to the dispute have exclusively the character of advice, and never have binding force.

ARTICLE 7

The acceptance of mediation can not, unless there be an agreement to the contrary, have the effect of interrupting, delaying, or hindering mobilization or other measures of preparation for war.

If it takes place after the commencement of hostilities, the military operations in progress are not interrupted in the absence of an agreement to the contrary.

ARTICLE 8

The *contracting* Powers are agreed in recommending the application, when circumstances allow, of special mediation in the following form:

In case of a serious difference endangering peace, the States at variance choose respectively a Power, to which they intrust the mission of entering into direct communication with the Power chosen on the other side, with the object of preventing the rupture of pacific relations.

For the period of this mandate, the term of which, unless otherwise stipulated, can not exceed thirty days, the States in dispute cease from all direct communication on the subject of the dispute, which is regarded as referred exclusively to the mediating Powers, which must use their best efforts to settle it.

In case of a definite rupture of pacific relations, these Powers are charged with the joint task of taking advantage of any opportunity to restore peace.

PART III. INTERNATIONAL COMMISSIONS OF INQUIRY

ARTICLE 9

In disputes of an international nature involving neither honor nor vital interests, and arising from a difference of opinion on points of fact, the *contracting* Powers deem it expedient *and* desirable that the parties who have not been able to come to an agreement by means of diplomacy, should, as far as circumstances allow, institute an international commission of inquiry, to facilitate a solution of these disputes by elucidating the facts by means of an impartial and conscientious investigation.

ARTICLE 10

International commissions of inquiry are constituted by special agreement between the parties in dispute.

The inquiry convention defines the facts to be examined; *it determines the mode and time in which the commission is to be formed* and the extent of the powers of the commissioners.

It also determines, if there is need, where the commission is to sit, and whether it may remove to another place, the language the commission shall use and the language the use of which shall be authorized before it, as well as the date on which each party must deposit its statement of facts, and, generally speaking, all the conditions upon which the parties have agreed.

If the parties consider it necessary to appoint assessors, the convention of inquiry shall determine the mode of their selection and the extent of their powers.

ARTICLE 11

If the inquiry convention has not determined where the commission is to sit, it will sit at The Hague.

The place of meeting, once fixed, can not be altered by the commission except with the assent of the parties.

If the inquiry convention has not determined what languages are to be employed, the question shall be decided by the commission.

ARTICLE 12

Unless an undertaking is made to the contrary, commissions of inquiry shall be formed in the manner determined by Articles *45 and 57* of the present Convention.

ARTICLE 13

Should one of the commissioners or one of the assessors, should there be any, either die, or resign, or be unable for any reason whatever to discharge his functions, the same procedure is followed for filling the vacancy as was followed for appointing him.

ARTICLE 14

The parties are entitled to appoint special agents to attend the commission of inquiry, whose duty it is to represent them and to act as intermediaries between them and the commission.

They are further authorized to engage counsel or advocates, appointed by themselves, to state their case and uphold their interests before the commission.

ARTICLE 15

The International Bureau of the Permanent Court of Arbitration acts as registry for the commissions which sit at The Hague, and shall place its offices and staff at the disposal of the contracting Powers for the use of the commission of inquiry.

ARTICLE 16

If the commission meets elsewhere than at The Hague, it appoints a secretary general, whose office serves as registry.

It is the function of the registry, under the control of the president, to make the necessary arrangements for the sittings of the commission, the preparation of the minutes, and, while the inquiry lasts, for the charge of the archives, which shall subsequently be transferred to the International Bureau at The Hague.

ARTICLE 17

In order to facilitate the constitution and working of commissions of inquiry, the contracting Powers recommend the following rules, which shall be applicable to the inquiry procedure in so far as the parties do not adopt other rules.

ARTICLE 18

The commission shall settle the details of the procedure not covered by the special inquiry convention or the present Convention, and shall arrange all the formalities required for dealing with the evidence.

ARTICLE 19

On the inquiry both sides must be heard.

At the dates fixed, each party communicates to the commission and to the other party the statements of facts, if any, and, in all cases, the instruments, papers, and documents which it considers useful for ascertaining the truth, as well as the list of witnesses and experts whose evidence it wishes to be heard.

ARTICLE 20

The commission is entitled, with the assent of the Powers, to move temporarily to any place where it considers it may be useful to have recourse to this means of inquiry or to send one or more of its members. Permission must be obtained from the State on whose territory it is proposed to hold the inquiry.

ARTICLE 21

Every investigation, and every examination of a locality, must be made in the presence of the agents and counsel of the parties or after they have been duly summoned.

ARTICLE 22

The commission is entitled to ask from either party for such explanations and information as it considers necessary.

ARTICLE 23

The *parties* undertake to supply the commission of inquiry, as fully as they may think possible, with all means and facilities necessary to enable it to become completely acquainted with, and to accurately understand, the facts in question.

They undertake to make use of the means at their disposal, under their municipal law, to insure the appearance of the witnesses or experts who are in their territory and have been summoned before the commission.

If the witnesses or experts are unable to appear before the commission, the parties will arrange for their evidence to be taken before the qualified officials of their own country.

ARTICLE 24

For all notices to be served by the commission in the territory of a third contracting Power, the commission shall apply direct to the Government of the said Power. The same rule applies in the case of steps being taken on the spot to procure evidence.

The requests for this purpose are to be executed so far as the means at the disposal of the Power applied to under its municipal law allow. They can not be rejected unless the Power in question considers they are calculated to impair its sovereign rights or its safety.

The commission will equally be always entitled to act through the Power on whose territory it sits.

ARTICLE 25

The witnesses and experts are summoned on the request of the parties or by the commission of its own motion, and, in every case, through the Government of the State in whose territory they are.

The witnesses are heard in succession and separately, in the presence of the agents and counsel, and in the order fixed by the commission.

ARTICLE 26

The examination of witnesses is conducted by the president.

The members of the commission may however put to each witness questions which they consider likely to throw light on and complete his evidence, or get information on any point concerning the witness within the limits of what is necessary in order to get at the truth.

The agents and counsel of the parties may not interrupt the witness when he is making his statement, nor put any direct question to him, but they may ask the president to put such additional questions to the witness as they think expedient.

ARTICLE 27

The witness must give his evidence without being allowed to read any written draft. He may, however, be permitted by the president to consult notes or documents if the nature of the facts referred to necessitates their employment.

ARTICLE 28

A minute of the evidence of the witness is drawn up forthwith and read to the witness. The latter may make such alterations and additions as he thinks necessary, which will be recorded at the end of his statement.

When the whole of his statement has been read to the witness, he is asked to sign it.

ARTICLE 29

The agents are authorized, in the course of or at the close of the inquiry, to present in writing to the commission and to the other party such statements, requisitions, or summaries of the facts as they consider useful for ascertaining the truth.

ARTICLE 30

The commission considers its decisions in private and the proceedings are secret.

All questions are decided by a majority of the members of the commission. If a member declines to vote, the fact must be recorded in the minutes.

ARTICLE 31

The sittings of the commission are not public, nor the minutes and documents connected with the inquiry published except in virtue of a decision of the commission taken with the consent of the parties.

ARTICLE 32

After the parties have presented all the explanations and evidence, and the witnesses have all been heard, the president declares the inquiry terminated, and the commission adjourns to deliberate and to draw up its report.

ARTICLE 33

The report is signed by all the members of the commission.

If one of the members refuses to sign, the fact is mentioned; but the validity of the report is not affected.

ARTICLE 34

The report of the commission is read at a public sitting, the agents and counsel of the parties being present or duly summoned.

A copy of the report is given to each party.

ARTICLE 35

The report of the commission is limited to a statement of facts, and has in no way the character of an award. It leaves to the parties entire freedom as to the effect to be given to the statement.

ARTICLE 36

Each party pays its own expenses and an equal share of the expenses incurred by the commission.

PART IV. INTERNATIONAL ARBITRATION

Chapter I. The System of Arbitration

ARTICLE 37

International arbitration has for its object the settlement of disputes between States by judges of their own choice and on the basis of respect for law.

Recourse to arbitration implies an engagement to submit in good faith to the award.

ARTICLE 38

In questions of a legal nature, and especially in the interpretation or application of international conventions, arbitration is recognized by the *contracting* Powers as the most effective, and, at the same time, the most equitable means of settling disputes which diplomacy has failed to settle.

Consequently, it would be desirable that, in disputes about the above-mentioned questions, the contracting Powers should, if the case arose, have recourse to arbitration, in so far as circumstances permit.

ARTICLE 39

The arbitration convention is concluded for questions already existing or for questions which may arise eventually.

It may embrace any dispute or only disputes of a certain category.

ARTICLE 40

Independently of general or private treaties expressly stipulating recourse to arbitration as obligatory on the *contracting* Powers, the said Powers reserve to themselves the right of concluding new agreements, general or particular, with a view to extending compulsory arbitration to all cases which they may consider it possible to submit to it.

Chapter II. The Permanent Court of Arbitration

ARTICLE 41

With the object of facilitating an immediate recourse to arbitration for international differences, which it has not been possible to settle by diplomacy, the *contracting* Powers undertake to *maintain the* Permanent Court of Arbitration, *as established by the First Peace Conference*, accessible at all times, and operating, unless otherwise stipulated by the parties, in accordance with the rules of procedure inserted in the present Convention.

ARTICLE 42

The Permanent Court *is* competent for all arbitration cases, unless the parties agree to institute a special tribunal.

ARTICLE 43

The Permanent Court sits at The Hague.

An International Bureau serves as registry for the Court. It is the channel for communications relative to the meetings of the Court; it has charge of the archives and conducts all the administrative business.

The *contracting* Powers undertake to communicate to the Bureau, *as soon as possible*, a certified copy of any conditions of arbitration arrived at between them and of any award concerning them delivered by a special tribunal.

They likewise undertake to communicate to the Bureau the laws, regulations, and documents eventually showing the execution of the awards given by the Court.

ARTICLE 44

Each *contracting* Power *selects* four persons at the most, of known competency in questions of international law, of the highest moral reputation, and disposed to accept the duties of arbitrator.

The persons thus selected *are* inscribed, as members of the Court, in a list which shall be notified to all the *contracting* Powers by the Bureau.

Any alteration in the list of arbitrators is brought by the Bureau to the knowledge of the *contracting* Powers.

Two or more Powers may agree on the selection in common of one or more members.

The same person can be selected by different Powers.

The members of the Court are appointed for a term of six years. These appointments are renewable.

Should a member of the Court die or resign, the same procedure is followed for filling the vacancy as was followed for appointing him. *In this case the appointment is made for a fresh period of six years.*

ARTICLE 45

When the *contracting* Powers wish to have recourse to the Permanent Court for the settlement of a difference which has arisen between them, the arbitrators called upon to form the tribunal with jurisdiction to decide this difference must be chosen from the general list of members of the Court.

Failing the direct agreement of the parties on the composition of the arbitration tribunal, the following course shall be pursued:

Each party appoints two arbitrators, *of whom one only can be its national or chosen from among the persons selected by it as members of the Permanent Court.* These arbitrators together choose an umpire.

If the votes are equally divided, the choice of the umpire is intrusted to a third Power, selected by the parties by common accord.

If an agreement is not arrived at on this subject each party selects a different Power, and the choice of the umpire is made in concert by the Powers thus selected.

If, within two months' time, these two Powers can not come to an agreement, each of them presents two candidates taken from the list of members of the Permanent Court, exclusive of the members selected by the parties and not being nationals of either of them. Drawing lots determines which of the candidates thus presented shall be umpire.

ARTICLE 46

The tribunal being thus composed, the parties notify to the Bureau their determination to have recourse to the Court, *the text of their compromis,* and the names of the arbitrators.

The Bureau communicates without delay to each arbitrator the compromis, and the names of the other members of the tribunal.

The tribunal assembles at the date fixed by the parties. *The Bureau makes the necessary arrangements for the meeting.*

The members of the *tribunal,* in the exercise of their duties and out of their own country, enjoy diplomatic privileges and immunities.

ARTICLE 47

The Bureau is authorized to place its offices and staff at the disposal of the *contracting* Powers for the use of any special board of arbitration.

The jurisdiction of the Permanent Court may, within the conditions laid down in the regulations, be extended to disputes between *non-contracting* Powers or between *contracting* Powers and *non-contracting* Powers, if the parties are agreed on recourse to this tribunal.

ARTICLE 48

The *contracting* Powers consider it their duty, if a serious dispute threatens to break out between two or more of them, to remind these latter that the Permanent Court is open to them.

Consequently, they declare that the fact of reminding the parties at variance of the provisions of the present Convention, and the advice given to them, in the highest interests of peace, to have recourse to the Permanent Court, can only be regarded as friendly actions.

In case of dispute between two Powers, one of them can always address to the International Bureau a note containing a declaration that it would be ready to submit the dispute to arbitration.

The Bureau must at once inform the other Power of the declaration.

ARTICLE 49

The Permanent Administrative Council, composed of the diplomatic representatives of the *contracting* Powers accredited to The Hague and of the Netherland Minister for Foreign Affairs, who will act as president, is charged with the direction and control of the International Bureau.

The Council *settles* its rules of procedure and all other necessary regulations.

It *decides* all questions of administration which may arise with regard to the operations of the Court.

It *has* entire control over the appointment, suspension, or dismissal of the officials and employees of the Bureau.

It *fixes* the payments and salaries, and controls the general expenditure.

At meetings duly summoned the presence of *nine* members is sufficient to render valid the discussions of the Council. The decisions are taken by a majority of votes.

The Council communicates to the *contracting* Powers without delay the regulations adopted by it. It furnishes them with an annual report on the labors of the Court, the working of the administration, and the expenditure. *The report likewise contains a résumé of what is important in the documents communicated to the Bureau by the Powers in virtue of Article 43, paragraphs 3 and 4.*

ARTICLE 50

The expenses of the Bureau shall be borne by the *contracting* Powers in the proportion fixed for the International Bureau of the Universal Postal Union.

The expenses to be charged to the adhering Powers shall be reckoned from the date on which their adhesion comes into force.

Chapter III. Arbitration Procedure

ARTICLE 51

With a view to encouraging the development of arbitration, the *contracting* Powers have agreed on the following rules, which are applicable to arbitration procedure, unless other rules have been agreed on by the parties.

ARTICLE 52

The Powers which have recourse to arbitration sign a compromis, in which the subject of the dispute is clearly defined, *the time allowed for appointing arbitrators, the form, order, and time in which the communication referred to in Article 63 must be made, and the amount of the sum which each party must deposit in advance to defray the expenses.*

The compromis likewise defines, if there is occasion, the manner of appointing arbitrators, any special powers which may eventually belong to the tribunal, where it shall meet, the language it shall use, and the languages the employment of which shall be authorized before it, and, generally speaking, all the conditions on which the parties are agreed.

ARTICLE 53

The Permanent Court is competent to settle the compromis, if the parties are agreed to have recourse to it for the purpose.

It is similarly competent, even if the request is only made by one of the parties, when all attempts to reach an understanding through the diplomatic channel have failed, in the case of—

1. A dispute covered by a general treaty of arbitration concluded or renewed after the present Convention has come into force, and providing for a compromis in all disputes and not either explicitly or implicitly excluding the settlement of the compromis from the competence of the Court. Recourse can not, however, be had to the Court if the other party declares that in its opinion the dispute does not belong to the category of disputes which can be submitted to compulsory arbitration, unless the treaty of arbitration confers upon the arbitration tribunal the power of deciding this preliminary question.

2. A dispute arising from contract debts claimed from one Power by another Power as due to its nationals, and for the settlement of which the offer of arbitration has been accepted. This arrangement is not applicable if acceptance is subject to the condition that the compromis should be settled in some other way.

ARTICLE 54

In the cases contemplated in the preceding article, the compromis shall be settled by a commission consisting of five members selected in the manner arranged for in Article 45, paragraphs 3 to 6.

The fifth member is president of the commission ex officio.

ARTICLE 55

The duties of arbitrator may be conferred on one arbitrator alone or on several arbitrators selected by the parties as they please, or chosen by them from the members of the Permanent Court of Arbitration established by the present Convention.

Failing the constitution of the tribunal by direct agreement between the parties, the course *referred to in Article 45, paragraphs 3 to 6, is followed.*

ARTICLE 56

When a sovereign or the chief of a State is chosen as arbitrator, the arbitration procedure is settled by him.

ARTICLE 57

The umpire is president of the tribunal ex officio.

When the tribunal does not include an umpire, it appoints its own president.

ARTICLE 58

When the compromis is settled by a commission, as contemplated in Article 54, and in the absence of an agreement to the contrary, the commission itself shall form the arbitration tribunal.

ARTICLE 59

Should one of the arbitrators either die, retire, or be unable for any reason whatever to discharge his functions, the same procedure is followed for filling the vacancy as was followed for appointing him.

ARTICLE 60

The tribunal sits at The Hague, unless some other place is selected by the parties.

The tribunal can only sit in the territory of a third Power with the latter's consent.

The place of meeting once fixed can not be altered by the tribunal, except with the consent of the parties.

ARTICLE 61

If the question as to what languages are to be used has not been settled by the compromis, it shall be decided by the tribunal.

ARTICLE 62

The parties are entitled to appoint special agents to attend the tribunal to act as intermediaries between themselves and the tribunal.

They are further authorized to retain for the defense of their rights and interests before the tribunal counsel or advocates appointed by themselves for this purpose.

The members of the Permanent Court may not act as agents, counsel, or advocates except on behalf of the Power which appointed them members of the Court.

ARTICLE 63

As a general rule, arbitration procedure comprises two distinct phases: pleadings and oral discussions.

The pleadings consist in the communication by the respective agents to the members of the tribunal and the opposite party of *cases, counter-cases, and, if necessary, of replies; the parties annex thereto all papers* and documents called for in the case. This communication shall be made *either directly or through the intermediary of the International Bureau, in the order* and within the time fixed by the *compromis.*

The time fixed by the compromis may be extended by mutual agreement by the parties, or by the tribunal when the latter considers it necessary for the purpose of reaching a just decision.

The discussions consist in the oral development before the tribunal of the arguments of the parties.

ARTICLE 64

A *certified copy* of every document produced by one party must be communicated to the other party.

ARTICLE 65

Unless special circumstances arise, the tribunal does not meet until the pleadings are closed.

ARTICLE 66

The discussions are under the control of the president.

They are only public if it be so decided by the tribunal, with the assent of the parties.

They are recorded in minutes drawn up by the secretaries appointed by the president. These minutes *are signed by the president and by one of the secretaries and* alone have an authentic character.

ARTICLE 67

After the close of the pleadings, the tribunal is entitled to refuse discussion of all new papers or documents which one of the parties may wish to submit to it without the consent of the other party.

ARTICLE 68

The tribunal is free to take into consideration new papers or documents to which its attention may be drawn by the agents or counsel of the parties.

In this case, the tribunal has the right to require the production of these papers or documents, but is obliged to make them known to the opposite party.

ARTICLE 69

The tribunal can, besides, require from the agents of the parties the production of all papers, and can demand all necessary explanations. In case of refusal the tribunal takes note of it.

ARTICLE 70

The agents and the counsel of the parties are authorized to present orally to the tribunal all the arguments they may consider expedient in defense of their case.

ARTICLE 71

They are entitled to raise objections and points. The decisions of the tribunal on these points are final and can not form the subject of any subsequent discussion.

ARTICLE 72

The members of the tribunal are entitled to put questions to the agents and counsel of the parties, and to ask them for explanations on doubtful points.

Neither the questions put, nor the remarks made by members of the tribunal in the course of the discussions, can be regarded as an expression of opinion by the tribunal in general or by its members in particular.

ARTICLE 73

The tribunal is authorized to declare its competence in interpreting the compromis, as well as the other *papers and documents* which may be invoked, and in applying the principles of law.

ARTICLE 74

The tribunal is entitled to issue rules of procedure for the conduct of the case, to decide the forms, *order*, and time in which each party must conclude its arguments, and to arrange all the formalities required for dealing with the evidence.

ARTICLE 75

The parties undertake to supply the tribunal, as fully as they consider possible, with all the information required for deciding the case.

ARTICLE 76

For all notices which the tribunal has to serve in the territory of a third contracting Power, the tribunal shall apply direct to the Government of that Power. The same rule applies in the case of steps being taken to procure evidence on the spot.

The requests for this purpose are to be executed as far as the means at the disposal of the Power applied to under its municipal law allow. They can not be rejected unless the Power in question considers them calculated to impair its own sovereign rights or its safety.

The Court will equally be always entitled to act through the Power on whose territory it sits.

ARTICLE 77

When the agents and counsel of the parties have submitted all the explanations and evidence in support of their case the president shall declare the discussion closed.

ARTICLE 78

The tribunal considers its decisions in private and *the proceedings remain secret.*

All questions are decided by a majority of the members of the tribunal.

ARTICLE 79

The award must give the reasons on which it is based. *It contains the names of the arbitrators; it is signed by the president and registrar or by the secretary acting as registrar.*

ARTICLE 80

The award is read out in public sitting, the agents and counsel of the parties being present or duly summoned to attend.

ARTICLE 81

The award, duly pronounced and notified to the agents of the parties, settles the dispute definitively and without appeal.

ARTICLE 82

Any dispute arising between the parties as to the interpretation and execution of the award shall, in the absence of an agreement to the contrary, be submitted to the tribunal which pronounced it.

ARTICLE 83

The parties can reserve in the compromis the right to demand the revision of the award.

In this case and unless there be an agreement to the contrary, the demand must be addressed to the tribunal which pronounced the award. It can only be made on the ground of the discovery of some new fact calculated to exercise a decisive influence upon the award and which was unknown to the tribunal and to the party which demanded the revision at the time the discussion was closed.

Proceedings for revision can only be instituted by a decision of the tribunal expressly recording the existence of the new fact, recognizing in it the character described in the preceding paragraph, and declaring the demand admissible on this ground.

The compromis fixes the period within which the demand for revision must be made.

ARTICLE 84

The award is not binding except on the parties in dispute.

When it concerns the interpretation of a Convention to which Powers other than those in dispute are parties, they shall inform all the signatory Powers in good time. Each of these Powers is entitled to intervene in the case. If one or more avail themselves of this right, the interpretation contained in the award is equally binding on them.

ARTICLE 85

Each party pays its own expenses and an equal share of the expenses of the tribunal.

Chapter IV. Arbitration by Summary Procedure

ARTICLE 86

With a view to facilitating the working of the system of arbitration in disputes admitting of a summary procedure, the contracting Powers adopt the following rules, which shall be observed in the absence of other arrangements and subject to the reservation that the provisions of Chapter III apply so far as may be.

ARTICLE 87

Each of the parties in dispute appoints an arbitrator. The two arbitrators thus selected choose an umpire. If they do not agree on this point, each of them proposes two candidates taken from the general list of the members of the Permanent Court exclusive of the members appointed by either of the parties and not being nationals of either of them; which of the candidates thus proposed shall be the umpire is determined by lot.

The umpire presides over the tribunal, which gives its decisions by a majority of votes.

ARTICLE 88

In the absence of any previous agreement the tribunal, as soon as it is formed, settles the time within which the two parties must submit their respective cases to it.

ARTICLE 89

Each party is represented before the tribunal by an agent, who serves as intermediary between the tribunal and the Government who appointed him.

ARTICLE 90

The proceedings are conducted exclusively in writing. Each party, however, is entitled to ask that witnesses and experts should be called. The tribunal has, for its part, the right to demand oral explanations from the agents of the two parties, as well as from the experts and witnesses whose appearance in Court it may consider useful.

PART V. FINAL PROVISIONS

ARTICLE 91

The present Convention, duly ratified, shall replace, as between the contracting Powers, the Convention for the pacific settlement of international disputes of the 29th July, 1899.

ARTICLE 92

The present Convention shall be ratified as soon as possible.

The ratifications shall be deposited at The Hague.

The first deposit of ratifications shall be recorded in a procès-verbal signed by the representatives of the Powers which take part therein and by the Netherland Minister for Foreign Affairs.

The subsequent deposits of ratifications shall be made by means of a written notification, addressed to the Netherland Government and accompanied by the instrument of ratification.

A duly certified copy of the procès-verbal relative to the first deposit of ratifications, of the notifications mentioned in the preceding paragraph, and of the instruments of ratification, shall be immediately sent by the Netherland Government, through the diplomatic channel, to the Powers invited to the Second Peace Conference, as well as to those Powers which have adhered to the Convention. In the cases contemplated in the preceding paragraph, the said Government shall at the same time inform the Powers of the date on which it received the notification.

ARTICLE 93

Non-signatory Powers which have been *invited to* the *Second* Peace Conference may adhere to the present Convention.

The Power which desires to adhere notifies its intention in writing to the Netherland Government, forwarding to it the act of adhesion, which shall be deposited in the archives of the said Government.

This Government shall immediately forward to all the other Powers invited to the Second Peace Conference a duly certified copy of the notification as well as of the act of adhesion, mentioning the date on which it received the notification.

ARTICLE 94

The conditions on which the Powers which have not been *invited to* the *Second* Peace Conference may adhere to the present Convention shall form the subject of a subsequent agreement between the contracting Powers.

ARTICLE 95

The present Convention shall take effect, in the case of the Powers which were not a party to the first deposit of ratifications, sixty days after the date of the procès-verbal of this deposit, and, in the case of the Powers which ratify subsequently or which adhere, sixty days after the notification of their ratification or of their adhesion has been received by the Netherland Government.

ARTICLE 96

In the event of one of the contracting *Powers wishing to* denounce the present Convention, *the* denunciation shall be notified in writing to the Netherland Government, *which shall* immediately communicate *a duly certified copy* of the notification to all the other Powers *informing them of the date on which it was received.*

The denunciation shall only have effect in regard to the notifying Power, *and one year after the notification has reached the Netherland Government.*

ARTICLE 97

A register kept by the Netherland Minister for Foreign Affairs shall give the date of the deposit of ratifications effected in virtue of Article 92, paragraphs 3 and 4, as well as the date on which the notifications of adhesion (Article 93, paragraph 2) or of denunciation (Article 96, paragraph 1) have been received.

Each contracting Power is entitled to have access to this register and to be supplied with duly certified extracts from it.

In faith whereof the plenipotentiaries have *appended their signatures to* the present Convention.

Done at The Hague, the *18th October, 1907*, in a single copy, which shall remain deposited in the archives of the Netherland Government, and duly certified copies of which shall be sent, through the diplomatic channel to the contracting Powers.

(*Here follow signatures.*)

10. TREATY OF PEACE, SIGNED AT PARIS, 30 MARCH, 1856, AND DECLARATION OF PARIS, ADOPTED BY SIGNATORIES THERETO

a. Treaty of Paris, 30 March, 1856 [1]

In the Name of Almighty God

Their Majesties the Queen of the United Kingdom of Great Britain and Ireland, the Emperor of the French, the Emperor of all the Russias, the King of Sardinia, and the Emperor of the Ottomans, animated by the desire of putting an end to the calamities of war, and wishing to prevent the return of the complications which occasioned it, resolve to come to an understanding with His Majesty the Emperor of Austria as to the bases on which peace might be reëstablished and consolidated, by securing through effectual and reciprocal guarantees, the independence and integrity of the Ottoman Empire.

For this purpose Their said Majesties have named as their Plenipotentiaries, that is to say:

(*Names of plenipotentiaries.*)

[1] *British and Foreign State Papers*, Vol. XLVI, pp. 8-26; see above, text, Chap. IX.

Which Plenipotentiaries, assembled in Congress at Paris,

An understanding having been happily established between them, Their Majesties the Queen of the United Kingdom of Great Britain and Ireland, the Emperor of Austria, the Emperor of the French, the Emperor of all the Russias, the King of Sardinia, and the Emperor of the Ottomans, considering that in the interest of Europe, His Majesty the King of Prussia, a signing Party to the Convention of the 13th of July, 1841, should be invited to participate in the new arrangements to be adopted, and appreciating the value that the concurrence of His said Majesty would add to a work of general pacification, invited him to send Plenipotentiaries to the Congress.

In consequence, His Majesty the King of Prussia has named as His Plenipotentiaries, that is to say:

(*Names of plenipotentiaries.*)

The Plenipotentiaries, after having exchanged their full powers, found in good and due form, have agreed upon the following Articles:—

ARTICLE I

From the day of the exchange of the ratifications of the present Treaty, there shall be peace and friendship between Her Majesty the Queen of the United Kingdom of Great Britain and Ireland, His Majesty the Emperor of the French, His Majesty the King of Sardinia, His Imperial Majesty the Sultan, on the one part, and His Majesty the Emperor of all the Russias, on the other part; as well as between their heirs and successors, their respective dominions and subjects, in perpetuity.

* * * * *

ARTICLE VII

Her Majesty the Queen of the United Kingdom of Great Britain and Ireland, His Majesty the Emperor of Austria, His Majesty the Emperor of the French, His Majesty the King of Prussia, His Majesty the Emperor of all the Russias, and His Majesty the King of Sardinia, declare the Sublime Porte admitted to participate in the advantages of the public law and system (concert) of Europe. Their Majesties engage, each on his part, to respect the independence and the territorial integrity of the Ottoman Empire; guarantee in common the strict observance of that engagement; and will, in consequence, consider any act tending to its violation as a question of general interest.

ARTICLE VIII

If there should arise between the Sublime Porte and one or more of the other signing Powers, any misunderstanding which might endanger the maintenance of their relations, the Sublime Porte, and each of such Powers, before having recourse to the use of force, shall afford the other Contracting Parties the opportunity of preventing such an extremity by means of their mediation.

ARTICLE IX

His Imperial Majesty the Sultan, having, in his constant solicitude for the welfare of his subjects, issued a Firman which, while ameliorating their condition without distinction of religion or of race, records his generous intentions toward the Christian populations of his Empire, and wishing to give a further proof of his sentiments in that respect, has resolved to communicate to the Contracting Parties the said Firman emanating spontaneously from his sovereign will.

The Contracting Powers recognize the high value of this communication. It is clearly understood that it cannot, in any case, give to the said Powers the right to interfere, either collectively or separately, in the relations of His Majesty the Sultan with his subjects, nor in the internal administration of his Empire.

ARTICLE X

The Convention of the 13th of July, 1841, which maintains the ancient rule of the Ottoman Empire relative to the closing of the Straits of the Bosphorus and of the Dardanelles, has been revised by common consent.

The Act concluded for that purpose, and in conformity with that principle, between the High Contracting Parties, is and remains annexed to the present Treaty, and shall have the same force and validity as if it formed an integral part thereof.

ARTICLE XI

The Black Sea is neutralized: its waters and its ports, thrown open to the mercantile marine of every nation, are formally and in perpetuity interdicted to the flag of war, either of the Powers possessing its coasts, or of any other Power, with the exceptions mentioned in Articles XIV and XIX of the present Treaty.

ARTICLE XII

Free from any impediment, the commerce in the ports and waters of the Black Sea shall be subject only to regulations of health, customs, and police, framed in a spirit favorable to the development of commercial transactions.

In order to afford to the commercial and maritime interests of every nation the security which is desired, Russia and the Sublime Porte will admit Consuls into their ports situated upon the coast of the Black Sea, in conformity with the principles of international law.

ARTICLE XIII

The Black Sea being neutralized according to the terms of Article XI, the maintenance or establishment upon its coast of military-maritime arsenals becomes alike unnecessary and purposeless; in consequence, His Majesty the Emperor of all the Russias and His Imperial Majesty the Sultan engage not to establish or maintain upon that coast any military-maritime arsenal.

ARTICLE XIV

Their Majesties the Emperor of all the Russias and the Sultan having concluded a Convention for the purpose of settling the force and the number of light vessels, necessary for the service of their coasts, which they reserve to themselves to maintain in the Black Sea, that Convention is annexed to the present Treaty, and shall have the same force and validity as if it formed an integral part thereof. It cannot be either annulled or modified without the assent of the Powers signing the Present Treaty.

ARTICLE XV

The Act of the Congress of Vienna having established the principles intended to regulate the navigation of rivers which separate or traverse different States, the Contracting Powers stipulate among themselves that those principles shall in future be equally applied to the Danube and its mouths. They declare that this arrangement henceforth forms a part of the public law of Europe, and take it under their guarantee.

The navigation of the Danube cannot be subjected to any impediment or charge not expressly provided for by the stipulations contained in the following Articles: in consequence, there shall not be levied any toll founded solely upon the fact of the navigation of the river, nor any duty upon the goods which may be on board of vessels. The regulations of police and of quarantine to be established for the safety of the States separated or traversed by that river shall be so framed as to facilitate, as much as possible, the passage of vessels. With the exception of such regulations, no obstacle whatever shall be opposed to free navigation.

ARTICLE XVI

With the view to carry out the arrangements of the preceding Article, a Commission, in which Great Britain, Austria, France, Prussia, Russia, Sardinia, and Turkey, shall each be represented by one delegate, shall be charged to designate and to cause to be executed the works necessary below Isaktcha, to clear the mouths of the Danube, as well as the neighboring parts of the sea, from the sands and other impediments which obstruct them, in order to put that part of the river and the said parts of the sea in the best possible state for navigation.

In order to cover the expenses of such works, as well as of the establishments intended to secure and to facilitate the navigation at the mouths of the Danube, fixed duties, of a suitable rate, settled by the Commission by a majority of votes, may be levied, on the express condition that, in this respect as in every other, the flags of all nations shall be treated on the footing of perfect equality.

ARTICLE XVII

A Commission shall be established, and shall be composed of delegates of Austria, Bavaria, the Sublime Porte, and Würtemberg (one for each of those Powers), to whom shall be added Commissioners from the three Danubian Principalities, whose nomination shall have been approved by the Porte. This Commission, which shall be permanent: 1. Shall prepare regulations of navigation and river police; 2. Shall remove the impediments, of whatever nature they may be, which still prevent the application to the Danube of the arrangements of the Treaty of Vienna; 3. Shall order and cause to be executed the necessary works throughout the whole course of the river; and 4. Shall, after the dissolution of the European Commission, see to maintaining the mouths of the Danube and the neighboring parts of the sea in a navigable state.

ARTICLE XVIII

It is understood that the European Commission shall have completed its task, and that the Riverain Commission shall have finished the works described in the preceding Article, under Nos. 1 and 2, within the period of two years. The signing Powers assembled in Conference having been informed of that fact, shall, after having placed it on record, pronounce the dissolution of the European Commission, and from that time the permanent Riverain Commission shall enjoy the same powers as those with which the European Commission shall have until then been invested.

ARTICLE XIX

In order to insure the execution of the regulations which shall have been established by common agreement, in conformity with the principles above declared, each of the Contracting Powers shall have the right to station, at all times, two light vessels at the mouths of the Danube.

*　*　*　*　*

ARTICLE XXII

The Principalities of Wallachia and Moldavia shall continue to enjoy, under the suzerainty of the Porte, and under the guarantee of the Contracting Powers, the privileges and immunities of which they are in possession. No exclusive protection shall be exercised over them by any of the Guaranteeing Powers. There shall be no separate right of interference in their internal affairs.

*　*　*　*　*

ARTICLE XXXIV

The present Treaty shall be ratified, and the ratifications shall be exchanged at Paris in the space of four weeks, or sooner if possible.

In witness whereof the respective Plenipotentiaries have signed the same, and have affixed thereto the seal of their arms.

Done at Paris, the thirtieth day of the month of March, in the year one thousand eight hundred and fifty-six.

> *Clarendon*
> *Cowley*
> *Buol-Schauenstein*
> *Hübner*
> *A. Walewski*
> *Bourqueney*
> *Manteuffel*
> *C. M. D'Hatzfeldt*
> *Orloff*
> *Brunnow*
> *C. Cavour*
> *De Villamarina*
> *Aali*
> *Mehemmed Djemil*

b. Declaration of Paris, 1856 [1]

Considering:

That maritime law, in time of war, has long been the subject of deplorable disputes:

That the uncertainty of the law and of the duties in this same matter gives occasion to differences of opinion between neutrals and belligerents which may cause serious difficulties and even conflicts:

That it is consequently advantageous to establish a uniform doctrine on so important a point:

[1] *British and Foreign State Papers*, Vol. XLVI, pp. 26-27; see above, text, Chap. V.

That the Plenipotentiaries assembled at the Congress of Paris cannot better respond to the intentions by which their Governments are animated than by seeking to introduce into international relations fixed principles in this respect:

The above-mentioned Plenipotentiaries, being duly authorized, resolved to concert among themselves as to the means of attaining this object; and, having come to an agreement, have adopted the following solemn Declaration:—

1. Privateering is and remains abolished:

2. The neutral flag covers enemy's goods, with the exception of contraband of war:

3. Neutral goods, with the exception of contraband of war, are not liable to capture under enemy's flag:

4. Blockades, in order to be binding, must be effective; that is to say maintained by a force sufficient really to prevent access to the enemy's coast.

The Governments of the undersigned Plenipotentiaries engage to bring the present Declaration to the knowledge of the States which have not been called upon to take part in the Congress of Paris, and invite them to accede to it.

Convinced that the maxims which they now proclaim cannot but be received with gratitude by the whole world, the undersigned Plenipotentiaries doubt not that the efforts of their Governments to obtain the general adoption thereof will be crowned with full success.

The present Declaration is not and shall not be binding except between those powers who have acceded or shall accede to it.

11. TREATY OF ALLIANCE FOR THE PRESERVATION OF THE BALANCE OF POWER, 1814 [1]

In the Name of the Most Holy and Undivided Trinity.

His Majesty the King of the United Kingdom of Great Britain and Ireland, His Imperial and Royal Apostolic Majesty the Emperor of Austria, King of Hungary and Bohemia, His Majesty the Emperor of All the Russias, and His Majesty the King of Prussia, have transmitted to the French Government proposals for concluding a General Peace, and being desirous, should France refuse the Conditions therein contained, to draw closer the ties which unite them for the vigorous prosecution of a War undertaken for the salutary purpose of putting an end to the miseries of Europe, of securing its future repose, by reëstablishing a just balance of Power, and being at the same time desirous, should the Almighty bless their pacific intentions, to fix the means of maintaining against every attempt the order of things which shall have been the happy consequence of their efforts, have agreed to sanction by a solemn Treaty, signed separately by each of the four Powers with the three others, this twofold engagement.

(Here the plenipotentiaries are named.)

The said Plenipotentiaries, after having exchanged their Full Powers, found to be in due and proper form, have agreed upon the following Articles:

ARTICLE I

The High Contracting Parties above named solemnly engage by the present Treaty, and in the event of France refusing to accede to the Conditions of Peace now proposed, to apply all the means of their respective States to the vigorous prosecution of the War against that Power, and to employ them in perfect concert, in order to obtain for themselves and for Europe a General

[1] British and Foreign State Papers, Vol. I, pp. 129-131; see above, text, Chap. IX.

Peace, under the protection of which the rights and liberties of all Nations may be established and secured.

This engagement shall in no respect affect the Stipulations which the several Powers have already contracted relative to the number of Troops to be kept against the Enemy; and it is understood that the Courts of England, Austria, Russia, and Prussia, engage by the present Treaty to keep in the field, each of them, one hundred and fifty thousand effective men, exclusive of garrisons, to be employed in active service against the common Enemy.

ARTICLE II

The High Contracting Parties reciprocally engage not to negotiate separately with the common Enemy, nor to sign Peace, Truce, nor Convention, but with common consent. They, moreover, engage not to lay down their Arms until the object of the War, mutually understood and agreed upon, shall have been attained.

* * * * *

ARTICLE V

The High Contracting Parties, reserving to themselves to concert together, on the conclusion of a Peace with France, as to the means best adapted to guarantee to Europe, and to themselves reciprocally, the continuance of the Peace, have also determined to enter, without delay, into defensive engagements for the protection of their respective States in Europe against every attempt which France might make to infringe the order of things resulting from such Pacification.

ARTICLE VI

To effect this, they agree that in the event of one of the High Contracting Parties being threatened with an attack on the part of France, the others shall employ their most strenuous efforts to prevent it, by friendly interposition.

ARTICLE VII

In the case of these endeavors proving ineffectual, the High Contracting Parties promise to come to the immediate assistance of the Power attacked, each with a body of sixty thousand men.

* * * * *

ARTICLE XV

In order to render more effectual the Defensive Engagements above stipulated, by uniting for their common defense the Powers the most exposed to a French invasion, the High Contracting Parties engage to invite those Powers to accede to the present Treaty of Defensive Alliance.

ARTICLE XVI

The present Treaty of Defensive Alliance having for its object to maintain the equilibrium of Europe, to secure the repose and independence of its States, and to prevent the invasions which during so many years have desolated the World, the High Contracting Parties have agreed to extend the duration of it to twenty years, to take date from the day of its Signature; and they reserve to themselves, to concert upon its ulterior prolongation, three years before its expiration, should circumstances require it.

The present Treaty shall be ratified, and the Ratifications exchanged within two months, or sooner if possible.

In witness whereof, the respective Plenipotentiaries have signed the same, and affixed thereto the Seal of their Arms.

Done at Chaumont this 1st of March, in the year of our Lord 1814.

(L.S.) *Castlereagh*

(L.S.) *Clement Wenceslaus Lothaire,*
Prince of Metternich

12. ACT OF THE HOLY ALLIANCE, 26 SEPTEMBER, 1815 [1]

In the Name of the Most Holy and Indivisible Trinity.

Their Majesties the Emperor of Austria, the King of Prussia, and the Emperor of Russia, having, in consequence of the great events which have marked the course of the three last years in Europe, and especially of the blessings which it has pleased Divine Providence to shower down upon those States which place their confidence and their hope on it alone, acquired the intimate conviction of the necessity of settling the steps to be observed by the Powers, in their reciprocal relations, upon the sublime truths which the Holy Religion of our Saviour teaches:

They solemnly declare that the present Act has no other object than to publish, in the face of the whole world, their fixed resolution, both in the administration of their respective States, and in their political relations with every other Government, to take for their sole guide the precepts of that Holy Religion, the precepts of Justice, Christian Charity, and Peace, which, far from being applicable only to private concerns, must have an immediate influence on the councils of Princes, and guide all their steps, as being the only means of consolidating human institutions and remedying their imperfections. In consequence, their Majesties have agreed on the following Articles:

Conformably to the words of the Holy Scriptures, which command all men to consider each other as brethren, the Three Contracting Monarchs will remain united by the bonds of a true and indissoluble fraternity, and, considering each other as fellow countrymen, they will, on all occasions and in all places, lend each other aid and assistance; and, regarding themselves toward their subjects and armies as fathers of families, they will lead them, in the same spirit of fraternity with which they are animated, to protect Religion, Peace and Justice.

In consequence, the sole principle of force, whether between the said governments or between their Subjcts, shall be that of doing each other reciprocal service, and of testifying by unalterable good will the mutual affection with which they ought to be animated, to consider themselves all as members of one and the same Christian nation; the three allied Princes looking on themselves as merely delegated by Providence to govern three branches of the

[1] *British and Foreign State Papers*, Vol. III, p. 211; see above, text, Chap. IX.

one family, namely, Austria, Prussia, and Russia, thus confessing that the Christian world, of which they and their people form a part, has in reality no other Sovereign than Him to whom alone power really belongs, because in Him alone are found all the treasures of love, science, and infinite wisdom, that is to say, God, our Divine Saviour, the Word of the Most High, the Word of life. Their Majesties consequently recommend to their people, with the most tender solicitude, as the sole means of enjoying that Peace which arises from a good conscience, and which alone is durable, to strengthen themselves every day more and more in the principles and exercise of the duties which the Divine Saviour has taught to mankind.

ARTICLE III

All the Powers who shall choose solemnly to avow the sacred principles which have dictated the present Act, and shall acknowledge how important it is for the happiness of nations, too long agitated, that these truths should henceforth exercise over the destinies of mankind all the influence which belongs to them, will be received with equal ardor and affection into this Holy Alliance.

Done in triplicate, and signed at Paris, the year of Grace 1815, 14/26 September.

(L.S.) *Francis*
(L.S.) *Frederick William*
(L.S.) *Alexander*

13. PROGRAM OF THE CONCERT OF EUROPE IN THE GREEK QUESTION; TREATY OF 6 JULY, 1827 [1]

In the name of the Most Holy and Undivided Trinity.

His Majesty the King of the United Kingdom of Great Britain and Ireland, His Majesty the King of France and Navarre, and His Majesty the Emperor of all the Russias, penetrated with the necessity of putting an end to the sanguinary struggle which, while it abandons the Greek Provinces and the Islands of the Archipelago to all the disorders of anarchy, daily causes fresh impediments to the commerce of the States of Europe, and gives opportunity for acts of Piracy which not only expose the subjects of the High Contracting Parties to grievous losses, but also render necessary measures which are burdensome for their observation and suppression.

His Majesty the King of the United Kingdom of Great Britain and Ireland, and his Majesty the King of France and Navarre, having, moreover, received from the Greeks an earnest invitation to interpose their mediation with the Ottoman Porte; and together with His Majesty the Emperor of all the Russias, being animated with the desire of putting a stop to the effusion of blood, and of preventing the evils of every kind which the continuance of such a state of things may produce;

They have resolved to combine their efforts, and to regulate the operation thereof by a formal Treaty, for the object of reëstablishing peace between the contending parties, by means of an arrangement called for, no less by sentiments of humanity, than by interests for the tranquillity of Europe.

For these purposes they have named their plenipotentiaries to discuss, conclude, and sign the said Treaty, that is to say:— ...

Who, having communicated to each other their full powers, found to be in due and proper form, have agreed upon the following articles.

[1] *British and Foreign State Papers*, Vol. XIV, p. 632; see above, text, Chap. IX.

ARTICLE I

The contracting Powers shall offer their mediation to the Ottoman Porte, with the view of effecting a reconciliation between it and the Greeks. This offer of mediation shall be made to that Power immediately after the ratification of the present treaty, by means of a joint declaration, signed by the plenipotentiaries of the Allied Courts at Constantinople; and, at the same time, a demand for an immediate armistice shall be made to the two contending parties, as a preliminary and indispensable condition to the opening of any negotiation.

ARTICLE II

The arrangement to be proposed to the Ottoman Porte shall rest upon the following bases:—

The Greeks shall hold under the Sultan as under a Lord paramount; and, in consequence thereof, they shall pay to the Ottoman Empire an annual tribute, the amount of which shall be fixed, once for all, by common agreement. They shall be governed by authorities whom they shall choose and appoint themselves, but in the nomination of whom the Porte shall have a defined right. In order to effect a complete separation between the individuals of the two nations, and to prevent the collisions which would be the inevitable consequence of so protracted a struggle, the Greeks shall become possessors of all Turkish property situated either upon the continent, or in the islands of Greece, on condition of indemnifying the former proprietors, either by an annual sum to be added to the tribute which they shall pay to the Porte, or by some other arrangement of the same nature.

ARTICLE III

The details of this arrangement, as well as the limits of the territory upon the continent, and the designation of the islands of the Archipelago to which it shall be applicable, shall be settled by a negotiation to be afterwards entered into between the High Powers and the two contending parties.

ARTICLE IV

The contracting Powers engage to pursue the salutary work of the pacification of Greece, upon the bases laid down in the preceding articles, and to furnish, without the least delay, their representatives at Constantinople with all the instructions which are required for the execution of the Treaty which they now sign.

ARTICLE V

The contracting Powers will not seek in these arrangements, any augmentation of territory, any exclusive influence, or any commercial advantage for their subjects, which those of every other nation may not equally obtain.

ARTICLE VI

The arrangements for the reconciliation and peace, which shall be definitively agreed upon between the contending parties, shall be guaranteed by those of the signing Powers who may judge it expedient or possible to contract that obligation. The operation and the effects of such guarantee shall become the subject of future stipulation between the High Powers.

ARTICLE VII

The present Treaty shall be ratified, and the ratifications shall be exchanged in two months, or sooner if possible.

In witness, &c.

Done at London, the 6th day of July, in the year of our Lord 1827.

Dudley

Le Prince De Polignac
Lieven

ADDITIONAL ARTICLE

In case the Ottoman Porte should not, within the space of one month, accept the mediation which is to be proposed to it, the High contracting parties agree upon the following measures:—

1. It shall be declared to the Porte, by their representatives at Constantinople, that the inconveniences and evils described in the Patent Treaty as inseparable from the state of things which has, for six years, existed in the East, and the termination of which, by the means at the command of the Sublime Ottoman Porte, appears to be still distant, impose upon the High contracting parties the necessity of taking immediate measures for forming a connection with the Greeks. It is understood that this shall be effected by establishing commercial relations with the Greeks, and by sending to and receiving from them, for this purpose, consular agents, provided there shall exist in Greece authorities capable of supporting such relations.

2. If, within the said term of one month, the Porte does not accept the armistice proposed in the first article of the Patent Treaty, or if the Greeks refuse to carry it into execution, the High contracting Powers shall declare to either of the contending parties which may be disposed to continue hostilities, or to both of them, that the said High Powers intend to exert all the means which circumstances may suggest, to their prudence, for the purpose of obtaining the immediate effects of the armistice of which they desire the execution, by preventing, as far as possible, all collision between the contending parties; and in consequence, immediately after the above-mentioned declaration, the High Powers will, jointly, exert all their efforts to accomplish the object of such armistice, without, however, taking any part in the hostilities between the two contending parties. Immediately after the signature of the present additional Article, the High contracting Powers will, jointly, transmit to the admirals commanding their respective squadrons in the Levant, conditional instructions in conformity to the arrangements above declared.

3. Finally, if, contrary to all expectation, the measures do not prove sufficient to procure the adoption of the propositions of the High contracting parties by the Ottoman Porte; or if, on the other hand, the Greeks decline the conditions stipulated in their favor, by the Treaty of this date, the High contracting Powers will, nevertheless, continue to pursue the work of pacification, on the bases upon which they have agreed; and, in consequence, they authorize, from the present moment, their representatives at London to discuss and determine the future measures which it may become necessary to employ.

The present additional article shall have the same force and validity as if it were inserted, word for word, in the treaty of this day. It shall be ratified, and the ratifications shall be exchanged at the same time as those of the said treaty.

In witness, &c.

Done at London, the 6th day of July, in the year of our Lord 1827.
Dudley

Le Prince De Polignac
Lieven

14. CONVENTION OF THE CONCERT OF EUROPE PROVIDING GUARANTEES FOR THE KINGDOM OF GREECE, 7 MAY, 1832 [1]

The Courts of France, Great Britain, and Russia, exercising the power conveyed to them by the Greek Nation, to make choice of a Sovereign for Greece, raised to the rank of an independent State, and being desirous of giving to that country a fresh proof of their friendly disposition, by the election of a Prince descended from a Royal House, the friendship and alliance of which cannot fail to be of essential service to Greece, and which has already acquired claims to her esteem and gratitude, have resolved to offer the Crown of the new Greek State to the Prince Frederick Otho of Bavaria, second son of His Majesty the King of Bavaria.

His Majesty the King of Bavaria, on his part, acting in the character of Guardian of the said Prince Otho during his minority, participating in the views of the three Courts, and duly appreciating the motives which have induced them to fix their choice upon a Prince of his house, has determined to accept the Crown of Greece for his second son the Prince Frederick Otho of Bavaria.

In consequence of such acceptance, and for the purpose of agreeing upon the arrangements which it has rendered necessary, their Majesties the King of the French, the King of the United Kingdom of Great Britain and Ireland, and the Emperor of all the Russias, on the one part, and His Majesty the King of Bavaria on the other, have named as their Plenipotentiaries, viz:

Who, after having exchanged their full powers, found to be in good and due form, have agreed upon and signed the following Articles:—

ARTICLE I

The Courts of Great Britain, France, and Russia, duly authorized for this purpose by the Greek nation, offer the hereditary Sovereignty of Greece to the Prince Frederick Otho of Bavaria, second son of His Majesty the King of Bavaria.

ARTICLE II

His Majesty the King of Bavaria, acting in the name of his said son, a minor, accepts, on his behalf, the hereditary Sovereignty of Greece, on the conditions hereinafter settled.

ARTICLE III

The Prince Otho of Bavaria shall bear the title of King of Greece.

ARTICLE IV

Greece, under the sovereignty of the Prince Otho of Bavaria, and under the guarantee of the three Courts, shall form a monarchical and independent State, according to the terms of the Protocol signed between the said Courts, on the 3rd of February, 1830, and accepted both by Greece and by the Ottoman Porte.

[1] *British and Foreign State Papers*, Vol. XIX, p. 33; see above, text, Chap. IX.

ARTICLE V

The limits of the Greek State shall be such as shall be definitely settled by the negotiations which the Courts of Great Britain, France, and Russia, have recently opened with the Ottoman Porte, in execution of the Protocol of the 26th of September, 1831.

ARTICLE VI

The three Courts having beforehand determined to convert the Protocol of the 3rd of February, 1830, into a definite Treaty, as soon as the negotiations relative to the limits of Greece shall have terminated, and to communicate such Treaty to all the States with which they have relations, it is hereby agreed that they shall fulfil this engagement, and that His Majesty the King of Greece shall become a Contracting Party to the Treaty in question.

ARTICLE VII

The three Courts shall, from the present moment, use their influence to procure the recognition of the Prince Otho of Bavaria as King of Greece, by all the Sovereigns and States with whom they have relations.

* * * * *

ARTICLE XII

In execution of the stipulations of the Protocol of the 20th of February, 1830, His Majesty the Emperor of all the Russias engages to guarantee, and their Majesties the King of the United Kingdom of Great Britain and Ireland and the King of the French engage to recommend, the former to his Parliament, the latter to his Chambers, to enable their Majesties to guarantee, on the following conditions, a loan to be contracted by the Prince Otho of Bavaria, as King of Greece:—

1. The Principal of the loan to be contracted under the guarantee of the three Powers shall not exceed a total amount of sixty millions of francs.

2. The said loan shall be raised by instalments of twenty millions of francs each.

3. For the present, the first instalment only shall be raised, and the three Courts shall each become responsible for the payment of one-third of the annual amount of the interest and sinking fund of the said instalment.

4. The second and the third instalments of the said loan may also be raised, according to the necessities of the Greek State, after previous agreement between the three Courts and His Majesty the King of Greece.

5. In event of the second and third instalments of the above-mentioned loan being raised in consequence of such an agreement, the three Courts shall each become responsible for the payment of one-third of the annual amount of the interest and sinking fund of these two instalments, as well as of the first.

6. The Sovereign of Greece and the Greek State shall be bound to appropriate to the payment of the interest and sinking fund of such instalments of the loan as may have been raised under the guarantee of the three Courts, the first revenues of the State, in such manner that the actual receipts of the Greek Treasury shall be devoted, first of all, to the payment of the said interest and sinking fund, and shall not be employed for any other purpose, until those payments on account of the instalments of the loan raised under

the guarantee of the three Courts, shall have been completely secured for the current year.

The Diplomatic Representatives of the three Courts in Greece shall be specially charged to watch over the fulfilment of the last-mentioned stipulation.

ARTICLE XIII

In case a pecuniary compensation in favor of the Ottoman Porte should result from the negotiations which the three Courts have already opened at Constantinople for the definite settlement of the limits of Greece, it is understood that the amount of such compensation shall be defrayed out of the proceeds of the loan which forms the subject of the preceding Article.

15. CONSTITUTION OF THE INTERNATIONAL LABOR ORGANIZATION [1]

Section I

ORGANISATION OF LABOUR

Whereas the League of Nations has for its object the establishment of universal peace and such a peace can be established only if it is based upon social justice;

And whereas conditions of labour exist involving such injustice, hardship and privation to large numbers of people as to produce unrest so great that the peace and harmony of the world are imperiled; and an improvement of those conditions is urgently required: as, for example, by the regulation of the hours of work, including the establishment of a maximum working day and week, the regulation of the labour supply, the prevention of unemployment, the provision of an adequate living wage, the protection of the worker against sickness, disease and injury arising out of his employment, the protection of children, young persons and women, provision for old age and injury, protection of the interests of workers when employed in countries other than their own, recognition of the principle of freedom of association, the organisation of vocational and technical education and other measures:

Whereas also the failure of any nation to adopt humane conditions of labour is an obstacle in the way of other nations which desire to improve the conditions in their own countries;

The HIGH CONTRACTING PARTIES, moved by sentiments of justice and humanity as well as by the desire to secure the permanent peace of the world, agree to the following:

CHAPTER I

Organisation

ARTICLE I

A permanent organisation is hereby established for the promotion of the objects set forth in the Preamble.

The original Members of the League of Nations shall be the original Mem-

[1] See above, text, Chap. XII.

bers of this organisation, and hereafter membership of the League of Nations shall carry with it membership of the said organisation.

ARTICLE 2

The permanent organisation shall consist of:

(1) a General Conference of Representatives of the Members, and,

(2) an International Labour Office controlled by the Governing Body described in Article 393.

ARTICLE 3

The meetings of the General Conference of Representatives of the Members shall be held from time to time as occasion may require, and at least once in every year. It shall be composed of four Representatives of each of the Members, of whom two shall be Government Delegates and the two others shall be Delegates representing respectively the employers and the workpeople of each of the Members.

Each Delegate may be accompanied by advisers, who shall not exceed two in number for each item on the agenda of the meeting. When questions specially affecting women are to be considered by the Conference, one at least of the advisers should be a woman.

The Members undertake to nominate non-Government Delegates and advisers chosen in agreement with the industrial organisations, if such organisations exist, which are most representative of employers or workpeople, as the case may be, in their respective countries.

Advisers shall not speak except on a request made by the Delegate whom they accompany and by the special authorisation of the President of the Conference, and may not vote.

A Delegate may by notice in writing addressed to the President appoint one of his advisers to act as his deputy, and the adviser, while so acting, shall be allowed to speak and vote.

The names of the Delegates and their advisers will be communicated to the International Labour Office by the Government of each of the Members.

The credentials of Delegates and their advisers shall be subject to scrutiny by the Conference, which may, by two-thirds of the votes cast by the Delegates present, refuse to admit any Delegate or adviser whom it deems not to have been nominated in accordance with this Article.

ARTICLE 4

Every Delegate shall be entitled to vote individually on all matters which are taken into consideration by the Conference.

If one of the Members fails to nominate one of the non-Government Delegates whom it is entitled to nominate, the other non-Government Delegate shall be allowed to sit and speak at the Conference, but not to vote.

If in accordance with Article 389 (3) the Conference refuses admission to a Delegate of one of the Members, the provisions of the present Article shall apply as if that Delegate had not been nominated.

ARTICLE 5

The meetings of the Conference shall be held at the seat of the League of Nations, or at such other place as may be decided by the Conference at a previous meeting by two-thirds of the votes cast by the Delegates present.

ARTICLE 6

The International Labour Office shall be established at the seat of the League of Nations as part of the organisation of the League.

ARTICLE 7

The International Labour Office shall be under the control of a Governing Body consisting of twenty-four persons, appointed in accordance with the following provisions:

The Governing Body of the International Labour Office shall be constituted as follows:

Twelve persons representing the Governments;

Six persons elected by the Delegates to the Conference representing the employers;

Six persons elected by the Delegates to the Conference representing the workers.

Of the twelve persons representing the Governments eight shall be nominated by the Members which are of the chief industrial importance, and four shall be nominated by the Members selected for the purpose by the Government Delegates to the Conference, excluding the Delegates of the eight Members mentioned above.

Any question as to which are the Members of the chief industrial importance shall be decided by the Council of the League of Nations.

The periodic office of the Members of the Governing Body will be three years. The method of filling vacancies and other similar questions may be determined by the Governing Body subject to the approval of the Conference.

The Governing Body shall, from time to time, elect one of its members to act as its Chairman, shall regulate its own procedure and shall fix its own times of meeting. A special meeting shall be held if a written request to that effect is made by at least ten members of the Governing Body.

ARTICLE 8

There shall be a Director of the International Labour Office, who shall be appointed by the Governing Body, and, subject to the instructions of the Governing Body, shall be responsible for the efficient conduct of the International Labour Office and for such other duties as may be assigned to him.

The Director or his deputy shall attend all meetings of the Governing Body.

ARTICLE 9

The staff of the International Labour Office shall be appointed by the Director, who shall, so far as is possible with due regard to the efficiency of the work of the Office, select persons of different nationalities. A certain number of these persons shall be women.

ARTICLE 10

The functions of the International Labour Office shall include the collection and distribution of information on all subjects relating to the international adjustment of conditions of industrial life and labour, and particularly the examination of subjects which it is proposed to bring before the Conference with a view to the conclusion of international conventions, and the conduct of such special investigations as may be ordered by the Conference.

It will prepare the agenda for the meetings of the Conference.

It will carry out the duties required of it by the provisions of this Part of the present Treaty in connection with international disputes.

It will edit and publish in French and English, and in such other languages as the Governing Body may think desirable, a periodical paper dealing with problems of industry and employment of international interest.

Generally, in addition to the functions set out in this Article, it shall have such other powers and duties as may be assigned to it by the Conference.

ARTICLE 11

The Government Departments of any of the Members which deal with questions of industry and employment may communicate directly with the Director through the Representative of their Government on the Governing Body of the International Labour Office, or failing any such Representative, through such other qualified official as the Government may nominate for the purpose.

ARTICLE 12

The International Labour Office shall be entitled to the assistance of the Secretary-General of the League of Nations in any matter in which it can be given.

ARTICLE 13

Each of the Members will pay the travelling and subsistence expenses of its Delegates and their advisers and of its Representatives attending the meetings of the Conference or Governing Body, as the case may be.

All other expenses of the International Labour Office and of the meetings of the Conference or Governing Body shall be paid to the Director by the Secretary-General of the League of Nations out of the general funds of the League.

The Director shall be responsible to the Secretary-General of the League for the proper expenditure of all moneys paid to him in pursuance of this Article.

CHAPTER II

Procedure

ARTICLE 14

The agenda for all meetings of the Conference will be settled by the Governing Body, who shall consider any suggestion as to the agenda that may be made by the Government of any of the Members or by any representative organisation recognised for the purpose of Article 389.

ARTICLE 15

The Director shall act as the Secretary of the Conference, and shall transmit the agenda so as to reach the Members four months before the meeting of the Conference, and, through them, the non-Government Delegates when appointed.

ARTICLE 16

Any of the Governments of the Members may formally object to the inclusion of any item or items in the agenda. The grounds for such objection shall be set forth in a reasoned statement addressed to the Director, who shall circulate it to all the Members of the Permanent Organisation.

Items to which such objection has been made shall not, however, be excluded from the agenda, if at the Conference a majority of two-thirds of the votes cast by the Delegates present is in favour of considering them.

If the Conference decides (otherwise than under the preceding paragraph) by two-thirds of the votes cast by the Delegates present that any subject shall be considered by the Conference, that subject shall be included in the agenda for the following meeting.

ARTICLE 17

The Conference shall regulate its own procedure, shall elect its own President and may appoint committees to consider and report on any matter.

Except as otherwise expressly provided in this Part of the present Treaty, all matters shall be decided by a simple majority of the vote cast by the Delegates present.

The voting is void unless the total number of votes cast is equal to half the number of the Delegates attending the Conference.

ARTICLE 18

The Conference may add to any committees which it appoints technical experts, who shall be assessors without power to vote.

ARTICLE 19

When the Conference has decided on the adoption of proposals with regard to an item in the agenda, it will rest with the Conference to determine whether these proposals should take the form: (a) of a recommendation to be submitted to the Members for consideration with a view to effect being given to it by national legislation or otherwise, or (b) of a draft international convention for ratification by the Members.

In either case a majority of two-thirds of the votes cast by the Delegates present shall be necessary on the final vote for the adoption of the recommendation or draft convention, as the case may be, by the Conference.

In framing any recommendation or draft convention of general application the Conference shall have due regard to those countries in which climactic conditions, the imperfect development of industrial organisation or other special circumstances make the industrial conditions substantially different and shall suggest the modifications, if any, which it considers may be required to meet the case of such countries.

A copy of the recommendation or draft convention shall be authenticated by the signature of the President of the Conference and of the Director and shall be deposited with the Secretary-General of the League of Nations. The Secretary-General will communicate a certified copy of the recommendation or draft convention to each of the Members.

Each of the Members undertakes that it will, within the period of one year at most from the closing of the session of the Conference, or if it is impossible owing to exceptional circumstances to do so within the period of one year, then at the earliest practicable moment and in no case later than eighteen months from the closing of the session of Conference, bring the recommendation or draft convention before the authority or authorities within whose competence the matter lies, for the enactment of legislation or other action.

In the case of recommendation, the Members will inform the Secretary-General of the action taken.

In the case of a draft convention, the Member will, if it obtains the consent of the authority or authorities within whose competence the matter lies, communicate the formal ratification of the convention to the Secretary-General and will take such action as may be necessary to make effective the provisions of such convention.

If on a recommendation no legislative or other action is taken to make a recommendation effective, or if the draft convention fails to obtain the consent of the authority or authorities within whose competence the matter lies, no further obligation shall rest upon the Member.

In the case of a federal State, the power of which to enter into conventions on labour matters is subject to limitations, it shall be in the discretion of that Government to treat a draft convention to which such limitations apply as a recommendation only, and the provisions of this Article with respect to recommendations shall apply in such case.

The above Article shall be interpreted in accordance with the following principle:

In no case shall any Member be asked or required, as a result of the adoption of any recommendation or draft convention by the Conference, to lessen the protection afforded by its existing legislation to the workers concerned.

ARTICLE 20

Any convention so ratified shall be registered by the Secretary-General of the League of Nations, but shall only be binding upon the Members which ratify it.

ARTICLE 21

If any convention coming before the Conference for final consideration fails to secure the support of two-thirds of the votes cast by the Delegates present, it shall nevertheless be within the right of any of the Members of the Permanent Organisation to agree to such convention among themselves.

Any convention so agreed to shall be communicated by the Governments concerned to the Secretary-General of the League of Nations, who shall register it.

ARTICLE 22

Each of the Members agrees to make an annual report to the International Labour Office on the measures which it has taken to give effect to the provisions of conventions to which it is a party. These reports shall be made in such form and shall contain such particulars as the Governing Body may request. The Director shall lay a summary of these reports before the next meeting of the Conference.

ARTICLE 23

In the event of any representation being made to the International Labour Office by an industrial association of employers or of workers that any of the Members has failed to secure in any respect the effective observance within its jurisdiction of any convention to which it is a party, the Governing Body may communicate this representation to the Government against which it is made and may invite that Government to make such statement on the subject as it may think fit.

ARTICLE 24

If no statement is received within a reasonable time from the Government in question, or if the statement when received is not deemed to be satisfactory by the Governing Body, the latter shall have the right to publish the representation and the statement, if any, made in reply to it.

ARTICLE 25

Any of the Members shall have the right to file a complaint with the International Labour Office if it is not satisfied that any other Member is securing the effective observance of any convention which both have ratified in accordance with the foregoing Articles.

The Governing Body may, if it thinks fit, before referring such a complaint to a Commission of Inquiry, as hereinafter provided for, communicate with the Government in question in the manner described in Article 409.

If the Governing Body does not think it necessary to communicate the complaint to the Government in question, or if, when they have made such communication, no statement in reply has been received within a reasonable time which the Governing Body considers to be satisfactory, the Governing Body may apply for the appointment of a Commission of Inquiry to consider the complaint and to report thereon.

The Governing Body may adopt the same procedure either of its own motion or on receipt of a complaint from a Delegate to the Conference.

When any matter arising out of Articles 410 or 411 is being considered by the Governing Body, the Government in question shall, if not already represented thereon, be entitled to send a representative to take part in the proceedings of the Governing Body while the matter is under consideration. Adequate notice of the date on which the matter will be considered shall be given to the Government in question.

ARTICLE 26

The Commission of Inquiry shall be constituted in accordance with the following provisions:

Each of the Members agrees to nominate within six months of the date on which the present Treaty comes into force three persons of industrial experience, of whom one shall be a representative of employers, one a representative of workers, and one a person of independent standing, who shall together form a panel from which the Members of the Commission of Inquiry shall be drawn.

The qualifications of the persons so nominated shall be subject to scrutiny by the Governing Body, which may by two-thirds of the votes cast by the representatives present refuse to accept the nomination of any person whose qualifications do not in its opinion comply with the requirements of the present Article.

Upon the application of the Governing Body, the Secretary-General of the League of Nations shall nominate three persons, one from each section of this panel, to constitute the Commission of Inquiry, and shall designate one of them as the President of the Commission. None of these three persons shall be a person nominated to the panel by any Member directly concerned in the complaint.

ARTICLE 27

The Members agree that, in the event of the reference of a complaint to a Commission of Inquiry under Article 411 they will each, whether directly concerned in the complaint or not, place at the disposal of the Commission all the information in their possession which bears upon the subject-matter of the complaint.

ARTICLE 28

When the Commission of Inquiry has fully considered the complaint, it shall prepare a report embodying its findings on all questions of fact relevant to determining the issue between the parties and containing such recommendations as it may think proper as to the steps which shauld be taken to meet the complaint and the time within which they should be taken.

It shall also indicate in this report the measures, if any, of an economic character against a defaulting Government which it considers to be appropriate, and which it considers other Governments would be justified in adopting.

ARTICLE 29

The Secretary-General of the League of Nations shall communicate the report of the Commission of Inquiry to each of the Governments concerned in the complaint, and shall cause it to be published.

Each of these Governments shall within one month inform the Secretary-General of the League of Nations whether or not it accepts the recommendations contained in the report of the Commission; and if not, whether it proposes to refer the complaint to the Permanent Court of International Justice of the League of Nations.

ARTICLE 30

In the event of any Member failing to take the action required by Article 405 with regard to a recommendation or draft Convention, any other Member shall be entitled to refer the matter to the Permanent Court of International Justice.

ARTICLE 31

The decision of the Permanent Court of International Justice in regard to a complaint or matter which has been referred to it in pursuance of Article 415 or Article 416 shall be final.

ARTICLE 32

The Permanent Court of International Justice may affirm, vary or reverse any of the findings or recommendations of the Commission of Inquiry, if any, and shall in its decision indicate the measures, if any, of an economic character which it considers to be appropriate, and which other Governments would be justified in adopting against a defaulting Government.

ARTICLE 33

In the event of any Member failing to carry out within the time specified the recommendations, if any, contained in the report of the Commission of Inquiry, or in the decision of the Permanent Court of International Justice, as the case may be, any other Member may take against that Member the measures of an economic character indicated in the report of the Commission or in the decision of the Court as appropriate to the case.

ARTICLE 34

The defaulting Government may at any time inform the Governing Body that it has taken the steps necessary to comply with the recommendations of the Commission of Inquiry or with those in the decision of the Permanent Court of International Justice, as the case may be, and may request it to apply to the Secretary-General of the League to constitute a Commission of Inquiry to verify its contention. In this case the provisions of Articles 412, 413, 414, 415, 417 and 418 shall apply, and if the report of the Commission of Inquiry or the decision of the Permanent Court of International Justice is in favour of the defaulting Government, the other Governments shall forthwith discontinue the measures of an economic character that they have taken against the defaulting Government.

CHAPTER III

General

ARTICLE 35

The Members engage to apply conventions which they have ratified in accordance with the provisions of this Part of the present Treaty to their colonies, protectorates and possessions which are not fully self-governing:

(1) Except where owing to the local conditions the convention is inapplicable, or

(2) Subject to such modifications as may be necessary to adapt the convention to local conditions.

And each of the Members shall notify to the International Labour Office the action taken in respect of each of its colonies, protectorates and possessions which are not fully self-governing.

ARTICLE 36

Amendments to this Part of the present Treaty which are adopted by the Conference by a majority of two-thirds of the votes cast by the Delegates present shall take effect when ratified by the States whose representatives compose the Council of the League of Nations and by three-fourths of the Members.

ARTICLE 37

Any question or dispute relating to the interpretation of this Part of the present Treaty or of any subsequent convention concluded by the Members in pursuance of the provisions of this Part of the present Treaty shall be referred for decision to the Permanent Court of International Justice.

CHAPTER IV

Transitory Provisions

ARTICLE 38

The first meeting of the Conference shall take place in October, 1919. The place and agenda for this meeting shall be as specified in the Annex hereto.

Arrangements for the convening and the organisation of the first meeting of the Conference will be made by the Government designated for the purpose in the said Annex. That Government shall be assisted in the preparation of the documents for submission to the Conference by an International Committee constituted as provided in the said Annex.

The expenses of the first meeting and of all subsequent meetings held before the League of Nations has been able to establish a general fund, other than the expenses of Delegates and their advisers, will be borne by the Members in accordance with the apportionment of the expenses of the International Bureau of the Universal Postal Union.

ARTICLE 39

Until the League of Nations has been constituted all communications which under the provisions of the foregoing Articles should be addressed to the Secretary-General of the League will be preserved by the Director of the International Labour Office, who will transmit them to the Secretary-General of the League.

ARTICLE 40

Pending the creation of a Permanent Court of International Justice disputes which in accordance with this Part of the present Treaty would be submitted to it for decision will be referred to a tribunal of three persons appointed by the Council of the League of Nations.

ANNEX

FIRST MEETING OF ANNUAL LABOUR CONFERENCE, 1919

The place of meeting will be Washington.

The Government of the United States of America is requested to convene the Conference.

The International Organising Committee will consist of seven Members, appointed by the United States of America, Great Britain, France, Italy, Japan, Belgium and Switzerland. The Committee may, if it thinks necessary, invite other Members to appoint representatives.

Agenda:
(1) Application of principle of the 8-hours day or of the 48-hours week.
(2) Question of preventing or providing against unemployment.
(3) Women's employment:
    a Before and after child-birth, including the question of maternity benefit;
    b During the night;
    c In unhealthy processes.
(4) Employment of children:
    a Minimum age of employment;
    b During the night;
    c In unhealthy processes.
(5) Extension and application of the International Conventions adopted at Bern in 1906 on the prohibition of night work for women employed in industry and the prohibition of the use of white phosphorus in the manufacture of matches.

Section II

GENERAL PRINCIPLES

ARTICLE 41

The High Contracting Parties, recognising that the well-being, physical, moral and intellectual, of industrial wage-earners is of supreme international importance, have framed, in order to further this great end, the permanent machinery provided for in Section I and associated with that of the League of Nations.

They recognise that differences of climate, habits and customs, of economic opportunity and industrial tradition, make strict uniformity in the conditions of labour difficult of immediate attainment. But, holding as they do, that labour should not be regarded merely as an article of commerce, they think that there are methods and principles for regulating labour conditions which all industrial communities should endeavour to apply, so far as their special circumstances will permit.

Among these methods and principles, the following seem to the High Contracting Parties to be of special and urgent importance:

First.—The guiding principle above enunciated that labour should not be regarded merely as a commodity or article of commerce.

Second.—The right of association for all lawful purposes by the employed as well as by the employers.

Third.—The payment to the employed of a wage adequate to maintain a reasonable standard of life as this is understood in their time and country.

Fourth.—The adoption of an eight hours' day or a forty-eight hours' week as the standard to be aimed at where it has not already been attained.

Fifth.—The adoption of a weekly rest of at least twenty-four hours, which should include Sunday wherever practicable.

Sixth.—The abolition of child labour and the imposition of such limitations on the labour of young persons as shall permit the continuation of their education and assure their proper physical development.

Seventh.—The principle that men and women should receive equal remuneration for work of equal value.

Eighth.—The standard set by law in each country with respect to the conditions of labour should have due regard to the equitable economic treatment of all workers lawfully resident therein.

Ninth.—Each State should make provision for a system of inspection in which women should take part, in order to insure the enforcement of the laws and regulations for the protection of the employed.

Without claiming that these methods and principles are either complete or final, the High Contracting Parties are of opinion that they are well fitted to guide the policy of the League of Nations; and that, if adopted by the industrial communities who are members of the League, and safeguarded in practice by an adequate system of such inspection, they will confer lasting benefits upon the wage-earners of the world.

16. STATUTE OF THE INTERNATIONAL COURT OF JUSTICE

ARTICLE I

The International Court of Justice established by the Charter of the United Nations as the principal judicial organ of the United Nations shall be constituted and shall function in accordance with the provisions of the present Statute.

CHAPTER I. ORGANIZATION OF THE COURT

ARTICLE 2

The Court shall be composed of a body of independent judges, elected regardless of their nationality from among persons of high moral character, who possess the qualifications required in their respective countries for appointment to the highest judicial offices, or are jurisconsults of recognized competence in international law.

ARTICLE 3

1. The Court shall consist of fifteen members, no two of whom may be nationals of the same state.

2. A person who for the purposes of membership in the Court could be regarded as a national of more than one state shall be deemed to be a national of the one in which he ordinarily exercises civil and political rights.

ARTICLE 4

1. The members of the Court shall be elected by the General Assembly and by the Security Council from a list of persons nominated by the national groups in the Permanent Court of Arbitration, in accordance with the following provisions.

2. In the case of Members of the United Nations not represented in the Permanent Court of Arbitration, candidates shall be nominated by national groups appointed for this purpose by their governments under the same conditions as those prescribed for members of the Permanent Court of Arbitration by Article 44 of the Convention of The Hague of 1907 for the pacific settlement of international disputes.

3. The conditions under which a state which is a party to the present Statute but is not a Member of the United Nations may participate in electing the members of the Court shall, in the absence of a special agreement, be laid down by the General Assembly upon recommendation of the Security Council.

ARTICLE 5

1. At least three months before the date of the election, the Secretary-General of the United Nations shall address a written request to the members of the Permanent Court of Arbitration belonging to the states which are parties to the present Statute, and to the members of the national groups appointed under Article 4, paragraph 2, inviting them to undertake, within a given time, by national groups, the nomination of persons in a position to accept the duties of a member of the Court.

2. No group may nominate more than four persons, not more than two of whom shall be of their own nationality. In no case may the number of candidates nominated by a group be more than double the number of seats to be filled.

ARTICLE 6

Before making these nominations, each national group is recommended to consult its highest court of justice, its legal faculties and schools of law, and its national academies and national sections of international academies devoted to the study of law.

ARTICLE 7

1. The Secretary-General shall prepare a list in alphabetical order of all the persons thus nominated. Save as provided in Article 12, paragraph 2, these shall be the only persons eligible.

2. The Secretary-General shall submit this list to the General Assembly and to the Security Council.

ARTICLE 8

The General Assembly and the Security Council shall proceed independently of one another to elect the members of the Court.

ARTICLE 9

At every election, the electors shall bear in mind not only that the persons to be elected should individually possess the qualifications required, but also that in the body as a whole the representation of the main forms of civilization and of the principal legal systems of the world should be assured.

ARTICLE 10

1. Those candidates who obtain an absolute majority of votes in the General Assembly and in the Security Council shall be considered as elected.

2. Any vote of the Security Council, whether for the election of judges or for the appointment of members of the conference envisaged in Article 12, shall be taken without any distinction between permanent and non-permanent members of the Security Council.

3. In the event of more than one national of the same state obtaining an absolute majority of the votes both of the General Assembly and of the Security Council, the eldest of these only shall be considered as elected.

ARTICLE 11

If, after the first meeting held for the purpose of the election, one or more seats remain to be filled, a second and, if necessary, a third meeting shall take place.

ARTICLE 12

1. If, after the third meeting, one or more seats still remain unfilled, a joint conference consisting of six members, three appointed by the General Assembly and three by the Security Council, may be formed at any time at the request of either the General Assembly or the Security Council, for the purpose of choosing by the vote of an absolute majority one name for each seat still vacant, to submit to the General Assembly and the Security Council for their respective acceptance.

2. If the joint conference is unanimously agreed upon any person who fulfils the required conditions, he may be included in its list, even though he was not included in the list of nominations referred to in Article 7.

3. If the joint conference is satisfied that it will not be successful in procuring an election, those members of the Court who have already been elected shall, within a period to be fixed by the Security Council, proceed to fill the vacant seats by selection from among those candidates who have obtained votes either in the General Assembly or in the Security Council.

4. In the event of an equality of votes among the judges, the eldest judge shall have a casting vote.

ARTICLE 13

1. The members of the Court shall be elected for nine years and may be re-elected; provided, however, that of the judges elected at the first election, the terms of five judges shall expire at the end of three years and the terms of five more judges shall expire at the end of six years.

2. The judges whose terms are to expire at the end of the above-mentioned initial periods of three and six years shall be chosen by lot to be drawn by the Secretary-General immediately after the first election has been completed.

3. The members of the Court shall continue to discharge their duties until their places have been filled. Though replaced, they shall finish any cases which they may have begun.

4. In the case of the resignation of a member of the Court, the resignation shall be addressed to the President of the Court for transmission to the Secretary-General. This last notification makes the place vacant.

ARTICLE 14

Vacancies shall be filled by the same method as that laid down for the first election, subject to the following provision: the Secretary-General shall, within one month of the occurrence of the vacancy, proceed to issue the invitations provided for in Article 5, and the date of the election shall be fixed by the Security Council.

ARTICLE 15

A member of the Court elected to replace a member whose term of office has not expired shall hold office for the remainder of his predecessor's term.

ARTICLE 16

1. No member of the Court may exercise any political or administrative function, or engage in any other occupation of a professional nature.

2. Any doubt of this point shall be settled by the decision of the Court.

ARTICLE 17

1. No member of the Court may act as agent, counsel, or advocate in any case.

2. No member may participate in the decision of any case in which he has previously taken part as agent, counsel, or advocate for one of the parties, or as a member of a national or international court, or of a commission of enquiry, or in any other capacity.

3. Any doubt on this point shall be settled by the decision of the Court.

ARTICLE 18

1. No member of the Court can be dismissed unless, in the unanimous opinion of the other members, he has ceased to fulfil the required conditions.

2. Formal notification thereof shall be made to the Secretary-General by the Registrar.

3. This notification makes the place vacant.

ARTICLE 19

The members of the Court, when engaged on the business of the Court, shall enjoy diplomatic privileges and immunities.

ARTICLE 20

Every member of the Court shall, before taking up his duties, make a solemn declaration in open court that he will exercise his powers impartially and conscientiously.

ARTICLE 21

1. The Court shall elect its President and Vice-President for three years; they may be re-elected.

2. The Court shall appoint its Registrar and may provide for the appointment of such other officers as may be necessary.

ARTICLE 22

1. The seat of the Court shall be established at The Hague. This, however, shall not prevent the Court from sitting and exercising its functions elsewhere whenever the Court considers it desirable.

2. The President and the Registrar shall reside at the seat of the Court.

ARTICLE 23

1. The Court shall remain permanently in session, except during the judicial vacations, the dates and duration of which shall be fixed by the Court.

2. Members of the Court are entitled to periodic leave, the dates and duration of which shall be fixed by the Court, having in mind the distance between The Hague and the home of each judge.

3. Members of the Court shall be bound, unless they are on leave or prevented from attending by illness or other serious reasons duly explained to the President, to hold themselves permanently at the disposal of the Court.

ARTICLE 24

1. If, for some special reason, a member of the Court considers that he should not take part in the decision of a particular case, he shall so inform the President.

2. If the President considers that for some special reason one of the members of the Court should not sit in a particular case, he shall give him notice accordingly.

3. If in any such case the member of the Court and the President disagree, the matter shall be settled by the decision of the Court.

ARTICLE 25

1. The full Court shall sit except when it is expressly provided otherwise in the present Statute.

2. Subject to the condition that the number of judges available to constitute the Court is not thereby reduced below eleven, the Rules of the Court may provide for allowing one or more judges, according to circumstances and in rotation, to be dispensed from sitting.

3. A quorum of nine judges shall suffice to constitute the Court.

ARTICLE 26

1. The Court may from time to time form one or more chambers, composed of three or more judges as the Court may determine, for dealing with particular categories of cases; for example, labor cases and cases relating to transit and communications.

2. The Court may at any time form a chamber for dealing with a particular case. The number of judges to constitute such a chamber shall be determined by the Court with the approval of the parties.

3. Cases shall be heard and determined by the chambers provided for in this Article if the parties so request.

ARTICLE 27

A judgment given by any of the chambers provided for in Articles 26 and 29 shall be considered as rendered by the Court.

ARTICLE 28

The chambers provided for in Articles 26 and 29 may, with the consent of the parties, sit and exercise their functions elsewhere than at The Hague.

ARTICLE 29

With a view to the speedy despatch of business, the Court shall form annually a chamber composed of five judges which, at the request of the parties, may hear and determine cases by summary procedure. In addition, two judges shall be selected for the purpose of replacing judges who find it impossible to sit.

ARTICLE 30

1. The Court shall frame rules for carrying out its functions. In particular, it shall lay down rules of procedure.

2. The Rules of the Court may provide for assessors to sit with the Court or with any of its chambers, without the right to vote.

ARTICLE 31

1. Judges of the nationality of each of the parties shall retain their right to sit in the case before the Court.

2. If the Court includes upon the Bench a judge of the nationality of one of the parties, any other party may choose a person to sit as judge. Such person shall be chosen preferably from among those persons who have been nominated as candidates as provided in Articles 4 and 5.

3. If the Court includes upon the Bench no judge of the nationality of the parties, each of these parties may proceed to choose a judge as provided in paragraph 2 of this Article.

4. The provisions of this Article shall apply to the case of Articles 26 and 29. In such cases, the President shall request one or, if necessary, two of the members of the Court forming the chamber to give place to the members of the Court of the nationality of the parties concerned, and, failing such, or if they are unable to be present, to the judges specially chosen by the parties.

5. Should there be several parties in the same interest, they shall, for the purpose of the preceding provisions, be reckoned as one party only. Any doubt upon this point shall be settled by the decision of the Court.

6. Judges chosen as laid down in paragraphs 2, 3, and 4 of this Article shall fulfil the conditions required by Articles 2, 17 (paragraph 2), 20, and 24 of the present Statute. They shall take part in the decision on terms of complete equality with their colleagues.

ARTICLE 32

1. Each member of the Court shall receive an annual salary.

2. The President shall receive a special annual allowance.

3. The Vice-President shall receive a special allowance for every day on which he acts as President.

4. The judges chosen under Article 31, other than members of the Court, shall receive compensation for each day on which they exercise their functions.

5. These salaries, allowances, and compensation shall be fixed by the General Assembly. They may not be decreased during the term of office.

6. The salary of the Registrar shall be fixed by the General Assembly on the proposal of the Court.

7. Regulations made by the General Assembly shall fix the conditions under which retirement pensions may be given to members of the Court and to the Registrar, and the conditions under which members of the Court and the Registrar shall have their traveling expenses refunded.

8. The above salaries, allowances, and compensation shall be free of all taxation.

ARTICLE 33

The expenses of the Court shall be borne by the United Nations in such a manner as shall be decided by the General Assembly.

CHAPTER II. COMPETENCE OF THE COURT

ARTICLE 34

1. Only states may be parties in cases before the Court.

2. The Court, subject to and in conformity with its Rules, may request of public international organizations information relevant to cases before it, and shall receive such information presented by such organizations on their own initiative.

3. Whenever the construction of the constituent instrument of a public international organization or of an international convention adopted thereunder is in question in a case before the Court, the Registrar shall so notify the public international organization concerned and shall communicate to it copies of all the written proceedings.

ARTICLE 35

1. The Court shall be open to the states parties to the present Statute.

2. The conditions under which the Court shall be open to other states shall, subject to the special provisions contained in treaties in force, be laid down by the Security Council, but in no case shall such conditions place the parties in a position of inequality before the Court.

3. When a state which is not a Member of the United Nations is a party to a case, the Court shall fix the amount which that party is to contribute towards the expenses of the Court. This provision shall not apply if such state is bearing a share of the expenses of the Court.

ARTICLE 36

1. The jurisdiction of the Court comprises all cases which the parties refer to it and all matters specially provided for in the Charter of the United Nations or in treaties and conventions in force.

2. The states parties to the present Statute may at any time declare that they recognize as compulsory *ipso facto* and without special agreement, in relation to any other state accepting the same obligation, the jurisdiction of the Court in all legal disputes concerning:

  a. the interpretation of a treaty;
  b. any question of international law;
  c. the existence of any fact which, if established, would constitute a breach of an international obligation;
  d. the nature or extent of the reparation to be made for the breach of an international obligation.

3. The declaration referred to above may be made unconditionally or on condition of reciprocity on the part of several or certain states, or for a certain time.

4. Such declarations shall be deposited with the Secretary-General of the United Nations, who shall transmit copies thereof to the parties to the Statute and to the Registrar of the Court.

5. Declarations made under Article 36 of the Statute of the Permanent Court of International Justice and which are still in force shall be deemed, as between the parties to the present Statute, to be acceptances of the compulsory jurisdiction of the International Court of Justice for the period which they still have to run and in accordance with their terms.

6. In the event of a dispute as to whether the Court has jurisdiction, the matter shall be settled by the decision of the Court.

ARTICLE 37

Whenever a treaty or convention in force provides for reference of a matter to a tribunal to have been instituted by the League of Nations, or to the Permanent Court of International Justice, the matter shall, as between the parties to the present Statute, be referred to the International Court of Justice.

ARTICLE 38

1. The Court, whose function is to decide in accordance with international law such disputes as are submitted to it, shall apply:
  a. international conventions, whether general or particular, establishing rules expressly recognized by the contesting states;
  b. international custom, as evidence of a general practice accepted as law;
  c. the general principles of law recognized by civilized nations;
  d. subject to the provisions of Article 59, judicial decisions and the teachings of the most highly qualified publicists of the various nations, as subsidiary means for the determination of rules of law.

2. This provision shall not prejudice the power of the Court to decide a case *ex aequo et bono*, if the parties agree thereto.

CHAPTER III. PROCEDURE

ARTICLE 39

1. The official languages of the Court shall be French and English. If the parties agree that the case shall be conducted in French, the judgment shall be delivered in French. If the parties agree that the case shall be conducted in English, the judgment shall be delivered in English.

2. In the absence of an agreement as to which language shall be employed, each party may, in the pleadings, use the language which it prefers; the decision of the Court shall be given in French and English. In this case the Court shall at the same time determine which of the two texts shall be considered as authoritative.

3. The Court shall, at the request of any party, authorize a language other than French or English to be used by that party.

ARTICLE 40

1. Cases are brought before the Court, as the case may be, either by the notification of the special agreement or by a written application addressed to the Registrar. In either case the subject of the dispute and the parties shall be indicated.

2. The Registrar shall forthwith communicate the application to all concerned.

3. He shall also notify the Members of the United Nations through the Secretary-General, and also any other states entitled to appear before the Court.

ARTICLE 41

1. The Court shall have the power to indicate, if it considers that circumstances so require, any provisional measures which ought to be taken to preserve the respective rights of either party.

2. Pending the final decision, notice of the measures suggested shall forthwith be given to the parties and to the Security Council.

ARTICLE 42

1. The parties shall be represented by agents.

2. They may have the assistance of counsel or advocates before the Court.

3. The agents, counsel, and advocates of parties before the Court shall enjoy the privileges and immunities necessary to the independent exercise of their duties.

ARTICLE 43

1. The procedure shall consist of two parts: written and oral.

2. The written proceedings shall consist of the communication to the Court and to the parties of memorials, counter-memorials and, if necessary, replies; also all papers and documents in support.

3. These communications shall be made through the Registrar, in the order and within the time fixed by the Court.

4. A certified copy of every document produced by one party shall be communicated to the other party.

5. The oral proceedings shall consist of the hearing by the Court of witnesses, experts, agents, counsel, and advocates.

ARTICLE 44

1. For the service of all notices upon persons other than the agents, counsel, and advocates, the Court shall apply direct to the government of the state upon whose territory the notice has to be served.

2. The same provision shall apply whenever steps are to be taken to procure evidence on the spot.

ARTICLE 45

The hearing shall be under the control of the President or, if he is unable to preside, of the Vice-President; if neither is able to preside, the senior judge present shall preside.

ARTICLE 46

The hearing in Court shall be public, unless the Court shall decide otherwise, or unless the parties demand that the public be not admitted.

ARTICLE 47

1. Minutes shall be made at each hearing and signed by the Registrar and the President.

2. These minutes alone shall be authentic.

ARTICLE 48

The Court shall make orders for the conduct of the case, shall decide the form and time in which each party must conclude its arguments, and make all arrangements connected with the taking of evidence.

ARTICLE 49

The Court may, even before the hearing begins, call upon the agents to produce any document or to supply any explanations. Formal note shall be taken of any refusal.

ARTICLE 50

The Court may, at any time, entrust any individual, body, bureau, commission, or other organization that it may select, with the task of carrying out an enquiry or giving an expert opinion.

ARTICLE 51

During the hearing any relevant questions are to be put to the witnesses and experts under the conditions laid down by the Court in the rules of procedure referred to in Article 30.

ARTICLE 52

After the Court has received the proofs and evidence within the time specified for the purpose, it may refuse to accept any further oral or written evidence that one party may desire to present unless the other side consents.

ARTICLE 53

1. Whenever one of the parties does not appear before the Court, or fails to defend its case, the other party may call upon the Court to decide in favor of its claim.

2. The Court must, before doing so, satisfy itself, not only that it has jurisdiction in accordance with Articles 36 and 37, but also that the claim is well founded in fact and law.

ARTICLE 54

1. When, subject to the control of the Court, the agents, counsel, and advocates have completed their presentation of the case, the President shall declare the hearing closed.

2. The court shall withdraw to consider the judgment.

3. The deliberations of the Court shall take place in private and remain secret.

ARTICLE 55

1. All questions shall be decided by a majority of the judges present.
2. In the event of an equality of votes, the President or the judge who acts in his place shall have a casting vote.

ARTICLE 56

1. The judgment shall state the reasons on which it is based.
2. It shall contain the names of the judges who have taken part in the decision.

ARTICLE 57

If the judgment does not represent in whole or in part the unanimous opinion of the judges, any judge shall be entitled to deliver a separate opinion.

ARTICLE 58

The judgment shall be signed by the President and by the Registrar. It shall be read in open court, due notice having been given to the agents.

ARTICLE 59

The decision of the Court has no binding force except between the parties and in respect of that particular case.

ARTICLE 60

The judgment is final and without appeal. In the event of dispute as to the meaning or scope of the judgment, the Court shall construe it upon the request of any party.

ARTICLE 61

1. An application for revision of a judgment may be made only when it is based upon the discovery of some fact of such a nature as to be a decisive factor, which fact was, when the judgment was given, unknown to the Court and also to the party claiming revision, always provided that such ignorance was not due to negligence.
2. The proceedings for revision shall be opened by a judgment of the Court expressly recording the existence of the new fact, recognizing that it has such a character as to lay the case open to revision, and declaring the application admissible on this ground.
3. The Court may require previous compliance with the terms of the judgment before it admits proceedings in revision.
4. The application for revision must be made at latest within six months of the discovery of the new fact.
5. No application for revision may be made after the lapse of ten years from the date of the judgment.

ARTICLE 62

1. Should a state consider that it has an interest of a legal nature which may be affected by the decision in the case, it may submit a request to the Court to be permitted to intervene.
2. It shall be for the Court to decide upon this request.

ARTICLE 63

1. Whenever the construction of a convention to which states other than those concerned in the case are parties is in question, the Registrar shall notify all such states forthwith.

2. Every state so notified has the right to intervene in the proceedings; but if it uses this right, the construction given by the judgment will be equally binding upon it.

ARTICLE 64

Unless otherwise decided by the Court, each party shall bear its own costs.

CHAPTER IV. ADVISORY OPINIONS

ARTICLE 65

1. The Court may give an advisory opinion on any legal question at the request of whatever body may be authorized by or in accordance with the Charter of the United Nations to make such a request.

2. Questions upon which the advisory opinion of the Court is asked shall be laid before the Court by means of a written request containing an exact statement of the question upon which an opinion is required, and accompanied by all documents likely to throw light upon the question.

ARTICLE 66

1. The Registrar shall forthwith give notice of the request for an advisory opinion to all states entitled to appear before the Court.

2. The Registrar shall also, by means of a special and direct communication, notify any state entitled to appear before the Court or international organization considered by the Court, or, should it not be sitting, by the President, as likely to be able to furnish information on the question, that the Court will be prepared to receive, within a time limit to be fixed by the President, written statements, or to hear, at a public sitting to be held for the purpose, oral statements relating to the question.

3. Should any such state entitled to appear before the Court have failed to receive the special communication referred to in paragraph 2 of this Article, such state may express a desire to submit a written statement or to be heard; and the Court will decide.

4. States and organizations having presented written or oral statements or both shall be permitted to comment on the statements made by other states or organizations in the form, to the extent, and within the time limits which the Court, or, should it not be sitting, the President, shall decide in each particular case. Accordingly, the Registrar shall in due time communicate any such written statements to states and organizations having submitted similar statements.

ARTICLE 67

The Court shall deliver its advisory opinions in open court, notice having been given to the Secretary-General and to the representatives of Members of the United Nations, of other states and of international organizations immediately concerned.

ARTICLE 68

In the exercise of its advisory functions the Court shall further be guided by the provisions of the present Statute which apply in contentious cases to the extent to which it recognizes them to be applicable.

CHAPTER V. AMENDMENT

ARTICLE 69

Amendments to the present Statute shall be effected by the same procedure as is provided by the Charter of the United Nations for amendments to that Charter, subject however to any provisions which the General Assembly upon recommendation of the Security Council may adopt concerning the participation of states which are parties to the present Statute but are not Members of the United Nations.

ARTICLE 70

The Court shall have power to propose such amendments to the present Statute as it may deem necessary, through written communications to the Secretary-General, for consideration in conformity with the provisions of Article 69.

17. CHARTER OF THE UNITED NATIONS

We the Peoples of the United Nations
Determined
> to save succeeding generations from the scourge of war, which twice in our lifetime has brought untold sorrow to mankind, and
> to reaffirm faith in fundamental human rights, in the dignity and worth of the human person, in the equal rights of men and women and of nations large and small, and
> to establish conditions under which justice and respect for the obligations arising from treaties and other sources of international law can be maintained, and
> to promote social progress and better standards of life in larger freedom,

And for These Ends
> to practice tolerance and live together in peace with one another as good neighbors, and
> to unite our strength to maintain international peace and security, and
> to ensure, by the acceptance of principles and the institution of methods, that armed force shall not be used, save in the common interest, and to employ international machinery for the promotion of the economic and social advancement of all peoples,

Have Resolved to Combine Our Efforts
to Accomplish These Ends
Accordingly, our respective Governments, through representatives assembled in the city of San Francisco, who have exhibited their full powers found to be in good and due form, have agreed to the present Charter of the United Nations and do hereby establish an international organization to be known as the United Nations.

CHAPTER I

PURPOSES AND PRINCIPLES

ARTICLE 1

The Purposes of the United Nations are:

1. To maintain international peace and security, and to that end: to take effective collective measures for the prevention and removal of threats to the peace, and for the suppression of acts of aggression or other breaches of the peace, and to bring about by peaceful means, and in conformity with the principles of justice and international law, adjustment or settlement of international disputes or situations which might lead to a breach of the peace;

2. To develop friendly relations among nations based on respect for the principle of equal rights and self-determination of peoples, and to take other appropriate measures to strengthen universal peace;

3. To achieve international cooperation in solving international problems of an economic, social, cultural, or humanitarian character, and in promoting and encouraging respect for human rights and for fundamental freedoms for all without distinction as to race, sex, language, or religion; and

4. To be a center for harmonizing the actions of nations in the attainment of these common ends.

ARTICLE 2

The Organization and its Members, in pursuit of the Purposes stated in Article 1, shall act in accordance with the following Principles.

1. The Organization is based on the principle of the sovereign equality of all its Members.

2. All Members, in order to ensure to all of them the rights and benefits resulting from membership, shall fulfil in good faith the obligations assumed by them in accordance with the present Charter.

3. All Members shall settle their international disputes by peaceful means in such a manner that international peace and security, and justice, are not endangered.

4. All Members shall refrain in their international relations from the threat or use of force against the territorial integrity or political independence of any state, or in any other manner inconsistent with the Purposes of the United Nations.

5. All Members shall give the United Nations every assistance in any action it takes in accordance with the present Charter, and shall refrain from giving assistance to any state against which the United Nations is taking preventive or enforcement action.

6. The Organization shall ensure that states which are not Members of the United Nations act in accordance with these Principles so far as may be necessary for the maintenance of international peace and security.

7. Nothing contained in the present Charter shall authorize the United Nations to intervene in matters which are essentially within the domestic jurisdiction of any state or shall require the Members to submit such matters to settlement under the present Charter; but this principle shall not prejudice the application of enforcement measures under Chapter VII.

CHAPTER II

MEMBERSHIP

ARTICLE 3

The original Members of the United Nations shall be the states which, having participated in the United Nations Conference on International Organization at San Francisco, or having previously signed the Declaration by United Nations of January 1, 1942, sign the present Charter and ratify it in accordance with Article 110.

ARTICLE 4

1. Membership in the United Nations is open to all other peace-loving states which accept the obligations contained in the present Charter and, in the judgment of the Organization, are able and willing to carry out these obligations.

2. The admission of any such state to membership in the United Nations will be effected by a decision of the General Assembly upon the recommendation of the Security Council.

ARTICLE 5

A Member of the United Nations against which preventive or enforcement action has been taken by the Security Council may be suspended from the exercise of the rights and privileges of membership by the General Assembly upon the recommendation of the Security Council. The exercise of these rights and privileges may be restored by the Security Council.

ARTICLE 6

A Member of the United Nations which has persistently violated the Principles contained in the present Charter may be expelled from the Organization by the General Assembly upon the recommendation of the Security Council.

CHAPTER III

ORGANS

ARTICLE 7

1. There are established as the principal organs of the United Nations: a General Assembly, a Security Council, an Economic and Social Council, a Trusteeship Council, an International Court of Justice, and a Secretariat.

2. Such subsidiary organs as may be found necessary may be established in accordance with the present Charter.

ARTICLE 8

The United Nations shall place no restrictions on the eligibility of men and women to participate in any capacity and under conditions of equality in its principal and subsidiary organs.

CHAPTER IV

THE GENERAL ASSEMBLY

Composition

ARTICLE 9

1. The General Assembly shall consist of all the Members of the United Nations.

2. Each Member shall have not more than five representatives in the General Assembly.

Functions and Powers

ARTICLE 10

The General Assembly may discuss any questions or any matters within the scope of the present Charter or relating to the powers and functions of any organs provided for in the present Charter, and, except as provided in Article 12, may make recommendations to the Members of the United Nations or to the Security Council or to both on any such questions or matters.

ARTICLE 11

1. The General Assembly may consider the general principles of cooperation in the maintenance of international peace and security, including the principles governing disarmament and the regulation of armaments, and may make recommendations with regard to such principles to the Members or to the Security Council or to both.

2. The General Assembly may discuss any questions relating to the maintenance of international peace and security brought before it by any Member of the United Nations, or by the Security Council, or by a state which is not a Member of the United Nations in accordance with Article 35, paragraph 2, and, except as provided in Article 12, may make recommendations with regard to any such questions to the state or states concerned or to the Security Council or to both. Any such question on which action is necessary shall be referred to the Security Council by the General Assembly either before or after discussion.

3. The General Assembly may call the attention of the Security Council to situations which are likely to endanger international peace and security.

4. The powers of the General Assembly set forth in this Article shall not limit the general scope of Article 10.

ARTICLE 12

1. While the Security Council is exercising in respect of any dispute or situation the functions assigned to it in the present Charter, the General Assembly shall not make any recommendation with regard to that dispute or situation unless the Security Council so requests.

2. The Secretary-General, with the consent of the Security Council, shall notify the General Assembly at each session of any matters relative to the maintenance of international peace and security which are being dealt with by the Security Council and shall similarly notify the General Assembly, or the Members of the United Nations if the General Assembly is not in session, immediately the Security Council ceases to deal with such matters.

1. The General Assembly shall initiate studies and make recommendations for the purpose of:

    a. promoting international cooperation in the political field and encouraging the progressive development of international law and its codification;

    b. promoting international cooperation in the economic, social, cultural, educational, and health fields, and assisting in the realization of human rights and fundamental freedoms for all without distinction as to race, sex, language, or religion.

2. The further responsibilities, functions, and powers of the General Assembly with respect to matters mentioned in paragraph 1(b) above are set forth in Chapters IX and X.

Subjects to the provisions of Article 12, the General Assembly may recommend measures for the peaceful adjustment of any situation, regardless of origin, which it deems likely to impair the general welfare or friendly relations among nations, including situations resulting from a violation of the provisions of the present Charter setting forth the Purposes and Principles of the United Nations.

1. The General Assembly shall receive and consider annual and special reports from the Security Council; these reports shall include an account of the measures that the Security Council has decided upon or taken to maintain international peace and security.

2. The General Assembly shall receive and consider reports from the other organs of the United Nations.

The General Assembly shall perform such functions with respect to the international trusteeship system as are assigned to it under Chapters XII and XIII, including the approval of the trusteeship agreements for areas not designated as strategic.

1. The General Assembly shall consider and approve the budget of the Organization.

2. The expenses of the Organization shall be borne by the Members as apportioned by the General Assembly.

3. The General Assembly shall consider and approve any financial and budgetary arrangements with specialized agencies referred to in Article 57 and shall examine the administrative budgets of such specialized agencies with a view to making recommendations to the agencies concerned.

Voting

1. Each member of the General Assembly shall have one vote.

2. Decisions of the General Assembly on important questions shall be made by a two-thirds majority of the members present and voting. These

questions shall include: recommendations with respect to the maintenance of international peace and security, the election of the non-permanent members of the Security Council, the election of the members of the Economic and Social Council, the election of members of the Trusteeship Council in accordance with paragraph 1 (c) of Article 86, the admission of new Members to the United Nations, the suspension of the rights and privileges of membership, the expulsion of Members, questions relating to the operation of the trusteeship system, and budgetary questions.

3. Decisions on other questions, including the determination of additional categories of questions to be decided by a two-thirds majority, shall be made by a majority of the members present and voting.

ARTICLE 19

A Member of the United Nations which is in arrears in the payment of its financial contributions to the Organization shall have no vote in the General Assembly if the amount of its arrears equals or exceeds the amount of the contribution due from it for the preceding two full years. The General Assembly may, nevertheless, permit such a Member to vote if it is satisfied that the failure to pay is due to conditions beyond the control of the Member.

Procedure

ARTICLE 20

The General Assembly shall meet in regular annual sessions and in such special sessions as occasion may require. Special sessions shall be convoked by the Secretary-General at the request of the Security Council or of a majority of the Members of the United Nations.

ARTICLE 21

The General Assembly shall adopt its own rules of procedure. It shall elect its President for each session.

ARTICLE 22

The General Assembly may establish such subsidiary organs as it deems necessary for the performance of its functions.

CHAPTER V

THE SECURITY COUNCIL

Composition

ARTICLE 23

1. The Security Council shall consist of eleven Members of the United Nations. The Republic of China, France, the Union of Soviet Socialist Republics, the United Kingdom of Great Britain and Northern Ireland, and the United States of America shall be permanent members of the Security Council. The General Assembly shall elect six other Members of the United Nations to be non-permanent members of the Security Council, due regard being specially paid, in the first instance to the contribution of Members of the

United Nations to the maintenance of international peace and security and to the other purposes of the Organization, and also to equitable geographical distribution.

2. The non-permanent members of the Security Council shall be elected for a term of two years. In the first election of the non-permanent members, however, three shall be chosen for a term of one year. A retiring member shall not be eligible for immediate re-election.

3. Each member of the Security Council shall have one representative.

Functions and Powers

ARTICLE 24

1. In order to ensure prompt and effective action by the United Nations, its Members confer on the Security Council primary responsibility for the maintenance of international peace and security, and agree that in carrying out its duties under this responsibility the Security Council acts on their behalf.

2. In discharging these duties the Security Council shall act in accordance with the Purposes and Principles of the United Nations. The specific powers granted to the Security Council for the discharge of these duties are laid down in Chapters VI, VII, VIII, and XII.

3. The Security Council shall submit annual and, when necessary, special reports to the General Assembly for its consideration.

ARTICLE 25

The Members of the United Nations agree to accept and carry out the decisions of the Security Council in accordance with the present Charter.

ARTICLE 26

In order to promote the establishment and maintenance of international peace and security with the least diversion for armaments of the world's human and economic resources, the Security Council shall be responsible for formulating, with the assistance of the Military Staff Committee referred to in Article 47, plans to be submitted to the Members of the United Nations for the establishment of a system for the regulation of armaments.

Voting

ARTICLE 27

1. Each member of the Security Council shall have one vote.

2. Decisions of the Security Council on procedural matters shall be made by an affirmative vote of seven members.

3. Decisions of the Security Council on all other matters shall be made by an affirmative vote of seven members including the concurring votes of the permanent members; provided that, in decisions under Chapter VI, and under paragraph 3 of Article 52, a party to a dispute shall abstain from voting.

Procedure

ARTICLE 28

1. The Security Council shall be so organized as to be able to function continuously. Each member of the Security Council shall for this purpose be represented at all times at the seat of the Organization.

2. The Security Council shall hold periodic meetings at which each of its members may, if it so desires, be represented by a member of the government or by some other specially designated representative.

3. The Security Council may hold meetings at such places other than the seat of the Organization as in its judgment will best facilitate its work.

ARTICLE 29

The Security Council may establish such subsidiary organs as it deems necessary for the performance of its functions.

ARTICLE 30

The Security Council shall adopt its own rules of procedure, including the method of selecting its President.

ARTICLE 31

Any member of the United Nations which is not a member of the Security Council may participate, without vote, in the discussion of any question brought before the Security Council whenever the latter considers that the interests of that Member are specially affected.

ARTICLE 32

Any Member of the United Nations which is not a member of the Security Council or any state which is not a Member of the United Nations, if it is a party to a dispute under consideration by the Security Council, shall be invited to participate, without vote, in the discussion relating to the dispute. The Security Council shall lay down such conditions as it deems just for the participation of a state which is not a Member of the United Nations.

CHAPTER VI

PACIFIC SETTLEMENT OF DISPUTES

ARTICLE 33

1. The parties to any dispute, the continuance of which is likely to endanger the maintenance of international peace and security, shall, first of all, seek a solution by negotiation, enquiry, mediation, conciliation, arbitration, judicial settlement, resort to regional agencies or arrangements, or other peaceful means of their own choice.

2. The Security Council shall, when it deems necessary, call upon the parties to settle their dispute by such means.

ARTICLE 34

The Security Council may investigate any dispute, or any situation which might lead to international friction or give rise to a dispute, in order to determine whether the continuance of the dispute or situation is likely to endanger the maintenance of international peace and security.

ARTICLE 35

1. Any Member of the United Nations may bring any dispute or any situation of the nature referred to in Article 34 to the attention of the Security Council or of the General Assembly.

2. A state which is not a Member of the United Nations may bring to the attention of the Security Council or of the General Assembly any dispute to which it is a party if it accepts in advance, for the purposes of the dispute, the obligations of pacific settlement provided in the present Charter.

3. The proceedings of the General Assembly in respect of matters brought to its attention under this Article will be subject to the provisions of Articles 11 and 12.

ARTICLE 36

1. The Security Council may, at any stage of a dispute of the nature referred to in Article 33 or of a situation of like nature, recommend appropriate procedures or methods of adjustment.

2. The Security Council should take into consideration any procedures for the settlement of the dispute which have already been adopted by the parties.

3. In making recommendations under this Article the Security Council should also take into consideration that legal disputes should as a general rule be referred by the parties to the International Court of Justice in accordance with the provisions of the Statute of the Court.

ARTICLE 37

1. Should the parties to a dispute of the nature referred to in Article 33 fail to settle it by the means indicated in that Article, they shall refer it to the Security Council.

2. If the Security Council deems that the continuance of the dispute is in fact likely to endanger the maintenance of international peace and security, it shall decide whether to take action under Article 36 or to recommend such terms of settlement as it may consider appropriate.

ARTICLE 38

Without prejudice to the provisions of Articles 33 to 37, the Security Council may, if all the parties to any dispute so request, make recommendations to the parties with a view to a pacific settlement of the dispute.

CHAPTER VII

ACTION WITH RESPECT TO THREATS TO THE PEACE, BREACHES OF THE PEACE, AND ACTS OF AGGRESSION

ARTICLE 39

The Security Council shall determine the existence of any threat to the peace, breach of the peace, or act of aggression and shall make recommendations, or decide what measures shall be taken in accordance with Articles 41 and 42, to maintain or restore international peace and security.

ARTICLE 40

In order to prevent an aggravation of the situation, the Security Council may, before making the recommendations or deciding upon the measures provided for in Article 39, call upon the parties concerned to comply with such provisional measures as it deems necessary or desirable. Such provisional measures shall be without prejudice to the rights, claims, or position of the parties concerned. The Security Council shall duly take account of failure to comply with such provisional measures.

The Security Council may decide what measures not involving the use of armed force are to be employed to give effect to its decisions, and it may call upon the Members of the United Nations to apply such measures. These may include complete or partial interruption of economic relations and of rail, sea, air, postal, telegraphic, radio, and other means of communication, and the severance of diplomatic relations.

Should the Security Council consider that measures provided for in Article 41 would be inadequate or have proved to be inadequate, it may take such action by air, sea, or land forces as may be necessary to maintain or restore international peace and security. Such action may include demonstrations, blockade, and other operations by air, sea, or land forces of Members of the United Nations.

1. All Members of the United Nations, in order to contribute to the maintenance of international peace and security, undertake to make available to the Security Council, on its call and in accordance with a special agreement or agreements, armed forces, assistance, and facilities, including rights of passage, necessary for the purpose of maintaining international peace and security.

2. Such agreement or agreements shall govern the numbers and types of forces, their degree of readiness and general location, and the nature of the facilities and assistance to be provided.

3. The agreement or agreements shall be negoitated as soon as possible on the initiative of the Security Council. They shall be concluded between the Security Council and Members or between the Security Council and groups of Members and shall be subject to ratification by the signatory states in accordance with their respective constitutional processes.

When the Security Council has decided to use force it shall, before calling upon a Member not represented on it to provide armed forces in fulfillment of the obligations assumed under Article 43, invite that Member, if the Member so desires, to participate in the decisions of the Security Council concerning the employment of contingents of that Member's armed forces.

In order to enable the United Nations to take urgent military measures, Members shall hold immediately available national air-force contingents for combined international enforcement action. The strength and degree of readiness of these contingents and plans for their combined action shall be determined, within the limits laid down in the special agreement or agreements referred to in Article 43, by the Security Council with the assistance of the Military Staff Committee.

ARTICLE 46

Plans for the application of armed force shall be made by the Security Council with the assistance of the Military Staff Committee.

ARTICLE 47

1. There shall be established a Military Staff Committee to advise and assist the Security Council on all questions relating to the Security Council's military requirements for the maintentance of international peace and security, the employment and command of forces placed at its disposal, the regulation of armaments, and possible disarmament.
2. The Military Staff Committee shall consist of the Chiefs of Staff of the permanent members of the Security Council or their representatives. Any Member of the United Nations not permanently represented on the Committee shall be invited by the Committee to be associated with it when the efficient discharge of the Committee's responsibilities requires the participation of that Member in its work.
3. The Military Staff Committee shall be responsible under the Security Council for the strategic direction of any armed forces placed at the disposal of the Security Council. Questions relating to the command of such forces shall be worked out subsequently.
4. The Military Staff Committee, with the authorization of the Security Council and after consultation with appropriate regional agencies, may establish regional subcommittees.

ARTICLE 48

1. The action required to carry out the decisions of the Security Council for the maintenance of international peace and security shall be taken by all the Members of the United Nations or by some of them, as the Security Council may determine.
2. Such decisions shall be carried out by the Members of the United Nations directly and through their action in the appropriate international agencies of which they are members.

ARTICLE 49

The Members of the United Nations shall join in affording mutual assistance in carrying out the measures decided upon by the Security Council.

ARTICLE 50

If preventive or enforcement measures against any state are taken by the Security Council, any other state, whether a Member of the United Nations or not, which finds itself confronted with special economic problems arising from the carrying out of those measures shall have the right to consult the Security Council with regard to a solution of those problems.

ARTICLE 51

Nothing in the present Charter shall impair the inherent right of individual or collective self-defense if an armed attack occurs against a Member of the United Nations, until the Security Council has taken the measures necessary to maintain international peace and security. Measures taken by Members in the exercise of this right of self-defense shall be immediately reported to the Security Council and shall not in any way affect the authority and responsibility of the Security Council under the present Charter to take at any time such action as it deems necessary in order to maintain or restore international peace and security.

CHAPTER VIII

REGIONAL ARRANGEMENTS

ARTICLE 52

1. Nothing in the present Charter precludes the existence of regional arrangements or agencies for dealing with such matters relating to the maintenance of international peace and security as are appropriate for regional action, provided that such arrangements or agencies and their activities are consistent with the Purposes and Principles of the United Nations.

2. The Members of the United Nations entering into such arrangements or constituting such agencies shall make every effort to achieve pacific settlement of local disputes through such regional arrangements or by such regional agencies before referring them to the Security Council.

3. The Security Council shall encourage the development of pacific settlement of local disputes through such regional arrangements or by such regional agencies either on the initiative of the states concerned or by reference from the Security Council.

4. This Article in no way impairs the application of Articles 34 and 35.

ARTICLE 53

1. The Security Council shall, where appropriate, utilize such regional arrangements or agencies for enforcement action under its authority. But no enforcement action shall be taken under regional arrangements or by regional agencies without the authorization of the Security Council, with the exception of measures against any enemy state, as defined in paragraph 2 of this Article, provided for pursuant to Article 107 or in regional arrangements directed against renewal of aggressive policy on the part of any such state, until such time as the Organization may, on request of the Governments concerned, be charged with the responsibility for preventing further aggression by such a state.

2. The term enemy state as used in paragraph 1 of this Article applies to any state which during the Second World War has been an enemy of any signatory of the present Charter.

ARTICLE 54

The Security Council shall at all times be kept fully informed of activities undertaken or in contemplation under regional arrangements or by regional agencies for the maintenance of international peace and security.

CHAPTER IX

INTERNATIONAL ECONOMIC AND SOCIAL COOPERATION

ARTICLE 55

With a view to the creation of conditions of stability and well-being which are necessary for peaceful and friendly relations among nations based on respect for the principle of equal rights and self-determination of peoples, the United Nations shall promote:

    a. higher standards of living, full employment, and conditions of economic and social progress and development;
    b. solutions of international economic, social, health, and related problems; and international cultural and educational cooperation; and
    c. universal respect for, and observance of, human rights and fundamental freedoms for all without distinction as to race, sex, language, or religion.

ARTICLE 56

All Members pledge themselves to take joint and separate action in cooperation with the Organization for the achievement of the purposes set forth in Article 55.

ARTICLE 57

1. The various specialized agencies, established by intergovernmental agreement and having wide international responsibilities, as defined in their basic instruments, in economic, social, cultural, educational, health, and related fields, shall be brought into relationship with the United Nations in accordance with the provisions of Article 63.

2. Such agencies thus brought into relationship with the United Nations are hereinafter referred to as specialized agencies.

ARTICLE 58

The Organization shall make recommendations for the coordination of the policies and activities of the specialized agencies.

ARTICLE 59

The Organization shall, where appropriate, initiate negotiations among the states concerned for the creation of any new specialized agencies required for the accomplishment of the purposes set forth in Article 55.

ARTICLE 60

Responsibility for the discharge of the functions of the Organization set forth in this Chapter shall be vested in the General Assembly and, under the authority of the General Assembly, in the Economic and Social Council, which shall have for this purpose the powers set forth in Chapter X.

CHAPTER X

THE ECONOMIC AND SOCIAL COUNCIL

Composition

ARTICLE 61

1. The Economic and Social Council shall consist of eighteen Members of the United Nations elected by the General Assembly.

2. Subject to the provisions of paragraph 3, six members of the Economic and Social Council shall be elected each year for a term of three years. A retiring member shall be eligible for immediate re-election.

3. At the first election, eighteen members of the Economic and Social Council shall be chosen. The term of office of six members so chosen shall expire at the end of one year, and of six other members at the end of two years, in accordance with arrangements made by the General Assembly.

4. Each member of the Economic and Social Council shall have one representative.

Functions and Powers

ARTICLE 62

1. The Economic and Social Council may make or initiate studies and reports with respect to international economic, social, cultural, educational, health, and related matters and may make recommendations with respect to any such matters to the General Assembly, to the Members of the United Nations, and to the specialized agencies concerned.

2. It may make recommendations for the purpose of promoting respect for, and observance of, human rights and fundamental freedoms for all.

3. It may prepare draft conventions for submission to the General Assembly, with respect to matters falling within its competence.

(*See above, Ch. IV, Art. 17, Par. 3*)

4. It may call, in accordance with the rules prescribed by the United Nations, international conferences on matters falling within its competence.

ARTICLE 63

1. The Economic and Social Council may enter into agreements with any of the agencies referred to in Article 57, defining the terms on which the agency concerned shall be brought into relationship with the United Nations. Such agreements shall be subject to approval by the General Assembly.

2. It may coordinate the activities of the specialized agencies through consultation with and recommendations to such agencies and through recommendations to the General Assembly and to the Members of the United Nations.

ARTICLE 64

1. The Economic and Social Council may take appropriate steps to obtain regular reports from the specialized agencies. It may make arrangements with the Members of the United Nations and with the specialized agencies to obtain reports on the steps taken to give effect to its own recommendations and

to recommendations on matters falling within its competence made by the General Assembly.

2. It may communicate its observations on these reports to the General Assembly.

ARTICLE 65

The Economic and Social Council may furnish information to the Security Council and shall assist the Security Council upon its request.

ARTICLE 66

1. The Economic and Social Council shall perform such functions as fall within its competence in connection with the carrying out of the recommendations of the General Assembly.

2. It may, with the approval of the General Assembly, perform services at the request of Members of the United Nations and at the request of specialized agencies.

3. It shall perform such other functions as are specified elsewhere in the present Charter or as may be assigned to it by the General Assembly.

Voting

ARTICLE 67

1. Each member of the Economic and Social Council shall have one vote.

2. Decisions of the Economic and Social Council shall be made by a majority of the members present and voting.

Procedure

ARTICLE 68

The Economic and Social Council shall set up commissions in economic and social fields and for the promotion of human rights, and such other commissions as may be required for the performance of its functions.

ARTICLE 69

The Economic and Social Council shall invite any Member of the United Nations to participate, without vote, in its deliberations on any matter of particular concern to that Member.

ARTICLE 70

The Economic and Social Council may make arrangements for representatives of the specialized agencies to participate, without vote, in its deliberations and in those of the commissions established by it, and for its representatives to participate in the deliberations of the specialized agencies.

ARTICLE 71

The Economic and Social Council may make suitable arrangements for consultation with non-governmental organizations which are concerned with matters within its competence. Such arrangements may be made with international organizations and, where appropriate, with national organizations after consultation with the Member of the United Nations concerned.

ARTICLE 72

1. The Economic and Social Council shall adopt its own rules of procedure, including the method of selecting its President.

2. The Economic and Social Council shall meet as required in accordance with its rules, which shall include provision for the convening of meetings on the request of a majority of its members.

CHAPTER XI

DECLARATION REGARDING NON-SELF-GOVERNING TERRITORIES

ARTICLE 73

Members of the United Nations which have or assume responsibilities for the administration of territories whose peoples have not yet attained a full measure of self-government recognize the principle that the interests of the inhabitants of these territories are paramount, and accept as a sacred trust the obligation to promote to the utmost, within the system of international peace and security established by the present Charter, the well-being of the inhabitants of these territories, and, to this end:

    a. to ensure, with due respect for the culture of the peoples concerned, their political, economic, social, and educational advancement, their just treatment, and their protection against abuses;

    b. to develop self-government, to take due account of the political aspirations of the peoples, and to assist them in the progressive development of their free political institutions, according to the particular circumstances of each territory and its peoples and their varying stages of advancement;

    c. to further international peace and security;

    d. to promote constructive measures of development, to encourage research, and to cooperate with one another and, when and where appropriate, with specialized international bodies with a view to the practical achievement of the social, economic, and scientific purposes set forth in this Article; and

    e. to transmit regularly to the Secretary-General for information purposes, subject to such limitation as security and constitutional considerations may require, statistical and other information of a technical nature relating to economic, social, and educational conditions in the territories for which they are respectively responsible other than those territories to which Chapters XII and XIII apply.

ARTICLE 74

Members of the United Nations also agree that their policy in respect of the territories to which this Chapter applies, no less than in respect of their metropolitan areas must be based on the general principle of good-neighborliness, due account being taken of the interests and well-being of the rest of the world, in social, economic, and commercial matters.

CHAPTER XII

INTERNATIONAL TRUSTEESHIP SYSTEM

ARTICLE 75

The United Nations shall establish under its authority an international trusteeship system for the administration and supervision of such territories as may be placed thereunder by subsequent individual agreements. These territories are hereinafter referred to as trust territories.

ARTICLE 76

The basic objectives of the trusteeship system, in accordance with the Purposes of the United Nations laid down in Article 1 of the present Charter, shall be:

 a. to further international peace and security;

 b. to promote the political, economic, social and educational advancement of the inhabitants of the trust territories, and their progressive development towards self-government or independence as may be appropriate to the particular circumstances of each territory and its peoples and the freely expressed wishes of the peoples concerned, and as may be provided by the terms of each trusteeship agreement;

 c. to encourage respect for human rights and for fundamental freedoms for all without distinction as to race, sex, language, or religion, and to encourage recognition of the interdependence of the peoples of the world; and

 d. to ensure equal treatment in social, economic, and commercial matters for all Members of the United Nations and their nationals, and also equal treatment for the latter in the administration of justice, without prejudice to the attainment of the foregoing objectives and subject to the provisions of Article 80.

ARTICLE 77

1. The trusteeship system shall apply to such territories in the following categories as may be placed thereunder by means of trusteeship agreements:

 a. territories now held under mandate;

 b. territories which may be detached from enemy states as a result of the Second World War; and

 c. territories voluntarily placed under the system by states responsible for their administration.

2. It will be a matter for subsequent agreement as to which territories in the foregoing categories will be brought under the trusteeship system and upon what terms.

ARTICLE 78

The trusteeship system shall not apply to territories which have become Members of the United Nations, relationship among which shall be based on respect for the principle of sovereign equality.

ARTICLE 79

The terms of trusteeship for each territory to be placed under the trusteeship system, including any alteration or amendment, shall be agreed upon by the states directly concerned, including the mandatory power in the case of territories held under mandate by a Member of the United Nations, and shall be approved as provided for in Articles 83 and 85.

ARTICLE 80

1. Except as may be agreed upon in individual trusteeship agreements, made under Articles 77, 79 and 81, placing each territory under the trusteeship system, and until such agreements have been concluded, nothing in this Chapter shall be construed in or of itself to alter in any manner the rights whatsoever of any states or any peoples or the terms of existing international instruments to which Members of the United Nations may respectively be parties.

2. Paragraph 1 of this Article shall not be interpreted as giving grounds for delay or postponement of the negotiation and conclusion of agreements for placing mandated and other territories under the trusteeship system as provided for in Article 77.

ARTICLE 81

The trusteeship agreement shall in each case include the terms under which the trust territory will be administered and designate the authority which will exercise the administration of the trust territory. Such authority, hereinafter called the administering authority, may be one or more states or the Organization itself.

ARTICLE 82

There may be designated, in any trusteeship agreement, a strategic area or areas which may include part or all of the trust territory to which the agreement applies, without prejudice to any special agreement or agreements made under Article 43.

ARTICLE 83

1. All functions of the United Nations relating to strategic areas, including the approval of the terms of the trusteeship agreements and of their alteration or amendment, shall be exercised by the Security Council.

2. The basic objectives set forth in Article 76 shall be applicable to the people of each strategic area.

3. The Security Council shall, subject to the provisions of the trusteeship agreements and without prejudice to security considerations, avail itself of the assistance of the Trusteeship Council to perform those functions of the United Nations under the trusteeship system relating to political, economic, social, and educational matters in the strategic areas.

ARTICLE 84

It shall be the duty of the administering authority to ensure that the trust territory shall play its part in the maintenance of international peace and security. To this end the administering authority may make use of volunteer forces, facilities, and assistance from the trust territory in carrying out the obligation towards the Security Council undertaken in this regard by the administering authority, as well as for local defense and the maintenance of law and order within the trust territory.

1. The functions of the United Nations with regard to trusteeship agreements for all areas not designated as strategic, including the approval of the terms of the trusteeship agreements and of their alteration or amendment, shall be exercised by the General Assembly.

2. The Trusteeship Council, operating under the authority of the General Assembly, shall assist the General Assembly in carrying out these functions.

CHAPTER XIII

THE TRUSTEESHIP COUNCIL

Composition

1. The Trusteeship Council shall consist of the following Members of the United Nations:

    a. those Members administering trust territories;

    b. such of those Members mentioned by name in Article 23 as are not administering trust territories; and

    c. as many other Members elected for three-year terms by the General Assembly as may be necessary to ensure that the total number of members of the Trusteeship Council is equally divided between those Members of the United Nations which administer trust territories and those which do not.

2. Each member of the Trusteeship Council shall designate one specially qualified person to represent it therein.

Functions and Powers

1. The General Assembly and, under its authority, the Trusteeship Council, in carrying out their functions, may:

    a. consider reports submitted by the administering authority;

    b. accept petitions and examine them in consultation with the administering authority;

    c. provide for periodic visits to the respective trust territories at times agreed upon with the administering authority; and

    d. take these and other actions in conformity with the terms of the trusteeship agreements.

The Trusteeship Council shall formulate a questionnaire on the political, economic, social and educational advancement of the inhabitants of each trust territory, and the administering authority for each trust territory within the competence of the General Assembly shall make an annual report to the General Assembly upon the basis of such questionnaire.

Voting

1. Each member of the Trusteeship Council shall have one vote.

2. Decisions of the Trusteeship Council shall be made by a majority of the members present and voting.

Procedure

ARTICLE 90

1. The Trusteeship Council shall adopt its own rules of procedure, including the method of selecting its President.

2. The Trusteeship Council shall meet as required in accordance with its rules, which shall include provision for the convening of meetings on the request of a majority of its members.

ARTICLE 91

The Trusteeship Council shall, when appropriate, avail itself of the assistance of the Economic and Social Council and of the specialized agencies in regard to matters with which they are respectively concerned.

CHAPTER XIV

THE INTERNATIONAL COURT OF JUSTICE

ARTICLE 92

The International Court of Justice shall be the principal judicial organ of the United Nations. It shall function in accordance with the annexed Statute, which is based upon the Statute of the Permanent Court of International Justice and forms an integral part of the present Charter.

ARTICLE 93

1. All Members of the United Nations are *ipso facto* parties to the Statute of the International Court of Justice.

2. A state which is not a Member of the United Nations may become a party to the Statute of the International Court of Justice on conditions to be determined in each case by the General Assembly upon the recommendation of the Security Council.

ARTICLE 94

1. Each Member of the United Nations undertakes to comply with the decision of the International Court of Justice in any case to which it is a party.

2. If any party to a case fails to perform the obligations incumbent upon it under a judgment rendered by the Court, the other party may have recourse to the Security Council, which may, if it deems necessary, make recommendations or decide upon measures to be taken to give effect to the judgment.

ARTICLE 95

Nothing in the present Charter shall prevent Members of the United Nations from entrusting the solution of their differences to other tribunals by virtue of agreements already in existence or which may be concluded in the future.

ARTICLE 96

1. The General Assembly or the Security Council may request the International Court of Justice to give an advisory opinion on any legal question.

2. Other organs of the United Nations and specialized agencies, which

may at any time be so authorized by the General Assembly, may also request advisory opinions of the Court on legal questions arising within the scope of their activities.

CHAPTER XV

THE SECRETARIAT

ARTICLE 97

The Secretariat shall comprise a Secretary-General and such staff as the Organization may require. The Secretary-General shall be appointed by the General Assembly upon the recommendation of the Security Council. He shall be the chief administrative officer of the Organization.

ARTICLE 98

The Secretary-General shall act in that capacity in all meetings of the General Assembly, of the Security Council, of the Economic and Social Council, and of the Trusteeship Council, and shall perform such other functions as are entrusted to him by these organs. The Secretary-General shall make an annual report to the General Assembly on the work of the Organization.

ARTICLE 99

The Secretary-General may bring to the attention of the Security Council any matter which in his opinion may threaten the maintenance of international peace and security.

ARTICLE 100

1. In the performance of their duties the Secretary-General and the staff shall not seek or receive instructions from any government or from any other authority external to the Organization. They shall refrain from any action which might reflect on their position as international officials responsible only to the Organization.
2. Each Member of the United Nations undertakes to respect the exclusively international character of the responsibilities of the Secretary-General and the staff and not to seek to influence them in the discharge of their responsibilities.

ARTICLE 101

1. The staff shall be appointed by the Secretary-General under regulations established by the General Assembly.
2. Appropriate staffs shall be permanently assigned to the Economic and Social Council, the Trusteeship Council, and, as required, to other organs of the United Nations. These staffs shall form a part of the Secretariat.
3. The paramount consideration in the employment of the staff and in the determination of the conditions of service shall be the necessity of securing the highest standards of efficiency, competence, and integrity. Due regard shall be paid to the importance of recruiting the staff on as wide a geographical basis as possible.

CHAPTER XVI

MISCELLANEOUS PROVISIONS

ARTICLE 102

1. Every treaty and every international agreement entered into by any Member of the United Nations after the present Charter comes into force shall as soon as possible be registered with the Secretariat and published by it.

2. No party to any such treaty or international agreement which has not been registered in accordance with the provisions of paragraph 1 of this Article may invoke that treaty or agreement before any organ of the United Nations.

ARTICLE 103

In the event of a conflict between the obligations of the Members of the United Nations under the present Charter and their obligations under any other international agreement, their obligations under the present Charter shall prevail.

ARTICLE 104

The Organization shall enjoy in the territory of each of its Members such legal capacity as may be necessary for the exercise of its functions and the fulfillment of its purposes.

ARTICLE 105

1. The Organization shall enjoy in the territory of each of its Members such privileges and immunities as are necessary for the fulfillment of its purposes.

2. Representatives of the Members of the United Nations and officials of the Organization shall similarly enjoy such privileges and immunities as are necessary for the independent exercise of their functions in connection with the Organization.

3. The General Assembly may make recommendations with a view to determining the details of the application of paragraphs 1 and 2 of this Article or may propose conventions to the Members of the United Nations for this purpose.

CHAPTER XVII

TRANSITIONAL SECURITY ARRANGEMENTS

ARTICLE 106

Pending the coming into force of such special agreements referred to in Article 43 as in the opinion of the Security Council enable it to begin the exercise of its responsibilities under Article 42, the parties to the Four-Nation Declaration, signed at Moscow, October 30, 1943, and France, shall, in accordance with the provisions of paragraph 5 of that Declaration, consult with one another and as occasion requires with other Members of the United Nations with a view to such joint action on behalf of the Organization as may be necessary for the purpose of maintaining international peace and security.

Nothing in the present Charter shall invalidate or preclude action, in relation to any state which during the Second World War has been an enemy of any signatory to the present Charter, taken or authorized as a result of that war by the Governments having responsibility for such action.

CHAPTER XVIII

AMENDMENTS

Amendments to the present Charter shall come into force for all Members of the United Nations when they have been adopted by a vote of two-thirds of the members of the General Assembly and ratified in accordance with their respective constitutional processes by two-thirds of the Members of the United Nations, including all the permanent members of the Security Council.

1. A General Conference of the Members of the United Nations for the purpose of reviewing the present Charter may be held at a date and place to be fixed by a two-thirds vote of the members of the General Assembly and by a vote of any seven members of the Security Council. Each Member of the United Nations shall have one vote in the conference.

2. Any alteration of the present Charter recommended by a two-thirds vote of the conference shall take effect when ratified in accordance with their respective constitutional processes by two-thirds of the Members of the United Nations including all the permanent members of the Security Council.

3. If such a conference has not been held before the tenth annual session of the General Assembly following the coming into force of the present Charter, the proposal to call such a conference shall be placed on the agenda of that session of the General Assembly, and the conference shall be held if so decided by a majority vote of the members of the General Assembly and by a vote of any seven members of the Security Council.

CHAPTER XIX

RATIFICATION AND SIGNATURE

1. The present Charter shall be ratified by the signatory states in accordance with their respective constitutional processes.

2. The ratifications shall be deposited with the Government of the United States of America, which shall notify all the signatory states of each deposit as well as the Secretary-General of the Organization when he has been appointed.

3. The present Charter shall come into force upon the deposit of ratifications by the Republic of China, France, the Union of Soviet Socialist Republics, the United Kingdom of Great Britain and Northern Ireland, and the United States of America, and by a majority of the other signatory states.

A protocol of the ratifications deposited shall thereupon be drawn up by the Government of the United States of America which shall communicate copies thereof to all the signatory states.

4. The states signatory to the present Charter which ratify it after it has come into force will become original Members of the United Nations on the date of the deposit of their respective ratifications.

ARTICLE III

The present Charter, of which the Chinese, French, Russian, English and Spanish texts are equally authentic, shall remain deposited in the archives of the Government of the United States of America. Duly certified copies thereof shall be transmitted by that Government to the Governments of the other signatory states.

In Faith Whereof the representatives of the Governments of the United Nations have signed the present Charter.

Done at the city of San Francisco the twenty-sixth day of June, one thousand nine hundred and forty-five.

18. CONSTITUTION OF THE FOOD AND AGRICULTURE ORGANIZATION OF THE UNITED NATIONS

PREAMBLE

The Nations accepting this Constitution, being determined to promote the common welfare by furthering separate and collective action on their part for the purposes of

raising levels of nutrition and standards of living of the peoples under their respective jurisdictions,

securing improvements in the efficiency of the production and distribution of all food and agricultural products,

bettering the condition of rural populations, and thus contributing toward an expanding world economy,

hereby establish the Food and Agriculture Organization of the United Nations, hereinafter referred to as the "Organization", through which the Members will report to one another on the measures taken and the progress achieved in the fields of action set forth above.

ARTICLE I

Functions of the Organization

1. The Organization shall collect, analyse, interpret, and disseminate information relating to nutrition, food and agriculture.

2. The Organization shall promote and, where appropriate, shall recommend national and international action with respect to

    a. scientific, technological, social, and economic research relating to nutrition, food and agriculture;

    b. the improvement of education and administration relating to nutrition, food and agriculture, and the spread of public knowledge of nutritional and agricultural science and practice;

c. the conservation of natural resources and the adoption of improved methods of agricultural production;

d. the improvement of the processing, marketing, and distribution of food and agricultural products;

e. the adoption of policies for the provision of adequate agricultural credit, national and international;

f. the adoption of international policies with respect to agricultural commodity arrangements.

3. It shall also be the function of the Organization

a. to furnish such technical assistance as governments may request;

b. to organize, in cooperation with the governments concerned, such missions as may be needed to assist them to fulfil the obligations arising from their acceptance of the recommendations of the United Nations Conference on Food and Agriculture; and

c. generally to take all necessary and appropriate action to implement the purposes of the Organization as set forth in the Preamble.

ARTICLE II

Membership

1. The original Members of the Organization shall be such of the nations specified in Annex I as accept this Constitution in accordance with the provisions of Article XXI.

2. Additional Members may be admitted to the Organization by a vote concurred in by a two-thirds majority of all the members of the Conference and upon acceptance of this Constitution as in force at the time of admission.

ARTICLE III

The Conference

1. There shall be a Conference of the Organization in which each Member nation shall be represented by one member.

2. Each Member nation may appoint an alternate, associates, and advisers to its member of the Conference. The Conference may make rules concerning the participation of alternates, associates, and advisers in its proceedings, but any such participation shall be without the right to vote except in the case of an alternate or associate participating in the place of a member.

3. No member of the Conference may represent more than one Member nation.

4. Each Member nation shall have only one vote.

5. The Conference may invite any public international organization which has responsibilities related to those of the Organization to appoint a representative who shall participate in its meetings on the conditions prescribed by the Conference. No such representative shall have the right to vote.

6. The Conference shall meet at least once in every year.

7. The Conference shall elect its own officers, regulate its own procedure, and make rules governing the convocation of sessions and the determination of agenda.

8. Except as otherwise expressly provided in this Constitution or by rules made by the Conference, all matters shall be decided by the Conference by a simple majority of the votes cast.

ARTICLE IV

Functions of the Conference

1. The Conference shall determine the policy and approve the budget of the Organization and shall exercise the other powers conferred upon it by this Constitution.

2. The Conference may by a two-thirds majority of the votes cast make recommendations concerning questions relating to food and agriculture to be submitted to Member nations for consideration with a view to implementation by national action.

3. The Conference may by a two-thirds majority of the votes cast submit conventions concerning questions relating to food and agriculture to Member nations for consideration with a view to their acceptance by the appropriate constitutional procedure.

4. The Conference shall make rules laying down the procedure to be followed to secure:

 a. proper consultation with governments and adequate technical preparation prior to consideration by the Conference of proposed recommendations and conventions; and

 b. proper consultation with governments in regard to relations between the Organization and national institutions or private persons.

5. The Conference may make recommendations to any public international organization regarding any matter pertaining to the purpose of the Organization.

6. The Conference may by a two-thirds majority of the votes cast agree to discharge any other functions consistent with the purposes of the Organization which may be assigned to it by governments or provided for by any arrangement between the Organization and any other public international organization.

ARTICLE V

The Executive Committee

1. The Conference shall appoint an Executive Committee consisting of not less than nine or more than fifteen members or alternate or associate members of the Conference or their advisers who are qualified by administrative experience or other special qualifications to contribute to the attainment of the purpose of the Organization. There shall be not more than one member from any Member nation. The tenure and other conditions of office of the members of the Executive Committee shall be subject to rules to be made by the Conference.

2. Subject to the provisions of paragraph 1 of this Article, the Conference shall have regard in appointing the Executive Committee to the desirability that its membership should reflect as varied as possible an experience of different types of economy in relation to food and agriculture.

3. The Conference may delegate to the Executive Committee such powers as it may determine, with the exception of the powers set forth in paragraph 2 of Article II, Article IV, paragraph 1 of Article VII, Article XIII, and Article XX of this Constitution.

4. The members of the Executive Committee shall exercise the powers delegated to them by the Conference on behalf of the whole Conference and not as representatives of their respective governments.

5. The Executive Committee shall appoint its own officers and, subject to any decisions of the Conference, shall regulate its own procedure.

ARTICLE VI

Other Committees and Conferences

1. The Conference may establish technical and regional standing committees and may appoint committees to study and report on any matter pertaining to the purpose of the Organization.

2. The Conference may convene general, technical, regional, or other special conferences and may provide for the representation at such conferences, in such manner as it may determine, of national and international bodies concerned with nutrition, food and agriculture.

ARTICLE VII

The Director-General

1. There shall be a Director-General of the Organization who shall be appointed by the Conference by such procedure and on such terms as it may determine.

2. Subject to the general supervision of the Conference and its Executive Committee, the Director-General shall have full power and authority to direct the work of the Organization.

3. The Director-General or a representative designated by him shall participate, without the right to vote, in all meetings of the Conference and of its Executive Committee and shall formulate for consideration by the Conference and the Executive Committee proposals for appropriate action in regard to matters coming before them.

ARTICLE VIII

Staff

1. The staff of the Organization shall be appointed by the Director-General in accordance with such procedure as may be determined by rules made by the Conference.

2. The staff of the Organization shall be responsible to the Director-General. Their responsibilities shall be exclusively international in character and they shall not seek or receive instructions in regard to the discharge thereof from any authority external to the Organization. The Member nations undertake fully to respect the international character of the responsibilities of the staff and not to seek to influence any of their nationals in the discharge of such responsibilities.

3. In appointing the staff the Director-General shall, subject to the paramount importance of securing the highest standards of efficiency and of technical competence, pay due regard to the importance of selecting personnel recruited on as wide a geographical basis as is possible.

4. Each Member nation undertakes, insofar as it may be possible under its constitutional procedure, to accord to the Director-General and senior staff diplomatic privileges and immunities and to accord to other members of the staff all facilities and immunities accorded to non-diplomatic personnel attached to diplomatic missions, or alternatively to accord to such other members of the staff the immunities and facilities which may hereafter be accorded to equivalent members of the staffs of other public international organizations.

ARTICLE IX

Seat

The seat of the Organization shall be determined by the Conference.

ARTICLE X

Regional and Liaison Offices

1. There shall be such regional offices as the Director-General with the approval of the Conference may decide.
2. The Director-General may appoint officials for liaison with particular countries or areas subject to the agreement of the government concerned.

ARTICLE XI

Reports by Members

1. Each Member nation shall communicate periodically to the Organization reports on the progress made toward achieving the purpose of the Organization set forth in the Preamble and on the action taken on the basis of recommendations made and conventions submitted by the Conference.
2. These reports shall be made at such times and in such form and shall contain such particulars as the Conference may request.
3. The Director-General shall submit these reports, together with analyses thereof, to the Conference and shall publish such reports and analyses as may be approved for publication by the Conference together with any reports relating thereto adopted by the Conference.
4. The Director-General may request any Member nation to submit information relating to the purpose of the Organization.
5. Each Member nation shall, on request, communicate to the Organization, on publication, all laws and regulations and official reports and statistics concerning nutrition, food and agriculture.

ARTICLE XII

Cooperation with Other Organizations

1. In order to provide for close cooperation between the Organization and other public international organizations with related responsibilities, the Conference may, subject to the provisions of Article XIII, enter into agreements with the competent authorities of such organizations defining the distribution of responsibilities and methods of cooperation.
2. The Director-General may, subject to any decisions of the Conference, enter into agreements with other public international organizations for the maintenance of common services, for common arrangements in regard to recruitment, training, conditions of service, and other related matters, and for interchanges of staff.

ARTICLE XIII

Relation to Any General World Organization

1. The Organization shall, in accordance with the procedure provided for in the following paragraph, constitute a part of any general international organization to which may be entrusted the coordination of the activities of international organizations with specialized responsibilities.

2. Arrangements for defining the relations between the Organization and any such general organization shall be subject to the approval of the Conference. Notwithstanding the provisions of Article XX, such arrangements may, if approved by the Conference by a two-thirds majority of the votes cast, involve modifications of the provisions of this Constitution: Provided that no such arrangements shall modify the purposes and limitations of the Organization as set forth in this Constitution.

ARTICLE XIV

Supervision of Other Organizations

The Conference may approve arrangements placing other public international organizations dealing with questions relating to food and agriculture under the general authority of the Organization on such terms as may be agreed with the competent authorities of the organization concerned.

ARTICLE XV

Legal Status

1. The Organization shall have the capacity of a legal person to perform any legal act appropriate to its purpose which is not beyond the powers granted to it by this Constitution.
2. Each Member nation undertakes, insofar as it may be possible under its constitutional procedure, to accord to the Organization all the immunities and facilities which it accords to diplomatic missions, including inviolability of premises and archives, immunity from suit, and exemptions from taxation.
3. The Conference shall make provision for the determination by an administrative tribunal of disputes relating to the conditions and terms of appointment of members of the staff.

ARTICLE XVI

Fish and Forest Products

In this Constitution the term "agriculture" and its derivatives include fisheries, marine products, forestry, and primary forestry products.

ARTICLE XVII

Interpretation of Constitution

Any question or dispute concerning the interpretation of this Constitution or any international convention adopted thereunder shall be referred for determination to an appropriate international court or arbitral tribunal in the manner prescribed by rules to be adopted by the Conference.

ARTICLE XVIII

Expenses

1. Subject to the provisions of Article XXV, the Director-General shall submit to the Conference an annual budget covering the anticipated expenses of the Organization. Upon approval of a budget the total amount approved shall be allocated among the Member nations in proportions determined, from time to time, by the Conference. Each Member nation undertakes, subject to the requirements of its constitutional procedure, to contribute to the Organization promptly its share of the expenses so determined.

2. Each Member nation shall, upon its acceptance of this Constitution, pay as its first contribution its proportion of the annual budget for the current financial year.

3. The financial year of the Organization shall be July 1 to June 30 unless the Conference should otherwise determine.

ARTICLE XIX

Withdrawal

Any Member nation may give notice of withdrawal from the Organization at any time after the expiration of four years from the date of its acceptance of this Constitution. Such notice shall take effect one year after the date of its communication to the Director-General of the Organization subject to the Member nation's having at that time paid its annual contribution for each year of its membership including the financial year following the date of such notice.

ARTICLE XX

Amendment of Constitution

1. Amendments to this Constitution involving new obligations for Member nations shall require the approval of the Conference by a vote concurred in by a two-thirds majority of all the members of the Conference and shall take effect on acceptance by two-thirds of the Member nations for each Member nation accepting the ammendment and thereafter for each remaining Member nation on acceptance by it.

2. Other amendments shall take effect on adoption by the Conference by a vote concurred in by a two-thirds majority of all the members of the Conference.

ARTICLE XXI

Entry into Force of Constitution

1. This Constitution shall be open to acceptance by the nations specified in Annex I.

2. The instruments of acceptance shall be transmitted by each government to the United Nations Interim Commission on Food and Agriculture, which shall notify their receipt to the governments of the nations specified in Annex I. Acceptance may be notified to the Interim Commission through a diplomatic representative, in which case the instrument of acceptance must be transmitted to the Commission as soon as possible thereafter.

3. Upon the receipt by the Interim Commission of twenty notifications of acceptance the Interim Commission shall arrange for this Constitution to be signed in a single copy by the diplomatic representatives, duly authorized thereto, of the nations who shall have notified their acceptance, and upon being so signed on behalf of not less than twenty of the nations specified in Annex I this Constitution shall come into force immediately.

4. Acceptances the notification of which is received after the entry into force of this Constitution shall become effective upon receipt by the Interim Commission or the Organization.

ARTICLE XXII

First Session of the Conference

The United Nations Interim Commission on Food and Agriculture shall convene the first session of the Conference to meet at a suitable date after the entry into force of this Constitution.

Languages

Pending the adoption by the Conference of any rules regarding languages, the business of the Conference shall be transacted in English.

Temporary Seat

The temporary seat of the Organization shall be at Washington unless the Conference should otherwise determine.

First Financial Year

The following exceptional arrangements shall apply in respect of the financial year in which this Constitution comes into force:

a The Budget shall be the provisional budget set forth in Annex II to this Constitution; and

b The amounts to be contributed by the Member nations shall be in the proportions set forth in Annex II to this Constitution: Provided that each Member nation may deduct therefrom the amount already contributed by it toward the expenses of the Interim Commission.

Dissolution of the Interim Commission

On the opening of the first session of the Conference, the United Nations Interim Commission on Food and Agriculture shall be deemed to be dissolved and its records and other property shall become the property of the Organization.

ANNEX I

Nations Eligible for Original Membership

AUSTRALIA	INDIA
BELGIUM	IRAN
BOLIVIA	IRAQ
BRAZIL	LIBERIA
CANADA	LUXEMBOURG
CHILE	MEXICO
CHINA	NETHERLANDS
COLOMBIA	NEW ZEALAND
COSTA RICA	NICARAGUA
CUBA	NORWAY
CZECHOSLOVAKIA	PANAMA
DENMARK	PARAGUAY
DOMINICAN REPUBLIC	PERU
ECUADOR	PHILIPPINE COMMONWEALTH
EGYPT	POLAND
EL SALVADOR	UNION OF SOUTH AFRICA
ETHIOPIA	UNION OF SOVIET SOCIALIST
FRANCE	REPUBLICS
GREECE	UNITED KINGDOM
GUATEMALA	UNITED STATES OF AMERICA
HAITI	URUGUAY
HONDURAS	VENEZUELA
ICELAND	YUGOSLAVIA

ANNEX II

Budget for the First Financial Year

The provisional budget for the first financial year shall be a sum of 2,500,000 U. S. dollars, the unspent balance of which shall constitute the nucleus of a capital fund.

This sum shall be contributed by the Member nations in the following proportions:

	Per cent
Australia	3.33
Belgium	1.28
Bolivia	.29
Brazil	3.46
Canada	5.06
Chile	1.15
China	6.50
Colombia	.71
Costa Rica	.05
Cuba	.71
Czechoslovakia	1.40
Denmark	.62
Dominican Republic	.05
Ecuador	.05
Egypt	1.73
El Salvador	.05
Ethiopia	.29
France	5.69
Greece	.38
Guatemala	.05
Haiti	.05
Honduras	.05
Iceland	.05
India	4.25
Iran	.71
Iraq	.44
Liberia	.05
Luxembourg	.05
Mexico	1.87
Netherlands	1.38
New Zealand	1.15
Nicaragua	.05
Norway	.62
Panama	.05
Paraguay	.05
Peru	.71
Philippines	.25
Poland	1.19
Union of South Africa	2.31
U. S. S. R.	8.00
United Kingdom	15.00
U. S. A.	25.00
Uruguay	.58
Venezuela	.58
Yugoslavia	.71
Provision for new Members	2.00
Total	100.00

19. CONSTITUTION OF THE WORLD HEALTH ORGANIZATION

THE STATES parties to this Constitution declare, in conformity with the Charter of the United Nations, that the following principles are basic to the happiness, harmonious relations and security of all peoples:

Health is a state of complete physical, mental and social well-being and not merely the absence of disease or infirmity.

The enjoyment of the highest attainable standard of health is one of the fundamental rights of every human being without distinction of race, religion, political belief, economic or social condition.

The health of all peoples is fundamental to the attainment of peace and security and is dependent upon the fullest co-operation of individuals and States.

The achievement of any State in the promotion and protection of health is of value to all.

Unequal development in different countries in the promotion of health and control of disease, especially communicable disease, is a common danger.

Healthy development of the child is of basic importance; the ability to live harmoniously in a changing total environment is essential to such development.

The extension to all peoples of the benefits of medical, psychological and related knowledge is essential to the fullest attainment of health.

Informed opinion and active co-operation on the part of the public are of the utmost importance in the improvement of the health of the people.

Governments have a responsibility for the health of their peoples which can be fulfilled only by the provision of adequate health and social measures.

ACCEPTING THESE PRINCIPLES, and for the purpose of co-operation among themselves and with others to promote and protect the health of all peoples, the contracting parties agree to the present Constitution and hereby establish the World Health Organization as a specialized agency within the terms of Article 57 of The Charter of the United Nations.

CHAPTER I. OBJECTIVE

ARTICLE 1

The objective of the World Health Organization (hereinafter called the Organization) shall be the attainment by all peoples of the highest possible level of health.

CHAPTER II. FUNCTIONS

ARTICLE 2

In order to achieve its objective, the functions of the Organization shall be:
  a to act as the directing and co-ordinating authority on international health work;
  b to establish and maintain effective collaboration with the United Nations, specialized agencies, governmental health administrations, professional groups and such other organizations as may be deemed appropriate;
  c to assist governments, upon request, in strengthening health services;

d to furnish appropriate technical assistance and, in emergencies, necessary aid upon the request or acceptance of governments;

e to provide or assist in providing, upon the request of the United Nations, health services and facilities to special groups, such as the peoples of trust territories;

f to establish and maintain such administrative and technical services as may be required, including epidemiological and statistical services;

g to stimulate and advance work to eradicate epidemic, endemic and other diseases;

h to promote, in co-operation with other specialized agencies where necessary, the prevention of accidental injuries;

i to promote, in co-operation with other specialized agencies where necessary, the improvement of nutrition, housing, sanitation, recreation, economic or working conditions and other aspects of environmental hygiene;

j to promote co-operation among scientific and professional groups which contribute to the advancement of health;

k to propose conventions, agreements and regulations, and make recommendations with respect to international health matters and to perform such duties as may be assigned thereby to the Organization and are consistent with its objective;

l to promote maternal and child health and welfare and to foster the ability to live harmoniously in a changing total environment;

m to foster activities in the field of mental health, especially those affecting the harmony of human relations;

n to promote and conduct research in the field of health;

o to promote improved standards of teaching and training in the health, medical and related professions;

p to study and report on, in co-operation with other specialized agencies where necessary, administrative and social techniques affecting public health and medical care from preventive and curative points of view, including hospital services and social security;

q to provide information, counsel and assistance in the field of health;

r to assist in developing an informed public opinion among all peoples on matters of health;

s to establish and revise as necessary international nomenclatures of diseases, of causes of death and of public health practices;

t to standardize diagnostic procedures as necessary;

u to develop, establish and promote international standards with respect to food, biological, pharmaceutical and similar products;

v generally to take all necessary action to attain the objective of the Organization.

CHAPTER III. MEMBERSHIP AND ASSOCIATE MEMBERSHIP

ARTICLE 3

Membership in the Organization shall be open to all States.

ARTICLE 4

Members of the United Nations may become Members of the Organization by signing or otherwise accepting this Constitution in accordance with the provisions of Chapter XIX and in accordance with their constitutional processes.

ARTICLE 5

The States whose governments have been invited to send observers to the International Health Conference held in New York, 1946, may become Members by signing or otherwise accepting this Constitution in accordance with the provisions of Chapter XIX and in accordance with their constitutional processes provided that such signature or acceptance shall be completed before the first session of the Health Assembly.

ARTICLE 6

Subject to the conditions of any agreement between the United Nations and the Organization, approved pursuant to Chapter XVI, States which do not become Members in accordance with Articles 4 and 5 may apply to become Members and shall be admitted as Members when their application has been approved by a simple majority vote of the Health Assembly.

ARTICLE 7

If a Member fails to meet its financial obligations to the Organization or in other exceptional circumstances the Health Assembly may, on such conditions as it thinks proper, suspend the voting privileges and services to which a Member is entitled. The Health Assembly shall have the authority to restore such voting privileges and services.

ARTICLE 8

Territories or groups of territories which are not responsible for the conduct of their international relations may be admitted as Associate Members by the Health Assembly upon application made on behalf of such territory or group of territories by the Member or other authority having responsibility for their international relations. Representatives of Associate Members to the Health Assembly should be qualified by their technical competence in the field of health and should be chosen from the native population. The nature and extent of the rights and obligations of Associate Members shall be determined by the Health Assembly.

CHAPTER IV. ORGANS

ARTICLE 9

The work of the Organization shall be carried out by:
a The World Health Assembly (herein called the Health Assembly);
b The Executive Board (hereinafter called the Board);
c The Secretariat.

CHAPTER V. THE WORLD HEALTH ASSEMBLY

ARTICLE 10

The Health Assembly shall be composed of delegates representing Members

ARTICLE 11

Each Member shall be represented by not more than three delegates, one of whom shall be designated by the Member as chief delegate. These delegates should be chosen from among persons most qualified by their technical competence in the field of health, preferably representing the national health administration of the Member.

ARTICLE 12

Alternates and advisers may accompany delegates.

ARTICLE 13

The Health Assembly shall meet in regular annual session and in such special sessions as may be necessary. Special sessions shall be convened at the request of the Board or of a majority of the Members.

ARTICLE 14

The Health Assembly, at each annual session, shall select the country or region in which the next annual session shall be held, the Board subsequently fixing the place. The Board shall determine the place where a special session shall be held.

ARTICLE 15

The Board, after consultation with the Secretary-General of the United Nations, shall determine the date of each annual and special session.

ARTICLE 16

The Health Assembly shall elect its President and other officers at the beginning of each annual session. They shall hold office until their successors are elected.

ARTICLE 17

The Health Assembly shall adopt its own rules of procedure.

ARTICLE 18

The functions of the Health Assembly shall be:

a to determine the policies of the Organization;

b to name the Members entitled to designate a person to serve on the Board;

c to appoint the Director-General;

d to review and approve reports and activities of the Board and of the Director-General and to instruct the Board in regard to matters upon which action, study, investigation or report may be considered desirable;

e to establish such committees as may be considered necessary for the work of the Organization;

f to supervise the financial policies of the Organization and to review and approve the budget;

g to instruct the Board and the Director-General to bring to the attention of Members and of international organizations, governmental or nongovernmental, any matter with regard to health which the Health Assembly may consider appropriate;

h to invite any organization, international or national, governmental or non-governmental, which has responsibilities related to those of the

Organization, to appoint representatives to participate, without right of vote, in its meetings or in those of the committees and conferences convened under its authority, on conditions prescribed by the Health Assembly; but in the case of national organizations, invitations shall be issued only with the consent of the government concerned;

i to consider recommendations bearing on health made by the General Assembly, the Economic and Social Council, the Security Council or Trusteeship Council of the United Nations, and to report to them on the steps taken by the Organization to give effect to such recommendations;

j to report to the Economic and Social Council in accordance with any agreement between the Organization and the United Nations;

k to promote and conduct research in the field of health by the personnel of the Organization, by the establishment of its own institutions or by co-operation with official or non-official institutions of any Member with the consent of its government;

l to establish such other institutions as it may consider desirable;

m to take any other appropriate action to further the objective of the Organization.

ARTICLE 19

The Health Assembly shall have authority to adopt conventions or agreements with respect to any matter within the competence of the Organization. A two-thirds vote of the Health Assembly shall be required for the adoption of such conventions or agreements which shall come into force for each Member when accepted by it in accordance with its constitutional processes.

ARTICLE 20

Each Member undertakes that it will, within eighteen months after the adoption by the Health Assembly of a convention or agreement, take action relative to the acceptance of such convention or agreement. Each Member shall notify the Director-General of the action taken and if it does not accept such convention or agreement within the time limit, it will furnish a statement of the reasons for non-acceptance. In case of acceptance, each Member agrees to make an annual report to the Director-General in accordance with Chapter XIV.

ARTICLE 21

The Health Assembly shall have authority to adopt regulations concerning:

a sanitary and quarantine requirements and other procedures designed to prevent the international spread of disease;

b nomenclatures with respect to diseases, causes of death and public health practices;

c standards with respect to diagnostic procedures for international use;

d standards with respect to the safety, purity, and potency of biological, pharmaceutical and similar products moving in international commerce;

e advertising and labelling of biological, pharmaceutical and similar products moving in international commerce.

ARTICLE 22

Regulations adopted pursuant to Article 21 shall come into force for all Members after due notice has been given of their adoption by the Health

Assembly except for such Members as may notify the Director-General of rejection or reservations within the period stated in the notice.

ARTICLE 23

The Health Assembly shall have authority to make recommendations to Members with respect to any matter within the competence of the Organization.

CHAPTER VI. THE EXECUTIVE BOARD

ARTICLE 24

The Board shall consist of eighteen persons designated by as many Members. The Health Assembly, taking into account an equitable geographical distribution, shall elect the Members entitled to designate a person to serve on the Board. Each of these Members should appoint to the Board a person technically qualified in the field of health, who may be accompanied by alternates and advisers.

ARTICLE 25

These Members shall be elected for three years and may be re-elected; provided that of the Members elected at the first session of the Health Assembly, the terms of six Members shall be for one year and the terms of six Members shall be for two years, as determined by lot.

ARTICLE 26

The Board shall meet at least twice a year and shall determine the place of each meeting.

ARTICLE 27

The Board shall elect its Chairman from among its members and shall adopt its own rules of procedure.

ARTICLE 28

The functions of the Board shall be:

a to give effect to the decisions and policies of the Health Assembly;

b to act as the executive organ of the Health Assembly;

c to perform any other functions entrusted to it by the Health Assembly;

d to advise the Health Assembly on questions referred to it by that body and on matters assigned to the Organization by conventions, agreements and regulations;

e to submit advice or proposals to the Health Assembly on its own initiative;

f to prepare the agenda of meetings of the Health Assembly;

g to submit to the Health Assembly for consideration and approval a general programme of work covering a specific period;

h to study all questions within its competence;

i to take emergency measures within the functions and financial resources of the Organization to deal with events requiring immediate action. In particular it may authorize the Director-General to take the necessary steps to combat epidemics, to participate in the organization of health relief to victims of a calamity and to undertake studies and research the urgency of which has been drawn to the attention of the Board by any Member or by the Director-General.

ARTICLE 29

The Board shall exercise on behalf of the whole Health Assembly the powers delegated to it by that body.

CHAPTER VII. THE SECRETARIAT

ARTICLE 30

The Secretariat shall comprise the Director-General and such technical and administrative staff as the Organization may require.

ARTICLE 31

The Director-General shall be appointed by the Health Assembly on the nomination of the Board on such terms as the Health Assembly may determine. The Director-General, subject to the authority of the Board, shall be the chief technical and administrative officer of the Organization.

ARTICLE 32

The Director-General shall be *ex officio* Secretary of the Health Assembly, of the Board, of all commissions and committees of the Organization and of conferences convened by it. He may delegate these functions.

ARTICLE 33

The Director-General or his representative may establish a procedure by agreement with Members, permitting him, for the purpose of discharging his duties, to have direct access to their various departments, especially to their health administrations and to national health organizations, governmental or non-governmental. He may also establish direct relations with international organizations whose activities come within the competence of the Organization. He shall keep Regional Offices informed on all matters involving their respective areas.

ARTICLE 34

The Director-General shall prepare and submit annually to the Board the financial statements and budget estimates of the Organization.

ARTICLE 35

The Director-General shall appoint the staff of the Secretariat in accordance with staff regulations established by the Health Assembly. The paramount consideration in the employment of the staff shall be to assure that the efficiency, integrity and internationally representative character of the Secretariat shall be maintained at the highest level. Due regard shall be paid also to the importance of recruiting the staff on as wide a geographical basis as possible.

ARTICLE 36

The conditions of service of the staff of the Organization shall conform as far as possible with those of other United Nations organizations.

ARTICLE 37

In the performance of their duties the Director-General and the staff shall not seek or receive instructions from any government or from any authority external to the Organization. They shall refrain from any action which might reflect on their position as international officers. Each Member of the Organization on its part undertakes to respect the exclusively international character of the Director-General and the staff and not to seek to influence them.

CHAPTER VIII. COMMITTEES

ARTICLE 38

The Board shall establish such committees as the Health Assembly may direct and, on its own initiative or on the proposal of the Director-General, may establish any other committees considered desirable to serve any purpose within the competence of the Organization.

ARTICLE 39

The Board, from time to time and in any event annually, shall review the necessity for continuing each committee.

ARTICLE 40

The Board may provide for the creation of or the participation by the Organization in joint or mixed committees with other organizations and for the representation of the Organization in committees established by such other organizations.

CHAPTER IX. CONFERENCES

ARTICLE 41

The Health Assembly or the Board may convene local, general, technical or other special conferences to consider any matter within the competence of the Organization and may provide for the representation at such conferences of international organizations and, with the consent of the government concerned, of national organizations, governmental or non-governmental. The manner of such representation shall be determined by the Health Assembly or the Board.

ARTICLE 42

The Board may provide for representation of the Organization at conferences in which the Board considers that the Organization has an interest.

CHAPTER X. HEADQUARTERS

ARTICLE 43

The location of the headquarters of the Organization shall be determined by the Health Assembly after consultation with the United Nations.

CHAPTER XI. REGIONAL ARRANGEMENTS

ARTICLE 44

a The Health Assembly shall from time to time define the geographical areas in which it is desirable to establish a regional organization.

b The Health Assembly may, with the consent of a majority of the Members situated within each area so defined, establish a regional organization to meet the special needs of such area. There shall not be more than one regional organization in each area.

ARTICLE 45

Each regional organization shall be an integral part of the Organization in accordance with this Constitution.

ARTICLE 46

Each regional organization shall consist of a Regional Committee and a Regional Office.

ARTICLE 47

Regional Committees shall be composed of representatives of the Member States and Associate Members in the region concerned. Territories or groups of territories within the region, which are not responsible for the conduct of their international relations and which are not Associate Members, shall have the right to be represented and to participate in Regional Committees. The nature and extent of the rights and obligations of these territories or groups of territories in Regional Committees shall be determined by the Health Assembly in consultation with the Member or other authority having responsibility for the international relations of these territories and with the Member States in the region.

ARTICLE 48

Regional Committees shall meet as often as necessary and shall determine the place of each meeting.

ARTICLE 49

Regional Committees shall adopt their own rules of procedure.

ARTICLE 50

The functions of the Regional Committee shall be:

a to formulate policies governing matters of an exclusively regional character;

b to supervise the activities of the Regional Office;

c to suggest to the Regional Office the calling of technical conferences and such additional work or investigation in health matters as in the opinion of the Regional Committee would promote the objective of the Organization within the region.

d to co-operate with the respective regional committees of the United Nations and with those of other specialized agencies and with other regional international organizations having interests in common with the Organization;

e to tender advice, through the Director-General, to the Organization on international health matters which have wider than regional significance;

f to recommend additional regional appropriations by the governments of the respective regions if the proportion of the central budget of the Organization allotted to that region is insufficient for the carrying out of the regional functions;

g such other functions as may be delegated to the Regional Committee by the Health Assembly, the Board or the Director-General.

ARTICLE 51

Subject to the general authority of the Director-General of the Organization, the Regional Office shall be the administrative organ of the Regional Committee. It shall, in addition, carry out within the region the decisions of the Health Assembly and of the Board.

ARTICLE 52

The head of the Regional Office shall be the Regional Director appointed by the Board in agreement with the Regional Committee.

ARTICLE 53

The staff of the Regional Office shall be appointed in a manner to be determined by agreement between the Director-General and the Regional Director.

ARTICLE 54

The Pan American sanitary organization represented by the Pan American Sanitary Bureau and the Pan American Sanitary Conferences, and all other inter-governmental regional health organizations in existence prior to the date of signature of this Constitution, shall in due course be integrated with the Organization. This integration shall be effected as soon as practicable through common action based on mutual consent of the competent authorities expressed through the organizations concerned.

CHAPTER XII. BUDGET AND EXPENSES

ARTICLE 55

The Director-General shall prepare and submit to the Board the annual budget estimates of the Organization. The Board shall consider and submit to the Health Assembly such budget estimates, together with any recommendations the Board may deem advisable.

ARTICLE 56

Subject to any agreement between the Organization and the United Nations, the Health Assembly shall review and approve the budget estimates and shall apportion the expenses among the Members in accordance with a scale to be fixed by the Health Assembly.

ARTICLE 57

The Health Assembly or the Board acting on behalf of the Health Assembly may accept and administer gifts and bequests made to the Organization provided that the conditions attached to such gifts or bequests are acceptable to the Health Assembly or the Board and are consistent with the objective and policies of the Organization.

ARTICLE 58

A special fund to be used at the discretion of the Board shall be established to meet emergencies and unforeseen contingencies.

CHAPTER XIII. VOTING

ARTICLE 59

Each Member shall have one vote in the Health Assembly.

ARTICLE 60

a Decisions of the Health Assembly on important questions shall be made by a two-thirds majority of the Members present and voting. These questions shall include: the adoption of conventions or agreements; the approval of agreements bringing the Organization into relation with the United Nations and inter-governmental organizations and agencies in accordance with Articles 69, 70 and 72; amendments to this Constitution.

b Decisions on other questions, including the determination of additional categories of questions to be decided by a two-thirds majority, shall be made by a majority of the Members present and voting.

c Voting on analogous matters in the Board and in committees of the Organization shall be made in accordance with paragraphs (*a*) and (*b*) of this Article.

CHAPTER XIV. REPORTS SUBMITTED BY STATES

ARTICLE 61

Each Member shall report annually to the Organization on the action taken and progress achieved in improving the health of its people.

ARTICLE 62

Each Member shall report annually on the action taken with respect to recommendations made to it by the Organization and with respect to conventions, agreements and regulations.

ARTICLE 63

Each Member shall communicate promptly to the Organization important laws, regulations, official reports and statistics pertaining to health which have been published in the State concerned.

ARTICLE 64

Each Member shall provide statistical and epidemiological reports in a manner to be determined by the Health Assembly.

ARTICLE 65

Each Member shall transmit upon the request of the Board such additional information pertaining to health as may be practicable.

CHAPTER XV. LEGAL CAPACITY, PRIVILEGES AND IMMUNITIES

ARTICLE 66

The Organization shall enjoy in the territory of each Member such legal capacity as may be necessary for the fulfilment of its objective and for the exercise of its functions.

ARTICLE 67

a The Organization shall enjoy in the territory of each Member such privileges and immunities as may be necessary for the fulfilment of its objective and for the exercise of its functions.

b Representatives of Members, persons designated to serve on the Board and technical and administrative personnel of the Organization shall similarly enjoy such privileges and immunities as are necessary for the independent exercise of their functions in connection with the Organization.

ARTICLE 68

Such legal capacity, privileges and immunities shall be defined in a separate agreement to be prepared by the Organization in consultation with the Secretary-General of the United Nations and concluded between the Members.

CHAPTER XVI. RELATIONS WITH OTHER ORGANIZATIONS

ARTICLE 69

The Organization shall be brought into relation with the United Nations as one of the specialized agencies referred to in Article 57 of the Charter of the United Nations. The agreement or agreements bringing the Organization into relation with the United Nations shall be subject to approval by a two-thirds vote of the Health Assembly.

ARTICLE 70

The Organization shall establish effective relations and co-operate closely with such other inter-governmental organizations as may be desirable. Any formal agreement entered into with such organizations shall be subject to approval by a two-thirds vote of the Health Assembly.

ARTICLE 71

The Organization may, on matters within its competence, make suitable arrangements for consultation and co-operation with non-governmental international organizations and, with the consent of the government concerned, with national organizations, governmental or non-governmental.

ARTICLE 72

Subject to the approval by a two-thirds vote of the Health Assembly, the Organization may take over from any other international organization or agency whose purpose and activities lie within the field of competence of the Organization such functions, resources and obligations as may be conferred upon the Organization by international agreement or by mutually acceptable arrangements entered into between the competent authorities of the respective organizations.

CHAPTER XVII. AMENDMENTS

ARTICLE 73

Texts of proposed amendments to this Constitution shall be communicated by the Director-General to Members at least six months in advance of their consideration by the Health Assembly. Amendments shall come into force for all Members when adopted by a two-thirds vote of the Health Assembly and accepted by two-thirds of the Members in accordance with their respective constitutional processes.

CHAPTER XVIII. INTERPRETATION

ARTICLE 74

The Chinese, English, French, Russian and Spanish texts of this Constitution shall be regarded as equally authentic.

ARTICLE 75

Any question or dispute concerning the interpretation or application of this Constitution which is not settled by negotiation or by the Health Assembly shall be referred to the International Court of Justice in conformity with the Statute of the Court, unless the parties concerned agree on another mode of settlement.

ARTICLE 76

Upon authorization by the General Assembly of the United Nations or upon authorization in accordance with any agreement between the Organization and the United Nations, the Organization may request the International Court of Justice for an advisory opinion on any legal question arising within the competence of the Organization.

ARTICLE 77

The Director-General may appear before the Court on behalf of the Organization in connection with any proceedings arising out of any such request for an advisory opinion. He shall make arrangements for the presentation of the case before the Court including arrangements for the argument of different views on the question.

CHAPTER XIX. ENTRY INTO FORCE

ARTICLE 78

Subject to the provisions of Chapter III, this Constitution shall remain open to all States for signature or acceptance.

ARTICLE 79

a States may become parties to this Constitution by
    (i) signature without reservation as to approval;
    (ii) signature subject to approval followed by acceptance; or
    (iii) acceptance.

b Acceptance shall be effected by the deposit of a formal instrument with the Secretary-General of the United Nations.

ARTICLE 80

This Constitution shall come into force when twenty-six Members of the United Nations have become parties to it in accordance with the provisions of Article 79.

ARTICLE 81

In accordance with Article 102 of the Charter of the United Nations, the Secretary-General of the United Nations will register this Constitution when it has been signed without reservation as to approval on behalf of one State or upon deposit of the first instrument of acceptance.

ARTICLE 82

The Secretary-General of the United Nations will inform States parties to this Constitution of the date when it has come into force. He will also inform them of the dates when other States have become parties to this Constitution.

IN FAITH WHEREOF the undersigned representatives having been duly authorized for that purpose, sign this Constitution.

DONE in the City of New York this twenty-second day of July 1946, in a single copy in the Chinese, English, French, Russian and Spanish languages, each text being equally authentic. The original texts shall be deposited in the archives of the United Nations. The Secretary-General of the United Nations will send certified copies to each of the Governments represented at the Conference.

Appendix B

BIBLIOGRAPHY

The bibliography which follows is highly selective. It would be impossible to render a bibliography of international organization complete without including vast ranges of material upon all topics in international history, law, and diplomacy. In addition, the literature of this field is growing and changing with great rapidity today. The titles found below have been included, therefore, only because they perform one or more of three functions, namely to indicate sources drawn upon for material used in the text; to indicate the scope of, and directions taken by, the literature in this field; or to indicate books especially significant and helpful for further study and reading. Secondary works readily available in English have been preferred but works in French and German are included also. No attempt has been made to list completely the many articles to be found in the technical journals of international law and politics and the general periodicals of public events; for these the student will be better served by himself consulting the indexes of those journals.

Of all the general works cited, the treatises by Eagleton, Mower, and Vinacke deserve special mention for the scope of attention given by them to all the institutions and practices of international government.

Works are usually cited, in the footnotes above, by the name of the author or by that name and a brief title; where special abbreviations are used they are indicated below. The works listed are arranged in accordance with their significance for topics discussed in the text, not merely alphabetically or in respect to their general importance.

§ 1

Introduction; Nature of International Organization; General

KREHBIEL, E., *Nationalism, War, and Society*. New York, 1916.

MOON, P. T., *Syllabus on International Relations*. New York, 1925.

League of Nations, *Handbook of International Organizations*. Geneva, 1938.

MASTERS, R. D., *Handbook of International Organizations in the Americas*. Washington, 1945.

ECKEL, P. E., *The Far East Since 1500*. New York, 1947.

HARLEY, J. E., *International Understanding*. Stanford, 1931.

HERSHEY, A. S., *Essentials of Public International Law and Organization*. New York, 1927 (2d. ed.).

HICKS, F. C., *New World Order*. New York, 1920.

HODGES, C., *Background of International Relations*. New York, 1931.

HOOVER, H., and GIBSON, H., *The Problems of Lasting Peace*. Garden City, 1942.

HUGHAN, J. W., *Study of International Government*. New York, 1923.

INGRAHAM, K., *Years of Crisis (1919-1945)*. New York, 1947.

(Lawyers of Canada and the United States), *The International Law of the Future*. Washington, 1944.

MARRIOTT, J. A. R., *European Commonwealth*. Oxford, 1918.

MOWER, E. C., *International Government*. Boston, 1931.

MUIR, R., *The Interdependent World and its Problems*. London, 1932.

SCHEVILL, F., *A History of Europe*. New York, 1938.

SCHMECKEBIER, L., *International Organizations in which the United States Participates*. Washington, 1935.

SCHÜCKING, W., *Die Organisation der Welt*. Tübingen, 1908.

SELIGMAN, E. R. A., ed., *Encyclopedia of the Social Sciences*. New York, 1930-1933.

SEYMOUR, C., *Diplomatic Background of the War*. New Haven, 1916.

VINACKE, H. M., *International Organization*. New York, 1934.

WOOLF, L. S., *International Government*. New York, 1916.

BALL, M. E., *The Problem of Inter-American Organization*. Stanford, 1944.

BUELL, R. L., *International Relations*. New York, 1932.

DUPLESSIX, E., *L'Organisation Internationale*. Paris, 1909.

EAGLETON, C., *International Government*. New York, 1932.

FAIRGREAVE, J., *Geography and World Power*. New York, 1917.

GARNER, J. W., *Political Science and Government*. New York, 1928.

GUGGENHEIM, P., *L'Organisation de la Société Internationale*. Neuchatel, 1944.

Rand, McNally, & Co., *Commercial Atlas of America; of Foreign Countries*. Chicago, 1921.

RENNER, G. T., *Global Geography*. New York, 1944.

The Statesman's Year-Book, New York.

Académie de Droit International. Receuil des Cours. Paris.

American Academy of Political and Social Science. *Annals*. Philadelphia.

American Institute of International Law, *Recommendations of Havana Concerning International Organization*, with Commentary by Scott, J. B. New York, 1917.

American Political Science Association, *American Political Science Review*.

American Society of International Law, *American Journal of International Law; Proceedings*, Washington.

Academy of Political Science, *Political Science Quarterly*, New York.

Carnegie Endowment for International Peace, *International Conciliation*. New York.

Comité du Livre, Annuaire Générale de la France et de l'Etranger. Paris.

Foreign Policy Association, *Publications*. New York.

Geneva Research Centre, *Geneva Special Studies*. Geneva, 1930-1941.

Public Opinion Quarterly, Princeton.

Office Centrale des Associations Internationales, *La Vie Internationale*. Brussels, 1912-1921.

Society of Comparative Legislation, *Journal of Comparative Legislation and International Law*, London.

World Peace Foundation, *International Organization*. Boston.

——, *Pamphlet Series*. Boston.

American Society for Public Administration, *Public Administration Review*. Chicago.

The American Mercury.

The New York Times.

Great Britain, Foreign Office, *British and Foreign State Papers*. London.

United States, Department of State, *The Department of State Bulletin*, Washington.

——, *Press Releases*. Washington.

——, *Register*. Washington.

§ 2

Nation States

BOWMAN, J., *The New World*. New York, 1928.

BUCK, P. W., and MASLAND, J. W., *Government of Foreign Powers*. New York, 1947.

BURNS, C. D., *The World of States*. London, 1917.

DOMINIAN, L., *Frontiers of Language and Nationality in Europe*. New York, 1917.

GOOCH, G. P., *Nationalism*. New York, 1921.

HOLDICH, T. H., *Political Frontiers and Boundary Making*. London, 1916.

JAMES, H. G., *The Republics of Latin-America*. New York, 1923.

MacIVER, R. N., *The Modern State*. London, 1926.

MALLORY, W. H., ed., *Political Handbook of the World*, 1947. New York, 1947.

MANCE, Sir H. O., *Frontiers, Peace Treaties, and International Organization*. New York, 1946.

MOWRER, P. S., *Balkanized Europe*. New York, 1921.

OGG, F. A., *European Government and Politics*. New York, 1939 (2d ed.).

ROSE, J. H., *Nationality in Modern History*. New York, 1916.

ROUÇEK, J. S., ed., *Government and Politics Abroad*. New York, 1947.

PILLSBURY, W. B., *The Psychology of Nationalism and Internationalism*. New York, 1919.

WELDON, T. D., *States and Morals*. London, 1946.

WHITTLESEY, D. S., *The Earth and the State*. New York, 1944.

WILLOUGHBY, W. W., and FENWICK, C. G., *Types of Restricted Sovereignty and of Colonial Autonomy*. Washington, 1919.

§ 3

International Intercourse; Private International Organization; Cosmopolitanism

CHISHOLM, G. G., *Handbook of Commercial Geography*. New York, 1928.

CLARK, G. N., *Unifying the World*. New York, 1920.

DELAISI, F., *Political Myths and Economic Realities*. London, 1925.

DONALDSON, J., *International Economic Relations*. New York, 1928.

EIJKMAN, P. H., *L'Internationalisme Scientifique*. The Hague, 1911.

ENKE, S., and SALERA, V., *International Economics*. New York, 1947.

FERRERO, G., *The Unity of the World*. New York, 1930.

HARTWIG, Th., *Der Kosmopolitische Gedanke*. Ludwigsburg, 1924.

HUBER, M., *Principles, Tasks, and Problems of the Red Cross*. Geneva, 1946.

MARVIN, F. S., *Unity of Western Civilization*. Oxford, 1922.

MATHEWS, B., ed., *World Brotherhood*. London, 1920 (?).

STREIT, C. K., *Where Iron Is There is the Fatherland*. New York, 1920.

WHITE, L. C., *Structure of Private International Organizations*. Philadelphia, 1933.

§ 4

International Politics

ARMSTRONG, H. F., ed., *The Foreign Policy of the Powers.* New York, 1935.
CULBERTSON, W. S., *International Economic Policies.* New York, 1925.
DEALEY, J. Q., *Foreign Policies of the United States.* New York, 1926.
ECKEL, P. E., *The Far East Since 1500,* New York, 1947.
FIFIELD, R. H., and PEARCY, G. E., *Geopolitics in Principle and Practice.* Boston, 1944.
FISK, G. M., and PEIRCE, P. S., *International Commercial Policies.* New York, 1923.
FOX, W. T. R., *The Super-Powers.* New York, 1944.
FRASER, H. J., *Foreign Trade and World Politics.* New York, 1926.
HOBSON, J. A., *Imperialism.* London, 1905.
MARKUS, J., *Grandes Puissances, Petites Nations, et le Problème de l'Organisation Internationale.* Geneva, 1946.
MOON, P. T., *Imperialism and World Politics.* New York, 1924.
POTTER, P. B., *The Freedom of the Seas in History, Law, and Politics.* New York, 1924.
SCHUMANN, F. L., *International Politics.* New York, 1941. (3d. ed.).
SHARP, W. R., and KIRK, G. L., *Contemporary International Politics.* New York, 1940.
SPYKMAN, N. J., *America's Strategy in World Politics.* New York, 1942.
TOWLE, L. W., *International Trade and Commercial Policy.* New York, 1947.
WILLIAMS, B. H., *Economic Foreign Policy of the United States.* New York, 1929.
WOOLF, L. S., *Economic Imperialism.* New York, 1921.

§ 5

International Law

BRIERLY, J. L., *The Law of Nations. London,* 1942 (3d. ed.).
Carnegie Endowment for International Peace, *The Classics of International Law.* Washington.
EDMUNDS, S. E., *The Lawless Law of Nations.* Washington, 1925.
FENWICK, C. G., *International Law.* New York, 1934.
FIELD, D. D., *Outlines of an International Code.* New York, 1876.
GARNER, J. W., *International Law and the World War.* New York, 1920.
———, *Prize Law during the World War.* New York, 1927.
HIGGINS, A. P., *The Binding Force of International Law.* Cambridge, England, 1910.
HYDE, C. C., *International Law.* Boston, 1945. (2d. ed.).
Institute of International Law, *Resolutions,* ed. by Scott, J. B. New York, 1916.
JITTA, D. J., *The Renovation of International Law.* The Hague, 1919.
KEETON, G. W., and SCHWARZENBERGER, G., *Making International Law Work.* London, 1939.
LAUTERPACHT, H., *The Function of Law in the International Community.* Oxford, 1933.
NATHAN, M., *The Renascence of International Law.* London, 1925.
NIPPOLD, O., *The Development of International Law after the World War.* Oxford, 1923.

Nussbaum, A., *Concise History of the Law of Nations.* New York, 1947.
Oppenheim, L. F. L., *International Law.* New York, 1944–(6th ed. by Lauter-
    pacht).
Potter, P. B., "International Law in the Twentieth Century", in *Twentieth
    Century Political Thought.* New York, 1946.
———, *A Manual Digest of Common International Law.* New York, 1932.
Ralston, J. H., *Democracy's International Law.* Washington, 1922.
Schwarzenberger, G., *International Law.* London, 1945–.
Wilson, G. G., *Handbook of International Law.* St. Paul, 1939 (3d. ed.).

§6
Diplomacy and Treaties
a (1). *Consular Organization and Practice*

American Foreign Service, *American Foreign Service Journal.* Washington.
Norton, H. K., *Foreign Office Organization.* Philadelphia, 1929.
Puente, J. I. y, *The Foreign Consul in the United States.* Chicago, 1926.
Stewart, I., *Consular Privileges and Immunities.* New York, 1927.
Stowell, E. C., *Consular Cases and Opinions.* Washington, 1909.
———, *Le Consul.* Paris, 1909.
Stuart, G. H., *American Diplomatic and Consular Practice.* New York, 1936.
United States, Department of State, *Consular Regulations.* Washington.
United States, Department of Commerce, *Consular Regulations of Foreign
    Countries.* Tariff Series Nos. 24, 24a, 24b. Washington, 1915-17.

a (2). *Diplomatic Organization and Practice*

Bernard, M., *Four Lectures on Diplomacy.* London, 1868.
Bourquin, M., *Dynamism and the Machinery of International Institutions.*
    Geneva, 1940 (*Geneva Special Studies,* Vol. XI, No. 5).
Foster, J. W., *Practice of Diplomacy.* New York, 1906.
Gallup, G. H., and Rae, S. F., *The Pulse of Democracy.* New York, 1940.
Guérard, A., *A Short History of the International Language Movement.*
    London, 1922.
Hershey, A. S., *Diplomatic Agents and Immunities.* Washington, 1919.
Hill, M., *Immunities and Privileges of International Officials.* Washington, 1947.
Mathews, J. M., *American Foreign Relations; Conduct and Policies.* New
    York, 1938 (2d. ed.).
Neilson, F., *How Diplomats Make War.* New York, 1915.
Ponsonby, A., *Democracy and Diplomacy.* London, 1915.
Poole, D. C., *The Conduct of Foreign Relations under Modern Democratic
    Conditions.* New Haven, 1924.
Reinsch, P. S., *Secret Diplomacy.* New York, 1922.
Satow, Sir E., *Guide to Diplomatic Practice.* New York, 1923 (3d. ed.).
United States, Department of State. *Diplomatic Instructions.* Washington.

a (3). *Good Offices and Mediation*

Franklin, W. M., *Protection of Foreign Interests.* Washington, 1946.
Melville, E. de, *Vermittlung und Gute Dienste.* Gotha, 1920.
Zanfiresco, J., *De la Médiation.* Paris, 1911.

b. Treaties

CRANDALL, S. B., *Treaties, their Making and Enforcement.* Washington, 1916.
JONES, M. J., *Full Powers and Ratification.* Cambridge, England, 1946.
MALLORY, W. M., comp., *Treaties... between the United States... and other Powers.* Washington, 1910 (Sen. Doc. 357:61st Cong., 2d Sess.).
McCLURE, W. M., *The International Executive Agreement.* New York, 1941.
McNAIR, Sir A. D., *The Law of Treaties.* New York, 1938.
MYERS, D. P., *Manual of Collections of Treaties.* Cambridge, Massachusetts, 1922.
ROXBURGH, R., *International Conventions and Third States.* London, 1917.
United States, Senate, *Ratification of Treaties* (in various countries). Washington, 1919 (Sen. Doc. 26, 66 Cong., 1 Sess.).
United States, Department of State. *Treaty Making Power in Various Countries.* Washington, 1919.
——, *Treaty Series.* Washington.
VISSCHER, P. de, *De la Conclusion des Traités Internationaux.* Brussells, 1943.
WILCOX, F. O., *Ratification of International Conventions.* London, 1935.

§7

International Conference

DUNN, F. C., *Practice and Procedure of International Conferences.* Baltimore, 1929.
GRUBER, G., *Internationale Staatenkongresse und Konferenzen.* Berlin, 1919.
HILL, N. L., *The Public International Conference.* Stanford, 1929.
HUNT, E. E., *Conferences, Committees, Conventions.* New York, 1925.
MOULTON, M., *A Structural View of the Conference as an Organ of International Coöperation.* New Brunswick, 1930.
O'DAVOREN, W., *Post-War Reconstruction Conferences.* London, 1943.
PARKES, J. W., *International Conferences.* Geneva, 1933.
PASTUHOV, V. D., *A Guide to the Practice of International Conferences.* Washington, 1945.
SATOW, Sir E. M., *International Congresses.* London, 1920.
SHENTON, H. N., *Cosmopolitan Conversation.* New York, 1933.
United States, *Department of State, List of Official International Conferences and Meetings.* Washington, monthly.
——, *Participation by the United States Government in International Conferences, July 1, 1941–June 30, 1945.* Washington, 1947.

§8

International Administration and Adjudication

a (1) and (2). International Administration

BERTHOUD, P., *Le Contrôle International de l'Exécution des Conventions Collectives.* Geneva, 1946.
BURNHAM, J., *The Managerial Revolution.* New York, 1941.
Carnegie Endowment for International Peace, *Conference on Training for International Administration.* Washington, 1944 (restricted circulation).
GAY, G. J., and FISHER, H. H., *Public Relations of the Commission for Relief in Belgium.* Stanford, 1929.

GLESINGER, E., *Nazis in the Woodpile*. Indianapolis, 1942.

HILL, N. L., *International Administration*. New York, 1931.

HOBSON, A., *The International Institute of Agriculture*. Berkeley, 1931.

HOSTIE, J., *The Communications and Transit Organization of the League of Nations*. Washington, 1948.

JONES, S. B., *Boundary Making*. Washington, 1945.

LANDIS, J., *The Administrative Process*. New Haven, 1938.

LEONARD, L. L., *International Regulation of Fisheries*. Washington, 1944.

MANCE, Sir H. Osborne, and WHEELER, J. E.,
International Telecommunications. New York, 1943.
International Air Transport. New York, 1943.
International River and Canal Transport. New York, 1944.
International Sea Transport. New York, 1945.
International Road Transport (Mance only). New York, 1947.

PINK, G., *The Conference of Ambassadors*. Geneva, 1942 (*Geneva Studies*, Vol. XII, Nos. 4-5.)

REIFF, H., *The United States and International Administrative Unions*. New York, 1937 (*International Conciliation*, No. 332).

REINSCH, P. S., *Public International Unions*. Boston, 1911.

ROGERS, W. C., *International Administration, A Bibliography*. Chicago, 1945.

SAYRE, F. B., *Experiments in International Administration*. New York, 1919.

United States, Department of State, *International Agencies in which the United States Participates*. Washington, 1946.

WEDGEWOOD, Sir R. L., and WHEELER, J. E., *International Rail Transport*. New York, 1946.

ZINK, H., *American Military Government in Germany*. New York, 1947.

b (1). *Inquiry and Conciliation*

HILL, N. L., *International Commissions of Inquiry and Conciliation*. New York, 1932 (*International Conciliation*, No. 278).

VULCAN, C., *La Conciliation dans le Droit International Actuel*. Paris, 1932.

EFREMOV, J. N., *La Médiation et la Conciliation Internationales*. La Flèche, 1925.

b (2). *International Adjudication*

American Arbitration Association, *The Arbitration Journal*. New York.

CARLSTON, K. S., *The Process of International Arbitration*. New York, 1946.

HABICHT, M., *Post-War Treaties for Pacific Settlement of International Disputes*. Cambridge, Masachusetts, 1931.

HUDSON, M. O., *International Tribunals Past and Future*. Washington, 1944.

RALSTON, J. H., *Law and Procedure of International Tribunals*. Stanford, 1926.

DE WOLF, F. C., *General Synopsis of Treaties of Conciliation, Judicial Settlement, Security, and Disarmament Actually in Force*. Washington, 1932.

§9

International Federation

a. Alliances; Balance of Power; Concert

DUPUIS, C., *Le Principe d'Equilibre et le Concert Européen*. Paris, 1909.

HANOTAUX, G., *La Politique de l'Equilibre*. Paris, 1914.

HEARNSHAW, F. J. C., *European Coalitions*. London, 1920.

HILL, N. L., *Post-War Treaties of Security and Mutual Guarantee*. New York, 1928 (*International Conciliation*, No. 244).

HOLLAND, T. E., *The European Concert in the Eastern Question*. Oxford, 1885.

KOUMANOUDI, K., *Traités d'Alliance*. Paris, 1901.

MOWAT, R. B., *The Concert of Europe*. New York, 1930.

PHILLIPS, W. A., *The Confederation of Europe*. London, 1914.

b. National Sovereignty and International Federation

BRIE, S., *Theorie der Staatenverbindungen*. Stuttgart, 1886.

KOROWICZ, M. S., *Souvereinté des Etats et l'Avenir du Droit International*, Paris, 1945.

LE FUR, L., *Bundesstaat und Staatenbund*. Breslau, 1902.

MATTERN, J., *State, Sovereignty, and International Law*. Baltimore, 1928.

MOUSKHELI, M., *Théorie Juridique de l'Etat Fédéral*. Paris, 1931.

TAYLER, W. L., *Federal States and Labor Treaties*. New York, 1935.

c. Constitution of International Federation

BRIDGMAN, R. L., *World Organization*. Boston, 1905.

COUDENHOVE-KALERGI, R. N., *Crusade for Pan-Europe*. New York, 1943.

DURAND, C., *Les Etats Fédéraux*, Paris, 1930.

EATON, H. O. (ed.), *Federation*. Norman, 1944.

EDGERTON, H. E., *Federation and Unions in the British Empire*. Oxford, 1911.

EWING, A. C., *The Individual, the State, and World Government*. New York, 1947.

GREAVES, H. R. G., *Federal Union in Practice*. London, 1940.

HART, A. B., *Introduction to the Study of Federal Government*. Boston, 1891.

LEDERMANN, L., *Les Précurseurs de l'Organisation Internationale*. Neuchatel, 1945.

MINOR, R. C., *Republic of Nations*. New York, 1918.

MOGI, S., *Problem of Federalism*. London, 1931.

NEWFANG, O., *World Government*. New York, 1942.

NOVIKOW, J., *Fédération de l'Europe*. Paris, 1901.

POLEY, A. P., *Federal Systems of the United States and the British Empire*. Boston, 1913.

REVES, E., *Anatomy of Peace*. New York, 1945.

SCOTT, J. B., *The United States of America: A Study in International Organization*. Washington, 1920.

STIMSON, F. J., *The Law of the Federal and State Constitutions*. Boston, 1908.

STREIT, C. K., *Union Now*. New York, 1939.

TRUEBLOOD, B. F., *The Federation of the World*. New York, 1899.

WHEARE, K. C., *Federal Government*. Oxford, 1947.

WYNNER, E., and LLOYD, G., *Searchlight on Peace Plans*. New York, 1944.

YORK, E., *Leagues of Nations*. London, 1919.

§ 10

Functions of International Organization

a. Procedure; International Legislation; Sanctions

DUNN, F. S., *Peaceful Change*. New York, 1937.

GIHL, T., *International Legislation*. New York, 1937.

HUDSON, M. O., *International Legislation*. Washington, 1931—.

KNUDSON, J. I., *Methods of International Legislation*. Geneva, 1928.

KOO, W., Jr., *Voting Procedures in International Political Organizations*. New York, 1947.

RICHES, C. A., *Majority Rule in International Organization*. Baltimore, 1940.

WILLIAMS, Sir J. F., *International Change and International Peace*. Oxford, 1932.

CLARK, E., *Boycotts and Peace*. New York, 1932.

DAVIES, Lord D., *The Problem of the Twentieth Century*. London, 1930.

FITE, E. D., *Government by Coöperation*. New York, 1932.

GOUBRAN, C., *Le Problème des Sanctions dans l'Evolution de l'Arbitrage International*. Paris, 1923.

HOGAN, A. E., *Pacific Blockade*. Oxford, 1908.

MITRANY, D., *The Problem of International Sanctions*. London, 1925.

NIJHOFF, M., ed., *War Obviated by an International Police*. The Hague, 1915.

POTTER, P. B., *Collective Security and Peaceful Change*. Chicago, 1937 (University of Chicago *Public Policy Pamphlets*, No. 24).

WEHBERG, H., *Theory and Practice of International Policing*, London, 1935.

WHEELER-BENNETT, J. W., *The Problem of Security*. London, 1927.

WILDE, P. S., *Sanctions and Treaty Enforcement*. Cambridge, Massachusetts, 1934.

b. Content; Subject matters; Peace

*ANGELL, Sir N., *The Great Illusion*. New York, 1910.

BEALES, A. C. F., *History of Peace*. London, 1931.

BOECKEL, F. B., *Between War and Peace*. New York, 1928.

CARTER, J., *Man is War*. Indianapolis, 1926.

COLLIN, C. C., *War Against War*. New York, 1917.

COULTON, G. G., *The Main Illusions of Pacifism*. Cambridge, England, 1916.

CRANE, F., *War and World Government*. New York, 1915.

CRILE, G. W., *A Mechanistic View of War and Peace*. New York, 1916.

CROSBY, O. T., *International War: Its Causes and Its Cure*. London, 1919.

CURTI, M. E., *Peace or War: The American Struggle, 1636-1936*. New York, 1936.

DICKINSON, G. L., *War: Its Nature, Cause, and Cure*. New York, 1923.

DURAS, V. H., *Universal Peace by International Government*. New York, 1908.

ENGELBRECHTS, H. C., and HANIGHEN, E. C., *Merchants of Death*. New York, 1934.

HOWE, F. C., *Why War?* New York, 1916.

MANDER, L. A., *Foundations of Modern World Society*. Stanford, 1941.

MARVIN, F. S., *Evolution of World Peace*. New York, 1921.

MORRIS, R. T., *The Way out of War: Biology of the Subject*. New York, 1918.

NICOLAI, G. F., *Biology of War*. London, 1919.

PERRIS, H. H., *War and Peace*. New York, 1911.

PORRITT, A., ed., *The Causes of War*. London, 1932.

POWERS, H. H., *Things Men Fight For*. New York, 1916.

RAMSAY, W. M., *Imperial Peace*. Oxford, 1913.

ROSE, J. H., *The Indecisiveness of Modern War*. London, 1927.

RUSSELL, B. A. W., *Why Men Fight*. New York, 1917.

TEAD, O., *The People's Part in Peace; Basis for a Sound Internationalism*. New York, 1918.

VEBLEN, T. B., *The Nature of Peace and the Terms of Its Perpetuation*. New York, 1917.

VESTAL, S. C., *The Maintenance of Peace*. New York, 1921.

WALLER, B. C., *Paths to World Peace.* London, 1926.
WEHBERG, H., *The Outlawry of War.* Washington, 1931.
WOODS, F. A., and BALTZLY, A., *Is War Diminishing.* New York, 1927.
WOOLF, L. S., *Intelligent Man's Way to Prevent War.* London, 1933.
WRIGHT, Q., *A Study of War.* Chicago, 1942.
NOEL-BAKER, P. J., *Disarmament.* London, 1926.
ENOCK, A. G., *The Problem of Armaments.* New York, 1923.
JOUHAUX, L., *Le Désarmement.* Paris, 1927.
MADARIAGA, S., *Disarmament.* Oxford, 1929.
WHEELER-BENNETT, J. W., *Reduction of Armaments.* London, 1925.

§ 11

History of International Organization

GARNER, J. W., *Recent Developments in International Law.* Calcutta, 1925.
HAYES, C. J. H., *The Historical Evolution of Modern Nationalism.* New York, 1931.
HIGGINS, A. P., *The Hague Peace Conferences.* Cambridge, England, 1909.
MARSTON, F. S., *The Peace Conference of 1944.* New York, 1944.
ter MEULEN, J., *Der Gedanke der Internationalen Organisation in seiner Entwicklung.* The Hague, 1917-1940.
PHILLIPSON, C., *International Law and Custom of Ancient Greece and Rome.* London, 1911.
RALSTON, J. H., *International Arbitration from Athens to Locarno.* Stanford, 1929.
SCOTT, J. B., *The Hague Peace Conferences.* Baltimore, 1909.
SHEPHERD, W. R., *Historical Atlas.* New York, 1929 (7th ed.).
TEMPERLEY, H. W. V., ed., *A History of the Peace Conference of Paris.* London, 1920-1924.
WALKER, T. A., *A History of the Law of Nations.* Cambridge, England, 1899.
VISVANATHA, S. V., *International Law in Ancient India.* Madras, 1925.
WHEATON, H., *History of the Law of Nations* (1648-1842). New York, 1845.
WRIGHT, R. F., *Medieval Internationalism.* London, 1930.

§ 12

The League of Nations

BOURNE, R. S. (comp.), *Towards an Enduring Peace.* New York, 1916.
POLLARD, A. F., *The League of Nations in History.* New York, 1918.
DUGGAN, S. P., ed., *The League of Nations.* Boston, 1919.
GOLDSMITH, R., *The League to Enforce Peace.* New York, 1917.
MARBURG, T., *Development of the League of Nations Idea.* New York, 1932.
BARTLETT, R. J., *The League to Enforce Peace.* Chapel Hill, 1944.
MILLER, D. H., *My Diary at the Peace Conference.* New York, 1928.
———, *Drafting of the Covenant.* New York, 1928.
RAY, J., *Commentaire du Pacte de la Société des Nations.* Paris, 1930-1935.
SCHÜCKING, W., and WEHBERG, H., *Die Satzung des Völkerbundes.* Berlin, 1931 (3rd ed.).
ENGEL, S., *League Reform.* Geneva, 1940 (*Geneva Special Studies*, Vol. XI, Nos. 3-4).
League of Nations, *Document*, Geneva.

KNUDSON, J. I., *History of the League of Nations*. Atlanta, 1938.

League of Nations, *Ten Years of World Coöperation*. Geneva, 1930.

GUGGENHEIM, P., *Der Völkerbund*. Leipzig, 1932.

MORLEY, F., *The Society of Nations*. Washington, 1932.

MYERS, D. P., *Handbook of the League of Nations*. Boston, 1935.

OTTLIK, G., ed., *Annuaire de la Société des Nations*. Lausanne, 1927-1938.

POTTER, P. B., *The League of Nations and Other International Organization*. Geneva, 1934 (*Geneva Studies*, Vol. V, No. 6).

BURTON, M. E., *The Assembly of the League of Nations*. Chicago, 1941.

POTTER, P. B., *Article XIX of the Covenant of the League of Nations*. Geneva, 1941 (Geneva Research Centre, *Geneva Studies*, Vol. XII, No. 2).

RICHES, C. A., *The Unanimity Rule in the League of Nations*. Baltimore, 1933.

CONWELL-EVANS, T. P., *The League Council in Action*. London, 1929.

League of Nations, Secretariat, *The Council of the League of Nations*, Geneva, 1938.

BRUGIÈRE, P. F., *La Sécurité Collective, 1919-1945*. Paris, 1946.

HIGHLEY, A. E., *The First Sanctions Experiment*. Geneva, 1938 (*Geneva Special Studies*, Vol. IX, No. 4).

de RESSEGNIER, G., *Les Sanctions Militaires de la Société des Nations*. Paris, 1930.

WILLIAMS, B., *State Security and the League of Nations*. Baltimore, 1927.

RUSSELL, F., *The International Government of the Saar*. Berkeley, 1926.

WAMBAUGH, S., *The Saar Plebiscite*. Cambridge, 1940.

RANSHOFEN-WERTHEIMER, E. F., *The International Secretariat*. Washington, 1945.

HILL, M., *Immunities and Privileges of International Officials*. Washington, 1947.

GREAVES, H. G. R., *The League Committees and World Order*. Oxford, 1931.

HALL, H. D., *Mandates, Dependencies and Trusteeship*. Washington, 1947 (?).

WRIGHT, Q., *Mandates under the League of Nations*. Chicago, 1930.

de ASCARATE, P., *League of Nations and National Minorities*. Washington, 1945.

BOUDREAU, F. G., "Health and World Organization," in *World Organization*, cited below.

RENBORG, B. A., *International Drug Control: A Study of International Administration by and through the League of Nations*. Washington, 1947.

Institut International de Coöperation Intellectuelle, *L'Institut International de Coöperation Intellectuelle, 1925-1946*. Paris, 1946 (?).

HILL, M., *The Economic and Financial Organization of the League of Nations*. Washington, 1946.

BERDAHL, C., *The Policy of the United States with Respect to the League of Nations*. Geneva, 1932.

BREGMAN, A., *La Politique de la Pologne dans la Société des Nations*. Paris, 1932.

COLCORD, S., *The Great Deception*. New York, 1923.

CORDIER, A. W., *European Union and the League of Nations*. Geneva, 1931, (*Geneva Studies*, Vol. II, No. 6).

DAVIS, K. W., *The Soviet Union and the League of Nations, 1919-1933*. Geneva, 1934 (*Geneva Special Studies*, Vol. V, No. 1).

EASTMAN, S. M., *Canada at Geneva*. Toronto, 1946.

FLEMING, D. F., *The United States and International Organization*. New York, 1938.

HUBBARD, U. P., *The Coöperation of the United States with the League of Nations*. New York, 1931 (*International Conciliation*, No. 274).

JÄCKH, E., and Schwarz, W., *Die Politik Deutschlands im Völkerbund*. Geneva, 1932.

KELCHNER, W. H., *Latin American Relations with the League of Nations*. Boston, 1929.

MANNING, C. A. W., *Policies of the British Dominions in the League of Nations*. Geneva, 1932.

MATSUSHITA, M., *Japan in the League of Nations*. New York, 1929.

MUNCH, P., *La Politique du Danemark dans la Société des Nations*. Geneva, 1931.

POTTER, P. B., *Permanent Delegations to the League of Nations*. Geneva, 1930 (*Geneva Studies*, Vol. I, No. 8).

ROLIN, H. A., *La Politique de la Belgique dans la Société des Nations*. Geneva, 1931.

SOWARD, H., *Canada and the League of Nations*. New York, 1932. (*International Conciliation*, No. 283).

League of Nations, *Report on the Work of the League During the War*, Geneva, 1945.

———, International Labor Office, *The First Decade*. Geneva, 1931.

International Labor Office, *Future Policy, Program, and Status of the International Labor Organization*. Montreal, 1944.

HUDSON, M. O., *The Permanent Court of International Justice, 1930-1942*. New York, 1943.

League of Nations, Permanent Court of International Justice, *Ten Years of International Jurisdiction*. Leyden, 1932.

BUTLER, H. B., *The Lost Peace*. London, 1941.

DAVIS, H. E., ed., *Pioneers in World Order*. New York, 1944.

DELL, R. E., *The Geneva Racket*. London, 1941.

Institute on World Organization, *World Organization: A Balance Sheet of the First Great Experiment*. Washington, 1942.

RAPPARD, W. E., *The Geneva Experiment*. London, 1931.

WEBSTER, C. K., *The League of Nations in Theory and Practice*. London, 1933.

ZIMMERN, Sir A. E., *The League of Nations and the Rule of Law*. London, 1939.

ZIMMERN, L. A., *Must the League Fail?* London, 1932.

§ 13

United Nations

BENTWICH, N. De M., *From Geneva to San Francisco*. London, 1946.

BOYD, A., *United Nations Organization Handbook*. London, 1946.

Commission to Study the Organization of Peace, *Publications*, New York.

DOLIVET, L., *The United Nations*. New York, 1946.

DULLES, E. L., *Bretton Woods Monetary Conference*. New York, 1944 (Foreign Policy Association, *Reports*, Vol. XX, No. 12).

FINER, H., *The United Nations Economic and Social Council*. Boston, 1946.

GALLOWAY, G. B., *Post-war Planning in the United States*. New York, 1942.

GOODRICH, L. M., and Hambro, E., *Charter of the United Nations*. Boston, 1946.

HARLEY, J. E., *Documentary Textbook of the United Nations*. Los Angeles, 1947.

HUDSON, M. O., and others, *The International Court*. Washington, 1945.

League of Nations, *The League Hands Over, Geneva,* 1946 (League Document: Gen. 1946. 1).

McCormick, T. C. T., ed., *Problems of the Post-War World.* New York, 1945.

Summers, R. E., comp., *Dumbarton Oaks.* New York, 1945.

United Nations, *Documents* and *Official Records.* New York.

———, Preparatory Commission, *Report.* London, 1945.

United States, Department of State, *The United Nations Conference of International Organization: Selected Documents.* Washington, 1946.

Universities Committee on Post-War International Problems, *Publications,* Boston.

Woodrow Wilson Foundation, *United Nations News.* New York.

Index

Adjudication, international: place in international organization, 14, 16, 154, 156, 164, 204, 206; international administration and, 14, 16, 132; good offices and mediation, 89, 154; arbitration as, 155; private claims, 157, 162; basis of settlement, 157, 159; composition of tribunal, 158; treaties providing for, 158; obligatory arbitration, 159; range of questions, 160, 162; national honor and vital interests, 160; domestic questions, 161; status of individual, 163; decision final, 163; and sovereignty, 190; International Court of Justice (UN), 164; historical development, 230, 231, 234, 237; Claims Commission, 234; Permanent Court of Arbitration, 234.

Administration, international: place in international organization, 14, 15, 131, 207, 234, 241; conference and, 132; diplomatic and consular activity and, 132; definition and interpretation, chart, 133; agency organization, supervision, control, 134-136, 143, 149; geographical aspects, 135, 146; personnel problems, 136, 146, 147; coördination of effort, 136, 146; objectives, 138; contribution to world peace, 138; subject matter analysis, table, 139-140; functions and procedure, table, 141, 142; financial support, 142, 149; appraisal, 144, 149; war-time conditions affecting, 145; membership in unions, 146; leadership function, 147; publicity and promotion, 147; regulations, issuance and enforcement, 148; headquarters and plant, 149; UN powers, 266; UN specialized agencies, 273.

Agreements: See Treaties.

Alliances: origin and function, 167; nature, 168; objects, 168, 172; legal aspects, 170; membership, 170; relation to balance of power, 170, 172; international concert, 173; historically inadequate, 195.

Ancient world: interstate organization, 229-231; international law, 235; arbitration, 237.

Arbitration: See Adjudication.

Armaments: manufacturers as warmongers, 41; foreign policy problem, 50;

peace through disarmament, 223; limitation of, 224, 245.

Balance of power: nature, 170, 175; forms, 171; value, 172; preservation through international concert, 173-177.

Bureaus, international: See Administration, international.

Boundaries: nations and, 33; boundary commissions, 234.

Claims Commission: 234.

Colonies: See Dependencies.

Commerce: See Intercourse, international.

Concert: international: formation, 172; grounds of opposition, 173; intervention as principal agency, 173, 178; security and revision, 174; consent gained by generalization of interests, 176; use of armed force, 178; guarantees and their enforcement, 178; evaluation, 180; obstacles, nationalism and commercial imperialism, 180, 182.

Concert of Europe: 241.

Conciliation: See Inquiry and Conciliation.

Conference, international: place in international organization, 115-130, 277; nature and function, 115, 116, 120; expression of results, 116, 119, 124; subjects, 117, 124, 128; peace conferences, 117, 124, 125; terminology, 117; evolution, 117, 126; administration and, 118; final consequences, 119; organization and conduct, 120, 129; value, 121, 126, 129; preparation, 121; membership, 122, 125, 128; sessions, debate, voting, 123; unanimity requirement, 124; equality of representation, 124; and sovereignty, 183; resolutions, 210.

Consular system: organization and practice, 67-75; origin and scope, 67, 75; personnel and equipment, 68, 70, 74; supervision and control, 69, 71, 74; diplomacy and, 69, 73; merchant consuls, 70; native consuls, 70; officers' powers and duties, 71-74; information service, 72; immunities, 73; tenure of office, 73; historical development, 231, 232, 233, 237.